JOSHUA BLAU

TOPICS IN HEBREWAND SEMITIC LINGUISTICS

JOSHUA BLAU

TOPICS IN HEBREW AND SEMITIC LINGUISTICS

THE MAGNES PRESS, THE HEBREW UNIVERSITY, JERUSALEM

Published with the assistence of
The Fund For Encouraging Scholars and Writers,
The President's Office

Distributed by The Magnes Press, P.O. 7695, Jerusalem 91076, Israel
Fax 972–2–5633370

IBN 965–493–006–4

Printed in Israel
Typesetting: Daatz, Jerusalem

To the Memory of Shoshana Bahat
Lover of the Hebrew Language and Friend

Contents

Preface

In this volume I have collected most of my papers written in English dealing with Hebrew and Semitic linguistics. I have excluded books and booklets, as well as summaries. Papers dealing with Arabic were not included in this volume, not in the least because my papers dealing with Middle Arabic have been published by The Magnes Press under the title *Studies in Middle Arabic and Its Judaeo-Arabic Variety*, Jerusalem 1988. This collection is the English pendant to the Hebrew volume *Studies In Hebrew Linguistics*, Jerusalem, The Magnes Press, 1996, in which my Hebrew papers dealing with Hebrew (and Semitic) linguistics were published, including the Hebrew translation of papers first issued in German. I do hope that this collection of my papers will convey to scholars something more than the mere sum of my various publications and that the indices will enable the reader to find his wish more easily. The papers, according to their very nature, deal with details. He who is interested to know how these items fit into the general frame, is referred not only to my publication *A Grammar of Biblical Hebrew*², Wiesbaden 1993 but also to the short treatise 'On the History and Structure of Hebrew', which opens this collection and has been especially written for it. The various papers have been brought up-to-date by additions and corrections attached to them; asterisks on the margin refer to these additions.

I would like to thank the various publishers who granted permission to republish these papers, and to The Magnes Press and its head, Dan Benovici, for publishing it, as well as to the Fund for Encouraging Scholars and Writers, The President's Office, for their assistance.

J. B.

INTRODUCTION

On the History and Structure of Hebrew[1]

The history of Hebrew (henceforth H) is unique not only on account of its long attested history of three millennia, but especially since it is the only language that after having ceased being spoken (for 1700 years!), has now become the mother tongue of some three million people. During its long history it has always been the language of Jewish culture and religion, and for this reason H in its various manifestations during the ages, despite the great differences between them, formed some kind of unity and has ever been intelligible to the Jewish intelligentsia: Jewish religion is to a great extent based on the two classical eras of H, viz. Biblical H (henceforth BH) and Rabbinical H (henceforth RH), the Bible and Rabbinical writings being the basis of Jewish education and study. The writings of the preceding periods of H were absorbed into Jewish culture of later ages, so that one may use the model of a one-way-window for describing the development of H, later H being incomprehensible to the speakers of earlier ages (just as one cannot look in from the outside through a one-way-window), whereas (almost) all the preceding types of H have been, as stated, understood by the Jewish intelligentsia (just as one may look out through a one-way-window). In other words, intelligibility within H is uni-directional: earlier layers are open to later, but not vice-versa. Accordingly, a Biblical scribe, for instance, would not well understand a mediaeval Rabbinical text, whereas an educated Israeli has no difficulty in apprehending a Biblical text or even, if taught the subject matter, a Rabbinical one. As a result, H in its different crystallizations over three thousand years, giving rise to diverse **linguistic** structures, has nevertheless (also) to be considered one **cultural** unity.

H belongs to the Canaanite family of Northwest Semitic (to which also Ugaritic,[2] Aramaic, etc. belong; cf. below pp. 308–31). As a Semitic tongue, its

[1] I am indebted to S. Hopkins for his advice in writing this paper.

[2] I do regard Ugaritic as a separate Northwest Semitic tongue; see below pp. 339–43

roots are in general constituted by consonants, especially its verbal roots, whereas the vowels, as a rule, only modify them in forming verbal and nominal themes. As a West Semitic language, its suffix conjugation (as *šɔmar* 'he kept') has become, already in BH, a veritable finite verb denoting the past, preserving (in BH solely) only vestiges of its stative use (e.g., *ᶜɔməqu* 'they are deep'), as reflected in East Semitic. Not having expanded the use of broken plurals and of the conative verbal theme *fāᶜala*, as have the Southwest Semitic tongues (e. g., Arabic, Ethiopic) and having shifted *w* in initial position to *y*, H belongs, as stated, to Northwest Semitic. Exhibiting e.g., the shifts *ā* > *ō* (>ɔ), *d̲* > *z*, *t̲* >*š* (cf. below pp. 50–103), *ḍ/ẓ* > *ṣ*, and showing further the vowels *i* — *i*, rather than *a* — *a*, in the active derived verbal themes (see below pp. 174–80), H forms a part of the Canaanite language family. Less conclusive is the derivation of many participles from the stem of the intransitive suffix conjugation (*qɔm, zɔqen, nišmɔr*) and the formation of verbal themes like *rɔmem* 'he exalted', rather than **riyyem*, in the hollow and geminate verbs (see below pp. 169–73), since they occur in Ugaritic as well.

BH is only to a limited extent attested in old inscriptions, as in the calendar of Gezer, from the tenth century B.C.E, written in the Old H script. The linguistic evaluation of these inscriptions is impeded by their quite extreme consonantal script, the vowel letters being used less frequently than in the Bible. The Bible itself, the main source for BH, is not easy to evaluate lingustically either, since it is made up of three distinct historical strata, viz. (in the order of their antiquity and importance) the consonantal text, the vowel letters, and the system of diacritical marks for vowels and cantillation. One has also to be very careful with the linguistic assessment of the (Greek and Latin) transcriptions of Biblical texts and words, since one has to take into account the intricacies of both the transcribed and the transcribing language (see below pp. 267–71).

The twenty-two letters of the H alphabet were originally purely consonantal. Some of them were polyphonic, viz. ש = *šin/śin* (see for details below pp 50ff.), further presumably ע = *ᶜ/ġ* and ח = *ḥ/x* (see *Polyphony*). This implies that the Israelites took over the alphabet from a dialect in which these pairs of consonants had coincided and that they preferred to make do with polyphony of ח ש ע, rather than introducing new letters. *Š/(ś>)s* remained (and still are, except in the Samaritan tradition), and *ḥ/x* and *ᶜ/ġ* coalesced > *ḥ* and ᶜ respectively. It stands to reason, as also demonstrated by deviating translations of the Septuagint, that the earliest layer of the text of the Bible contained consonants only, vowel letters arising later by changes in pronunciation, as well as by subsequent additions and perhaps even intentional orthographic reform. These vowel letters were increasingly utilized by the scribes of the Bible (cf. also below pp. 21–25) and became even more frequent in RH. Yet, since they were a rather restricted aid for enabling the exact reading of the holy text, especially after H had ceased being a living tongue in the second half of first millennium C. E., vowel and cantillation marks were introduced, which, however, were based on a much older and generally reliable tradition. Nevertheless, sometimes later linguistic features were introduced in place of those that had fallen into disuse, especially whenever no express tradition to the contrary existed and the consonantal text was ambiguous. A case in point is the internal passive of *qal*, which is preserved only whenever the consonantal text did not permit its vocalization as *nif*^{c}*al*. The most elaborate vocalization (and cantillation) system and the only one utilized today is the Tiberian. It marks vowel quality only (rather than quantity), distinguishes between open and closed *e* (in the Babylonian vocalization system open *e* and *a* have coincided) and is characterized by the shift of *u* to *ɔ*, thus coinciding with *ɔ*< *ā*, contrary to the other vocalization systems. The use of ָ *qamaṣ* to mark *ɔ* both when it developed from short *u* and long *ā* is one of the main proofs that Tiberian vocalization does not mark the quantity of vowels.

Even if one takes into consideration the elimination of ancient linguistic features by late vocalization, BH, although stretching over many hundreds of years and originating from different parts of Palestine, reflects a surprisingly uniform language. This is due to its being a standardized literary tongue, stemming, it seems, from the scribal school of Jerusalem. Nevertheless, one has to distinguish between poetry and prose, as well as between early, classical and late poetry, further between classical and late prose, without going into details and differentiating between historical, legal, etc., prose. Thus poetry uses archaic features: *inter alia*, it still utilizes the longer forms of the prepositions אֱלֵי 'to', עֲלֵי 'on', עֲדֵי 'until', restricts the use of the definite article, of the relative pronoun and the object marker (all of which, it seems, were absent from the earliest layers of H) and adds the endings *-i*/*-o* to nouns in construct (*-i* in other cases as well). Early poetry has, among other things, preserved the short prefix conjugation to mark past even when not following "conversive" *wāw* (as *yaṣṣeḇ* 'he set' Deut. xxxii:8). Late prose, after the destruction of the first Temple (586 B.C.E.), *inter alia*, prefers אֲנִי 'I' to אָנֹכִי. It stands to reason that in this era, besides Aramaic, the dialect spoken by the authors and scribes was the precursor of RH, which was to become in the first half of the first millennium C.E. the second classical language of H, perhaps spoken in southern Judaea. In the period of the Judaean kingdom, this dialect was overshadowed by the speech of Jerusalem. After the destruction of the first Temple, the latter's standing deteriorated, and therefore, late biblical prose, although imitating biblical style, reflects the forerunners of RH and an Aramaic adstratum, as, e.g., the tendency to mark the direct object by *lə*.

RH, a dialect of which is already reflected by some of the Bar-Kokhba letters (round 132 C.E.), is the language of the writings of the *tannaim*, who, *inter alia*, composed the *Mishna* and the *Tosefta*, probably redacted in the second half of the second century C.E. It reflects decisive Aramaic influence, since Aramaic was by that time spoken not only exclusively in Galilee but also, together with the spoken form of RH, in Judaea. The texts written in RH are, as a rule, unvocalized, and their pronunciation is transmitted orally, exhibiting many a difference between the various traditions. Since late scribes copying Mishnaic, etc., manuscripts were better versed in BH than in RH grammar, they often changed RH forms to BH ones, so that genuine RH has to be reconstructed from reliable manuscripts, rather than from printed editions. Thus, in RH proper the difference between final ן-/ם- has been neutralized, and e.g., אָדָם 'man' is spelt in reliable manuscripts אדן, a form which is totally absent from the printed edition. When round 1900 H was revived as a spoken language, RH was only known in the form in which it appears in the printed editions, i.e., adapted to a great extent to BH, so that the morphology of Israeli H (henceforth IH) was, almost exclusively, based on BH.

After the disastrous failure of the Bar-Kokhba revolt (132–35 C.E.), the population of Judaea was decimated, and the rabbis and their disciples moved north to Galilee, bringing with them the southern Tannaitic literature written in RH. Here they became quicky assimilated to the Aramaic-speaking environment, and in one or two generations spoken H became altogether extinct (perhaps with the exception of dispersed and culturally rather unimportant settlements in the south of Judaea). Late RH (henceforth LRH) came now into being, used alongside of Aramaic, which had become the only spoken language. It is already a pure literary tongue, since, as stated, H had ceased being spoken. It is used by the *amoraim*, whose most conspicuous work, of decisive cultural importance, was the two Talmuds (the Palestinian and the Babylonian, redacted c. the 5th cent. C.E.), written in Aramaic and LRH, both Aramaic and LRH having Palestinian/Western and Babylonian/Eastern varieties. LRH already reflects the common characteristics of the various forms of literary H not backed by spoken H. All these forms of literary H which arose during the 1700 years in which H was not spoken, exhibit different mixtures of the preceding periods of H, especially of BH and RH, as well as the influence of the vernacular. This applies to LRH as well: it cannot be dubbed genuine RH, since it reflects BH admixture (as the use of attributive הַזֹּאת 'this' [feminine]). Already RH proper was exposed, as stated, to the decisive influence of Aramaic, which, being the only spoken language, asserted itself even more strongly in the LRH period.

Although H, from the time of the Bar-Kokhba revolt had ceased being spoken, it continued to undego changes, since it was constantly used in writing. The amalgation of BH and RH, characteristic of mediaeval H, applies even to the **puristic** BH of Spanish H poetry, since even this variety of H contains a few RH elements and reflects the impact of the spoken language (in this case, of Arabic, which, however, influenced H not only as spoken tongue but in its literary form as well, cf. the use of וְאִם 'although', mirroring Classical Arabic وَإِنْ. However, whereas Spanish H poetry tried to abstain from loan-translations, prose works from the same cultural area, i.e., the Islamic world, especially scientific and philosophical translations from Arabic, teem with such loan translations (some of which have extended into modern IH).

Yet the mediaeval layers of H changed not only by amalgamation of existing elements and under the impact of external influence, but also according to regular patterns of analogical formation (see E. Goldenberg in *Encyclopaedia Judaica*[2], supplementary entries, s.v. *Hebrew, Medieval*). This was brought about by the needs of artistic embellishment and was carried out, contrary to changes in a living tongue, in a premeditated manner.

The revival of H as a spoken language around 1900 C.E. had been made possible by a unique concatenation of various factors. There were still sufficient numbers of Jews steeped in traditional society and therefore intimately familiar with H; certain sections of the Zionist movement were inspired by the idea of reviving H as the national spoken language; and in Palestine around 1900 C.E. no secular standard language was in use among the whole Jewish population, which spoke a plethora of different colloquials. So it came about that H became once more a spoken language, after it had ceased being spoken for some seventeen centuries. And what we said of the common characteristics of the various forms of literary H not being backed by spoken H that they all reflect different mixtures of the preceding periods of H, especially of BH and RH, as well as the influence of the vernaculars, also applies to IH, although it is backed now by H as mother tongue: IH too is an amalgamated language, some sort of *Mischsprache*. Its morphology, no doubt the most characteristic part of any language, is based, in the main, on BH, yet reflects also RH influence (as the disappearance of conversive *waw*, the use of *šel*, and the formation of geminate verbs according to the pattern of regular verbs; in these cases, the trend toward simplification was also instrumental). Yet not only is IH a fusion of elements from several previous layers, but is still, theoretically at least, open toward its ancient layers and freely draws upon them (see Z. Ben-Ḥayyim,

Leshonenu La^cam 4, fascs. 2–3 [1952–53], pp. 143ff.), as if the various strata of H were arranged side by side (in contradistinction to languages that have developed "naturally" and have, therefore, their layers stratified, so to speak, one above the other, so that there is no productive derivation from older strata). The impact of various vernaculars on preceding forms of H is paralleled in the case of IH by the influence of Standard Average European: in the first stages, especially Yiddish and Russian, but also French and German exerted their influence, later English journalese has become more prominent, making IH more and more a European tongue in matters of phraseology.

Thus far we have presented a bird's-eye view of the exceptional external history of H. We shall now deal with some aspects of its internal structure. Predictably enough, we start with BH and shall only occasionally deviate to other periods, especially to RH and IH.

As to phonetics, BH possesses, as do, more or less, the later layers of H, allophones of the stops *b, g, d, k, p, t*, being after vowels pronounced as spirants, viz. *ḇ, ḡ, ḏ, ḵ, p̱, ṯ*. Yet the automatic shift of these stops to spirants after vowels has been preserved in word initial only when following a word with vocalic ending in external close juncture. Otherwise (for details see *Hebrew Linguistics* pp. 280ff.), the spirant allophones are about to become phonemes (לָקַחַתְּ 'you [fem. sg.] took' as against לָקַחַת 'to take'; also the very same word may be used with alternating plosive and spirant pronunciation, as קָרְבָּן 'sacrifice', yet Ez. 40:43 קָרְבַן). The realization of the phonemic status of *b, g, d, k, p, t* is of the utmost importance for the understanding of the BH vowel system, particularly as to the correct evaluation of *shwa*, which, as well known, reflects both zero and *ə*: since the plosive/spirant pronunciation does not necessarily depend on being preceded by zero vowel/*ə* (according to the Tiberian tradition as a rule pronounced *a*) respectively, one will not analyse *ə* as a phoneme, as if an opposition zero: *ə* existed, and rather consider their alternation to be subphonemic, the more so since *ə* shifts to zero (cf. also below pp. 210–17) and *vice versa*.

It was at a rather late stage that laryngals/pharyngals (viz. א, ע, ה, ח) became weakened and lost their ability to be doubled and developed ultra-short qualitative variants for *ə*; for details of the behaviour of laryngals/pharyngals see *Hebrew Linguistics* pp. 17ff. In RH laryngals and pharyngals were apparently preserved in the villages, but weakened in the towns in the vicinity of Hellenistic centres.

As to vowels, a feature characteristic of Canaanite dialects in general is the shift *ā* > *ō*. Since exceptions preserving the original *ā* are quite frequent (see *Hebrew Linguistics* pp. 25–30), it stands to reason that this shift was conditioned, occurring, it seems, in stressed syllables only. This explains why words pronounced quickly without stress did not partake in this shift and how in words which in some forms contained stressed *ā*, in others unstressed *ā*, *ā* could have spread by analogy over the whole paradigm in some words, while in other words it was the shifted *ō* which was extended. By rigorous analysis of the syllables containing *ō*, an early stage of stress can be reconstructed (see below pp. 120–22).

A quite late feature is the pretonic lengthening of *a* in open syllables (and sometimes also of *i*), and it is well possible that it reflects a reaction to the decisive Aramaic influence that late BH underwent. Through Aramaic influence speakers of H had lost their ability to pronounce short vowels in open unstressed syllables; accordingly, in order to preserve them, they lengthened them (the so-called pretonic lengthening; or doubled the consonant following them; for details see below pp. 106ff.).

Very important is the diachronic treatment of stress (for details see below pp. 104–25), because by means of a quite simple assumption a plethora of seemingly chaotic features turn out to be systematic and neatly regulated (although the regularity was often blurred by analogy). Words stressed in pause on their ultima have, as a rule, elided their final short vowels, whereas those stressed on their penult in pause have preserved their final syllables. Accordingly, if one adds the elided final vowels to words stressed in pause on their ultima, one can reconstruct a stage in which the great majority of the H vocabulary was stressed on the penult, and this in turn suggests the former existence of a stage of **general penult stress** (which was preceded by the period of stress suggested by the shift *ā* > *ō*, see above). The different behaviour of pausal forms which, as a rule, preserved the original penult stress (as שָׁמָ'רוּ 'they kept' < *šāmā'rū*) as against context forms in which the stress passed to the ultima (as שָׁמְרוּ'; the long vowel in the first syllable is due to pretonic lengthening, thus indicating that the stress shift to the ultima is even later than pretonic lengthening) stems from the different length of the penult. In pausal form, owing to pausal lengthening, the penult was long and long vowel in an open stressed penultimate syllable, as a rule, preserved the stress, whereas the shift of stress from short open penult had become a veritable sound shift, resulting in the elision of unstressed short vowels in the penultimate syllable. At the time of this shift to the ultima, pretonic lengthening of open syllables, itself a late feature, ceased operating and unstressed short vowels in the penultimate syllable were reduced to *shwa*, rather than lengthened, as is the case in Aramaic and presum-

[3] The following stemma may illustrate this development: in pause **šama'rū* > (pretonic langthening) **šāma'rū* >(pausal langthening) *šāmā'rū*; in context **šama'rū* >**šāma'rū* >**šāməru'*.

ably through the influence of Aramaic (see pp. 112–13). It was against this background that forms like שָׁמְרוּ' arose, see above, further יָדְךָ' 'your hand' < *yāda'ḵā (cf. pausal יָדֶ'ךָ), אֲנִי' "I" < *ʾa'nī (cf. pausal אָ'נִי).[3]

Another late feature in the vowel system is the attenuation of *a* to *i* in closed unstressed syllables, especially when preceding another *a*. The inverse shift of *i* to *a* in stressed closed syllables, the so-called Philippi's Law, has been claimed to be an early feature, according to Philippi himself even Proto-Semitic. Evidence, however, shows that it is a rather late special characteristic of Hebrew (the same shift, e.g., in Aramaic, being due to parallel development), even later than pausal lengthening (see below pp. 36ff.), but preceding attenuation, as proven by nouns like **marbiṣ* 'place of breach', in the absolute preserving its original form מַרְבֵּץ, yet in construct exhibiting מִרְבַּץ, which arose by a twofold shift: first * *marbiṣ* changed, through Philippi's Law, to * *marbaṣ*, and then, through attenuation, to מִרְבַּץ. Similarly, the tendency to shift the stress from closed syllables to an open ultima is later than Philippi's Law, as indicated by עַתָּה' 'now', in pause עָ'תָּה, still paroxytone, derived from עֵת 'time', i.e., originally *ʿi'ttā, to change through Philippi's law (in stressed syllable!) to *ʿa'ttā, and then shifting the stress to the ultima (see *Hebrew Linguistics*, pp. 15–16).[4]

As a rule, sound shifts are considered the main force effecting sound changes, whereas analogic formation is regarded as bringing about smaller alterations only. Yet sometimes analogy happens to crowd out the effects of sound shift, so that only some scattered vestiges of the latter enable us to reconstruct it. Two such cases in BH are the sound shifts *uy* > *ī* and *iw* > *ū*, which, as a rule, through analogy, were levelled out to *ū* and *ī* respectively (see for details pp. 185ff.).

Sometimes, the assumption of sound shift and/or analogy does not suffice for the understanding of a linguistic feature and one has to resort to the supposition of hyper-correction; thus I am inclined to interpret nouns of the type of בְּאֵר 'well' (see pp. 250ff.).

One of the characteristics of BH vocalization is that absolute nouns in

[4] At this stage it is expedient to present a synopsis of the relative chronology of some of the sound shifts mentioned:

1. *ā* > *ō*.
2. General penult stress.
3. Pausal lengthening.
4. Omission of final short vowels.
5. Philippi's Law (it cannot be proven whether the omission of final short vowels in absolute nouns precedes Philippi's Law or is later, see below p. 40, n. 11).
6. Pretonic lengthening (which, because of the likely influence of Aramaic, has to be considered late)
7. Stress shift to the ultimate; pretonic reduction; attenuation.

stressed closed final syllables exhibit *qamaṣ* as against *pataḥ* in verbs, presumably because the final short vowels disappeared in verbs earlier; for details see *Hebrew Linguistics* pp. 72–76 and below pp 31–32; 273ff.

An important feature of BH morphology is the presence of the final vowel *qamaṣ* in pronouns like יָדְךָ, הֵנָּה, אַתָּה and in verbal forms like שָׁמַרְתָּ, owing to its original *anceps* character, for which see also pp. 142–43. In RH the forms are שָׁמַרְתָּה, יָדָךְ, הֵן, אַתָּה/אַתְּ respectively, partly, at least, owing to Aramaic influence. IH, as usual, continues the BH features, yet it uses for 'they (fem.)' RH הֵן (yet, in contradistiction to RH, where הֵן denotes both masculine and feminine, it is limited to the feminine).

Interesting is the addition of the definite article to the attributive demonstrative pronoun following a substantival head preceded by the definite article (type הַיָּד הַזֹּאת 'this hand'; as against יָד זוֹ in RH, reflecting, surprisingly enough, archaic features both in form, זוֹ as against זֹאת, and in the absence of the pleonastic definite article from both the substantival head and the demonstrative pronoun. In IH both constructions alternate.

The BH tense system denoting facts consists of four finite forms: the simple and "conversive" suffix conjugation and the simple and "conversive" prefix conjugation, the "conversive" forms being preceded by *wə/wa* respectively. It is a moot question whether the verbal forms originally denoted aspects or time. In classical BH prose, at any rate, these forms seem to mark time, since the difference between the simple suffix and the "conversive" (as a rule short) prefix conjugation, both referring to the past, and between the simple prefix and the "conversive" suffix conjugation (which contains secondary forms stressed on the ultima, like 'וְשָׁמַרְתָּ' 'and you will keep'; cf. below pp. 199ff.), both referring to the future/present, depends on the syntactical environment only: as a rule, whenever we find the use of *w* 'and' possible, the "converted" forms are applied, otherwise the simple forms. In poetry, however, the use of tenses is quite free, presumably owing to intentional archaism as well as pseudo-archaism (cf. below pp. 208ff., 260 ff.). Quite different are the tense systems in RH and IH. In both the "conversive" forms have disappeared. In RH the prefix conjugation is mainly modal, and the active participle is used to mark future/present, whereas in IH the participle refers to the present and the prefix tense to the future.

In BH the number of subordinate clauses is somewhat limited, and the boundary lines between main and subordinate clauses blurred. In RH and IH main and subordinate clauses are clearly distinguished, and a plethora of subordinate clauses exist, in IH not only under the influence of RH but also by the impact of Standard Average European.

The Monophthongization of Diphthongs as Reflected in the Use of Vowel Letters in the Pentateuch

The medial diphthongs ay and aw were not simultaneously monophthongized. First aw shifted to ô, while under the same conditions ay was still preserved. This state of affairs is reflected in the spelling of the Pentateuch, the oldest layer of the Bible: medial ṣērê is spelled almost exclusively with yôd only when it developed from ay, and then it is almost invariably followed by yôd; whereas medial ḥôlam with wāw is used much less regularly, being spelled not infrequently without wāw even when it developed from ô, and marked by wāw, though less often, even when it reflects historical â.

There is hardly an element in biblical studies or Semitics in general in which Jonas Greenfield has not taken a personal interest. I therefore offer him this brief study, a side issue in diachronic biblical phonology.

It is my thesis that the medial diphthongs *ay* and *aw* were not simultaneously monophthongized. First *aw* shifted to *ô*, while, under the same conditions, *ay* was still preserved. Only later was *ay* monophthongized to *â* under the very same conditions that had previously caused *aw* to shift to *ô*, thus creating the (historically incorrect) impression that the two diphthongs were simultaneously monophthongized.

The different rate of monophthongization need not surprise one. Instances of discrepancy in the behavior of diphthongs are well known. A case in point is Biblical Aramaic, in which also *aw* shifted to *ô* while *ay* was preserved in certain positions.[1]

Author's note: The system for transliteration of Biblical Hebrew used in this article is my own.

1. See, e.g., H. Bauer and P. Leander, *Grammatik des Biblisch-Aramäischen* (Halle, 1927) 37–38; S. Segert, *Altaramäische Grammatik* (Leipzig, 1975) 125ff.

The difference in the rate of monophthongization is reflected in the use of *matres lectionis* in the Pentateuch. The orthography of the Pentateuch was apparently fixed earlier than the spelling of the other books of the Bible;[2] it therefore reflects an earlier period of Hebrew. On the assumption that it still exhibits a stage of pronunciation in which medial *ay*, in contradistinction to medial *aw*, was preserved, we can recognize a regular pattern of what would otherwise seem to be arbitrary spelling habits.

The main difference between the behavior of the medial *ṣērê* and *ḥôlam* is twofold. Almost exclusively, medial *ṣērê* is spelled with *yôd* only in cases in which it developed from the diphthong *ay*, and then it is almost invariably spelled that way.[3] Medial *ḥôlam* with *wāw*, on the other hand, is used much less regularly; not only may it be spelled without *wāw* even if it developed from *aw*, but it may also, though less often, be marked by *wāw* when it reflects historical *â*. A convincing explanation of this different behavior of *ṣērê yôd* and *ḥôlam wāw* is that, when the orthography of the Pentateuch was fixed, medial *ay* had not yet become monophthongized, so that *yôd* had not yet become a vowel letter marking medial *ṣērê*; medial *aw*, however, had already shifted to *o*, so that *wāw* had already developed to indicate medial *ô*.

Admittedly, cases of long *ô* not arising from monophthongization are much more frequent than cases of long *ê* not stemming from *ay*. Yet even the somewhat restricted occurrence of long *ê* not due to monophthongization seems statistically significant, sufficiently so to establish that, at the time the orthography of the Pentateuch was fixed, medial *ay* was still a diphthong. The almost constant use of *yôd* marking medial *ṣērê* < *ay* points in the same direction. For details see below.

Some details should now be cited concerning the use of medial *ṣērê yôd* < *ay* in the Pentateuch. It clearly prevails in the plural/dual of nouns

2. See, e.g., F. I. Andersen and A. D. Forbes, *Spelling in the Hebrew Bible* (BibOr 41; Rome, 1986; hereafter AF) 313–14. Throughout this paper I have gratefully utilized the extensive statistics contained in that work. I believe that J. Barr's review (in *JSS* 33 [1988] 122–31) does not do justice to AF, which, of course, like every scholarly treatise, does have its weak points. Mainly, for my purposes, I missed the subdivision into groups of biblical books in many an orthographic type. *Obiter dictu*, on pp. 98–100, §3.4.3, AF mistook the Sephardic pronunciation used in the scholarly literature for the Tiberian as reflected in Masoretic vocalization. According to the latter, every *qāmeṣ*, pronounced according to the Sephardic pronunciation *a* or *o*, reflects a vowel like *å*, as against *ḥôlam o*. Therefore, according to the Tiberian tradition, *wāw* could not mark *qāmeṣ* [*qāṭān*]. Cf. also Y. Yahalom, *Leš* 52 (1988) 131 n. 54. At any rate, Barr's own book on biblical spelling (*The Variable Spellings of the Hebrew Bible* [Schweich Lectures of the British Academy, 1986; Oxford, 1989]) was of much less use for my purpose than AF.

3. Deviations either reflect special conditions or are statistically irrelevant; for some details see below.

preceding pronominal suffixes, as well as in prepositions with "plural" pronominal suffixes.[4]

Spellings like גּוֹיֵהֶם (four times in the Pentateuch; no cases with *plene* spelling are attested) reflect the well-known tendency to avoid double *yôd*. If this were a purely orthographic feature, one would assume that later, after the medial *ay* had shifted to *ê*, the original spelling *גּוֹיֵיהֶם was replaced by גּוֹיֵהֶם because of this tendency. It is also possible that **gōyayhem* was contracted comparatively early by dissimilation, and this is reflected in the orthography of the Pentateuch.[5]

Yet not only is medial *ê* < *ay* in nouns spelled so often with *yôd* that exceptions become statistically irrelevant,[6] but medial long *ê* which has not developed from *ay* is almost invariably written without *yôd*, thus attesting that *yôd* was not yet used to mark *ê* at the time the orthography of the Pentateuch was fixed. This is the case with nouns III-*yôd*, such as *miqnêhū* < **miqnayuhū* 'his cattle' and *śadêhū* < *śadayuhū* 'his field',[7] in which *ê* is not marked with *yôd* because the monophthongization of *ayu* occurred too early to affect even the spelling habits of the Pentateuch; this is also the case with nouns II-*wāw*/*yôd*, such as גֵּר, כֵּן, מֵת, נֵר, עֵד, רֵק.[8]

4. See AF, 170–73, types 13–14, and the analysis, 135ff., §5.5.4.

5. For the dissimilation of *yay*, cf., e.g., Bauer and Leander (*Grammatik*, 204, end), who treat the haplology of *ayayya*.

6. Nothing can be inferred from rare defective spellings of verbs III-*yôd* such as וְהִפְרֵתִי, 'and I shall make fruitful' because it may reflect original **wĕhip̄rītī* < **wĕhip̄riytī*. As to pronominal suffixes following imperfect forms (as -*ē* [*hū*]), their etymon is more obscure. They may represent, e.g., short *i*; see, e.g., E. König, *Lehrgebäude der hebräischen Sprache* (Leipzig, 1885) 2.443 (cf. also G. Bergsträsser, *Hebräische Grammatik* [Leipzig, 1918–1929] 2.24, end; repr. Hildesheim, 1986, in one volume); at the time the spelling of the Pentateuch was fixed, *ṣērê* stemming from short *i* presumably represented a short vowel, the change being qualitative only. The same applies apparently to *ḥôlam* arising from short *u*. Accordingly, we will not deal with them in the framework of this paper. As to these pronominal suffixes following imperfect forms of verbs iii *yôd* (as in יִקְנֵהוּ), the origin of this form is not clear either: thus, the indicative might have influenced the short imperfect (**yiqnayuhū* might have affected **yiqnayhū*); the indicative itself was spelled defectively, because (see below) the monophthongization of *ayu* occurred too early to be reflected even in the orthography of the Pentateuch; moreover, ordinary verbs might have had an effect on III-*yôd*. Cf. also H. Bauer and P. Leander (*Historische Grammatik der hebräischen Sprache des Alten Testamentes* [Halle, 1922] 421), who derived it from short *i*.

7. Since the pronominal suffix -*ēhū* occurs with nouns III-*yôd* only, it was not influenced by other nouns. On the other hand, the spelling of, e.g. מַרְאֵיהֶן 'their appearance' has been adjusted to the spelling of plural nouns.

8. Although these nouns must be derived synchronically from roots II-*wāw*/*yôd*, their origin is not entirely clear. I would opt for deriving them partly from *awi*/*ayi*, partly from biliteral roots; cf. my "Origins of Open and Closed *e* in Proto-Syriac," *BSOAS* 32 (1969) 4. At any rate, (p. 302) they contain long *ṣērê*, since it is preserved even when remote from stress. Only outside the Pentateuch is *plene* spelling attested. On the other hand, while רֵק has to be derived from **rayiq* (if it is not originally biliteral), I am inclined to trace רֵיקָם (! invariably with *yôd*) back to **rayqam* because of its fixed *plene* spelling (a third pattern is reflected by רֵיק < **riyq*).

In living languages one cannot always draw a sharp line between the preservation of diphthongs and monophthongization.[9] Even in dialects that preserve diphthongs they may be monophthongized in quick and unclear speech, and a dialectologist may come up against serious difficulties in the attempt to distinguish diphthongs from long vowels. Prepositions, by nature, are pronounced less distinctly than nouns, especially prepositions whose task is to indicate relations which, in languages with case systems, are represented by cases. This clearly applies to the preposition אֶל, which partly denotes what is referred to in Indo-Germanic tongues by the dative. Therefore, for example, *ᵓilayhum was apt to shift to אֲלֵיהֶם more quickly than the *ay* in nouns was monophthongized. This is probably why some two-thirds of the occurrences of ᵓ*el* with pronominal suffixes in the Pentateuch[10] are spelled without *yôd*, presumably because at the time the orthography of the Pentateuch was fixed, *ᵓ*ilay-* preceding pronominal suffixes had already shifted to ᵓ*ilê*, whereas *ay* in general was still preserved.[11]

Since the preposition ᶜ*al* 'on' has a more independent meaning than ᵓ*el*, which, as stated, often indicates relation only (as do cases), its *ay* preceding pronominal suffixes was much less contracted; that is why only about 15 percent of its occurrences in the Pentateuch[12] are spelled defectively, much less than in the case of ᵓ*el*, yet much more than with ordinary nouns. In other words, first *ay* in ᵓ*el* was monophthongized, later in ᶜ*al*, and only later still was it affected in ordinary nouns.

It is well known that long *ḥôlam* emerged in Hebrew both by monophthongization of *aw* and by shift of stressed *â* to *ô*. Even in the Pentateuch, the feminine plural suffix *ôt* < *ât*, for example, is spelled in almost one-third of its occurrences with a *wāw*;[13] this minority of occurrences,[14] a substantial one, to be sure, proves that *aw* had already shifted to *ô*, and *wāw* developed to a *mater lectionis* marking medial *ô*.

9. See O. Jastrow's important observations in *Die mesopotamisch-arabischen* qəltu *Dialekte*, vol. 1: *Phonologie und Morphologie* (Wiesbaden, 1978) 77–78.

10. See AF, 171.

11. The third of the occurrences of ᵓ*elē* spelled plene probably reflects later adaptation to the spelling of nouns. In the other books of the Bible, *plene* spelling prevails, because in these books *ay* in general had been monophthongized and *yôd* had developed to be used as a vowel letter indicating medial *ṣērê*.

12. See AF, 172.

13. See AF, 11. Here are some other cases of *ô* < *â*: זְרוֹעַ is spelled with *wāw* four times in the Pentateuch; לָשׁוֹן only once; קוֹל (AF, 46–48) in the absolute singular is as a rule spelled plene, but with pronominal suffixes and in the plural it is spelled defectively (which indicates that its etymon is *qāl*, rather than *qawl*). In דּוֹר, too, *plene* spelling prevails.

14. The plene spelling of הֲלוֹא 'is not?' as against לֹא 'not' (AF, 186–87) is surprising. Perhaps it represents not (only) interrogative הֲ + לֹא, but (also) affinity with Biblical Aramaic

ô < *aw* is as a rule spelled with *wāw*. In some cases the *plene* spelling is so conspicuous that deviations from it need not be statistically significant. This is the case, for example, with יוֹם (only יְמִים in Num 9:22 is spelled defectively), שׁוֹר, תּוֹרָה, מוֹעֵד (spelled defectively in only seven of its very numerous occurrences), as well as in verbs I-*wāw* in *Hiphil*,[15] and *Niphal* past and participle. Sometimes, however, the minority of occurrences of defective spelling is conspicuous enough to indicate that *aw* had already shifted to *ô*. Thus תּוֹלְדוֹת occurs twenty-nine times in the Pentateuch, twenty-three of them with *plene* spelling and six defective (more than twenty percent!). This, together with the use of *wāw* in a substantial minority of occurrences to mark *ô* < *â*, leaves no doubt that, by the time the orthography of the Pentateuch was fixed, *aw* had already become monophthongized[16] and *wāw* had become a vowel letter to mark medial *ô*.[17]

אֱלוֹ 'lo' (see, e.g., Bauer and Leander, *Grammatik*, §71a; and the literature cited in W. Gesenius and F. Buhl, *Hebräisches und aramäisches Handwörterbuch über das Alte Testament* [16th ed.; Leipzig, 1915], Aramaic part, s.v. אֱלוֹ); in that case, the *ḥôlam* might reflect original *aw*.

The etymon of the verbal theme called *Polel* of II-*wāw*/*yôd* and geminate verbs (see AF, 196, type 45) is obscure (see my "Studies in Hebrew Verb Formation," *HUCA* 42 [1971] 147–51); in addition, one must take into consideration the possibility of vocalizing defectively spelled geminate verbs as *Piel* (see Bergstrasser, *Hebräische Grammatik* 2.140). (pp. 169–73)

15. The defective spelling of אסף, etc. reflects a different history; see Bergsträsser, *Hebräische Grammatik* 2.79.

16. In contradistinction to *ay*.

17. Whereas *yôd* had not yet become a vowel letter indicating medial long *ṣērê*.

Non-Phonetic Conditioning of Sound Change and Biblical Hebrew

1.

THE TIME-HONORED discussion of the problem of the non-phonetic conditioning of sound change has been intensified through the recent emergence of generative phonology. Whereas the orthodox neogrammarian position, as well as that of "autonomous" phonemics, only allow for strict phonetic conditioning of sound change, "systematic" generative phonology posits that phonetic changes may also take place in environments whose specification requires reference to non-phonetic morphophonemic and/or (superficial) grammatical structure.[1] In the following I shall attempt to view this problem from the vantage-point of some sound changes in Biblical Hebrew.

2.

Many scholars,[2] correctly in my opinion, allow for paradigmatic resistance to sound change. According to this view, functionally significant sounds may be preserved, although "blindly operating" sound change should have changed them. Sounds behave differently if they are the sole markers of a certain

1. See, e.g., Postal (1968, pp. 231–260).

2. See, e.g., Horn (1923, pp. 118–120), who (in pp. 131–133) deals with the history of research; Malkiel (Lehmann-Malkiel, 1968, p. 68); Szemerényi (1968, pp. 3–38); Anttila (1972, p. 80).

grammatical category, and sound changes are delayed if homonymy would result. In short, sound changes do not take place irrespective of the needs of communication. They do not operate blindly, endangering mutual understanding.

2.1

Indeed, Biblical Hebrew exhibits a rather clear case of paradigmatic resistance to sound change, preserving a functionally significant sound. As is well known, the second person singular personal pronouns, as a rule, are *'attā* (masc.): *'att* (fem.), the corresponding pronominal suffixes (used in genitive and accusative function) *-kā : -ēk,* etc., the corresponding suffixes marking the persons of the perfect *-tā* : *-t*. Whereas the final vowel of the feminine has disappeared, that of the masculine remained, no doubt owing to paradigmatic pressure, since the omission of the masculine final vowel would have entailed the disappearance of any difference between masculine and feminine.[3] One would not attribute the preservation of the final vowel in the masculine forms to the greater stability of the *a*-vowel.[4] In other Semitic languages (e.g., in Aramaic and Arabic dialects), it is the feminine final vowel *i* that, as a rule, exhibits greater stability,[5] thus proving that the main factor for the preservation

3. As a matter of fact, the pronominal suffixes exhibiting the vowel *ē* preceding the *k* in the feminine would have preserved the functional difference between masculine and feminine even if the masculine had lost its final vowel (except for forms in which the pronominal suffixes are preceded by a long vowel, as "your father"-*'āḇīḵā : 'āḇīk*). It stands to reason that the preservation of the final vowel in the masculine in pronominal suffixes as well is due to the analogy of the personal pronoun and the perfect (and pronominal suffixes preceded by long vowel).

4. Though it might have influenced the preservation of the final vowel in the masculine rather than in the feminine. The main reason for the preservation of one of the final vowels was paradigmatic pressure, and in Hebrew (contrary to other Semitic tongues, see below) it was the *a*-vowel that was preserved, perhaps because of its greater stability. At any rate, in Hebrew *a* is more stable than *i/u*, as demonstrated by its behavior in open pretonic syllables: whereas *u* (always) and *i* (often) are reduced, *a* is always lengthened. In many Arabic dialects too (called by J. Cantineau *différentiel*) *a* is more stable.

5. The particulars are rather complicated, including, e.g. in Syriac, the preservation of the final *-ī* in orthography only. For our purpose we shall cite the behavior of the pronominal suffixes in Baghdadi (according to Blanc, 1964, pp. 64–65): in the Jewish dialect, after bases ending in a consonant the final vowel is omitted in both masculine and feminine, since the difference in gender is sufficiently indicated by the vowel preceding *k*; after bases terminating in a vowel, however, in which no vowel difference preceding *k* obtains between masculine and feminine, only the masculine loses its final vowel, the feminine being *-ki*, a clear example of paradigmatic blocking of the omission of a functionally necessary vowel. In the Christian dialect, however, through the influence of the perfect suffixes *katabet:katabti*, as well as of the pronominal suffixes after bases ending in a vowel (cf. also note 3 above), the feminine pronominal suffix of the second person has always the form *-ki* (and in the Muslim dialect >*-č*).

of one of the final vowels was paradigmatic pressure, phonetic parameters
* being at most secondary.[6]

2.2

It goes without saying that the principle of paradigmatic resistance to sound change has to be applied judiciously. Even *prima facie* clear cases of blocking of changes of functionally important sounds may, on closer inspection, turn out rather to exhibit ordinary sound change. Thus it has been claimed[7] that third person feminine singular perfect forms of *verba IIIy* like *hāyāt* ("she was") with preservation of the final *t* (as against its regular omission, e.g., in *kātəbā*, "she wrote") is due to paradigmatic pressure. Had the *t* shifted to zero, the allegedly regular feminine form **hāyā* would have become identical with the corresponding masculine. It is, however, more likely[8] that originally it was only the feminine ending *-at* that shifted to *-ā*, whereas *-āt* preserved its *t*. Therefore, in this case, the preservation of the *t* is regular, rather than due to paradigmatic pressure.

2.3

As is well known, case endings are especially apt to be omitted, in both Semitic and non-Semitic languages. This omission of the case endings is due to multiple causation. For example, in Neo-Arabic the dropping of the case endings was due to the intertwinement of many factors:[9] the disappearance of the final short vowels, the analogical extension of pausal forms lacking case endings, and also the prevalence of more frequent forms over less common ones (e.g., the prevalence of the *-īna*/*-ayna* endings in the sane masculine plural/dual over the *-ūna*/*-āni* endings). Yet this process was conditioned by the low functional yield of the case endings, partly due to substitutes[10] preceding the

6. Grotzfeld (1964, p. 54) posits for the perfect suffixes in the Arabic dialect of Damascus an originally short final vowel in the masculine as against a long vowel in the feminine (**ta* : **tī*). His view is based on the fact that traces of a long final vowel are preserved in Classical Arabic in the feminine form but not in the masculine. Therefore, he regards the preservation of the final *-ī* as original rather than secondary, due to a tendency for differentiation and the influence of the imperfect/imperative ending *-ī*. This, however, is not very likely. Nöldeke (1904, p. 20) adduced decisive proof for *-tā* originally terminating in a long vowel. That Classical Arabic has not preserved traces of this long vowel is insignificant. Thus, in the perfect suffix of the second person plural traces of a long final vowel have been preserved in Classical Arabic in the masculine (*katabtumūhu*), but not in the feminine; though, as demonstrated by Nöldeke (1904, pp. 24–25), it terminated in a long vowel as well.

7. See, e.g., Bauer-Leander, 1922, p. 411.

(p. 128) 8. See Blau (forthcoming a, p. 2).

9. For particulars see Blau (1965, pp. 168–169).

10. As were prepositional phrases in the case of Romance languages (see Havers, 1931, p. 198) and word order in the case of Arabic.

disappearance of the case ending and thus becoming one of the factors of its disappearance,[11] and partly due to the redundancy of the case endings.[12]

This conditioning of the omission of the case endings is reflected in their preservation in adverbial function, attested in both Semitic[13] and non-Semitic[14] languages. Whereas in general the case endings were redundant, in the special case of adverbial function they continued to be necessary markers of this grammatical category and were therefore preserved. This is the case in Biblical Hebrew in adverbs terminating in *-ām*:[15] *ḥinnām* ("in vain"), *yômām* ("by day"), *rêqām* ("in vain").

2.3.1

Another case of the preservation of an otherwise disappearing sound in adverbial function in Biblical Hebrew is the rather marginal preservation of *-at*, which otherwise (cf. Section 2.2) shifted to *-ā*: *moḥŏrāt* ("the morrow"), frequently used as a noun, presumably to be interpreted as an original adverb,[16] further *rabbat* ("much"), which as an adverb is attested in Psalms only, yet its occurrence in late prose as a noun ("many," 2Chr 30:17, 18) demonstrates that it was not limited to poetry. It stands to reason that this *-at* ending in adverbial function is due to multilinear development, to the preservation of the *-at* of the feminine ending, because it was reinterpreted as marking adverbial function and therefore preserved, and further to the existence of an original adverbial ending *-at* of different origin, which, in the light of Arabic *rubbata/rabbata* ("sometimes") is, at least in the case of *rabbat*, quite likely,[17] even if in Hebrew it reflects Aramaic influence.

3.

Yet the not strictly phonetic conditioning of sound change may be, it seems, demonstrated in more conspicuous cases as well. According to the view of the

11. See Havers (1931, p. 198).

12. For the problem of the redundancy of case endings cf. Blau (1977a, pp. 4–8).

13. Cf. for Arabic Blau (1965, pp. 170, 216, 217); for Aramaic Bauer-Leander (1927, pp. 205b, 254o, 244r).

14. See, e.g., Anttila (1972, p. 80).

15. It stands to reason that these words did not terminate in a simple accusative, but (also) in an adverbial ending. This is indicated by the El-Amarna transcription (137:21) *ri-ḳa-mi* exhibiting a final short vowel. The omission of such a final short vowel in Hebrew is also demonstrated by the oxytone stress of these words (see Blau, 1976, p. 30).

16. Cf. Brockelmann (1908–13, I, p. 409, where also instances for Aramaic are cited), and Bauer-Leander (1927, p. 254o and p. 225r, where a different and unconvincing explanation is provided).

17. See Barth (1913, p. 18 and 1913–14, p. 307).

strict conditioning of phonetic changes, a phonetic change affects the sound concerned in all the positions in which it is operating. Let us assume that in a certain language the allophones A_1 and A_2 exist. Later (stage II), another sound (B) shifts to A_1: B>A_1. Now (stage III) another sound change affects A_1, let us say: A_1>C. According to the view that sound changes only require reference to phonetic information, A_1 has to shift to C in all its occurrences, both in environments in which it alternated with A_2 and in those in which it developed from B. Yet I would like to submit that this is not the only possibility. The other is that the sound shift A_1>C affects only the phoneme A_1 that arose from B, without changing A_1 that is the allophone of A_2. In this case, the speaker differentiates between the phoneme A_1, which is not restricted to a special environment, and the allophone A_1, which he recognizes by its restriction to special environments and its alternation with A_2 in other environments. Synchronically, therefore, I am inclined to posit for stage II a phoneme A_1 (the historical continuation of B) and the allophones A_1 and A_2.

3.1

It seems that (late) Biblical Hebrew reflects such a case of identical phonemes and allophones with only the phonemes being affected by a sound change. It can be proved[18] that, at least at the time of the Septuagint translation of the Pentateuch, Biblical Hebrew still possessed *ǵ* and *ḫ* (which later shifted to ʿ and *ḥ* respectively). We do not, to be sure, know the exact date of the spirantization of *(b), g, (d), k, (p,t)*.[19] It stands to reason, however, that it had already taken place at the time of the translation of the Septuagint. Accordingly, one has to posit that besides the phonemes /*ǵ*/and /*ḫ*/, the allophones [*ǵ*] and [*ḵ*] (of /*g*/ and /*k*/) also already existed, although the latter were practically identical to the former. Later, when the phonemes *ǵ* and *ḫ* shifted to ʿ and *ḥ*, the phonetically identical allophones were not affected.

3.2

This interpretation of the facts may be buttressed by Eastern Syriac and Modern Hebrew. In Eastern Syriac,[20] *ḥ* has shifted to *ḫ*, and, as is ususal, post-vocalic *b, g, d, k, p, t* have been spirantized. Yet the coexistence of *ḫ* and spirantized *k* has not led to any significant confusion between the two. Similarly, in literary and colloquial standards of Modern Hebrew as used by Ashkenazim *w* has shifted to *v* and *ḥ* to *x*, alongside *v*/*x* which are the

* 18. See Blau (forthcoming b).
19. See Kutscher (1964–65, pp. 49–58).
20. See Blau (1970, p. 16).

allophones[21] of *b*/*k*, respectively. Nevertheless, this has not led to any significant amount of confusion between the phonemes *v*/*x* and the phonetically identical allophones.

4. *

On the other hand, I think that recent proposals as to the excessive abstractness of sound changes are exaggerated. *Inter alĭa,* it has been claimed that grammatical classes, as parts of speech, have as such direct influence on sound change.[22] It is very difficult for me to accept such a claim. It is, in my opinion, hard to imagine that a sound shift should be blocked in a certain grammatical category without any historical, phonetic, or functional reasons, or analogical formation. In the following, I shall cite two cases exhibiting different phonetic treatment of grammatical categories in Biblical Hebrew, for which, on closer inspection, however, functional reasons or analogical formation may be made very likely. I am of course well aware that this does not refute the possibility of the influence of grammatical categories on sound change. It cautions one, however, against rushing into unwarranted conclusions.[23]

4.1

In Biblical Hebrew, as is well known, absolute nouns in stressed closed syllables exhibit long vowels, in contrast to the verbs which exhibit short *

21. In my opinion, in the literary and colloquial standards of Modern Hebrew occlusive and spirantized *b, g, d, k, p, t* have to be analyzed as allophones and the spirantized allophones *ḇ ḵ* (as against *v*<*w*; *ḥ*<*ḥ*) must not be analyzed as separate phonemes. Although oppositions such as *sapa* (<*sappa*, "couch"): *sap̱a* (<*śāpā*, "lip, language") do exist, in cases like *piḵa* ("your mouth")/*bəpiḵa* ("in your mouth") or *tap̱ar* ("he sewed")/*yitpor* ("he will sew") *p-p̱* are felt by the educated speaker at least as allophones. In fact, I advocate a more "abstract" phonemic analysis, or the mixing of levels between phonemics and morphophonemics; though this does by no means indicate that I plead for generative phonology. At any rate, I have the impression that too much attention has been paid to Modern Hebrew substandard, at the expense of Modern Hebrew standard (though, of course, the linguistic analysis of Modern Hebrew substandard is perfectly legitimate).

22. See, e. g., Postal (1968, pp. 231ff). In the domain of Semitics this view was mainly upheld by the Italian school of Semitics; see recently Aspesi (1977), who quotes Garbini several times; further Garbini (1978, p. 52).

23. Even Anttila (1972, p. 79), who states that "one frequently finds a different treatment of the same sound on the categorial verb-noun axis," prudently remarks that "perhaps in some such cases we have different chronology rather than real grammatical conditioning." And Aspesi, in the conclusion of his paper (1977, p. 401), propounds the view that the alleged sound shift *s*(*š*)>*h* did not operate outside certain morphological classes, because this would have involved too far reaching changes in the phonological system. Although this argument is hardly convincing, it shows that even Aspesi felt discomfort at the assumption that a sound shift be limited to a certain morphological class without any (in this case, functional) reason.

vowels in this position. It stands to reason[24] that the different behavior of verbs is due to the fact that final short vowels disappeared in verbs before they were dropped in absolute nouns, so that the vowel between the second and third radical consonants came comparatively early to stand in a closed syllable and was not lengthened. The reason[25] for the earlier dropping of the final short vowels in verbs was that they were functionally redundant. Whereas the final short vowels in nouns were the only markers of the case endings: the *-a* ending of the third person singular masculine perfect was altogether redundant, not standing in any opposition; and the *-u* ending of the indicative **yaqtulu* in contrast to the zero ending of the jussive **yaqtul* was redundant, since the opposition indicative: jussive was sufficiently indicated by the different stress, i.e. **yaqtúlu*:**yáqtul*.[26] In other words: in the case of the dropping of the case endings in the absolute noun there was paradigmatic resistance to the omission of the final short vowels (see Section 2 above), but in verbs the final short vowels were either totally redundant or not the sole markers of the "moods,"
* and therefore they were affected by the regular sound change.

4.2

The sound structure of the imperative, as it is exhibited in *qal*, is exceptional. According to the general penultimate stress that once prevailed in Biblical Hebrew,[27] one would have expected **qútul*/**qítil*/**qátal*, which could not have regularly shifted to **qətúl*/**qətíl*/**qətál*. Again, one should not simply resort to the assumption of grammatical conditioning. Some scholars attributed the special behavior of the imperative to the loss of stress of this grammatical category.[28] This, however, is unlikely,[29] not only because one would then have expected similar behavior in the imperative with pronominal suffixes (as *kotḇēhū*), which is not the case, but also because the imperative in *nip̄ʿal (hiššāmēr)* is normally stressed and exhibits pretonic lengthening. The

(pp. 273–74) 24. See for particulars Blau (1968, pp. 36–37), where (in note 44) it is refuted that the different vocalization was due to either different stress or to the rare occurrence of verbs in pausal position. Cf. also Blau (1977–78, p. 147).

25. The reasons adduced by Blau (1968, p. 37, note 45) are not convincing.

(p. 275) 26. This difference in stress stems from a period in which penultimate stress generally prevailed. The assumption of such a stress period is, in my opinion, the most powerful explanation of the phonetics of Biblical Hebrew, and is the cardinal point upon which the understanding of Biblical vocalization pivots (cf. Blau, 1976, p. 30). For the reason of the preservation of the final *-a*
(pp. 262–63) of the cohortative **aqtula* cf. Blau (1977b, pp. 29–30).

27. See the preceding note.

28. So, e.g., Bergsträsser (1918–29, I, p. 115). For the shortening of the imperative in general see Horn (1923, pp. 32–40).

29. Cf. also Blau (1977–78, p. 149).

simplest explanation of the special behavior of the imperative *qal* is that it was restructured according to the imperfect (*kəṯōḇ* according to *yiḵṯōḇ*; cf. also *qûm*, rather than the expected **qom*, restructured according to *yāqûm*, and *qûmî*, etc.; cf. also Arabic *('u)ktub*, restructured according to the imperfect *yaktub*-). At any rate, one need not assume grammatical conditioning of these vowel structures.

5.

I have tried to show that sound change is not always strictly phonetically conditioned. I have demonstrated on the strength of biblical material that functionally significant sounds may be preserved in positions in which they are, as a rule, omitted (Section 2), and that phonemes are apt to behave differently from phonetically identical allophones (Section 3). On the other hand, I do not consent to the often expressed opinion that sound changes may be limited to certain grammatical classes to the exclusion of others, without any historical, phonetic, or functional reasons, or analogical formation. I am convinced that accurate analysis of such alleged cases is apt to discover special reasons that led to the restriction of a certain sound change to a special grammatical class. In Section 4 two such alleged cases occurring in Biblical Hebrew were treated, and the reasons underlying them analyzed.

BIBLIOGRAPHY

Anttila, R. 1972. *An Introduction to Historical and Comparative Linguistics*. New York.

Aspesi, F. 1977. "Sistema fonematico 'complessivi' e sistemi fonematici 'morfologici': un' interpretazione di alcuni fatti semitici." *Istituto Orientale di Napoli: Annali* 37:393–401.

Barth, J. 1913. *Die Pronominalbildung in den semitischen Sprachen*. Leipzig.

———. 1913–14. "Assyrisches *iš*, hebr.- aram. *t* als Adverbialendung." *Zeitschrift für Assyriologie und verwandte Gebiete* 28:307–309.

Bauer, H. and P. Leander. 1922. *Historische Grammatik der hebräischen Sprache des Alten Testaments*. Halle.

———. 1927. *Grammatik des Biblisch-Aramäischen*. Halle.

Bergsträsser, G. 1918–29. *Hebräische Grammatik*. Leipzig.

Blanc, H. 1964. *Communal Dialects in Baghdad*. Cambridge, Mass.

Blau, J. 1965. *The Emergence and Linguistic Background of Judaeo-Arabic*. Oxford.

Blau, J. 1968. "Some Difficulties in the Reconstruction of 'Proto-Hebrew' and 'Proto-Canaanite'." *In Memoriam P. Kahle, Beiheft zur Zeitschrift für die alttestamentliche Wissenschaft,* 103:29–43. Berlin.

_____. 1970. "Bəʻayot bahistorya šel hallašon haʻiḇrit." *In Memory of G. Alon, Essays in Jewish History and Philology,* pp. 9–23. Tel Aviv.

_____. 1976. *A Grammar of Biblical Hebrew.* Wiesbaden.

_____. 1977a. "The Beginnings of the Arabic Diglossia, A Study of the Origins of Neoarabic." *Afroasiatic Linguistics,* vol. 4, issue 4. Malibu.

_____. 1977b. "Marginalia Semitica." *Israel Oriental Studies* 7:14–32.

_____. 1977–78. "'Osep maʼamarav šel mizraḥan ḥašuḇ." *Ləšonenu* 42:146–151.

_____. Forthcoming a. "The Parallel Development of the Feminine Ending *-at* in Hebrew and Some Semitic Languages."

_____. Forthcoming b. "On Polyphony in Biblical Hebrew." *Proceedings of the Israel Academy of Sciences and Humanities.*

Brockelmann, C. 1908–13. *Grundriss der vergleichenden Grammatik der semitischen Sprachen.* Berlin.

Garbini, G. 1978. "Pensieri su Ebla (ovvero: le uova di Babilonia)." *Istituto Orientale di Napoli* 38:41–52.

Grotzfeld, H. 1964. *Laut- und Formenlehre des Damaszenisch-Arabischen.* Wiesbaden.

Havers, W. 1931. *Handbuch der erklärenden Syntax.* Heidelberg.

Horn, W. 1923. *Sprachkörper und Sprachfunktion²*, Leipzig.

Kutscher, Y. 1964–65. "Meḥqar haššemit haccəponit-maʻaraḇit bəyameynu." *Ləšonenu* 29:47–58, 115–128.

Lehmann, W. P. and Y. Malkiel. 1968. *Directions for Historical Linguistics.* Austin, Texas.

Nöldeke, T. 1904. *Beiträge zur semitischen Sprachwissenschaft.* Strassburg.

Postal, P. M. 1968. *Aspects in Phonological Theory.* New York.

Szemerényi, O. 1968. "Methodology of Genetic Linguistics." *Methoden der Sprachwissenschaft, (Enzyklopädie der geisteswissenschaftlichen Arbeits-methoden, 4).* Eds. H. Schnelle *et al.* München-Wien.

Additions and Corrections

to **p. 27**.*5*: See p. 262.§5.2

to **p. 28**.*2*: As well known, the nominal patterns *paᶜl*/*piᶜl* are mixed up, because of the action of Philippi's law and attenuation. On the other hand, the verbal patterns **yigl* > *yigɛl* (jussive of *qal*) and **yagl* > *yɛgɛl* (jussive of *hifᶜīl*) are clearly differentiated, presumably through paradigmatic pressure, to distinguish the two verbal patterns from each other (*pace* H. Birkeland, *Akzent und Vokalismus im Althebräischen*, Oslo 1940, p. 28).

to **p. 30**.*n. 18*: See 'On Polyphony in Biblical Hebrew'. *Proceedings of the Israel Academy of Science and Humanities*, 6:2, Jerusalem 1982, pp. 74–75. Cf. also the fact that in the dialect of Ḥassānīya in Mauritania *ṯ* appears only in some positions unvoiced, viz. in word final, in immediate contact with an unvoiced consonant and when doubled, as a rule, however, voiced, yet without ever being mistaken for *ḏ*; see D. Cohen, *Le Dialecte arabe* Ḥassānīya *de Mauritanie*, Paris 1963, p. 13, and, in his wake, Fischer & Jastrow, p. 251.–6ff.

to **p. 31**.*§4*: In the dialect of Jibla in the Arabian Peninsula the *a* of the nominal pattern *faᶜil* is preserved (*hazil* 'emaciated'), yet in the same verbal pattern (perfect of first verbal theme) it changes to *i* (*hizil* 'he became emaciated'); see Fischer & Jastrow, p. 107:19ff. Could it be that the assimilation of *a* to *i* started in those conjugated forms of the perfect in which it was unstressed, to be then transferred to stressed *a*?

to **p. 31**.*–2*: Read 'in stressed closed final syllables' for 'in stressed closed syllables'.

to **p. 32**.*§4.1*, *end*: In Syriac, doubled final vowels are sometimes preserved in nouns, yet always simplified in verbs (Nöldeke, *Syriac* 18–19). It stands to reason that the fact that verbs *mediae infirmae* in Syriac as a rule do not double their second radical (except when preceded and followed by a short vowel; Nöldeke, *Syriac* 122), did not enable the analogical restitution of the doubling, in contradistinction to nouns.

On Pausal Lengthening, Pausal Stress Shift, Philippi's Law and Rule Ordering in Biblical Hebrew[1]

* ABSTRACT: Philippi's Law operated much later than generally assumed. It was preceded by:

1. Pausal lengthening; and
2. Pausal stress shift to the last syllable.

Therefore, *pataḥ* that arose through Philippi's Law from *i* did not change through pausal lengthening to *qamaṣ*. For example, pausal *wayyílik, which through pausal stress shift became *wayyilík, ultimately became *wayyēláḵ* with final *pataḥ* rather than *qamaṣ*, because pausal lengthening had ceased operating. Similarly, *milk, shifting through Philippi's Law to *malk, did not change to *mālk (>*māleḵ), but remained *malk (>*méleḵ*), because pausal lengthening had ceased operating.

1. The strict application of sound shifts and rigorous rule ordering is apt to clarify the conditions of phonetic behavior, which, *prima facie*, seems to be without any conditioning. Since, however, the regular behavior of sound shifts is affected by analogy, the results obtained are sometimes rather intricate.

1.1. Our starting point for the understanding of biblical phonology is the assumption that, in biblical Hebrew, general penult stress once prevailed.[2] This theory, in my opinion, is the most powerful explanation avail-

1. I would like to thank my friend Professor Richard Steiner, who, acting as moderator of a symposium on stress in biblical Hebrew at Yeshiva University, New York, in December 1979, asked me about pausal *wayyēlák* as against the context form *wayyélek*, and so initiated this paper. I am grateful to him also for his sympathetic attitude during later stages. My friend Simon A. Hopkins read an early version of this paper and called my attention, *inter alia*, to the omission of an appropriate reference to Sarauw (1939). Needless to say, I alone am responsible for the views expressed.

(pp. 202ff.) 2. See Blau (1976, p. 30), further e.g. Blau (1971a, pp. 18ff.), where (p. 19, note 8)
(pp. 104ff) additional literature is cited, further Blau (1978, pp. 91ff.).

able; with a single assumption it accounts for the position of stress in the majority of words, as attested in the later stage of biblical Hebrew, preserved by the Masorah. Words which have preserved their final vowels, have, in fact, kept their penult stress in general (e.g. *'ākálnû* 'we ate', *qā́mû* 'they rose') or at least in pause (e.g. *'ākā́lā* 'she ate', *šîrékā* 'your song'), whereas those stressed on their ultima, as a rule, have lost their final vowel and now end in a consonant (as *dābā́r* < **dabáru* 'thing', *'ākál* < **'akála* 'he ate'). Pausal forms like *'ākā́lā*, *šîrékā*, as against context forms like *'ākəlā́*, *šîrəkā́*, show that the original place of stress was preserved more faithfully in pause in words ending in a vowel, whereas in context it shifted to the ultima.

2. Yet, contrary to the general tendency towards the preservation of penult stress in pause in vowel-final words and its secondary shift to ultima in context, a minority of examples is attested in consonant-final words ending with original penult stress in context as against secondary ultima stress in pause, for example:[3]

Non-Pausal		*Pausal*
wayyā́šob	'and he returned'	*wayyāšṓb*
wayyā́mot	'and he died'	*wayyāmṓt*
wayyḗšeb	'and he sat'	*wayyēšḗb*
**wayyiggā́mel*	'and he was weaned'	*wayyiggāmál*
**wayyinnā́peš*[4]	'and he rested'	*wayyinnāpáš*
wayyḗlek	'and he went'	*wayyēlák*
wayyḗred	'and he went down'	*wayyērád*
wayyṓmer	'and he said'	*wayyōmár*
wayyṓkal	'and he ate'	*wayyōkál*[5]

3. The words cited can easily be found with the help of a concordance; words not attested as such in the Bible, yet to be reconstructed as such from other words of the same form, are (also) marked by an asterisk. The use of a macron and a circumflex is in accordance with the method of transliteration used in *Hebrew Annual Review* and does not indicate that the vowels marked are indeed (historically) long or that those unmarked are in fact (historically) short.

4. As a matter of fact, the context form of this word has been influenced by its pausal form, being stressed on its ultima, i.e. only *wayyinnapḗš* exists.

5. For this exceptional pausal stress, cf. e.g. Böttcher (1866–68, I, p. 294, par. 489.3); Ewald (1870, p. 192, par. 92f); König (1881–97, II, p. 521); Brockelmann (1908–13, I, p. 106, par. 43p.κ.γγ), who, however, considers the ultima stress of the pausal forms to be more original; Bergsträsser (1918–29, I, p. 163, par. 29i), in whose opinion the pausal stress on the ultima is secondary, assuming that first, under circumstances difficult to specify, the original penult stress passed to the ultima and was later limited to pausal forms; Bauer-Leander (1922, p. 186, par. 13g, h), who also consider this pausal stress to be secondary, in their opinion being due to the influence of the imperfect form without consecutive *wāw* on the less frequent pausal forms with *wāw* (it is, however, difficult to understand why the influence of the *wāw*-less forms should have been stronger than that of the context forms

2.1. The last six examples adduced in par. 2 are exceptional in another sense as well: the stressed syllable in pause is short, containing *pataḥ*[6] rather than *qamaṣ*: *wayyiggāmál, wayyināpáš, wayyēlák, wayyērád, wayyōmár, wayyōkál*. This feature of stressed pausal *pataḥ* is attested in other cases as well in which the stress of the *pataḥ* is original:[7] *bat* 'daughter', *gat* 'winepress', *'aṭ* 'softly', *'ad* 'perpetuity' (exhibiting *segol* after connecting *wāw*: *wā'ed*), *bāz* 'spoil' (but Num 31:32 *bāz*), *qaš* 'straw' alongside of *qāš*, *sap* 'threshold' alongside of *sāp*, *mas* 'corvée' alongside of *mās*; Gen 16:8 *bôráḥat* 'fleeing', Ps 107:35 *máyim* 'water' with *'etnaḥ* not preceded by *'ole wəyored*, whereas Prov 30:16 *máyim* with *'etnaḥ* follows *'ole wəyored* (yet at the end of the verse in Ps 107:35 *māyim* with *qamaṣ* occurs) and, accordingly, one *may* interpret also the first *segol* of the pausal segolate type *mélek* as originally short, since it corresponds to the *pataḥ* of *bôráḥat/máyim*. This is especially so since, in the Babylonian vocalization, pausal forms of the type *dâšan, mârad, 'âšar* (but also *'ā́šar*), *tip'árat* (but also *tip'ārat*) are attested with historically short *a* in the stressed pausal syllable;[8] *tēláknā* 'they (fem.) will go', *tiššākábnā* 'they

---

with consecutive *wāw*); Lambert (1938, p. 66, par. 154), who regards the pausal stress as more original; Joüon (1947, p. 80, par. 32e); Meyer (1966–72, I, p. 92, par. 21.3b), who, similar to Blau (1976, p. 40, par. 11.5.1), does not account for the passing of the original penult stress to the ultima in pause. Sarauw (1939, pp. 80, 85), who deals with *yēlḗk/yḗlák*, rather than with *wayyḗlek/wayyēlák*, posits original *yēlḗk* for pause, *yēlák* for context.

6. Long *pataḥ* is very exceptional, cf. e.g. Bergsträsser (1918–29, I, p. 60). Aartun (1967), who deals with short *a* in stressed syllables in general, does not treat the special problem of pausal *pataḥ*. Cf. also Blau (1968).

7. Cf. Böttcher (1866–68, I, pp. 297–98, par. 492) and Ewald (1870, p. 192, par. 92f), who both call attention to the *pataḥ* stemming from *ē/i*, as do also Lambert (1938, p. 65) and König (1881–97, II, pp. 534, 537–38). See also Bergsträsser (1918–29, pp. 160–61), who deals with the differences between the Tiberian and the Babylonian vocalizations; Bauer-Leander (1922, pp. 232–33), who regard these pausal forms as original context forms, yet treat monosyllabic nouns separately; Joüon (1947, p. 79, par. 32b), where, however, pausal *tikbádnā* is erroneous; Sarauw (1939, pp. 77f). I have not especially dealt with cases of *'etnaḥ* after *'ole wəyored*, since, not marking the division of a verse into two halves, this *'etnaḥ* does not always entail pausal lengthening (as it occurs sometimes even with *'etnaḥ* not following *'ole wəyored* in Psalms, Job, and Proverbs; yet such cases were expressly mentioned).

8. For the Babylonian forms, see Bergsträsser (1918–29, p. 161, par. 29), Yeivin (1968, p. 193), and Yeivin (1972–73, p. 33, par. 44). On the other hand, as shown by the cited sources, Babylonian (originally) long *ā* may correspond to the first Tiberian *segol* of segolates, as Babylonian *rā́ša'* to Tiberian *réša'*, Babylonian *tā́ben* to Tiberian *tében* in pause, the differences being due to various analogical formations. The extent of analogical formations among segolates is also reflected by the limited number of Babylonian *qēṭal* forms, corresponding to Tiberian *qḗṭel*, see Yeivin (1972–73, p. 189, par. 477); cf. also Sarauw (1939, pp. 85–86); and in general Leander (1912, p. 190). For Samaritan Hebrew, see Ben Ḥayyim (1977, p. 188, par. 4.1.3.4). Cf. further Tiberian forms like *nḗpel, sḗter, šḗbeṭ* in context, as against pausal *nā́pel, sā́ter, šā́beṭ*, or *nébel/nḗbel* in context, *nā́bel* in pause, further e.g. *néṣaḥ/nḗṣaḥ* in context, in pause always *néṣaḥ*, or *yḗša'*, even with small disjunctive accent (and in pause) *yḗša'*.

will be ravished', *tə'akkâsnā* 'they will tinkle', *tiśbâ'nā* 'they will be satisfied', *tiqšâbnā* 'they will pay attention', *teḥĕrâšnā* 'they will be deaf', *hētáz* 'he cut off', *hēpár* 'he broke', *qāmâl* 'it decayed', *wāmâttî* 'and I shall die' (as against pausal *mā́tnû*), *zāqántî* 'I have become old', Prov 24:30 *'ābártî* 'I have passed' (with *'etnaḥ* without preceding *'ole wəyored*, and similarly in the following three cases: Job 34:5 *ṣādáqtî* 'I am righteous', Job 42:6 *wəniḥámtî* 'and I repent', Ps 102:26 *yāsádtā*)—further *'ākáltî* 'I ate', *niṣṣálnû* 'we have been saved', *dibbártā* 'you have spoken', *dibbârtî* 'I have spoken', *higgâdtā* 'you have told', *higgâḏtî* 'I have told', *šibbártā* 'you have broken', *miggârtā* 'you have hurled'; *hiṣṣálnû* 'we have saved', *ḥērâptā* 'you have reproached', *heḥĕrâmtî* 'I have banned', *heḥĕrâmnû* 'we have banned', *hošbártî* 'I have been shattered'; *hāšáb* 'bring back!', *hāšá'* 'besmear', *tālán* 'lodge!' (so after *'al* 'not' expressing prohibition in pause, Judg 19:20, yet also in context in Job 17:2, used as an indicative), *ləhābár* 'to purify', *'al tə'aḥár* 'do not delay' (three times, as against Eccl 5:3 *'al tə'aḥḗr* in context), *wayyaggáš* 'and he brought', Job 13:21 *harḥáq* 'remove!' (with *'etnaḥ* without preceding *'ole wəyored*), *'al teḥĕráš* 'do not be silent' (but also *teḥĕraš*).[9] *

3. The pausal forms cited in par. 2 and even more particularly in par. 2.1, are, *prima facie*, a medley of examples without a common denominator. Yet, in our opinion, they can all be understood by paying careful attention to the relative chronology (diachronic rule ordering) and conditioning of the relevant sound changes. Since, however, some of these rules are affected by widespread analogy, the results, as generally in language (see par. 1), are not quite clear-cut.

3.1. As we have observed (see par. 2), in a minority of cases the original penult stress is preserved in context forms only, whereas the pausal forms have ultima stress. All the examples have a closed ultima; accordingly, we can record the sound shift: IN PAUSE THE PENULT STRESS SHIFT-

9. For various verbal forms exhibiting *a* in the Babylonian vocalization, cf. Yeivin (1968, pp. 470, 506). I do not count *pataḥ*, where even the context form should have exhibited *qamaṣ*, the most conspicuous case being *'amīlâm* 'I shall annihilate(?) them' in Ps 118:10, 11, 12 where even the context form should have terminated in *-lām* (with *qamaṣ*). Cf. also the exceptional context form Neh 9:5 *mərômâm* with final *pataḥ*. Are these forms due to dissimilation of the Tiberian *qamaṣ*, i.e. *å*, from the *m* (just as *yåm* 'sea' even in construct and *ṣåb* 'lizard'; 'litter' are due to assimilation), i.e. the *pataḥ* is originally long (just as the *qamaṣ* of *yåm* at least in construct has to be considered originally short)? This, however, is already outside the scope of this paper, as are nouns which exhibit stressed *pataḥ* (originally long, it seems) due to assimilation to a following ' (type *'arbá'* 'four', see Blau (1968).

ED TO THE CLOSED ULTIMA,[10] but was preserved when the ultima was open.

3.2. The shift of the pausal stress to closed ultima (par. 3.1.), however, does not account for the short stressed pausal syllable (par. 2.1, beginning). Of necessity, we have to posit that THE PAUSAL STRESS SHIFT TO CLOSED ULTIMA IS LATER THAN PAUSAL LENGTHENING, since only this assumption explains why these syllables were not affected by pausal lengthening. When pausal stress had reached the closed ultima, pausal lengthening had ceased operating; accordingly, the closed ultima, now affected by pausal stress, continued having a short vowel.

3.3. We have not yet accounted for the reason that many forms cited in par. 2 exhibit *pataḥ* in pause as against *segol* (ultimately stemming from *i*) in context: *wayyiggāmál*, *wayyinnāpáš*, *wayyēlák*, *wayyērád*, *wayyōmár*. Since in these forms *a* for original *i* occurs in closed stressed syllables, and it is according to Philippi's Law that *i* shifted to *a* in closed stressed syllables, we have to posit that PHILIPPI'S LAW CONTINUED OPERATING DURING THE PAUSAL STRESS SHIFT TO CLOSED ULTIMA.

3.4. Accordingly, first pausal lengthening ceased operating, then the pausal stress shift to closed ultima occurred, at which stage Philippi's Law Law was still operating.[11] This assumption fully accounts for the behavior of the pausal forms cited in par. 2. Original **wayyílik*[12] (short imperfect

10. In all the examples cited in par. 2 the penult is open. However, it stands to reason that pausal stress shifted to a closed ultima even from a closed penult, see par. 4.1.4, note 27.

11. This does not, however, imply that Philippi's Law *started* operating at this stage only. *Obiter dictum*, it *may* well be that Philippi's Law continued operating longer than generally assumed, viz. even when final short vowels were dropped in the absolute. Generally, it is claimed that during the operation of Phillipi's Law, nouns in the absolute still preserved the case vowels, whereas in construct they had already dropped them. This claim is based on absolute forms like *zāqḗn* 'old' still exhibiting *ē*, allegedly because at the time of the action of Philippi's Law it still had the form **zaqinu*, *i* being an open syllable; see e.g. Blau (1976, p. 36, par. 9.3.4). As a matter of fact, nouns not ending in a double consonant (like **bitt>*batt>bat* 'daughter') never ended in a short stressed *i* in a closed syllable to be affected by Philippi's Law. Before the case endings were dropped, the *i* occurred in an open syllable (type **zaqínu*); at the same time as they were dropped, the *i* was compensatorily lengthened, type *zāqēn* (cf. Blau 1976, p. 31) and therefore was not affected by Philippi's Law, even if it still operated, because it did not influence long vowels.

12. For the sake of simplicity I write *wayyilik* rather than *wayyalik*, without implying that the (original) *a* had already at that stage shifted to *i* (presumably by assimilation). It is outside the scope of this paper to treat the problem whether the *segol* of *wayyēlek* derives from *i* or, as Ben-Ḥayyim (1978, p. 103) thinks, from *a*.

with "conversive" *wāw*), for example, first shifted in pause (where, by pausal lengthening, it had already become **wayyḗlik*) to **wayyēlík*, then becoming, by dint of Philippi's Law, *wayyēlák*. The final short *a* was not lengthened, since pausal lengthening had already ceased operating.

4. Contextual forms with *a* from original *i* are to be explained as the result of analogy. Thus, for example, it stands to reason that the characteristic vowel of the imperfect *qal* of *'.k.l.* 'to eat' was *i*, as preserved in several pausal forms, e.g., *yokḗlû*.[13] Accordingly, one expects the context form to be **wayyôkel*, rather than *wayyôkal*. The latter is due to analogy, *inter alia*, of the pausal form, and the same applies, for example, to non-pausal *tērád, tālán*.[14]

4.1. Analogical formation interfered extensively with the words cited in par. 2.1. We shall treat them in groups:

4.1.1 Monosyllabic nouns with *a* originally ending in a double consonant

Some of these nouns, no doubt, exhibit original *i*: *bat*, derived from the masculine **bin* 'son'; *gat*, as indicated by the cuneiform proper nouns *Gimtu, Ginti, Giti*; presumably also *'ad*, as indicated by the *segol* of *wā'ed*, which arises from *i* after laryngals and pharyngals;[15] and *sap*, cognate with Akkadian *sippu* (also 'threshold'). On the other hand, *mas* seems to have original *a*, in the light of El-Amarna *massa*, and so also *qaš*, in light of Aramaic *qaššā*, borrowed into Arabic as *qašš*, and cf. also middle Hebrew *qaššīn*; Syriac *qeššā* does not disprove an original *a*, since the *e* may be due to assimilation to the *š*. Nevertheless, it is quite noteworthy that (perhaps with the exception of *qaš*, if *qaššīn* is, indeed, the correct pronunciation) *all* these nouns have *i* preceding suffixes and that I have not found a single noun that has *a* preceding suffixes and *a* in pause. Accordingly, it stands to reason that the occurrence of *a* (as against *ā*) in pause is somehow connected with the original pattern *qill* (*mas* and *qaš*

13. It is beyond the scope of this paper to tackle the problem of whether the *i/e* is original or rather arose by dissimilation from *u*: **'okul>*'okil*.

14. It stands to reason that *i* in final closed stressed syllables of verbs in context shifted to *e* (*segol*), rather than to *a*, see Blau (1971b, pp. 155–56), and Blau (1976, pp. 36–37, (pp. 177–78) note 2). Therefore, these context forms cannot be considered to reflect the exclusive impact of Philippi's Law. For additional cases of the intrusion of *a* into context forms, cf. the Babylonian vocalization of forms like *hapqad* or *yēlak*, see Yeivin (1968, pp. 470, 506, par. 23.27, 30.2), and Yeivin (1972–73, pp. 100, 109, par. 234, 265). A form like pausal *wayyḗšeb*, rather than *wayyēšáb*, is due to the impact of the contextual form.

15. This interpretation, in my opinion, is much more likely than if we were to posit original **wā'ad*, i.e. Tiberian *wà'ad*, and to assume that the *a* changed to *e* through the impact of the preceding *å*. As a rule, it is only a *following å* that changes a *preceding a* to *e* (type *heḥåg<*haḥåg* 'the feast').

being due to analogy). The question of how this connection arose can be answered by investigating the relative chronology of Philippi's Law and pausal lengthening:

a) Let us assume, for argument's sake, that Philippi's Law preceded pausal lengthening. In this case the original pattern *qill* would have become *qall* in both context and pause by the influence of Philippi's Law to lengthen later in pause to *qāll*. Accordingly, original *qill* would have had the following forms: *qall* (in absolute[16] and construct), *qāll* (in pause), *qillīm* (preceding stressed suffix, where Philippi's Law could not apply). These forms would have been identical to the original *qall* forms, except for those preceding stressed suffixes, which would be *qallīm*, etc. This paradigm does not provide an explanation why original *qall* should have a much greater tendency to preserve pausal *qāll*, whereas original *qill* tends towards pausal *qall* (with *pataḥ*). Accordingly, the supposition that Philippi's Law preceded pausal lengthening seems to be fallacious.

b) Therefore let us assume that PAUSAL LENGTHENING PRECEDED THE OPERATION OF PHILIPPI'S LAW. In this case, by pausal lengthening *qill* became *qēll* in pause.[17] Then Philippi's Law began to operate, changing *qill* in both absolute[16] and construct to *qall*, but not affecting pausal *qēll*, because Philippi's Law only applies to SHORT *i*. The differences between original *qall* and *qill* were, accordingly, quite conspicuous:

Original *qall*: *qall* (in absolute and construct), *qāll* (in pause), *qallīm*.
Original *qill*: *qall* (in absolute[16] and construct), *qēll* (in pause), *qillīm*.

Since the difference between pausal *qēll* and contextual *qall* was too great, the pausal form was replaced by the contextual one; and since pausal lengthening ceased being productive (except by analogy), pausal *qall* was not lengthened to **qāll*.

Since this interpretation of the facts is the only one that accounts for pausal *qall* (with *pataḥ*) deriving from original *qill*, we are inclined to posit that pausal lengthening, indeed, preceded Philippi's Law. Since pausal lengthening in Aramaic is rather marginal, presumably to a great extent due to Hebrew influence,[18] it stands to reason that it is not due to

16. As a matter of fact, the absolute *qill*, through Philippi's Law, shifted to *qell* (with
(p. 177) *segol*) rather than to *qall*, see Bergsträsser (1918–29, I, p. 149, par. 26i), Blau (1971b, p. 155), and Blau (1976, pp. 36–37, note 2). Later this *qell* often shifted to *qēll*. At this stage we find nouns of the type *qēn* 'nest', construct *qan*. Then, either the absolute prevailed (type *lēb* 'heart', construct *lēb*), or the construct prevailed (type *bat*, construct *bat*). Since we are dealing with the later type only, for the sake of simplicity I have simply posited *qall* for the absolute.

17. Forms like pausal *šāmēăʿ* 'he heard' demonstrate that *i* shifted to *ē* by pausal lengthening.

18. See Bauer-Leander (1927, p. 23, par. 5d), Segert (1975, pp. 142–43, par. 3.9.9.5).

common Northwest Semitic heritage, but rather a special Hebrew development.[19] Accordingly, the even later Philippi's Law cannot be common Northwest Semitic heritage either, but developed in Hebrew separately.[20]

4.1.2. Segolate nouns

It has been surmised[21] that segolate nouns of the pattern *qéṭel* (with *segol* in both syllables) that are derived from original *qiṭl* have pausal *qéṭel*, whereas the *qéṭel* nouns that are derived from original *qaṭl* form pausal *qā́ṭel*. In the main, this seems to be correct, although analogical formation has greatly interfered with this situation.[22] The different behavior of *qéṭel*<*qiṭl*, and *qéṭel*<*qaṭl* is easily accounted for by the assumption that pausal lengthening preceded Philippi's Law. *Qiṭl* first became **qēṭl* (>*qḗṭel*) in pause, which, because of the long *ē*, was not affected by Philippi's Law; later, in context, *qiṭl* changed through Philippi's Law to *qaṭl* (>*qéṭel*). Original *qaṭl*, on the other hand, through pausal lengthening changed in pause to *qāṭl* (>*qā́ṭel*). Since the dif-

19. *Pace* Sarauw (1939, p. 107).

20. Philippi regarded his law even as Proto-Semitic. See against this assumption Brockelmann (1908–13, I, pp. 147–48), and Bergsträsser (1918–29, p. 149, par. 26h), who considered this sound shift to be Northwest Semitic, as did Leander (1912, p. 186) and Blake (1950, p.83). Sarauw (1939, pp. 76–80), on the other hand, recognized that pausal lengthening preceded Philippi's Law but postponed Philippi's Law until after Origines! Sarauw based his claim on the fact that Origines (and other Greek sources) transcribed *pataḥ* deriving from *i* by *epsilon*, since he interpreted every *epsilon* as reflecting *i*. This, however, is fallacious. Brønno's lists of Tiberian *pataḥ* corresponding to *epsilon* in the Hexapla (1943, pp. 262–280; without agreeing to all his interpretations) clearly show that *epsilon* often transcribes *original pataḥ*; so *'ad* 'till' is transcribed both αδ (Ps 28:9, 46:10; 89:47) and εδ (Ps 18:38); *'al* 'not!' is transcribed by ελ eight times, etc. Though the usual claim that Philippi's Law preceded the dropping of case endings in the absolute is erroneous (see above, note 11), there is no indication for its very late action either. Sarauw (1939, p. 78), to be sure, is correct in demonstrating that it is later than the elision of the glottal stop in *yārētī* 'I was afraid', etc., yet this elision is by no means late, see Blau (1975, p. 68). At any rate, Philippi's Law is earlier than the tendency characteristic of the fourth Proto-Hebrew stress period (for which see Blau 1976, pp. 32–34; this stress period, to be sure, is later than pretonic lengthening, see p. 33 for ultima, rather than penult, stress). During this period original **'áttā* 'now' had become *'attā́*. Yet **'áttā* itself arose from **'íttā* (from *'ēt* 'time' < **'itt*) through the action of Philippi's Law on the originally stressed first syllable, which became unstressed only during the fourth Proto-Hebrew stress period. Accordingly, Philippi's Law is earlier than this stress period.

21. See e.g. Sarauw (1939, pp. 84–85), Joüon (1947, p. 79, par. 32b; p. 236, par. 96c), as against Bauer-Leander (1927, p. 566, par. 72e), who posit pausal *qāṭel* for original *qiṭl* as well.

22. Only faint traces of original contextual *e* (*segol*) alongside of pausal *ē* (*ṣere*) have been preserved: contextual *dibber* 'he spoke' exhibiting final *segol* that arose from *i* through Philippi's Law (see Blau 1971, p. 155), whereas pausal *dibbēr* was not affected by Philippi's (p. 177)
Law, because pausal lengthening preceded it. Similarly, contextual *kibbes* 'he washed' has *segol* (alongside *kibbēs*, to be sure) as against pausal *kibbēs*.

ference between contextual *qaṭl* and pausal *qēṭl* was both quantitative and qualitative, whereas the difference between contextual *qaṭl* and pausal *qāṭl* was quantitative only, the great dissimilarity between *qaṭl* and *qēṭl* was levelled down and contextual *qaṭl* (>*qéṭel*) was used in pause as well. However, this situation, as stated, was greatly changed by widespread analogical formation, which, *inter alia*, entailed pausal *qāṭel* alongside of contextual *qēṭel*, and even more surprisingly, contextual *qēṭel* alongside of pausal *qeṭel* (although we would have expected just the op-
* posite, i.e. contextual *qeṭel* and pausal *qēṭel*).[23]

4.1.3. Plural feminine forms

At least some of the 2nd/3rd person plural feminine forms with *pataḥ* arose from original *i*, as *tiššākabnā*, *tə'akkasnā*, *tēlaknā*, and perhaps also some other *qal* forms, if they exhibit original *i*- imperfects. According to Philippi's Law, only the contextual forms should have exhibited *a*, whereas, because of the preceding pausal lengthening, the pausal forms should have contained *ē*. Since the differences were again both quantitative and qualitative, they were levelled out by the intrusion of the contextual forms into pausal position (and, in other cases, by the prevalence of the pausal forms, as in the case of *pi'el*, in which *ē* prevailed, also through the influence of other members of the paradigm containing *ē*). Similarly, at least many of the perfect forms cited in the next group with stressed pausal *pataḥ* contain original *i*, as *hētaz*, *hēpar*, *dibbartā* and other *hip'īl* and *pi'el* forms,[24] as well as *qal* forms like *qāmal*, *wāmattî*,
* *zāqantî*. *Hošbartî* may be taken as a hint that the passive perfect forms originally had *i* in their second syllable (**huqṭila*, **quṭṭila*,**quṭila*).[25]

4.1.4. Stressed *pataḥ* in closed ultima

The last group comprises words which, BOTH IN CONTEXT AND IN PAUSE, bear stress on *pataḥ* in their closed ultima (and this is the reason I have dealt with them separately and not together with par. 2). Yet it stands to reason that these imperative and shortened imperfect forms (including both jussive and *wāw*-imperfect)[26] were originally stressed on

23. For the extent of analogical formation in segolate nouns, cf. note 8 above.

(pp. 174–80) 24. For original *i* in these verbal forms, cf. Blau (1971b, pp. 152–58).

25. As in Arabic and Aramaic, *pace* Bauer-Leander (1922, p. 284a).

26. The *wāw*-imperfect forms treated in this paragraph have closed penult. This is the reason that, in contradistinction to the forms dealt with in par. 2 above, they are stressed on their final syllables even in context (see below). I have included the construct infinitive *ləhābar* as well in this group because of its formal identity with the imperative (cf. e.g. in verbs III-guttural, forms like *hiššama'*, rather than *hiššāmēă'* 'to be heard'), as if it originally ended in the last radical, rather than in a case ending. It is outside the scope of this paper to examine the question whether this identity is original or rather due to the analogy of the imperative.

their penult. Since these forms from their very beginning ended in their last radical, during the general penult stress period they were stressed on their penult, i.e. **hášib*, **háši'*, **tə'áḥir*,[27] *wayyággiš*,[27] *hárḥiq*. The stress shifted first in pause to the ultima, in accordance with the rule that shifted pausal stress to a closed ultima. The ultima contained *i*,[28] which, in accordance with Philippi's Law, shifted in the now stressed syllable to *a*. Since pausal lengthening had already ceased operating, the short *a* remained in pause. Later, stress shifted to the last syllable in the contextual forms also in forms with closed penult (like *harḥēq*), since words ending in two closed syllables are invariably stressed on their final syllables, i.e. on the second closed syllable. The contextual ultima stress in forms with open penult (like *hāšēb*) is due to the analogy of the ordinary (unshortened) imperfect. Yet the *wāw*-imperfect forms were less affected by this analogy and often preserved their original stress on the penult, when it was open (like *wayyāšeb*).

5. Third person singular feminine *qal* perfect has the pausal form *qāṭā́lā*, originally (after the pausal lengthening) **qaṭā́lat*. If, at the time of the pausal shift to closed final syllables, the final *t* had not yet been deleted, it would have affected **qaṭā́lat* to become **qaṭālát* (and later **qaṭālā́*). Accordingly, the dropping of the final *t* in the third person singular feminine of the perfect precedes the pausal shift to closed final syllables.

5.1. The same applies to the dropping of the (originally consonantal) *-h* of the terminative *-āh*. If, at the time of the pausal shift to closed ultima, nouns of the type *báytah* 'home' still ended in *-h*, they would have been affected by the pausal shift. Accordingly, pausal *bā́ytā*, etc., demonstrate that the dropping of the final *-h* of terminative *-āh* preceded the pausal stress shift.

6. This is the relative chronology established:

6.1. PAUSAL LENGTHENING. This shift preceded the pausal stress shift, since vowels that became stressed by the pausal stress shift were not

27. These examples are of special importance, since, having a closed penult, they reflect the pausal stress shift to closed ultima from *closed* penult, thus demonstrating that this stress shift obtained for both open *and closed* penult, cf. note 10 above. It stands to reason that these pausal forms, due to pausal lengthening, originally had long stressed penult syllables **tə'ā́ḥir*, **wayyā́ggiš*, **hā́rḥiq*). Later, however, when these syllables became unstressed, their long vowel was shortened.

28. If *teḥĕraš* indeed belongs to this group and is not due to the analogy of original *i*-imperfect forms, it was originally **táḥriš*, according to Barth's Law of the imperfect prefixes of *qal*.

affected by it. It also preceded Philippi's Law, since vowels lengthened by pausal lengthening did not undergo the shift *i*>*a* (**mēlk*, for example, did not shift to **mālk*), because this *i* was first lengthened, so that Philippi's Law did not apply to it.

6.2. DROPPING OF THE FINAL *-T* OF THE THIRD PERSON FEMININE SINGULAR PERFECT SUFFIX *-AT* AND OF THE FINAL *-H* OF THE TERMINATIVE *-AH*.

This dropping preceded the pausal stress shift, since otherwise pausal **qatā́lat* and **bā́ytah* would also have been affected by the pausal stress shift. The (relative) chronological relation between the dropping of *-t*/*-h* and pausal lengthening is not established.

6.3. PAUSAL STRESS SHIFT TO CLOSED ULTIMA

6.4. PHILIPPI'S LAW. It was (still) operating after the pausal stress shift, since in words like *wayyēlā́k* it affected the syllable that became stressed by the pausal stress shift. This, however, does not imply that Philippi's Law only started operating after the pausal stress shift.[29]

29. For other particulars of relative chronology related to Philippi's Law see note 20 above.

BIBLIOGRAPHY

Aartun, K. 1967. "Althebräische Nomina mit konserviertem kurzem Vokal in der Hauptdrucksilbe." *Zeitschrift der Deutschen Morgenländischen Gesellschaft* 117:247–65.

Bauer, H. - P. Leander. 1922. *Historische Grammatik der hebräischen Sprache des Alten Testamentes.* Halle.

_____. 1927. *Grammatik des Biblisch-Aramäischen.* Halle.

Ben-Ḥayyim, Z. 1977. *The Literary and Oral Tradition of Hebrew and Aramaic amongst the Samaritans. V. Grammar of the Pentateuch.* Jerusalem.

_____. 1978. "Hirhurim ʿal maʿareket hattənuʿot bəʿiḇrit." *Studies in the Bible and the Ancient Near East Presented to S. E. Loewenstamm.* Ed. Y. Avishur and J. Blau, I, pp. 93–105. Jerusalem.

Bergsträsser, G. 1918–29. *Hebräische Grammatik.* Leipzig.

Blake, F. R. 1950. "The Apparent Interchange between *a* and *i* in Hebrew." *Journal of Near Eastern Studies* 9:76–83.

Blau, J. 1968. "Bibelhebräische Nomina, die auf *pataḥ* - *ʿayin* enden." *Zeitschrift der Deutschen Morgenländischen Gesellschaft* 118:257–58.

_____. 1971a. "Marginalia semitica I." *Israel Oriental Studies* 1:1–35.

_____. 1971b. "Studies in Hebrew verb formation." *Hebrew Union College Annual* 42:133–58.

_____. 1975. "ʿAl bəʿayot bitḥum hahaṭʿama baʿiḇrit haqqəduma." *Baruch KurzweilMemorial Volume*, pp. 62–73. Ed. M. Z. Kaddari, A. Saltman, and M. Schwarcz. Tel Aviv.

_____. 1976. *A Grammar of Biblical Hebrew.* Wiesbaden. *

Böttcher, F. 1866–68. *Ausführliches Lehrbuch der hebräischen Sprache.* Leipzig.

Brockelmann, C. 1908–13. *Grundriss der vergleichenden Grammatik der semitischen Sprachen.* Berlin.

Brønno, E. 1943. *Studien über hebräische Morphologie und Vokalismus.* Leipzig.

Ewald, H. 1870. *Ausführliches Lehrbuch der hebräischen Sprache des Alten Bundes*[8]. Göttingen.

Joüon, P. 1947. *Grammaire de l'hébreu biblique*[2]. Rome.

König, E. 1881–97. *Historisch-kritisches Lehrgebäude der hebräischen Sprache.* Leipzig.

Lambert, M. 1938. *Traité de grammaire hébraïque.* Paris.

Leander, P. 1912. "Der kampf zwischen Philippi's gesetz und dem systemzwange in der hebräischen sprachgeschichte." *Le Monde Oriental* 6:185–92.

Meyer, R. 1966–72. *Hebräische Grammatik.* Berlin.

Sarauw, C. 1939. *Über Akzent und Silbenbildung in den älteren semitischen Sprachen.* København.

Segert, S. 1975. *Altaramäische Grammatik.* Leipzig.

Yeivin, I. 1968. *Hanniqqud habbab̲li umasoret hallašon hammištaqep̄et mimmennu.* Jerusalem (doctoral thesis).

_____. 1972–73. *Masoret hallašon ha'ib̲rit hammištaqep̄et banniqqud habbab̲li.* Jerusalem.

Additions and Corrections

to **p. 36.***1*: For the chronology of Philippi's Law see also *Hebrew Linguistics*, pp. 12–16, where p. 13. n.23 C. Saraw's late fixing of the law to the third century C.E. is mentioned. K. Beyer, *Die aramäischen Texte vom Toten Meer*, Göttingen 1984, pp. 140–41 fixed it even to a later date, to the eighth century C.E., later than the attenuation, which he attributes to the third century C.E. Yet not only prove forms like the constructs מִרְבַּץ, מִשְׁבַּר (from מַרְבֵּץ, מַשְׁבֵּר, with dissimilation in the first syllable) that attenuation is later than the action of Philippi's Law (see *Hebrew Linguistics*, pp. 15–16), but transcriptions like *asarmōt*, *salpaad*, *asabia* for חֲצַרְמָוֶת, צְלָפְחָד, יוֹשִׁבְיָה in the Septuagint demonstrate the occurrence of Philippi's Law in the third century B.C. (see ibid., p.14).

to **p. 38**.*7*: Read *baz* 'spoil' for *bāz*.

to **p. 38**.*8*: Delete *sāp* (being based on inferior readings).

to **p. 38**.*9*: Delete *mās*.

to **p. 38**.*10*: For *mayim* cf. I. Ben-David, *Contextual and Pausal Forms in Biblical Hebrew*, Jerusalem 1995 (in Hebrew), p. 2ll, n. 40.

to **p. 38**.*-3*: Read *ᶜaśar* for *ᶜašar*.

to **p. 38**.*n. 8. end*: For a comprehensive synchronic description of this feature see I. Ben-David, *Leshonenu* 47 (1983), pp. 232–247. From the diachronic point of view, this alternation is quite surprising (see infra §4,1,2, end), since one would have expected *segol* in context (owing to Philippi's law) and *ṣere* in the pause (where the action of Philippi's law was prevented by pausal lengthening). As demonstrated by Ben-David, sometimes in the pause *segol* and *qamaṣ* interchange. It seems that *nāpel*, etc. reflect original *qaṭl* forms, *nēpel*, etc. being due to attenuation, which affected not only closed syllables totally unstressed but also words which, in the context of the sentence, had lost their stress.

to **p. 39**.*12*: Delete הָשְׁבַּרְתִּי, since it is attested by inferior manuscripts only; see below addition to **p. 44**.24–25.

to **p. 39**.*18*: Delete "(but also ...)!", since תֶּחֱרַשׁ (this is the intende form) Ps. 39.13 is only attested in inferior versions. The short *a* of אַל תֶּחֱרַשׁ is also corroborated by Origines's ελθαρες.

to **p. 44**.*9*: See addition referring to p. 38 n. 8, end.

to **p. 44**.*24-25*: Since pausal הָשְׁבַּרְתִּי is attested by inferior manuscripts only, the main version being הָשְׁבָּרְתִּי, nothing can be inferred as to the original structure of passive perfect forms.

to **p. 47**: middle: Blau, J. 1978 = This volume, pp. 104–19.

"Weak" Phonetic Change and the Hebrew *śîn*

0. Introduction

THIS ARTICLE originally arose out of the author's attempt to restate the
* current, "conservative" view on the existence of a third unvoiced non-emphatic sibilant in Hebrew, and, of course, in Proto-Semitic, viz. the *śîn,* against suggestions raised recently. Yet it soon became clear that the analysis of alleged exceptional sound correspondences of the Hebrew sibilants, claimed by some scholars, has to be based on the examination of the problem of exceptional sound correspondences in the Semitic languages in general, i.e., on what we shall in this paper dub "weak phonetic change." Since, it seems, the notion of "weak phonetic change" and its cautious handling is of great importance not only for the elucidation of the status of the Hebrew *ś* in particular, but for comparative Semitic studies in general, I eventually decided to begin this article with a somewhat long exposition on weak phonetic change, and to deal with the special problem of the Hebrew (and Proto-Semitic) *ś* later.

1. "Weak Phonetic Change"

As is well known, occasional deviations from regular sound correspondences are well attested in Semitic languages in general and in

Hebrew in particular. This gives rise to two problems: a theoretical one, concerning the origins of these deviations, and a practical one, concerning how far they authorize scholars to jump to conclusions and apply exceptional sound correspondences for the etymological interpretation of difficult words, thus elucidating abstruse passages.

Malkiel, in a brilliant essay (1962), has focused attention on the cooperation of three forces in the emergence of unexpected sound correspondences, viz. what he dubs *"weak phonetic change," spontaneous sound shift* and *lexical contamination.* Phonetic changes tend to be regular to the extent that they occur in clearly delimited speech communities. Since, however, most communities (including those speaking Semitic languages) tend to be fluid, irregularities occur, considered by Malkiel to be due to weak sound change. In the following, however, we shall prefer to speak of dialect mixture and borrowing, and use the term "weak phonetic change" to designate the result of the cooperation of dialect mixture and borrowing, spontaneous sound shift and lexical contamination. There exists no general agreement on the definition of "spontaneous sound shift," which, at any rate, seems to include dissimilation, assimilation (at least at a distance), metathesis and haplology. Lexical contamination, the third factor contributing to the emergence of weak phonetic change, is, in my opinion, especially important for Semitic languages. Since in Semitic tongues the majority of roots are triliteral, the number of possible combinations is more limited than in other languages and, therefore, the number of roots which by pure chance are similar in sound and form is relatively quite high. These roots tend to attract each other: a "sporadic"[1] sound shift occurs when a word, attracted by another word which belongs to the same semantic field, assimilates itself to it in form as well. Similarly, words similar in sound and related in meaning may assimilate themselves in meaning, so that the meaning of one word is specialized through the influence of the other.[2] It stands to reason that it is, *inter alia,* through this attraction that Semitic tongues exhibit a great number of triliteral roots related in meaning, exhibiting identical first and second radicals and differing in the third only,[3] thus making the impression that the third radical exhibits only phonetic alternation. In other,

1. This is the term used by Fraenkel (1898, p. 61), who was the first to pay systematic attention to this phenomenon.

2. See Fraenkel (1898, p. 62).

3. Like Hebrew *prd, prz, prṭ, prk, prm, prs, prʿ, prṣ, prq, prr, prś, prš.* For this phenomenon cf. recently the judicious remarks of J. Kuryłowicz (1973, pp. 6, 12).

though admittedly less conspicuous cases, words of similar (or allegedly similar) meaning, differing either in their first, or sometimes in their second radical,[4] give the impression that the first or second radical, respectively, exhibits a mere phonetic alternation, the basic meaning being expressed by the other radicals. For all these reasons, one must be careful not to jump to conclusions because of the occurrence of what seems to be irregular sound correspondence and disregard the typical features in favor of deviant and random features. One has always to bear in mind that the great majority of words in the various Semitic languages reflect sound correspondences due to regular sound shift, and it would be against any sound method to overlook them because of the existence of exceptional sound correspondences, which are due to weak phonetic change. Not only is the Semitic linguist obliged to assign to regular sound correspondence its proper place and not to exaggerate the importance of irregular sound correspondence, but the Semitic philologist must not light-heartedly apply weak sound change for the elucidation of difficult passages. The prospects that a word whose meaning is not sufficiently clear does indeed exhibit a weak sound change are rather limited and, therefore, one cannot be careful enough. In the following we shall deal with some cases of real and alleged weak sound changes in various Semitic languages.

1.1 Aramaic ṣ Corresponding to Proto-Semitic ð̣

The Proto-Semitic (PS) consonant which is continued by Modern Standard Arabic *ḍ*[5] is represented in Early Aramaic by *q* and in later Aramaic by . Yet, alongside this regular correspondence, another, much more restricted one exists, viz. that of the Aramaic *ṣ*, corresponding to PS ð̣. In Blau (1970a, pp. 60–63), I have collected about fourteen cases of such abnormal correspondence. Many of these cases can be interpreted as originating in spontaneous sound shift, i.e., caused by the dissimilating

4. Thus, e.g., Haupt (1906), *inter alia*, connected *wqr, nqr, sqr, q'r,* and *'kr, wkr, nkr, mkr, škr, k'r;* Moscati (1947, p. 135)—*brr, b'r, btr,* further *infra ksl, kšl, ktl* proposed by Vollers (1894). It goes without saying that many of these alleged affinities are rather dubious. Yet cf. also rather established cases like Arabic *'lk, 'lk, lwk,* denoting "to chew, to champ the bit."

* 5. And which, in all likelihood, in PS was something like ð̣ˡ; cf. Steiner's (forthcoming) work on the lateral pronunciation of ð̣ and *ś*, to be edited by the American Oriental Society.

effect of *ǵ*, *ḥ*, and *r*.[6] Other cases may be due to lexical contamination, e.g. *ṣmd—ḍmd*. At least in one case (*npṣ*—"to shake [off]"), it is difficult to find any sound that could have caused dissimiliation or to discover a lexeme with which it could have blended; therefore, one may perhaps attribute its origins to an Aramaic dialect in which *ḍ* had shifted to *ṣ*, rather than to *q/ʿ*. In other cases, the *ṣ* may be due to the joint operation of dissimilation, lexical contamination and dialect mixture.[7]

1.2 Ugaritic *ǵ* Corresponding to PS *θ*

Another famous case of irregular sound correspondence is that of Ugaritic *ǵ* to PS *θ*.[8] Gordon (1965, pp. 27–28) went so far as to posit, on the strength of five such correspondences acknowledged by him, an additional PS consonant. Since, however, weak phonetic change is a quite widespread phenomenon in Semitic languages, we are either obiiged to posit additional PS consonants in every case or, what makes much more sense, not to postulate an additional PS sound in the case of Ugaritic *ǵ* corresponding to PS *θ*.[9] In the light of the quite composite character of the dialectal structure of Ugaritic, the weak sound change Ugaritic *ǵ* < PS *θ* can easily be interpreted as due to dialect mixture.[10] On the other hand, I have not found cases which cannot be explained otherwise.[11]

6. As *ḥṣr* ("grass"), occurring in Sefîre (whereas Judeo-Aramaic *ḥăṣīrā* may be considered a Hebrew loan as well).

7. Thus *ṣbr* ("to heap up"), attested not only in Judeo-Aramaic but outside it as well (for particulars see Blau, 1970a, pp. 60–63), could have originated in an Aramaic dialect in which *ṣ*, rather than *q/ʿ*, was the reflex of PS *ḍ*; the *ṣ* could be due to the dissimilatory effect of *r*; and it could exhibit the lexical contamination of the reflex of PS *ḍbr* and *ṣbr*. *

8. For the whole complex of the problem of Ugaritic *ǵ*, see also Dietrich-Loretz (1967).

9. It has been claimed, to be sure, that for reasons of symmetry, a third lateralized dental existed in PS (see Cantineau, 1960, pp. 16, 55, 287), and it could be reflected by the sound correspondence *θ—ǵ*. Yet symmetry is a rather weak argument (and Cantineau himself was more reserved about it, cf. p. 287, which was written in 1951–52, as against the other passages from 1941) and the fact that it is allegedly reflected by Ugaritic alone makes it even less likely.

10. Cf. Blau (1968, p. 525a, note 18).

11. Rather extreme is Rössler's attitude (1961), who altogether denied the existence of the sound correspondence PS *θ* = Ugaritic *ǵ*. After finding different etymologies for most words allegedly exhibiting this sound correspondence, he accepted only two *prima facie* cases, viz. *ǵmʾ* and *yqǵ* and attributed them, however, to clerical error. Yet the occurence of such clerical errors in exactly a way that led to the assumption of a nonexisting sound shift, would be quite a coincidence. Cf. also Jirku (1964, pp. 481–482).

Even the clearest case, viz. *ǵm'* ("to be thirsty"), *can* be interpreted as due to a blend of *ẓm'* with *ǵmy*.[12] The other cases are even less certain: Gordon (1965, text 127:42), *ištm'. wtqǵ udn* ("hear and . . . ear") is interpreted (in the wake of Isa 50:4 *yāʿîr lî 'ōzen lišmōăʿ*, "he wakens my ear to hear") as "be alert (of ear)," the Gt imperative of *yqẓ/yqǵ*. This is by no means impossible, yet not certain at all. One must not overlook the differences between the Ugaritic text and the biblical passage: the latter not only uses the root *ʿwr*, rather than *yqṣ*, but also speaks of God awakening man's ear, rather than of someone being awakened as to his ear. Therefore, one has to take into serious consideration Aistleitner's proposal (1965) to interpret *tqǵ* as "incline";[13] cf. the frequent biblical phrase *hiṭṭā 'ōzen* ("he inclined his ear"), parallel to *šāmaʿ* ("he heard"). As to *nǵr* ("to watch"), Rainey (1970) has adduced strong arguments for its correspondence with PS *nθr*.[14] On the other hand, Loewenstamm (1971) has convincingly shown that *nǵr may* be interpreted as a secondary root, parallel to Ugaritic *ǵyr* ("to watch") = Hebrew *ʿwr* ("to watch"), which, according to this view, has to be separated from Ugaritic and

12. In Arabic, various extensions of what seems to be the bilateral root *ǵm* are attested: *ǵamy* ("fainting"), *ǵym* ("to be clouded, be affected with burning thirst"); the original meaning was, it seems, "to be covered," which developed to denote both fainting and thirst.

13. His suggestion, however, was not accepted because of the quite impossible etymology proposed by him: he compared the Ugaritic word with Arabic *ṣǵy* ("to incline"), as if Ugaritic *q* could correspond to Arabic *ṣ*! Yet even without a convincing etymology, one must not discard the possibility of *tqǵ* denoting inclination. Tentatively only, I propose to interpret it as G imperative of *tqǵ*. A trace of this *tqǵ* ("to incline") has perhaps been preserved in Biblical Hebrew *tqʿ*. *tqʿ*, as a rule, denotes "to thrust, to clap, to blast" and it stands to reason that, in this sense, it is onomatopoetic (cf. Blau, 1955, p. 344). Yet in Exod 10:19 *wayyiśśā 'et hā'arbe wayyitqāʿēhû yammā sûp* ("and it carried the locusts and . . . into the Red Sea") it may denote "it inclined, turned them into the Red Sea," and thus be related to our *tqǵ*. *Prima facie*, the use of *h locativus* (*yammā*) corroborates this interpretation, since *tqʿ*, as a rule, governs the preposition *bə-* (the phrase *tāqaʿ kap lə-* seems to be of different origin, literally meaning "to clap hands *for* someone"). Caquot (1974, pp. 207–208) identified Ugaritic *tqǵ* with Hebrew *tqʿ* in the Middle Hebrew *tāqaʿ libbō lə'āḇîw šebaššāmayim*, interpreted by him as "he extended his heart to his celestial father." He also compares (Caquot *et al.*, 1974, p. 571, note x) biblical *tāqaʿ 'ōhel* ("to pitch a tent"). Yet, despite the existence of *nāṭā 'ōhel*, literally "to spread out the tent" (e.g. Gen 31:19), it seems much more likely to interpret *tāqaʿ 'ōhel* as an abbreviation of *tāqaʿ yitdôt hā'ōhel* ("to drive the pegs of the tent"). And as to the Middle Hebrew phrase, it must not be separated from Talmud Bab., *Yebamot*, 109b *tōqēăʿ 'aṣmō lidḇar hălāḵā*, exhibiting an identical construction and perhaps denoting "(forcefully) inserting himself/forcing himself into the decisions of the religious law," but by no means "extending himself . . . ". At any rate, both expressions are vague (cf. also Ben-Yehuda, 1948, s.v.) and cannot be used for the elucidation of the Ugaritic word. For *tāqaʿ kap* see *supra*.

14. Cf. also Rainey (1971, pp. 157–158).

Hebrew *'wr* ("to arouse").[15] Ultimately, the decision between these two intepretations depends on how one assesses the frequency of the sound shift PS θ > Ugaritic *ǵ*, and accordingly, as to the problem we are treating, we move in a vicious circle. *ǵr* ("mountain") is generally compared with Aramaic *ṭûr* ("mountain") and Hebrew *ṣûr* ("rock"). Yet Rössler (1961, pp. 165–167) has quite convincingly demonstrated that the affinity of these words is rather doubtful, since the Hebrew word denotes "rock" rather than "mountain," and no common Semitic word for "mountain" exists.[16] As to *mǵy* ("to reach, arrive"), its connection with Aramaic *mṭ'* is rather dubious, since one would have expected the Ugaritic word to terminate in '. Moreover, the expected form *mẓ'* is also attested in Ugaritic, and, therefore, it stands to reason that *mǵy* is of different origin.[17] *ǵlm*, etc. (Gordon, 1965, Krt 19; 125:50; 51:vii:54) has been interpreted by many as denoting "covering, darkness." Yet even if this interpetation proves to be correct, it can easily be derived from Hebrew *'lm* ("to hide"), presumably related to Ugaritic *ǵlp* ("to envelop"); see Ginsberg (1946). Since, as we have seen, the correspondence PS θ—Ugaritic *ǵ* is so restricted,[18] one will not hasten to elucidate obscure words like *ǵlm*, etc. with its help, the more so since in Gordon (1965, text 51:VII:54–55) *ǵlmt* is parallel to *ẓlmt*, the real correspondence of PS θ.[19] *

---

15. Incidentally, in Middle Hebrew *n'r* in *nip'al* ("to awake") is attested (and perhaps Judg 16:20), thus exhibiting the alteration *'wr:n'r* in the sense of "to awake."

16. Rössler's own etymology (p. 167) for *ǵr*, though possible, is unverifiable. He claims that it corresponds to Arabic *ǵawr* ("lowland"). This could be buttressed by several words denoting both "lowland, etc." and "mountain, etc.", occurring in Semitic languages (see Nöldeke, 1910, pp. 83–84). Rössler himself compared Hebrew *gib'ā* ("hill") and *gābîă'* ("cup"), which, however, are less convincing; the more so, since *gābîă'* may be an Egyptian loan word (see Koehler-Baumgartner, 1967ff, s.v.). Nöldeke (1910, pp. 83–84) adduces, *inter alia*, Christian Palestinian Aramaic *gəlîmā* ("valley, hill"). As to Arabic *ḥawṣā'u* ("deep well" and "elevation") adduced by Nöldeke, see also Fischer (1965, p. 59, note 1). (I do not understand his exact reasons for his opposition to Nöldeke's etymology; he may perhaps be referring to the second etymology proposed by Nöldeke.)

17. For particulars, see Blau (1972, pp. 67–72). (pp. 231–36)

18. It is perhaps limited to one case, viz. *ǵm'* (which may be due either to dialectal borrowing or presumably to lexical contamination).

19. For want of additional material it is impossible to say whether the alternation of *k—zz* in one word in Khurrian (see Soden, 1967, pp. 291–294) has significance for our phenomenon. As to the spelling with *ẓ* for *ṭ*, Dietrich *et al.* (1975) explained it as due to Khurrian influence as well. I have the impression that the seven words spelled in this way (in ten occurrences) have to be divided into two groups. Two words occur in the archaizing text UT 77 in Gordon (1965) (cf. for this Blau, 1970a, p. 43, note 3) and, although according to

1.3 Ugaritic *θ* Corresponding to PS *š́*

Another weak phonetic change in Ugaritic is the correspondence of Ugaritic *θ* to what seems to be PS *š́*. The only conspicuous case is Ugaritic *ḥθbn* ("account"), exhibiting *θ* as second radical, supported by Egyptian *ḥśb* ("to reckon up"), since Egyptian *ś* may correspond to Semitic *θ*, yet not to Semitic *š́*. Aramaic *ḥš́b* ("to reckon up, to consider"), however, points to original *š́*, as does also Arabic *ḥsb*, whereas Hebrew *ḥš́b* may be derived from both *ḥθb* and *ḥš́b*. Since in loan words Ugaritic *θ* may represent *š́*, it may be borrowed in Ugaritic.[20] This, however, does not explain Egyptian *ś*. Degen (1971) therefore suggested to consider this root (which is absent from Akkadian) to be ultimately an Egyptian loan word in all the Semitic languages in which it is attested. This would explain the exceptional sound correspondence Egyptian *ś*—Ugaritic *θ*—Hebrew *š́*. *š́* in the Aramaic dialects is a Hebrew loan, and Arabic *ḥsb* an Aramaic loan. This theory, however, despite its ingenuity, is not without problems. Such a long chain of borrowings, though by no means impossible, is *prima facie,* somewhat unlikely. Moreover, *ḥš́b* is attested in quite a considerable number of Aramaic dialects,[21] and this makes the assumption of a Canaanite loan somewhat dubious. Even the assumption of an Aramaic loan in Arabic is less likely than it would seem *prima facie*. Not only is Arabic *ḥsb* early and amply attested and appears in many derivations (see, e.g., Lane, 1863–93, s.v.), but Goldziher (1889, p. 41) has quite convincingly suggested that Arabic *ḥasab* ("noble descent") originally denotes the enumeration of the noble deeds of the ancestors. If this etymology proves true, it would show how deeply *ḥsb* and its derivations are rooted in Arabic. The autochthonous character of Arabic *ḥsb* becomes even more likely, if one accepts Nöldeke's derivation (1910, p.

---

the lucid exposition of Dietrich *et al.* (1975), the shift *ẓ* > *ṭ* is not attested in Ugaritic texts, I still think that it occurred in Ugaritic, because the simplest explanation of the use of *ẓ* instead of *ṭ* in 77 is still the assumption of pseudo-correction (see Blau, 1970a, p. 43). All the other occurrences of the spelling with *ẓ* instead of *ṭ* occur in one group of texts. I am inclined to interpret it by the assumption that the shift of *ẓ* > *ṭ* underlies this group of texts also. In this group, there was a tendency to mark the sound *ṭ* more by the letter *ẓ* (which was also pronounced *ṭ*) than by the letter *ṭ*, and this is the reason for the occurrence of this special spelling in this group of texts. Similarly, the Ge'ez letter *ẓ*, from the point of view of the history of the alphabet, continues South-Arabic *ð* rather than *ẓ*, and *š́* in the Canaanite
* alphabet occupies the place of *θ*, as exhibited by Ugaritic.

20. See Blau-Greenfield (1970, p. 13).

21. For particulars see Koehler-Baumgartner (1953, Aramaic part, s.v. *ḥš́b*).

59, note 3) of Arabic *ḥizb* ("party, sect"), Ge'ez *ḥezb* ("people, clan, tribe") from *ḥisb* (cf. also Jeffery, 1938, pp. 108–109). Nöldeke calls attention to the alternation of the roots *ḥsb—ḥzb* in Ge'ez (cf. also *infra*), and his derivation may be buttressed by the occurrence of *ḥzb* in Epigraphic South-Arabic not only in the sense of "people" (so Conti Rossini, 1931, s.v.) and "fighting band" (so Jamme, 1962, s.v.), but also in that of "quantity, number" (Jeffery, 1938, pp. 108–109). An ingenious solution was proposed by Rainey:[22] he assumed the existence of two originally different, but quite similar roots; viz., *ḥθb* ("to reckon") and *ḥšb* ("to think"), which later have fallen together in the various languages. This suggestion can be buttressed by the likely etymology Egyptian *ḥθb* has on the one hand, and Hebrew *ḥšb* has on the other. (Which, admittedly, can be interpreted not only as exhibiting original *ḥšb* but also *ḥθb*.) Sethe (1916, p. 77; also quoted by Brockelmann, 1928, s.v. *ḥšb*) has quite convincingly derived the Egyptian word "to reckon" from "to break," whereas the original meaning of "to think" might have been "to tie" (cf. Hebrew *ḥēšeb*, "girdle"), since the connection between "to tie" and "to think" is well attested.[23] This assumption of the double root *ḥθb* ("to reckon")—*ḥšb* ("to think") can be accomodated to the occurrence of Ge'ez *ḥsb* ("to reckon, to consider") and *ḥzb* ("to consider") by supposing that *ḥsb*, originally denoting "to reckon" only, arose from *ḥθb*, whereas *ḥzb* ("to consider") has to be derived from *ḥšb*.[24] On the other hand, Epigraphic South-Arabic *ḥzb* ("people," or "fighting band," and "number, quantity") is not without difficulties for Rainey's thesis. The meaning "people, fighting band" can, to be sure, be derived (just as Ge'ez *ḥezb*, "people, class, tribe") from the postulated original meaning of *ḥšb* ("to think," viz. "to tie").[25] Yet the derivation of "quantity, number" from the postulated original *ḥθb* denoting reckoning[26] is phonetically ticklish, since it is much more difficult to imagine a phonetic shift *θb* > *zb*

22. First in Rainey (1971, p. 159) somewhat cautiously. In the first (Hebrew) version of this article he had not yet proposed this thesis. Cf. also Rainey (1974, p. 185, note 10).

23. See the literature adduced in Blau (1957, p. 101, and especially note 5). Cf. also Arabic *'aqada* ("to tie"), *'i'taqada* ("to believe"), and further in Gesenius (1835ff, s.v. *ḥšb*).

24. One must not simply assume the shift *ḥšb* > *ḥsb* (according to Ge'ez sound shift *š* > *s*) > *ḥzb*, since *ḥzb* occurs in Epigraphic South-Arabic as well, in which (see the literature adduced in Blau, 1970a, p. 111, note 4) *š* did not shift to *s*. Accordingly, one would rather postulate *šb* > *žb* (since no phoneme *ž* exists in Epigraphic South-Arabic) > *zb*.

25. For the semantic shift cf., e.g., Arabic *'uṣba* ("party") from *'aṣaba* ("to bind").

26. Cf. Nöldeke (1910, p. 59, note 3), who derived also the meaning "party" from "reckoning," assuming, however (see *supra*), original *ḥisb* < *ḥišb*.

(*ḥiθb > ḥizb) than šb > zb (*ḥišb > ḥizb). If one nevertheless accepts Rainey's thesis (as I am inclined to do), the most satisfactory solution seems to be to assume that *ḥizb* ("people, fighting band") arose from *ḥšb* ("to tie") and then attracted **ḥθb* ("reckoning").

All the other cases of Ugaritic *θ* corresponding to PS *š* are dubious. It stands to reason (see Blau-Greenfield, 1970, p. 12) that Virolleaud was right in connecting the Ugaritic epithet *gθr* with the Akkadian epithet *gašru* ("strong, powerful"), since both sense and usage exactly fit. Soden (1965ff, s.v.) has suggested to connect it with Arabic *jsr* ("to be bold, courageous"), which, however, cannot reflect PS *θ*, but either *š* or *s*. The meaning of the Arabic root, although it does not exactly tally, is close enough. Therefore, one will either accept the equation Akkadian *gašru* — Arabic *jsr* and consider Ugaritic *gθr* an Akkadian loan in which Ugaritic *θ* transcribes Akkadian *š* (see Blau-Greenfield, 1970, p. 13), or regard the (partial) similarity of Arabic *jsr* as being due to chance only. As to Gordon (1965, text 128:I:2) *mẓ(?)ma. yd.mθkt*, Greenfield (1969, p. 96,) was right in remarking that it occurs in a doubtful context. It is, as a rule, translated "the thirsty she took by the hand." Yet *mẓma*, if the reading is correct, does not exactly denote "thirsty," but rather "the parched one," as, in fact, Ginsberg (in Pritchard, 1958) translates, being the passive participle of the D form. One would rather expect simple "thirsty"; in Hebrew, at any rate, the parallel **məṣummā'* does not exist. Moreover, the attempt to compare Ugaritic *yd mθkt* with Hos 7:5 *māšaḵ yādô 'et lôṣəṣîm* is not convincing. The verse is difficult and its meaning dubious. But even if it meant "he stretched out his hand with scorners," i.e. "made common cause with them," it does not mean "he supported the scorners (who needed help)," as the alleged context in Ugaritic requires. Even the sentence structure is different, since the Ugaritic construction would be paralleled by Hebrew **lôṣəṣîm yād māšaḵ*. More plausible would be to compare *Klmw* 13 (cf. Ginsberg, 1946) *w'nk.tmkt.mškbm.lyd* ("and I supported the *mškbm*"), *tmk* denoting not only "to hold (firmly)," as does Hebrew *mšk* (see Yalon, 1963, p. 80) and Arabic *msk*, but also "to support." Yet Hebrew *mšk* (and Arabic *msk*) do not exhibit the meaning of "support." Accordingly, in light of the dubious text, the lack of any comparable use of *mšk*, and the necessity of postulating weak sound change, one would rather refrain from comparing *mθkt* with *mšk*. Greenfield (1969) has also correctly remarked that for Ugaritic *dθ* (which has been interpreted as "to tread, trample down") an adequate etymology is provided by Arabic *dyθ* ("to abase"), so that it need not be connected with PS *dwš/dyš*. Caquot *et al.* (1974, p. 436, note f), on the other hand, compared it to the rare Arabic *daθθa*. Nothing certain can be stated as to Ugaritic *gbθt*. (For the occurrence of this and other Ugaritic words, see the various Ugaritic glossaries.) It is generally interpreted as "humps" of the *ibrm*, which may denote "bulls," the *gbθt* of the *ibrm* being parallel to the *qrnm* of the *θrm*, i.e., "the horns of the oxen." Yet it is not certain that *gbθt* really denotes "humps," and not another conspicuous part of the body of the *ibrm*, and even if it does, its connection with Middle Hebrew *gbš* ("to heap up") is rather dubious. Moreover, it is difficult to state what kind of *š* is exhibited by *gbš*, since it is attested, in the form of *gbš*, only once in Judeo-Aramaic (see Kutscher, in Koehler-Baumgartner, 1967ff, s.v. *dabbešet* [!]), where, accordingly, it may have been borrowed from Hebrew. Hebrew *šillûḥîm* ("dowry") in 1 Kgs 9:16, *prima facie*, has a clear etymology, viz. from *šlḥ* ("to send"), being the parting gift of the father to his daughter when sending her away. Yet in Ugaritic "to send" is *šlḥ*, while "dowry" (parallel to *mlg*, "dowry") is *θlḫ*. Accordingly, despite the *prima facie* certain etymology, Ugaritic *θlḫ* and Hebrew *šillûḥîm* have to be separated from Ugaritic, Hebrew, and Aramaic *šlḥ*. Were not Ugaritic *šlḥ* attested, one would connect *θlḫ* with "to send," in spite of the existence of Aramaic *šlḥ* (as did, in fact, Driver, 1956, s.v., who, however, misread the word as *θlḥ*), and would assume weak sound change, an additional proof of how careful one has to be not to rush to postulating exceptional sound shifts. Ugaritic *ngθ* and *ngš*, both denoting "to approach, meet,"[27] are, it seems, doublets, either original, inherited ones[28] or originally roots with similar, yet nevertheless different meanings, which were attracted to one another, perhaps also by the interference of other roots.[29] Ugaritic *θθ* ("six"), *θdθ* ("sixth") do not,

27. Ullendorff (1962, p. 340) attributed the meaning of "to press, drive, overwhelm" to *ngš*. Yet in Gordon (1965, text 52:68) only the meaning "to approach, meet" is suitable.

28. Cf., e.g., Mühlau-Volck's rather fanciful assumption (1890, s.v. *ng'*) that roots exhibiting *ng* as their first radicals have the basic meaning of "to push, beat," as Hebrew *ngh*, *ngḥ*, *ngl*, *ngn*, *ngp*, *ngś*, *ngš*, also *nhg*, and Arabic *njnj*, *njl*, *njh*, *njš*, *njr*, *nj'*. Much more likely is Streck's view (quoted in Gesenius-Buhl, 1915, s.v. *ngś*) that *ngś* and *ngš* are secondary offshoots of one root denoting "to tread."

29. Thus, e.g., Arabic *njθ*, *inter alia* denoting "to seek, investigate," may be influenced not only by *njš*, which, among other meanings, denotes "to seek" as well, but also by the very frequent *bḥθ*, which governs the preposition of *'an*, as does *njθ*. It is even possible that at first *njθ* was influenced by *bḥθ*, and then *njš* was influenced by *njθ*. At any rate, it seems that Gordon's assumption (1965, s.v. *ngθ*) that Ugaritic *ngθ* denotes "to seek," does not fit text 75:1:40, where Baal has already met the "devourers." One would rather interpret it as "to approach." In Gordon (1965, *'nt:* pl. x: V:4, 17) the text is not clear enough, whereas in

of course, exhibit an exceptional sound shift *š* > *θ*, despite their correspondence to PS *šdθ* (as preserved by Epigraphic South-Arabic), since the initial *θ* is due to assimilation to the final one. Similar assimilation is well attested in Ugaritic, where the *š*-prefix of the causative verbal form is assimilated to *θ* as first radical (see Gordon, 1965, p. 34). Compare also the assimilation of the *θ* of **šādiθ* to the initial *š* in Arabic *sādis* < **šādiš* ("sixth"). As to Ugaritic *θlθ* ("three") and its correspondence to PS *ś*, see (p. 244) Blau (1972, p. 80); as to Ugaritic *iθ* ("being") as against Arabic *laysa* ("is (pp. 222–25) not"), see Blau (1972, pp. 58–61). In the wake of al-Yasin (1952, p. 110), Ugaritic *θrm* ("to eat, dine") is generally connected with Iraqi Arabic *θaram* ("to cut food in pieces"). If this connection is correct (pay attention to the difference in meaning!), it may be buttressed by Classical Arabic *θarama*, as a rule denoting "to break the teeth," according to Landberg (1920–42, s.v. *θlm*), yet al-Azharī, quoted by ibn Manẓūr (1955–56, s.v.), states that it means, like *raθama* and *ratama*, any sort of breaking. On the other hand, *šrm* ("to break") is attested in Syriac and, in the form *srm* (marginally, to be sure) in Arabic.[30] One would perhaps posit a PS doublet *θrm—šrm* ("to break"), which may or may not be connected with Ugaritic *θrm* ("to eat, dine"). Ugaritic *θnn* denotes some kind of soldier (see Gordon, 1965, s.v.). Aistleitner's interpretation (1965, s.v.) as "lancer" and its connection with the PS root *šnn*, originally meaning "tooth," is a mere *etymologicum*. Dahood (1965, p. 332) connected Ugaritic *yθn* and Hebrew *yāšān* ("old") with Arabic *'asina* ("to be filthy"), as was usual before the discovery of Ugaritic.[31] Yet the divergence in form (Ugaritic *θ*, i.e. PS *θ*, as against Arabic *s* representing PS *š*) and the lack of real identity in meaning (Ugaritic and Hebrew "old" as against Arabic "stinking water") makes this connection rather precarious. The meaning of Ugaritic *θ'r* ("to arrange, serve food") is certain, yet its etymology is completely obscure, and Gordon (1965) is, in our opinion, right in simplv adducing the meaning without any addition.

Gordon (1965, text 49:II:6, 27) would maintain that both "to seek" and "to approach" fit the context. So "to approach" seems clearly to be attested, whereas "to seek" is dubious. It may, of course, be parallel to Arabic *njθ*, if in Arabic the meaning "to seek" is not secondary, as suggested. On the other hand, the meaning of "seeking" might have emerged secondarily in Ugaritic as well through the interference of *bqθ* ("to seek").

30. Brockelmann (1928, s.v. *šrm*) and Aistleitner, (1965, s.v. *θrm*) cite it in the second form; I have found it in the fifth form in ibn Manẓūr (1955–56, s.v. *srm*).

31. See especially Nöldeke (1910, p. 203). One would like to add Arabic *wasina* ("to faint because of the stench of the well"), because it is closer in form to *yšn/yθn*.

For various attempts at etymology, see, e.g., Aistleitner (1965, s.v.), Rin (1968, p. 73), Caquot *et al.* (1974, p. 157, note f; p. 160, note t). Yet any etymological connection is so dubious that one would methodologically refrain from assuming any exceptional sound correspondence. The same applies to the etymologies suggested by Dahood (1965, p. 331, note 60) for *kpθ*, presumably denoting "earth," and by de Moor (1969, p. 107b) for the proper noun *pθpθ*. Etymology is a rather uncertain domain, even if one sticks to the accepted sound shifts.

1.4 Ugaritic ẓ Corresponding to PS ð

Other weak sound changes that have been postulated for Ugaritic are even less attested and therefore, methodologically, one should refrain from using them to explain unclear passages. Thus, in order to explain difficult *ẓu*, de Moor (1968, p. 213, note 3) claimed that the use of the letter *ẓ* in correspondence to PS *ð* is not restricted to Gordon (1965), text 75 (where, in my opinion at least [Blau, 1968, p. 525a], it exhibits an archaic (pp. 341–42)
trait of marking *ð*, which had already disappeared in the contemporary language), but is attested in additional cases as well. He cites three occurrences, none of which, however, supports his claim. Ugaritic *ḥẓr* ("court") corresponds to Arabic *ḥaẓīra*, Judeo-Aramaic *ḥuṭrā* ("sheepfold"), and presumably also to Ge'ez *ḥaṣūr* ("hedge").[32] In the light of Epigraphic South-Arabic *ḥḏr* ("abode") and *mḥḏr* ("vestibule"), Hebrew *ḥāṣēr* ("court") could, to be sure, be derived from *ḥðr* as well.[33] Yet the Ugaritic parallel in exactly the same sense and usage, buttressed by Arabic and Aramaic correspondence, conclusively proves its derivation from PS *ḥθr*.

32. *Pace* Koehler-Baumgartner (1967ff, s.v. III *ḥṣr*). It is more likely that the Ge'ez word exhibits original *θ*, rather than *ṣ*, because of the greater frequency of **ḥθr* in a local sense. The constant spelling with *ṣ*, rather than with *ḍ*, makes the assumption of the root **ḥðr* for Ge'ez somewhat unlikely. This **ḥðr*, on the other hand, is well attested in Epigraphic South-Arabic *ḥḏr* ("abode") and *mḥḏr* ("vestibule") (see Conti Rossini, 1931, s.v.), thus showing again that different roots with related meanings may develop in the same direction even without any blend. Accordingly, the occurrence of **ḥðr* in this sense in Ge'ez would not be unexpected altogether. Moreover, the derivation of *ḥaḏīra* ("enclosure, village") and *maḥḏara* ("room") in South Arabic dialects (see Landberg, 1920–42 and 1901, s.v.) from **ḥðr* is quite likely. Yet since *ð* and *θ* have fallen together, these words *may* exhibit the root *ḥθr* as well.

33. As, no doubt, Hebrew *ḥāṣēr* ("settlement which has no wall about it") has to be derived from *ḥðr*. Cf., e.g., Orlinsky (1939, pp. 24–26), Malamat (1962, p. 147), Rodinson, (1957, p. 116), Loewenstamm and Blau (1957ff, s.v.).

Ugaritic *ẓrw* ("resin") corresponds, to be sure, to Arabic *ḍarw/ḍirw* and Epigraphic South-Arabic *ḍrw* on the one hand, and Syriac *ṣarwâ* on the other. Yet the latter is apparently a loan word (see Kutscher, 1976, p. 25, note 54), and the former are *perhaps* due to blending with *ḍrw* ("to bleed") (see Blau, 1970a, pp. 61–62). And the derivation of *ẓrw* from PS *θrw* is conclusively demonstrated by Galilean Aramaic *ṭrw* (see Kutscher, 1976, p. 25). The third root cited by de Moor, *ǵẓy*, which denotes something like "to entreat with gifts," has no clear etymology. Therefore, one would consent to the way adopted by Gordon (1965, s.v.), who elucidated its meaning by *parallelismus membrorum* and refrained from any etymology. Any attempt[34] to connect it with Arabic *ǵḍy*, *ǵḍḍ* ("to be dark [night], contract the eyelids, lower [the eyes], blink") not only presupposes a phonetic correspondence *ẓ*—*ḍ* for which no certain example exists, but also a semantic connection which is more than precarious.[35] Accordingly, one would not accept de Moor's proposal to explain the difficult and unclear *ẓu* by the assumption of a nonexisting sound-correspondence *ẓ*—*ḍ*.

1.5 Ugaritic *δ* Corresponding to PS *ś*/*θ*

One should not also consent to the interpretation of Ugaritic words containing *δ* as corresponding, without any constraints, to PS *ś* or even to PS *θ*.[36] The only case in which Ugaritic *δ* does correspond to PS *ś* is when immediately preceding *d*. The phonetic reason for this can be easily understood. After the Ugaritic sound *δ* had shifted to *d* and, therefore, the letter *δ* had become obsolete (cf. Blau, 1968, pp. 523 ff.), the letter *δ* came to be used mostly in Hurrian words, denoting a sound presumably like *ž*.[37] Therefore, since *ś* immediately preceding *d* became voiced, it was

34. De Moor establishes the connection "to wink at a person," hence "to try to please him with presents"; Aistleitner (1965, s.v.), "to bear patiently," hence "to put in favorable mood"; Caquot *et al.* (1974, p. 194, note o), "to darken, close the eyes," hence "to connive."

35. I have the feeling that, using exceptional sound correspondence and fancy semantic connection, one could establish an etymology for everything.

(p. 339) 36. Cf., e.g., Blau (1968, p. 523, note 5), where additional literature is cited (including Cross, 1962, p. 249); further Sauren-Kestemont (1971, p. 205, note 58), who rely on Aistleitner (1965).

37. This pronunciation may be reflected by the Akkadian transliterations of the personal name *δmrhd* by *ši-im-rad-du* and *zi-im-rad-du;* cf. also Gröndahl (1967, p. 14).

sometimes spelled with the letter *ð* in such cases. A certain case for all practical purposes, is *kðd,* alongside of *kšd;* it probably arose in immediate contact with the *d* in an infinitive form like **kišdum* > **kiðdum.*[38] Another possible case is *aðddy,* if it corresponds to Hebrew *'ašdôdî* (see Cross-Freedman, 1964, p. 49). In all the other cases the suggestions proposed for *ð* corresponding to PS *š* (or *θ*) are, in my opinion, imaginary. The place name *ðbl* simply does not correspond to PS *θbl;*[39] nor does *ðrt/ðhrt* ("vision") have any connection with Hebrew and Aramaic *šwr/šhr* or Arabic *shr.*[40] *ðd,* exhibiting *ð* not immediately preceding *d,* does not, it seems, denote "mountain," but either "territory, premises" (see Gordon, 1965, s.v.) or "tent" (compare Caquot *et al.*, 1974, p. 121, note d with additional literature), so that its connection with Akkadian *šadû* is precarious even from the semantic point of view.[41] *ðd* ("breast") is a nursery word and, therefore, of exceptional formation: in Ugaritic *ðd, θd,* and *zd* alternate, in Hebrew *šad* < **θad* and *dad* (cf. Nöldeke, 1910, p. 121, note 1).

1.6 Hebrew *d* Corresponding to PS *ð*; Other "Weak" Correspondences of Hebrew *z/d*

As is well known, the regular reflex of PS *ð* is Hebrew *z*. In the following, I shall deal with Hebrew *d* as a reflex of PS *ð*,[42] also mentioning some cases in which it is dubious whether Hebrew *z/d* correspond to PS *z/ð/d*. *d* as reflex of PS *ð* is attested in Hebrew *ndr* ("to vow"), occurring alongside the regular *nzr* ("to consecrate");[43] *qdr* ("to be dark"); *ḥdl* ("to cease")

38. For such an infinitive cf. *ni-iḫ-rum* in the quadrilingual word list in Nougayrol *et al.* (1968, p. 241). This seems more likely than to assume a clerical error with Caquot *et al.* (1974, p. 242, note r). For a different view, see Held (1962, p. 285, note 4).

39. *Pace* Cross (1962, note 74), Cross-Freedman (1964, note 78).

40. *Pace* Cross (1962, note 74), Aistleitner (1965, s.v.), followed by Sauren-Kestemont (1971, note 74).

41. *Pace* Aistleitner (1965, s.v.), Cross (1962, note 74), Sauren-Kestemont (1971, note 74). By the way, one should by no means compare (*pace* Aistleitner, 1965, Sauren-Kestemont, 1971) Arabic *sadd,* since the meaning "mountain" is secondary only, the primary meaning being "anything that closes and obstructs"; cf. Lane (1863–93, s.v.).

42. For particulars see the biblical dictionaries, especially Gesenius-Buhl (1915), who adduce important additional literature and, further, Brockelmann (1928). See also Gesenius-Buhl (1915, s.v. *d*) and further Bauer (1934), who postulated borrowing from what he termed "Ṣafonic dialects"; see against him Garbini (1960, pp. 194–196).

43. Cf. also Ginsberg (1945, p. 161, note 8), who tentatively suggests a blend of *nðr* with *ndb.*

(cf. Thomas, 1957); *dll* ("to be low, languish"), perhaps alternating with *zll* ("to be worthless");[44] perhaps also *dlq* ("to burn, pursue"), if it really corresponds to Arabic *ðlq*, originally "to sharpen," which, *inter alia*, denotes "to light, do quickly" (see Kopf, 1958, p. 170). The cases enumerated may be due to the dissimilatory effect of *r/l*, shifting *ð* to *d*,[45] yet they may reflect dialect mixture as well, through the influences of dialects in which, as in Aramaic and Ugaritic, *ð* had shifted to *d*. In the case of *dll*, at least,[46] the possibility of lexical contamination must not be overlooked either. For the lack of any dissimilatory factor, one would interpret Hebrew *qippôd* ("owl/hedgehog")[47] in the light of Arabic *qunfuð/qunfað*,[48] either by assuming that it was borrowed from a dialect in

44. Against the historical identification of these two roots see, however, Nöldeke (1900, p. 157), who connects Hebrew *dll* with Syriac *dallīl* ("few"), *dəlīl* ("easy"), positing PS *dll*. In note 157, he calls attention to how secondary semantic developments may mislead: from Arabic *dll*, a separate homonymous root *dalāl* denoting "to direct, indicate" (undoubtedly without any connection whatever with our *dll/ðll/zll*) is derived, originally meaning "indication by gesture," then "boldness, coquetishness." This meaning is quite close to Syriac *zallīl* ("debauched"), although these two words exhibit independent development of two completely unrelated roots. It is quite important to keep the possibility of such developments in mind and not to jump to far-reaching conclusions, involving violation of well-established sound correspondences.

45. This is, it seems, Nöldeke's opinion (1886, p. 729, note 1), if I understand him correctly, where he deals with *qdr*, *ndr*, *ḥdl*. Brockelmann (1908–13, I, p. 237) speaks expressly of dissimilation, mentioning *ndr*, *ḥdl*. Fraenkel (1886, p. xiv) speaks of exceptions from regular sound shifts in general, referring to *ḥdl*, *qdr*, *dll*. Cf. also note 61.

46. For the possible existence of PS *dll*, see note 44. This root might have been blended with PS *ðll* which is certainly preserved in Arabic *ðll*.

47. The *ô* of *qippôd* is originally short, see Ben-Ḥayyim (1946, p. 193). The *n* of Arabic *qunfuð* could not have influenced the original *ð* of *qippôd*, since it is secondary only, due to dissimilation; cf. for this feature Blau (1970a, p. 127). The identification of Hebrew *qippôd* with hedgehog is problematic and at least in most of its occurrences in the Bible it denotes some kind of owl; see, e.g., Driver (1921, p. 383); Aharoni (1935), who, however, is in some particulars somewhat inconsistent (cf. Aharoni, 1938, p. 470); Ben-Yehuda (1948ff, s.v.); Aḥiṭuv, *Encyclopaedia Biblica*, 1976, s.v. In Syriac too (cf. also Ben-Yehuda, 1948ff), *qupdā* may denote not only "hedgehog," but "owl" as well, see Payne Smith (1879–1901, s.v.), who connects these meanings (though not *expressis verbis*), and Brockelmann, (1928, s.v.) who wrongly separates them. For the reason why these words denote both "hedgehog" and "owl," see, e.g., Aharoni (1935, p. 160); Driver (1921, p. 383); Ben-Yehuda (1948ff); Feliks (1955–56, s.v. *qippôd*).

48. As far as I can see, *qunfuð* occurs in the sense of "hedgehog" only. This does not, however, contravene its affinity with biblical *qippôd*, even if the latter denotes "owl" only, since, as demonstrated by Syriac, "hedgehog" and "owl" are related, see the preceding note, *in fine*. In the light of the variation in the vocalization of this word (*qunfU/Að*) and its occurrence with *d* as well (*qunfud*), one could regard it as an Aramaic loan word, as does Jeffery (1938, p. 179); he, however, relies on the secondary *n* only, although it occurs in

which PS δ has shifted to *d*,[49] or by assuming the existence of a doublet or even a triplet. The latter would consist of (1) *qpd*, from which Hebrew *qippôd* and perhaps Aramaic *qupdâ* are derived; (2) *qpδ*, the root of Arabic *qunfuδ*[50] and perhaps of Hebrew *qippôz*, Aramaic *qup̄dâ* and Ge'ez *q^u^enfez;* and perhaps (3) *qpz*, if Hebrew *qippôz* is really related and Ge'ez *q^u^enfez* stems from it. (And perhaps even *qpṣ*.)

Because of the existence of Aramaic and Arabic *zmr* it is generally assumed that Hebrew *zmr* ("to make music, to sing") reflects PS *zmr*. Yet Zimmern (1917, p. 95, cited by Brockelmann, 1928, s.v.) has tentatively suggested that Hebrew and Aramaic *zmr* are borrowed from Akkadian (and Arabic *zmr* was again borrowed from Aramaic).[51] Since Akkadian *z* can reflect both PS *z* and *δ*, *zmr* may, if Zimmern's thesis proves true, be derived from both original **zmr* and **δmr*. Now Ugaritic *δmr* ("to play music")[52] has been discovered (Gordon, 1965, text 602:3). Thus, * Loewenstamm (1969)[53] postulated *δmr* as the original root, to become *zmr* in Hebrew and Akkadian, whereas in Aramaic and Arabic it exhibits loan words.[54] Another possibility would be to assume that *zmr* ("to sing")

original Arabic words as well, as *ḥanẓ*, see Blau (1970a, p. 127). I do not understand why, according to Garbini (1960, p. 196), the alternation of *δ* and *d* in *qunfuδ* suggests original *d*. Does he consider it an Aramaic loan word with original *d*, which had become spirantized after the vowel? Against this interpretation one could adduce Hommel's claim (1879, pp. 401ff), that "hedgehog" is a mammal known in Proto-Semitic (this could also be claimed against the assumption that Hebrew *qippôd* is a loan word; Hebrew *qippôd*, however, may be due to dialect mixture, rather than to borrowing, though the difference is somewhat slight). Moreover, it occurs early in Arabic poetry, see Hommel (1879, p. 339). If, in fact, *qunfūδ* were an Aramaic loan, one could derive the Hebrew, Aramaic, and Arabic words simply from *qfd*. In this case, however, one should consider Hebrew *qippôz* not related and Ge'ez *q^u^enfez* an Aramaic loan (with spirantized *d* > *z*) or an Arabic one, as indeed Geyer (1905, p. 118, note 2), on whom Jeffery relies, seems to assume.

49. Fraenkel (1886, p. XIV) regarded *qippôd* as an Aramaic loan.

50. So far, I have not found the root *qpδ* attested outside *qunfuδ* in Arabic, despite Růžička (1909, p. 133) where read *taqanfaδa*, a denominative verb derived from *qunfuδ*, for *taqaffaδa*.

51. If Epigraphic South-Arabic *zmr*, quoted by Koehler-Baumgartner (1967ff, s.v.), really existed (I could not verify it, nor is it mentioned in Müller's additions [1963, p. 308] to Koehler-Baumgartner [1953], where it is lacking)—it would, of course, invalidate Zimmern's suggestion to some extent. That Arabic *zmr* is an Aramaic loan word was already claimed by Schwally (1898, pp. 133–134).

52. *zmr* in this sense is not attested in Ugaritic, *pace* Koehler-Baumgartner (1967, s.v.), since it occurs in a completely obscure context. (In Koehler-Baumgartner, 1953, it was still adduced with a question mark.) Cf. also Loewenstamm (1969).

53. Incidentally, Loewenstamm did not know of Zimmern's proposal and only cited Schwally's view as to Arabic *zmr* being an Aramaic loan word.

54. He went so far as to assume that no homonymous root *δmr* (from which, as a rule, Hebrew *zimrā* in the phrase *'ozzî wəzimrāt YHWH* is derived) exists. He postulated *one*

with *z* in PS, and Ugaritic *δ* is due to the blend of two roots.[55] It is even possible that Ugaritic *δmr* ("to sing") is a scribal error, since in the same text *δmr* ("strength, might") occurs twice. At any rate, the case of *zmr* clearly demonstrates how intricate the etymology might be and how imperative it is to collect evidence piecemeal.

Another case of a Hebrew word whose etymology seemed perfectly clear till the discovery of Ugaritic is *ḥzy* ("to see") (cf. Blau, 1970b, pp. 439–440 for particulars), viz. PS *ḥzw*. Yet in Ugaritic *ḥdy* ("to see") is attested, which, it seems, reflects PS *ḥδw* from which, *inter alia,* Arabic *ḥiδā'a* ("opposite") and Hebrew *ḥāze* ("breast") are derived. Since the semantic shift "opposite" > "to see" is well attested,[56] it is easy to derive Hebrew *ḥzy* ("to see") from **ḥδw*. This was the reason that Ginsberg (1938, p. 210, note 3) proposed the following ingenious solution: Hebrew *ḥzy* ("to see") stems from PS *ḥδw* ("to be opposite" > "to see"), and no PS *ḥzw* exists at all. Hebrew *ḥzw* (later > *ḥzy*) was borrowed into

---

root *δmr* ("to praise in cultic song"), from which *zimrā,* standing parallel to *'oz* ("strength, might"), is derived in the sense of "the glory given to God in cultic song." Loewenstamm's thesis may be buttressed by the fact that in the morning prayer of "*yištabbaḥ*" in the phrase *kī ləḵā nā'ē . . . šīr ušḇāḥā hallēl wəzimrā 'oz umemšālā . . . bərāḵôt wəhôdā'ôt* ("because chant and laud, praise and song, strength and power . . . benedictions and thanks befit you"), "song" and "strength" are parallel. Loewenstamm calls attention to Ps 59:18 *'uzzī 'ēleḵā 'ăzammērā* ("my strength I sing to you"), where "strength" and "song" are also connected, and interprets *'ozzī wəzimrāt* accordingly. Yet although this interpretation is, no doubt, possible (cf. the papers pro and con of Good [1970] and Parker [1971]), it is by no means necessary. One may well claim that the phrase *'uzzī 'ēleḵā 'ăzammērā* is not a primary phrase exhibiting both *'oz* and *zimrā,* but rather a secondary one, some sort of play on words, imitating *'ozzī wəzimrāt,* which, though originally exhibiting *zimrā* ("strength, might"), was understood as "praise." Moreover, *δmr* ("to be strong") does not completely rely on Epigraphic South-Arabic, for which Loewenstamm has convincingly demonstrated that *δmr* having the sense of "strength" cannot be proved. As to the Samaritan gloss *zimrā* = "strength" (see Ben-Ḥayyim, 1957ff, II, pp. 96–97, 457, quoted also by Greenfield, 1964, p. 265), one may, to be sure, argue that it arose from the interpretation of *'ozzī wəzimrāt.* Yet cf. also Arabic *δimr, δamir, δamir* ("clever and brave") and Ugaritic *δmr* ("hero") (see, e.g., Caquot *et al.,* 1974, p. 159, note m; p. 217, note n). Moreover, one must not lose sight of the possibility that, as suggested by Montgomery, (1951, p. 289), (*'ozzī wə*)*zimrāt* is etymologically related to Syriac *dmr* ("to awe, wonder"). At any rate, this etymology is not less likely than that propounded by Brockelmann (1928, s.v.). Accordingly, I am inclined to postulate for Biblical Hebrew an additional root *zmr,* originally *δmr,* in the sense of "to be strong" (or "to be inspired with awe").

55. See Blau-Greenfield (1970, p. 12). One could imagine that it was through the influence of *δmr* ("to pronounce solemnly"), as preserved in Epigraphic South-Arabic (see Beeston, 1950, p. 265) and Ge'ez, that *zmr,* when used in the sense of "to sing publicly," shifted to *δmr.*

56. Cf., e.g., the Arabic synonyms *muqābala* and *mu'āyana* (see, e.g., Pollak, 1931, p. 102), and *'iyān* and *muwājaha* (ibn Manẓur, 1955–56, s.v. *'yn,* p. 302b).

Aramaic, from which again Arabic *ḥāzī* ("diviner") was borrowed. Yet despite its ingenuity, it is not easy to consent to this theory. Aramaic *ḥzw* (see also Koehler-Baumgartner, 1953, Aramaic part, s.v.) is so well attested that the assumption of a loan word is at least dubious,[57] and even Arabic *ḥāzī* is not as isolated as it would *prima facie* seem (see, e.g., Landberg, 1920–42, s.v.). Therefore, in my opinion, it is much more likely that PS *ḥzw* ("to see") and *ḥðw* ("to be opposite") coexisted in PS, and at a certain, still undefinable time, the latter developed into "to see." Hebrew *ḥzy* may, therefore, on principle, be regarded as the continuation of both roots. (See Gordon, 1965, s.v. For why **ḥzw* is more likely, see Blau, 1970b, p. 443, note 101.)

Another Hebrew root the etymology of which seemed fairly well established till the discovery of Ugaritic is *zrʿ* ("to sow"). It was generally derived from PS *zrʿ*, although Epigraphic South-Arabic *ðrʿ* ("seed") was already known.[58] As is often the case in Semitic linguistics, it was Nöldeke (1910, p. 164),[59] exhibiting his usual sober judgment, who determined (rightly, in my opinion) the relation between the forms with initial *ð* and initial *z:* he derives Arabic *ðura* ("holcus sorghum") from *ðurʿa*, stemming from *ðrʿ* as preserved in Arabic *ðaraʿa* and Geʿez *zarʿa* ("to scatter, to sow") (and, one may add, Epigraphic South-Arabic *ðrʿ*), which is related to Hebrew *zārā*, Arabic *ðarā*, Aramaic *dərā* and Geʿez *zarawa* ("to scatter, winnow") and which is to be separated from Arabic *zaraʿa*, Aramaic *zəraʿ* and Hebrew *zāraʿ*.[60] With the discovery of Ugaritic *ðrʿ* ("to sow"), the vantage point from which Hebrew *zrʿ* was looked on changed. Baumgartner (in Koehler-Baumgartner, 1953, Aramaic part, s.v. *zrʿ*, following H. Bauer), posited PS *ðrʿ*, and considered, somewhat hesitantly to be sure, Aramaic *zrʿ* as a Canaanite loan word, as did also

57. It is interesting to note that Wagner (1966, pp. 53–54), on the contrary, considers Hebrew *ḥzy* to be an Aramaic loan word. In the light of Ugaritic *ḥdy* and the occurrence of Hebrew *ḥzy* in pre-exilic writings, one would rather prefer the possibility (also considered by Wagner) that it is genuine Hebrew, yet its more frequent occurrence is due to Aramaic influence.

58. See Conti Rossini (1931, s.v.). It is noteworthy to remark that Stehle (1940, p. 513) and Beeston (1962, p. 13) do not adduce *ðrʿ* among the cases of exceptional sound correspondence of Epigraphic South-Arabic *ð* to PS *z* (in my opinion, rightly so, see *infra*).

59. Yet he adduced only Arabic *ðrʿ* and Geʿez *zarʿa* ("to scatter, sow"), without referring to Epigraphic South-Arabic.

60. Landberg (1920–42, s.vv. *ðry*, *zrʿ*, especially p. 940), in accordance with his method of "great" etymology, which connects roots exhibiting similar radicals (cf. *supra*), expressly opposed Nöldeke and connected all these roots, as did also, e.g., Mühlau-Volck (1890, s.vv. *zrʿ*, I *zrr*).

Aro (1964).[61] This, however, is less likely than Loewenstamm's suggestion (1962) that Ugaritic *ðr'*, which does not denote "to sow" only, but also "to winnow, disperse," is due to a blend of PS *zr'* ("to sow") and *ðrw* ("to winnow, disperse"). One may tentatively add that South Semitic (Epigraphic South-Arabic, Arabic, Ge'ez) *ðr'* ("to disperse, sow"), which is no doubt related to **ðrw*, has also presumably received the meaning of "sowing" by semantic attraction to *zr'* ("to sow").

Hebrew *zrq* ("to throw"), no doubt, corresponds to PS *zrq*. It could however, also reflect **ðrq*, cf. Arabic *ðrq*, which, however (*pace* Gesenius-Buhl, 1915, s.v. *zrq*), does not denote "to throw," but "to dung" (see Blau, 1970a, p. 49, note 9. Aramaic *drq* is not, it seems, a genuine form, see note 61.) It is not unlikely that *zrq-ðrq* constitute a PS doublet. For Hebrew *zky* ("to be pure"), see the literature cited in Blau (1970a, p. 49, note 9). Hebrew *giddep̄* ("to revile, blaspheme") is related not only to Syriac, Judeo-Aramaic and Christian Aramaic *gaddep̄* in the same sense, but, it seems, also to Ge'ez *gdf* ("to throw,[62] repudiate"), on the one hand, and to Epigraphic South-Arabic, *gðf* ("to blaspheme") on the other. (See Stehle, 1940, p. 513, and note 60, without, however, consenting to all the correspondences adduced there.) If, in the light of Epigraphic South-Arabic *gðf*, one postulated PS *gðp*, one should regard Hebrew *giddep̄* as an Aramaic loan word, since PS *gðp* should be reflected by Hebrew **gzp̄*.[63] Yet Ge'ez *gdf*, in my opinion, proves the *d* to be

61. Aro also, with similar hesitation, suggested that Arabic *zr'* is a Canaanite loan word. Another possibility, according to this theory, would be to consider the Arabic word an Aramaic loan word. Both Baumgartner and Aro cited Aramaic *dr'*: Baumgartner as Judeo-Aramaic, Aro as Aramaic without qualifications. As a matter of fact, *dr'* (just as *drq*) is restricted to various Targumic texts, and the question arises of how reliable these forms are, especially since *zr'-dr'* (and *zrq-drq*) alternate. Fraenkel (1905) regarded both verbs as due to dissimilation of *z* > *d* in the vicinity of *r* (see *supra*, note 45). Kutscher (1967, p. 173) and Koehler-Baumgartner (1967ff, s.v. *zrq*) however, regarded *drq* as hyper-Aramaism and *dr'* (Koehler-Baumgartner 1967ff, s.v. *zr'*) as a dubious form; I am inclined to accept this view (*pace* Blau, 1970a, p. 48, note 9) in light of Exod 19:13 Targum Neofiti and Paris 110 *yzdrqwn*, Kahle (1930, p. 56) *yzdrqn*, as against British Museum add. 27031 *ydryqwn;* Exod 9:8 Neofiti *wyzrwq* as against British Museum *wydrqynyh*.

62. For the semantic shift "to throw" > "to curse" cf. Nöldeke (1910, p. 47, note 3), Fraenkel (1886, p. 228), Gesenius-Buhl (1915, s.v. *gdp*), Blau-Loewenstamm (1970, p. 9, note 13). Cf. also Nöldeke (1952, s.v. *'abana*, "to speak evil of"), if I am correct in deriving it from "to throw stones." In this case, it would exhibit an additional relic of Semitic **'abn* ("stone") in Arabic, besides that cited by Nöldeke (1886, p. 724).

63. So hesitantly Fraenkel (1886, p. 228), who connected the Hebrew word with Arabic *qaðafa* ("to throw"). Yet later (1898, p. 74) he, silently, accepted Barth's etymology (1893, p. 28), who compared Arabic *jdb* ("to disapprove") and assumed alternation of *p-b* as third radical, thus postulating original *d* for *giddep̄*. Nöldeke (1910, p. 62) also changed his mind

original, since the Ge'ez word cannot be considered an Aramaic loan,[64] because Ge'ez has well preserved the presumably original meaning of *gdp*, viz. "to throw" (see note 62), which, as far as I know, is not attested in any Aramaic dialect. Accordingly, one would rather postulate at least two PS related roots, presumably even more, viz. (in the light of Ge'ez) *gdp*[65] and (cf. Epigraphic South-Arabic) *gδp*, with which *qδp*, as occurring in Arabic, is related. Aramaic *gaddep̄* may reflect both **gdp* and **gδp*.[66]

Hebrew *gzm* ("to cut"; in the Bible, in derivations only) has many correspondences to roots in various Semitic languages which reflect PS *gzm*. Yet in different languages reflections of what seems to be PS *gzm*, *gδm*, and *gdm* with a similar meaning are well attested,[67] exhibiting either genuine variations in PS or later attraction of originally different roots. Hebrew *dlp* ("to drip") corresponds to roots in Semitic tongues reflecting PS *dlp*. Yet in Middle Hebrew and Judeo-Aramaic *zlp* ("to sprinkle, pour") is attested, as well as in Syriac in similar meaning,[68] presumably

---

and hesitantly suggested the possibility of different roots attracting each other for Arabic-Ge'ez-Tigre *qδf*, *ǵδf*, *ǵdf*, *ḥdf*, *jδf*, *jdf*. Wagner (1966, p. 39) considered Hebrew *giddep* an Aramaic loan, and consistently assumed the same for Arabic *jaddafa* and Ge'ez *gadafa*. For the latter see *infra*.

64. In Ge'ez, PS *δ* is reflected by *z*, rather than by *d*.

65. Somewhat complicated is the case of Arabic *jaddafa*. In Classical Arabic it denotes "to deny a favor," rather than "to blaspheme." It was Golius who, relying on Hebrew *giddep*, interpreted Arabic *jaddafa* in the sense of blaspheming (see Lane, 1863–93, s.v.), and from here it passed to European works dealing with etymology (as Gesenius-Buhl, 1915, s.v.; Wagner, 1966; Koehler-Baumgartner, 1967ff, s.v.; Barthélemy, 1935ff, s.v.; yet not in Brown *et al.*, 1907, s.v.). In the sense of blasphemy I know it only from dialects—its first attestation, so far as I know, being Bocthor, adduced by Dozy (1881, s.v.); see also Barthélemy (1935ff, s.v.) and Spiro (1895, s.v.). In the dialects it may well be an Aramaic loan; cf. Féghali (1920, p. 257; 1922, pp. 15, 27) for Lebanese *ǵaddef* (Féghali, by the way, also postulates for Classical Arabic *jaddafa* the meaning of blaspheming); Frayha (1947, s.v. *ǵaddaf*). The original meaning of *jaddafa* ("to deny a favor") may well have been "to cut," a sense preserved by Arabic *jadafa*, and originally it may not be related to Ge'ez *gadafa*, "to throw" > "to blaspheme."

66. *gdp* ("to scrape"), attested in Mandaic (see Drower-Macuch, 1963, s.v.) and in Middle Hebrew (see, e.g., Jastrow, 1903, s.v.) continues, it seems, *gdp* ("to cut"), rather than *gdp* ("to throw").

67. See, e.g., Gesenius-Buhl (1915) and Brown *et al.* (1907), s.v. *gzm*; Stehle (1940, p. 514); Brockelmann (1928, s.vv. *gdm*, *gzm*); Soden (1965ff, s.v. *gadāmu*); further Landberg (1920–42, s.v. *jdm*). Cf. also the alternation of *gdd*, *gδδ*, *gzz* (see Mühlau-Volck, 1890, s.v. *gdd*; Koehler-Baumgartner, 1967ff, s.v. Landberg, 1920–42, s.v.). Cf. also Arabic *jadafa* ("to cut") in note 65 above, and Greenfield (1958, p. 210, note 20), who also mentions *gd'*/*gz'*.

68. See, e.g., Gesenius-Buhl (1915); Brown *et al.* (1907); Koehler-Baumgartner (1967ff); Brockelmann (1928, s.v. *dlp*); Levy (1867–68 and 1876–89); Jastrow (1903); Payne Smith (1879–1901); Brockelmann (1928, s.v. *zlp*).

not a genuine doublet, but due to attraction of *dlp* by a root like *zlḥ* ("to shed, to sprinkle").[69]

2. Hebrew and PS *ś*

There exists an ever-growing literature dealing with non-voiced, non-emphatic sibilants in Semitic languages in general and in Hebrew in particular. Many of these studies, in one way or another, pivot upon the fact that in the Hebrew alphabet *ś* is the only phoneme[70] marked polyphonically rather than by a special letter.[71] On the other hand, the tradition for the existence of *ś* is well established and the main lines of development, as traditionally explained (see, e.g. Bergsträsser, 1918–29, I, pp. 6, 88) and also accepted by us, are quite clear: the Hebrew alphabet stems from a language in which *š* and *ś* have merged, presumably in *š*. Since the Hebrews did not add new letters to the accepted alphabet, they used *š* (ש) polyphonically, for both *š* and *ś*.[72] And, indeed, comparison with other Semitic languages clearly demonstrates the genuine character of the differentiation between *š* and *ś* in Hebrew, today pronounced *š* and *s*, respectively (except by Samaritans, who pronounce both of them as *š*), and establishes the separate existence of *ś*, different from both PS *š* and *s*. *ś*, i.e. the letter spelled ש and pronounced *s*, exhibits a regular correspondence to many other Semitic languages, different from the sound correspondence of both *š* (i.e. the letter spelled ש and pronounced *š*) and *s* (i.e., the letter *samek*, pronounced *s*). *s* invariably corresponds to *s* in

69. Cf., e.g., Levy (1876–89); Brockelmann (1928, s.v.). Otherwise Greenfield (1958, p. 210).

70. The spirant variants of *b, g, d, k, p, t* are allophones only.

71. Additional letters of the Hebrew alphabet, to be sure, might have been polyphonic. If ʿ and *ḥ*, in fact, marked two different sounds till the end of the second century B.C.E., viz. ʿ/*ġ* and *ḥ*/*ḫ* respectively (see, e.g., Bergsträsser, 1918–29, I, pp. 36–38), they have to be regarded as polyphonic for that period. Yet this fact, if correct, has to be inferred and has not been handed down by living tradition as in the case of *ś*. On the other hand, even *ś* is not pronounced today as a phonetic entity differing from other sounds of the Hebrew alphabet, but as *s* like *samek*.

72. As a rule, it is postulated that the pronunciation of *ś* was closer to *š* than to *s*, and therefore ש, the letter marking *š*, was chosen to represent *ś* (see e.g., Bergsträsser, 1918–29, I, p. 42). Yet it is not impossible that ש was chosen by the impact of the language from which the Hebrew alphabet was borrowed. In this language ש was used for marking not only original *š*, but also *ś*. Therefore, since Hebrew words containing *ś* corresponded to words of that language spelled with ש, ש was used for marking *ś*, even if *ś* happened to be closer to *s* than to *š*. Cf., for the similar choice of Arabic *ṭ*/ʿ for marking *ẓ*/*ġ* respectively through the influence of Nabatean Aramaic, Blau (1970a, pp. 59–60).

other Semitic languages, š corresponds to š in most Semitic languages, with the exception of Arabic and Ge'ez (and later Assyrian), in which it appears as *s*. *ś* is exhibited by *š* in Akkadian, Ugaritic, Arabic, and Ethiopic, by a special letter in Epigraphic South-Arabic (and by a special sound in Modern South-Arabic) and is spelled in early Aramaic with ש, in later Aramaic with *samek*. The simplest and most reasonable interpretation of the special correspondence of Hebrew *ś* is the assumption of a separate PS phoneme *śîn*, which continued its existence in South Arabic, as well as in early Aramaic and (in a changed form) in Arabic and Ge'ez and, of course, in early Hebrew. Exceptions to regular sound correspondence are, to be sure, attested. They have, however, to be carefully balanced against regular sound correspondences and reduced, as far as possible, to their proper dimensions, the more so, since, as we have seen in Section 1 above, deviations from regular sound correspondence occur with other Hebrew (and Semitic) sounds as well.

2.1 Critical Analysis of Vollers (1894)

In many ways, one may regard Vollers (1894) as the prototype of works disregarding typical sound development in favor of deviant and random features. This article is now, for all practical purposes, forgotten. Yet it deserves careful consideration, since it demonstrates to what extremes the negligence of sound philological method may lead, even though this paper reflects great erudition and acumen, or perhaps because of these qualities. Its main thesis is the division of the Semitic languages into two groups, one exhibiting sibilants and their variants ("the S-group"), the other occlusives and their variants ("the T-group"). It is based on a long series of comparisons of words in which the S-group and the T-group allegedly interchange, often stemming from a somewhat uncurbed fantasy. Thus Arabic *šariba* ("to drink") is related to *θirb* ("fat") (p. 191); Hebrew *šāgag* ("to go astray, commit sin") to Arabic *θajja* ("to flow strongly") and *miθajj* ("voluble orator"), allegedly because the Hebrew word denotes sin committed by quick and negligent speech! (p. 193); Hebrew *sətāw* ("winter," i.e. "the period of rain") is connected with *šātā* ("to drink") (pp. 201–202; on p. 209 this correspondence is adduced as a certain case); Hebrew *kesel* ("loins") is, on the one hand, related to *kōtel* ("wall," originally "to be compact") (p. 193), and on the other, to *kāšal* ("to stumble, stagger") (p. 202); Hebrew *šmm* (*inter alia*, "to be appalled") allegedly corresponds to Aramaic (and, one may add, to Hebrew) *tmh* ("to be astounded") and Arabic *whm, thm* ("to imagine"), although the latter is doubtlessly secondary (p. 194). One would not be surprised when, on the strength of such comparisons, Vollers, *inter alia*, arrives at the conclusion (p. 171) that irregular correspondences of sibilants are almost as frequent as the regular ones, and reconstructs a phase in which *s* was the only unvoiced non-emphatic sibilant (p. 210), which only later shifted, under yet unspecified conditions, to *š*. So, in Vollers' opinion (pp. 211–212), the ancient *sb'* ("to be satiated") coexisted in Hebrew with the later, originally southern, *šb'*. Eventually, *sb'* prevailed, and this is the reason for ש in such words being pronounced as *s*. *ś*, in Vollers' opinion, never existed, and one must not (p. 213) infer from Epigraphic South-Arabic s_3 that PS had three non-emphatic unvoiced sibilants. In Vollers' opinion, it is the result of the collision of two speech communities. We shall, however, see in the following (Section 3 below) that deviations from regular sound shift of sibilants occur in a minority of cases only, and they have to be interpreted as due to special reasons. Accordingly, for PS, as accepted, a series of three unvoiced non-emphatic sibilants has to be postulated, viz. *s, š, ś*.

2.2 Critical Analysis of Gumpertz (1953)

Gumpertz (1953, pp. 33–50; English summary, p. iii) has reconstructed a somewhat similar development of unvoiced non-emphatic sibilants. If I understand him properly,[73] he too postulates one sibilant of this kind, the pronunciation of which, however, was with a bilateral lisp.[74]

73. Cf. Ben-Ḥayyim's judicious remarks (1955, pp. 165–166).

74. He even claims that different pronunciations of *š* and *ś* cannot be established until the time of the *naqdānîm*, and that the first authentic testimony for the difference between the pronunciation of ש and *samek* can be traced to Jerome only. Cf. against this view the judicious remarks of Kutscher (1955, p. 361). On the other hand, the core of Gumpertz' paper on the pronunciation of ש is quite important for the history of the pronunciation of this letter, since it demonstrates that all over Europe, with the exception of Arabic-speaking Spain, the pronunciation of ש as *ś* was entirely unknown in the early Middle Ages.

3. Critical Analysis of Magnanini (1974)

In a recent article, Magnanini (1974) also arrives at the conclusion that no PS *ś* existed. In the main part of his paper, Magnanini analyzes 93 Arabic roots containing *š*, which, according to the current view, should correspond to PS and Hebrew *ś*. He also collected ten cases of Arabic *s* corresponding to Hebrew *ś*, rather than to Hebrew (and PS) *s*/*š*. Taken altogether, he examined 103 cases and found that only 35 exhibit "regular" sound correspondence, as against 68 "irregular" cases. From this extreme irregularity he infers that PS *ś* is a ghost phoneme.

3.1 Attestations of PS *ś* outside Hebrew

Even before we scrutinize the alleged irregular correspondence of Hebrew *ś* and Arabic *š*, we want to stress that the existence of PS *ś* by no means depends on Hebrew only. It is attested in South Arabic as well, further in Proto-Sinaitic inscriptions, as well as in transcriptions exhibited by Egyptian texts, the al-Amarna letters from Jerusalem (see Diem, 1974, pp. 228ff) and by Old Akkadian (Diem, 1974, p. 248).

3.2 Unvoiced Non-Emphatic Sibilants in Epigraphic South-Arabic

Magnanini was, it seems, aware of this problem. Therefore, in a somewhat summarizing way,[75] he cites eleven cases from Epigraphic South-Arabic and, adding that they could easily be augmented, infers from them that the third unvoiced non-emphatic sibilant exhibits an innovation. Yet, even before analyzing these examples, one must not lose sight of the fact that the texts mentioned above, even without the Hebrew and Epigraphic South-Arabic evidence, postulate the existence of PS *ś*.

From the eleven cases cited by Magnanini from Epigraphic South-Arabic, four contain s_1 (as a rule, and in my opinion correctly, considered to represent PS *š*). Three of them allegedly correspond to PS *s*: *'*s_1*r*,

75. He adduces LaSor (1957–58) and Beeston (1962), yet not Cantineau (1935–45), Stehle (1940), Beeston (1951).

which, however, is due to an error of Conti Rossini, 1931, s.v. (see Stehle, 1940, p. 524, note 185), the correct reading being *'*s_3*r* (s_3 is, as a rule, and correctly in my opinion, identified with PS *s*), which thus reflects regular sound correspondence. *hrs*$_1$ is identified by many with Hebrew *hrs;* yet its correlation with s_1*trs*$_1$, i.e., an *'ištaf'al* form, makes one assume that the *h* of *hrs*$_1$ may be the prefix of *hf'l* (cf. Jamme, 1962, p. 13b, where additional literature is cited). The third, and last, example is the proper noun *ḥs*$_1$*n,* which allegedly corresponds to Hebrew *ḥsn* ("to be strong"). This correspondence, however, is wholly imaginary.[76] The fourth example with s_1, the proper noun (!) *dws*$_1$, allegedly corresponds to the Hebrew proper noun *dîśôn,* exhibiting the exceptional sound correspondence Epigraphic South-Arabic s_1 = Hebrew (and PS) *ś.* Yet the Hebrew proper noun is *dîšôn,*[77] thus exhibiting a completely regular sound correspondence. Moreover, there is no need whatsoever for the Hebrew and Epigraphic South-Arabic proper nouns to be in fact related.[78]

Magnanini cites three cases of s_2 corresponding to Hebrew (and PS) *š,* rather than to the expected *ś.* Yet all of them are dubious. For *ws*$_2$*':* see, e.g., Beeston (1951, p. 16) and Jamme (1962, p. 38a);[79] for s_2*'w:* Beeston (1951, p. 16) and Müller (1963, p. 316); for s_2*ft:* Müller (1963, p. 316).[80]

From the four cases cited for s_3, which should correspond to PS *s,* one, allegedly exhibiting the correspondence s_3 = Hebrew *š* (viz. s_3*wd* = Hebrew *šēd*), is completely imaginary: see for the various possibilities of the origin of the Hebrew word the biblical dictionaries s.v., especially Brown *et al.* (1907). Moreover, Hebrew *šēd* in the sense of "lord," rather than "demon," is a mere *etymologicum.* The other three adduced cases with s_3 allegedly correspond to Hebrew *ś.* The only possible case of exception from regular sound correspondence among them is perhaps Epigraphic South-Arabic *ḥs*$_3$*r* and Hebrew **ḥaśrā/*ḥăšērā,* yet even it is

76. The Epigraphic South-Arabic proper noun could, for instance, correspond to Arabic *ḥasan* ("beautiful"), a very frequent proper noun in Arabic, if the latter exhibits PS *ḥšn.* Incidentally, Conti Rossini (1931, s.v.) connected these two words, yet mixed them up again with Hebrew *ḥsn* as well, thus apparently misleading Magnanini.

77. In Conti Rossini (1931, s.v.) *dîšôn* is spelled correctly yet the other Hebrew proper noun, *dîšān,* is erroneously spelled *dîśān* with *ś,* and this, perhaps, misled Magnanini.

78. Thus the Hebrew one may reflect original *θ* (cf., e.g., Gesenius-Buhl, 1915, s.v.).

79. I would like to add that in Middle Hebrew, *siyya'* (originally *śiyya'*) denotes "to aid."

80. Incidentally, Hebrew *šāpat* ("to set on the fire, establish"), with which Magnanini compares this word, exhibits, it seems, PS *θ*, both if it corresponds to Ugaritic *θpd* ("to put") or—what is, in my opinion, more likely—if it is a denominative verb, derived from a noun from the root *θpy,* denoting the stone supporting the kettle.

by no means certain.[81] Compare Stehle (1940, p. 536), who adduces Beeston's view, for *'r*s_3; and pp. 536–537, for *'*s_3*b*.

The inference to be drawn from these cases is quite simple: as Stehle (1940), Cantineau (1935–45), LaSor (1957–58), and Beeston (1951 and 1962) have demonstrated, the Epigraphic South-Arabic sibilants reflect completely regular sound correspondence, as also exhibited by the examples cited by Magnanini.

3.3 Correspondences of Hebrew and Arabic Sibilants

The correspondences Magnanini adduced for Arabic *š* and Hebrew *ś* are not irregular either. The allegedly irregular character of the correspondence of Hebrew *ś* originates in etymologies which are partly based on loan words, on dissimilations, on quite unlikley semantic shifts (disregarding much more likely ones), and even on mere errors. A small number of *possible* (but by no means *necessary*) irregular correspondences remain. But these, however, should be discarded, because they contravene regular sound shift and are not necessary. In one case only, viz. Hebrew *śwq* = Arabic *šwq* ("to desire"), there is, it seems, a genuine deviation from sound shift.[82] I have, in the following, arranged the material according to Hebrew roots, because it is much easier to check the etymology with the help of the biblical, rather than Arabic, dictionaries. I have also divided the material according to the sound correspondences which they exhibit.[83]

81. For the Epigraphic South-Arabic word, cf. Stehle (1940, p. 537). According to Magnanini himself, the Hebrew word corresponds to Arabic *ḥšr* as well, so that one should posit a triple irregular correspondence, viz. Epigraphic South-Arabic s_3 (as a rule reflecting PS *s*), Hebrew (and PS) *ś*, and Arabic *š* (corresponding, as a rule, to PS *ś*)! Moreover, the Hebrew word *may* denote the (heavenly) sieve and correspond to Ugaritic *ḫθr*, thus exhibiting original *θ*.

82. One could hardly consent to Brockelmann (1908–13, I, p. 167), who, in the main, follows Barth (1893, p. 46), that the Arabic *š* is due to assimilation to the following *q*. Fraenkel (1898, p. 80), on the other hand, suggests lexical contamination.

83. As a rule, I am citing roots or, in the case of the clear nominal character of the root, the noun. Magnanini, as a rule (yet see *šemeš*, *'eśer*, *resen*, *šōrēr*, *kāsûăḥ*, etc., further *II w/y* roots, as *ṭwś*) adduces roots in the third person sing. masc. of *qal*, even of nominal roots like *šāpan*. As a rule, I do not adduce the meanings, if they can easily be found in the biblical dictionaries for Hebrew and the usual dictionaries for Arabic. Magnanini cites the meaning of the Arabic verb, the Hebrew meaning being quoted after "(ebr)" (see, e.g., *resen*, *šōrēr*, *'eśer*). As a rule, however, "(ebr)" is missing, giving the impression that the Arabic verb

3.3.1

Hebrew *ś* corresponding to Arabic *š*, as stated by Magnanini himself:[84] *'rś; ḥpś*, for which Magnanini cites two Arabic correspondences, viz. *ḥfš*, which seems to be appropriate, and *ḫfš*, the meaning of which does not fit at all;[85] *ṭwś; kārēś; ngś* (cf. also note 28); *nś'; 'eśeb; 'eśer; prś; pśy; pś'*, whose correspondence with Arabic *fšġ*, however (cf. Koehler-Baumgartner, 1953, s.v.), is rather dubious; *qaśwā; śb'; śhd; śṭn* (cf. also Blau, 1970a, p. 103); *śyb; śyd; śmḥ; śimlā; śn'; śrg; śrd; śrṭ; śry; śrq; śtr*, altogether 26 cases. Add to them two cases in which Magnanini wrongly connects Hebrew *ś* with Arabic *s*, rather than with Arabic *š*, viz. Hebrew *bśm* as against Arabic *bašām* ("spice") (for the problem of Arabic *bšm*, see Gesenius-Buhl, 1915, s.v., who adduced Lagarde's view); and Hebrew *bśr*, which is connected by Magnanini not only correctly with Arabic *bšr*, but also with *bsr*, which, however, has a totally unsuitable meaning ("to frown"). (For its Semitic correspondences see Brockelmann, 1928, s.v. *bsr*.) Magnanini also adduces three cases in which *ś* and *s* alternate in the Hebrew root, corresponding to Arabic *š*. This has to be interpreted as reflecting original Hebrew *ś*, *s* being due to later orthographic habit: *grś/s*, *ḥrś/s*, and *ś/sbk* (see Blau, 1970a, p. 114, and p. 115, respectively). Magnanini connects Hebrew *s'r* with Arabic *šġr*. Yet the Hebrew root alternates with *ś'r*. Moreover, the correspondence with Arabic *šġr* is very dubious and, therefore, it is rather uncertain whether in this case too Hebrew *ś* is matched by Arabic *š* (cf. Blau, 1970a, p. 115, especially note 5). An additional case of Hebrew *ś* corresponding to Arabic *š* is Hebrew *qimmôś* as against Arabic *qummāš*; yet Magnanini adopts the inferior reading *qimmōš*.[86]

---

denotes the meanings of the Hebrew one as well. In most cases I have not called attention to it. Similarly, I have not corrected small deviations. Even if the etymologies of the current biblical dictionaries differ from those proposed by Magnanini, I have not, as a rule, referred to them, contenting myself with stating that Magnanini's etymology is not necessary.

84. As in etymologies in general, not all the cases cited are certain. Yet since Magnanini agreed to these etymologies, I have, as a rule, adduced them without comment. I have, however, omitted Hebrew *qəśîṭā* since the meaning of the proposed Arabic *qšṭ* was too different (the etymology of the Hebrew word being, in fact, unknown), further *śḥṭ*, which does not fit Arabic *šḥṭ* in meaning. For *śyn* read **šyn*, only preserved as *kətīḇ*, the *š* being proven by the secondary root *štn* (cf. also Middle Hebrew *šeten* "urine"), corresponding to *θ*, *inter alia* in Arabic *maθāna*, which has given rise to the secondary root *mθn* and is felt as derived from it.

85. For particulars see Blau (1955, p. 342 and note 1) and Wagner (1966, pp. 59–60).

86. For *qimmôś* with *ś* see the biblical dictionaries; *ś* is also the reading of the Aleppo Codex and Ms. Leningrad B19a.

3.3.2

Besides *bśm* and *bśr*, treated above, Magnanini claims in nine additional cases that Hebrew *ś* corresponds to Arabic *s*. Yet in three cases only is this correspondence in any way likely, and on the strength of such narrow evidence one will hardly jump to the conclusion that the sound correspondence of Hebrew *ś* is not constant. The three cases are: *ḥśp*, which, however, may reflect a blend of *ḥśp* with *ḥsp*, since it corresponds to Ugaritic *ḥsp* (see also Blau, 1970a, pp. 124, 134); *rpś*, which Magnanini collates with Arabic *rfs* which, however, may itself very well correspond to Hebrew *rms*;[87] and *śbr*.[88] So even in these cases, which are the most likely ones, it is rather dubious that Hebrew *ś*, in fact, is matched by Arabic *s*. Even less certain are the other cases. If *miśpāḥ* ("bloodshed") really corresponds to Arabic *sfḥ* ("to pour out"), the spelling with *ś* should be considered secondary on the strength of **sāpîăḥ* ("shower"), spelled with (original) *s* (cf. Blau, 1970a, p. 123). The meaning of Hebrew *śdd* ("to harrow") can hardly be connected with Arabic *sdd* ("to be right"), nor can Hebrew *śāde* ("field") be connected with Arabic *sdw* ("to extend," especially hand). Expressions like *laylun musaddan* ("extended night," see Dozy [1881, s.v.]) are rare and, it seems, secondary. Arabic *sikkīn*, corresponding to Hebrew *śakkîn*, is an Aramaic loan word (see Fraenkel, 1886, p. 84). Hebrew *śkk* alternates with *skk*, Arabic *skk* corresponding to the latter, *škk* to the former (cf. also Blau, 1970a, p. 116). As to Hebrew *śəmāmît* ("a kind of lizard"), it is dubious whether it can be connected with Arabic *samm* ("poison").[89]

3.3.3

Magnanini also attempts to show the late character of Hebrew *ś* by

87. In Biblical Hebrew *rpś* and *rps* alternate. It stands to reason that the *ś* is original and the *s* due to the impact of *rms*; see Blau (1970a, p. 122), following Barth and Fraenkel (see Blau, 1970a, note 39).

88. For the possibility of Arabic *š*, rather than *s*, corresponding to the *ś* in this word see e.g., the literature cited in Brockelmann (1928, s.v. *I sbr*), and cf. also. Ginzberg (1934) and Wagner (1966, p. 108). Personally, I would vote for dialectal Arabic *šbr* ("to look") as the most likely correspondence for Hebrew *sbr*. Cf. also Landberg (1920–42, s.v., *šbr*) and further Classical *šbr* ("to measure by span"), admittedly a denominative verb, wrongly connected with Hebrew *šbr* by Magnanini (see *infra* Section 3.3.3, end).

89. And even if so, one must not lose sight of the fact that the latter is an Aramaic loan word, as surmised, because of the inconsistency of its vowel, by Fraenkel (1886, p. 262). For the problem of *samm* cf. also Blau (1970a, pp. 119–120).

the alleged correspondence of Arabic *š* with Hebrew *š*, rather than with *ś*. As mentioned in 3.3 above, however, among Magnanini's examples there is only one really convincing case, viz. Hebrew and Arabic *šwq* ("to desire"). In eleven other cases the correspondence is possible, but by no means necessary. Again, the basis of the deviant correspondence is so narrow that one would not, on the strength of it, jump to the conclusion that the sound correspondence Arabic *š*—Hebrew *ś* is not regular. The cases are: *'šr*, compared by Magnanini with Arabic *'šr*, though it may correspond to Arabic *ysr*,[90] exhibiting regular sound correspondence; **ḥašrā/ḥăšērā* (see also Kutscher, 1957, p. 252, but cf. note 81 above); *ḥăšaš* ("chaff"), not necessarily corresponding to Arabic *ḥašīš*, but rather to *ḥuθθ* (see Gesenius-Buhl, 1915, s.v.); *nšl* possibly matched by Arabic *nsl*, rather than by *nšl*;[91] Arabic *ntš*, which according to Magnanini corresponds to Hebrew *ntš*,[92] is, in my opinion, best interpreted as reflecting alternation of the third radical of roots beginning with *nt*, as exhibited by Hebrew *ntš*, *nts*, *ntṣ*, *nt'*, ultimately originating in PS *ntś* (cf. also Wagner, 1966, p. 85); similarly Arabic *'qš*, allegedly matched by Hebrew *'qš*, presumably exhibits alternation of the third radical of roots beginning with *'q* (cf. Syriac *'qs*, Arabic *'qṣ*; for *possible* additional cases, see Gesenius, 1835ff, s.v.; Mühlau-Volck, 1890, s.v. *'qb*), ultimately going back to PS *'qś*, which may be reflected by Syriac *'qs* as well (*pace* Brockelmann, 1928, s.v.); *pwš/pyš*; *qrš*; *šbb*;[93] *šwṭ*; *šôrēr*.

In the following cases, the exceptional sound correspondence Hebrew *š*—Arabic *š* (which, by the way, is not always certain) is, it seems, due to the dissimilatory effect of an additional sibilant in the Arabic root (for particulars cf. *infra* Section 4.3): *šzr*; *šḥṣ*; *šemeṣ*; *šemeš*; *šsp*. In other cases, the assumption of Arabic *s* corresponding to Hebrew *š* is, in my opinion, much likelier than Arabic *š*: a clear mistake is that Hebrew *ḥbš* is matched by Arabic *ḥbš*, since its Arabic correspondence is, no doubt, *ḥbs*; Hebrew *ḥwš* ("to feel")[94] corresponds to Arabic *ḥss* in the same sense;

90. For the alternation of ' and *y* as first radical see, e.g., Nöldeke's masterly paper (1910, pp. 202–206), where the alternation of initial *w/y* is treated as well.

91. Cf. also Arabic *sll* corresponding to Hebrew *šll* ("to draw out"). Arabic *nšl* was even considered by Fraenkel (1886, p. 88) an Aramaic loan, yet his arguments are not convincing. By no means would one interpret the *š* of *nšl* as being due to an *ad hoc* dissimilation (*pace* Brockelmann, 1908–13, I, p. 167; cf. also Landberg, 1920–42, s.v.).

92. According to Fraenkel (1886, p. 137), Arabic *ntš* is an Aramaic loan, a somewhat unlikely supposition in the light of the existence of Ge'ez *nšt* with metathesis.

93. Besides the biblical dictionaries see also Fraenkel (1898, pp. 80–81), Koehler-Baumgartner (1953, Aramaic part, s.v. *šəbīb*), Wagner (1966, pp. 111–112). Cf. also Beeston (1951, p. 11).

94. I assume that Magnanini had this meaning of *ḥwš* in mind, since the meanings ad-

Hebrew *neḥšāl* exhibits formal and semantic similarity not only with Arabic *ḥšl/ḫšl*, as proposed by Magnanini, but also with *ḥsl/ḫsl* (and even with *ḥθl*); Hebrew *r'š* is matched not only by Arabic *r'š*, but also by Arabic *r's* (which is, admittedly, less frequent); Hebrew *šibbōlet* ("ear of grain") must not be derived from Arabic *šbl* ("to grow"), since the latter is clearly a denominative from *šibl* ("whelp"). Although Arabic *sunbula* ("ear of grain") may well be an Aramaic loan (see Jeffery, 1938, pp. 178–179), the Arabic correspondence of Hebrew *šbl* seems to be *sbl* (see the biblical dictionaries); for Hebrew *šeger* ("offspring") cf. the literature adduced by Gesenius-Buhl (1915, s.v.), and especially Fraenkel (1886, p. 114, note 1). Besides, one has to take the possibility into consideration that *šeger* denotes "womb" rather than "offspring" (see Feigin, 1926, p. 44); as to Hebrew *šḥṭ*, according to ibn Sida (cited in Landberg, 1901, p. 388), Arabic *sḥṭ* has to be preferred to Arabic *šḥṭ* (see also Landberg, 1920–42 s.vv. *sḥṭ, šḥṭ;* Beeston, 1951, p. 11); Arabic *šṭf* is not the genuine correspondence of Hebrew *šṭp*, but rather an Aramaic loan,[95] as also hinted by its restricted dialectal attestation (see Barthélemy, 1935ff, s.v.; further Almkvist, 1925, p. 57, note 1). On the other hand, Arabic *sṭf* (see the literature adduced in Gesenius-Buhl, 1915, s.v. *šṭp*), which *prima facie* may reflect the genuine correspondence of Hebrew *šṭp*, is very restricted as well and may reflect a loan word adapted to Arabic;[96] Hebrew *šrg* simply does not exist.

In other cases it is Arabic *θ*, rather than alleged *š*, that corresponds to Hebrew *š:* Arabic *qašš*, corresponding to Hebrew *qaš* ("chaff"), is an Aramaic loan (see Fraenkel, 1886, p. 137), and if one insists that Hebrew *qšš* ("to gather") is related to an Arabic verb in the sense of collecting, rather than being a denominative verb from *qaš*, meaning "to gather stubble" (*qšš* in Zeph 2:1 is obscure), one would prefer to connect it with Arabic *qθθ;* Hebrew *ḥrš* does not correspond to Arabic *ḥrš* nor to *ḫrš*, but to *ḥrθ;* Hebrew *'šš* ("to be wasted away"), if it is related to an Arabic verb

---

duced "to have fear, be shaken, agitated" (cf. Syriac *ḥss*, "feeling, pain, agitation") fit homonymous *ḥwš* ("to haste") less well. *ḥwš* ("to haste") reflects PS *š* as well, as demonstrated by its Ugaritic parallel. Accordingly, it must not be connected with Arabic *ḥθθ*, *pace* Barth, cited, e.g., by Gesenius-Buhl (1915, s.v.).

95. For its occurrence in (Jewish and Samaritan) Aramaic see Ben-Ḥayyim (1957ff, II, p. 477a).

96. For such adaptations cf. Blau (1970a, pp. 101–102). I have also played with the idea of regarding *šṭp* as *šaf'ēl* of *ṭpp*, from which also Hebrew *nṭp* ("to drop, drip") is derived; cf. also Ben-Yehuda (1948ff, p. 7056, note 1).

denoting "to be lean," one would rather choose *ǵθθ*, and not *'śś*, for it; Hebrew *šāpān* corresponds to PS *θpn*, as proved by the *Śḥeri*[97] word *θufun;*[98] Hebrew *šql* corresponds to Arabic *θql* since Arabic *šql* is an Aramaic loan (see Fraenkel, 1886, p. 197); for *šyn* cf. above note 84.

In the following cases, although no clear Arabic correspondences to the Hebrew roots can be suggested, it is clear that Magnanini's proposals, exhibiting Arabic *š* as against Hebrew *š*, are not sound: Hebrew *ḥlš* ("to defeat"), presumably originally "to weaken," since it also has the meaning "to be weak," has been connected by Magnanini (so also alternatively by Zorell, 1949ff, s.v.) with Arabic *ḥlš* ("to mow"). Yet the Arabic word is dialectal,[99] and the difference in meaning together with the marginal attestation of the Arabic word (without mentioning the irregular sound corresondence, since this would imply *petitio principii*) makes any connection rather unlikely.[100] Hebrew *ḥšk* ("to be, grow dark") allegedly corresponds to Arabic *ḥšk* ("to be filled"), yet "to be filled" originally refers to the udder, being derived from *ḥišāk* ("a piece of wood preventing a kid from sucking the udder"), related to Hebrew *ḥśk* ("withhold") (see, e.g., Gesenius-Buhl, 1915; Koehler-Baumgartner, 1967ff, s.v. *ḥśk;* Brockelmann, 1928, s.v. *ḥsk*). Hebrew *'nš* ("to punish") must not be connected with Arabic *'nš*, since the latter does not denote "to torture" (*pace* Magnanini), which, incidentally, does not match either, but rather "to seize the neck of the enemy in fighting," which, in my opinion, fits even less. Hebrew *rḥš* is connected with Arabic *rḥš;* yet the Arabic verb, quite a marginal one, is suspect of being an Aramaic loan.[101] Hebrew *ršm* must not be compared with Arabic *ršm*, as proposed

97. Fresnel (1838a, p. 514, note 1) calls this language "Ehhkili," i.e., Eḥkili, which he spells in Arabic with *ḥ*. This language (see Fresnel, 1838b, p. 79, note 2 and Maltzan, 1873, p. 225) was dubbed *Šḥauri* by the Austrian expedition, and is called *Śḥeri* by Johnstone (1970, p. 296; 1972, p. 1, note 1; 1975, pp. 2–3).

98. See Fresnel (1838a, p. 514, note 1). For Proto-Sinaitic cf. Albright (1948, p. 21, note 71).

99. As expressly noted by Zorell (1949ff). See, e.g., Dozy (1881), Hava (1899), Wahrmund (1876), Barthélemy (1935ff), Denizeau (1960), Landberg (1920–42), s.v.

100. I am playing with the thought of deriving this dialectal *ḥlš* from Aramaic *šlḥ* ("to strip off"). For the metathesis postulated cf. Christian Palestinian Aramaic *ḥlš*. For the semantic shift (Arabic *ḥlš* denotes also "to pull out"): Hebrew *ḥlṣ*, *qal*—"to draw off (a sandal)"; *pi'el*—"to pull out (stones)"; *nšl*—"to slip off (iron); draw off (sandal)"; *šll*—"to draw out (sheaves); spoil, plunder"; *šlp*—"to draw off (sandal)," related to Arabic *slb* ("to plunder, take off [garment]"). Cf. also Neo-Syriac *šlḥ* ("to be naked, lose hair"). (Arabic *ḥlš* also denotes "to pull out beard," see Dozy, 1881, s.v.).

101. See Brockelmann (1928, s.v. *rḥš*); cf. also Landberg (1920–42, p. 1219, note 1). By the way, Barth (1893, p. 48) connected Aramaic *rḥš* with Arabic *ršḥ*, without knowing that

by Magnanini, not even with *rsm* (though exhibiting regular sound correspondence), since both, in all likelihood, are Aramaic loans (see Fraenkel, 1886, pp. 137, 250), the latter, in all likelihood, due to adaptation to Arabic (see above note 96). Hebrew *š'p* ("to gasp, pant after, be eager for," perhaps also "to persecute") can hardly be compared with Arabic *š'f* ("to be afraid, to hate"), because of the semantic gap separating the latter even from the (uncertain) sense "to persecute," nor can Hebrew *šbḥ* ("to praise") be compared with Arabic *šbḫ* ("to extend [hands]"), which is by no means special to prayer. Hebrew *šāḇēă'*, compared with Arabic *šabi'a*, is, it seems, due to printer's error. Magnanini compares Arabic *šbr* ("to measure") with Hebrew *šbr*, having possibly "to buy grain" in mind. The gap in meaning, however, makes this assumption quite unlikely; moreover, Arabic *šbr* may perhaps be related to Hebrew *śbr* (see above note 88). Hebrew *šlḥ* ("to send") must not be compared with Arabic *šlḥ* ("to throw off," also "to strip off"), because the Arabic verb is an Aramaic loan.[102] Arabic *šmr* does not exhibit meanings which could possibly be connected with Hebrew *šmr*. Hebrew *šp'* must not be related to Arabic *šf'*, because the latter has the basic meaning "to join," from which all the other meanings are derived. Barth's proposal (1902, p. 51) to connect Hebrew *šp'* with Arabic *sbġ* is very attractive; it is not easy to justify the comparison of Hebrew *'ešnāḇ* ("window") with Arabic *šnb* ("to be cold"), despite Zorell (1949ff, s.v.).

3.3.4

Magnanini also adduces cases of irregular Arabic correspondence to Hebrew *s*, viz. Arabic *š*. The current, and, in my opinion, correct view is that in these cases the spelling with *s* is late and arose after the original *ś* had merged with *s* (cf. Blau, 1970a, pp. 114ff). We have already mentioned (in 3.3.1) cases of the spelling with the original *ś* still attested alongside the later *s*. We shall now cite three other cases, in which the only attested spelling is with *s*, so that, *prima facie*, one could be more in-

ibn Janāḥ (1873–75, s.v., *rhš*) proposed the same for Hebrew *rhš*. In my opinion, however, Fraenkel (1898, p. 80) was right in opposing Barth's (and, one may add, ibn Janāḥ's) proposal, since it combines two irregularities, i.e., exceptional sound correspondence and metathesis.

102. Even Fīrūzabādī in his *Qāmūs* dubs it *sawādī*; cf., e.g., Féghali (1920, pp. 241, 246).

clined to consider an irregular sound correspondence Hebrew *s*—Arabic *š* possible: Magnanini ingeniously connects Hebrew *nissā* ("to try") with Arabic *nšw* ("to smell"); yet despite the ingenuity of this proposal I doubt its validity, even without taking the irregular sound correspondence into account: in Classical Arabic, at least, this meaning developed in a quite different direction, viz. "to get dizzy (from wine), to get wind (of news)," and just as in Hebrew the meaning of "smelling" is totally absent, so too in Classical Arabic is that of "trying" absent. Hebrew *rss* and Arabic *ršš*, in fact, match in both form and meaning. Yet the possibility obtains that they are unrelated onomatopoetic words (see Blau, 1970a, p. 115). The third word is *sətāw* ("winter"), which, however, is spelled in Old Aramaic with *ś* and, therefore, its Hebrew spelling (*hapax legomenon!*) has, by necessity, to be regarded as late (cf. Blau, 1970a, p. 115).

In other cases, the alleged correspondence of Arabic *š* to Hebrew *s* is quite unlikely because of the gap of meaning: Arabic *ḫšn* ("to be rough, hard, coarse"; so also Brown *et al.*, 1907, s.v.) fits Hebrew *ḥāsôn* ("strong") much less than Arabic *ḥṣn* ("to be unaccessible", see e.g., Gesenius-Buhl, 1915; Brockelmann, 1928, s.v.). Arabic *kšm* has only the meaning of "to cut off the nose," which matches Hebrew *ksm* ("to shear, clip") fairly well. Nevertheless, in the light of many alternating forms, as Hebrew and Arabic *gzm*, Middle Hebrew and Arabic *gdm*, Arabic *jðm*, Arabic and Hebrew *qsm*, one would rather refrain from positing irregular sound correspondence. Hebrew *sḥp* denotes "to prostrate, wash away," whereas Arabic *šḥf* designates "to skin"; a connection between the two is possible, but by no means convincing. Although Arabic *sifl* is an Aramaic loan (see Fraenkel, 1886, pp. 67–68), no Arabic *šafal* exists (*pace* Magnanini) to match Hebrew *sepel*. The alleged connection between Hebrew *sam* ("spice") and Arabic *šamma* ("to smell") is quite intricate (see Blau, 1970a, pp. 119–120), and it becomes even more opaque if one connects it with *śəmāmît* (see 3.3.2 above and note 89). I have not found any meaning like "to shed, dilate" for Arabic *šrḥ*, and, therefore, it does not fit Hebrew *srḥ* ("to overhang, expand"). We have already seen in 3.3.3 above that Arabic *'šš* ("to be lean") does not fit Hebrew *'šš* ("to be wasted away"); by no means does it match Hebrew *'ss* ("to press"), not only because of the difference in meaning, but also since Arabic *'ss* ("to press," *'i'tassa*, "to press the udder of a camel," see Fīrūzabādī's *Qāmūs*, s.v.) is attested, exhibiting the regular sound shift.

In other cases too, one would prefer to postulate regular, rather than irregular, sound correspondence: Arabic *ḥms* ("to irritate") *may* be compared with Hebrew *ḥms* ("to treat violently"); accordingly; there is no reason to prefer Arabic *ḥmš* ("to maltreat, offend"), even *ḫmš* ("to slap, cut off"). Nor would one prefer to compare Arabic *ḥšl*, which is only an alternative form of *ḥsl*, with Hebrew *ḥsl*, and therefore, one would not connect the Hebrew word with Arabic *ḫšl* either. Hebrew *ksḥ* ("to cut away") fits Arabic *ksḥ* (generally, "to sweep away, remove," also used in connection with thorns—*kasaḥa šawka-š-šajarati*, "he removed the thorn of the tree"), but not *kšḥ*, which denotes "to drive away," rather than "to peel." I would prefer to connect Hebrew *mss* (and also *msy*) with Arabic *tamāsā* ("to be melted"; see Saadya's translation of Exod 16:21), rather than with *mšš*. I do not understand why Magnanini compares Arabic *ršn* ("to put the hand in the vessel") with Hebrew *resen* ("halter"), rather than Arabic *rasan* ("halter"), for which cf. Fraenkel (1886, pp. 100–101), Landberg (1920–42, s.v.). No Hebrew *sn'* ("to hate") exists, the regular correspondence of Arabic *šn'* being always Hebrew *śn'*.

As these examples demonstrate, the sound correspondences of the Hebrew sibilants are almost always regular, a few only exhibit *possible* irregularity, and in even fewer (perhaps only in *təšûqā*) is irregular sound correspondence really likely.

4. Critical Analysis of Diem (1974)

In a very closely reasoned article, Diem (1974), following others,[103] claims that in Biblical Hebrew (i.e., in the dialect of Jerusalem), *ś*, the PS character of which he admits, had shifted to *š*, to change afterwards to *s* through the interference of Aramaic. Kutscher's arguments against Garbini's similar views were well known to Diem (1974, p. 246). Kutscher (1965, pp. 40ff) called attention to the existence of many Hebrew roots spelled with *ś* without parallels in Aramaic. Why, then, he asked, on good grounds in my opinion, did the Masoretes read ש as *s* in these cases, for many of which it can be demonstrated by comparison with other Semitic languages that the ש does not correspond to PS *š*? Against this argument Diem suggests that it is of little consequence if no Aramaic parallel is known for this or that Hebrew word, since the vocabulary of Aramaic, especially of Official Aramaic, is attested to a small extent only. The

103. He quotes (p. 224, especially notes 11 and 13) G. Garbini and K. Beyer. Similar arguments have already been adduced by Tur-Sinai in his remarks to Ben-Yehuda (1948ff, p. 6777b).

absence of attestations need not indicate that Aramaic in fact lacked these words. Diem analyzes five words adduced by Kutscher (1965), apparently at random, as words lacking Aramaic parallels and claims that four of them have Aramaic parallels indeed. Diem, however, did not take into account one decisive factor, viz. that of frequency. According to Diem's theory, bilingual Jews, speaking both Hebrew and Aramaic,[104] identified Hebrew words containing original *ś*, already pronounced as *š*, with the parallel Aramaic ones and started pronouncing them in an Aramaic way, substituting *s* for original *ś*, because of the higher prestige of Aramaic. Yet the influence of an Aramaic word could not make itself felt unless it was frequent enough to influence the parallel Hebrew word. If the Hebrew word was much more frequent, the influence of Aramaic was, for all practical purposes, excluded. Thus for instance, despite the occurrence of an Aramaic parallel to Hebrew *śimlā* ("garment") in the Aramaic Uruk text, it is very difficult to conceive that this rare Aramaic word could have influenced the pronunciation of the frequent Hebrew one. Even less conceivable is Aramaic influence on Hebrew *śmḥ* ("to rejoice"), even if it is related to Syriac *ṣmḥ* ("to send out rays"). In this case, a real difference obtains in both meaning ("to rejoice" as against "to send rays") and form (Hebrew *ś*, allegedly pronounced *š*, as against Aramaic *ṣ*; the latter, at most, should have changed the Hebrew sibilant to *ṣ*, and the existence of Hebrew *ṣmḥ*, "to grow," should not have prevented this change). Therefore, in this case at least, the assumption of Aramaic influence is altogether impossible. Moreover, as ill luck would have it, in the Hebrew original of Kutscher (1965), viz. *ləšonenu* 29:119 (1964–65), Kutscher cited another example, which, apparently by oversight, has been omitted from the English translation: *śāde* ("field"). This extraordinarily frequent Hebrew word is altogether absent from Aramaic, and even if it should eventually be detected in an Aramaic text, the high frequency of the Hebrew word as against the Aramaic one (which has not yet been detected and perhaps never will!) rules out the possibility of any Aramaic influence on the pronunciation of the Hebrew word. And *śāde* is not the only word of this kind. Even more conspicuous is the case of *'āśā* ("to do, make"), which is so frequent in the Hebraic group of languages and characteristic of them that Ginsberg (1970, p. 111) considered it "the simplest mark by which this group may be distinguished both from other

104. For the possibility, tentatively suggested by Diem (1974, p. 245) that the pronunciation of *ś* as *s* came into being after Hebrew had already become a dead language, see *infra* 4.5.

Canaanite ones and from the rest of the Semitic languages." Even if, by some chance, this verb should be detected in an Aramaic dialect, it is quite inconceivable that the Aramaic verb with such low frequency should have influenced such a frequent Hebrew verb. Accordingly, Diem's hypothesis cannot account for the occurrence of many conspicuous Hebrew words containing *ś* (i.e., spelled with ש and pronounced *s*). Therefore, by necessity one should concur with the accepted view that Hebrew *ś*, corresponding to other Semitic languages in a way often different from the reflection of Hebrew *š* and *s*, has to be considered genuine and that its pronunciation as *s* arose without Aramaic influence.

4.1 Hebrew Words with Sibilants Differing from Aramaic

That the pronunciation of the Hebrew sibilants is not due to the impact of Aramaic is also hinted by *śəʿārûm* ("they were acquainted with them") in Deut 32:17, the *ś* of which is established by Arabic *šaʿara* ("to perceive"); if there had been Aramaic influence one would have expected **šəʿārûm*, in the light of the frequent Aramaic *šaʿēr* ("to estimate") (cf. in Hebrew, Prov 23:7), which could have been easily adapted to the Deuteronomic passage (in the sense of "to calculate"). Or why should obscure *niśqad*, Lam 1:14, be spelled with *ś*, despite the existence of the frequent Hebrew *šqd* ("to watch")?! By necessity, we have to postulate the existence of a (genuine) tradition which made the Masoretes establish *ś*, rather than *š*, in these cases.

There exist other indications as well which contravene the assumption of far-reaching Aramaic influence on the pronunciation of Hebrew sibilants. There exists at least one clear-cut case of Hebrew *s* in a word influenced by Aramaic corresponding to Aramaic *š*: Nöldeke (1910, p. 37, note 3) has made a very good case for Hebrew *kns* being a homonymic verb. Genuine Hebrew *kns*, denoting "to enter," very frequent in Middle Hebrew in *nifʿal*, occurs in Isa 28:20 *wəhammassēḵā ṣārā kəhitkannēs* ("and the covering is [too] narrow, when one enters it") and *miḵnəsê* ("trousers") is derived from it. In late Biblical Hebrew[105] and in Middle Hebrew, this root was attracted by Aramaic *knš* ("to collect"), and *kns* acquired the meaning of "to collect." So in this case not only was

105. See, e.g, Gesenius-Buhl (1915, s.v. II *kns*); Nöldeke (1910) mentions Middle Hebrew only.

Aramaic not powerful enough to make Hebrew *kns* be pronounced *knš*, but Hebrew imposed upon "to collect" the pronunciation with *s*, because of the existing Hebrew root, rather than *knš* as in Aramaic.[106]

In this connection, it is worthwhile to call attention to obscure *štm* (Num 24:3, 15) which, in the light of Diem's thesis, one would have expected to exhibit *ś* through the influence of Aramaic *stm* (see Jastrow, 1903, s.v.), *sṭm* (see Brockelmann, 1928, s.v.), *sdm* (see Drower-Macuch, 1963, s.v.) ("to stop up"), the more so since Hebrew *śtm* is attested (see Blau, 1970a, p. 121, note 35). Accordingly, one would discard the theory of decisive Aramaic influence on the pronunciation of Hebrew sibilants.

4.2

Accordingly, we cannot accept Diem's main thesis that it was through Aramaic influence that, in some cases, שׂ came to be pronounced as *s*. Now we shall proceed to analyze some of his quite impressive collateral proofs in a somewhat different light.

4.3 Irregular Sound Correspondences of Hebrew *š*

Diem (1974, pp. 246–247) calls attention to the existence of Hebrew *š*, where, according to its correspondences with other Semitic languages, one would rather have expected *ś*. These cases, in Diem's opinion, have to be interpreted as exhibiting original *ś*. Yet because of the want of Aramaic parallels, *š*, which in genuine Hebrew, in Diem's opinion, had superseded *ś*, had been left and not changed to *s*. Diem himself (pp. 246–247, note 120) felt the weakness of his position, since in these cases he accepted the *argumentum ex silentio* of the absence of Aramaic parallels, yet not in the case of Hebrew *ś*. More important, however, in our opinion, is the uncertain and marginal character of this *š*. In the wake of Yahuda (1903, especialy pp. 707ff), Diem adduces eight words allegedly exhibiting *š*, where one would have expected *ś*, five of which, however, exhibit another sibilant alongside *š*, so that the deviation from regular

106. It is interesting to note that in Codex Kaufmann *niḵnəsā* ("she entered") is spelled with *ś* (and final *'alep*), presumably through the influence of Aramaic *knš*; see Blau (1970a, p. 25).

sound correspondence may well be due to dissimilation.[107] As to the remaining three words, the etymology of Hebrew *nāḥāš* ("snake") is by no means clear, cf., e.g., Nöldeke (1904, p. 133, note 4) or Fraenkel (1898, p. 80); Hebrew *šuppû* ("they have become lean") may be connected, to be sure, with Arabic *šff* ("to be transparent"), yet the meeting of two deviations, viz. Hebrew *š* corresponding to Arabic *š*, and a Hebrew *IIIy* verb to an Arabic *media geminata*, makes one cautious. One would altogether discard Yahuda's interpretation of *šəlûḥôt* ("shoots, branches"), Isa 16:8, since it may easily be derived from *šlḥ* ("to send"), cf. Ps 80:12 *təšallaḥ qəṣîrêhā 'ad yām* ("she sent her boughs unto the sea"), Jer 17:8 *wə'al yūḇal yəšallaḥ šorāšāw* ("and it sends out its roots by the river"). (See the biblical dictionaries s.v., who, justly in our opinion, did not even care to quote Yahuda on this passage.) It would have been more expedient to quote a deviant correspondence like Hebrew *təšūqā* ("longing") = Arabic *šawq*, in exactly the same meaning and usage (see 3.3 above and note 82). Yet the marginal existence of such deviant correspondence does not prove anything. One must not forget that exceptional correspondences have been claimed also, e.g., for Aramaic *š*, as for Aramaic *nəšaq* = Hebrew *nāšaq*, if it is really related to Arabic *našaqa* ("to smell") (see, e.g., Barth, 1893, pp. 46–47; Fraenkel, 1898, pp. 79–80; Barth, 1902, p. 58); Aramaic *riḥšā* ("reptile"), if it really corresponds to Arabic *rāšiḥ* (see Barth, 1893, p. 48; Fraenkel, 1898, p. 80; Barth 1902, p. 58); Aramaic *nešbā* ("net"), if related to Arabic *našiba* ("to stick") (see Fraenkel, 1886, p. 120; Barth, 1893, p. 50). Although this exceptional correspondence (Aramaic *š*—Arabic *š*) is not less established than Hebrew *š*—Arabic *š*, it cannot be inferred from it that Aramaic or Arabic *š* have come into being through foreign influence. Weak phonetic change is well attested in Semitic languages (cf. Section 1), accordingly, nothing can be inferred from marginal deviations in sound correspondence for Hebrew *š* either.

107. For such dissimilations cf. the literature adduced by Gesenius-Buhl (1915, s.vv. *šemeš, šrš*); Koehler-Baumgartner (1953, Aramaic part, s.v. *šəmaš*). Yahuda (1903, pp. 708–709, note 1) also cites Hebrew *ššp* = Arabic *ššf*. On the other hand, Hebrew *ḥāšaš* = Arabic *ḥašīš* (p. 708), cf. also *supra* 3.3.3, does not exhibit dissimilation, since in roots *mediae geminatae* this feature does not occur. Other cases exhibiting dissimilations are: Hebrew *šzr* = Arabic *šzr* (see the literature adduced in Blau, 1975, p. 28, notes, 8, 9); Hebrew *šḥz* = Arabic *šḥδ*. That Diem did not pay attention to the possibility of dissimilation is more surprising, since Yahuda (p. 708) expressly mentioned the occurrence of two sibilants in the words adduced by him.

4.4 The Shift θ > š in the Neo-Aramaic dialect of Lower Ṭiyārī

One of the main reasons for Diem's refusal to accept the shift θ > š at face value while positing rather θ > ś > š (and later, through Aramaic interference, š > *s* in some of its occurrences), is his assumption that θ does not shift to š if another sibilant without a kettle sound ("Kesselgeräusch") exists (Diem, 1974, pp. 225–226, p. 247). Yet the shift θ > š is attested under these circumstances in at least one living, though admittedly quite marginal, Semitic tongue, which, however, suffices to prove the possibility of this shift. In the Neo-Aramaic dialect of Lower Ṭiyārī, for which, to be sure, no well-established texts exist, what was once the spirant allophone of *t*, viz. θ, under conditions which still have to be established, has shifted to š. Nöldeke (1896, p. 303) has correctly considered this to be probably the same sound shift that changed PS θ in
* Hebrew and Akkadian into š.[108]

4.4.1

In his endeavor to refute the possibility of the shift θ > š (if another sibilant without kettle sound exists), Diem (1974, pp. 247ff) has collected important material for the shift θ > *s*[109] and θ > ś. Yet one must not lose sight of the fact that the only shift of θ attested by Diem in living dialects is to *s*, whereas its shift to ś (which is necessary for Diem's theory, see 4.4 above) is based only on Diem's reconstruction of Hebrew, Proto-Sinaitic and, relying on D. O. Edzard, of Akkadian. Therefore, *prima facie*, one should not exclude the shift θ > š (even if it were not attested, see 4.4 above) more than θ > ś, the more so, since PS ś was, it seems, a lateral sound (Steiner, forthcoming). As to Egyptian transcriptions, despite the sound proofs adduced by Diem (pp. 230ff) that they distinguish between š and ś/θ (by the way, also between š and the other sibilants) one can only infer from them that for the Egyptian ear ś and θ seemed to be close; they do not, however, prove that θ had, in fact, shifted to ś. Moreover, Aro

108. Cf. also Maclean (1901, p. X), Lidzbarski (1894, pp. 226, 236–237), Nöldeke (1868, p. 46), further Stoddard (1855, p. 75), Maclean (1895, p. 338).

109. In passing, I would like to add that in the Arabic dialect of Daragōzü as well, θ has shifted to *s*, see Jastrow (1973, p. 15).

(1959, p. 323, note 1), despite Diem's qualifications (p. 247, note 122), has made very sound observations on the possible different phonetic character of Semitic *s*, which, in my opinion, well explain the shift *θ* > *š*. He calls attention to the series of unvoiced non-emphatic sibilants in Semitic consisting of three members (*s*, *ś*, *š*), as against the single voiced *z*. He surmises therefore, that Semitic *s* was especially "sharp" and, accordingly, unsuitable for serving as the sibilant counterpart of *θ*. In Aro's opinion, for languages that had only one unvoiced sibilant, like Hittite and Greek, it was Old Semitic *š* that was felt as the closest correspondence to their sibilant(s) and therefore the Hittites spelled their *s* with Akkadian *š* and the Greeks accepted *šîn* as the sign of their *sigma*.[110] In this connection, it is not without interest to remember[111] that early Arabic transcriptions from Spanish invariably transcribe the Spanish *s* by Arabic *š*. It seems that the Spanish *s* was apico-alveolar. Therefore, the Arabic ear identified it with Arabic *š*, and Arabic *s* with Spanish *z*, *ç* (a predorsodental affricate). This transcription cautions us not to jump to conclusions on the strength of transcriptions, and this also applies to the transcriptions utilized by Garbini (1971). Thus, in our opinion (*pace* Diem, 1974, pp. 247–248, following Edzard), the use of Old Akkadian *ś* to mark PS *θ* does not prove that *θ* shifted to *ś* in Old Akkadian, since PS *š* is also marked in Old Akkadian by *ś* (see Aro, 1959, p. 328). Accordingly, Old Akkadian *ś* for PS *θ* *may* reflect *θ* > *š* as well, and, in the light of later Akkadian, this is not unlikely.

4.4.2

In our opinion, Diem has not taken into consideration the admittedly few texts written in an Ugaritic alphabet of approximately 22 letters, which, *inter alia*, reflect the graphemic development *š*/*θ* > *θ* (see Greenfield, 1969, who adduced additional literature, p. 96, note 20). In all probability, this has to imply that, in the language reflected by these texts, PS *š*, *ś*, and *θ* coincided in *š*. One could, to be sure, imagine a starting point different from the language reflected by the majority of

110. Yet one must not lose sight of the fact that the situation in Greek was rather complicated (cf. the use of *san* in some Greek dialects); see, e.g., Jeffery (1961, pp. 27ff). Cf. also Nöldeke (1904, pp. 125–126). At any rate one would not consent to Garbini's opinion (1971, p. 37), that Greek *sigma* demonstrates that Northwest-Semitic *š* was pronounced *s*.

111. See, e.g., Fischer (1917, p. 50), Steiger (1932, pp. 200ff, especially p. 202).

Ugaritic texts (in which š and ś have become one sound) and claim that the development was rather:

Stage I š, ś, θ
Stage II š, ś (since θ > ś), i.e. different from the majority of Ugaritic texts
Stage III š (since ś > š).

This, however, in light of the majority of Ugaritic texts, is less likely than to assume:

Stage I š, ś, θ
Stage II š, θ, (since ś > š) as also reflected by the majority of Ugaritic texts, i.e., at this stage, all the Ugaritic texts still reflected a common lingual type
Stage III š (since θ > š in the minority of texts).

Greenfield (1969, p. 96, note 18), on the strength of the evidence from Hittite and Hurrian (and perhaps also Akkadian) words and names, even suggested that in Ugaritic also, as exhibited by the majority of texts, θ was only a historical spelling, since θ had already phonetically merged with š. At any rate, at least some Ugaritic texts seem to reflect the sound shift θ > š, contrary to Diem's thesis, and the mere fact that in Akkadian transcriptions š marks Ugaritic θ,[112] indicates that š was not phonetically as far from θ as Diem wants us to believe.

4.5 Hebrew š Could Not Shift to s through Aramaic Influence

Diem (1974, p. 245) mentions the possibility that Hebrew ś, then still pronounced š, shifted, under Aramaic influence, to s after Hebrew had already become a dead language. In my opinion, however, this assumption is almost inconceivable. It implies that Hebrew, a dead language of great prestige, serving as the sacred tongue of the synagogue, was so much influenced by the spoken vernacular, viz. Aramaic, that in the syn-

112. Though one must not overemphasize the importance of these transcriptions either. Rainey (1971, p. 156), at any rate, considers it a mechanical transcription.

agogal reading the letter ש was overdifferentiated and, in cases in which it corresponded to Aramaic *s*, was no longer pronounced *ś*, but rather *s*. No similar cases are known to me from Jews having Arabic as their mother tongue, also a closely related Semitic language (though admittedly, Aramaic is even more closely related), and it is not due to chance that Diem could only adduce one allegedly similar case, in which people with Arabic as their mother tongue learning Syriac, pronounce *dahḇā* as *dahabā*, *ðahabā* and *ðahbā* thus restoring either an omitted vowel or *ð* (or both) in the wake of Arabic *ðahab*. Yet the resemblance of these cases is deceptive. The introduction of (synchronically) wrong vowels, through the influence of Arabic, into unvocalized Syriac is simply due to lack of knowledge. And as to the pronunciation of *d* as *ð*, one must not lose sight of the fact that in Syriac these consonants are allophones. He who learns Syriac is taught, according to certain rules, to pronounce the letter *d* sometimes as *d* and sometimes as *ð*. In a case like ours he may, under the impact of his mother tongue, pronounce *ð* contrary to the rules. Quite different is the case of Hebrew ש. Diem claims that the letter ש, which, in his opinion, should in genuine Hebrew *always* be pronounced *ś*, was overdifferentiated under the influence of the Aramaic mother tongue, and, in reading, was sometimes correctly pronounced *ś*, yet in other cases *s*. This would exhibit a real overdifferentiation of the reading of a letter in a dead language, whereas in the case of Syriac *d*/*ð*, the double reading is a part of the system of the dead language, yet it was wrongly applied through the influence of the mother tongue.

The assumption that Hebrew was already a dead language when it underwent the alleged (partial) shift *ś* > *s* under the influence of Aramaic is impossible to accept for historical reasons as well. Even if one discards the spelling of words containing original *ś* with *s* in the masoretic text as late changes (although this seems quite unlikely), this spelling is attested in the Dead Sea Scrolls from the first century B.C.E., and since the Bar Kosiba letters written in Middle Hebrew prove that Hebrew continued to be a living tongue until the Bar Kosiba revolt (132–35 C.E.) by necessity the alleged shift *ś* > *s*, if it occurred at all, took place when Hebrew was still a living tongue.

4.6 "The *šibbōlet* Incident"

Diem (1974, pp. 242–243) accepted Speiser's interpretation (1942) of the *šibbōlet* incident, viz. that in the dialect of Ephraim *θ* had become *s*,

since original **θibbōlet* shifted to *sibbōlet*. This interpretation, however, despite its ingenuity, fails because it is pivoted upon the rare Judeo-Aramaic *θublā* ("ear of corn"), whereas all the other linguistic evidence indicates that this word begins with PS *š*, rather than with *θ*. Yet Fraenkel (1905), in a short notice,[113] correctly in my opinion, regarded this word as a learned Aramaicizing formation,[114] so that there is no way to postulate
* *šibbōlet* with initial *θ*. Therefore, one would have to return to the simple literal interpretation of the *šibbōlet* incident, viz. that in the language of Ephraim, all the unvoiced non-emphatic sibilants had fallen together in
* *s*.[115]

5. Conclusion

We have tried to demonstrate that the Hebrew pronunciation of *ś* is based on living tradition, rather than on Aramaic influence, since it is attested in very frequent words (as *'śy*, "to do, make"), which are totally absent from Aramaic (and even if they occurred, would have been too rare to exert any influence). Besides dealing with some marginal issues, we have tried to show that the shift *θ* > *š*, even when another unvoiced non-emphatic sibilant exists, is in fact attested in at least one living dialect, and vestiges of it may be reflected in various extinct Semitic tongues. We also dealt *in extenso* with the problem of "weak phonetic change" due to dialectical mixture (including borrowing), dissimilation and lexical contamination, and attempted to demonstrate how imperative it is for sound linguistic interpretation to keep "weak phonetic change" in its proper limits and not to lose sight of its marginal character as against regular sound shift.

In this paper, I have often opposed views of my colleagues. Yet, paraphrasing Schuchardt's words,[116] one must not forget that it is thanks to their willingness to deal with thorny problems of Semitic sound cor-

113. Kutscher (1967, p. 174), without knowing of Fraenkel's notice, arrived at the same conclusion.

114. One may add, out of over-self-assertion (see Blau, 1970a, p. 48, note 9).

115. According to Brockelmann (1908–13, I, p. 132), who cites Littmann (1902, p. 11) and Bauer (1926, p. 8), this is the case in the Arabic dialect of Nablus as well. Yet one would be prudent to refrain from connecting it with the dialect of Ephraim, the more so since the same phenomenon obtains in Judeo-Arabic Maghrebine dialects (see, e.g., Cohen, 1912, p. 24). The same applies to later Ge'ez (see, e.g., Brockelmann, 1908–13, p. 133) and, according to some scholars (see Soden, 1952, p. 30), to Middle and New Assyrian as well.

116. See Spitzer (1922, p. 338).

respondence in general and of Hebrew sibilants in particular that progress in scholarship is achieved. This paper is founded on the views of its predecessors, both on those to which it assented and those from which it differed, and I am glad to express my indebtedness to them.

Addendum

Sheer oversight on my part is responsible for the omission of due references, when dealing with Hebrew *d* corresponding to Proto-Semitic *ð* (section 1.6), to C. Rabin's important and stimulating paper "La Correspondance *d* Hébreu—*ḏ* Arabe," *Mélanges Marcel Cohen,* The Hague, 1970, pp. 290–297. At this stage, it was not possible to include them in the body of this paper and space prohibits a detailed consideration of all his 32 etymological suggestions. From the cases in which Rabin assumes influence of "liquids and *r*," I have dealt with *dll* (Rabin no. 12), *dlq* (Rabin 13), *ḥdl* (Rabin 18), *ndr* (Rabin 21) and *qdr* (Rabin 27). Since I did not treat Middle Hebrew, Mishnaic (*sukkā*) *mədublelet* is outside the scope of our treatise. I have not been convinced by his suggestions as to *dōhēr* (8, since "horses of noble descent," in my opinion, does not fit Judg 5:22), *dlḥ* (11, since original *d* is firmly established by Akkadian and Sham'ali), *drb* (15; cf. also Gesenius-Buhl, 1915), *ne'dar* (24, since both *ġdr* and *ta'aððara* denote "to remain behind," and the latter must not be preferred to the former), *'ēder* (25, the etymology of which is considered by Rabin himself as doubtful), and *śədērā* (29, the original *d* of which is sufficiently established by Akkadian). The other derivations (with the exception of *gdm,* for which cf. Section 1.6) do not convince, since they postulate not only a "weak" sound change, but exceptional semantic correspondence as well (or correspond to a Hebrew root exhibiting *z;* see 9). Therefore, I do not accept Rabin's assumption that *ð* shifts to *d* in the vicinity of labials. In some cases, the accepted correspondence to Arabic *ḏ* is not worse (though also not better) than that proposed by Rabin with *ð* (as 14, Arabic *damdama* as against Rabin's *ðamā*). *pḥd* (26) is, it seems, an Aramaic loan.

BIBLIOGRAPHY

Abbreviations:

BASOR = *Bulletin of the American Schools of Oriental Research*
JAOS = *Journal of the American Oriental Society*
VT = *Vetus Testamentum*
ZDMG = *Zeitschrift der deutschen morgenländischen Gesellschaft*

Aharoni, I. 1935. "qippôd." *ləšonenu* 6:137–163.

———. 1938. "On some animals mentioned in the Bible." *Osiris* 5:461–478.

Aistleitner, J. 1965. *Wörterbuch der ugaritischen Sprache*. Berlin.

Albright, W. F. 1948. "The early alphabetic inscriptions from Sinai and their decipherment." *BASOR* 110:6–22.

Almkvist, H. 1925. "Kleine Beiträge zur Lexikographie des Vulgärarabischen." *Le Monde Oriental* 19:V–XIV; 1–186.

Al-Yasin, I. 1952. *The Lexical Relation between Ugaritic and Arabic*. (Shelton Semitic Monograph Series I). New York.

Aro, J. 1959. "Die semitischen Zischlaute (*ṯ*), š, ś und s und ihre Vertretung im Akkadischen." *Orientalia* N.S. 28, pp. 321–335.

———. 1964. "Gemeinsemitische Ackerbauterminologie." *ZDMG* 113: 471–480.

Barth, J. 1893. *Etymologische Studien*. Berlin.

———. 1902. *Wurzeluntersuchungen*. Leipzig.

Barthélemy, A. 1935ff. *Dictionnaire Arabe-Français, Dialectes de Syrie*. Paris.

Bauer, H. 1934. "Zu den Ras-Schamra Texten 1929." *Orientalistische Literaturzeitung* 37:474–475.

Bauer, L. 1926. *Das palästinische Arabisch*[4]. Leipzig.

Beeston, A. F. L. 1950. "Notes on Old South Arabian lexicography II." *Le Muséon* 63:261–268.

———. 1951. "Phonology of the Epigraphic South Arabian unvoiced sibilants." *Transactions of the Philological Society*, pp. 1–26.

———. 1962. *A Descriptive Grammar of Epigraphic South Arabian*. London.

Ben-Ḥayyim, Z. 1946. "ləharḥaḇat hallašon ulətiqqunah." *ləšonenu* 14:190–197.

———. 1955. Review of Gumpertz *mibṭa'ey śəp̱atenu. Kirjath Sepher* 30:163–172.

———. 1957ff. *'iḇrit va'aramit nosaḥ šomron.* Jerusalem.

Ben-Yehuda, E. 1948ff. *millon hallašon ha'iḇrit.* Jerusalem.

Bergsträsser, G. 1918–29. *Hebräische Grammatik.* Leipzig.

Blau, J. 1955. "Etymologische Untersuchungen auf Grund des palaestinischen Arabisch." *VT* 5:337–344.

———. 1957. "Über homonyme und angeblich homonyme Wurzeln." *VT* 7: 98–102.

———. 1968. "On problems of polyphony and archaism in Ugaritic spelling." *JAOS* 88:523–526.

———. 1970a. *On Pseudo-Corrections in Some Semitic Languages.* Jerusalem.

———. 1970b. "he'arot lə'ocar hammillim šebbammiqra." *seper Yosef Braslavy,* pp. 439–443. Ed. Israel Ben-Shem. Jerusalem.

———. 1972. "Marginalia Semitica II." *Israel Oriental Studies* 2:57–82.

———. 1975. "Philological notes on the Bible based on medieval Judaeo-Arabic." *Shnaton, An Annual for Biblical and Ancient Near Eastern Studies* 1:27–31.

Blau, J. and J. C. Greenfield. 1970. "Ugaritic glosses." *BASOR* 200:11–17.

Blau, J. and S. E. Lowenstamm. 1970. "'ugaritit *ṣly* 'qillel'." *ləšonenu* 35:7–10.

Brockelmann, C. 1908–13. *Grundriss der vergleichenden Grammatik der semitischen Sprachen.* Berlin.

———. 1928. *Lexicon Syriacum*². Halle.

Brown, F., S. R. Driver, and C. A. Briggs. 1907. *A Hebrew and English Lexicon of the Old Testament.* Oxford.

Cantineau, J. 1935–45. "La 'mutation des sifflantes' en sudarabique." *Mélanges Gaudefroy-Demombynes,* pp. 313–323. Cairo.

———. 1960. *Études de linguistique arabe.* Paris.

Caquot, A. 1974. "Notes de lexicographie ougaritique."*Actes du Ier Congrès International de Linguistique Sémitique et Chamito-Sémitique* (1969, Paris), pp. 203–208. Eds. A. Caquot and D. Cohen. The Hague.

Caquot, A. *et al.* 1974. *Textes ougaritiques, I, Mythes et légendes.* Paris.

Cohen, M. 1912. *Le parler arabe des Juifs d'Alger.* Paris.

Conti Rossini, C. 1931. *Chrestomathia arabica meridionalis epigraphica.* Rome.

Cross, F. M. 1962. "Yahweh and the God of the Patriarchs." *Harvard Theological Review* 55:225–259.

Cross, F. M. and D. N. Freedman. 1964. "The name of Ashdod." *BASOR* 175:48–50.

Dahood, M. 1965. "Hebrew-Ugaritic lexicography III." *Biblica* 46:311–332.

Degen, R. 1971. Review of Koehler-Baumgartner *Hebräisches und aramäisches Lexikon zum Alten Testament*³, I, Leiden, 1967. *Orientalistische Literaturzeitung* 66:259–273.

Denizeau, C. 1960. *Dictionnaire des parlers arabes de Syrie, Liban et Palestine.* Paris.

Diem, W. 1974. "Das Problem von שׂ im Althebräischen und die kanaanäische Lautverschiebung." *ZDMG* 124:221–252.

Dietrich, M. and O. Loretz. 1967. "Untersuchungen zur Schrift- und Lautlehre des Ugaritischen (I): Der ugaritische Konsonant ǵ." *Welt des Orients* 4:300–315.

Dietrich, M., O. Loretz, and J. Sanmartín. 1975. "Untersuchungen zur Schrift- und Lautlehre des Ugaritischen (III)." *Ugarit-Forschungen* 7:103–108.

Dozy, R. P. 1881. *Supplément aux dictionnaires arabes.* Leyde.

Driver, G. R. 1921. "The meaning of קאת and קפד in Hebrew." *Journal of Theological Studies* 22:382–383.

———. 1956. *Canaanite Myths and Legends.* Edinburgh.

Drower, E. S. and R. Macuch. 1963. *A Mandaic Dictionary.* Oxford.

Encyclopaedia Biblica V. 1976. Jerusalem.

Féghali, M. T. 1920. "Études sur les emprunts syriaques dans les parlers arabes du Liban." *Mémoires de la Société de Linguistique de Paris.* 27:210–248; 257–282.

———. 1922. "Études sur les emprunts syriaques dans les parlers arabes du Liban (suite et fin)." *Mémoires de la Société de Linguistique de Paris.* 28:13–42.

Feigin, S. 1926. "Word Studies." *American Journal of Semitic Languages and Literature* 43:44–53.

Feliks, Y. 1955–56. *haḥay šel hattanak̲.* Tel Aviv.

Fischer, A. 1917. *Zur Lautlehre des Marokkanisch-Arabischen.* Leipzig.

Fischer, W. 1965. *Farb- und Formbezeichnungen in der Sprache der altarabischen Dichtung.* Wiesbaden.

Fraenkel, S. 1886. *Die aramäischen Fremdwörter im Arabischen.* Leiden.

———. 1898. "Zum sporadischen Lautwandel in den semitischen

Sprachen." *Beiträge zur Assyriologie und semitischen Sprachwissenschaft* 3:60–86.

———. 1905. "Zu Zeitschrift 58, S. 954 Z.6." *ZDMG* 59, p. 252 (*sic!*).

Frayha, A. 1947. *mu'jam al-'alfaẓ al-'āmmiyya fi-l-lahja-l-lubnāniyya.* Beirut.

Fresnel, F. 1838a. "Quatrième lettre sur l'histoire des Arabes avant l'Islamisme." *Journal Asiatique* (June), pp. 497–544.

———. 1838b. "Note sur la langue hhymiarite (!)." *Journal Asiatique* (July), pp. 79–84.

Garbini, G. 1960. *Il semitico de nord-ovest.* Naples.

———. 1971. "The phonetic shift of sibilants in Northwestern Semitic in the first millennium B.C." *Journal of Northwest Semitic Languages* 1:32–38.

Gesenius, W. 1835ff. *Thesaurus philologicus criticus.* Lipsia.

Gesenius, W. and F. Buhl. 1915. *Handwörterbuch.* Leipzig.

Geyer, R. 1905. *Zwei Gedichte von al-'a'šā.* Vienna.

Ginsberg, H. L. 1938. "A Ugaritic parallel to 2 Sam. 1:21." *Journal of Biblical Literature* 57:209–213.

———. 1945. "Psalms and inscriptions of petition and acknowledgment." *Louis Ginzberg Jubilee Volume,* pp. 159–171. Eds. A. Marx *et al.* New York.

———. 1946. *The Legend of King Keret.* New Haven.

———. 1970. "The Northwest Semitic languages." *The World History of the Jewish People, II, Patriarchs,* pp. 102–124. Tel Aviv.

Ginzberg, Louis. 1934. "Beiträge zur Lexikographie des Jüdisch-Aramäischen." *Monatsschrift für Geschichte und Wissenschaft des Judentums* 78:23–25.

Goldziher, I. 1889. *Muhammedanische Studien I.* Halle.

Good, E. M. 1970. "Exodus XV;2." *VT* 20:358–359.

Gordon, C. H. 1965. *Ugaritic Textbook.* Rome.

Greenfield, J. C. 1958. "Lexicographical notes I." *Hebrew Union College Annual* 29:203–228.

———. 1964. "Samaritan Hebrew and Aramaic in the Work of Prof. Zev Ben-Ḥayyim." *Biblica* 45:261–268.

———. 1969. "Amurrite, Ugaritic and Canaanite." *Proceedings of the International Conference on Semitic Studies,* pp. 92–101. Jerusalem.

Gröndahl, F. 1967. *Die Personennamen der Texte aus Ugarit.* Rome.

Gumpertz, Y. F. 1953. *miḇṭa'ey śəpatenu.* Jerusalem.

Haupt, P. 1906. "Die semitischen Wurzeln QR, KR, XR." *American Journal of Semitic Languages and Literature* 23:241–252.

Hava, J. G. 1899. *Arabic-English Dictionary*. Beirut.

Held, M. 1962. "The YQTL-QTL (QTL-YQTL) sequence of identical verbs in Biblical Hebrew and Ugaritic." *Studies and Essays in Honor of A. A. Neuman*, pp. 281–290. Eds. M. Ben-Horin *et al.* Leiden.

Hommel, F. 1879. *Die Namen der Säugetiere bei den südsemitischen Völkern*. Leipzig.

Ibn Janāḥ, M. 1873–75. *The Book of Hebrew Roots*. Ed. A. Neubauer. Oxford.

Ibn Manẓur, M. 1955–56. *lisān al-'arab*. Beirut.

Jamme, A. 1962. *Sabaean Inscriptions from Maḥram Bilqis (Mârib)*. Baltimore.

Jastrow, M. 1903. *A Dictionary of the Targumim, the Talmud Babli and Yerushalmi, and the Midrashic Literature*. New York.

Jastrow, O. 1973. *Daragözü (Erlanger Beiträge zur Sprach- und Kunstwissenschaft 46)*. Nürnberg.

Jean, C. F. and J. Hoftijzer. 1965. *Dictionnaire des inscriptions sémitiques de l'ouest*. Leiden.

Jeffery, A. 1938. *The Foreign Vocabulary of the Qur'ān*. Baroda.

Jeffery, L. H. 1961. *The Local Scripts of Archaic Greece*. Oxford.

Jirku, A. 1964. "Der Buchstabe Ghain im Ugaritischen." *ZDMG* 113:481–482.

Johnstone, T. M. 1970. "A definite article in the modern South Arabian Languages." *Bulletin of the School of Oriental and African Studies* 33:295–307.

———. 1972. "The languages of poetry in Dhofar." *Bulletin of the School of African Studies* 35:1–17.

———. 1975. "The modern South Arabian languages." *Afro-Asiatic Linguistics*, Vol. I, No. 5, pp. 1–29.

Kahle, P. 1930. *Masoreten des Westens* II. Stuttgart.

Koehler, L. and W. Baumgartner. 1953. *Lexicon in Veteris Testamenti libros*. Leiden.

———. 1967ff. *Hebräisches und aramäisches Lexikon zum Alten Testament*³. Leiden.

Kopf, L. 1958. "Arabische Etymologien und Parallelen zum Bibelwörterbuch." *VT* 8:161–215.

Kuryłowicz, J. 1973. *Studies in Semitic Grammar and Metres.* London.

Kutscher, Y. 1955. "'al *mibṭa'ey śəpatenu* ləGumpertz." *Tarbiẓ* 24:355–368.

———. 1957. "lammillon hammiqra'i." *ləšonenu* 21:251–258.

———. 1965. "Contemporary studies in North-Western Semitic." *Journal of Semitic Studies* 10:21–51.

———. 1967. "Mittelhebräisch und Jüdisch-Aramäisch im neuen Köhler-Baumgartner." *VT Supplement* 16:158–175.

———. 1976. *Studies in Galilean Aramaic.* Ramat Gan.

Landberg, C. 1901. *Études sur les dialectes de l'Arabie méridionale, I. Ḥaḍramoût.* Leide.

———. 1920–42. *Glossaire Daṯînois.* Leide.

Lane, E. W. 1863–93. *An Arabic-English Lexicon.* London.

LaSor, W. S. 1957–58. "The sibilants in Old South Arabic." *The Jewish Quarterly Review* N.S. 48:161–173.

Levy, J. 1867–68. *Chaldäisches Wörterbuch über die Targumim.* Leipzig.

———. 1876–89. *Wörterbuch über die Talmudim und Midraschim.* Leipzig.

Lidzbarski, M. 1894. "Beiträge zur Grammatik der neuaramäischen Dialekte." *Zeitschrift für Assyriologie und verwandte Gebiete* 9:224–263.

Littmann, E. 1902. *Neuarabische Volkspoesie.* Berlin.

Loewenstamm, S. E. 1962. "The Ugaritic fertility myth—the result of a mistranslation." *Israel Exploration Journal.* 12:87–88.

———. 1969. "The Lord is my strength and my glory." *VT* 19:464–470.

———. 1971. "mi məpaḥed mippəney haššiṭa habbalšanit?" *ləšonenu* 36:67–70.

Loewenstamm, S. E. and J. Blau. 1957ff. *'ocar ləšon hammiqra.* Jerusalem.

Maclean, A. J. 1895. *Grammar of the Dialects of Vernacular Syriac.* Cambridge.

———. 1901. *A Dictionary of the Dialects of Vernacular Syriac.* Oxford.

Magnanini, P. 1974. "Sulla corrispondenza consonantica arabo /š/ ebraico /ś/." *Annali dell'Istituto Orientale di Napoli* 34:401–408.

Malamat, A. 1962. "Mari and the Bible: some patterns of tribal organization and institutions." *JAOS* 82:143–150.

Malkiel, Y. 1962. "Weak phonetic change, spontaneous sound shift, lexical contamination." *Lingua* 11:263–275. (Reprinted in Malkiel, 1968, *Essays on Linguistic Themes*, pp. 33–45, Berkeley and Los Angeles.)

Maltzan, H. v. 1873. "Dialectische Studien über das Mehri im Vergleich mit verwandten Mundarten." *ZDMG* 27:225–231.

Montgomery, J. A. 1951. *A Critical and Exegetical Commentary on the Books of Kings* (ICC). Ed. H. S. Gehman. Edinburgh.

Moor, J. C. de. 1968. "Murices in Ugaritic mythology." *Orientalia* 37:212–215.

———. 1969. Review of Franke Gröndahl, *Die Personennamen der Texte aus Ugarit*, 1967. *Bibliotheca Orientalis* 26:105a–108a.

Moscati, S. 1947. "Il biconsonantismo nelle lingua semitiche." *Biblica* 28:113–135.

Mühlau, F. and W. Volck. 1890. *Wilhelm Gesenius' hebräisches und aramäisches Handwörterbuch über das Alte Testament*. Leipzig.

Müller, W. W. 1963. "Altsüdarabische Beiträge zum hebräischen Lexikon." *Zeitschrift für die alttestamentliche Wissenschaft* 75:304–316.

Nöldeke, T. 1868. *Grammatik der neusyrischen Sprache*. Leipzig.

———. 1886. Review of F. Delitzsch, *Prolegomena eines neuen hebräisch-aramäischen Wörterbuchs zum Alten Testament*, 1886. *ZDMG* 40:718–743.

———. 1896. Review of Lidzbarski's *Die neuaramäischen Handschriften*, 1896; Sachau's *Skizze des Fellichi-Dialekts von Mosul*, 1895; Maclean's *Grammar of the Dialects of Vernacular Syriac*, 1895. *ZDMG* 50:302–316.

———. 1900. Review of F. Schulthess, *Homonyme Wurzeln im Syrischen*. Berlin. 1900. *ZDMG* 54:152–164.

———. 1904. *Beiträge zur semitischen Sprachwissenschaft*. Strassburg.

———. 1910. *Neue Beiträge zur semitischen Sprachwissenschaft*. Strassburg.

———. 1952. *Belegwörterbuch zur klassischen arabischen Sprache*. Berlin.

Nougayrol, J., E. Laroche, C. Virrolleaud, and C. Schaffer (eds.). 1968. *Ugaritica V*.

Orlinsky, H. M. 1939. "*ḥāṣēr* in the Old Testament." *JAOS* 59:22–37.

Parker, S. B. 1971. "Exodus XV:2 again." *VT* 21:373–379.

Payne Smith, R. 1879–1901. *Thesaurus Syriacus*. Oxford.

Pollak, F. 1931. "Beiträge zum arabischen Lexikon II." *Wiener*

Zeitschrift für die Kunde des Morgenlandes 38:100–124.
Pritchard, J. B. 1958. *The Ancient Near East: An Anthology of Texts and Pictures*. Princeton.
Rainey, A. F. 1970. "haššiṭa habbalšanit—ləvay šeyincəruha." *ləšonenu* 35:11–15.
———. 1971. "Observations on Ugaritic grammar." *Ugarit-Forschungen* 3:151–172.
———. 1974. "The Ugaritic texts in *Ugaritica 5*." *JAOS* 94:184–194.
Rin, S. 1968. *'alilot ha'elim*. Jerusalem.
Rodinson, M. 1957. "Ḫṣṣtn, royaume d'Imru-l-qais." *Groupe linguistique d'études chamito-sémitiques* 7:114–116.
Rössler, O. 1961. "Ghain in Ugaritischen." *Zeitschrift für Assyriologie und verwandte Gebiete* 54:158–172.
Růžička, R. 1909. "Konsonantische Dissimilation in den semitischen Sprachen." *Beiträge zur Assyriologie und semitischen Sprachwissenschaft* VI/4:1–268.
Sauren, H. and G. Kestemont. 1971. "Keret, roi de Ḫubur." *Ugarit-Forschungen* 3:181–221.
Schwally, F. 1898. "Lexikalische Studien." *ZDMG* 52:132–148.
Sethe, K. 1916. "Von Zahlen und Zahlwörtern bei den alten Ägyptern und was für andere Völker und Sprachen daraus zu lernen ist." *Schriften der Gesellschaft der Wissenschaft Strassburg*, 25.
Soden, W. v. 1952. *Grundriss der Akkadischen Grammatik*. Rome.
———. 1965ff. *Akkadisches Handwörterbuch*. Wiesbaden.
———. 1967. "Kleine Beiträge zum Ugaritischen und Hebräischen." *VT Supplement* 16:291–300.
Speiser, E. A. 1942. "The Shibboleth incident (Judges 12:6)." *BASOR* 85:10–13.
Spiro, S. 1895. *An Arabic-English Vocabulary of the Colloquial Arabic of Egypt*. Cairo-London.
Spitzer, L. (ed.). 1922. *Hugo Schuchardt-Brevier*. Halle.
Stehle, D. 1940. "Sibilants and emphatics in South Arabic." *JAOS* 60:507–543.
Steiger, A. 1932. *Contribución a la fonética del Hispano-Árabe y de los arabismos en el ibero-romanico y el siciliano*. Madrid.
Steiner, R. Forthcoming. "The case for fricative-laterals in Proto-Semitic." *American Oriental Series* 59.
Stoddard, D. T. 1855. *Grammar of the Modern Syriac Language*. (American Oriental Society's Proceedings V). London.

Thomas, D. W. 1957. "Some observations on the Hebrew root חדל." *VT Supplement* 4:8–16.

Ullendorf, E. 1962. "Ugaritic marginalia II." *Journal of Semitic Studies* 7:339–351.

Vollers, K. 1894. "Arabisch und Semitisch, Gedanken über eine Revision der semitischen Lautgesetze." *Zeitschrift für Assyriologie und verwandte Gebiete* 9:165–217.

Wagner, M. 1966. "Die lexikalischen und grammatikalischen Aramäismen im alttestamentlichen Hebräisch." *Beihefte zur Zeitschrift für die alttestamentliche Wissenschaft* 96. Berlin.

Wahrmund, A. 1876. *Handwörterbuch der neu-arabischen und deutschen Sprache, I, Neu-arabisch——deutscher Teil.* Giessen.

Yahuda, A. S. 1903. "Hapax Legomena im Alten Testament." *The Jewish Quarterly Review* 15:698–714.

Yalon, H. 1963. "mašaḵ bammiqra." *qunṭrəsim lə'inyəney hallašon ha'iḇrit*[2] 2:76–80.

Zimmern, H. 1917. *Akkadische Fremdwörter als Beweis für babylonischen Kultureinfluss.* Leipzig.

Zorell, F. 1949ff. *Lexicon Hebraicum et Aramaicum Veteris Testamenti.* Rome.

Additions and Corrections

to **p. 50**.*8*: G. Garbini, *Il Semitico Nordoccidentale*, Roma 1988, p. 106, n. 18, added to his paper from 1964 'Il consonantismo dell'ebraico attraverso il tempo' an additional remark, in which, since I postulated the existence of śīn for Hebrew, he castigated me for being addicted to **nationalistic linguistics**(!) because I dared to restate the current(!) conservative view that Hebrew śīn did exist, contrary to Garbini's view. I do not have to stress the absurdity of finding any connection between the existence or absence of a certain phoneme in any language and nationalism, be it linguistic or not-linguistic. Will anyone regard an Italian who postulated an additional phoneme for his language, as nationalistic?! Yet the sad thing is that Garbini, instead of coming to grips with the material I presented in this paper, simply dismisses it, does not change his view from 1964, and invents the excuse of nationalism.

to **p. 52**.*n. 5*: In the meantime, Steiner's work has been published (1977).

to **p. 53**.*n. 7, end*: Cf. also Steiner, op. cit., pp. 149ff., who allows for more conditioning phones causing this sound shift.

to **p. 55**.*-1*: This analysis is followed, in the main, by Sivan, pp. 17-18.

to **pp. 55–56**.*n. 19*: This analysis is followed, in the main, by Sivan, p. 18.

to **p. 63**.*4* : This analysis is followed, in the main, by Sivan, pp. 18-19.

to **p. 65**.*14*: Cf. Sivan, p. 16.

to **p. 70**.*n. 71*: See *Polyphony, passim.*

to **p. 71**.*23*: C. Landberg, *Études sur les dialectes de l'Arabe méridionale, ii, Daṯīnah*, Leiden 1909, p. 500, to be sure, consents to Vollers.

to **p. 88**.*14*: The shift θ > š is also attested (as I learn from S. Hopkins) in the Arabic dialect of Chad, see Fischer & Jastrow, p. 50.

to **p. 92**.*7*: Accordingly, I consider P. Swigger's proposition (*JSS* 26. [1981]) to be unfounded, since it is based on the alleged Proto-Semitic form **θibbolet*.

to **p. 92**.*10*: A. F. L. Beeston (*JSS* 24.175-77 [1979]) considers my proposition that all the unvoiced non-emphatic sibilants had fallen together in *s* to lack the virtue of economy; in his opinion, the assumption that not only *š* but *ś* also had shifted to *s* does not take into account that it would have led to an alarmingly high incidence of homonymy. Yet the history of Semitic languages does attest to the survival of one unvoiced non-emphatic sibilant; this is the case in Gᶜez, see Brockelmann, i 133, E. Mittwoch, 'Die traditionelle Aussprache des Äthiopischen', *Mitteilungen des Seminars für orientalische Sprachen*, ii (pp. 126-248), p. 136, and in Maghrebine dialects, see Fischer & Jastrow, pp. 50.-3; 253.1. Beeston's own proposal is based on Modern South Arabian *seblit* 'ear of corn', which, in his opinion, indicates Proto-Semitic **sblt*. This, however, is erroneous, since in Mehri, for instance, *s* may correspond to Proto-Semitic *š*, presumably by the influence of Arabic,. as e.g., in the words corresponding to Arabic سبي 'to capture', سكن 'to settle', سوّي 'to level', سكر 'to be drunk', and also تسع 'nine', which has in Mehri the forms of *tîsa, sê, sât*.

Hebrew Stress Shifts, Pretonic Lengthening, and Segolization: Possible Cases of Aramaic Interference In Hebrew Syllable Structure

1 One of the main problems of the historic investigation of Biblical Hebrew is to determine the extent of Aramaic influence exerted on it. Recently, even the claim has been raised that Biblical Hebrew, as transmitted by the Masoretes, exhibits an amalgamate of Hebrew and Aramaic elements, the task of the Hebrew philologist being to clear the Hebrew component from Aramaic superstructure.[1] Yet, outside the frame of such excessive claims,[2] it is imperative to attempt to establish the extent of Aramaic influence. In the following we shall try to examine cases of *possible* Aramaic interference in Biblical Hebrew syllable structure (which, however, must by no means be regarded as established). In order to avoid the pitfalls of atomistic procedure, we shall at first try to establish the framework of Biblical Hebrew syllable structure in its entirety, in order to investigate later possible cases of Aramaic interference.

2 Biblical Hebrew syllable structure and stress pattern may be described as follows:

A. OPEN ULTIMA

a. Short open penult: the ultima is stressed, as *kāṭəḇā* 'she wrote," *kāṭəḇū* "they wrote", *dāgəḵā* "your fish", *'ănī* "I"; exceptions: *miḏbárā* "to the wilderness"; *šəmāránī* "he kept me", *tóhū* "wilderness". Sometimes the short penult has been lengthened and, according to Ac, it is stressed: *miḏbārā*, *šəmārānū* "he kept us", and one will interpret similarly forms like *dāgēnū* "our fish" as exhibiting long *ē* (as in the plural).

b. Closed penult: the penult is stressed: *kāṭaḇtā* "you wrote"; exceptions: *'attā* "you", *ʿattā* "now", as well as various forms of perfect with *wāw* con-
(pp. 199ff.) secutive (v. *Israel Oriental Studies* 1.15 ff. [1971], further many nouns like *malkā* "queen" and verbal forms like *higlā* "he exiled".

c. Long open penult: the penult is stressed: *'āḇīḵā* "your father", *hēqīmū*

[1] V. Beyer, 1969.

[2] V. later note 4.

"they erected", *bānītī* "I built", *qāmū* "they stood up"; exceptions: *'ānōkī* "I", as well as some forms of perfect with *waw* consecutive, v. *Israel Oriental Studies, ibid.*, further many nouns like *ḥōmā* "wall" and verbal forms like *hāyā* "he was".

B. CLOSED ULTIMA

a. Short open penult: the ultima is stressed: *kəṭóḇ* "write!", in other cases the originally short stressed penult was lengthtened and accordingly (v. Bc) remained stressed: *wayyikkāṭeḇ* "and it was written" (through the influence of *yikkāṭéḇ* "it will be written", exhibiting long *ā* by sound shift, viz. through pretonic lengthening; cf. *infra*).

b. Closed penult: the ultima is stressed, e.g. imperfect and imperative of *hifʿil, piʿel, hitpaʿel.*

c. Long open penult: sometimes the penult is stressed: *wayḇārek̲* "and he blessed", *wayyōšaʿ* "and he helped"; in other cases the ultima: imperfect, imperative and perfect forms like *yəḇārék̲, bārék̲, bērék̲*; *yāqīm, yāqém, hāqém, hēqīm*, further nouns like *ḥāsīḏ* "pious".

This short and by necessity perfunctory mainly synchronic description of Hebrew syllable structure (which, on purpose, omits e.g. construct forms, having weak stress or no stress at all) reflects a rather confused picture: it is almost impossible to predict word stress according to syllable structure. Yet it is possible, as if by magic, to introduce order into this apparent chaos. Through *one single assumption* it is possible to explain the stress of the great majority of Hebrew words. Therefore this assumption has to be regarded as the most powerful explanation of the interdependence of stress and syllable structure, a veritable pivot on which everything hinges. Let us add to the Hebrew words the final short vowels which, according to comparative grammar, were lost in Hebrew, and then, without changing the traditional place of stress, *the great majority of words exhibit stress on penult*. Those which are today stressed on the ultima have, as a rule, lost final short vowels, the addition of which makes them stressed on the penultima. And those which are today stressed on the penult, have, as a rule, preserved their final syllable. Accordingly, we assume a **period of general penult stress.**[3] Therefore, words like *hēqīmā, hēqīmū,*

[3] For the history of research v. *Israel Oriental Studies* 1. 19, note 8 (1971). — By the (p. 203)
assumption that only stressed *ā* shifted to *ō*, even an older stage of Hebrew stress can be reconstructed. As a rule, parallel to the stress in vogue in the pronunciation of Classical Arabic, a stress structure is posited according to which the penult was stressed when long; otherwise the antepenult (for particulars v. Blau, 1970, pp. 31–32). It can, however, be de- *
monstrated that, in Arabic at least, this stress structure is not original. Accordingly, no *
proof for the existence of this stress system in Hebrew can be adduced either. Therefore, the shift of only stressed *ā* to *ō* can also be accounted for by a different theory, assuming penult stress when the penult syllable contained a long vowel, or even a short one if the short vowel

tāqīmī, hāqīmū, 'ănáḥnū, 'ālḗhā, 'árṣā, etc., which have preserved their final syllable, are still stressed on their penult, whereas words like *dāḇār, yāqūm, śādē, gālā, yiglē, kāṭáḇ, yiḵtóḇ, dāgā*, which have lost their final short vowels (< **dabáru*, **yaqūmu*, **śadáyu*, **galáya*, **yigláyu*, **katába*, **yaktúbu*, **dagátu*), exhibit now ultima stress, yet, by addition of the elided final short vowels, also attest to the existence of a general penult stress before the elision of the final short vowels. Since this theory of a general penult stress is so powerful that, by the simple addition of the elided final short vowels, it explains stress in the majority of Hebrew words, every other analysis of the stress has to adjust itself to it. Therefore, in the following we shall deal with exceptions from this theory, i.e. with words exhibiting stress on their ultima, although they have not elided their final vowels, as well as with words with penult stress despite the elision of their final short vowel, — from the vantage point of this theory. At this juncture, however, it will be more expedient to treat first the problem of pretonic lengthening, to deal afterwards with Biblical Aramaic syllable structure and then only with the cases of exceptional stress position in Biblical Hebrew and also in Biblical Aramaic.

3 One of the most conspicuous features of syllable structure in Biblical Hebrew is, it seems, the general preservation of originally short vowels, especially of *a*, in pretonic open syllables. This is, in a sense, the cardinal point upon which the structure of Biblical Hebrew pivots, thorougly differentiating it from Aramaic,[4] in which short vowels in this position were, as a rule, elided. Yet the most surprising thing is that these pretonic vowels were not only preserved, but even lengthened.

REMARK: So surprising was this fact that some scholars even tried to explain it away by regarding these vowels as short, v. Grimme, 1896,

was not preceded by a long vowel. If, however, the short penult was preceded by a long vowel, the long vowel was stressed. Thus according to both the accepted and newly proposed theory (we shall call the latter "Maghrebine stress system", because it bears strong resemblance with the stress structure to be posited for ancient Maghrebine dialects) *maqāmu* will be stressed on the penult, *kātibu* on the antepenult. Yet *kataba* was, according to the accepted theory, stressed on the antepenult, according to the "Maghrebine", however, on the penult.
* For particulars v. Blau, 1975, pp. 62–70.

4 Beyer, 1969, as a matter of fact, did not pay attention to this crucial difference between the Hebrew and the Aramaic morphological structure. Would he have done so, he would have perhaps not overemphasized the role of Aramaic influence on Masoretic Hebrew. — Birkeland, 1940, pp. 8 ff. has recognized the importance of the preservation of originally short pretonic vowels. He has, however, identified it with the pretonic lengthening of open short vowels. Yet it is by no means clear whether these vowels were preserved because they were lengthened or rather they were preserved and ultimately lengthened (v. *infra*; so even according to Birkeland). Therefore, one will rather consider the preservation of these vowels to be the cardinal point and deal with their lengthening as an additional problem.

p. 34, or half-long, Joüon, 1923, p. 23. Yet since C. Brockelmann's paper, ZA 14.343 (1899), it has been commonplace to consider these vowels to be long, v. e.g. Brockelmann, 1908–13, I, p. 101, Bergsträsser, 1918–29, I, p. 117. Brockelmann's argumentation is, to be sure, fallacious: he relies on Syriac (Nestorian) and Arabic loans of Hebrew proper nouns, exhibiting long pretonic vowels. Yet the lengthening may be due to Syriac, which could only thus (or by the reduplication of the following consonant) preserve vowels in open unstressed syllables. And the same applies to Arabic loans adduced by Brockelmann, since they did not pass into Arabic directly, but *via* Aramaic; for particulars v. Blau, 1968, p. 31. (p. 268)
Nevertheless, the lengthening of pretonic originally short vowels in open syllables is well established. Judaeo-Arabic *fāsūq* 'verse (in the Scriptures)' exhibits long *ā*, as demonstrated by occasional spelling with *alif* and by the plurals *fawāsīq/fawāsiq*, v. Blau, 1965, p. 164. This word entered Judaeo-Arabic directly from Hebrew, not only because the parallel Aramaic word (according to the dictionaries at least) is *pəsūqā* with *shwa* after the *p*, but also because it would have been taken over into Arabic with the (feminine) ending *a/ā*; accordingly it attests to pretonic lengthening in Hebrew. Moreover, pretonic lengthening is also exhibited by the oldest layer of the Septuagint, viz. the Pentateuch (3rd century B.C.): η always marks long *ē* in it, and η occurs in pretonic open syllables as well, as Ησαυ, Κηδαρ, thus establishing the existence of pretonic lengthening as early as the third century B.C. And the lengthening of originally short pretonic vowels in open syllables can be demonstrated by internal evidence as well: words like *wəḵāṭaḇtī, kāṭəḇū, dāgəḵā, 'ānōḵī* exhibit long *ā* in their first syllable, as demonstrated by their preservation despite distance from the place of the stress .This *ā* had become lengthened at a previous stage, when it stood in the pretonic syllable: **wəḵāṭáḇtī, *kāṭáḇū, *dāgáḵā, *'ānṓḵī*; for particulars v. infra § 6. *

4 It is a moot question what caused pretonic short vowels in open syllables not only to be preserved, but even lengthened (whereas in Aramaic, for instance, they are reduced). In the main, there are two major trends attempting to explain this feature. One considers it, despite internal differences, a purely phonetic fact. One will not accept the view that these now pretonic vowels were lengthened during a preceding period in which they bore the main stress; cf. e.g. C. Brockelmann's judicious remark against it, *ZDMG* 94. 367 ff. (1940). On the other hand, it is not impossible that the lengthening was due to secondary stress, as assumed by Sarauw, 1939, p. 66, in his masterly work on stress and syllable structure in Semitic languages. Nevertheless, one must not lose sight of Brockelmann's strictures, according to which Sarauw's theory

implies that the secondary stress in a form like *qāṭál(a)* (and as one may add, also e.g. *qəṭāláni* and *qāṭəlū*, originally *qāṭalū*) was stronger than the main stress, which was not strong enough to lengthen its vowel (Brockelmann, *ibid.*, p. 348). Moreover, the supposition of the Hebrew secondary stress is in its entirety based on Hebrew pretonic lengthening and thus moving in a vicious circle, since, *pace* Sarauw, *ibid.*, p. 15, in Geʿez only long vowels and vowels in closed syllables bear a secondary stress, v. Mittwoch, 1925, p. 160. On the other hand, one will hardly concur with Brockelmann's other criticism (*ibid.*), that pretonic lengthening in *living* Hebrew would have made it a slow and cumbersome language, exhibiting long vowels only: in the Neo-Aramaic dialect of Ṭur ʿAbdin, in Ṭuroyo, there is, in fact, a plethora of phonemically long syllables, including pretonic ones. This demonstrates that a great number of phonemically long syllables is by no means impossible in living languages (cf. *BSOAS* 31. 606–607 [1968]). As to their phonetic aspect, in Ṭuroyo vowel length is more or less regulated by their position in respect of the stress (v. ibid.); yet the quality even of vowels remote from the stress demonstrates that they are phonemically long. It stands to reason that the situation in Biblical Hebrew was quite similar. Phonemically long vowels were, it seems, actualized in different lengths, according to their position in respect to stress. It is by no means impossible that the Tiberian vocalization system which, as is well known, marks only quality of vowels, neglected their quantitative aspect, because it was regulated more or less automatically.

Cantineau, 1932, p. 132, regarded the lengthening of pretonic vowels as being due to a phonetic process as well, viz. to the rhythm. He even cited some, in his opinion parallel, instances from the Arabic dialect of Palmyre, exhibiting *faʿūl* > *fāʿūl*; later, however, Cantineau himself came to regard these cases as due to morphological assimilation, v. Brockelmann, *ibid.*, p. 349. Nevertheless, according to T.M. Johnstone, *BSOAS* 24. 250 f. (1961), in the Arabic Dōsiri dialect in bisyllabic words the ultimate syllable of which contains a long vowel and the penult is a short syllable containing *a*, there is a tendency to lengthen the penult (*ʿāǧūz*, *xāḏēt*); yet alongside the lengthened form, the unlengthened form occurs as free variant. As a matter of fact, I have noted the lengthening even when the ultimate syllable, though long, does not contain a long vowel (p. 293, note 1 *sāraḥt*), and even in closed (!) penult (*tārwa*; p. 292, note 4 *sārraḥt*). Therefore, this feature needs further elucidation. Nevertheless, one will have to admit the mere phonetic possibility of pretonic lengthening, without, however, losing sight of the fact that so far it is only attested as a marginal, optional feature, whereas in Biblical Hebrew it is one of the main traits of syllable structure.

The other trend explains pretonic lengthening as being due to Aramaic influence; v. Brockelmann, *ZA* 14. 343 ff. (1899), *idem*, 1908–13, I, p. 101.

Through Aramaic impact Jews lost the ability of pronouncing short vowels in open unstressed syllables. Accordingly (just as did speakers of Maghrebine dialects in loans from classical Arabic)[5] they lengthened these vowels. Brockelmann, and in his wake Bergsträsser, 1918–29, I, p. 117, §21k, propounded that this lengthening is peculiar to scholarly, rather than living, pronunciation of Hebrew, after it had already ceased being a living language. This, however, can be proved as fallacious. We know from the Bar Kokhba letters written in Middle Hebrew that Hebrew in its Middle Hebrew form continued living till then (2nd century A.D.). These letters were written in Middle Hebrew, because Middle Hebrew was the spoken language. Had the writers intended to use literary Hebrew, they would have written in Biblical Hebrew. Pretonic lengthening, however, is attested by the transcription of proper nouns in the Septuagint (v. §3, remark) about half a millenium earlier.

H. Bauer, on the other hand, suggested a very early date for this Aramaic interference in Hebrew syllable structure (v. e.g. Bauer-Leander, 1922, p. 237g′). Yet this assumption is based on Bauer's thesis that Hebrew is a "mixed" language, a hypothesis which was rejected by the majority of scholars; cf. e.g. the short, but just strictures raised by Bergsträsser, 1918–29, II, p. iii, note 1, who mainly emphasized that Bauer's thesis implies that the systems of the two languages that mingled, i.e. of Hebrew and Aramaic, were preserved partly almost without change. Besides, as Brockelmann (*ZDMG* 94. 348) observed, this would presume that in Aramaic vowels were reduced as early as 1400 B.C., and this is at least unlikely. I am calling attention to that in the Aramaic of Sham'al (eighth century B.C.) short pretonic vowels in open syllable were, it seems, preserved, v. Dion, 1974, pp. 104–105, and in the Aramaic incantation in cuneiform found in Uruk (about third century B.C.) vowels otherwise reduced or dropped appear as full vowels (although they have, it seems, to be interpreted as half-vowels, v. Blau, *IOS* 1. 27–28). Moreover, this thesis pre- (pp. 211–12)

[5] One will, *mutatis mutandis*, compare the Ṭuroyo syllable structure. Among its long vowels a relatively high percentage arose from short ones when the following double consonant became simple. It stands to reason that at the time when these consonants had become simple, the speakers of Ṭuroyo were unable to pronounce short vowels in open unstressed syllables and, therefore, lengthened them (in their case, without external influence; cf. the similar lengthening of vowels in Biblical Hebrew and Biblical Aramaic preceding historically double *r* and certain laryngals/pharyngals that had become simple. One will consider the vowel changes attested in these cases as exhibiting originally quantitative difference, *pace* Brockelmann, 1918–13, I, p. 198, § iβ, who, following Grimme 1896, p. 77, interpreted them as qualitative changes due to assimilation: were this the case, this assimilation should have occurred preceding originally simple r/laryngal/pharyngal as well. Why then are these alleged assimilations restricted to historically double consonants?! Moreover, *qamaṣ* rather becomes *pataḥ* by assimilation to these simple consonants [e.g. *wayyāsar*, *wayyānaḥ*, etc., as against *wayyāqom*], rather than *vice versa*).

supposes that both languages that mixed, i.e. Hebrew and Aramaic, already reduced short vowels in open syllables, Aramaic even in pretonic syllables, both in those preceding the pretonic ones. Thus, according to Bauer's thesis one needs must posit that e.g. *dəḇārīm* "things" was in Hebrew already pronounced *dəḇarīm*,[6] rather than **daḇarīm*. Had according to this theory Hebrew still preserved the first *a* in *daḇarīm*, in a position in which it could not stand in Aramaic, it would have lengthened it as well, in order to make Arameans able to pronounce it: **dāḇārīm*. It is, however, highly unlikely that short vowels in this position were already reduced so early in Canaanite in general and in Hebrew in particular.

The same objection may be raised against Birkeland's (1940, pp. 10 f.) claim that it was the immigrant "bedouin" Israelites who had preserved and lengthened pretonic vowels, whereas the native sedentary Canaanite population reduced it. Moreover, Brockelmann (*apud* Birkeland, ibid., p. 126) correctly observed that according to Birkeland's hypothesis the Canaanites lengthened pretonic vowels in their attempt to adjust their speech to that of the Israelites, and afterwards this adjusted pronunciation, exhibiting long pretonic vowels, was taken over by the Israelites. It goes without saying that this construction is too complex to be accepted.

One will rather assign the lengthening of pretonic vowels, if it was in fact due to Aramaic impact, to the period of the second Temple (*terminus ante quem*: third century B.C., as exhibited in the transcription of proper nouns in the Pentateuch translation of the Septuagint), when Hebrew, in its Middle Hebrew form, was a living language (v. *supra*), but profoundly influenced by Aramaic (and, of course, also influencing Aramaic). It stands to reason that in this period the speakers of Hebrew lost the ability of pronouncing short vowels in open unstressed syllables, and therefore lengthened them. At this time, such vowels in the syllables preceding the pretonic one were, it seems, already reduced. Accordingly, it was in pretonic syllables only that this lengthening occurred.

5. We shall now analyse the syllable structure and stress pattern of Biblical Aramaic, compared with Biblical Hebrew. It may be described as follows (I am, in the main, following Birkeland, 1940, p. 3):

A. OPEN ULTIMA

As a rule the penult is stressed.

a. Short open penult: the penult is stressed (as against stressed ultima in Biblical Hebrew): *kəṯáḇū* "they wrote", *šəḇúqū* "*let*!" Exceptions: *status*

[6] I am transcribing *ḇ* for convenience only, without presupposing that *b* in postvocalic position had already become spirantized at this period.

emphaticus forms like **šəmā* "the name"; further *dənā* "this", *'ănā* "I", *'ărū, 'ălū* "behold", *ḥĕyī* "live!"; nouns like *rəḇū* "greatness", nouns like *kāṯəḇā* "writing" (fem.), nouns with pronominal suffixes and verbal forms like *bənā* "he built", *tehĕwē* "she will be", *'ezē* "heated" (with *e* in the penult).

b. Closed penult, the penult is stressed (as in Hebrew): *'éllę* "these", *yəḏá'tā* "you knew", *śāmtā* "you put"; exceptions: *himmō* "they", perhaps influenced by its synonym *himmōn*; verbal forms like *haglī* "he took into exile", *status emphaticus* forms like *malkā* "the king"; nouns with pronominal suffixes.

c. Long open penult, the penult is stressed (as in Hebrew): *qāmū* "they rose"; exceptions: *status emphaticus* forms like *yōma* "the day"; nouns with pronominal suffixes; nouns like *'ēṭā* "counsel", *bəhīlū* "hurry".

B. CLOSED ULTIMA

a. Short open penult, the ultima is stressed (as in Hebrew): *bəṭeláṯ* "it ceased", *yisgəḏún* "they will prostrate", *bārəḵēṯ* "I blessed", *šabbəḥēṯ* "I praised", *gəḇár*, *'ĕnāš* "man"; exceptions: segolate nouns like *męlęḵ* "king", cf. also *'ĕḏáyin* "then".

b. Closed penult: as in Hebrew, the ultima is stressed: *'innūn, 'innīn, himmōn* "they", *hašlēm* "complete!", *naddát* "she fled", etc.

c. Long open penult: as in Hebrew, sometimes the penult is stressed, as *sāpaṯ* "it (fem.) was fulfilled", *hăqēmeṯ* "I set up"; in other cases the ultima: *hoqīmáṯ* "(was) set up", *pərīsáṯ* "she was divided", *yəqūmūn* "they will rise", *yədūrān* "they (fem.) will dwell".

As in the case of Hebrew, this short and by necessity perfunctory mainly synchronic description of Biblical Aramaic syllable structure reflects a quite confused picture, which does not enable to predict word stress according to syllable structure. Again, as it was with Hebrew, it is possible to introduce order into this apparent chaos by the assumption of a period of general penult stress (as propounded by Cantineau, 1932): words that have not lost final short vowels, as *kətābū, šəḇuqū, 'ēllę, yeda'tā, śamtā, qāmū, sāpaṯ, haqēmeṯ*, have preserved their penult stress, while words that have lost their final short vowels, as *gəḇar, rəḇū, kāṯəḇā, malkī, rēšáh, bənā, tehĕwē, 'ezē, yisgəḏūn, yəqūmūn, yedūrān* (> **gəḇáru, *rəḇūtu, *kāṯəḇátu, *malkíya, *rēšáha, *bənáya, *tehewíyu, *'ezíyu, *yisgəḏúna, *yəqūmúna, *yəḏūrána*)[7], are now stressed on their ultima. As in the case of Hebrew, exceptions occur, i.e. words stressed on their ultima, although they have not lost a final vowel, and those with penult stress despite the elision of their final vowels; yet we shall have, because of the power of the theory of a general penult stress, to consider these exceptions, as in the

7 I am transcribing in a way which involves as few changes as possible, in order to emphasize the point in question. This, however, must not be taken as sign for any sort of relative chronology.

case of Hebrew, from the vantage point of the theory of penult stress. Before doing so, however, we shall raise the question whether the general penult stress in both languages arose independently or has rather to be interpreted as due to one wave. This question, however, has to remain without answer, since nothing certain can be stated as to the causes of this parallel development. To quote Cantineau, 1931, p. 98 "Une pareille innovation est-elle une trace d'une période commune araméo-hébraïque? Ou s'est-elle faite indépendentment dans les deux langues? Est-ce une innovation spontanée? Ou est-elle due à l'influence des langues parlées sur la côte et dans l'hinterland immédiat par les peuples que les Araméens et les Canaanéens ont trouvés installés avant eux en ces contrées?". And one may add: is it due to contact between Hebrew and Aramaic? Nothing certain can be said. I only want to call attention to the fact that penult stress occurred independently several times in the history of Semitic languages, as it was e.g. the case in Nestorian Syriac, v. e.g. Nöldeke, 1898, p. 39.

6 There is quite a considerable number of words in Hebrew with ultima stress, although they have not elided their final vowels. The most conspicuous series among them are words that, according to the theory of general penult stress, should habe been stressed on their open penult containing a short vowel, rather than on their open ultima, which in fact bears the stress, whereas the historical short vowel in the open penult has been reduced: *yiḵtəḇū*, *niḵtəḇā*, *'ănī*, *dāgəḵā*, *kāṭəḇā*, *kāṭəḇū*, rather than **yiḵtóḇū*, **niḵtóḇā*, **'ánī*, **dāgéḵā*, **kāṭáḇā*, **kāṭáḇū* (corresponding to the pausal forms **yiḵtōḇū*, *niḵtōḇā*, *'ānī*, *dāgēḵā*, *kāṭāḇā*, *kāṭāḇū*). As the three last examples show, the antepenult containing *qameṣ*, original *pataḥ*, does not change. This must needs be interpreted that the shift from the original penult (which is attested by the pausal forms as well) has taken place *after* pretonic vowels had been lengthened. Accordingly, if I am correct in assigning pretonic lengthening to the period of the second Temple before the third century B.C. (v. §4, end), this shift of stress from the penult to the ultima occurred even later, presumably in the last centuries B.C., when the influence of Aramaic had become even stronger. Since the shift of stress from the penult to the ultima occurred in Biblical Aramaic as well under very similar (though by no means identical) conditions (v. §7), it may well be due to Aramaic influence, though the tendency for ultima stress could have arisen in both languages independently. In both languages, through the elision of final short vowels, the majority of words was no longer stressed on the penult, but rather on the ultima. The rhythm of these words could have acted as catalysator, arising the tendency of oxytone stress. On the other hand, I am rather inclined to attribute the change in syllable structure that occurred at this period, to Aramaic influence. As we have seen, one of the main dif-

ferences between Aramaic and Hebrew syllable structure is (v. §4) that in Aramaic short vowels in pretonic open syllables are reduced, in Hebrew however lengthened. Yet at this period the historical vowel in the open penult has been reduced in *yiḵtəḇū, niḵtəḇā, 'ănī, dāgəḵā, kāṭəḇā, kāṭəḇū* in Hebrew as in Aramaic, presumably under Aramaic impact.

Till now we have dealt with the shift of stress from short vowels in open penult to open ultima. This shift occurs so regularly that it may be considered a veritable sound shift. Exceptions occur only in verbs with pronominal suffix of the first person sg. of the type *šəmārání* (which, however, may be influenced by the rhythm of segolate nouns like *báyit* "house"), further by *miḏbárā*, which, * however, alternates with *miḏbārā*, exhibiting the spreading of a pausal form to context position (and one will interpret similarly the long penult vowel in *šəmārānū* and presumably also in *dāgēnū* [sg.]). A similar veritable sound shift is the shift from closed penult to closed ultima, as reflected in many forms of the imperative, the jussive and the imperfect with *waw consecutive* without suffixes, which all terminated originally in the last radical (the "short" imperfect, also called apocopate, had originally double function, that of the jussive and the past; the function of the past has in the main been preserved after *waw consecutive*; cf. e.g. *Israel Oriental Studies* 1. 22–23 [1971]). The imperative (pp. 206–07) and the jussive, under the influence of the imperfect, have not preserved penult stress even if it fell on an open syllable (as *hōréḏ, yōréḏ*). After *waw consecutive*, however, penult stress is often preserved on open syllables (type *wayḇárẹḵ*), but never on closed ones (type *wayqaddéš*). Even pausal forms did not preserve * the penult stress in words of this syllable structure.

I do not know of cases of the preservation of penult stress on open syllables containing short vowels in words with closed ultima. In contradistinction to words with such penult syllable, but with open ultima (v. *supra*), no traces of this stress structure have been preserved. Since, as far as I know, words with this syllable structure are only attested in certain imperative, jussive and imperfect form with *waw consecutive*, the almost general shift of stress to the ultima may be due to the impact of the imperfect as well: jussive *yikkāṭéḇ*, originally **yikkáṭeḇ*, through the influence of the imperfect *yikkāṭéḇ* (and, at any rate, the pretonic lengthening of the jussive *yikkĀṭéḇ* has to be attributed to the impact of the imperfect, since at this period pretonic lengthening had ceased operating, v. *supra*). As to the imperative *qal*, one has to take into account the possibility, that it was originally phonemically (but not phonetically) monosyllabic. I wonder whether the frequent imperative *hiššámẹr* "be aware!" with penult stress is influenced by the frequent *hiššāmer ləḵā* with rhythmical retraction of the stress preceding a monosyllable or rather a residue of penult stress with secondary lengthening of the originally short vowel.

Till now we have dealt with regular stress shift from the penult to ultima. Yet in words with open ultima, exhibiting closed penult (v. § 2Ab) or long open penult (v. § 2Ac) as well as in words with closed ultima, exhibiting long open penult (as *waybārẹk* as against *wayḥārēp̄*; cf. § 2Bc) only a tendency for the shift of stress from the penult to the ultima exists. In the case of the first and second person sg. masc. of the perfect with *waw consecutive* this tendency has been "grammaticalized": the ordinary perfect has preserved penult stress, that with *waw*, in these persons, as a rule, exhibits stress on the ultima. This differentiation is late: despite the shift of stress to the ultima the original pretonic syllable, now being antepretonic, exhibits a (historically not original) long vowel, thus attesting to pretonic lengthening being older that this stress shift: *wəḵāṯaḇtī*.

7 As to the Biblical Aramaic words exhibiting ultima stress, although they have not elided their final vowels, they have to be interpreted as due to the tendency to oxytone stress as well.[8] In contradistinction to Hebrew, however, in words with open ultima, as a rule, the stress is preserved on short open penult (v. § 5Aa; exceptions: *dənā*, *'ănā*, *'ărū*, *'ălū*). As in Hebrew, oxytone stress obtains in words exhibiting closed penult and closed ultima (v. § 5Bb). As in Hebrew, short open penult lost its stress when the ultima was closed (cf. § 5Ba); *bəṭelát* (with rather surprising preservation of the pretonic vowel, which is, at least historically, short), *tiqpát* (with loss of the pretonic short vowel) < **təqípaṭ*, *nepqāṭ* < **nəpáqaṭ*; late forms in late Aramaic dialects like *nəp̄áqaṭ* are not, it seems, traces of the old form, but rather restitution through the influence of *nəp̄aq* (cf. Cantineau, 1931, pp. 93–94, Birkeland, 1940, p. 3, who, however, express different opinions. Birkeland goes as far as to reject because of the third pers. sg. fem. of the perfect Cantineau's thesis of a general penult stress in Biblical Aramaic, yet one will hardly follow him). The penult stress of closed or and even more of long open syllables of words with open ultima (§5Ab, c) is in Biblical Aramaic regular, much more so than in Hebrew. In words with closed ultima and long open penult only a tendency to ultima stress obtains (as in Hebrew; cf. § 5Bc): *hŏqīmáṭ*, *pərīsáṭ*, as against *sāp̄aṭ*.

As these examples demonstrate, despite the great similarity in the general trend of Biblical Hebrew and Biblical Aramaic at this period of tendency to oxytone stress and identity in many details, there exist important differences in details. Hebrew was, to be sure, at this time decisively influenced by Aramaic. Yet one must not lose sight of the decisive fact that Hebrew was still a living tongue (in its Middle Hebrew form) and bilingual speakers of Hebrew and

[8] Nouns in *status emphaticus* have to be analysed differently, since they lost their final short vowel; v. Cantineau, 1931, p. 92. Less convincingly Birkeland, 1940, p. 2.

Aramaic were speakers versed in two languages, and not just Arameans speaking Hebrew. And Hebrew was not only influenced by Aramaic, but also influenced it, as reflected by various phenomena in Judeo-Aramaic and Christian Palestinian Aramaic.

8 Till now, we have not yet dealt with the so-called segolate nouns in the framework of Biblical Hebrew and Biblical Aramaic syllable structure and stress pattern. Recently, they have been treated in several important publications (Spitaler, 1968; Malone, 1971; Muraoka 1976; Steiner, 1976). Here I am only interested in the inclusion of segolation in the framework of general stress shift, the cardinal point of which is the assumption of general penult stress in both Biblical Hebrew and Biblical Aramaic.

Malone, 1971, e.g. p. 61, connects the stress shift of **náhar* to *nahár* with that of e.g. **zi'b* > **zīḇ* to *zə'ēḇ*. This view was rightly criticized by Muraoka, 1976, p. 230b, because it ignores the existence of general penult stress.. Muraoka assumes that Hebrew epenthesis had its origin in Aramaic as well, yet it became felt in Hebrew later than the influence of the Aramaic stress shift. This, however, involves considerable chronological difficulties. Epenthesis is already attested in the Septuagint, whereas it is likely that the tendency to oxytone shift is later (v. §6). It stands to reason that, for pure phonetic causes, epenthesis arose in a part of the segolates immediately with the elision of final short vowels. Accordingly, I would rather assume that the different behaviour of Hebrew (mainly forms like *męlęḵ*) and Aramaic (mainly forms like *ṣəlém*) segolates is due to the different morphophonemic status[9] of the segolates. In both Hebrew and Aramaic, after the final short vowels had been omitted, epenthesis took place and phonetically the formerly monosyllabic segolates had become bisyllabic. This is the reason for Hebrew segolates in the Septuagint being transcribed as bisyllabic. Yet Hebrew segolates were morphophonemically monosyllabic. This is the reason for their transcription by Origines as monosyllabic[10] and the alternation of monosyllabic and bisyllabic forms in Jerome's transcriptions. Therefore, as a rule, segolate nouns in Hebrew were not affected by the tendency to oxytone stress, although they phonetically exhibited stressed

[9] Malone, 1971, p. 62b operated with the notion of morphophonemic representation of segolates. He, however, attributed original monosyllabic morphophonemic representation of segolates to Aramaic, assuming that originally the stress shift preceded epenthesis, in Aramaic, however, by analogical reshaping, a morphophonemic change occurred, permuting the descriptive order of stress shift and epenthesis. We have seen, however, that presumably epenthesis preceded the tendency to oxytone stress, rather than vice versa. Therefore, the conduct of the segolates in Aramaic can easily be accounted for, and it is Hebrew that needs special explanation.

[10] This explanation is more powerful than the assumption of a different dialect, since it explains also the vacillation of Jerome's transcriptions, v. infra.

short penult in open syllable, which, at this time, contravened Hebrew syllable structure (§ 6): morphophonematically they were monosyllabic and stressed on their only syllable.[11] It is even dubious whether segolates ever became in Hebrew morphophonematically bisyllabic;[12] Jerome's transcription, at any rate, suggest that they remained morphophonemically monosyllabic. In Aramaic, on the other hand, the epenthetic vowel became morphophonemically counted, making these nouns also morphophonemically bisyllabic. Therefore, they were influenced by the general tendency to oxytone stress, according to which (§ 7) short open penult lost its stress in words with closed ultima.[13]

[11] For epenthetic vowels not being morphophonemically counted cf. e.g. dialectal Arabic *bikitbu* "they will write": would the epenthetic (second) *i* count, it would have attracted the stress (as it does in the speech of some speakers; v. Blanc, 1953, pp. 28–29). — Segolate nouns ending in ' exhibit in Hebrew two different forms: one with total loss of the ' (*ḥeṭ* "sin", the ' still spelt after the *ṭ*), the other with epenthesis *pęlę* "wonder", the ' still spelt after the second *e* and once *perhaps* also pronounced. If in fact epenthesis arose immediately with the elision of short final vowels (as I think it happened), *pęlę* could have arisen by real epenthesis, the ' being once pronounced. It could have, however, originated by analogy to "sound" segolates. It stands to reason that, contrary to Malone, 1971, pp. 71–72, nouns of the type of *bęḵę* "weeping" are not due to sound shift (an epenthetic vowel *ę* preceding *y* being unlikely) but rather to analogy (a possibility also taken into account by Malone). With Barth, 1894, p. 21, I am inclined to consider nouns like *bęḵę* as original *fi'al* forms: **bekę* with stress on the ultima. Barth, correctly in our opinion, explains the shift of *e* to *ę* as parallel to the shift of *pe'ęl* to *pę'ęl* in "sound" nouns (*neḏęr-nęḏęr*); cf. the vacillation *qęṣę* — *qeṣę*. He does not, however, account for the shift of the stress to the penult. This has to be attributed to the analogy of segolate nouns. Bauer-Leander, 1922, p. 579q' (quoted by Malone) posit analogy as well, yet without assuming an original *pi'al* nominal theme. Yet without this assumption is is difficult to account for the final *h* occurring in the consonantal text (*bkh*, rather than *bky*). Though we think that (phonetic) segolization arose with the elision of final short vowels, it stands to reason that analogical formations triggered by it were much later, too late to find expression in the consonantal text.

[12] Because of the early attestation of epenthesis, on the one hand, and the late attestation of monosyllabic forms, on the other, I prefer this explanation to that offered Blau, 1970, p. 38.

[13] One of the main reasons of Spitaler, 1968, p. 194, for deriving the shift of stress to the epenthetic vowel in the ultima in Aramaic exclusively by analogy, rather than by sound shift, is his sceptical attitude to the possibility of stressed epenthetic vowels in Semitic languages. Yet we have already seen (note 11, beginning) that forms like *bikitbu* do exist. Moreover, the existence of such forms is well attested in Maghrebine dialects in once monosyllabic "(segolate") nouns now stressed on their final, once epenthetic vowel (like *šhar* "month"; v. e.g. Brockelmann, 1908–13, p. 86). These forms arose, in my opinion, because of the old Maghrebine stress according to which words of the type *fa'al* are oxytone, a process quite similar to what happened in Aramaic. — Malone, 1971, pp. 59–60, derives both nouns of the type *zə'eḇ* "wolf" and *gəḏl* "kid" by assuming that epenthesis occurred in them earlier. (pp. 250ff.) As to type *zə'eḇ*, cf. against it *Israel Oriental Studies* 7. 17 ff. (1977). As to type *gəḏl*, we accept, more or less, Malone's explanation. It stands to reason that with the elision of final short vowels monosyllabic nouns, now terminating in two consonants, developed epenthetic

Steiner, 1976, attributes construct forms like *ḥădár* in Hebrew to the earlier disappearance of final short vowels in the construct. If, however, Hebrew segolates remained morphophonemically monosyllabic, one would not expect absolute and construct forms to differ. Moreover, the tendency to ultima stress is later than the omission of final short vowels even in the absolute. Accordingly, one will explain the occurrence of forms like *ḥădàr* in construct, rather than in the absolute, according to Siever's assumption (quoted by Steiner, 1976, p. 5) that construct forms, being unstressed, were only influenced by the rhythm of their context.[14]

9 To sum up: the theory that in both Biblical Hebrew and Biblical Aramaic once a general penult stress prevailed is the most powerful explanation which accounts for such a wide range of forms that seeming exceptions from it have to be analysed from the vantage point of this theory. Most of these exceptions are accounted for by tendency to ultima stress which shifted the stress in both languages in forms that did not elide final short vowels and, therefore, according to the theory of general penult stress still bore stress on the penult, to the ultima. This shift occurred after pretonic lengthening in Hebrew, as demonstrated by the existence of lengthened historically pretonic vowels in now antepretonic syllables (as: *wəḵāṭaḇtí*, *kāṭəḇū́*), presumably by Aramaic influence (which is also felt in pretonic lengthening), it seems in the last centuries B.C. The reduction of short pretonic syllables (as: *kāṭəḇū́* < **kāṭábū*) also attests to Aramaic influence. Yet for all the Aramaic influence, differences in syllable structure and stress pattern remained between Aramaic and Hebrew, still a living tongue at this time. For phonetic causes, it stands to reason that segolization occurred in both languages immediately with the omission of short final vowels. At any rate, it is already attested in the Septuagint. The tendency to oxytone stress, being later than pretonic lengthening, must needs be later

vowels. In many cases, however, such epenthetic forms alternated with even phonetically monosyllabic forms (e.g. **málęk* — **malk*); yet in the case of nouns of the type of *gəḏī*, both forms, i.e. **gáḏiy* — **gaḏy*, gave rise to **gáḏī*. The long final vowel *ī* (as against the short vowel in *męlęḵ*), was even morphophonemically counted and, therefore, attracted the stress. For an additional possibility v. Steiner, 1976, p. 14, note 30; yet the reduction of the first vowel militates against a too early date.

[14] Steiner, 1976, p. 6, claims that the shift of stress from etymological vowel to epenthetic vowel in proper nouns, which do not occur in construct, weakens Sievers's theory seriously. Yet Steiner himself (p. 14) allows for the possibility that these proper nouns denoting place names were borrowed from the dialects of the cities to which they refer. As to the timbre of the epenthetic vowel, in my opinion, *pace* Steiner, 1976, p. 15, it was *ę*, lowered to *a* in the vicinity of *r* and laryngals. *səgan* does not cause difficulties, because, being an Akkadian loan, it passed through Aramaic to Hebrew. The occurrence of epenthesis preceding a final consonant fits Sievers's theory, not less than others.

than the much earlier omission of final short vowels not only in the construct but in the absolute as well. Accordingly, the occurrence of the shift of stress to the originally epenthetic vowel in segolate nouns in Hebrew in the construct, rather than in the absolute, cannot be attributed to the earlier elision of final short vowels in the construct, but rather to rhythmic reason, the construct being unstressed. Because in both Biblical Hebrew and Biblical Aramaic the tendency to oxytone stress is later than epenthesis, which has for phonetic reasons to be postulated in some segolates at least with the omission of short final vowels, the general penult stress of Hebrew segolates cannot be accounted for by the assumption that the tendency to oxytone stress ceased operating before epenthesis. One will rather assume that segolate nouns, though phonetically bisyllabic, remained morphophonematically monosyllabic. This also explains their monosyllabic form in Origines's transcriptions as well as their vacillation in Jerome's writings.

BIBLIOGRAPHY

Barth, J., 1894. *Die Nominalbildung in den semitischen Sprachen*[2], Leipzig.

Bauer, H.–Leander, P., 1922. *Historische Grammatik der hebräischen Sprache*, Halle.

Bauer, H.–Leander, P., 1927. *Grammatik des Biblisch-Aramäischen*, Halle.

Bergsträsser, G., 1918–29. *Hebräische Grammatik*, Leipzig.

Beyer, K., 1969. *Althebräische Grammatik*. Göttingen.

Birkeland, H., 1940. *Akzent und Vokalismus im Althebräischen*. Oslo.

Blanc, H., 1953. *Studies in North Palestinian Arabic*. Jerusalem.

Blau, J., 1965. *The Emergence and Linguistic Background of Judaeo-Arabic*. Oxford.

Blau, J., 1968. "Some Difficulties in the Reconstruction of 'Proto-Hebrew' and 'Proto-Canaanite' ", *In Memoriam Paul Kahle*, Berlin, pp. 29–43.

Blau, J., 1970. "הערות לגלגלי ההטעמה בעברית הקדומה", *Hayyim Schirmann Jubilee Volume*, Jerusalem, pp. 27–38.

Blau, J., 1975. "על בעיות בתחום ההטעמה בעברית הקדומה", *Baruch Kurzweil Memorial Volume*, Tel-Aviv–Ramat-Gan, pp. 62–73.

Brockelmann, C., 1908–13. *Grundriss der vergleichenden Grammatik der semitischen Sprachen*, Berlin.

Cantineau, J., 1931. "De la place de l'accent de mot en Hébreu et en Araméen biblique", *Bulletin d'études orientales de l'Institut Français de Damas* 1. 81–98.

Cantineau, J., 1932. "Élimination des syllabes brèves en Hébreu et en Araméen biblique", *Bulletin d'études orientales de l'Institut Français de Damas* 2. 125–44.

Dion, P.–E., 1974. *La langue de Ya'udi*, Ottawa.

Grimme, H., 1896. *Grundzüge der hebräischen Akzent- und Vokallehre*, Freiburg.

Joüon, P., 1923. *Grammaire de l'Hébreu biblique*. Rome.

Malone, J. L., 1971. "Wave Theory, Rule Ordering, and Hebrew-Aramaic Segolation", *Journal of the American Oriental Society* 91. 44–66.

Mittwoch, E., 1925. "Die traditionelle Aussprache des Äthiopischen", *Mitteilungen des Seminars für orientalische Sprachen zu Berlin, 2. Abteilung, Westasiatische Studien*, pp. 126–248.

Muraoka, T., 1976. "Segolate Nouns in Biblical and Other Aramaic Dialects", *Journal of the American Oriental Society* 96. 226–235.

Nöldeke, T., 1898. *Kurzgefasste syrische Grammatik*[2]. Leipzig.

Sarauw, C., 1939. *Über Akzent und Silbenbildung in den älteren semitischen Sprachen*, København.

Spitaler, A., 1968. "Zum Problem der Segolisierung im Aramäischen", *Studia Orientalia in memoriam C. Brockelmann = Wissenschaftliche Zeitschrift der Martin-Luther-Universität Halle-Wittenberg, Gesellschafts- und sprachwissenschaftliche Reihe*, Heft 2/3, 17. 193–199.

Steiner, R., 1976. "On the Origin of the *ḥeḏer* ~ *ḥăḏár* Alternation in Hebrew", *Afroasiatic Linguistics*, vol. 3, 5. 1–18.

ZA* = *Zeitschrift für Assyriologie und verwandte Gebiete.

Additions and Corrections

to **p. 105**.*n. 3.5*: See *Hebrew Linguistics*, pp. 45-46, and cf. also *Grammar*. pp. 30ff.

to **p. 105**.*n. 3.6*: See *Studies*, pp. 297-305

to **p. 106**.*n. 3.7*: See *Hebrew Linguistics*, pp. 54-62

to **p. 107**.*end of remark*: The alternation of pretonic lengthening and pretonic doubling (*Grammar* 32.1ff.) also attests to the length of pretonic open syllables.

to **p. 113**.*10-12*: For a detailed analysis of the vowel structure of nouns terminating in the so-called ה locale see *Hebrew Linguistics*, pp. 89-93.

to **p. 113**.*23-24*: As a matter of fact, oxytone pausal forms reflect a special pausal stress shift, see supra

Some Remarks on the Prehistory of Stress in Biblical Hebrew

1 The cardinal point upon which the reconstruction of stress in Old Hebrew (and perhaps the understanding of Biblical phonology itself) pivots is the recognition that at a certain period of the history of Biblical Hebrew general penultimate stress prevailed. Since most of the words stressed on their last syllables have lost their final short vowels, whereas words that have not lost final vowels are, as a rule, stressed on their penult, the assumption of a period with general penultimate stress at one blow accounts for the stress in the majority of Biblical words. Moreover, it provides an excellent vantage point from which the exceptions, mainly words stressed on their last syllables, although they have not lost their final vowels, can be
* treated. I have dealt with this problem several times, v. e.g. *Schirmann,*
(pp. 199–208) pp. 27-38; Blau, *Grammar,* pp. 30-34; *idem, IOS* 1 (1971) 15-24.

2 In the following, I would like to treat some marginal issues connected with the history of Biblical stress, i.e. two periods preceding and following respectively the period which, in our opinion, was of decisive importance, viz. that of general penult stress. First (par. 3) we shall deal with the earliest Proto-Hebrew period which can be reconstructed (Blau, *Grammar,* p. 30, §9.1.1). We have already treated the problems connected with that period
* in a Hebrew paper (*Kurzweil,* pp. 62-70) and shall summarize the view expressed there. Later (par. 4), we shall deal with the last (fifth) period that has been posited for the development of the Hebrew stress in which, allegedly, final consonant clusters were opened by auxiliary unstressed vowels, thus giving rise to new words with penult stress, so that the Hebrew stress system arrived at the stage transmitted by the Masoretes (Blau, *Grammar,* p. 34, §9.1.5).

3 The earliest Proto-Hebrew period to be reconstructed is dependent on the shift $\bar{a} > \bar{o}$. It stands to reason that this shift was limited to stressed syllables.[1] Accordingly, a stress period can be reconstructed in which the syllables in which now $\bar{o}$ arising from $\bar{a}$ are attested, were stressed and those in which $\bar{a}$ subsisted were unstressed (if one disregards cases of analogy).

* [1] Cf. the detailed reasoning *Alon,* pp. 9-14.

As far as a stress period is reconstructed from the presence and absence of the shift $\bar{a} > \bar{o}$,[2] a stress system is posited which is accepted in the usual reading of literary Arabic, i.e. (with the exception of the ultima) the last long syllable is stressed; if the word lacks long syllables, either (according to the system adopted)[3] the antepenult syllable or the one preceding it or the very first syllable is stressed. This stress system is also very often posited for Proto-Semitic,[4] no doubt through the influence of the accepted reading of literary Arabic. Yet since M. Lambert's pioneering article on the Arabic stress in 1897(!)[5] we know for certain that the usual reading of literary Arabic is of late provenance and reflects the adaptation of the stress system characteristic of the (Syrian-) Lebanese dialect group. In these dialects, in fact, as a rule, the last long syllable is stressed, and in default of such a syllable the stress recedes. Since this stress system is late even in Neo-Arabic (v. below), the reconstruction of such a stress pattern for Hebrew has to rely on its own merits. As a matter of fact, it accounts satisfactorily for the behaviour of $\bar{a}/\bar{o}$ in Hebrew. Its existence is, nevertheless, not demonstrated, since its distribution may be explained by a different supposition.

It stands to reason that the stress system as preserved in Syrian-Lebanese dialects is later than the stress system characteristic of Maghrebine (Western) dialects.[6] The main features of the Maghrebine stress pattern are:

1. If the last syllable is not preceded by a long vowel, it is the last syllable that bears the stress: *'aswád.*

[2] So Bergsträsser I, p. 143, §25a (referring to p. 114, §21b), Blau, *Grammar*, p. 30, §9.1.1.

[3] For the various systems of retracting the stress v. Sarauw, p. 35. *Schirmann*, p. 31, I opted for retracting the stress, in default of long syllables, to the antepenult, because such a stress is attested in Egyptian transcriptions, v. Albright, p. 20, §32, p. 39, §AVI. Yet one has to beware of inferring too much from loan-words, which may exhibit not only stress characteristic of the borrowing tongue, but also, by pseudo-correction, what the speaker of the borrowing language regards as peculiar to the language from which he borrows. Moreover, no certainty exists as to the identity of the stress pattern of Hebrew and the Canaanite dialects reflected in the Egyptian transcriptions. Accordingly, it is more prudent to leave these transcriptions out of account for the reconstruction of the early Hebrew stress system. *

[4] V. e.g. Bergsträsser, p. 114, §21b, Bauer-Leander, p. 177, §12f, Moscati, pp. 65-67. Moscati relies on Akkadian as well, yet even he (p. 66, §10.6) expresses some qualifications because of our limited knowledge. For further material cf. *Kurzweil*, p. 63, n. 8.

[5] M. Lambert, 'De l'accent en arabe', *JA*, ixe Sér., Tom x (novembre-décembre 1897), pp. 402-13. For the history of research v. J. Blau, *BSOAS* 35 (1972) 476-77. *

[6] See Blau, *BSOAS* 35 (1972) 476-78. I am using the term "Maghrebine stress system" as some sort of abbreviation, since it would be more accurate to speak of the "ancient Maghrebine stress system", because in modern dialects the Eastern stress system was superimposed on the Maghrebine one. *

2. A long vowel preceding the last syllable attracts the stress. Pay attention that only long vowels attract the stress but not closed syllables (whereas in the Eastern stress system and in the usual way of stressing literary Arabic both open syllables containing long vowels and closed syllables containing short vowels function as long syllables): *lábis*.

3. From two long vowels it is the first that is stressed, and the second, being unstressed, is shortened: *ṣanádiq*.

For early Hebrew a stress system may be posited according to the first two features of the Maghrebine stress pattern,[7] which satisfactorily accounts for the shift of stressed $\bar{a} > \bar{o}$ both in nouns of the type **lašānu* > *lāšōn* with penult stress and those of the type **kāhinu* > *kōhēn* with antepenult stress, exhibiting stress on the long vowel preceding the last syllable (feature 2). Accordingly, for the time being, we are unable to reconstruct the details of the early Hebrew stress system. It remains a moot question whether words like **mišmar(u)*, **katab(a)* were stressed on their first or second syllable in accordance with the Eastern or Western stress pattern respecitvely. The only certain fact seems to be that, in accordance with both systems, words of the type **lašānu* were stressed on their second syllable, whereas words of the type **kāhinu* exhibited antepenult stress.

4. In the preceding section we have attempted to show that it is not possible to reconstruct the details of a certain stress system on the basis of the sound shift $\bar{a} > \bar{o}$. At least two stress patterns, viz. that resembling the way literary Arabic is stressed, based on the stress of Eastern Arabic dialects, and that similar to the stress system obtaining in Western dialects, fit the data of the shift $\bar{a} > \bar{o}$. In the following I shall attempt to show that two ways of interpretation apply to an additional stress period as well, in this case, however, the accepted interpretation seems less likely than that which I am going to propose.

At a certain period of the history of the Biblical stress quite a strong inclination towards the stressing of the last syllable obtained. In words with certain syllable structure, in fact, the shift of penult stress to the ultima

[7] The third feature does not fit the behaviour of $\bar{a}/\bar{o}$, as exhibited by $\bar{a}$ in words of the type **śimālīy* > *śəmālī* "on the left". If $\bar{a}$ were stressed, as it should be according to feature 3, it would have shifted to $\bar{o}$. Nevertheless, nothing can be inferred about the absence or presence of a possible historical link between early Hebrew stress pattern according to the lines suggested here and the Western Neo-Arabic stress system. For even if such a link existed, the absence of feature 3 in Hebrew as against its presence in Neo-Arabic would not surprise, since
* feature 3 may reflect later development; cf. *Kurzweil*, p. 65, §1.2.1.

became a veritable sound shift. This was the case in words with open *short* stressed penultimate syllables, which were either lengthened or lost the stress, to be transferred to the ultima.[8] Yet one important case of exceptions exists: words that originally terminated in consonant clusters exhibit penult stress on the now open short penult syllable: *ná'ar* "boy". Therefore, I assumed[9] that at the time when the stress shift from open penult syllables with short vowel operated, these words still terminated in consonant clusters. It was only later, when this stress shift stopped operating, that these final consonant clusters were opened. Therefore, I posited a special, last, period in which final consonant clusters were opened, giving rise to open stressed penult syllables containing short vowels.

There exists, however, a more powerful explanation, which at the same time solves an additional problem, viz. that of the Greek transcriptions in the Septuagint and the Hexapla and the alternation of monosyllabic and disyllabic forms in Jerome's transcriptions. Both Greek transcriptions reflect earlier stages of "segolate" nouns than exhibited by the Tiberian tradition: the Septuagint (III — I century B.C.) still preserves in the *qatl* theme the original *a,* as Ιωχαβεδ as against Tiberian *yōḵeḇed,* and Origenes, though much later than the Septuagint (185-254 A.D.), reflects even an earlier stage, without auxiliary vowel opening the final consonant cluster, as γαβρ = Tiberian *geḇer* "man". It is, to be sure, possible that later Origenes reflects a dialect in which segolates behaved in a more archaic way than in the earlier dialects exhibited in the Septuagint. Nevertheless, this is not a very powerful explanation, and it does not account for the alternation of monosyllabic and disyllabic forms in Jerome's (4th century A.D.!) transcriptions. I am therefore propounding that the anaptyctic vowel

[8] Cf. *Schirmann*, pp. 37-38, §6; Blau, *Grammar*, pp. 32-34, §9.1.4. *

[9] V. *Schirmann*, p. 38, §7; Blau, *Grammar*, p. 34, §9.1.5. One will not claim that the stress passed from short vowels in open penult only to l o n g vowels in o p e n ultima, yet not to closed ultima, and it was therefore that segolates were not affected by this stress shift. As a matter of fact, I do not know of certain cases of stress shift to closed ultima. Sarauw, p. 26, cites the proper noun *bāśəmat;* yet the preservation of the final *t* attests to a name of foreign extraction. One could adduce imperative forms like *šəmor,* instead of the expected **šómor*. Yet the main factor in the emergence of this form was analogy to the imperfect *yišmor*, as demonstrated by the absence of pausal **šómor*. Besides, even segolate forms bear stress on the ultima when terminating in long vowels in open ultima, as *pərī* "fruit", *yəhī* "let it be". For segolates *II'* v. *IOS* 7 (1977) 17-23. As to some marginal cases of segolates stressed on the ultima (type: *dəḇaš;* Bauer-Leander, pp. 579-80), they exhibit in fact change of stress to closed ultima; yet they may reflect Aramaic influence. Nevertheless, the existence of segolate forms terminating in *-ū* with stress on the penult (type: *tóhū;* see, e.g., Bauer-Leander pp. 576-77, §72g') forces us not to content ouselves with attributing the special behaviour of the segolates to their final closed syllable but look for another explanation. * (pp. 250–56)

in segolates was phonologically irrelevant. Accordingly it could in transcriptions be omitted or marked, and it is therefore that the transcriptions of the Septuagint marked it, whereas it is absent in Origenes's Hexapla and not fixed in Jerome's transcriptions, not because the Hexapla and Jerome reflect an earlier stage. Since these auxiliary vowels were phonologically irrelevant, they were not stressed but rather the short vowel preceding them even in a system which did not permit short vowels in open syllables to be stressed, since phonologically these short vowels stood in closed syllables, *qodeš* "sacredness" for instance phonologically exhibiting *qodš* with the *o* in a doubly closed syllable.[10]

If this explanation is valid, as I believe it is, one will have to dispense with the assumption of a last period in the history of the Hebrew stress in which the segolate forms arose. One will rather assume that these forms existed already earlier, yet their auxiliary vowel separating the consonant cluster was phonologically irrelevant, also as to the stress system. It is even dubious whether segolates ever became in Hebrew morphophonemically disyllabic. Jerome's transcriptions, at any rate, suggest that they remained morphophonemically monosyllabic.

BIBLIOGRAPHY

Albright. . . . .W.F. Albright, *The Vocalization of the Egyptian Syllabic Orthography,* American Oriental Series 5, New Haven 1934.

Alon. . . . .J. Blau, "Problems in the History of Hebrew" (in Hebrew), *In Memory of Gedaliahu Alon, Essays in Jewish History and Philology* (Tel-Aviv 1970), pp. 9-23.

Bauer-Leander. . . . .H. Bauer & P. Leander, *Historische Grammatik der hebräischen Sprache des Alten Testaments,* Halle 1922.

Bergsträsser. . . . .G. Bergsträsser, *Hebräische Grammatik,* Leipzig 1918-29.

Blanc. . . . .H. Blanc, *Studies in North Palestinian Arabic* (Oriental Notes and Studies 4), Jerusalem 1953.

Blau, *Grammar*. . . . .J. Blau, *A. Grammar of Biblical Hebrew* (Porta Linguarum Orientalium *N.S. XII*), Wiesbaden 1976.

Kurzweil. . . . .J. Blau, "Problems of Word-Stress in Ancient Hebrew" (in Hebrew), *Baruch Kurzweil Memorial Volume,* Tel-Aviv — Ramat-Gan 1975, pp. 62-73.

[10] For auxiliary vowels being phonologically irrelevant and therefore non existent as to the stress cf. e.g. **bíktbū* > *bíkitbū* in Arabic dialects in which the stress system would have demanded *bikítbū*, if the second *i* were phonologically relevant; see, e.g., Blanc, pp. 28-29. Cf.
(p. 115) also *IOS* 8 (1978) 102.

Moscati. . . . .S. Moscati, ed., *An Introduction to the Comparative Grammar of the Semitic Languages* (Porta Linguarum Orientalium *N.S. VI*), Wiesbaden 1964.

Sarauw. . . . .C. Sarauw, *Über Akzent und Silbenbildung in den älteren semitischen Sprachen* (Det. Kgl. Danske Videnskabernes Selskab. Historisk-filologiske Meddelelser *xxvi*, 8), København 1939.

Schirmann. . . . .J. Blau, "Notes on Changes in Accent in Early Hebrew" (in Hebrew), *Hayyim (Jefim) Schirmann Jubilee Volume* (Jerusalem 1970), pp. 27-38.

Additions

to **p. 120**.*14*: = *Hebrew Linguistics*, pp. 41–53.
to **p. 120**.*22*: = *Hebrew Linguistics*, pp. 54–62.
to **p. 120**.*n.1*: = *Hebrew Linguistics*, pp. 25–30
to **p. 121**.*n. 3 .1*: = *Hebrew Linguistics*, pp. 44–45.
to **p. 121**.*n. 5.2*: = *Studies*, pp. 297–98.
to **p. 121**.*n. 6.1*: = *Studies*, pp. 297–99.
to **p. 122**.*n. 7.7*: = *Hebrew Linguistics*, p. 57. §1.2.1.
to **p. 123**.*n. 8*: = *Hebrew Linguistics*, pp. 51–52.
to **p. 123**.*n. 9.1*:= *Hebrew Linguistics*, p. 52.

The Parallel Development of the Feminine Ending *-at* in Semitic Languages[1]

Many Semitic languages exhibit the tendency to drop the *t* of the feminine ending *-at* in the absolute, leading to an exceptional morphological alternation *a* in the absolute: *-at* in the construct. Although, as a rule, exceptional morphological facts most strongly attest to inherited features, the exceptional morphological alternation *a* : *at* in various Semitic languages has to be interpreted as due to parallel development, because it arose at different times in different languages and because of many differences in details. It was because of the basic similarity of the Semitic languages that they developed in the same direction even in small details, making it the more arduous to differentiate between common heritage and parallel development. The bulk of the paper is devoted to the analysis of the constraints of the loss of *t* in *-at* in the various Semitic languages, stressing the differences between them in detail.

1. One of the fundamental difficulties of comparative linguistics, which
* pertains to its very essence, is the question of parallel development. This problem and its bearing on comparative Indo-European grammar were treated by A. Meillet, 1958, pp. 36–43, in his celebrated paper *Note sur une difficulté générale de la grammaire comparée*. His main thesis is that, without the intervention of important historical events, the dialects of a language incline to develop in the same direction even without mutual contact. If this is true in Indo-European grammar, the more so in Semitic linguistics, because of the basic similarity of the various Semitic languages.[2] In the following we shall deal with a very conspicuous case of parallel development, viz. with the tendency of the feminine ending *-at* to lose its *t* in final position in various Semitic languages. This surprising conformity of many Semitic tongues must be interpreted as due to parallel development, not only because it occurred in them at different times, but also owing to many differences in details. This is the more surprising since it is generally assumed that it is exceptional morphological facts that most strongly attest

(pp. 318–20) (1) I have dealt very briefly with this problem in Blau, 1978b, §5.1.4; (see Bibliography); for the history of the feminine suffix in Classical Arabic cf. Blau, 1980.

* (2) Cf. also Blau, 1969, pp. 39 ff.

to the affinity of languages (*v.*, e.g., Meillet, 1952, p. 58). In this case, in Hebrew and in some other Semitic dialects an anomalous morphological alternation *-a* in the absolute: *-at* in the construct occurs. Yet this exceptional morphological fact does not demonstrate the affinity of the languages involved, because it arose, for the reasons mentioned, independently, owing to parallel development.

1′ In the following, we shall analyse the loss of the *t* of the feminine ending in various Semitic languages, starting with Hebrew.

2. In Hebrew both absolute nouns and third person sing. fem. of the perfect, originally terminating in the feminine ending *-at*, exhibit *t*-less ending, i.e., they terminate in *qameṣ* marked by the mater lectionis *h* (with the exception of *naʿărā* "girl" in the Pentateuch where the ktiv is constantly *nʿr*). The only important exception is exhibited by IIIy verbs, which in the Bible usually terminate in the third person sing. fem. of the perfect in *-əṯā*, exceptionally in *-āṯ*; the latter ending prevails in Middle Hebrew. * In the domain of the nouns, exceptions exhibiting final *t* in the absolute are marginal, as a rule limited to archaic poetry or proper nouns, which presumably reflect different dialects (*v.* the grammars). The only frequent noun terminating in prose in *-t* is *moḥŏrāṯ*, presumably to be interpreted as an original adverb (*v.* Brockelmann, 1908–13, I, p. 409); in this connection *rabbaṯ* "much" has to be mentioned, which as adverb is attested in the Psalms only, yet its occurrence in late prose as noun ("many" [cf. *harbē* "much, many"] 2 Chr. 30:17, 18) demonstrates that it was not limited to poetry. *-at* ending in adverbs may be due to multilinear development, to the preservation of the feminine ending in adverbs (so Brockelmann, *ibid.*; I consider it reasonable that, whereas the feminine ending *-t* after *a* was redundant and therefore apt to be elided, it was, when felt as an adverbial morpheme, functional and therefore retained; for a similar status of the adverbial ending *-an* in Arabic dialects cf. Blau, 1965, p. 170) and to the existence of an adverbial ending *-at* of different origin, which, in the light of Arabic *rubbata/rabbata* "sometimes," is at least in the case of *rabbat* quite likely (*v.* Barth, 1913, p. 18; *idem, Zeitschrift für Assyriologie und verwandte Gebiete* 28.307 [1913–14]), even if it reflects in Hebrew Aramaic influence. *mənāṯ* "portion," *qəṣāṯ* "end" are presumably also due to Aramaic impact. At any rate, since the preservation of *-t* in nouns is quite marginal, due to special function (adverbs), style (archaic poetry) and loans (proper nouns), we shall not take it into account when dealing with the constraints of the disappearance of *-t*. On the other hand, the preservation of *t* in verbs IIIy is general and any theory has to account for it.

It seems that it was only *-aṯ* that developed into *a*, whereas *-āṯ* was preserved. This is the reason for the preservation of forms like *gālāṯ*, which later, by analogy of forms like *kāṯəḇā*, developed to *gālәṯā* in Biblical Hebrew, but did not change in Middle Hebrew (cf. Harris, 1939, pp. 57–59, §§33–34). In verbs, in which the III*y* verbs form a powerful group, often exerting influence on other verbal groups, rather than being influenced (cf.par.5), the *-āṯ* ending did not drop its *t* by the impact of verbs terminating in *-aṯ* > *ā*. Yet in nouns III*y* the ending *-āṯ*, which should have been preserved,[3] became *-ā* through the influence of the other feminine nouns and by back formation from the masculine (as *qāṣę̄* "end," which, on the basis of forms like *qāṣēhū* "his end," felt as consisting of **qāṣ* plus the pronoun *-ēhū*, was analysed as exhibiting the base **qāṣ* plus the suffix *-ę̄*; from this base a new feminine was formed: **qāṣ* plus *-ā*: *qāṣā*).

We have reconstructed a sound shift according to which only the feminine ending *-aṯ*, but not *-āṯ*, elided its *t*. Whereas the short quantity of the *a* is a constraint for this sound shift, there is no difference whether or not it was stressed. According to the theory of a general penult stress (cf.
(pp. 105ff.) * Blau, 1978a) nouns terminating in *-at(u)* exhibited stressed *a* (type: **dagắtu* > **dāgắṯ*), the perfect 3. pers. fem. sing. unstressed *a* (type: *katắbat*), and after both stressed and unstressed *a -t* was elided. In the next paragraph we shall deal with the behavior of the feminine ending *-at* in Phoenician and also broach the question of whether or not it has bearing on Hebrew.

As to the phonetic process, after Birkeland's judicious remarks (1940a, p. 119; cf. also 1940b, p. 98, note 1), there is, to my mind, no doubt that Hebrew *-at*[4] did not shift to *-ah* (to become finally *-a*). This has, to be sure, often been suggested in the wake of this phenomenon in Classical Arabic, yet even in Classical Arabic this shift is by no means as well attested as it is

(3) If we assume that in the oldest stage of stress in Hebrew a system similar to the ancient
* Maghrebine stress system prevailed (*v.* Blau, 1975, pp. 68–70). If this assumption proves correct, the shift *ā* > *ō* was limited to this period. Since however (pace Blau, *ibid.*) the elision of *y* in verbs III*y* has to be assigned to the, later, general penult stress period (because, otherwise, *gālā* would have been stressed on its penult), it was no longer affected by the shift *ā* > *ō* and, therefore, *-āt* did not shift to *-ōt* (I am not dealing with originally biradical verbs terminating in a long vowel, which eventually were absorbed by verbs III*y*). On the other hand, if we posit a stress similar to that accepted in the reading of Classical Arabic (*v.* Blau, *ibid.*), the shift *ā* > *ō* continued during the general penult stress period. Accordingly, *-āt* should have shifted to *-ōt* in both nouns and verbs III*y*. In the latter, it stands to reason that it became *-āt* later by the influence of the other perfect forms (*v.* Blau, *ibid.*).

(4) It stands to reason that *-atu* shifted directly to *-ā*, without an intermediate stage *-āt*. Had *-atu* given rise to *-āt*, the *t* would have been preserved after long *ā*. Therefore, one will have to posit *-atu* > *ā*, with the omission of the *t* together with the omission of the final case vowel.

generally claimed. Nevertheless, from the pure phonetic point of view, the passage *-t* > *-h* is well possible, cf., e.g., Kruisinga, 1925, p. 22, §§49–50. Yet, except in proper nouns, *h* in Hebrew is elided in internal open juncture only, *v.* Blau, 1976, pp. 24–25. Had, therefore, *t* in fact passed into *h*, the *h* would have been preserved. Accordingly, it seems that final *t* was pronounced without explosion, thus becoming inaudible (for the phonetic process cf., e.g., Kruisinga, 1925, p. 51, §105). As a rule, such a final *t* was analogically restored from cases in which it occupied medial position (*kāraṯ* "he cut down" was influenced, e.g., by *kārəṯū* "they cut down," etc.) as well as because of the word's connection with the root with final *t* (e.g., root *krt*). As to the feminine ending, although the *t* was preserved in medial position (e.g., in the construct), it was functionally superfluous, because the feminine was sufficiently marked by the *-a* of the ending *-at*. Similarly: the final *-t* of *-at* in pronouns was elided, *v.* Harris, 1939, pp. 53–54, §28 (without agreeing to the date proposed by him).

3. In Phoenician, as a rule, *-at* is preserved in nouns, yet the *t* is elided in * perf. 3. pers. fem. sg. It is generally assumed (cf. Harris, 1939, pp. 57–58, §33; pp. 67–68, §44) that the *t* was elided in Phoenician when the verb suffix differed from the noun suffix in that the noun suffix was not yet final but was followed by case endings or that in Phoenician there was a constraint of stress for the preservation of *t*, yet the unstressed verb suffix lost its *t*. In the latter case (pace Harris, who assumes quite a different stress system) the conditions in Phoenician were different from those in Hebrew (par.2), which elided final *t* of the feminine ending both after stressed and unstressed *a*. As a matter of fact, the assumption of an independent parallel development in Phoenician and Hebrew does not involve any difficulties, not only because, as we shall see, the elision of *t* in *-at* occurred independently in many Semitic dialects, but also because, in my opinion, J. Friedrich (*v.*, e.g., 1951, p. 1) was right in holding that the characteristics of the Canaanite dialects did not emerge in a Proto-Canaanite prehistoric period but arose, in historical times, presumably from Northwest Semitic, through mutual contact in accordance with the wave theory and (and this is the point that interests us) through parallel development. Therefore, should even Harris's first surmise prove right, viz. that the elision of final *-t* took place in verbs, when it was not yet final in nouns because of the following case endings, this does not necessarily imply that in Hebrew the elision of *-t* took place in two stages, first in the verb together with the Phoenician, then in nouns after they had dropped the case endings. Nor is it necessary, according to Harris's other assumption, that the elision of final *-t* reached Phoenician early, when nouns still

terminated in case endings, Hebrew later only when they had already dropped final short vowels. The dropping of *-t may* in Hebrew be an entirely independent development, separated from the Phoenician development in both space and time. Because of the possibility of independent development, the preservation of *-at* in the El-Amarna verbal form *a-ba-da-at*[5] does not necessarily prove that the elision even in Hebrew (the more so in Phoenician) was later than 1365, since the Hebrew dialect reflected in the Bible and that mirrored in the quoted El-Amarna letter from Jerusalem may well have developed along different lines. Nevertheless, this terminus post quem is for Hebrew quite reasonable.

Only in some Neo-Punic colonial forms of the Phoenician is the elision of *t* in feminine nouns attested (*v.*, e.g., Harris, 1939, p. 68, §44). It is possible that these forms stem from a Phoenician dialect in which *-t* in nouns was elided by the shift by which it was omitted in Hebrew. It is, however, much more likely that these forms reflect a late parallel development of the elision of *-t* in the absolute of the feminine ending *-at*.

4. Nothing certain can be stated as to Moabite. As to the perfect, no forms of the third pers. sg. fem. are attested. As to nouns, it is generally posited that the absolute ending *-at* has been preserved in Moabite. I do not deny that this is well possible; yet the evidence is much less clear than one would prima facie imagine.

Among absolute nouns terminating in the feminine suffix *-t* in the Mešaᶜ inscription, *št* "year" (lines 2; 8) clearly does not attest to the preservation of *-at*, since, as proved by the assimilation of the *n* (**šant* > **šatt*), it exhibits the feminine suffix *-t* immediately following the preceding consonant (in which case Hebrew too preserves the final *-t*, presumably because it was functionally essential: its elision would have entailed the total loss of the feminine suffix, whereas even after the loss of the *-t* of *-at* feminine was still sufficiently marked by *-a*). Therefore, one wonders whether or not other nouns terminating in the absolute in the feminine suffix *-t* have not to be analyzed as exhibiting *-t* following consonant, rather than *-at*. This seems to be the case at least for (line 28) *mšmᶜt* (if it is an absolute), according to Hebrew *mišmaᶜat*, "subjects," and Middle Hebrew *šaḥărīṯ* "morning" suggests for *hšḥrt* (line 15) the ending *-īt*. The somewhat dubious *ryt* (line 12) *may* perhaps exhibit **rīt*, and *if mʾt* (line 29) occurring after a lacuna, in fact means "hundred", it *may* still be derived from original **miʾt*, as preserved in Ugaritic *mi̊t* and Gᶜez *məʾət*. Even *hbmt* "the high place of worship" (line 3) *may* exhibit **bamt* or **bāmt*,

(5) Jerusalem 288:52. Brockelmann, 1908–13, I, p. 571, wrongly cites *abada* with the loss of the *-t*.

cf. Akkadian *bāmtu* "back." *hmslt* (line 26), if singular, of necessity exhibits the feminine ending *-at*, since the preceding *l* is doubled (root *sll*); yet it seems prima facie not less likely to parse it as a plural "(I made) the roads (along Arnon)." Accordingly, no clear evidence for the preservation of *-at* in Moabite can be found.

The only indication for the preservation of this ending is ex silentio, and one will have to admit how careful one must be when relying on such an argument: if Moabite *-at* had in fact changed to *-a*/*-ā*, indicated in script by *-h*, one would expect to come across some cases of feminine nouns terminating in *-h* in the Mešaᶜ inscription. The only possible case of feminine *-h* is the place name *qrḥh* (lines 3; 21; 24; 25), which, on the strength of the assumption that final *-h* in script cannot mark the feminine suffix in this inscription, is generally interpreted as terminating in *-ō* (cf. line 14 *nbh* — Hebrew *neḇō*). If it really was something like *qorḥā*, the pun Isa. 15:2 with *qorḥā* "baldness" is even more powerful than generally assumed. Nevertheless, the lack of clear cases of a feminine ending marked by *-h* in the Mešaᶜ inscription makes the assumption quite attractive that Moabite preserved final *-at* in nouns. One has, however, to remember that this is only an unverified supposition, still awaiting verification.

REMARK: At any rate, the use of the vowel letter *-h* to mark final *-a* is attested in Moabite by *bnh* "he built" (line 18). Even if this application of *h* had developed from the feminine ending, it would easily be explained in Moabite by Hebrew influence (just as Canaanite orthography influenced Aramaic as well; cf. Cross-Freedman, 1952, p.6). Yet, as we have seen (par. 2), in Hebrew the feminine ending was never *-ah* and the use of *h* as vowel letter is presumably due to its elision in **mah* "what," in terminative *-h* and pronominal suffixes.

5. For both geographical and chronological reasons we should now deal with Aramaic. Since, however, the situation in Aramaic and in Arabic is very much the same and the situation in Arabic is better documented, it seems more expedient to treat Arabic first.

In Classical Arabic *-at* is always preserved in the perfect, yet in nouns the *t* subsists in context forms only; in the pause, however, which, of course, is possible in the absolute only, it becomes *-ah*, as demonstrated by orthography (which in Arabic spells pausal forms only), by tradition and by rhyming with words terminating in *-ah*. The feminine plural always terminates in *-āt*, in both context and pausal forms.

As to the phonetic process, it seems, prima facie, that the *t* shifted to *h*.

This, however, is by no means as certain as generally assumed (*v.* Birkeland, 1940b, p. 98). According to the Classical Arabic pausal system no short vowels exist in pause. The preservation of short vowels in pause is only possible by the pronunciation of *h* after them. Accordingly, the pausal feminine ending might have phonetically developed *-at* > *-ah* (cf. the marginal occurrence of the feminine ending *-ah* in some Arabic dialects, *v.*, e.g., Cantineau, 1936–37, pp. 19–20); but the pausal form *-ah* may also reflect the shift *-at* > *-a*, the functionally necessary *-a* being preserved by the "pausal" *h* (cf. Brockelmann, 1908–13, I, p. 48, §37 dβ).

How did it happen that it was in the perfect 3. pers. sg. fem., a form which already in Proto-Semitic terminated in final feminine *-t*, that the *-t* was preserved, as against its omission in nouns where in Proto-Semitic and in context forms in Classical Arabic it is followed by case endings? As far as known to me, it was Birkeland only (1940b, p. 97) who asked this question. His answer, however, can hardly satisfy. He admits that according to sound shift *ḍarabat* "she beat" should have shifted to **ḍarabah*. This pausal **ḍarabah*, however, could have represented both the context forms *ḍaraba* "he beat" and *ḍarabahū* "he beat him". Therefore the functional load of the *t* was too heavy to disappear. This theory, however, has several flaws. First, it is quite dubious whether *ḍarabahū* has a pausal form like **ḍarabah*, *v.* Birkeland himself (1940b, pp. 42–43). Moreover, even if *ḍarabat* had shifted to **ḍarabah* and the latter could have been misunderstood as representing the pausal form of *ḍarabahū*, one will hardly grant that this ambiguity (which, by the way, occurs with transitive verbs only) is more misleading than the ambiguity of *malikah* "queen," the pausal form of *malikatun*, etc., which could also be misunderstood as representing the pausal form of *malikahū* "his king" (accusative). (Admittedly, this ambiguity is too limited, viz. to nouns from which a feminine form is derived by dint of *-at*.) Therefore, even if we do not take into consideration the fact that Birkeland's theory does not account for the almost identical situation in Aramaic (cf. par. 6), one can hardly accept it even for Arabic alone.

In my opinion, the situation in Arabic (and, as we shall see, in Aramaic) has to be explained by interaction between sound shift and analogy. According to the original sound shift every pausal *-at* shifted to *ah* (either directly or indirectly, *v.* above). It also bore upon words terminating in *-at* with radical *t*, as *minḥat* "chisel," *nukat* "spots," *kafat* "he withheld,"[6] yet the

(6) Aspesi (1977, p. 394) is wrong in positing that every final *t* (as, e.g., in *bayt* "house") was affected by this sound shift. His explanation that this sound shift only operated in morphological morphemes is not only precarious because it limits on principle sound shifts (pp. 26ff.) to morphological classes (cf. in general Blau, 1979), but not necessary as well, *v.* the immediate sequence.

analogy of forms with nonfinal *t*[7] and their connection with the root restored the *t*.

On the other hand, it stands to reason that *-āt* was not influenced by this sound shift from its very beginning. This is, to my mind, clearly demonstrated by the preservation of the feminine plural suffix *-āt* in every environment (for exceptions *v.* Rabin, 1951, p. 206, Birkeland, 1940b, p. 96). One will not accept Birkeland's proposal (1940b, p. 98) that, e.g., ***kātibāh***, the alleged pausal form of ***kātibāt*** "writing" (fem. plur.) according to sound shift, would have been misunderstood as the pausal form of ***kātibāhu*** "his two writers". Not only does this explanation not account for Aramaic, but it is highly artificial, ***kātibāhu*** being a rather marginal form.

Therefore, as a result of sound shift nouns terminating in *-at* in general shifted in the pause to *-ah*; yet nouns from roots III*w/y* exhibiting long *ā* preceding the *t*, should have kept their *t* in every context. We would have expected the pausal forms to be ***malikah*** "queen" on the one hand, ****fatāt*** "girl" on the other. Yet, because of the rather marginal standing of nouns from roots III*w/y*, they were influenced by the ordinary nouns and by their analogy their *t* shifted to *h* in pause even after long *ā*: ***fatāh***, spelt, according to the accepted pausal spelling, with final *h*.

Quite different was the development of verbs. According to sound shift ordinary verbs (type: ***katabat***) should terminate in pause in *-ah* (type: ****katabah***), verbs III*w/y* in *-āt* (type: ****ramāt***). In the domain of verbs, however, the status of roots III*w/y* is rather strong, much more so than among nouns. Therefore, verbs III*w/y* are not only apt to preserve their special affixes, but even sometimes influence other verbal classes. Thus, for instance, Brockelmann, 1908–13, I, p. 559, §260Ab, cites cases of the penetration of imperative suffixes of verbs III*y* into the other verbal classes in some Arabic dialects; p. 567, §260Cg, similar cases in the imperfect; p. 571, §262b ; p. 574; p. 575 in the perfect (cf. also a similar case in Tigre pp. 574–75). In Hebrew, the imperfect and the imperative with suffixes have been influenced by verbs III*y* (p. 641, §273Eb), as well as geminate verbs (p. 637, §272Ge); this class of verbs has undergone the influence of verbs III*y* in Arabic as well (p. 633, rem. 2; pp. 633–34). Not all the examples cited by Brockelmann are to the same extent cogent; together, however, they serve as a quite impressive model of the influence of verbs III*w/y*, and cf. now also Jastrow, 1978, e.g., pp. 241 f.

(7) In nouns terminating in the feminine ending *-at*, the influence of forms with non-final *t* was less strong even in nouns directly derived from corresponding masculine nouns (as in all adjectives and in substantives like ***malikat*** "queen" derived from ***malik*** "king"), since the masculine forms did not contain the *t* ending either and the feminine nouns were sufficiently differentiated from them by *-a* even without *t*.

On this background, the different development of the verbs in Arabic will easily be understood. According to sound shift, *katabat* "she wrote" should have shifted in pause to **katabah*, yet verbs III*w/y* should have terminated in pause in *-at*: **ramāt* "she threw". (One has to keep in mind that the structure of Classical Arabic permits closed syllables with long vowels in pause.) Through the influence of verbs III*w/y* that preserved *-āt* in pause, *-at* was also preserved in pause in all verbs (type: *katabat*). Later, through the influence of the context form (and also of the ordinary verb) pausal **ramāt* was superseded by *ramat*, which thus became the only form in both context and pause. At this time, however, the pausal shift *at* > *ah* had already ceased operating.

REMARK: Since closed syllables containing long vowel occur in pause only when the context form exhibits long vowel in open syllable (type: *kitāb* "book" in pause, *kitābun* in context), but not if the context form exhibits closed syllable (type: *ramat*; *lam yaqum* "he stood not up" in both context and pause, though one would have expected pausal **ramāt, *lam yaqūm*), it may be claimed that the pausal forms were derived from the context forms *after* long vowels in closed syllables had been shortened in them. In this case, of course, the pausal form would from the very beginning have contained short vowel (type: *ramat*) and no reason would have existed for the preservation of the *t*. Nevertheless, such an assumption does not explain all the forms involved. The shortened vowel is preserved as short even if the syllable is opened in sandhi: *lam yaqumi -l-waladu, ramati -l-bintu*, and these forms must be explained by the analogy of the usual context forms, since sandhi-forms have always existed. Accordingly, there is no difficulty in the assumption that the context forms influenced the pausal forms as well. Cf. also the dual *ramatā*, instead of **ramātā*, through the influence of *ramat*. Moreover, forms of the type *qāḍin* "judge" have as pausal forms not only *qāḍ*, with the usual dropping of *tanwīn -in*, but also *qāḍī*, and it is this form that prevails in most dialects. It stands to reason that original **qāḍīn* was shortened to *qāḍin* in context, because of the occurrence of a long vowel in a closed syllable, yet preserved in pause, to become eventually, by the dropping of the *n* of the *tanwīn, qāḍī*. This makes the existence of an original **ramāt* in pause very likely. The only other explanation offered for pausal *qāḍī* is, as far as known to me, that of Birkeland (1940b, p. 70), who posits a context form **qāḍiyun* still with the preservation of the *y*, which in pause developed to *qāḍī*. In my opinion, this explanation is less likely. Yet even on the strength of it, one will have to posit **ramayat* for the period in which **qāḍiyun* still subsisted, which, according to the usual sound shifts, had to shift to *ramat* in context, yet to **ramāt* in pause, in accordance with our assumption of an original pausal **ramāt*.

5′ In most modern Arabic dialects nouns in absolute terminate in *-a* (without taking imāla, etc., into consideration), in the perfect in *-at* (again, without taking imāla, etc. into consideration). In some dialects, (a weak) *h* follows the absolute ending *-a*, *v.* Cantineau, 1936–37, pp. 19–20 (*v.* par. 5). In the ancient dialect of Ṭayyiʾ the *t* of the feminine plural ending *-āt* is dropped in pause, *v.* Rabin, 1951, p. 206, §z, Birkeland, 1940b, p. 96 (*v.* par. 5). Accordingly, if my theory is correct, one would expect the *-at* ending of the perfect to drop as well (if one does not posit an independent later shift *-āt* > *a*). Yet nothing is known as to this ending in the Ṭayyiʾ dialect. In the modern dialect of Šammar, the likely descendant of the Ṭayyiʾ, however, the dropping of the final *t* is attested both in verbs and the plural *-āt* (where the *t* is sometimes replaced by a weak *y*). Yet the dropping of the final *t* in the feminine plural ending *-āt* (and its passage to a weak *h*) is attested in additional dialects in which the *t* of the feminine suffix of the perfect is, as usual, preserved (for details *v.* Cantineau, 1936–37, pp. 20–21; 132–33). For forms like *katabah* "she wrote" in Yemenite dialects, in all likelihood due to the analogy of nouns with pronominal suffixes, *v.* M.M. Bravmann, *Tarbiṣ* 13:177 (1941–42); Diem, 1973, p. 90, and now Jastrow, 1978, p. 251. *

6. In Aramaic, as in Arabic, *t* is preserved in the verb and the feminine plural, yet dropped in the absolute singular, as it is in Classical Arabic in pause and in Arabic dialects in general. It stands to reason to posit for Aramaic a development similar to that in Arabic: *-at* developed to *-ā*; *-āt* did not change. Therefore the *t* was preserved in singular nouns terminating in *-āt* (contrary to Arabic; type: *qəṣāṯ* "part"), in plural feminine nouns and in verbs IIIy; from the latter the preservation of the *t* spread over all the verbal classes. It is worthwhile to mention that through the influence of ordinary nouns terminating in *-at*, the *t* was dropped also in the absolute of nouns terminating in *-ūt*/*-īt*. For the not unusual preservation of the *-t* in adverbials terminating in *-at*, etc. (*v.*, e.g., Brockelmann, 1908–13, I, pp. 409; 493) cf. supra par. 2.

REMARK: According to a general penult stress to be postulated for Biblical Aramaic at least (cf. Blau, 1978a), nouns were stressed on the *a* of the feminine ending *-at* (type: **rabbắtu* "big"), verbs on the preceding syllable (type: **katắbat*). One could claim that only stressed *-at* lost its *t*. This, however, is prima facie unlikely, since, as a (pp. 110ff.)

rule, consonants after stressed vowels are more clearly pronounced (cf. Jesperson, 1913, p. 121).

6′ The loss of the final *t* of perfect 1st and 3rd feminine in Babylonian Jewish Aramaic is to be explained as extension of the forms with enclitics in which the *t* was assimilated; *v.* Boyarin, 1976, p. 22, note 24.[8]

7. In all the modern South Arabian languages the *t* of the feminine ending is preserved; in the language of Socotri, however, it passes to *-h* in both nouns and verbs(!) (*v.* Johnstone, 1975, pp. 15; 20), an additional proof for the extent of independent parallel development.

8. To sum up: We have seen that many Semitic languages exhibit the tendency to drop the *t* of the feminine ending *-at*. Yet despite the prima facie exceptional character of this feature and its similarity in the various dialects, the differences in details and even more the gap in time force us to the assumption of independent parallel development.

February 1979

BIBLIOGRAPHY

Aspesi, Francesco, 1977. "Sistema fonematica 'complessivo' e sistemi fonetici 'morfologici': un' interpretazione di alcuni fatti semitici. *Instituto Orientale di Napoli, Annali.* 37:393–401.

Barth, Jacob, 1894. *Die Nominalbildung in den semitischen Sprachen,*[2] Leipzig.

1913. *Die Pronominalbildung in den semitischen Sprachen.* Leipzig.

Birkeland, Harris, 1940a. *Akzent und Vokalismus in Althebräischen.* Oslo.

1940b. *Altarabische Pausalformen.* Oslo.

Blau, Joshua, 1965. *The Emergence and Linguistic Background of Judaeo-Arabic.* Oxford.

1969. "Some Problems of the Formation of the Old Semitic Languages in the Light of Arabic Dialects." *Proceedings of the International Conference on Semitic Studies held in Jerusalem,* 1965. Jerusalem, pp. 38–44.

1975. "ʿal brʿayot bitḥum hahaṭʿama baʿivrit haqrduma." *Baruch Kurzweil Memorial Volume.* Ramat Gan, pp. 62–73.

1976. *A Grammar of Biblical Hebrew.* Wiesbaden.

1978a. "Hebrew Stress Shifts, Pretonic Lengthening, and Segolization: Possible Cases of Aramaic Interference in Hebrew Syllable Structure." *Israel Oriental Studies.* 8:91–106.

1978b. "Hebrew and North-West Semitic." *Hebrew Annual Review.* 2:21–44.

1979. "Non-Phonetic Conditioning of Sound Change and Biblical Hebrew." *Hebrew Annual Review.* 3:7–15.

1980. "Ḥawla shurūṭ taḥawwul at-tā ʾilā hā fī -l-waqf fī -l-luġa al-fuṣḥā. *Abḥāth fī -l-luġa wa-l-uslūb.*" 2:1–5.

Boyarin, Daniel, 1976. "The Loss of Final Consonants in Babylonian Jewish Aramaic." *Afroasiatic Linguistics* III, 5:19–23.

Brockelmann, Carl, 1908–13. *Grundriss der vergleichenden Grammatik der semitischen Sprachen.* Berlin.

(8) *UT* 49:IV:27 *mhrtt* as against *ibid.*: 38 *mḥrṯh* does not, pace *UT* 34. §5.40, exhibit context form as against pausal form, but rather feminine form without pronominal suffix as against masculine form with pronominal suffix.

Cantineau, Jean. 1936–37. "Etudes sur quelques parlers des nomades arabes d'Orient." *Annales de l'institut d'études orientales*. 2:1–118; 3:119–237.
Cross, Frank M. — Freedman, David N., 1952. *Early Hebrew Orthography*. New Haven.
Diem, Werner, 1973. *Skizzen jemenitischer Dialekte*. Beirut.
Friedrich, Johannes, 1951. *Phönizisch-Punische Grammatik*. Roma.
Harris, Zellig S., 1939. *Development of the Canaanite Dialects*. New Haven.
Jastrow, Otto, 1978. *Die mesopotamisch-arabischen qəltu-Dialekte*, I. Wiesbaden.
Jesperson, Otto, 1913. *Lehrbuch der Phonetik*[2]. Leipzig-Berlin.
Johnstone, T.M., 1975. "The Modern South Arabian Languages." *Afroasiatic Linguistics*. I, 5:1–29.
Kruisinga, E., 1925. *A Handbook of Present-Day English, I. English Sounds*[4]. Utrecht.
Meillet, Antoine, 1952. *Linguistique historique et linguistique générale* II. Nouveau tirage. Paris.
——— 1958. *Linguistique historique et linguistique générale* I. Nouveau tirage. Paris.
Rabin, Chaim, 1951. *Ancient West-Arabian*. London.
UT = Gordon, Cyrus H. 1965. *Ugaritic Textbook*. Roma.

Additions and Corrections

to **p. 126**.*19*: For cases of parallel development see, e.g., *ZAL* 25. (1993), 95–99.

to **p. 126**.*n. 2*: = *Studies*, 362ff.

to **p. 127**.*15*: In Middle Hebrew, however, this feature does not, it seems, reflect the archaic Biblical ending; it is due to later development, see *Hebrew Linguistics*, 250–55.

to **p. 128**.*15*: The *t* was elided ater the shift of long vowels to short ones in final closed syllables (e.g. יָקֹם: יָקוּם) had ceased operating and הָיַת*, etc. had been analogically restored to הָיֵת (just as **qŭm* was restored to קוּם).

to **p. 128**.*n. 3.2*: = *Hebrew Linguistics*, 60–62.

to **p. 129**.*16*: In Phoenician the *t* is elided in verbs even after long vowels, i. e., even in III*y* verbs, see Z. S. Harris, *Development of the Canaanite Dialects*, New Haven 1939, pp. 58–59, §34. This too, it seems, distinguishes Phoenician from Hebrew.

to **p. 135**.*22*: Interestingly enough, in the Yemenite dialect of an-Naḏīr (Jabal Rāziḥ) feminine **determinate** nouns terminate also in the absolute (i.e., when determinate by the definite article) in *-et*, indeterminate ones in *ah* (P. Behnstedt, *Die Dialekte der Gegend von Ṣaᶜdah* [*Nord-Jemen*], Wiesbaden 1987, p. 162), whereas verbs end in *a* (op. cit. 28.-2). Since determination may be marked by the definite article, by the construct state, and by the annexation of pronominal suffixes and the two last forms exhibit *-et*, one is wonders whether the use of *-et* with nouns preceded by the definite article could reflect the influence of the two other ways of determination.

Remarks on the Development of Some Pronominal Suffixes in Hebrew

ABSTRACT: The paradigmatic pressure for the preservation of the final vowels of pronominal suffixes after long vowels, where gender opposition could not be marked by the preceding vowel, was strong enough to create in rabbinic Hebrew, in Aramaic, and in Arabic, dialect doublets, viz., suffixes without final vowel after originally short vowels (as rabbinic Hebrew *yāḏāḵ* 'your hand'), and those with final vowels after long vowels (as *yāḏeḵā* 'your hands').

1. In *Hebrew Annual Review*, R. C. Steiner (1979), among a plethora of stimulating observations, dealt with the 2ms and 3fs pronominal suffixes in biblical and rabbinic Hebrew. In the following, I would like to consider these features from somewhat different angles.

2. As to the 2ms pronominal suffix, in biblical Hebrew in context it invariably terminates in *-ḵā*, e.g. *yāḏəḵā* 'your hand', in pause either in *-āḵ*, e.g. *lāḵ* 'to you', or, as a rule, in *-eḵā*, e.g. *yāḏeḵā*. In rabbinic Hebrew, on the other hand, its usual form is *-āḵ*, e.g. *yāḏāḵ*, after bases ending in a vowel *-ḵā*, e.g. *yāḏeḵā* 'your hands' (for particulars, see Steiner 1979, p. 158). The prevalence of the *-āḵ* type in rabbinic Hebrew reflects an Aramaism, according to Ben-Ḥayyim (1954, pp. 63f); Steiner (p. 162) mentions as an additional factor the tendency of biblical Hebrew pausal forms to spread into nonpausal positions in rabbinic Hebrew. Both explanations, however, cannot be considered decisive, Ben-Ḥayyim's view, because the distribution of *-āḵ* in rabbinic Hebrew differs significantly from that in Aramaic (as pointed out by Steiner, pp. 161–2), Steiner's suggestion, because pausal forms terminating in *-āk̲* (such as *lāk̲*) are quite restricted in biblical Hebrew.

3. Accordingly, Steiner (p. 163) submitted that it was analogy to the distribution of the 3fs pronominal suffix *-āh/-hā* in biblical and rabbinic Hebrew that limited the borrowing of Aramaic *-āk̲* (or the spread of pausal *-āk̲*) to positions where *-āh* was already present, and blocked its spread to environments in which *-hā* was used. Accordingly, **yādā́kā*[1] changed to *yādāk̲* on the analogy of *yādāh*, but *yādek̲ā* remained, influenced by *yādehā*. This, of course, raises the problem of the distribution of the 3fs pronominal suffix in biblical and rabbinic Hebrew.

4. It is generally recognized that the 3fs pronominal suffix after originally short vowels (which have now disappeared) has the form *-āh* (e.g. *yādāh*), after long vowels[2] *-hā* (e.g. *yādehā*). We owe it to Steiner's insight (pp. 163–64) that originally also forms terminating in a consonant preceding the pronominal suffix governed *-hā*, e.g. *kiʿăsattā* 'she angered her', being synchronically identical with **kiʿăsathā*.[3]

Cantineau (1937) accounted for the distribution of this and other (also Aramaic and colloquial Arabic) pronominal suffixes by positing a rule of quantitative vowel harmony in Proto-Semitic, according to which the length of the vowel in a monosyllabic pronominal suffix is determined by the length of the base-final vowel. After a short base-final vowel, then, the *a* of the 3fs pronominal suffix was short and, hence, subject to apocope; after a base-final long vowel or diphthong, the *a* of the 3fs pronominal suffix was long and, hence, not deletable.[4]

I do not consider Cantineau's theory well-grounded, not so much because of Steiner's stricture (p. 171) that it fails to explain why the apocopated allomorph (in our case *-āh*) is not found after bases ending in a consonant in Proto-Hebrew (it may easily be included in Cantineau's hy- *

1. I prefer to posit the rabbinic Hebrew etymon **yādā́kā*, basing myself on biblical Hebrew pausal forms, see Steiner (p. 162, n. 10) and especially Kutscher (1963, p. 277), contrary to Steiner (p. 163), who derives *yādāk̲*, etc. from *yādəkā*, etc. Nevertheless, this reconstruction is not without problems, see Haneman (1980, pp. 39–62).

2. And those features, mainly imperfect forms (e.g. *yiqṭəlehā*), which have been analogically restructured through the influence of III-y verbs, exhibiting long *e* preceding the pronominal suffix (such as *yiglehā*, root *gly*). These features have to be mentioned in any synchronic description due to their frequency.

3. It should be noted that *-āh* later intruded into forms after original consonants. This is the case, e.g., after the short imperfect and the imperative. Accordingly, Steiner's (p. 166) wording "only bases which ended in a short vowel in Proto-Hebrew select the allomorph *-āh* in Masoretic Hebrew" needs qualification.

4. I have adopted Steiner's wording (pp. 170–71).

pothesis, by positing a rule of quantitative *syllable* harmony), but rather because of a diametrically opposed tendency obtaining in classical Arabic. As demonstrated by Fischer (1926), the 3ms pronominal suffix in classical Arabic terminates in a long vowel (*-hū*) after short(!) vowels, in a short vowel (*-hu*) after long(!) vowels (and often also after closed syllables), i.e. quantitative vowel disharmony (or even syllable disharmony) obtains. This does not disprove Cantineau's theory; yet it makes it much less likely.

Steiner (pp. 171–72), as an alternative to Cantineau's theory, suggests that apocope was blocked in cases where it would have created an impermissible cluster, i.e., two consonants at the end of the syllable (CVC*h*) or vowel length plus consonant at the end of the syllable (CV:*h*). Yet this theory is not flawless either. It is, to be sure, based on the correct supposition (cf. Steiner, p. 168) that, before the loss of case-endings and mood-endings in Proto-Hebrew, syllables could not terminate in two consonants nor could long vowels occur in closed syllables. *Yet with the loss of final short vowels such syllables became permissible.* This means that, at the time of the apocope of the final vowel of the 3fs pronominal suffix (which in all probability coincided with the general loss of final short vowels[5]), such syllables became permissible, so that no blocking took place.

5. In my opinion, the various forms of the 3fs pronominal suffix result from the rules of the elision of *h* in open juncture (i.e., when two morphemes form a single stress unit), their gist being that, after short vowels, *h* in this position was elided, yet after long vowels it was preserved (see Blau 1974, pp. 21–24; 1976, pp. 24–25). Accordingly *mar'ehā* 'her sight' with long *e* preceding the *h* preserved the *h*, yet *lahā*, with short *a* preceding the *h*, has become *lā* (as Num 32:42). Yet not only did the ending *-ā* mark feminine (*yaldā*[6] being understood as 'girl', rather than 'her boy'), but, because of forms like *'ăb̲îhā*, etc., *h* was considered characteristic of 3fs and therefore again added: *lāh*. When directly preceded by a consonant, the *h* was, as a rule, assimilated to it: *ki'ăsattā*.

6. Still, along with Steiner (p. 163, cf. above par. 3), one could interpret the distribution of the 2ms pronominal suffix in rabbinic Hebrew as being due to analogy with the 3fs pronominal suffix. Steiner (pp. 163–64) has even succeeded in demonstrating convincingly that *higgî'atk̲ā* 'it has reached you, it's yours' is a genuine rabbinic Hebrew form, corresponding to *ki'ăsattā*,

5. One could claim that final (even long) vowels of pronouns were elided even before the change of the syllable structure rules; cf. infra par. 7. Yet even later, with the change of syllable structure, one would have expected the blocking to cease and the final vowel to drop.

6. It is very likely that the feminine ending in Hebrew never terminated in *h*, see Blau (pp. 128–29) (1980, pp. 19–20).

synchronically identical with **ki ʿăsathā*.[7] Nevertheless, despite the possibility of such an analogical formation, I would like to submit a more powerful theory, which also explains the distribution of other, Aramaic and colloquial Arabic, pronominal suffixes. I submit that paradigmatic resistance often blocked the elision of functionally significant final vowels of pronominal suffixes. In rabbinic Hebrew, after words originally terminating in short vowels,[8] the 2ms pronominal suffix was sufficiently differentiated from the feminine one without taking the final *-ā* of *-ḵā* into consideration; therefore, it was elided (**yādáḵā* : *yādēḵ* > *yādāḵ* : *yādēḵ*). Yet, after long vowels (and original consonants) these pronominal suffixes differed only in the final *-ā* (*pîḵā* : *pîḵ*); accordingly, it was preserved.

The case of the 2s pronominal suffix in some Arabic dialects, e.g. Cairo (and Damascus), is similar. After original short vowels (e.g. *ʿandak* : *ʿandik* 'with you') the final vowels, being functionally insignificant, have been elided. Yet, after long vowels (type *fîk* : *fîki* 'in you') the elision of the final *-i* of the 2fs suffix would have destroyed the masculine : feminine opposition; therefore it was preserved. In contradistinction to Hebrew, presumably by analogy to the *-î* suffix of the imperfect (e.g. *taktubî*), it was the *-i*, rather than the *-a* of the masculine, that was preserved. *

In the Arabic dialect of the Bani Ḵâled of Transjordan, one of the rather limited number of dialects in which the final *-ā* of the 3fs pronominal

7. Cohen (1981, p. 51, n. 7), to be sure, did not accept Steiner's arguments, discarding the possibility of analogy to a nonexistent feature. In my opinion, however, forms like *ki ʿăsattā* and **ki ʿăsathā* are, indeed, synchronically identical, as claimed by Steiner. Nor are Cohen's other strictures convincing. *Higgîʿatḵā* is, indeed, a single form, yet such forms are in general not frequent. Cohen has, to be sure, discovered one(!) form terminating in *-tāḵ*, yet the later intrusion of *-āḵ* into forms after original consonants parallels the intrusion of *-āh* into this position, see note 3 above. On the other hand, Cohen's (1981, p. 17) own explanation, that the special vocalization of *higgîʿatḵā* results from it being a halakhic term which denoted dedication to Temple property, has to be taken into consideration. As a matter of fact, Cohen has discovered *-kā* also in expressions of curse. Nevertheless, Steiner's explanation is more attractive.

8. Throughout this paper we have taken it for granted that in Proto-Semitic the system of cases did not differ in absolute and construct (including *status pronominalis*), the construct also having full inflection. For particulars, see Blau (1978, pp. 129b–30a), and Steiner (1979, p. 166, n. 20). Against the theory that nominative and accusative had zero ending in construct, cf. Hebrew prepositions terminating in *-a* preceding pronominal suffixes: *lāḵ bāḵ*, *ʾōtāḵ*; for these, see Steiner (1979, p. 170, n. 30). If, in Hebrew at least, the accusative had in fact terminated in zero, Hebrew prepositions with pronominal suffixes would not behave differently from nouns. Only the assumption that the accusative preceding pronominal suffixes was marked by *-a* accounts for the preference of *-a* in prepositions, which originally were adverbial accusatives, whereas in nouns the various case endings alternated. *

suffix *-hā* is not preserved in every position, this pronominal suffix has the form *-a*^{h} (e.g. *be*^{i}*ta*^{h} 'her house') after originally short vowels, *-ha* (type *'abûha* 'her father') after long vowels (Cantineau, 1936-37, pp. 78; 184; Cantineau, 1937, pp. 156–58). One will assume that the final *-a* in *'abûha*, etc., has been preserved in order to differentiate these forms from *'abû*^{h} ('his father'; for which see Cantineau, 1936-37, p. 180).

In the Arabic dialects of the 'Ömûr, the Slût and the Sirḥân, the 1s pronominal suffix after verbs has the form *-an* after originally short vowels, yet that of *-ni* after long ones (type *yönṭûni* 'they will give me'; Cantineau, 1936-37, pp. 73–75, 176; Cantineau, 1937, pp. 157–58). It seems that in forms in which *-ni* was attached to the 2/3mpl forms of the imperfect, the final *-i* was preserved in order to differentiate these forms from the corresponding imperfect forms without pronominal suffix (to differentiate *yönṭûni* from *yönṭûn* 'they will give'). By analogy to these forms, the *-i* was preserved after long vowels in general.

In some cases, in accordance with the redundant character of language, both members of the functionally significant opposition of final vowels were retained. Thus in Official Aramaic, after long vowels, both the 3ms and the 3fs pronominal suffixes preserve their final vowels, e.g. *'ăḇûhî* : *'ăḇûhā*. (After short vowels the opposition between the pronouns is marked by the vowel preceding *-h*, e.g. *rēšēh* : *rēšah* 'his head':'her head.')

7. In order to understand how this paradigmatic pressure operated (cf.
(pp. 26–29) also Blau, 1979, pp. 7–10), it is worthwhile to observe it in living languages. In the following, I cite one of the finest works on Arabic dialectology that has appeared in the 1970s, viz. Jastrow (1978, pp. 217–18), as to the paradigmatic pressure exercised on the perfect 1s : 2ms : 2fs in modern Arabic dialects. In classical Arabic this paradigm has the form *qataltu* : *qatalta* : *qatalti*. In some Arabic dialects, in fact, despite the paradigmatic pressure, all these forms merged into one (Tunis: *qtalt*). In other dialects, the full opposition has been preserved (Dêr iz-Zôr: *qataltū* : *qatalt* : *qataltī*). In other cases, the 1s and 2ms again merged, but not the 2ms and 2fs (Damascus: *'atalt : 'atalt : 'ataltī*), or alternatively, the 2ms and 2fs merged, while the 1s remained different (Morocco: *qtelt* : *qteltī* : *qteltī*). Accordingly, paradigmatic pressure creates certain tendencies, which, however, may suffer many exceptions. Thus, in biblical Hebrew, the pausal masculine and feminine *lak̲* have coincided, and, e.g., in Tunisian Arabic, in which the opposition of gender in the second person has altogether disappeared, it is the original feminine pronominal suffix *-(i)k* that serves for both genders.

Yet, for the somewhat erratic character of the preservation and omission of the final vowels of pronominal suffixes, we have also to take into consideration that these vowels were anceps.[9] Accordingly, on the one hand, no real sound shift existed necessitating their deletion. On the other hand, in morphemes as frequently used as the pronominal suffixes are, even final long vowels may be omitted, not only in languages which elide their final short vowels, but also in those which keep them. A case in point is classical Arabic, which, as is well known, preserves even short final vowels. Nevertheless, it *may* elide even final long vowels in pronominal affixes. Thus, the original form of *-tum*, *-kum*, *-hum* in classical Arabic was, no doubt, *-tumū, -kumū, -humū.* Preceding *waṣla*, to be sure, this "reappearing" *-u* is spelt without vowel letter, but this is due to its being always in a closed syllable. Forms of the type *katabtumûhu* 'you wrote it' clearly demonstrate the length of this vowel, which nevertheless, was generally elided, whereas other vowels (as in the feminine forms *-tunna, -kunna, -hunna*) were preserved. This is also the case with Hebrew, Aramaic and colloquial Arabic pronominal suffixes. We have already mentioned the omission of the final vowel even where it is functionally significant (biblical Hebrew pausal *lāḵ*). On the other hand, the final vowel may be preserved, even where it has no function. So, e.g., in Official Aramaic, the gender opposition in the second person singular after originally short vowels is *-āḵ* : *-ēḵî*, the final *-î* of the 2fs being preserved in every position, and this is also the case in some Arabic dialects (Negev, cf. Blanc, 1970, pp. 130–31, especially n. 35). In most Arabic dialects, the final vowel of the 3fs pronominal suffix *-hā* is not elided.

8. Nevertheless, in spite of deviations and inconstancies (for particulars, from a different point of view, see Cantineau, 1937), the paradigmatic pressure for the preservation of the final vowels of pronominal suffixes after long vowels (where gender opposition could not be marked by the preceding vowel) was strong enough to create allomorphs in many cases, viz., suffixes without final vowels after originally short vowels, and suffixes with final vowels after long vowels. Such doublets *may* have even become productive, favoring similar rhythmical structures.[10]

9. *Pace* Steiner (1979, pp. 168–69, n. 27), I consider these final vowels, as customary, to be anceps. For the (occasional) length of the perfect affix *-tā*, for instance, see the decisive proofs adduced by Nöldeke (1904, p. 20), thus making also the anceps character of the *a* of *'anta, -ka* more than likely. For the length of the *a* of the perfect affix *-tinna/-tunna*, see Nöldeke (1904, pp. 24–25), which thus demonstrates the length of the *a* of *'antinna/'antunna* and *-kinna/-kunna* (and even of *(-)hinna/(-)hunna*). For Arabic *hummā*, cf. Jastrow (1978, p. 128)—if not influenced by the dual, cf. the literature cited in Blau (1966-67, p. 134, n. 8).

10. In some cases other factors operated. We have already dealt with the 3fs pronominal suffix in Hebrew (par. 5), which, in our opinion, was affected by the rules of the elision of *h* in open juncture.

BIBLIOGRAPHY

Ben-Ḥayyim, Z. 1954. *Studies in the Traditions of the Hebrew Language*. Madrid-Barcelona.

Blanc, H. 1970. "The Arabic Dialect of the Negev Bedouins." *The Israel Academy of Sciences and Humanities, Proceedings* IV, 7:112–50. Jerusalem.

Blau, J. 1966–67. *A Grammar of Christian Arabic*. Louvain.

_______. 1974. " 'Iyyunim bətorat hakkinnuyim (kolel 'et hayyiddua') bilšonot šemiyot." *Henoch Yalon Memorial Volume*, pp. 17–45. Eds. E. Y. Kutscher *et al.* Ramat Gan.

_______. 1976. *A Grammar of Biblical Hebrew*. Wiesbaden.

_______. 1978. "Kinnuyey nistar wənisteret bənun ubil'adeha bə'ibrit hammiqra." *Eretz Israel* 14:125–31.

_______. 1979. "Non-Phonetic Conditioning of Sound Change and Biblical Hebrew." *Hebrew Annual Review* 3:7–15.

_______. 1980. "The Parallel Development of the Feminine Ending *-at* in Semitic Languages." *Hebrew Union College Annual* 51:17–28.

Cantineau, J. 1936–37. "Etudes sur quelques parlers de nomades arabes d'Orient." *Annales de l'institut d'études orientales* 2:1–118; 3:119–237.

_______. 1937. "Une alternance quantitative dans des pronoms suffixes sémitiques." *Bulletin de la Société Linguistique de Paris* 38:148–64.

Cohen, H. 1981. *Kinnuyey hammušša hehabur 'el happo'al bilšon hammišna 'al pi ktab yad Kaufman.* Master's thesis, Tel Aviv University.

Fischer, A. 1926. "Die Quantität des Vokals des arabischen Pronominalsuffixes *hu (hi)*." In *Oriental Studies Dedicated to Paul Haupt*, pp. 390–402. Leipzig.

Haneman, G. 1980. *Torat hassurot šel ləšon hammišna*. Tel Aviv.

Jastrow, O. 1978. *Die mesopotamisch-arabischen qəltu-Dialekte* I. Wiesbaden.

Kutscher, E. Y. 1963. "Ləšon ḥazal." In *Seper Henoch Yalon*, pp. 246–80. Jerusalem.

Nöldeke, T. 1904. *Beiträge zur semitischen Sprachwissenschaft*. Strassburg.

Steiner, R. C. 1979. "From Proto-Hebrew to Mishnaic Hebrew: the History of *-kā* and *-hā*." *Hebrew Annual Review* 3:157–74.

Additions

to **p. 139**.*-4ff.*: For an important analysis of Cantineau's theory from a quite different point of view see O. Jastrow, "Une question embarassante" — Jean Cantineau über das Pronominalsuffix 3. sg. m. in den arabischen Dialekten' in *Festgabe für Hans-Rudolf Singer*, Frankfurt 1919, pp. 167–74.

to **p. 141**.*13ff.*: Cf. also W. Diem, 'Vom Altarabischen zum Neuarabischen. Ein neurer Ansatz', *Leslau Festschrift* (pp. 297–308), p. 301. [Diem, in this stimulating paper, replete with important findings, claims that first the case endings disappeared because of their redundancy and only afterwards were short final vowels in context omitted. I wholeheartedly consent to the important role played by redundancy, see already *Emergence* 245, yet I do think that the case endings vanished by the concatination of various **concurrent** factors (what Y. Malkiel dubbed multiple causation or plurilinear development). Diem infers from the vowel harmony of the short vowel preceding *-ka* 'your' that the case endings had already lost their function when the final short *-a* was still existent; one should, however, posit not only early **-kī* (as does Diem himself) but also original **-kā* with long final vowel (still preserved in Classical Arabic in context position: Sibawayhi II 323:17 أُعْطِيكَاهُ 'I shall give it to you'). I do not understand the relevance of the preservation of the tanwin in the interior of syntagmas for Diem's thesis, since, at any rate, as posited by Diem himself, the endings were not elided in the interior of syntagmas. By the way, for the ending *-u* in Yemenite dialects cf. *Studies* 285–87, *ZAL* 25.98–99 (1993), for the ending *-in Emergence* 247.13 ff.].

to **p. 141**.*n. 83*: = *Hebrew Linguistics*, pp. 101–02

Redundant Pronominal Suffixes Denoting Intrinsic Possession

In the first part of his paper "The Idea of 'Possession' in Linguistic Expression, A Significant Use of the Possessive Pronoun"[1] the late M. M. Bravmann dealt with the "pregnant" use of possessive pronouns in cases like וְדָבַק בְּאִשְׁתּוֹ 'and he cleaves unto his wife' Gen. 2:24, instead of the expected ...בְּאִשָּׁה '...unto a woman'. Compare also Iraqi Arabic *yāx^ed̲ marta* 'he takes a wife' (literally '... his wife') and Qurʾān 2:232 يَنْكِحْنَ أَزْوَاجَهُنَّ 'they marry "their" husbands'. He further adduced expressions of Arabic مَرْبُوطٌ بِرُمَّتِه 'tied with "his" neck-rope'; وُضِعَ عَلَى سَرِيرِه 'he was laid upon "his" bed'; كُفِّنَ فِي أَثْوَابِه 'he was shrouded in "his" garments'; فَلْيَتَبَوَّأْ مَقْعَدَهُ 'he shall take up "his" seat';[2] رُمِيَ بِحَجَرِه 'he was thrown with "his" stone'; Bagdadi Judeo-Arabic *qay^ᶜbni ḥōšū* 'he built "his" house', as well as some Ethiopic examples. In the second part of his paper, entitled 'Various Semantic Characteristics of the Concept "to have"', Bravmann compared this usage of the possessive pronoun for the expression of the concept 'to possess' in cases like *^ᶜ^endī b^entī* 'I have "my" daughter', *akū jīrān^em* 'they have a neighbor', literally 'there is their neighbor'.

I would like to consider this extraordinarily interesting collection of examples from an additional vantage point. All the nouns adduced by Bravmann exhibiting a *prima facie* redundant possessive pronouns are substantives, generally or at least in the special context in which they are, presupposed, so that, being implied, they need not be introduced to those who share in the discourse. Men have wives, women husbands, people have homes, neighbors, and daughters, dead men are laid on beds, shrouded in garments, prisoners are tied with neck-ropes, persons in certain situations take up seats, and every person meets an adequate adversary, denoted by the metaphor of being thrown with stones. In the wake of Levy-Bruhl,[3] these nouns are often dubbed inalienable. This

[1] This paper appeared in its final form in Bravmann's *Studies in Semitic Philology*, Leiden 1977, pp. 357–73; but its first part was already published in *Le Muséon* 85 (1972), pp. 269–74.

[2] A parallel passage is Ibn Saad, *Biographien Muhammeds, seiner Gefährten und der späteren Träger des Islams*, Leiden 1904ff., 12:10, ll. 3–4 مَنْ حَلَفَ عَلَى مِنْبَرِي كاذبًا ... فَلْيَتَبَوَّأْ مَقْعَدَهُ مِنَ النَّار 'he who swears falsely on my pulpit..., shall take up "his" seat of fire'. Similarly p. 12:20.

[3] See H. (B.) Rosén, *Lingua* 8 (1959), p. 267, n. 6.

term has the great advantage of being suggestive and perfectly fits the parts of body, nouns like husband, wife, daughter, and so forth. On the other hand, its clear overt references make its use somewhat difficult for nouns like bed, garment, neck-rope, seat, which cannot easily be decribed as something "the ownership of which is not transferable." E. H. Bendix,[4] speaks, in the main, of inherent nouns as against accidental ones, yet he also mentions the opposition objective: subjective, and further, intrinsic: extrinsic. [The late] R. Hetzron[5] speaks of 'intimate possessions'. In the following, I shall use the term 'intrinsic possession', because it suggests not only parts of the body, parts of a whole and relatives, but everything that naturally belongs to a given context.

Since nouns intrinsically possessed, in contradistinction to ordinary, extrinsic nouns, need not be introduced to those who take part in conversation, they often behave in a haphazard manner. Being implied in the situation, they need not be referred to exactly.[6] Therefore, sometimes the singular is used instead of the exact number, as Ps. 115:5–6 פֶּה לָהֶם...אַף לָהֶם 'they have "mouth"... they have "nose"'. [Cf. in Hebrew Jeremiah 7:33 נִבְלַת הָעָם הַזֶּה 'the corpses of this nation'; 9:7 לְשׁוֹנָם 'their tongues'. Therefore, one need not wonder (*pace* A. Spitaler, *Oriens* 15 (1962), p. 114, n. 1, E. Y. Kutscher, in: *Current Trends in Linguistics*, 6 (1971), p. 381; the case of *mlk mṣryn* 'kings of Egypt', adduced by Kutscher, is different) at the singular Ezra 5:10 שֻׁם גֻּבְרַיָּא 'the names of the men'; the same applies to Daniel 3:27 בְּגֶשְׁמְהוֹן 'in their bodies' (*pace* H. Bauer–P. Leander, *Grammatik des Biblisch-Aramäischen*, Halle 1927, also referred to by Kutscher, loc. cit., who consider it distributive, and T. Muraoka, *JSS* 11 (1966), pp.155–56, who dubs it "numberless"). This feature occurs in Arabic as well, cf. in Judaeo-Arabic the examples of the use of the singular for the dual with the double parts of the body adduced J. Blau, דקדוק הערבית־היהודית של ימי־הביניים², Jerusalem 1980, p. 102, §124ב, further e.g., R. David ben Abraham ben Rambam, ספר פרקי אבות עם פירוש בלשון ערבי, ed. B. H. Ḥânân, Alexandria 1900–1901, p. 26b.16 גבינהם 'their foreheads']. Similarly, in Classical Arabic the plural, and sometimes the singular, replaces the dual of such nouns denoting single members of the body, preceding a pronominal suffix in the dual, as

[4] E. H. Bendix, *Componential Analysis of General Vocabulary: The Semantic Structure of a Set of Verbs in English, Hindi, and Japanese*, Bloomington, Ind. 1966. I am indebted to [the late] E. Rubinstein for calling my attention to this work.

[5] *The Gunnän-Gurage Languages*, Studi di Semitistica e del Vicino Oriente Antico, Ricerche 12, Instituto Orientale di Napoli, Napoli 1977, p. 119.

[6] I hope to deal *in extenso* with the following features in a monograph treating intrinsic possession in Arabic and Hebrew [I have, so far, only treated the feature *qulûbuhumâ JSAI* 12 (1989), pp. 16ff. In the meantime, W. Diem has published an important paper on our subject 'Alienable und inalleniable Possession im Semitischen', *ZDMG* (1986), pp. 227–91].

قُلُوبُهُمَا (sometimes also قَلْبُهُمَا) ‘the hearts of them both’. [For details see ‘Two Studies in Sibawayhi’s Kitâb’, *JSAI* 12 (1989), pp. 1–30, especially pp. 16–30]. Often intrinsic nouns, which according to context are expected to be accompanied by a possessive pronoun, instead exhibit the definite article, as Qurʾān 4:23, where between names of relatives that govern possessive pronominal suffixes two nouns defined by the definite article (or more accurately, defined by a genitive determined by the definite article) are inserted: حُرِّمَتْ عَلَيْكُمْ أُمَّهَاتُكُمْ وَبَنَاتُكُمْ وَأَخَوَاتُكُمْ وَعَمَّاتُكُمْ وَخَالَاتُكُمْ وَبَنَاتُ الأَخِ وَبَنَاتُ الأُخْتِ وَأُمَّهَاتُكُمُ الَّتِي أَرْضَعْنَكُمْ وَأَخَوَاتُكُمْ مِنَ الرَّضَاعَةِ وَأُمَّهَاتُ نِسَائِكُمْ ... ‘forbidden to you are your mothers and daughters, your sisters, your aunts paternal and maternal, “the” brother’s daughters, “the” sister’s daughters, your mothers who have given suck to you, your suckling sisters, your wives’ mothers ...’. Moreover, even indefinite nouns may replace expected definite nouns with a possessive pronominal suffix, as Mal. 1:6 בֵּן יְכַבֵּד אָב ‘a son honors (his) father’.

Here, however, we are interested in the inverse phenomenon namely, the use of possessive pronouns even in contexts in which one would not have expected them. Since intrinsic nouns are firmly anchored in context, they are so regularly accompanied by references to this context that in some languages they regularly govern possessive pronouns.[7] An additional reason for the use of possessive pronouns with intrinsic nouns, related with the connection of intrinsic nouns with their context, but by no means identical with it, is the tendency toward concreteness: intrinsic nouns, especially parts of the body (but not only they), are conceived by the speaker only in connection with their owners, rather than as such.[8] [Cf. also Leviticus 6:3 וְלָבַשׁ הַכֹּהֵן מִדּוֹ בַד ‘and the priest shall put on **his** linen garment’]. In some cases, as in those of proleptic pronominal suffixes in Akkadian and Aramaic (type *aḫātīšu ša S.* ‘S’s sister’; ‘אבוהי די א’ ‘A’s father’,[9] the prevalence of this feature with intrinsic nouns is, it seems, due to the

[7] V. W. Havers. *Handbuch der erklärenden Syntax*, Heidelberg 1931, pp. 111–12, § 92, where further literature is quoted.

[8] Loc. cit.

[9] The connection of this feature with intrinsic nouns was, correctly in my opinion, stated by Havers, *Wörter und Sachen* 12 (1929), pp. 170–71 (also quoted in his *Handbuch*..., pp. 112, 239). It is a pity that his observation has not been heeded by Semitists. At any rate, the analysis of the examples cited by M. Z. Kadari, *Proceedings of the International Conference of Semitic Studies*, Jerusalem 1969, pp. 109–10; T. Nöldeke, *Kurzgefasste syrische Grammatik*[2], Leipzig 1898, pp. 155–56, 158; M. Schlesinger, *Satzlehre der Grammatik des babylonischen Talmuds*, Leipzig 1928, p. 66 § 39; H. Bauer & P. Leander, *Grammatik des Biblisch-Aramäischen*, Halle 1927, p. 314j, demonstrates the prevalence of intrinsic possession in this construction, making the historical connection between this construction and intrinsic nouns quite likely. For this feature in the Arabic dialect of Djidjelli see below.

tendency toward concreteness only, since the possessor to which the proleptic pronoun refers has not yet been mentioned.

In other cases, however, multiple causation for the use of (a special form of) possessive pronouns[10] with intrinsic nouns obtains. Thus in Modern Hebrew two sets of possessive pronouns are used: synthetic pronominal suffixes, relatively often attached to intrinsic nouins, and analytic שֶׁל forms. H. Rosén[11] was the first who called attention to the same substantives being used in intrinsic sense with pronominal suffixes (type בְּנוֹתַי 'my daughters'), in extrinsic usage with שֶׁל (type בָּנוֹת שֶׁלִּי 'my girls'), interpreting the difference in usage as primarily marking the opposition intrinsic: extrinsic. U. Ornan,[12] however, has demonstrated that שֶׁל forms occur with substantives used in a less common meaning, in our case בָּנוֹת in the sense of 'girls'. Consider, for example, אוֹצָר. In its usual sense 'treasure' it takes pronominal suffixes: אוֹצָרֵנוּ 'our treasure'. But in its exceptional usage 'treasury' it takes pronominal suffixes: הָאוֹצָר שֶׁלָּנוּ 'out treasury', אוֹצָר being in both senses an extrinsic noun.

Nevertheless, the use of intrinsic nouns with pronominal suffixes is not without connection with their intrinsicality. In spoken Modern Hebrew, a tendency toward the use of שֶׁל forms, at the expense of pronominal suffixes, obtains. In Biblical Hebrew, on the other hand, pronominal suffixes are always used. Accordingly, since one of the most important factors influencing Modern Hebrew is Biblical Hebrew, nouns occurring in the Bible with pronominal suffixes[13] tend to be used in literary Modern Hebrew with pronominal suffixes as

[10] According to J. H. Greenberg, in C. N. Li, *Word Order and Word Order Change*, Austin 1975, pp. 41–42, Austronesien and Amerindian languages have for intrinsic nouns (Greenberg uses "inalienables"), typically body parts and kinship terms, possessive affixes (type: head-my), whereas extrinsic possession is expressed by a superordinate possessed noun in apposition to the noun designating the actual possessed object (type: dog my-animal; one cannot say 'my dog' directly). Historically, Greenberg adds, it is the intrinsic nouns that retain the earlier construction. In my opinion, the reason for the survival of the earlier construction with intrinsic nouns is that, because of their firm connection with the context and tendency towards concreteness, they have been so often used in (the earlier) possessive construction that the new possessive construction did not supersede it in them. Cf. however, n. 15 below.
Greenberg also mentions Egyptian Arabic *ʾabi* 'my father' as against *bēt batāʿi* 'my house'; it seems, however, that the situation in Egyptian Arabic is more complicated (see W. Spitta, *Grammatik des arabischen Vulgärdialectes von Ägypten*, Leipzig 1880, pp. 262–63), though intrinsicality is one of the most important factors determining the use of pronominal suffix. Cf. the use of pronominal suffix in Djidjelli below.

[11] עברית טובה¹, Jerusalem 1957, pp. 137–38; עברית טובה², Jerusalem 1967, pp. 149–50; cf. also *BSL* 53 (1957–58), pp. 321–22.

[12] In: *Fourth World Congress of Jewish Studies: Papers*, Jerusalem 1968, Hebrew lectures, II, pp. 117–22.

[13] I am simplifying the issue. As a matter of fact, the development was more intricate since the use of pronominal suffixes in later layers of Hebrew influenced Modern Hebrew as well.

well, whereas other nouns are more exposed to the influence of the spoken language and exhibit שֶׁל forms. This is the reason (besides the important principle of differentiation, rightly stressed by Ornan) that nouns in their usual meaning, influenced by Biblical Hebrew, govern pronominal suffixes, whereas in their exceptional meaning, occurring only rarely or not at all in the Bible, they are followed by שֶׁל forms. Since intrinsic nouns *because of their intrinsicality* are very often used in the Bible with pronominal suffixes, they are used so in literary and even spoken Modern Hebrew as well, in contradistinction to their usage in exceptional extrinsic meanings. Thus intrinsicality does bear, though indirectly, upon the use of pronominal suffixes with intrinsic nouns.

As we have seen, one of the characteristics of intrinsic nouns is their tendency (because of their firm connection with the context and tendency toward concreteness) to govern possessive pronouns even in contexts in which they are redundant. This is, no doubt, at least one of the main factors that caused the nouns cited by Bravmann to be used with pronominal suffixes. Wives cannot be imagined without their husbands,[14] men without their wives, daughters without parents, neighbors without their neighbors, homes without their inhabitants. Similarly, other nouns must in certain situations be connected with their possessors, as neck-ropes with the person tied, beds with the person lying on them, shrouds with the dead, seats with the persons sitting on them, and stones with the persons who are pelted with them. It is because of this tight connection with the possessor that these nouns may exhibit pronominal suffixes even when according to strict logic these pronouns are redundant.

In the following I shall cite additional cases of such "redundant" pronouns with intrinsic nouns, dividing them into three groups. First, I shall adduce cases in which the use of the possessive pronoun may be due to both the intrinsic nouns being firmly anchored in the context and to the tendency toward concreteness. Then I shall treat cases which, it seems, reflect concreteness only. Finally, I shall deal with ramifications of the concept "to possess", which were also treated separately by Bravmann.

1. Redundant possessive pronouns due, besides other possible reasons, to the firm connection of intrinsic nouns with the context and a tendency toward concreteness (as are the examples cited by Bravmann in the first part of his

[14] The husband is also mentioned as possessor in Gen. 29:28 וַיִּתֶּן־לוֹ אֶת־רָחֵל בִּתּוֹ לוֹ לְאִשָּׁה 'he gave him Rachel his daughter to be his wife', לוֹ לְאִשָּׁה constituting a separate syntagmeme 'a wife for him'. Cf. also Gen. 29:29 וַיִּתֵּן לָבָן לְרָחֵל בִּתּוֹ אֶת־בִּלְהָה שִׁפְחָתוֹ לָהּ לְשִׁפְחָה 'and Laban gave Rachel his daughter Bilhah his maid to be her maid', לָהּ לְשִׁפְחָה denoting 'a maid for her'; similarly 29:24 וַיִּתֵּן לָבָן לָהּ אֶת־זִלְפָּה שִׁפְחָתוֹ לְלֵאָה בִתּוֹ שִׁפְחָה 'and Laban gave her Zilpah his maid to be Leah his daughter's maid' (which seems more convincing than to regard לְלֵאָה בִתּוֹ as apposition to לָהּ).

paper). In the Arabic dialect of Djidjelli in Algeria, and in the Berber substratum, too, some nouns denoting relationship are always used with pronominal suffixes, even in cases like *būh qahwāi ʾubnu ṣeiyād* 'the (literally: his) father is coffee-house keeper and the (literally: his) son is fisherman'.[15] In Biblical Hebrew redundant pronominal suffixes occur in adverbials of limitation, governed by an adjective/participle either in the absolute or in construct. The absolute is attested in 2 Sam. 15:32 קָרוּעַ כֻּתָּנְתּוֹ 'with his coat rent'; Neh. 4:12 וְהַבּוֹנִים אִישׁ חַרְבּוֹ אֲסוּרִים עַל מָתְנָיו וּבוֹנִים 'and the builders every one had his sword girded by his side and built'. For the construct see Prov. 14:2 נְלוֹז דְּרָכָיו 'one who is perverse in his ways'. In other cases the adjective/participle may be analyzed as either absolute or construct: 2 Sam. 9:13; Isa. 1:30; 30:27; Amos 2:16; Prov. 19:1. In all cases one would have rather expected the adverbial to be indeterminate, such as נְלוֹז דְּרָכִים*, literally 'one who is perverse as to ways', rather than 'as to his ways'.[16] Observe that the (secondary) pronominal suffix of דְּרָכָיו does not determinate the construct נְלוֹז, which according to the context and the parallel הוֹלֵךְ בְּיָשְׁרוֹ has to be analyzed as indeterminate.[17] Compare perhaps also Gen. 41:14, 2 Sam. 12:20 וַיְחַלֵּף שִׂמְלֹתָיו 'and he changed "his" apparel'.[18]

2. In the following cases the use of redundant pronouns with intrinsic nouns is due to tendency toward concreteness, rather than to context: In Djidjelli with certain kinship terms proleptic pronouns are used (see above for such pronouns in Akkadian and Aramaic), as *lūsetha ddi-zīn^{e}b* 'the sister-in-law of Ẓ'.[19] The pronominal suffix seems redundant with certain nouns denoting time as well, as Hebrew כֶּבֶשׂ (אֶחָד) בֶּן שְׁנָתוֹ (see the concordance) 'one lamb of the first year'.

[15] For additional examples, see P. Marçais, *Le parler arabe de Djidjelli*, Paris n.d., p. 406. Intrinsic nouns denoting body parts tend to use the earlier constructions in Djidjelli (cf. n. 10 above), viz., pronominal suffixes and the construct. Yet surprisingly enough the construct is especially frequent with nouns denoting body parts used in figurative sense; for particulars see ibid., pp. 415–16.

[16] In classical Arabic, as a rule, accusatival adverbials of limitation are indeterminate. Yet, after adjectives/participles in construct, adverbials of limitation are introduced by the definite article, whereas in the so-called *naᶜt sababī* construction, in which the adverbial of limitation in the surface construction has the function of the subject of the adjective/participle, it invariably governs a pronominal suffix.

[17] One could, of course, read נְלוֹז in the absolute and thus account for its being indeterminate. Yet not only is a similar phenomenon attested with בֶּן שְׁנָתוֹ (see below), but this phenomenon is well attested with the improper construct in classical Arabic — which, as mentioned in n. 16, exhibits a genitive with definite article, rather than with pronominal suffix. It is even possible that the fact that the genitive in improper construct does not make the *nomen regens* definite arose through the perhaps secondary determination of the genitive.

[18] This phrase, however, may also be interpreted as expressing possession: 'made change: he has an apparel'. In Gen. 19:12 an indeterminate kinship term alternates with two determinate ones: חָתָן וּבָנֶיךָ וּבְנֹתֶיךָ "son-in-law", "your" sons and "your" daughters'. Interesting is 2 Sam 15:30 וְרֹאשׁ לוֹ חָפוּי 'and he had his head covered', rather than וְרֹאשׁוֹ חָפוּי.

[19] For further examples, see Marçais, *Djidjelli*, p. 421.

Note again that the (secondary) possessive pronoun does not determine בֵּן, which serves as an apposition to the indefinite כֶּבֶשׂ. Compare classical Arabic سارا لَيْلَتَهُما وَيَوْمَهُما 'they went day and night'; أَنَّ اللّهَ قَدْ فَرَضَ عَلَيْهِمْ خَمْسَ صَلَوات في يَوْمِهِمْ ولَيْلَتِهِمْ 'that God has prescribed them five prayers every day and night';[20] and Akkadian *ina ḫarpīšu* 'in summer'.[21]

3. Ramifications of the concept 'to possess': El-Amarna 20:8–9 *ana aššatīšu ana bēlti Miṣri ana leqê* 'in order to take for him a wife to become the lady of Egypt', the underlying structure being 'to make him: he has a wife'. Similarly 27:17–18 *undu aššatī ša ērišu aḫūiā inandunmāme* 'as soon as my brother gives a wife for me whom I want', the underlying structure being 'makes me: I have a wife'. In other cases the *ša* phrase precedes *aššatu* with a pronominal suffix referring back to it:[22] 20:16 *ša aḫīia aššassu ša māt Miṣri bēlassu anandin*, literally "the wife of my brother, the lady of Egypt I shall give', that is 'I shall send a wife for my brother to become the lady of Egypt', the underlying structure being 'I shall make: my brother has a wife, Egypt a lady'. Similarly 29:28 *ša aḫīia ša arammuš aššassu mārtī attannaššu* 'to my brother whom I love I have given my daughter as wife', the underlying structure being 'I have made: my brother has my daughter as wife'; and so also 21:13–14. In the examples adduced from El-Amarna 'wife' exhibits a redundant pronominal suffix, as in וְדָבַק בְּאִשְׁתּוֹ, cited by Bravmann, and in *UT Krt 12–13 aṯt.ṣdqh.lpq mtrḫt.yšrh* 'he could not find "his" rightful wife, "his" proper spouse', being the surface structure of 'he could not get: he has a lawful wife ...'. So also Jud. 21:21 וַחֲטַפְתֶּם לָכֶם אִישׁ אִשְׁתּוֹ 'and catch every man "his" wife'; 21:22 לֹא לָקַחְנוּ אִישׁ אִשְׁתּוֹ 'we have not taken each man "his" wife', the underlying structure being 'to make (by catching, taking): you/we have wives'.

One would also like to mention here the Hebrew phrase בָּנָה בֵיתוֹ 'he built his house' (for example 1 Kgs. 3:1; 7:1; 9:15; Jer. 22:13; Prov. 9:1; 14:1), although בֵּיתוֹ may also be analyzed as an object of result; the underlying structure would then be 'he made through building: he had a house'.[23] Even less certain is whether נָטַע/תָּקַע אָהֳלוֹ 'he pitched "his" tent' has to be interpreted as being the surface structure of 'he made by pitching: he had a tent', since 'his tent' may be analyzed as an ordinary object (not necessarily an object of result): he has a

[20] See H. Reckendorf, *Die syntaktischen Verhältnisse des Arabischen*, Leiden 1895–98, p. 391.

[21] For this and other examples in Akkadian, see B. Landsberger, *JNES* 8 (1949), p. 288. Landsberger, however, considers them determinate by situation because — in contradistinction to Hebrew and especially Arabic — the pronominal suffix does not refer to the subject.

[22] Cf. von Soden, *Grundriss*, p. 193, j-l.

[23] Cf. Baghdadi Judeo-Arabic *qayᵉbni ḥōšū* 'he built "his" house' (cited above from Bravmann), which, pace Bravmann, must therefore be analyzed as expressing possession rather than exhibiting the "pregnant" use of possessive pronouns.

tent, which he pitches wherever he camps. On the other hand, indefinite אֹהֶל does occur in such phrases: Jer. 6:3 אֵלֶיהָ יָבֹאוּ רֹעִים וְעֶדְרֵיהֶם תָּקְעוּ עָלֶיהָ אֹהָלִים סָבִיב 'shepherds with their flocks will come unto her, they will pitch tents against her round about'. Compare further Ps. 104:21 וּלְבַקֵּשׁ מֵאֵל אָכְלָם 'to ask "their" food from God' (='to ask: they have food'); 104:27 לָתֵת אָכְלָם בְּעִתּוֹ 'to give food in due time',[24] and perhaps also 105:11 = 1 Chr. 16:18 לְךָ אֶתֵּן (אֶת) אֶרֶץ כְּנָעַן חֶבֶל נַחֲלַתְכֶם 'unto you shall I give the land of Canaan, "your" lot of inheritance'.

In the examples here adduced the pronominal suffix may be interpreted as "dative": "to take/give him a wife', 'to build himself a house', 'to pitch himself a tent', 'to give him food, inheritance', 'to ask food for himself'. It stands to reason that if in Biblical Hebrew datival pronominal suffixes in fact exist, they arose, partly at least, through the decisive influence of intrinsic nouns with pronominal suffixes in ramifications of the concept 'to possess'. At any rate, all the examples adduced by C. Brockelmann,[25] exhibit, as Brockelmann realized, the concept 'to possess', the possessed being, as I would like to add, an intrinsic noun:[26] Num. 12:6 אִם יִהְיֶה נְבִיאֲכֶם "if you have a prophet'; Jud. 4:9 לֹא תִהְיֶה תִּפְאַרְתְּךָ עַל הַדֶּרֶךְ 'you will not attain honor on your way'; Job 6:10 וּתְהִי עוֹד נֶחָמָתִי "I shall yet have comfort'. Brockelmann adds as a ramification of this construction Exod. 2:9 אֶתֵּן אֶת שְׂכָרֵךְ 'I shall give you reward' (= 'I shall make: you have reward'). The same applies to two Ugaritic passages, cited by S. E. Loewenstamm,[27] *UT* 67:I:20–21 *šb*^{c} *ydty.bṣ*^{c} 'I have seven portions of a bowl'; 2Aqht:I:26–27 *wykn.bnh bbt.šrš.bqrb hklh* 'and he will have a son in (his) house, a scion in the midst of his palace'. Loewenstamm rightly remarks that Ps. 115:7 יְדֵיהֶם ... רַגְלֵיהֶם 'they have hands ... they have feet, cited by Brockelmann[28] as one-term clauses, should not be separated from what Loewenstamm terms "datival usage' and what we prefer to call 'expressing the concept of possession with intrinsic nouns', treated by Brockelmann in the passage cited.[29] I am inclined to interpret similarly the classical Arabic phrase[30]

24 Cf Sefîre I B 38 (Old Aramaic) הן לתהב לחמי 'if you do not give "my" provisions'.

25 *Grundriss der vergleichenden Grammatik der semitischen Sprachen*, Berlin 1908–13, 2:263, §182b.

26 Yet Exod. 3:21, cited by Brockelmann, חֵן הָעָם 'favor with the people' is a *genitivus objectivus*, חנן being a transitive verb.

27 *Leshonenu* 38 (1973–74), pp. 149–50.

28 *Grundriss*, 2:40, §21g. The other two examples, Eccl. 5:14 and Gen. 22:24, adduced by Brockelmann as denoting possession, exhibit intrinsic nouns as well. It is, however, very dubious whether they can in fact be interpreted as denoting possession (Brockelmann himself contents himself by adding them as "perheps" pertinent).

29 Loc. cit.

30 أ. صالحاني، رَنّات المَثالث وَالمَثاني فِي رِوايات الأغاني، بيروت ١٩٣٢, I, p. 18, 5f.b. (=p. 19, 8f.b.).

وَأَخَذَتِ الأَرْضُ زِينَتَها, literally and the soil took its ornament', that is, 'and the soil adorned itself', its deep structure being 'and the soil made: it had ornament'.

I have endeavored to cite additional examples besides those adduced by Bravmann for redundant pronominal suffixes, both in what he terms "pregnant" usage and in those usages expressing the concept "to possess". We have seen that in all examples, in those quoted by Bravmann and in those added, the nouns governing the possessive pronoun were intrinsic substantives which, being firmly anchored in the context and/or tending toward concreteness, very often govern pronominal suffixes, even when the latter seem redundant. I had hoped that I would have been given the opportunity to discuss this additional view with Dr. Bravmann personally. It happened, however, that these lines are published in the volume dedicated to his memory. יְהֵא זִכְרוֹ בָּרוּךְ.

Studies in Hebrew Verb Formation

A. *The Hebrew Cohortative and its Semitic Correspondences*

1. In the first part of this paper I shall endeavor to examine the possible Semitic correspondences to the Hebrew cohortative, formed by an *-â* (ָה) suffix attached to *yqtl*. It goes without saying that every investigation of this kind has to be based on W. L. Moran's masterly paper dealing with Early Canaanite *yqtla*.[1] At first I shall treat the main usages of the Hebrew cohortative and those secondary uses that may further the examination of its Semitic correspondences, and thereafter the various Semitic languages.

2. *Hebrew*:

For all practical purposes, the Hebrew cohortative is limited to the first person.[2] Its main usages are:

2.1. "Direct"[3] volitive, denoting wish, request, demand, etc., as *ʾăḵappərâ*, "I will appease" (Gen. 32:21).

2.2. "Indirect"[3] volitive, due to a sort of *consecutio temporum* (or, more exactly, sequence of moods), after a preceding direct volitive, as after an imperative *hāḇîʾâ lî waʾōḵēlâ*, "bring me and I will/that I may eat" (Gen. 27:4).[4]

2.3. Because of (real or putative) parallel occurrences in other Semitic languages, it will be expedient to examine two additional usages:

2.3.1. After consecutive *waw*, i. e., referring to the past, the cohor-

[1] W. L. Moran, "Early Canaanite *yaqtula*," *Orientalia* N.S. 29 (1960), pp. 1–19 (henceforward: Moran).

[2] For some unimportant exceptions see, e. g., S. R. Driver, *A Treatise on the Use of the Tenses in Hebrew* . . .[3] (Oxford, 1892), p. 51, n. 1.

[3] For the terms "direct/indirect" see P. Joüon, *Grammaire de l'hébreu biblique*[2] (Rome, 1947), pp. 307 ff., 314 ff.

[4] Whether or not the "indirect" cohortative represents a main clause (as I would prefer) or a subordinate one, is outside the scope of this paper; see, e. g., Driver (n. 2), pp. 64 ff., E. Kuhr, *Die Ausdrucksmittel der konjunktionslosen Hypotaxe in der ältesten hebräischen Prosa* (Leipzig, 1929), pp. 46 ff.; H. M. Orlinsky, *Jew. Quart. Rev.*, N.S. 31 f. (1940–42), *passim*.

tative is mainly restricted to the late portions of the Bible.[5] Accordingly, putative or real parallel usages in another Semitic language cannot be supported by the Hebrew.

2.5.2. In some cases, the cohortative is attested in conditional clauses.[6] One is inclined to distinguish between its occurrence in (the protasis and/or apodosis of) asyndetic conditional clauses and that in *ʾim* clauses. The former, which is not infrequent, has to be interpreted as a subclass of two successive volitives (§ 2.2), as a rule connected by *wə*, between which, at least according to our linguistic feeling,[7] a certain adverbial relation obtains, be it final or conditional.[8] But we are here interested in the occurrence of the cohortative in *ʾim* clauses. This seems to be very rare; I have noted only two cases, in both of which special conditions prevail. [8] *ʾim ʾessaq šâmayim šâm ʾâttâ wəʾaṣṣîʿâ šəʾôl hinnekkâ.* [9] *ʾeššâ ḵanfê šâḥar ʾeškənâ bəʾaḥărît yâm.* [10] *gam šâm yâdəḵâ tanḥênî* . . . "if I ascend up into heaven, you are there; if I go down to hell, behold, you are (there); if I lift the wings of the morning (?) and dwell in the uttermost parts of the sea, even there will your hand take hold of me" (Ps. 139:8–10); the cohortative occurs twice in asyndetic protasis, which, to be sure, is paralleled by a preceding *ʾim* clause. ([4] *ʾădabbêrâ* . . . *ʾaḥbîrâ* . . . *wəʾânîʿâ* . . .) *ʾim ʾădabbərâ lô yêḥâśeḵ kəʾêḇî wəʾaḥdəlâ ma-mminnî yahălok* "(Let me speak . . . let me heap up (?) . . . and let me shake . . .) Though I speak, my grief is not calmed, and (though) I cease, what. . . ." (Job 16:[4–]6); a cohortative following *ʾim* is in fact attested, it may, however, be due to attraction to preceding "direct" cohortatives and also influenced by the following asyndetic conditional clause, containing a cohortative. As to the occurrence of the cohortative in the apodosis of *ʾim* clauses (as in Gen. 43:4), it reflects ordinary direct cohortative, by no means influenced by the preceding *ʾim* clause. Accordingly, one will, at the most, consider cohortative in syndetic conditional clauses as a quite marginal phenomenon in biblical Hebrew and refrain from using it as support for alleged parallel features in related dialects.

[5] See G. Bergsträsser, *Hebräische Grammatik II* (Leipzig, 1929), p. 23. It is more frequent in IQIsa than in the masoretic text; see E. Y. Kutscher, *The Language and the Linguistic Background of the Isaiah Scroll* (in Hebrew), (Jerusalem, 1959), p. 251; Ḥ. Yalon, *Studies in the Dead Sea Scrolls* (in Hebrew), (Jerusalem, 1967), pp. 22 f.

[6] See, e. g., E. Kautzsch–A. E. Cowley, *Gesenius' Hebrew Grammar*[2] (Oxford, 1910), p. 320, §108e; Driver (n. 2), pp. 174 ff.

[7] It is again outside the scope of this paper to broach the subject of whether or not these constructions exhibit genuine conditional clauses.

[8] For the close affinity of these senses, cf. Kuhr (n. 4), pp. 55 ff., who also quotes Bergsträsser (n. 5), §10k[e] (pp. 49–50).

3. *Early Canaanite*:

3.1. As to the origin of the Hebrew cohortative, in the main, two (pp. 262–23) theories have been advanced, both connecting it with forms of classical Arabic. According to some,[9] it corresponds to the Arabic energic *yqtlan*,[10] whereas others associated it (as to its form, at least) with the Arabic subjunctive *yqtla*.[11] Now, since the publication of Moran's paper (§1), the possibility of deriving the Hebrew cohortative from the energic is out of the question. Moran has demonstrated the existence and range of usage of *yqtla* in Early Canaanite, corresponding to quite a surprising degree to that of the Hebrew cohortative, on the one hand,[12] and the separate occurrence of the energic in that language,[13] on the other. Accordingly, if any Arabic form does correspond to the Hebrew cohortative, only the subjunctive is in question.[14]

3.2. In his paper, Moran has analyzed sixty-six Amarna letters (from the early 14th century B. C.) from Byblos. Of the 74 occurrences of *yqtla* in these letters, 36 exhibited a direct volitive (see §2.1) and 13 an indirect one (see §2.2), i. e. almost two thirds of the examples correspond exactly to the main usages of the Hebrew cohortative (to be sure, with one notable exception: the Hebrew cohortative is limited to the first person, whereas Early Canaanite *yqtla* is spread over the whole paradigm).

One could explain most of these occurrences as ventive,[15] all the more since in nine cases they terminate in *–am* (although final *–m* is admittedly often otiose in these letters).[16] This interpretation, how-

[9] See, e. g., C. Brockelmann, *Grundriss* . . . I, 1908, p. 557; Bergsträsser (n. 5), p. 24.

[10] This would imply that the Hebrew cohortative is a pausal form that has superseded the context form. The pausal shift *–an*>*–â* (*yqtlan*>*yqtlâ*) is, to be sure, attested only in Arabic; yet according to many scholars the feminine ending *–â*, spelled *–h*, is due to a similar pausal shift peculiar to Arabic: *–at*>*–ah*>*â* (though the evidence of the Mesha inscription, spelling **banâ* "he built" with final *h*, while preserving *–at*, does not favor this interpretation, it does not actually refute it; see for particulars and further literature F. M. Cross–D. N. Freedman, *Early Hebrew Orthography* . . . (New Haven, 1952), p. 6).

[11] See, e. g., H. Bauer–P. Leander, *Historische Grammatik der hebräischen Sprache* . . . (Halle, 1922), pp. 273, 301, 306 f.; Joüon (n. 3), p. 315, n. 1.

[12] See infra, §3.2.

[13] See Moran, p. 9, n. 1.

[14] See infra, §6. I. J. Gelb, Sequential Reconstruction of Proto-Akkadian, *Assyriological Studies 18* (Chicago, 1969), p. 101, however, posits that Hebrew *yqtla* is the result of conflation of *–an* of the energic and *–a* of what he calls subjunctive. He does not, however, take into account the separate occurrence of the energic in Early Canaanite.

[15] See Moran, p. 7.

[16] See Moran, p. 2, n. 1.

ever, is precluded by a twofold opposition permeating these letters:[17] in contradistinction to volitive *yqtla*, *yqtlu* states a simple fact;[18] and the indirect volitive (denoting purpose or intended result in a paratactic sentence structure) invariably[18a] continues a direct volitive, whereas such a paratactic purpose clause following a verb stating a fact exhibits *yqtlu*. This closely coherent pattern of the usage of *yqtla*, comprising almost two thirds of all its occurrences in these letters, cannot be explained as reflecting a ventive, but has to be accounted for as exhibiting the native speech of the scribes, which, in this special point, almost exactly corresponded to Hebrew usage.

3.3. One wonders, however, how it came about that the scribes of these highly official letters composed in Akkadian transferred the speech pattern of their native Canaanite language almost exactly into their writings. Moran[19] calls these *yqtla* forms ventives which have been equated with Canaanite *yqtla*. Yet one would have expected occasional deviations from the proper Akkadian use of the ventive in the direction of the Canaanite volitive rather than a well-knit structure of Canaanite usage. These El-Amarna letters from Byblos exhibit the contact between Akkadian, the language of prestige, and the "inferior" Canaanite. Whenever speakers of such an inferior tongue come in contact with a superior one, they try to imitate the language of prestige. Since, however, their knowledge of the latter is insufficient, they fall back into their native idiom. Thus it happens that forms of the inferior language alternate with those of the superior one.[20] Only in very vulgar texts do the forms of the inferior language prevail, since these texts are written, as a rule, in a vulgar tongue with only some admixture of the language of prestige. In this case, and in this

[17] See Moran, pp. 7 ff.

[18] See Moran, p. 8. I have noted only one exception of *yqtlu* used to mark prohibition: *lâ yaqulu šarru bêlia* "the king, my lord, shall not be negligent!" (EA 140:5, as against *lâ taqûl* [EA 139:5], exhibiting jussive). *[ilu]amana ilu ša šarri bêlika tidinu bašta* "Amon, the God of the king, your lord, shall give strength" (EA 71:4 f.; 86:3–5) *tidinu* has, so it seems, to be interpreted as plural of the jussive rather than singular of the indicative, the subject *[ilu]amana* standing also for *[ilu]bêlit ša [ālu]gubla* "Baʿalat of Byblos"; cf. the full expression *[ilu]amana u [ilu]bêlit ša [ālu]gubla tidinu baštaka* (EA 87:5–7; 95:3–5).

[18a] Yet, see Moran, p. 10, n. 2 for exceptions.

[19] P. 2.

[20] In such cases, one invariably meets with a third class of phenomena, viz., pseudocorrect, including hypercorrect, features. They are not lacking in these letters either, see, e. g., pseudocorrect *qatlâti* alongside Akkadian *qatlâku* and Canaanite *qatalti*; see F. M. Th. Böhl, *Die Sprache der Amarnabriefe* . . . (Leipzig, 1909), pp. 45 ff. — For a general theory of pseudocorrect features and their occurrence in Semitic languages see J. Blau, *On Pseudo-Corrections in Some Semitic Languages* (Jerusalem, 1970). This, however, is largely outside the scope of this paper.

case only, it is possible to realize the patterns of usage of the inferior language. The Amarna letters discussed here, however, can by no means be considered such very vulgar texts. Since they exhibit highly official correspondence, one would have expected, in the worst case, Akkadian intermingled with Canaanite elements, rather than prevalence of closely coherent patterns of Canaanite features. One would have anticipated that these texts, as a rule, exhibit proper Akkadian usage of the ventive, deviating only occasionally with the application of Canaanite *yqtla*. How did it happen that the Canaanite volitive *yqtla* prevailed over the Akkadian ventive *yqtla(m)*, and that the Canaanite indicative *yqtlu* superseded the Akkadian *yqtlu*, thus almost accurately reflecting the Canaanite verbal structure in these official Akkadian texts?

The explanation of this baffling situation seems to be that these letters reflect the contact between Akkadian and Canaanite only indirectly. Through this contact, presumably, a sort of pidgin Akkadian arose, containing Canaanite elements, and it became the recognized "chancellory language."[21] Into this language various Canaanite forms had penetrated, like the volitive *yqtla*, because of its similarity to the Akkadian ventive, and the indicative *yqtlu*, because of its formal closeness to the Akkadian subjunctive. Having become a part of the chancellory language, they were no more regarded as representatives of the inferior language, which was, as far as possible, to be avoided, but rather as an accepted feature of that chancellory mixed tongue. Since, however, the Canaanite forms were backed by the mother tongue of these scribes, whereas the Akkadian features were foreign phenomena, the former became more frequent at the expense of the latter. So it came about that *yqtl* forms with *–a(m)/–u* ending, as a rule, represent Canaanite volitive/indicative rather than Akkadian ventive/subjunctive, thus enabling Moran to reconstruct the Early Canaanite verbal pattern. This situation, however, did not arise through superimposition of Canaanite features on Akkadian forms through direct contact of these languages. This contact, at first, gave rise to the emergence of an accepted chancellory language, which originally, so we presume, contained only a limited number of Canaanite features. After these features had thus become a part of the accepted chancellory language, they eventually prevailed, as they were backed by the Canaanite mother tongue.[21a]

[21] P. Artzi arrived at similar results (if I am interpreting him correctly) when analyzing the glosses in the El-Amarna tablets; see his paper in *Bar-Ilan, Annual of Bar-Ilan University* . . . I (Ramat-Gan–Jerusalem, 1963), p. 50 (English summary, p. xvii).

[21a] It is even possible that at the time of the composition of the Amarna letters

3.4. This quite complicated pattern of the emergence of the chancellory language obliges us to assume a more sceptical attitude towards the different occurrences of *yqtla* than does Moran. Though one will wholeheartedly accept Moran's brilliant analysis of *yqtla* as direct/indirect volitive, both because of its almost complete correspondence with the Hebrew cohortative and its twofold opposition to *yqtlu*,[22] one will maintain a much more reserved attitude towards the other classes of *yqtla* than does Moran:[23] they lack parallels in other Semitic languages, notwithstanding Moran's attempt to demonstrate such parallels; they do not exhibit a system of opposition as does volitive *yqtla*; and they are much less frequent. Accordingly, one will explain them as being due to (correct or misunderstood) Akkadian usage and/or as reflecting stock expressions[24] of the chancellory language, which arose out of false equations, etc., of Akkadian and Canaanite features that have become productive.[25] In the following we shall deal with the additional classes adduced by Moran:

(p. 272) short vocalic verbal suffixes had already disappeared (cf. J. Blau, in *In Memoriam P. Kahle* (Berlin, 1968), p. 35, n. 31), being preserved as an archaism only in the "scribal language." This would, of course, make it even more difficult to evaluate Amarna letters syntactically.

[22] Theoretically, one may even claim that volitive *yqtla* does not exhibit living usage either in all its occurrences. One could imagine that in the Early Canaanite of Byblos as well as in Hebrew *yqtla* was limited to the first person, and its occurrence in the other persons in the Amarna letters of Byblos was due to its misunderstood equation with the Akkadian ventive, which had become productive in the chancellory language. Yet one will readily admit that it is simpler to assume a difference in usage between Hebrew and Early Canaanite. The original usage might have been in the first person, as in Hebrew, but was afterwards extended to the other persons; or it might have been used in the whole paradigm, to be limited later in Hebrew to the first person. If *yqtla* does occur in Old Akkadian and there also in other persons (see §5), the second assumption is more likely; see also Bauer–Leander (n. 11), p. 301, Anm. 3. For the restriction of the volitive to the first person in Greek see J. Wackernagel, *Vorlesungen über Syntax* I² (Basel, 1926), p. 233. Moreover, the occurrence of *–â* in the Hebrew imperative (second person!) also hints at this ending not being restricted to the first person. One is prima facie inclined to consider the imperative with *–â* a secondary formation through the influence of the cohortative (see H. Birkeland, *Akzent und Vokalismus*, Oslo, 1940, p. 127), and this influence could prevail much more easily if the imperfect *–â* was not restricted to the first person.

[23] Moran expresses doubts (p. 13), yet he is inclined to consider most cases representing living usage.

[24] As taken into account by Moran himself (p. 17), but on a rather restricted level.

[25] For the possibility of pseudocorrect and of other features becoming productive, cf., e. g., J. Blau, *A Grammar of Christian Arabic . . .*, p. 150, §47.

3.4.1. Nothing certain can be said about the alleged occurrence of *yqtla*, asyndetically dependent on a verb of fear (Moran, p. 14, §C). Moran, to be sure, is correct in claiming that this usage is quite consistent with the volitive character of *yqtla*. Only one example of this usage is attested, however, and it is based, as ill fortune would have it, on restoration. Moreover, pace Moran, nothing can be inferred from Arabic, since the Arabic subjunctive in general, and after verbs of fear in particular, is restricted to syndetic clauses.[26]

3.4.2. I am not inclined to regard the occurrence of *yqtla* in conditional clauses (Moran, p. 14, §D) as reflecting living usage either. Moran quotes four occurrences in the protasis, two of them after *inûma*, one after *u* following a question (in this case, however, reading and interpretation are uncertain), and one asyndetic following its apodosis. From the nine cases of *yqtla* in the apodosis, six follow a syndetic protasis (four times *šumma*, twice *inûma*), in one case (i) the protasis is wanting altogether and the interpretation is dubious, and in the remaining two cases (g, h) the alleged apodosis is connected by *u* to a preceding imperative/prohibition; accordingly, one will prefer to interpret them as indirect volitives.[27] Thus, in the main, *yqtla* is attested in syndetic conditional clauses (eight out of nine more or less certain cases). Since, pace Moran, pp. 15 f., nothing parallel in other Semitic languages is to be found,[28] and it is somewhat difficult to con-

[26] Cf. §6.1. For an additional case after a verb of fear preceding a pronominal suffix, see Moran, p. 18, §3.

[27] As to Hebrew, see §2.3.2; as to Arabic, §6.2.2, n. 46.

[28] As to Hebrew, cf. §2.3.2. As to Arabic, one should refrain from comparing the frequent occurrence of the Arabic jussive in both the protasis and the apodosis of conditional clauses (pace Moran, p. 15, and, e. g., M. M. Bravmann, *Studies in Arabic and General Syntax* (Le Caire, 1953), p. 131, §103). The so-called jussive (better apocopate) in many Semitic languages denotes not only jussive, but refers to the "past" as well (cf. Akkadian *iprus*, Hebrew *wayyqtl*, Arabic *lam yqtl*). Accordingly, I am inclined to interpret conditional "jussive," alternating with the "perfect" *qtl(a)*, as referring to the past in a way similar to *qtl(a)* (otherwise H. Fleisch [n. 43], p. 66). On the contrary, Hebrew jussive in asyndetic (!) conditional clauses reflects its volitive sense (cf. supra, n. 8), whereas it seems that the rather few examples of Hebrew jussive in syndetic conditional clauses exhibit exceptions, as attested in other cases as well; see Driver (n. 2), pp. 212 ff., Appendix II. Nor does Arabic subjunctive occur in conditional clauses. Moran (p. 15, nn. 4 and 5) refers to W. Wright–W. Robertson Smith–M. J. de Goeje, *A Grammar of the Arabic Language* II³ (Cambridge, 1898), pp. 36 ff., and mentions the restriction that the subjunctive appears only in the second member of a compound protasis/apodosis, the first member containing a jussive. This opinion of his is based on Wright, p. 40c; Wright, however, was wrong in his parsing, since *fa/wa* continuing the jussive (Moran omitted this necessary condition that the subjunctive is invariably introduced by *fa/wa*) intro-

nect the conditional with the volitive usage, one will refrain from regarding conditional *yqtla* as a living feature and rather interpret the partial consistency of its usage[29] as reflecting stock expressions occurring in the chancellory language.

3.4.3. Moran himself (p. 17) is inclined to interpret three occurrences of *yqtla* referring to the past (Moran, p. 16, §E)[30] and five in clauses introduced by *inûma* "as to (the fact)" (Moran, p. 16, §F) as not reflecting Canaanite usage and explains the cases after *inûma* as inherited stock expressions. He hesitates, however, as to three other occurrences which refer to the past and tries to explain them as expressing actual result after a clause in the first person. Yet on the assumption of an artificial chancellory language, which originated both from the Akkadian language of prestige and the Canaanite vernacular, and in which various (even not living) features might have become productive, one will be reluctant to attribute these features to living Canaanite.

3.4.4. The same applies to some *yqtla* forms preceding pronominal suffixes, in which Moran (p. 19, note 1) is inclined to assume potential meaning.

3.5. To sum up, we wholeheartedly accept Moran's main thesis that in the Early Canaanite of Byblos the principal usages of *yqtla* closely corresponded to that of the Biblical cohortative. In both the main use was that of direct and indirect volitive, the only important distinction being that in Hebrew its usage was restricted to the first person, whereas in Byblian it permeated the whole paradigm. We differ, however, from Moran in the estimate of the general character of the language of these Amarna letters. In our opinion they were written in an artificial chancellory language which originally arose by the contact of the Akkadian language of prestige with the Canaanite mother tongue, and in which later various, even artificial, features became productive. Only such an assumption explains how it happened that the opposition between the Canaanite indicative *yqtlu* and the volitive *yqtla* has been preserved in these texts to a high degree. Since these features, because of their formal similarity to Akkadian sub-

---

duces a hypotactic, rather than a paratactic, construction, expressing a conditioned result (cf. H. Reckendorf, *Arabische Syntax* (Heidelberg, 1921), p. 461, line 2, and also infra §6.2.2, n. 46). — For an additional case of *yqtla* occurring after *šumma* and preceding a pronominal suffix see Moran, p. 18, §4, where *yqtla* occurring in two parallel *šumma* clauses is quoted.

[29] See Moran, pp. 15 f.

[30] The Hebrew cohortative form referring to the past is late and cannot, therefore, be adduced as support for such a usage; see supra §2.3.1.

junctive/ventive, had penetrated the original chancellory language, they had become an accepted feature of that chancellory mixed tongue, and, ultimately, being backed by the mother tongue of the scribes, in many a case they superseded the Akkadian rival forms. Against this very complex background of interchanging Akkadian, Canaanite and artificial forms that had become productive one will hesitate to admit that other occurrences of *yqtla* represent Canaanite usage as well.

4. *Ugaritic*:

Nothing certain can be elicited from the unvocalized Ugaritic script, in which even *matres lectionis* are almost totally lacking. Alleged *yqtla* can only be discerned in *verba tertiae alef*,[31] yet not only do these putative examples lack any special sense, since some denote volition and others fact, but their very existence depends on the interpretation of the alef signs, a well-known moot question in Ugaritic grammar.[32] Accordingly, pending new material, one will have to forgo any attempt to elucidate this subject. Nothing can, for the time being at least, be inferred from the spelling of *y* in *verba III y* either; cf. the partly conflicting views as to imperative terminating in *y* Gordon, UT §§9.20; 13.53 and Blau-Loewenstamm [n. 32], p. 27.

5. *Akkadian*:

In Akkadian (with the exception of Old-Akkadian, v. infra), be it for phonetic[33] or other reasons, no vestiges of *yqtla* occur.[34]

It is in Old Akkadian, in which vestiges of final *-a* are attested,[35] that one could expect traces of *yqtla*. I. J. Gelb, *Materials for the Assyrian Dictionary* II^2 (Chicago, 1961), pp. 170 f. has found *iprusa* in a group of Sargonic texts. Though one will reject his identification

[31] Cf. C. H. Gordon, *UT*, p. 72.

[32] Cf. most recently D. Marcus, *Journal of the Ancient Near Eastern Society* . . . 1 (1968), pp. 50 ff., where additional literature is quoted, J. Blau–S. E. Loewenstamm, *Ugarit-Forschungen* 2 (1970), pp. 19 ff. — Gordon, *UT*, p. 72, n. 1, does not accept Herdner's view that *yqra* might be a jussive with the final alef sign reflecting the preceding vowel. In his opinion this fails to reckon with the shift *a*>*e*. Yet, without entering into details, even if one postulates this shift (cf. against it Blau–Loewenstamm, ibid., p. 23), one may assume that it was eliminated in the jussive through the analogy of the jussive forms with vocalic suffix and the indicative. — For further details on Ugaritic *yqtla*, cf. G. Garbini, *Il Semitico di nord-ovest* (Napoli, * 1960), p. 144, n. 3.

[33] See Chr. Sarauw, *Über Akzent und Silbenbildung* . . . (København, 1939), p. 123.

[34] The ventive *iprusa* is, of course, only a late development of *iprusam*.

[35] See I. J. Gelb, *Materials for the Assyrian Dictionary*, II^2 (Chicago, 1961), pp. 146 ff.

of *iprusa* with Arabic *yqtla*,[36] which has a quite different function (v. §6.1), one will also hesitate to accept Kienast's[37] proposal to interpret this *iprusa* as mimationless ventive, since ventive without mimation would not be something exceptional even in this early period. For other arguments in favor of Old Akkadian *yqtla*, see Gelb.[37a] *Prima facie*, one is inclined to agree with Th. Jacobsen's analysis[38] that the *–a* suffix presents the subject as "willing," "approachable," and this would constitute a bridge to the volitive in West Semitic. Moreover, Jacobsen has, at least in Old Babylonian, also found one case of *–a* ending formally and by translation clearly differentiated from the ventive.[39] Accordingly, pending further discoveries, one is inclined to postulate Proto-Semitic *yqtla*, which perhaps presented the subject as "willing," to develop later, in Canaanite at least, into a volitive.

6. *Arabic*:

6.1. The usage of Arabic *yqtla* is different. It is restricted to subordinate clauses only,[40] more exactly to subordinate clauses expressing desire, demand, purpose, etc. The problem is, of course, to establish the connection between the volitive use of Hebrew and Canaanite and the Arabic subjunctive.

6.2. It seems quite unlikely that, despite the formal identity and the affinity of usage, there is no historic relationship between these two types of usage. We shall, therefore, consider two possibilities only: has the volitive developed from the subjunctive or the subjunctive from the volitive?

6.2.1. It seems somewhat unlikely that the volitive developed from the subjunctive.[41] To be sure, one will not attach too much weight to the cases of the subjunctive limited to comparatively late Arabic and conclude that the subjunctive is late; yet if the predecessor of the volitive does occur in Akkadian (§5), one will be inclined to regard

[36] See B. Kienast, *Orientalia* 29 (1960), pp. 152–3, n. 2.

[37] Ibid.

[37a] Supra (n. 14), pp. 102 ff. But his view that Old Akkadian *iprusa* was used in subordinate clauses in accordance with the usage of the Akkadian subjunctive carries no conviction.

[38] *JNES* 19 (1960), p. 110 and n. 12. Fleisch (n. 43), p. 67, had no knowledge of Jacobsen's article and arrived at different results.

[39] Jacobsen, ibid., according to whom *iprusa* in Old Babylonian is characteristically used before a ventive, etc., element.

[40] *lan* "not" referring to the future and governing *yqtla* is due to later development: <*lâ ʾan*.

[41] So, e. g., S. Moscati, . . . *Comparative Grammar* . . . (Wiesbaden, 1964), p. 135 (§16.32); Joüon (n. 3), p. 315, n. 1; Gelb (n. 14), p. 100.

the volitive function of *yqtla* as the original one. Moreover, had the volitive developed from the subjunctive, one would have expected the volition to be expressed by the (new) voluntative preceded by the original conjunction (which now should have become a pleonastic mark of volition).[42]

6.2.2. Accordingly, it stands to reason, as it has been surmised several times,[43] that the volitive sense is the original one. Parallels for the development of the subjunctive from the volitive are known from other languages.[44] Moreover, even the ways of this development seem to be quite clear. When denoting demand, desire, etc., the use of *yqtla* as subjunctive developed from clauses in whose paratactic original form *yqtla* was used to express volition.[45] Clauses of purpose might also have originated from the indirect volitive.[46]

7. *Conclusion*:

If Jacobsen is right in his assumption that *yqtla* in Old Akkadian presents the subject as "willing," "approachable" (§5), it stands to reason that *yqtla* constitutes a part of the Proto-Semitic verbal system.

[42] Cf., e. g., in modern Arabic dialects the use of *ta* < *ḥattâ* ("until," "in order") as a "cohortative" particle (see, e. g., J. Blau, *Syntax . . . von Bîr-Zêt* (Walldorf-Hessen, 1960), pp. 235–6), or in French that of *que* ("qu'il vienne").

[43] See, e. g., H. Reckendorf, *Die syntaktischen Verhältnisse des Arabischen* (Leiden, 1895–1898), p. 60; most recently H. Fleisch in his stimulating paper '*yaqtula* cananéen et subjonctif arabe,' *Wissenschaftliche Zeitschrift der M. Luther Universität Halle-Wittenberg* 17 (1968), fasc. 2/3, pp. 65–76.

[44] See, e. g., F. Sommer, *Vergleichende Syntax der Schulsprachen* (Leipzig–Berlin, 1931), pp. 84, 85, note; M. Regula, *Grundlegung und Grundprobleme der Syntax* (Heidelberg, 1951), p. 142.

[45] See especially Fleisch (n. 43), p. 74: *ʾašartu ʾilayhi an lâ yafʿala*, originally *"I advised him: he shall not do it!", which eventually developed to "I advised him not to do it."

[46] The indirect volitive, Gen. 27:4 (see §2.2) corresponds to Arabic *ʾîtinî bihâ faʾâkula*; cf. Joüon (n. 3), p. 315, n. 1, who derives, however, the volitive from the subjunctive (see supra, n. 41). I know well that there is an important notional difference between Hebrew and Arabic (cf. also Kuhr [n. 4], pp. 46–7, n. 5): the latter does not necessarily follow a volitive/jussive/imperative, but may be preceded by any main clause the content of which is uncertain (like interrogation or condition); moreover, this *fayaqtula* denotes conditioned result, rather than purpose, etc. Nevertheless, pace Fleisch (n. 43), p. 67, one will not, because of the *synchronic* differences, deny the *historical* connections between these Hebrew and Arabic constructions. One will rather interpret the Arabic construction as an original indirect volitive, which developed into a purpose clause, to become ultimately a conditioned result. The last development must not surprise us since the main characteristic of Arabic syntax is fixed regulation of possibilities of usage and the exact delimitation of domains of signification of the syntactic means of expression (see G. Bergsträsser, *Einführung in die semitischen Sprachen* (München, 1928), p. 135). See also §8 *Excursus*.

In Canaanite it is used as (direct and indirect) volitive (§3), a usage easily to be derived from the "willing" of the subject, whereas the Hebrew adhortative has become limited to the first person (§§2; 3.4, n. 22). In Arabic this volitive has been restricted to subordinate clauses expressing desire, demand, purpose, etc. (§6.2.2).

If the assumption that *yqtla* is Proto-Semitic proves correct, it may influence our notion of the Proto-Semitic verbal system. As is well-known, it is a moot question whether or not the indicative *yqtlu* has to be accounted a Proto-Semitic feature. If in Proto-Semitic *yqtla* existed alongside *yqtl*, it would stand to reason that *yqtlu* too was a part of the Proto-Semitic verbal system. Since, because of its occurrence in Akkadian, Gᶜez (and Berber),[47] *iparras/yəqattəl* seems to have existed in Proto-Semitic as well, one is inclined to assume a Proto-Semitic verbal system in which *yqtlu* and *iparras/yəqattəl*[48] coexisted, presumably in a rather similar meaning. In most West-Semitic dialects *yqtlu* prevailed;[49] in Gᶜez, however, it was the latter that had been superseded.[50] In Akkadian as well, *iparras* got the upper hand and relegated *yqtlu* (i. e., *iprusu*) to its secondary functions, viz. to subordinate clauses.[51]

8. *Excursus*:

Fleisch,[52] *passim*, attaches great importance, for the reconstruction of the original usage of *yqtla*, to the occurrence of *yqtlu* in

[47] See most recently H. Polotsky, in *The World History of the Jewish People*, I 1, *At the Dawn of Civilization* ed. E. A. Speiser (Tel-Aviv, 1964), p. 111.

[48] So W. v. Soden, in *Akten des 24. internationalen Orientalisten-Kongresses* ... (Wiesbaden, 1959), p. 264. One will not concur with F. Rundgren's qualifications in his ... *Abriss der Aspektlehre* (Stockholm, 1961), p. 110 (where read p. 263, rather than p. 253), who demands comparison of systems, rather than of isolated features. The linguist, attempting to reconstruct a "proto-language," is obliged to trace isolated features occurring in the extant dialects of that language and to attribute them to it, if he has reason to assume that they were inherited, rather than that they arose independently. He will, of course, attempt to reconstruct the system as well; his success, however, will depend on the amount of information available. It is rather questionable whether preconceived notions on the development of systems is the correct way of reconstruction.

[49] Presumably, because *yəqattəl* was felt to belong to the D-verbal pattern.

[50] One must not interpret the jussive *yəkrī* in Gᶜez as representing ancient **yqtlu*, but rather ancient *yqtl* (<**yikriy*); cf. F. Praetorius, *Äthiopische Grammatik* (Karlsruhe–Leipzig, 1886), p. 47. Accordingly, one has to assume that *yqtlu* has disappeared from Gᶜez altogether.

[51] So J. Kuryłowicz, *L'apophonie en sémitique* (Wrocław–Warszawa–Kraków, 1961), p. 53, who considers, however, *iparras* a total innovation. For the fact that the indicative is renewed, the older form being preserved in subordinate clauses, cf., e. g., M. Cohen, *Le système verbal sémitique* ... (Paris, 1924), p. 38; Blau (n. 42), p. 100, n. 6.

[52] Supra, n. 43, passim; so already *MUSJ* 27 (1947 f.), pp. 42 f., 55 f.

syntactic environments in which classical Arabic uses *yqtla*. It is, however, difficult to concur with his views. First, he exaggerates the importance of this criterion, because he does not always rigorously distinguish between the form of subjunctive and the notion of purpose.[53] Even in classical Arabic not every purpose is expressed by the subjunctive; cf., e. g., circumstantial clauses indicating a future state.[54] This applies also to the use of *yqtlu* in asyndetic clauses of purpose (examples 11–16 out of a total of the 16 examples adduced by Fleisch of *yqtlu* instead of classical *yqtla*; pp. 69 f.). We have to conceive of the intrusion of the original volitive *yqtla* into subordinate clauses expressing purposefulness as a long development, one that did not comprise all occurrences of subordinate purposefulness. This happened to asyndetic clauses, at least according to the opinion of the school of Basra,[55] and also, it seems, after *kaymâ*[56] (Fleisch's examples nos. 5, 8, 9, pp. 68 f.). Accordingly, out of the 16 examples only seven remain.

Even more important is a second point. Fleisch (n. 43, p. 75) is of the opinion that the use of *yqtlu* instead of *yqtla* exhibits a more archaic stage than classical Arabic. Whereas in classical Arabic the originally volitive *yqtla* has developed into a subjunctive, *yqtlu* instead of *yqtla*, according to Fleisch, reflects a stage in which the volitive had not yet shifted to a subjunctive, but was abandoned before that shift had taken place. Therefore, the usage of *yqtlu* after *ʾan*, etc., exhibits an older stage in which no subjunctive existed. This interpretation of these scattered occurrences of *yqtlu*, rather than *yqtla*, however, is by no means the only possible explanation. C. Rabin,[57] who considers asyndetic object clauses a Western feature,[58] regards the use of *yqtlu* after *ʾan* in Western sources[59] not as a Western feature proper,

[53] Cf. Reckendorf (n. 43), p. 730; also Joüon (n. 3), p. 307, n. 1, p. 309, n. 2, who distinguishes between cohortative/jussive mood and cohortative/jussive form.

[54] See, e. g., Wright, etc. (n. 28), pp. 19 f.

[55] See A. Ibn al-Anbârî, *Die grammatischen Streitfragen* . . ., ed. G. Weil (Leiden, 1913), Arabic text, p. 233 (§77).

[56] Cf. the literature adduced by Fleisch himself (n. 43), p. 72; further Blau (n. 25), p. 263, n. 5. According to M. Ullmann, *Wörterbuch der klassischen arabischen Sprache*, I, Wiesbaden, 1970, s. v. *kaymā*, the indicative after *kaymā* exhibits *licentia poetica*. This, however, may reflect archaic usage.

[57] *Ancient West-Arabian* (London, 1951), pp. 186 f. (§13nn).

[58] Ibid., pp. 185 f. (§13kk).

[59] All seven relevant examples quoted by Fleisch are either of Western origin (5) or their author is unknown (2). On the other hand, Rabin's sources speak only of asyndetic object clauses, whereas *yqtlu* after *ʾan* in the examples adduced by Fleisch occurs twice in prepositional clauses. One will, however, regard the influence of asyndetic clauses in the case of *min qabli ʾan* (example no. 3) as possible, since asyndetic clauses after (*min*) *qabl* are well attested, see Blau (n. 25), p. 505, n. 61. On the other hand, *yqtlu* after *min ʾan* (example no. 7) does not fit Rabin's theory well,

but assumes that these Western authors, being accustomed to asyndetic clauses with *yqtlu*, used it in the unfamiliar ᵓ*an*-clause as well. Even if one does not agree with Rabin's view, one will not attempt to refute it (as Fleisch does)[59a] by claiming that *yutimmu* itself (in ᵓ*arâda yutimmu* "he wanted to complete") is unintelligible, since, because of the subjunctive *yqtla*, one would have expected *yutimma*. This claim is based on mixing up the form of the subjunctive with the notion of purpose, as if every such notion had to be marked by the subjunctive and the latter were not conditioned by certain syntactical environments.[60] Moreover, one could easily conceive that the verbal system of *yqtl–*, exhibiting the opposition "nonjussive" *yqtlu* : "jussive" *yqtl*, arose out of the system featuring the opposition indicative *yqtlu*: subjunctive *yqtla* : "jussive" *yqtl*. The elimination of *yqtla* in favor of *yqtlu* might have arisen through the influence of *yqtlu* preceded by ᵓ*an* in clauses not denoting purpose.[61] This explanation is corroborated by the fact that all the seven pertinent examples adduced by Fleisch contain ᵓ*an* rather than other conjunctions.[62] One therefore hesitates to connect the shift of volitive *yqtla* to subjunctive with the occurrence of *yqtlu* in syntactic environments which necessitate *yqtla* in classical Arabic.

---

since asyndetic *min*-clauses are attested only in late sources, see Blau (n. 25), p. 506, n. 63. One could claim that *yqtlu* spread from object clauses to prepositional clauses, but this assumption, however, would be rather artificial.

[59a] Supra, n. 43, p. 76, n. 10.

[60] I. e., the conjunctions ᵓ*an*, *li*, *kay*, *ḥattâ*, etc., or the negation *lan*.

[61] The so-called ᵓ*an* ᵓ*al-muxaffafa*. As a matter of fact, the Arab grammarians did see the connection of the occurrence of *yqtlu* after ᵓ*an* with ᵓ*an* ᵓ*al-muxaffafa* (so Fleisch himself [n. 43], pp. 71 f.), yet, of course, on the synchronic level only, since they had no historical perspective.

[62] We do not deal here with *kaymâ*-clauses, since with these the subjunctive is limited to some dialects of classical Arabic (see n. 56). As to *fa* governing *yqtlu* in conditioned results, where classical Arabic demands *yqtla* (see Nöldeke, *Zur Grammatik* . . ., p. 71; Fleisch [n. 43], p. 76, n. 5), it is, of course, due to the influence of the "connective" *fa*, which does not affect the following *yqtl–* and is much more frequent. One even wonders whether these few examples (as was stated, only seven of Fleisch's sixteen are relevant) in fact exhibit an actual linguistic stage, or, with six out of the seven occurring in ancient poetry and only one being a Quranic variant, rather are the result of poetic license owing to metre or rhyme (this applies, as a matter of fact, only to five occurrences, since in one, example no. 7, the change of *yqtlu* into *yqtla* does not entail any change in the metre). Fleisch (n. 43, p. 76, n. 10, end), to be sure, excludes such a possibility, since poetic license must not affect the basic rules of grammar. Yet if one allows for some relenting of linguistic standards regarding the use of the subjunctive in the wake of ᵓ*an* ᵓ*al-muxaffafa*, one could well imagine that, owing to the exigencies of the metre (or rhyme), the indicative was used instead of the subjunctive.

B. *The Origins of the Pôlel/Pôᶜel Themes of the Verba 2–w/y and 2–gem.: a Case of Plurilinear Development*

1. There is a plethora of studies of the origins of these verbal themes, either in the form of separate articles or included in more comprehensive studies or even in grammars. The classical study concluding the research of the 19th century (though one will call many of its results into question) is J. Barth's *Die Pôlêl-Conjugation und die Pôlāl-Participien*,[63] which also contains a very useful bibliographical survey. The bibliography was brought up-to-date by H. Fleisch,[64] who quotes Barth in extenso. One would like to add only H. L. Ginsberg's short remark in *AJSL* 46 (1929–30), p. 137, esp. note 1, and Wolfenson's article,[65] omitted by Fleisch. The problem of these verbal forms has also been treated since the appearance of Fleisch's book, yet, as a rule, without directing attention to new points of view; see, e. g., R. Meyer.[66] Important, however, are the short remarks of Kuryłowicz[67] and Morag[68] on our subject.

[63] In *Semitic Studies in Memory of A. Kohut* (Berlin, 1897), pp. 83–93. The great merit of Barth's article is that he has recognized the ultimate connection of the verbal themes treated with Arabic infinitives like *baynûna, daymûma*, etc., which exhibit the reduplication of the last radical in verba 2 *w-y* (though he was not the first to do so; see infra, n. 72). On the other hand, as mentioned, the results reached by Barth are by no means certain. He did rely too much on the affinity of the above-mentioned Arabic infinitives. Yet Akkadian forms like *tukinnâ* from *kwn*, not mentioned by Barth, also exhibit the doubling of the last radical in 2 *w-y*; cf. Sarauw [A, n. 33], pp. 43 f. Also the fact that the *piᶜel*, etc., of the verba 2-gem. is often formed as if from strong verbs was emphasized too much by Barth (p. 85); it stands to reason that *pôᶜel*, etc. forms from 2-gem. verbs were more frequent in biblical Hebrew than the vocalization discloses. As Bergsträsser (A, n. 5), II 140 (§27r) recognized, the distinction between *piᶜel* and *pôᶜel* forms of the 2-gem. is partly based on accidental scriptio plena and defectiva, respectively, so that one should assume more original *pôᶜel* forms. Since in later Hebrew *piᶜel* forms prevail (cf., e. g., M. Z. Segal, *Diqdûq leshôn hammishnâ* (Tel-Aviv, 1935/6), p. 148), the Masoretes were, it seems, inclined to vocalize in accordance with them, when the consonantal skeleton enabled them to do so. The main weak point of Barth's article is, however, that he rejected the Syriac evidence too casually in his endeavor to derive both the *pôlel* of the verba 2-*w/y* and the *pôᶜel* of the verba 2-gem. from one source. In this part, full reference to Fleisch is found in n. 64, to Goliger in n. 69, and to Morag in n. 68.

[64] H. Fleisch, *Les verbes à allongement vocalique interne en sémitique* . . . (Paris, 1944), pp. 10 ff. (cf. p. 10, n. 1). The scope of Fleisch's work is, of course, different; nevertheless, he treats our problem in extenso, because of the possibility (ultimately rejected by him) that Hebrew verbal forms with *ô* after the first radical exhibit "vocalic lengthening."

[65] L. B. Wolfenson, *The piᶜlēl in Hebrew*, *JAOS* 27 (1906), 303–316.

[66] R. Meyer, *Hebräische Grammatik* I (Berlin, 1966), p. 112, §27.2.

[67] Supra, A, n. 51, pp. 46 f. (§60).

[68] In *Tarbiz* 26 (1956/7), p. 351, n. 13.

2. Despite the widely divergent views expressed on the origins of these verbal themes, one may, in principle, distinguish between two ways of thought. According to one, the verbal theme containing *ô* after the first radical arose in one of these verbal classes (either 2–*w*/*y* or 2–gem.) and it spread to the other verbal class through analogy. This is, e. g., the view of Barth, Wolfenson, and Meyer. The other group, on the contrary, maintains a separate origin for the *pôlel* in the verba 2–*w*/*y*, and the *pôʿel* in the 2–gem. This view is expressed, e. g., by Fleisch. An intermediate opinion is held by M. Goliger,[69] who assumed that these verbal forms arose by reciprocal analogy. In the following I shall try to show that the development was plurilinear[70] and presumably many factors converged in giving rise to these verbal forms.

3. Every analysis of the Hebrew forms has to take into account the parallel Aramaic ones. This is the more important since Hebrew *ô* is historically ambiguous, because it may be derived from *â* or *aw*. In Aramaic, on the other hand, historical *â* is reflected by *â* only, whereas original *aw* is either retained (so in Syriac in open syllables) or monophthongized into *ô*. Accordingly, parallel Aramaic forms are apt to remove, partly at least, the equivocality inherent in the Hebrew forms. We shall, therefore, begin with the Aramaic forms,[71] though they are, in contradistinction to the Hebrew ones, quite marginal.

3.1. Aramaic forms with *aw*/*ô* after the first radical and reduplication of the third in verba 2–*w*/*y* (type Syriac *ʾeṯbawrar* from *bwr*; Christian Aramaic *gôḇeḇ* from *gwb*) are, despite their uncommonness, well attested. They may be derived, as Barth, p. 91, assumes, from *qaṭṭel* (i. e., *qawwel*) of verba 2–*w*, which, out of aversion to double *w*, shifted to *qawlel*, or directly from *qawlel* with reduplication of the third radical, as Fleisch, pp. 35 ff., and, following him, Morag, p. 35, n. 13, assume. As a matter of fact, the differences between both interpretations are quite minimal, since even if one derives this form directly from a theme with doubled third radical, the comparatively frequent occurrence of the reduplication of the third radical in these verbs is, no doubt, due to the aversion of doubling the medial *w*.[72]

[69] In *RSO* 17 (1938), p. 100.

(pp. 279) [70] For this term cf. *In Memoriam P. Kahle* (Berlin, 1968), p. 42. In many respects I find myself in agreement with Morag, who also distinguishes between the reflex of Aramaic *ô* as against *â*, as it was done partly already by Fleisch (n. 64), pp. 26 ff.

[71] For details concerning the various Aramaic dialects, see Fleisch (n. 64), pp. 26 ff.; Morag (n. 68), p. 351.

[72] That the consonant preceding or following *w*/*y* is often doubled and not *w*/*y*, was already discovered before Barth by M. Lambert in his important short remark, *REJ* 24 (1892), p. 107, n. 2.

3.2. Yet Aramaic forms with *aw/ô* after the first radical are attested in verba 2–gem. as well, though they are generally even rarer than the corresponding forms of 2–*w/y* verbs; they are absent altogether in Christian Palestinian Aramaic. Nevertheless, Fleisch's contention that this feature in 2–gem. verbs is altogether secondary, is, it seems, erroneous. To be sure, he may be correct (pp. 28 f.) in considering biblical Aramaic *ʾeštômam* a Hebrew loan; yet his attempt also to regard as secondary five (!, as against one occurrence in the 2–*w* class) cases attested in Syriac, since they are either derived from nouns containing *u* or occur alongside ordinary *ʾetqaṭṭal*, is unconvincing. The question is why is this feature much more frequent in verba 2–gem. than in others. Why are denominative verbs from nouns containing *u*, and parallel *ʾetqawṭal* and *ʾeṯqaṭṭal* themes relatively frequent in 2–gem. verbs? One is inclined to attribute this feature to the special qualities of this class, viz. either its affinity to the 2–*w/y*[73] or to the doubling of the second radical. According to the first alternative, one will consider these forms remodelled after the pattern of 2–*w*. A quite similar view is held by those who regard these forms as exhibiting a *qawṭel* pattern. Since this pattern arose presumably in roots 2–*w*,[74] these 2–gem. forms have also to be considered as ultimately influenced by the 2–*w* verbs. Yet one could very well explain these forms as arising in 2–gem. verbs proper without external influence. As is well known,[75] in reduplicated roots certain consonants[76] are apt to be dissimilated into *w* and, with *a*, form the diphthong *aw*. Moreover, the so-called 12th Arabic verbal theme *ʾiqṭawṭala*, has to be derived, it seems, from *ʾiqṭalṭala*,[77] exhibiting the spread of such dissimilations to all the forms. Similarly, one could easily conceive that in the verba 2–gem. *aw* first arose in certain roots, containing consonants apt to be dissimilated into *w*, and spread afterwards to the whole paradigm, whatever the radicals were.

3.3. Even more restricted is the use of *â* after the first radical in verba 2–*w/y* and 2–gem. (type *lâṭeṭ*, root *lwṭ*; *lâfef*, root *lff*); as far

[73] Fleisch, p. 21, to be sure, is sceptical about the mutual influence of these two verbal classes. Yet his doubts are unfounded; cf., e. g., Barth, p. 85, n. 2; Bergsträsser (A, n. 5) II, pp. 108(c); 134(bc); 140(q); and many of the verbs quoted pp. 170–72 (as *bwz–bzz, nwd–ndd, swr–srr, swk–skk, ṣwr–ṣrr*).

[74] Cf., e. g., Goliger, p. 99; Kuryłowicz (A, n. 51), p. 46 (§60).

[75] It is somewhat peculiar that, as far as I know, this explanation has not yet been offered.

[76] This is the case with *l* (as *məṭalṭelet* > *məṭôṭelet*), *m* (*šamšəmânâ* > *šawšəmânâ*), *b* (*kabkab* > *kawkab*), *f* (*ṭafṭâf* > *ṭôṭâf*); see R. Růžička, *BA* 6:4 (1907), pp. 42, 76, 107, 129.

[77] See C. Brockelmann, *Grundriss* . . . I, p. 519.

as is known to me,[78] it occurs only in Aramaic Targums having Babylonian vocalization. The simplest explanation for this feature is that it arose in the 2–gem. through dissimilation (type *sabbaba*>*sâbaba*),[79] and then it spread to the 2–*w/y*, an explanation often offered for Hebrew *pôᶜel/pôlel*. This assumption is corroborated by forms like *mitrab̲reb̲*>*mitrâreb̲*, exhibiting the same type of dissimilation. Fleisch, p. 28,[80] on the other hand, considers this feature secondary, a sort of pseudocorrection out of over-self-assertion,[81] which was modelled after the Hebrew forms, according to the pattern Hebrew *ô* : Aramaic *â*. This interpretation, however, is, to some extent at least, contradicted by the fact that in postbiblical Hebrew as preserved in Babylonian vocalization (i. e., in the same vocalization in which such Aramaic forms were preserved) there are attested forms with *â* after the first radical in verba 2–gem. and 2 *w/y* (with reduplication of the final radical). Because these Hebrew forms are restricted to the same tradition of vocalization as that in which the corresponding Aramaic forms occur, one will consider the Hebrew forms originating in the Aramaic.[82] This would imply that, according to Fleisch, at first *ô* in these verbs was supplanted by *â* through Hebrew influence (more correctly, as a reaction against Hebrew); later, however, the difference between Aramaic and Hebrew was again blurred by the substitution of Hebrew *ô* by *â*, this time through Aramaic influence. This is, of course, not entirely impossible. One could claim that, at first, when the position of Hebrew was secure, Aramaic forms with *â* arose; then, as the status of Aramaic became more and more important, Aramaic *â* spread to Hebrew as well. Nevertheless, this assumption is, it seems, too intricate to be convincing.

There is, however, another possibility. One may interpret these forms in the 2–gem. verbs as original *qâtala* themes (corresponding to the third verbal theme in Arabic). It is assumed that originally this theme had intensive meaning and served alongside the *qattal* (*piᶜel*) theme. As a rule, it was superseded by *qattal*; in the verba 2–gem., however, in which *qattal* involved difficulties of pronunciation (because of the twofold repetition of one sound), it subsisted to some extent.

[78] Yet Morag, p. 351, n. 13, speaks of "some Aramaic dialects."

[79] So for instance C. Brockelmann, *Grundriss* . . . I, p. 246 (§90d), and Morag, ibid.

[80] Yet on p. 34 he speaks of secondary dissimilation of the reduplication.

[81] For this term cf. my *Pseudo-corrections in Some Semitic Languages* (Jerusalem, 1970), pp. 15–16.

[82] So Morag, p. 352, who has adduced quite convincing, though only circumstantial, evidences.

The same applies to the verba 2–*w*/*y*, in which the type *qâwala* was superseded by *qâlala*,[83] perhaps also through the influence of the 2–gem. These explanations are not necessarily mutually exclusive; different developments may have converged in giving rise to the same verbal themes.

4. In Hebrew, as mentioned above, *ô* is even more ambiguous than in Aramaic. Accordingly, all the derivations proposed for both Aramaic *aw*/*ô* and *â* forms apply to Hebrew *pôlel*/*pôᶜel* as well. We may well claim that these themes originated from one basic form and even prove that all their manifestations can be derived from it. But even if we manage to show how this form might have developed, we cannot be sure whether the actual process took place exclusively along these lines.[84] The very possibility of plurilinear development does not permit us to reconstruct the actual development with any certainty.[85] The more so in our case in which plurilinear development is not a mere possibility, but, because of the corresponding Aramaic forms, a high probability: it stands to reason that the Aramaic forms containing *â* after the first radical are historically different from those exhibiting *aw*/*ô*. Accordingly, one has to content oneself with stating that the development might have been so without being able to prove it.

Therefore all we can do is to state that the Hebrew verbal themes *pôlel*/*pôᶜel* of the 2–*w*/*y* and 2-gem. verbs might have arisen in either of these classes and then spread to the other, or it might have originated in both of them independently, though even in this case later mutual influence is very likely. On the other hand, these forms might have developed at the very beginning through reciprocal analogy. A plethora of forms may underlie these verbal themes,[86] among them at least one containing *aw* after the first radical in the 2–*w* class (because of the Aramaic *aw*/*ô* forms and Egyptian *śwbb*),[87] and one accounting for the Aramaic *â* forms.

83 In this case one should assume that there was aversion not only against double *w* (see n. 72), but also against a long vowel followed by *w*.

84 Cf. *In Memoriam P. Kahle*, pp. 42 f. (pp. 279f.)

85 Even features that explain only a part of the manifestations (like those explaining either the Aramaic *aw*/*ô* or the *â* forms, but not both of them), have to be taken into consideration, since some manifestations may have originated in one feature, others in another.

86 For particulars cf. the analysis of the Aramaic forms.

87 If Egyptian *śwbb* corresponds, in fact, to Old Canaanite *šawbaba* (H. Bauer–P. Leander, *Grammatik des Biblisch-Aramäischen* (Halle, 1927), pp. 146 f., Fleisch, 12 f., especially p. 13, n. 1), we would have a proof that at least in part of the verba 2-*w* *ô* has to be derived from *aw*.

C. *The Original Vocalization of the Perfect of Hebrew Piᶜel and Hifᶜîl: Another Case of Plurilinear Development*

1. It is generally assumed[88] that the original vocalization of the perfect of the Hebrew *piᶜel* and *hifᶜîl* was according to the pattern *a–a–a*, i. e., *qattala* and *haqtala*, and weighty arguments have been adduced in favor of this assumption. Here and there, however, different views have been expressed. Thus A. Ungnad[89] upheld the view that the original vocalization of these verbal themes (and of the *nifᶜal*) was *i–a–a*, i. e., *qittala, hiqtala* (and *niqtala*). N. H. Tur-Sinai[90] has even said that the original vocalization was *i–i–a*, i. e., *qittila* and *hiqtila*, and he has proved his point by many conclusive arguments. Nevertheless, his views were not accepted, mainly, it seems, because the evidence for pattern *a–a–a* likewise seems decisive. The solution of the problem posed by the fact that weighty evidences obtain in favor of both patterns (i. e., *a–a–a* and *i–i–a*),[91] seems to be that these verbal themes should not be derived from one pattern, but rather * originate, at least, in two (i. e., in *a–a–a* and *i–i–a*); again a case of plurilinear development.[92]

In the following we shall first (§2) adduce arguments for the pattern *a–a* (*–a*), then for *i–i* (*–a*)[93] (§3); finally (§4) we shall describe the general background of the plurilinear development in these themes.

2. The following evidence exists for the pattern *a–a*; to be sure, some features adduced to exhibit original *a–a* may be explained differ-

[88] Cf. both the Hebrew and comparative Semitic grammars. For the whole problem cf. also A. Ungnad, *BA* 5:3 (1905), p. 250.

[89] *BA* 6:3 (1907), pp. 55 ff. H. L. Ginsberg, *BASOR* 98, 1945, p. 17, also postulates *i* for the first syllable of the perfect of the Hebrew *piᶜel* and *hifᶜîl*, and assumes that Phoenician *yifᶜil* arose because of this *i*. He also postulates *i* for the first syllable of the imperative, through the alleged influence of the perfect. This, however, is not very likely, since the influence of the imperfect on the imperative was, it seems, stronger than that of the perfect.

[90] In the main, he published his views (under the name H. Torczyner) as early as 1910 (*ZDMG* 64, pp. 269 ff.). I am quoting him from the improved Hebrew edition in his *Hallašôn wehassefer, kerekh hallašôn*² (Jerusalem, 1954), pp. 256–283.

[91] As to the pattern *i–a–a*, assumed by Ungnad and Ginsberg, it is, prima facie, due to a blend of *a–a–a* and *i–i–a*.

[92] As far as I am aware, such a development was not surmised by the scholars dealing with this problem. Only Tur-Sinai (n. 90), p. 261, polemizing against proofs for the pattern *a–a*, mentioned it as theoretical possibility, yet abandoned it entirely in the following discussion.

[93] Henceforth we shall disregard the final *a* since it is identical in both patterns and shall deal only with the first two vowels, *a–a* and *i–a*, respectively. The first vowel will be marked by I (i. e., Ia and Ii, respectively), the second by II (i. e., IIa and IIi).

ently, others apply only to the first or the second vowel. Nevertheless, considered together, they constitute a rather impressive evidence for this pattern.

2.1. Arabic and ancient Ethiopic have the pattern *a–a* in both verbal themes. As regards Hebrew proper, since it stands to reason that the *hitpaᶜel* originates in *hitqattal,*[94] it may be taken as a further hint (but not more than that) for original *qattala.*[95]

> NOTE. Nothing can be inferred from isolated Hebrew *naššanî* "he made me forget" (Gen. 41:51), a pronunciation presumably chosen more clearly to bring out the play on the name *Mənaššê.*

2.2. Original Ia is indicated by *pôᶜel/pôlel* of the 2–gem./2–*w*/*y* verbs (whether we assume a < *qawᶜala/qawlala* or a < *qâᶜala/qâlala* development; see Part B) for the *piᶜel* and by forms of the type of *hôlîd* < *hawlîd* of the 1–*w* verbs for the *hifᶜîl.* It may be claimed that these forms arose through analogy to the imperfect, yet this is not very likely. It may also be that the *hifᶜîl* of verba 1–laryng. of the type *wəhaʾăḇadtî* exhibits remnants of an original Ia.

2.3. About half of the occurrences of perfect *piᶜel* 3d pers. sing. masc. exhibit IIa.[96] It stands to reason that these forms reflect original IIa rather than an impact of the perfect of other verbal themes (like the *qal*).

2.4. In the *hifᶜîl* of the 2–gem. verbs forms of the type *hesaḇ* prevail.[97] Since it is unlikely that this IIa is due to analogy, one will consider it as evidence for original IIa in the *hifᶜîl.*[98]

> NOTE. The proofs for *a–a* adduced by A. Ungnad, *BA* 5:3 (1905), p. 250, are not convincing. It is more than doubtful that the West Semitic perfect is related to the Akkadian present; accordingly, no evidence can be brought from Akkadian *uparras.* The *piᶜel* of 3–*y* (type *gillâ*) need not represent original **gillaya,* since also **gilliya* would have developed into *gillâ* (cf., e. g., Bergsträsser (A, n. 5), I, p. 99[i]). The Arabic dialects do not prove more than classical Arabic. Even the Hebrew infinitive absolute *qattôl* does not prove anything, since it may be regarded as a secondary formation of *qattel* in analogy with *qal qatôl.*

94 Cf. Bergsträsser (A, n. 5), p. 100(k).

95 Quite differently Tur-Sinai (n. 90), pp. 272 f.

96 For the prevalence of IIa in the Babylonian vocalization see §3.2.

97 Cf. Bergsträsser (A, n. 5), II, 137(k).

98 As to *e*<Ii in the first syllable, it is perhaps due to a blend of ****hâsaḇ*** with ***heseḇ*<*hisib** (cf. §3.3).

3. The following evidence exists for the pattern *i–i* (with qualifications similar to those mentioned in §2 for *a–a*); as will be seen (§3.4), the pattern *i–i* originates in *u–u*.

3.1. Ii in the *hifᶜîl* is, it seems, attested already in El-Amarna (see §3.5, where also IIi is dealt with); in the *piᶜel*, in Phoenician (cf. e. g., Z. S. Harris, *A Grammar of the Phoenician Language* (New Haven, 1936), p. 42; J. Friedrich, *Phönizisch-punische Grammatik* (Roma, 1951), p. 62).[99] Phoenician **yiqtil*, corresponding to Hebrew *hifᶜîl*, is also easier to explain by the assumption of Ii (see Z. S. Harris, *Development of the Canaanite Dialects* (New Haven, 1939), p. 74 [§55], Ginsberg [n. 89]), but this assumption is by no means necessary; cf. Friedrich, p. 64 (§147).

Ii is commonly considered an "attenuation" of *a* in closed, unstressed syllable. But it seems that this assumption is fallacious. It stands to reason (see especially Bergsträsser [A, n. 5], I, p. 146 f.) that attenuation is quite a late phenomenon, as exhibited by the differences between Tiberian and Babylonian vocalizations and rather late transcriptions. Accordingly it is impossible to accept the view that it occurred as early as the period of El-Amarna.[100]

In order to escape this difficulty, Bergsträsser ([A, n. 5], II, p. 97) explained *qittal* as due to the vowel sequence *i–a*, as occurring also in the imperfect *qal* (Barth's law: *yiqtal* as against *yaqtul/yaqtil*). Yet this explanation is not convincing either. Even if Barth's law operated outside the imperfect *qal*, it is restricted to prefixes,[101] which excludes the perfect *piᶜel*. Had it operated generally, even outside the prefixes, *qal qatala* should have shifted to **qital*. (For the operation of Barth's law in open syllables, cf. *yêqal*.) Moreover, A. Bloch, *ZDMG* 117

[99] The Phoenician forms also exhibit IIi, which may, however, be due to analogy to the imperfect. This may apply to "East Canaanite" *qattil*; see Garbini (A, n. 32, end), pp. 126, 135.

[100] P. Leander's claim (*ZDMG* 74 (1920), p. 64) for the remote age of attenuation is based only on the *hifᶜîl* occurring in El-Amarna, since the occurrence of *i* in the prefix of imperfect *qal* may easily be explained by Barth's law (see infra) and the extent of *i* of the prefix through analogy. F. R. Blake, *JNES* 9 (1950), pp. 82 f., regards the attenuation as a general North-West Semitic law, since it occurs in Aramaic as well. Since, however, attenuation is very late in Hebrew, one will prefer to interpret it as being due to Aramaic influence. Besides, the attenuation might have occurred in different languages independently; compare its occurrence in Arabic dialects (the so-called *taltala*), and see for it, e. g., C. A. Ferguson, *Language* 35 (1959), p. 621. The assumption of H. Bauer–P. Leander, *Historische Grammatik* ... (Halle, 1922), p. 194(x), that the attenuation is old is contradicted by the next paragraph which shows numerous irregularities. Their attempt, following Brockelmann, to explain these irregularities as reflecting fluctuating shades, can be considered as an emergency device only.

[101] The above-mentioned *taltala* (see n. 100), is restricted to affixes.

(1967), pp. 22 ff., has made it quite likely that Barth's law is general * West Semitic, since it occurs in Arabic as well. Had it occurred outside imperfect *qal*, one would have expected to find traces of it in Arabic as well (admittedly an argumentum ex silentio).

3.2. Whereas the perfect of the *piᶜel*, as a rule, exhibits either IIa or IIi>*e*, there are three verbs that have *ę* (for particulars see Bergsträsser [A, n. 5], II, p. 95[d]). As far as is known to me, no convincing explanation has been offered for this feature. I would like to propose that, through Philippi's law, original IIi had shifted to *ę*.

As is well known (cf., e. g., Bergsträsser [A, n. 5], I, p. 149[h]), according to Philippi's law, *i* in a closed stressed syllable shifted to *a*. As a rule, however, this shift occurs only a) in a closed penult syllable bearing the main stress; b) in a closed ultimate syllable with secondary stress (i. e., in the construct). In very few cases only (as in **bint*>*bat̲*), did *i* in closed ultimate syllable bearing the main stress shift to *a*. (This occurred only in the absolute state of those nouns that, like **bint*, terminated in two consonants; other absolute nouns, like **ᶜiṣu*> *ᶜeṣ*, containing *i* in open syllables, were not affected by Philippi's law, which was operative before the loss of case vowels in absolute nouns). As a rule, absolute nouns terminating in (original) two consonants exhibit, according to the Tiberian vocalization, *ę* (**karmill*>*karmęl*), and even more often *e* (**libbu*>*leb̲*); in the Babylonian vocalization, however, ⌐ (corresponding to Tiberian *a* and *ę*) is used. One is inclined to interpret the situation as follows: According to the Babylonian vocalization, *i* in every closed stressed syllable shifted to ⌐ (i. e., to the sign corresponding to Tiberian *a* and *ę*). According to the Tiberian vocalization, *i* shifted to *a* in closed syllables, being either ultimate and bearing secondary stress, or penult and bearing main stress. If the closed syllable was ultimate and bore the main stress, * *i* shifted to *ę*. It was, however, in relatively few cases only, that this *ę* was preserved. As a rule, it shifted again to *e*.

The same happened, it seems, in verbs. Verbs (like constructs, in contradistinction to absolute nouns) had already lost their final vocalization and, accordingly, terminated in closed syllables. This fact is borne out by *a* in final syllables in verbs (like *kâtab̲*) as against *â* in absolute nouns (as *dâb̲âr*). Accordingly, verbs were affected by Philippi's law. In Babylonian vocalization, original *i* shifted to ⌐; this is one of the main reasons that verbs in Babylonian vocalization very often exhibit ⌐ as against Tiberian *e*.[102] This Tiberian *e* arose from *ę*<*i*. Only in a few cases was this *ę* preserved, viz. in the *piᶜel*

[102] See I. Yeivin, *The Babylonian Vocalization* . . . (Thesis), Jerusalem, 1968 (in Hebrew), pp. 289 f. (§xi.21).

of three verbs. Accordingly, these verbs have to be interpreted as exhibiting original Ii.

3.3. The pattern *i–i* is also exhibited by the *hifʿîl* of 2–*w/y* (type *hêqîm*).[103] In this case it is entirely impossible to claim attenuation, since this phenomenon is limited to closed syllables. One will somehow connect with this perfect pattern participles of the type *mêqîm*, which is already attested in "East Canaanite."[104] Ii is also attested by perfect *hifʿîl* of 2–gem. (type *hêsab̲/hêseb̲*).[105]

3.4. To Tur-Sinai we owe ([n. 90], pp. 270 f.) the insight that the perfect of *piʿel/hifʿîl*, exhibiting an *i–i* pattern, corresponds to the Akkadian stative *purrus/šuprus*, exhibiting an *u–u* pattern. As Tur-Sinai (see also pp. 265 ff.) has recognized, Akkadian *u–u* becomes in Hebrew *i–i*, as borne out, e. g., by the Akkadian loan word *kussû* "seat," which became *kissê* in Hebrew.[106]

3.5. Tur-Sinai (p. 270) has also recognized that forms of the type *dubir* "he led," occurring in El-Amarna, have to be interpreted as ancient *piʿel* forms, i. e., *dubbir*.[107] One is inclined to regard them as intermediate forms, exhibiting the transitional stage from *quttul* (as preserved in Akkadian) to *qittil* (i. e., *qittel*, as exhibited by Hebrew).[108] For the Phoenician forms, see §3.1, especially note 99.

[103] According to this view, both the imperfect and the perfect of 2-*w/y* contained original *î*. Therefore, the spread of this *î* to almost the whole paradigm of the *hifʿîl* of the strong verb is much easier to understand.

[104] See W. L. Moran, in *The Bible and the Ancient Near East; Essays in Honor of W. F. Albright*, ed. G. E. Wright (Anchor Edition: New York, 1965), p. 71. If this participle is in fact connected with the perfect, one will regard the prefix vowel as original and not derive it, as did Moran, p. 82, n. 104.

[105] *hêseb̲* may also exhibit original Ii, but it may also be due to the impact of the imperfect. Type *hêsab̲* is more frequent than *hêseb̲* even in Tiberian vocalization.

[106] For the shift of *u* to *i* see in detail Kutscher (A, n. 5), pp. 356 ff. Kuryłowicz (A, n. 51), p. 62 (§79), to be sure, claims that the Assyrian stative forms *parrus/šaprus* are more original. Yet *purrus/šuprus* are attested in Old Akkadian; see I. J. Gelb, *Materials for the Assyrian Dictionary* II² (Chicago, 1961), p. 174.

[107] A plethora of explanations have been proposed for these forms, all of them much less likely than Tur-Sinai's. F. M. Th. Böhl, *Die Sprache der Amarnabriefe* . . . (Leipzig, 1909), p. 45(i), following H. Zimmern, considers them as a blend of Akkadian *purrus* and Canaanite *qattil*, and similarly Brockelmann, *Grundriss* . . . I, p. 583 (f α, end). According to E. Ebeling, "Das Verbum der El-Amarna Briefe," *BA* 8:2 (1910), pp. 62 f., they exhibit the influence of Canaanite *pôʿel* on the stative with doubled second radical, whereas P. Dhorme, *RB* 23 (1914), p. 41, regards them as simple *qâtala* = *pôʿel*. Fleisch (B, n. 64), pp. 22 f., explains them as *qawtala*; against this see Garbini (A, n. 32), p. 127, n. 2.

[108] One will assume that forms like *dubbir* were stressed on the first syllable. *u* was preserved in the first, stressed syllable but shifted to *i* in the unstressed second syllable.

If *ḫi-iḫ-bi-e* (EA 256:7) does correspond to Hebrew *hęḥbî*(ʾ) "he hid," it represents the *i–i* pattern of the *hifʿîl*.[109]

3.6. IIi is also exhibited by *ê* after the second radical of the 1st/2nd person of *piʿel/hifʿîl* of 3–ʾ (type: *qinnêṯî/hôṣêṯî*). One necessarily interprets this *ê* as <*i*ʾ (since *a*ʾ would have resulted in *â*). The same *ê* in *nifʿal* (type: *nimṣêṯî*) is, to be sure, explained as being due to the analogy of 3–*y*: in the *nifʿal* of 3–*y*, in fact, *ê* prevails. This explanation cannot, however, apply to the *piʿel/hifʿîl*, since in 3–*y*, as a rule, they exhibit *î* after the second radical (being also due to IIi?).

4. Since there exists weighty evidence both for the pattern *a–a* and *i–i*, the inevitable conclusion is that not only the perfect of *qal* had different patterns (*qatala*, *qatila*, *qatula*), but that of the derived verbal themes as well.[110] Hebrew *piʿel* and *hifʿîl* preserved vestiges of both patterns. The original form of the Hebrew *i–i* pattern was *u–u*, as preserved in the Akkadian stative, which shifted to *i–i* owing to the shift of *u* to *i* in closed unstressed syllables, attested in many languages of the "Fertile Crescent."

One need not be surprised by the correspondence of the Akkadian stative with the West Semitic perfect. While many scholars consider these two forms in the *qal* as historically related, Bergsträsser (A, n. 5), II, pp. 11 (especially n. 3); 13 f., has adduced weighty evidence for the assumption that this affinity was not complete: the stative corresponds to the "neutric" perfects *qatila* and *qatula*, whereas *qatala* stands apart. In my opinion,[111] exactly the same relation obtains in the *piʿel* and *hifʿîl*: whereas the *a–a* pattern stands apart, the *i–i* (<*u–u*) theme corresponds to the Akkadian stative.[112]

[109] I am inclined to assume that, owing to the final long vowel (*î*), *hiḥbî* was differently stressed than *dubbir*, and this accounts for both *u* shifting to *i*. At first **ḫuḫbu*ʾ was stressed on the first syllable, and *u* in the second unstressed one shifted to *i*. Then this *i* was lengthened and attracted the stress; now it was the first *u* that shifted to *i*. A similar explanation accounts for the Hebrew type *ʾillêm*<**ʾullum* "mute." First, it seems, the first syllable was stressed, and in the second unstressed one *u* shifted to *i*; then the stress shifted to the second syllable, and now also the first *u* shifted to *i* (so pace Kutscher (A, n. 5), p. 365).

[110] It may well be that the imperfect of the derived verbal themes had different patterns as well. To investigate this is, of course, beyond the scope of this paper.

[111] H. Zimmern, *ZA* 5 (1890), pp. 1 ff., already surmised that the stative corresponds to the West Semitic perfect in the derived verbal themes as well (see especially p. 6, n. 1), and J. A. Knudzon agreed with him (*ZA* 7, 1892, p. 43).

[112] It is difficult to know whether the different patterns in the derived verbal themes had different meanings, as they had in the *qal*. Prima facie, I would assume that the development was not unlike that proposed by Kuryłowicz (A, n. 51), pp. 74 f., to wit, that originally the *u–u* pattern had passive function. Both patterns, the active *qattala/haqtala* and the passive *quttula/huqtula*, coexisted. Then the new

Yet whereas the different patterns of the *qal* were preserved in many Semitic languages, they disappeared in the derived verbal themes.[113] It seems that only in Hebrew clear vestiges of different patterns in the perfect in the *piᶜel*[114] and *hifᶜil* were preserved, reflecting another case of plurilinear development.

Additions and Corrections

to **p. 163**.*n. 32.9*: See also Sivan, pp. 68–69.

to **p. 174**.*17*: S. Izre'el, *IOS* 8.74–78 (1978) accepts the assumption of the *i- i* pattern, yet (77.n. 244) expresses doubts as to the origins of the *a — a* pattern. I do not understand what made A. F. Rainey (*Canaanite in the Amarna Tablets*, Leiden 1996, II, p. 310) claim that it impossible that *qittil* developed from *quttil*.

to **p. 175**.*20*: The *a* in these cases is due to Philippi's law, see addition to p. 177.29.

to **p. 177**.*1*: The occurrence of this feature in Arabic, to be sure, may also be due to parallel development.

to **p. 177**.*29*: Since clear tendency obtains for using פָּעַל in the pause, yet פִּעֵל in context (see E. Qimron, *Leshonenu* 50 [1983–84], p. 80), I prefer now to posit a general shift of *i* to *a* and consider the shift *i* > *ę* to be exceptional.

---

passive *quttila/huqtila* arose and superseded the old passive, which assumed active meaning and was, as a rule, entirely supplanted. Later the new passive became *quttal/huqtal*, and it was only then that the old one assumed the form *quttil/huqtil* and later *qittil/hiqtil*. It goes without saying that this development is by no means certain in any way. For the preservation of the old *quttul*-adjectives as *qittel* in Hebrew, see Tur-Sinai (n. 90), pp. 265 ff., Kutscher (A, n. 5), p. 365.

[113] Perhaps because they were identical in meaning, cf. the preceding note.

[114] It is very difficult to say anything certain about the regulation, on the synchronic level, of the alteration of Hebrew *qittel* and *qittal*; cf. for it C. Rabin, *Leshonenu* 32 (1967/8), pp. 12 ff.

On Some Vestiges of Univerbalization of the Units and Tens of the *Cardinalia* 21–99 in Arabic and Hebrew

Already medieval philologists recognized that the *Cardinalia* 11–19 have become univerbalized in Arabic and Hebrew. Sībawayhi (eighth century; I 86, 11–14) states: *fa-ʾidhā zidta ʿala- l-ʿasharati shayʾan min ʾasmāʾi ʾadna- l-ʿadadi fa-ʾinnahū yujʿalu maʿa -l-ʾawwali- sman wāḥidan istikhfāfan wa-yakūnu fī mawḍiʿi -smin munawwanin wa-dhālika qawluka ʾaḥada ʿashara dirhaman wa-thnā ʿashara dirhaman wa-ʾiḥdā ʿashrata jāriyatan fa-ʿalā hādha yujrā mina -l-wāḥidi ʾila -l-tisʿati* 'if you add to ten one of the low numbers, it coalesces with the first [number] into one word [so as] to make [the pronunciation] easy, and it comports as a [single] noun terminating in *tanwīn*. So you say 'eleven *dirham*', 'twelve *dirham*' and 'eleven slave girls'. Thus is the usage of the numbers one to nine [i.e. from eleven to nineteen]'.

More sophisticated is Ibn Janāḥ's (eleventh century; 384, 23–385, 3; cf. the Hebrew translation I 397, 14–17), view on Hebrew, no doubt, because the structure of Hebrew is much less homogeneous than that of Arabic, which was decisively influenced by analogy: *fa-ʾin ʿarrafta mā bayna-l-ʿăśārā ʾila -l-ʿeśrīm mina -l-ʿadadayni -lladhayni yujʿalāni -sman wāḥidan ʾadkhalta -l-taʿrīfa fī -l-ʿadadi -l-thāni kamā qīla wayyiqrā Yehōshūaʿ ʾel shənēm he-ʿăśār ʾīsh* (Joshua IV, 4) *wə-hū bi-shnēm he-ʿăśār* (I Kings XIX, 19) *li-ʾanna tarkībahū laysa bi-maḥḍin. wa-ʾin shiʾta ʾadkhaltahū ʿala -l-ʿadadi-l-ʾawwali tashbīhan lahū bi-mā tarkībuhū maḥḍun ka-mā qīla u-bha-sh-shānā hā-ʾaḥat ʿeśrē bə-yeraḥ būl* (I Kings VI, 38) 'and if you make definite the numerals from ten to twenty which coalesce into one noun, you add the definite [article] to the second numeral, as: 'and Joshua called the twelve men'; 'while he was with the twelfth', because its coalescence is not genuine. And if you wish, you may add it to the first numeral, making it similar to [words exhibiting] genuine coalescence, as it was said: 'and in the eleventh year in the month Bul'.

There are indications that the numerals 11–19 exerted an influence on the numerals 21–99, consisting of tens and units, and these numerals too were, to some extent, univerbalized. Again, the structure of Arabic is much clearer, because of the decisive influence of analogy, whereas the picture of multi-layered Biblical Hebrew is somewhat blurred. The following features hint at the univerbalization of 21–99 in Arabic:

1. As is well known, the units in Arabic always precede the tens, even if all the other numerals stand in descending order (as *'alfun wa-tis 'u -mi'atin wa-khamsun wa-thalāthūna* '1935').

2. The numbered noun may be repeated after each numeral; yet, it is, as a rule, not repeated after the unit preceding a ten. The various grammars adduce examples exhibiting this feature, yet without usually stating it explicitly. They content themselves with saying that the substantive may be repeated after each numeral. And even Reckendorf, *SV* (275–8), who expressly states that the noun is not repeated after units connected with tens, does not repeat his statement in his later *Syntax* (207, 2), contenting himself with the remark that the numbered noun is repeated after the various numeral elements. For example v. Reckendorf, *ibid.*; Wright, II, 239B / C; Ewald, II, 99, 3; as well as e.g. Tabari, I, 813, 7: *khamsu -mi'ati sanatin wa-thalāthun wa-'ishrūna sanatan* '523 years'; further *ibid.* 8[a] *mi'atay (!) sanatin wa-sittun wa-sittūna sanatan* '266 years'.

3. On the other hand, there is no indication of the univerbalization of the numbers 21–99 in Classical Arabic from the use of the definite article, since it is attached to both numerals (type: *'al-sittu wa-l-sittūna* 'the 66'). In Middle Arabic, to be sure, the definite article may be added to the first digit only (v. Blau, p. 382, §266.1, where in note 57 additional literature is adduced), as e.g. (v. Blau, *ibid.*) *al-tis'a wa-tis'īn* 'the 99'. Yet this phenomenon is not restricted to units and tens, cf. (*ibid.*) *al-thalāthmiya wa-thamāniya 'ashar* 'the 318' (if this number has not become univerbalized, because of denoting the number of the fathers of the church). At

any rate, this phenomenon is already outside Classical Arabic proper. As stated, the situation in Biblical Hebrew is much less clear.

1. Thus, as is well known, the numbers may be arranged either in ascending order (as, e.g. *shebha' wə-'eśrīm u-mē'ā* [Esther I, 1] '127', where of course, the order being ascending, the unit precedes the ten) or, more usually, in descending order, according to which the tens precede the units, as: *shesh mē'ōt wə-shishshīm wā-shesh* (I Chron. IX, 13), '666'; the units, however, *may* also precede the tens even when the numbers are arranged in descending order, presumably through the influence of the numbers 11–19: *wə-'elef u-shbha' mē'ōt wa-ḥămishshā wə-shibh'īm* (Ex. XXXVIII, 25) '1775'; *wə-'et hā-'elef u-shbha' ha-m-mē'ōt wa-ḥămishshā wə-shibh'īm, ibid.* 28 (pay attention to the article wanting with the units and tens!) 'the 1775'; *shesh mē'ōt ḥāmesh wə-shibh'īm* (Nu. XXXI, 37) '675'; *shəbha' mē'ōt ḥămishshā wə-shibh'īm* (Ezra II, 5) '775'. Cf. also *mə'at 'elef wə-'eḥād wa-ḥămishshīm 'elef* (Nu. II, 16) '151.000'. Nevertheless, one must not attach too much importance to this discontinuity in descending order, since discontinuity of another sort occurs elsewhere: *shənayim wə-'eśrīm 'elef shəlōshā wə-shibh'īm u-mātayim* (Nu. III, 43) '22,273'.

2. As to the repetition of the numbered noun, the picture emerging from Biblical Hebrew is not clear either. There occur, to be sure, numerous cases of repetition of the counted noun after every number, yet less so, between the unit and the ten, thus hinting at their univerbalization: *ḥāmesh wə-tish'īm shānā u-shmōnē mē'ōt shānā* (Gen. V, 17) '895 years' and similarly 18; 20; 23; 25; 26; 27. Cf. also Nu. II, 16, quoted *supra*. However, not only may the numbered noun be repeated between the unit and the ten *ḥāmesh shānīm wə-shishshīm shānā* (Gen. V, 15) '65 years', and similarly XII, 4, but it is also sometimes repeated, while lacking between other numerals, as if these constituted a unit: *shebha' shānīm wə-'arba'īm u-m'at shānā* (Gen. XLVII, 28) '147 years'. Nevertheless, one must admit that the omission of the numbered noun between unit and ten is more frequent.
3. Nothing can be inferred from the omission of the definite article between tens and units. This feature, to be sure, is attested (*'ad yōm hā-'eḥād wə-'eśrīm la-ḥodesh,* Ex. XII, 18, 'till the twenty-first of the month'). It is,

however, not restricted to units and tens (*ʾet ha-ḥamishshīm u-māṭayim ʾish,* Nu. XVI, 35, 'the two hundred and fifty men').

To sum up: The fixed position in Classical Arabic of the units before the tens, even in descending order, as well as the customary omission of the repeated numbered noun between units and tens, hints at (the beginnings of) their coalescence into one word. These features, to be sure, occur in Biblical Hebrew as well, yet here they are by no means fixed. Accordingly, one may, at the most, speak of contradictory tendencies in Biblical Hebrew, one of them being the tendency towards univerbalization of units and tens.

ABBREVIATIONS

Blau = J. Blau, *A Grammar of Christian Arabic . . .*, Louvain 1966–67.

Ewald = G.H.A. Ewald, *Grammatica critica linguae arabicae,* Lipsiae 1831–33.

Ibn Janāḥ = *Le livre des parterres fleuris, grammaire hébraique en arabe* d'Abou 'l-Walid Merwan ibn Djanah, ed. J. Derenbourg, Paris 1886. Its Hebrew translation is *Sefer ha-Riqma,* ed. M. Wilensky–D. Tene, Jerusalem 1964.

Reckendorf = H. Reckendorf, *Die syntaktischen Verhältnisse des Arabischen,* Leiden 1895–98.

Reckendorf, Syntax = H. Reckendorf, *Arabische Syntax,* Heidelberg 1921.

Sībawayhi = *Le Livre de Sībawayhi . . .*, ed. H. Derenbourg, Paris 1881-89.

Ṭabari = *Annales* auctore . . . M . . . Al-Ṭabari, ed. . . . M.J. de Goeje, Lugd. Bat. 1879–1901.

Wright = W. Wright, *A Grammar of the Arabic Language . . .*[3], Cambridge 1896–98.

Marginalia Semitica I

1. ARABIC / HEBREW *uyC*[1] > *îC*; *iwC* > *ûC*

As a rule, sound shifts are considered the main force effecting sound changes, whereas analogic formation is regarded as bringing about smaller alterations only in the operation of sound shifts. Yet, as is well known,[2] sometimes analogy happens to crowd out the effects of sound shift, so that only some scattered vestiges of the latter enable us to reconstruct it. In the following we shall undertake to postulate some sound shifts in Arabic and Hebrew, basing ourselves on some rather effaced traces of their action. We shall start with the most conspicuous one, to proceed to those less marked.

1.1. ARABIC *uyC* > *îC*. On the one hand, cases like **buyḍ* > *bîḍ* "white" (plural), **buyd* > *bîd* "deserts"[3] indicate the shift *uyC* > *îC*, on the other, numerous cases like **yuybisu* > *yûbisu* "he will make it dry", the feminine elative forms *fuʿlâ* of roots *mediae yâ* *ṭûbâ* "the best", *kûsâ* "the shrewdest", *ḍûqâ* "the narrowest"[4] suggest the shift *uyC* > *ûC*. It is, of course, methodologically * unsound to simply juxtapose both shifts, as does Fleisch 123, without trying to differentiate between them.[5] Since it is impossible to assign them to different periods, it stands to reason that only one of them exhibits genuine sound

1 C = consonant. More exactly: when not followed by vowel, since these shifts, also, act when *y*/*w* stand in word final. In Arabic *u* preceding *y* shifts to *i*, even if *y* is followed by a vowel. Nothing can be inferred as to the behaviour of *iw* in Arabic and of both shifts in Hebrew, when *y*/*w* precede a vowel; for particulars see below.

2 See, e.g., Bauer-Leander 54, §q.

3 Kuryłowicz 21 is, it seems, wrong in interpreting *mudîr* as being due to this sound shift.

4 These adjectives are quoted by Lane 1901b, and also by Brockelmann I, 190, Rem. 1. As to *ṭûbâ*, only in the sense of "best" does it exhibit the sound shift we are dealing with, since in the meaning of "blessed he..." it is an Aramaic loan, see S. Fraenkel, *De vocabulis... in Corano peregrinis* (Leiden 1880), p. 24 and A. Jeffery, *The Foreign Vocabulary of the Qur'ân* (Baroda 1938), *s.v.*

5 This also applies to the earlier editions of Socin-Brockelmann, e.g. the seventh edition (1913), p. 21, § 13d. On the other hand, Fleisch (*ibid.*, note 1) correctly interpreted *uyC* > *û* as being due to the pattern. One will, however, reject his claim that *bîḍ* is due to the tendency of conserving the radical *yâ* as far as possible. J. Barth, *Jubelschrift... des Dr. I. Hildesheimer*, (Berlin 1890), p. 151, note 1 assumes that in Arabic *uy* shifted to *û*.

shift, the other being due to analogical formation. And, as it has already been stated,[6] it is the more frequent sound change (*viz.* *uyC* > *ûC*) that is due to analogical formation: forms like *yûbisu*, *ḍûqâ* are influenced by the pattern exhibiting *u* as its characteristic vowel, whereas the genuine sound shift *uyC* > *îC* has been preserved but in a few patterns.

REMARK: *u* preceding *y* shifts to *i* also if *y* is followed by a vowel (see Socin–Brockelmann 21, § 13e, Kuryłowicz 21); e.g. **marmûyun* > *marmîyun*, spelt *marmiyyun* "thrown"; **tabannuyun* > **tabanniyun* (> *tabannin* "adopting"); **ruqûyun* > *ruqîyun*, spelt *ruqiyyun* "to ascend"; **ᶜuṣûyun* > *ʿuṣîyun*, spelt *ʿuṣiyyun* "sticks". Through patternizing, in some patterns forms with *u* occur alongside those with *i* and are more frequent than they, as *ʿuyûn* / *ʿiyûn* "eyes", *buyayt* / *biyayt* "small house".

1.2 HEBREW *uyC* > *îC*. This shift has left two vestiges only, *viz.* in two passive *Qal* imperfect form s of *verba mediae yâ*,[7] which, as is well known,[8] form these forms (as well as *Hofʿal*) as if from *verba primae yâ*: Gen. l 26 *wayyîśęm* (so also *kthîbh* Gen. xxiv 33) "he was laid" < **wayyuyśęm*; Exod. xxx 32 *yîsâḵ* "it will be poured" < **yuysâḵ*. One will consent to the opinion expressed by Bauer–Leander 201–202[9] that these forms reflect genuine sound shift, whereas the usual forms like *yûṣar*, etc.[10] "it is formed" do not exhibit a sound shift *uyC* > *û*, but are due to analogical formation.[11]

[6] See, e.g., Brockelmann I, 190 (quoted also by Bauer-Leander 202, note 1), the later editions of Socin-Brockelmann (as in the 12th one from 1948), as well as Kuryłowicz 21. Kuryłowicz 22 (who also quotes the rarer forms *ṭîbâ*, *kîsâ* and *ḍîqâ*) explains the shift *uy* > *û* as being due to morphological treatment. This is, of course, only another name for patternizing owing to analogical formation.

[7] J. Barth, *loc. cit.*, Bergsträsser II, 152, § 28t were, in our opinion, right in positing a *mediae y* root *syk* "to anoint, pour".

[8] See, e.g., Bergsträsser II, 154, § 28v*.

[9] Cf. also P. Leander, *OLZ* XXVIII (1965). p. 687. Similarly also Kuryłowicz 22, § 27. The first who expressed this opinion was, it seems, J. Barth, *loc. cit.*

[10] Bauer-Leander speak of *û* occurring in "some cases". This, however, is an understatement: *û* is the rule, having crowded out the results of the genuine sound shift, but for the vestiges mentioned; and even one of them subsisted in *kthîbh* only, being superseded in *qrê* by *û*.

[11] *Pace* Bergsträsser I, 97, who regards *uy* > *û* as genuine sound shift; see against him Kuriłowicz 22, § 27 (by the way, the main reason for nouns like *bârûṯ* not exhibiting that shift is, it seems, that, by metanalysis, *-ûṯ* developed into a suffix apt to be added to every kind of nouns, not to *tertiae w* alone; cf. Barth 412, 413ff). Against correcting *wayyîśęm* and *yîsâḵ* into *wayyûśam* and *yûsâḵ* respectively, thus disregarding a form occurring twice (and, one may add, once in *kthîbh*) in Pentateuch, see, e.g. Nöldeke, BSS 39; yet his supposition of a metaplastic *Nifʿal* of *primae y* is far from convincing. The same applies also to Bergsträsser II, 154, *in fine*, who surmises that these irregular forms of *mediae y* have been newly formed from *mediae y* according to the proportion *û*:*î*.

1.3 HEBREW *iwC*>*ûC*. I would like to propose that the genuine shift of *iwC* in Hebrew is *û*, as exhibited by *yûḵal* "he will be able", being the *a*-imperfect *Qal* of original *wkl*, i.e. < **yiwkal*, and *tûqaḏ* "she will burn", which occurs five times alternating with *tîqaḏ*.[12] As a rule, however, through the analogy of the pattern *yifʿal*, the pattern *yîʿal* (as already once *tîqaḏ*) prevailed, conveying the impression of *iw* shifting to *î*;[13] it was only *yûḵal* that, owing to its extraordinary frequency, was not influenced by analogy at all, whereas *tûqaḏ* due to analogy already alternates with *tîqaḏ*. *

REMARK: If our supposition as to the shift *iwC*>*ûC* in Hebrew (and Arabic, see § 1.4) is correct, forms like *qîmâ* "rising up" (and Arabic *qîma* "value") cannot be interpreted as genuine *qiṭla* patterns. They have

[12] For *tûqaḏ* as Qal cf. J. Barth, *ZDMG* XLVIII (1894), pp. 13–14. Once also *yêqaḏ*; cf. for it Bauer-Leander 195, § b'; p. 383, on the one hand, Bergsträsser 126, §d, note k, on the other.

[13] It is, of course, methodologically unsound to postulate the shifting of *iw* both to *î* and *û*, as do Brockelmann I, 601, R. Meyer, *Hebräische Grammatik* (Berlin 1966), Vol. I, p. 99 (cf. also Bauer-Leander 382, note 3). Bergsträsser I, 97 and Kuryłowicz 22, § 27 only admit *iw* > *î*. As to the words adduced by Bergsträsser (§f), all of them exhibit *iwy*, which, through assimilation, shifts to *iyy* (as **kiwy* > *kiyy* > *kî* "burning"; cf. in Arabic *kayy* < **kawy*); Bergsträsser himself allows for this possibility. According to Kuryłowicz the most striking indication of the shift *iw* > *iy* > *î* is the coincidence of *verba tertiae w* with those *tertiae y* "in the derived classes". If I am understanding it correctly, "the derived classes" designate the derived patterns of the verb, i.e. all the verbal patterns with the exception of *Qal*; if this is, in fact, Kuryłowicz's intention, he mistook the Hebrew verbal system for the Arabic one, since it is only in the latter that the supersession of *tertiae w* is limited to the derived verbal patterns, whereas in Hebrew they were crowded out altogether. One need not, however, ascribe the disappearance of *verba tertiae w* to *iw*, shifting to *î*. The elision of both *w* and *y* between short vowels and, it seems, at least in some cases between short and long vowels, yielding the same products of contraction (see for particulars in Hebrew e.g. Bergsträsser I, 99-102, for Arabic e.g. Fleisch 122 ff.), sufficiently accounts for the merger of *verba tertiae w* and *y*. Bergsträsser II, 78, § 14f postulates for *u*-perfect an *a*-imperfect with *u* as vowel of prefix (i.e. *Yufʿal*). Yet, besides the general unlikeliness of this assumption, there is no indication whatsoever for an *u*-perfect of *yqd* (see Birkeland 95). Birkeland himself assumes (p. 100) that in Proto-Semitic the vowel of prefix was influenced by the surrounding consonants, especially by the first radical consonant. Thus he explains Hebrew *yûḵal*, etc. and Arabic dialectal forms (see below) like *yûqaf*. Yet his theory pivots upon the supposition that imperfect, imperative and infinitive with elision of *w* is not limited to forms with *i* after the second radical consonant (pp. 92ff.). This, however, is, it seems, fallacious. In cases in which Birkeland postulates an *original a*-imperfect and does not allow for the influence of laryngals and pharyngals (see especially p. 94), the genuineness of *i* is held up by nouns containing *i* as their characteristic vowel (like Arabic *mawḍiʿ* "place", *hiba* "gift", Hebrew *dêʿâ* "knowledge", *mizbêᵃḥ* "altar", *maftêᵃḥ* "key"; since in the imperative and apocopate forms of the verb without suffixes the laryngals/pharyngals [and sometimes *r*] occurred in the same syllable as the vowel, they influenced it, whereas in nouns, owing to case endings [and in *hiba* because of the feminine ending], the vowel stood in a separate syllable).

to be considered either as original bi-literal patterns or as being due to the impact of *mediae y* (cf., *mutatis mutandis*, late Biblical Hebrew *qiyyam* "to fulfil" and Arabic *qayyim* "manager", the last form being due to the shift *awî* 〉 *ayî* 〉 *ayyi* in the middle of a morpheme). *If* the shift *iw* 〉 *û* also acted when preceding a vowel (other than *a*) one would interpret words like Hebrew *ʿânî* 〈 **ʿanîwu* "poor" and Arabic *ʿaliyy^{un}* (= *ʿalîy^{un}*) 〈 **ʿalîw^{un}* "high" as being due to the analogy of *tertiae y*.

* 1.4 ARABIC *iwC* 〉 *ûC*. Whereas Arabic dialectal forms like *yûqaf* (see for them e.g. Brockelmann I, 598, § 268 cβ, Birkeland 92f., Rabin 158) amply occur, being due, it seems, to this sound shift, it cannot, however, be directly attested in Classical Arabic. This is the reason why, as far as my knowledge goes, without exception, *iwC* 〉 *îC* is regarded as the genuine sound shift[14] (cf. also § 1.3, above, Remark). There exists, however, an important indication for *iwC* 〉 *ûC*: the fact that (with the exception of *faʿila*, *yafʿalu* and a few verbs containing laryngal / pharyngal) *verba tertiae w* in the imperfect of the first verbal pattern invariably exhibit *yafʿû*, as against *yafʿî* in *verba tertiae y*.[15] One is inclined to suggest that this situation arose by *u/iy* and *i/uw* in word final shifting to *î* and *û* respectively. Accordingly, both **yafʿiy* and **yafʿuy* became *yafʿî*, as against *yafʿû* originating from both **yafʿiw* and **yafʿuw*. This supposition is corroborated by an additional fact. As Barth has pointed out (see p. 123, § 79f.),[16] some nouns from roots *tertiae w* exhibit *i* as characteristic vowel (as *diʿwat*), thus indicating an imperfect **yafʿiwu*.

REMARK A: If the shift *iw* 〉 *û* was limited to cases in which no vowel followed the *w*, one would assume that the apocopate imperfect **yafʿiw* and the imperative **'ifʿiw* shifted to **yafʿû* / **ifʿû* respectively (to become finally **yafʿu* / **'ifʿu*); the indicative **yafʿiwu* was then influenced by these forms. *If*, however, one posits this sound shift even when the *w* is followed by a vowel (a supposition that cannot be corroborated by any other facts), then the indicative too developed to *yafʿû* by genuine sound shift.

REMARK B: On the face of it, forms like *nîrân*, plural of *nâr* (*mediae w*) "fire", *ʿîdân*, plural of *ʿûd* "piece of wood" contravene our shift: **niwrân* / **ʿiwdân* should have shifted to ** nûrân* / **ʿûdân* respectively. Yet the historical development was, it seems, different. It stands to reason that *-ân*

[14] See, e.g., Brockelmann I, 190, Brockelmann-Socin 21, § 13d, Kuryłowicz 21 (where omit, however, *mabîʿ*), Fleisch 122, § 24d.

[15] It is much more venturesome to infer anything from the fact that in *verba mediae infirmae yafûʿ* is limited to *verba mediae w*, *yafîʿ* to *mediae y*, since the influence of bi-literal patterns on these verbs was much stronger.

[16] On the other hand, one will hardly consent to the views expressed by Barth 190, § 127e; see also Kuryłowicz 22, § 26.

served, as in many Semitic languages, in Arabic as well, as a plural ending added to the singular base (cf. Brockelmann I, 450). If the singular base contained *a*, it was dissimilated to *i* (as *'ax* "brother", plural *'ixwân* < **'axwân*). Accordingly, *nâr* gave rise to *nîrân* < **nârân*. Then this pattern became productive and caused also forms like *'îdân*, without action of dissimilation.

As to *fi'lat* seemingly infringing our shift as well (as *thîrat*, plural of *thawr* "ox"), they have to be regarded as secondary forms of *fi'lân* (as *thîrân*); cf. also *'ixwat*, occurring alongside *'ixwân*.

2. ARABIC *ḍâl*, HEBREW *ṣe'ĕlîm*, SYRIAC *'âlâ* "*Zizyphus Lotus*"

Since the days of the great Abulwalîd Marwân ibn Djanâḥ[1] it is commonplace[2] to explain Hebrew *ṣę'ĕlîm* Job xl:21, 22 as *Zizyphus Lotus* in accordance with Arabic *ḍâl*. It is now[3] also generally recognized that *'âlâ* (as a rule spelt

1 He lived in the first half of the eleventh century.

2 Gesenius in his *Thesaurus... s.v.* quoted Ibn Djanâḥ's *Lexicon*, *s.v.*, *in extenso*; the latter did not only recognize the relationship of the Arabic and Hebrew words, but he also brilliantly demonstrated the fallaciousness of the accepted interpretation, viz. *ṣę'ęlîm* = *ṣəlâlîm* "shadows". Since Gesenius's days the correspondence of *ṣę'ĕlîm* with *ḍâl* is generally recognized, see the various biblical dictionaries. As far as I am aware, only F. Zorell *s.v.*, following L. Fonck, *Streifzüge durch die biblische Flora*, (Freiburg i. Br. 1900), pp. 96f., expressed himself against this identification. Yet Löw 135, basing himself on Arabic material, refuted Fonck's objections. On the other hand, Gesenius *ibid.* was wrong in claiming that already Saadia recognized the correspondence of *ṣę'êlîm* with *ḍâl*, as if translating Job xl 21 *taḥta -ḍ-ḍâl* "under the lotus". As a matter of fact, Saadia translated *taḥta-l-miẓalla*, *i.e.* he derived this word from "shadow" (see Saadia ben Josef al-Fayyoûmî, *Oeuvres complètes*, ed. J. H. Derenbourg – M. Lambert, (Paris 1893–1900), Vol. V, *Version arabe du livre de Job*, ed. W. Bacher, *ad locum*. Cf. also R. Ecker, *Die arabische Job-Übersetzung des Gaon Saadja ben Josef al-Fajjûmî...* (München 1962), p. 21, where note 49 Ecker is, however, wrong in claiming that ibn Djanâḥ derives our word from "shadow" as well, also mentioning the interpretation of "lotus". As a matter of fact, Ibn Djanâḥ admits the *grammatical* possibility of *ṣę'ĕlîm* being identical with *ṣəlâlîm*, yet he rejects it owing to the context and *parallelismus membrorum*). It seems that in the manuscript used by Gesenius the plural *maẓâll* was used instead of the singular (cf. for this form e.g. Ecker 282, note 6), *ḍ* being spelt for the *ẓ*, as usual in Judaeo-Arabic (see, e.g., my *Emergence*, p. 76), i.e. المضال, which he mistook for الضال. In Jewish exegesis and lexicography Ibn Djanâḥ's insight was immediately accepted by a man like Ibn Gikatila (second half of the eleventh century); see W. Bacher's edition of his translation and commentary to Job (Budapest 1908/1909, Offprint from *Festschrift... A. Harkavy* (St. Petersburg 1908), pp. 221–272, *ad locum*). On the other hand, the traditional Jewish interpretation (as it was already in the *Targum*) remained that of "shadow" (see, e.g., Rashi, Abraham ibn Esra, Gersonides), even in such a late commentary as *Məṣûdat Ṣiyôn* (seventeenth century, by David Altschul and his son Yekhiel Hillel Altschüler).

3 Thanks to I. Löw, *Aramäische Pflanzennamen* (Leipzig 1881), p. 275. Correct Koehler-Baumgartner[1] *s.v.* accordingly!

with *âlaf* after the *ʿê*) corresponds to these nouns in Syriac. Nevertheless, each noun in itself exhibits some minor problems.

2.1. ARABIC *ḍâl*. It is attested without consonantal *alif* only,[4] though the original form was, no doubt, **ḍa'l*. Since, as recognized by Spitaler,[5] consonantal *alif* in this position was not pronounced in vernacular, the tradition was apt to become incertain, if the *alif* was not preserved in other favourable forms. So did it come about that the original form disappeared from Classical Arabic, although according to its rules consonantal *alif* should have been retained in this position.

2.2. HEBREW *ṣę'ĕlîm*. In contradistinction to the *qaṭl* pattern in Arabic and Syriac, this word exhibits in Hebrew, on the synchronic level at least, the *qiṭl* pattern. Accordingly, in modern (Israeli) Hebrew the singular was revived according to this pattern: *ṣə'êl*.[6] The problem is whether or not there is any historical link between *qaṭl* in Arabic and Syriac, and *qiṭl* in Hebrew. *Prima facie*, there are two alternatives: either the various Semitic languages reflect different, originally unconnected patterns,[7] or the Hebrew vocalization is erroneous: the original pattern was *qaṭl* in Hebrew as well, and the genuine vocalization should have been (in accordance with *rôš* "head", plural *râšîm*) singular **ṣôl*, plural **ṣâlîm*.[8] Nevertheless, it seems that one could make out a case for the Hebrew form, as it is vocalized, as being the genuine continuation of the original *qaṭl* pattern, and for **ṣôl* as non-existent.

There is no unanimity among scholars as to the exact conditions under which Hebrew **ra'š* shifted to *rôš* (and, therefore, **ṣa'l* should have developed to **ṣôl*), yet it is not difficult to show the difference between these two words, according to some views. According to Bergsträsser I, 163–164, § 30c (where

[4] As expressly stated, e.g., by *Lisân al-ʿarab, s.v.* It is due to some sort of etymological hyper-correction that many scholars spell this word with consonantal *alif*, e.g. Nöldeke, Mand. 17, note 5, Brockelmann, LS 503, *s.v.* "*'âlâ*", E. König, *Hebräisches und aramäisches Wörterbuch zum Alten Testament*[6] (Leipzig 1936), *s.v.* "*ṣę'ęlîm*".

[5] *Bibliotheca Orientalis* XI (1954), p. 32, note 5.

[6] See I. Avinery, *Proceedings of the Academy of the Hebrew Language* XV (1967/1968), p. 15, idem, *Yad hallâšôn* (Tel Aviv 1964) *s.v.* Nevertheless, it is by no means certain that *ṣə'êl* is not a ghost word. First, it may well be that forms like *bə'êr* "well" are due to blend of the singular **bêr* and the plural **bə'ârôt*. In this case, since the plural of lotus was of a different pattern, see below, its development might have been different (if it was not influenced by words like *bə'êr*). Second, it stands to reason that it had in singular a feminine ending, see below. At any rate, Avinery (*ibid.*) is wrong when simply identifying *ṣę'ĕlîm* with *bę'ĕrôṯ bę'ęrôṯ* (*ḥêmâr*) Gen. xiv 10, since the last passage has to be interpreted as *status constructus* (cf. *ḥămešęṯ ḥămešęṯ šəqâlîm* Num. iii 47; *middahărôṯ dahărôṯ 'abbîrâw* Judg. v 22).

[7] As the case is with *rôš*, etc. in various Semitic languages, see the rather extreme view expressed by J. Friedrich, *Orientalia* XII (1943), p. 18; cf. also J. Blau, *BSOAS* XXXII (1969), p. 2, § 2.1.

[8] See A. Spitaler, *Bibliotheca Orientalis* XI (1954), p. 32, note 5.

he modified the view expressed I, 89, § 15b; cf. also Birkeland 40), for instance, this shift arose in the *status constructus*, where the *alef* preceded the tautosyllabic final consonant, and analogically spread to other forms. In this case, of course, it is not difficult to account for **ṣa'l* not shifting to **ṣôl*: this was due to the prevalence of those forms in which the *alef* was not followed by the final consonant and was, therefore, preserved. This predominance might have been due to the fact that, as it has been emphasized by the late Akiba Schlesinger,[9] *ṣę'ĕlîm* belongs to the plural pattern of botanical and zoological etc. species, formed by *-îm* from monosyllabic bases with feminine ending, without adding *a* after the second radical (*i.e.* like **šiqmâ* "sycomore", plural [as a rule] *šiqmîm*, rather than **šəqâmîm*). Accordingly, the plural **ṣa'lîm*, being rather similar to the singular, might have influenced it, whereas **rə'âšîm* (> *râšîm*), having a pattern different from the singular, did not change it. Moreover, if the singular, in fact, terminated in feminine ending (*i.e.* **ṣa'lâ*),[10] then it was not affected by the shift stressed *a'* > *â* > *ô* at all, because the *alef* did not precede the tautosyllabic final consonant.

The same holds good for the theory that it was during a general penultimate stress period that stressed *a'* (and stressed *a'* only) had shifted to *â* and then (since during this period this shift continued to act) to *ô*.[11] Not only did, of course, according to this theory as well the plural **ṣa'lîm* < **sa'lîma* not change, and was, being similar to the singular, apt to influence it, but the singular **ṣa'látu* (later >**ṣa'lâ*), exhibiting unstressed *a'*, also preserved its *alef*, whereas **rá'šu* > **râšu* > **rôšu* (later > *rôš*) lost it.

We have tried to establish that, whereas **ra'š* had shifted to *rôš*, the singular of "lotus" was not **ṣôl*, and **ṣa'lîm* itself did not change. Afterwards it shifted to **ṣi'lîm* and futher to *ṣę'ęlîm*, just as e.g. **ya'sup* shifted to **yi'suf* and further to *yę'ĕsof*.[12] Accordingly, *ṣę'ĕlîm*, though synchronically exhibiting the *qiṭl* pattern, is historically genuine continuation of *qaṭl*.

2.3. SYRIAC *ʿâlâ*. As a rule, non final *a'* shifts to East and West Syriac *e*. Nöldeke, Mand. 17, note 5 surmised that in our word and in *ʿânâ* "cattle", *a* was retained through the influence of ʿ (so also C. Brockelmann, *Syrische*

[9] See A. Schlesinger, *Researches in the Exegesis and Language of the Bible*, Publications of the Israel Society for Biblical Research V, Jerusalem 1962, pp. 50–51 (Hebrew).

[10] Job xl 21 *yəsukkûhû ṣę'ĕlîm* "lotus trees screen it" does not prove *ṣę'ĕlîm* being masculine. Basing themselves on Jer ii 19 and Job xix 15, the grammars (see, e.g., Gesenius-Kautzsch p. 161, § 60a) claim that 3. pers. fem. plur. imperfect with suffixes is *tiqṭəlû*; since, however, 3. pers. fem. plur. imperfect is often superseded by the masc. (see, e.g., Joüon 459, § 150c), *yiqṭəlû* may be used for fem. plur. with or without suffixes.

[11] See the author's paper in the *J. Schirmann Jubilee Volume* (Jerusalem 1969; Hebrew). For the period of general penult stress in Hebrew cf. below, § 5.6.

[12] For this sound shift see, e.g., Bergsträsser I, 90–91, § 15d (without, however, accepting all his examples).

Grammatik[7], Leipzig 1955, p. 36, § 59). Since, however, such an exceptional shift of *a*' to *â* is also exhibited by *mânâ* "vessel" and perhaps by *bâṭar* "after", one is inclined to postulate an older sound shift *a*' > *â*, the shift to *e* being later. *Mânâ* and *bâṭar* were affected by the earlier shift because of their great frequency, *ʿâlâ* and *ʿânâ* because of the preceding ʿ which occasioned the early dissimilation of the *âlaf*. For particulars see *BSOAS* XXXII (1969), p. 3, § 2.2.

3. HEBREW *ḥâṣîr* "reed" A ghost-word; hebrew *riḇṣâ* "irrigation"

3.1. Basing himself on Syriac *ḥêrê* "reeds" (spelt with *âlaf* after the *ḥêṭ*), the etymological *pendant*, it seems, of Hebrew *ḥâṣîr*,[1] I. Löw, in his monumental *Flora der Juden* (I, 581–582), proposed the meaning "reed" for Hebrew *ḥâṣîr* as well. Thus he added another signification to the two meanings already accepted of *ḥâṣîr*, *viz.* "grass" and "leeks" (Num. xi 5). Because of Löw's authority, his proposal was accepted by the various editions (all the three) of Koehler–Baumgartner. Yet *ḥâṣîr* "reed" is, it seems, a ghost-word.

3.2. Philologically, for positing the new meaning of *ḥâṣîr*, Löw is mainly relying upon Isa. xxxv 7:

7a	וְהָיָה הַשָּׁרָב לַאֲגַם
7b	וְצִמָּאוֹן לְמַבּוּעֵי מָיִם
7c	בִּנְוֵה תַנִּים רִבְצָה[2]
7d	חָצִיר לְקָנֶה וָגֹמֶא

In Löw's opinion, the juxtaposition of *ḥâṣîr* with *qânê* and *gómę* shows that *ḥâṣîr* is an aquatic plant as well. He assumes, following S. Grünberg, that *lə* in 7d designates "and". Accordingly, 7d means "reed *and* stalk and rush". The assumption that *lə* designates (at least here) "and" is, however, rather unlikely. Its real meaning becomes immediately clear, if temporarily one omits 7c: *lə*, governed by *wəhâyâ*, which occurs in the three parallel verses 7a, b, and d, describing that something characteristic of desert will become something typical of abundance in water. *Ḥâṣîr* denotes grass growing under the worst conditions,

[1] The correspondent root in Arabic is *xḍr* "green" (not *ḥḍr*, as Zorell *s.v.*), cf. also Akkadian *xaṣartum* "green wool, (green) dry mucus"; see F. Schulthess, *ZA* XIX (1905/1906), p. 127, and W. Fischer, *Farb- und Formbezeichnungen in der Sprache der altarabischen Dichtung*... (Wiesbaden 1965), p. 116. Accordingly, *ḥêrê* has to be interpreted as **ḥa'rê* < **ḥaʿrê* < **ḥaḍrê*. Yet in some Aramaic dialects *ṣ* is attested as second radical. In Judaeo-Aramaic this could be due to Hebrew influence, but not in *Sfire* (A 28). Here it exhibits, it seems, the well known "weak" sound change, Aramaic *ṣ* corresponding to Arabic *ḍ*. This, however, is beyond the scope of this paper.

[2] I am adopting the reading of *h* without *mappîq*. For particulars see below.

without water at all, even on roofs (*ḥâṣîr gaggôṯ* Isa. xxxvii 27; II Kgs. xix 26; Ps. cxxix 6), which thus becomes the type of what is quickly perishing (cf., *pace* Löw, Job viii 12 "it withers before every *ḥâṣîr*"). It is the sign of utter dearth that in the vicinity of springs and wadis, where, in normal times, stalk and rush is growing, one hopes to find perhaps some grass. This is the reason why I Kgs. v 18 Ahab and Obadiah are looking for grass in the vicinity of springs and wadis, and not, as Löw claims ("perhaps"), because *ḥâṣîr* is an aquatic plant. Accordingly, one would render Isa. xxxv 7a,b, and d:

7a: And the parched ground will become a pool;
7b: and the thirsty land (will become) springs of water;
7d: and grass (the sign of dearth, will become) stalk and rush (*i.e.*, even dry places, where grass only grew, will become as much watered that reed and stalk will supplant grass).

One need not wonder why 7c interrupts the parallel verses 7b and 7d.[3] Such interruptions are common in biblical poetry. Cf. e.g. Deut. xxxii 42:

42a	אַשְׁכִּיר חִצַּי מִדָּם
42b	וְחַרְבִּי תֹּאכַל בָּשָׂר
42c	מִדַּם חָלָל וְשִׁבְיָה
42d	מֵרֹאשׁ פַּרְעוֹת אוֹיֵב

i.e.,
42a I will make my arrows drunk with blood;
42b and my sword shall devour flesh;
42c with the blood of the slain and of the captives;
42d from the head of the leaders (?) of the foe.

As a rule,[4] 42c is considered continuation of 42a, and 42d of 42b. Accordingly, 42b interrupts the continuity of *middâm* 42a and its apposition *middam* 42c, and 42c intervenes between 42b and its attributive preposional phrase in 42d. Since, however, both 42c and 42d begin with the preposition *min*, one could consider 42c and 42d continuation of 42a; in this case, only 42b would disconnect the appositional (42c) and attributive (42d) prepositional phrase from 42a. Yet *a* being parallel to *c*, and *b* to *d* is not unusual in Biblical poetry,[5] whereas *a* being continued by *c* and *d* (just as *a* and *b* being continued by *d*, as we assumed for Isa. xxxv 7) is exceptional.

3.3. We have endeavoured to explain Isa. xxxv 7a,b, and d. We still have

[3] Prepositions may not only be separated from the governing verb, but they may be omitted altogether in parallel members, see, e.g., Gesenius-Kautzsch 384hh.

[4] See, e.g., S. R. Driver, *An Introduction to the Literature of the Old Testament*, Meridian Library edition (New York 1956), p. 364.

[5] See, e.g., Driver, *loc. cit.*

to interpret 7c *binwê ṯannîm riḇṣâ*. According to the parallelism, it has to signify desert turning into abundance of water. *Tannîm* are well known as dwelling in deserts (see, e.g., Jer. ix 10; x 22). Accordingly, *riḇṣâ* has to be the antonym of *nəwê ṯannîm* "abode of jackals", the symbol of desolation, i.e. it will denote "irrigation, irrigated land", the symbol of fertility and prosperity (cf., e.g., the usage of *gan râwę* "watered garden" Isa. lviii 11; Jer. xxxi 12; cf. also *mašqę* "irrigation, i.e. well-irrigated" Gen. xiii 10). This interpretation is corroborated by the verb *rbṣ*, used, as recognized by N. H. Tur-Sinai (in Ben Yehuda 6399b, note 1; cf. already, J. Levy, *Wörterbuch über die Talmudim und Midraschim...*², Berlin–Wien 1924, Vol. IV, p. 421b), in Biblical Hebrew in *Qal* Gen. xlix 25; Deut. xxxiii 13 in the phrase *təhôm rôḇęṣęṯ tâḥaṯ* "the abyss that overflows in the deep". Tur-Sinai rightly connected this root with Middle Hebrew *ribbeṣ* "to sprinkle, water".[6] Cf. also Syriac *rəḇaṣ* "to water", which then passed into Arabic and from there into Turkish.[7]

Accordingly, we interpret *riḇṣâ* (spelt with final *h* as *mater lectionis*)[8] as a feminine noun denoting "irrigation, irrigated land", being a *hapax legomenon.* Many manuscripts, to be sure, read *riḇṣâh* (with *mappîq* in the *h*, exhibiting its consonantal function). One has, however, the impression that this reading is secondary: since *reḇęṣ* occurs three times in the Bible, twice (Isa. lxv 10; Prov. xxiv 15) parallel to *nâwę*, our *riḇṣâ* was interpreted as *reḇęṣ* with pronominal suffix. In this connection it is interesting to note that 1 Qumran Isaiah Scroll *a* went as far as to substitute *reḇęṣ* for *riḇṣâ*! The ordinary manuscripts, however, did not dare to dispense with the *h* altogether, but contented

[6] One will not pay too much attention to *ribbeṣ* denoting irrigation by sprinkling. First, there are, it seems, still vestigial uses of *ribbeṣ* designating full watering, see H. Albeck, *Sedęr Zərâ'îm* (Jerusalem–Tel Aviv 1958), pp. 346/7, and S. Lieberman, *Tosefta Ki-Fshuṭah...*, *Order Zera'im* (New York 1955), p. 155 (referring to lines 42–43). Second, the semantic transition from abundant watering to sprinkling is an easy one, cf. e.g. Hebrew *šâṭaf*, denoting both (over)flowing and rinsing, and especially the Arabic loans in Turkish quoted in the next note.

[7] Cf. Brockelmann, LS, *s.v.*, who separates *rbṣ* "to water" from *rbṣ* "to press", cf. already Th. Nöldeke, *ZA* XXX (1951/1916), p. 116. M. T. Féghali, *Etudes sur les emprunts syriaques dans les parlers arabes du Liban* (Paris 1918), p. 52 (= *Mémoires de la Société de Linguistique de Paris* XXVII [1920], p. 268), idem, *Contes, légendes, coutumes populaires du Liban* (Paris 1930), p. 135, note 1, and A. Barthélemy, *Dictionnaire Arabe-Français, Dialectes de Syrie...* (Paris 1935→), *s.v.* "*rbṣ*", however, connect both meanings, with reason, as it seems. Cf. also A. Frayha, *A Dictionary of Non-Classical Vocables* (Beirut 1947), *s.v.*, and C. Landberg, *Glossaire Daṯînois* (Leiden 1920–1942), *s.v.* As to alleged Classical Arabic *barbaṣa*, lacking in most dictionaries, it is adduced in al-Fîrûzâbâdî's *Qâmûs*. As to *rbṣ* in Turkish, see A. Tietze, "Direkte arabische Entlehnungen im anatolischen Türkisch", in *Mélanges Jean Deny* (Ankara 1958), p. 279, § 72. It is interesting to note that in some places in Turkey it denotes abundant, in others insufficient irrigation.

[8] This is also the reading of Rashi, as well as of some twenty manuscripts.

themselves with interpreting the word as being derived from *reḇęṣ* with pronominal suffix. It is a pity that biblical dictionaries accepted this secondary reading.

Accordingly, we suggest to interpret Isa. xxxv 7 as follows: "And the parched ground will become a pool, and the thirsty land springs of water, in the abode of jackals (there will be) irrigation, grass (will become) stalk and rush".

3.4. We have endeavoured to show that *ḥâṣîr* does not denote "reed" either Isa. xxxv 7, the main basis of Löw's contention, or I Kgs. xviii 5; Job viii 12. The same applies to Isa. xliv 4, quoted by Löw (and, following him, by Koehler–Baumgartner). In the preceding verse God promises to bless Israel by watering dry ground. Accordingly, וְצָמְחוּ בְּבֵין חָצִיר כַּעֲרָבִים עַל־יִבְלֵי־מָיִם "they will grow among grass (i.e. at former dry places, where grass served as the only vegetation) as poplars by water courses", because the former dry places will become well watered.

Since *ḥâṣîr* nowhere designates "reed", one will beware of emending with Löw Ps. x 8, where the wicked is described as sitting (*bəma'raḇ*) *ḥăṣêrîm* to *ḥăsîrîm*, especially since the plural of *ḥaṣîr* is nowhere attested.[9]

3.5. Already the Septuagint interpreted *ḥâṣîr* Isa. xxxv 7 as *ḥâṣêr* "court", and so also Isa. xxxiv 13. It was followed[10] by many ancient (as Ibn Djanâḥ) and modern scholars (see the biblical dictionaries). As to Isa. xxxv 7, we hope to have shown the fallaceousness of this assumption. But Isa. xxxiv 13 as well, *ḥâṣîr* (as well as "the abode of jackals", see above) is used as a symbol of desolation:

13a	וְעָלְתָה אַרְמְנֹתֶיהָ סִירִים
13b	קִמּוֹשׂ וָחוֹחַ בְּמִבְצָרֶיהָ
13c	וְהָיְתָה נְוֵה תַנִּים
13d	חָצִיר לִבְנוֹת יַעֲנָה

"And thorns will come up in her palaces, nettles and brambles (will be) in her fortresses, and it will be an abode of jackals, and grass (suitable) for (the pasture of) ostriches (?) (will be there)".

9 Since the semantic field of *ḥăṣêrîm* "settlements" has contact with that of *midbâr* (see Isa. xlii 11) and of *kęręm* (see Cant. vii 12–13), both of which are connected with ambushes (Lam. iv 19; Judg. xxi 20), it *may* simply denote lurking places in such settlements.

10 Isa xxxiv 13 1 Qumran Isaiah Scroll *a* reads *ḥâṣêr*, no doubt a *lectio facilior*, cf. Kutscher 26, 179–180.

4. Aramaic Calque in Hebrew and Middle Arabic in the Field of Verbal Patterns

4.1. When dealing with lexical interference, U. Weinreich (*Languages in Contact*..., New York 1953, p. 50) mentions a "mild type" of it, which occurs, when a sign is changed on the model of a cognate in a language in contact, without effect on the content (as when *vakátsye* "vacation" becomes *vekeyšn* in American Yiddish). In his important article "Aramaic Calque in Hebrew" (*Tarbiz* XXXIII [1963/1964], p. 121, § 4) E. Y. Kutscher states that as a result of this interference, in Semitic languages the root may be changed and, as a matter of fact, a new root arises. In the following, we shall treat of changes in the pattern of the verb in Hebrew and Middle Arabic by the impact of Aramaic, thus pointing out a special subdivision of calque in Semitic languages.

4.2. This is the wording of Isa. xliv 21:

21a	זְכָר־אֵלֶּה יַעֲקֹב
21b	וְיִשְׂרָאֵל כִּי עַבְדִּי־אָתָּה
21c	יְצַרְתִּיךָ עֶבֶד־לִי אַתָּה
21d	יִשְׂרָאֵל לֹא תִנָּשֵׁנִי

Remember this, o Jacob, and Israel, for you are my servant,
I have formed you, you are my servant, o Israel, you...

It is quite clear that 21b is parallel to 21c, and 21a to 21d. Accordingly, 21d, being parallel to "Remember this, o Jacob", has to denote "o Israel, you must not forget me". This alone should suffice, as already stressed by Ibn Djanâḥ in his dictionary, *s.v.*, for taking *tinnâšênî* in the sense of a transitive verb denoting "you forget me" and discard its interpretation as "you will be forgotten by me". Moreover, the latter explanation involves difficulties not only with regard to the content, but also linguistical ones, since it supposes the use of pronominal suffix, having, as a rule, the function of direct object after verbs, as denoting the agent of a passive verb.[1] Nevertheless, as ill luck would have it, most biblical dictionaries prefer the interpretation "you will be forgotten by me",[2] and only a few commentaries and grammars emend our verb to

[1] Such a usage is not attested at all. Even other usages of pronominal suffixes instead of prepositional phrases (see, e.g., the literature quoted by Gesenius-Buhl, *s.v.*) are not certain, see Nöldeke, Mand. 397, note 1.

[2] See the different editions of Gesenius's dictionary, further König, Zorell; cf. also e.g. Bauer-Leander 344h. Among the traditional Jewish interpreters this is e.g. the view of Rashi; accordingly Gesenius (in his *Thesaurus, s.v.*) is wrong in attributing to him (calling him Yarḥî) the interpretation "you will forget me". It was, perhaps, the influence of Gesenius's *Thesaurus* that made the explanation "you will be forgotten by me" prevail.

tinšênî (*Qal*).[3] Very few only accept the Masoretic text, nevertheless interpreting it as "you will forget me".[4]

Prima facie, it seems that in genuine biblical style the *Qal* of *nšy* is used for expressing "forgetting". In Aramaic, however, *'Eṭpəʿel* was current.[5] Since in many cases Aramaic *'Eṭpəʿel* corresponded to Hebrew *Nifʿal* (e.g. in the roots *bhl*, *bny*, *ml'*, *ʿqr*, *qr'*, *šmʿ*), having the same, or almost the same, meaning, these verbal patterns were considered as identical by bi-lingual speakers of Hebrew and Aramaic. Accordingly, in Hebrew the *Nifʿal* of *nšy* was modelled after Aramaic *'Eṭpəʿel* in the sense of "forgetting".[6]

4.3. The basic linguistic structure of Christian Arabic and Judaeo-Arabic texts, exhibiting Middle-Arabic features, is rather similar. Yet whereas most of the Judaeo-Arabic texts belong to the second millennium, there is a plethora of Christian-Arabic texts of South-Palestinian derivation of much earlier origin. These texts date from the eighth century onwards, when Aramaic was still a living language. Therefore, traces of living Aramaic influence are not rare in

[3] See, e.g., Gesenius-Kautzsch 369, § 117x. Gesenius-Buhl also mentions the emendation *tiṭṭšênî*, which is also accepted by Koehler-Baumgartner[1].

[4] So e.g. Ben-Yehuda, *s.v.*, further all the ancient translations, including, of course (see below) the Aramaic ones. F. Delitzsch, *Biblischer Kommentar über den Propheten Jesaia...*[2] (Leipzig 1869) quotes Hitzig's opinion, who compares medial usage in Greek and Latin (yet he is not aware of the similar usage of *nizkar* "he remembered" in Middle Hebrew); Delitzsch, however, does not consent to Hitzig's view. S. D. Luzzatto in his commentary to Isaiah, attached to his Italian translation of it (Padua 1855–1867), regards it as a transitive verb, quoting a view which compares not only Greek and Latin, but also Aramaic. He admits that he thought to emend to *tinšênî*, yet he arrives at the conclusion that the prophet used *Nifʿal* "for the splendour of language", in order that the word should be in accordance with Aramaic. It is well possible that Luzzatto had already Aramaic calque in mind.

[5] See, e.g., Brockelmann, LS, *s.v.*, E. S. Drower – R. Macuch, *A Mandaic Dictionary* (Oxford 1963), *s.v.*, M. Jastrow, *A Dictionary of the Targumim, the Talmud Babli and Yerushalmi, and the Midrashic Literature* (New York 1903), *s.v.*

[6] For the *'Eṭpəʿel* of *nšy* in Samaritan Aramaic cf. Z. Ben-Ḥayyim, *The Literary and Oral Tradition of Hebrew and Aramaic amongst the Samaritans* (Jerusalem 1957), Vol. II, p. 593, l. 17, note, and see especially idem, *Lešonenu* XV (1946/1947), pp. 78–79. It is interesting to note that in Samaritan Hebrew, no doubt through the influence of Aramaic, *škḥ* "to forget" is similarly used in *Nifʿal*, as against *Qal* in the Jewish Hebrew Bible, see Ben-Ḥayyim, *op. cit.* III, 1 (Jerusalem 1961), p. 33, line 2 (read so instead of line 1!), note; p. 99, line 9, note. H. B. Rosén, in his stimulating lecture *The Comparative Assignment of Certain Hebrew Tense Forms* (Offprint from *Proceedings of the International Conference on Semitic Studies*, Jerusalem 1965), pp. 13–14, considers *tinnāšênî* a *Qal* imperfect feature, corresponding in form to the Akkadian present (*iparras*). We have, however, seen, that such an assumption is superfluous. Moreover, this assumption does not hold good for the other verb quoted by him either, *viz.* for *nṭy*, since its *Nifʿal* is attested in past as well (Num. xxiv 6). Rosén wonders (*ibid.*, note 14) whether or not this feature is exhibited also by *ml'*; yet its *Nifʿal* is attested in participle as well (Cant. v 2).

Christian-Arabic texts.[7] Accordingly, whenever Christian-Arabic and Judaeo-Arabic differ, it is expedient to investigate whether or not this is due to the presence of Aramaic influence in Christian-Arabic and its absence in Judaeo-Arabic.

4.3.1. In Middle-Arabic in general, the internal passive has, at least partly, been superseded by the reflexive verbal forms.[8] Among the latter, the eighth form is more frequently used than the seventh form as the passive of the first in Christian-Arabic of South-Palestinian origin (as e.g. *'ixtadam* "to be worshipped"), whereas in Judaeo-Arabic the seventh form is more frequent in this function (as *'infataḥ* "to be opened").[9] The reason for the higher frequency of the eighth form, formed by *-t-* infix, in Christian-Arabic is, presumably, due to the influence of Aramaic. In Aramaic the passive is marked by *t*-forms in general, the passive of the *Qal* (i.e. of the pattern corresponding in function to the first form) by *'Eṭpəʿel*. Because the latter and the Arabic eighth form were similar in both form and function, and because in many roots Aramaic *'Eṭpəʿel* corresponded to the Arabic eighth form, these verbal patterns were considered identical by bi-lingual speakers of Aramaic and Arabic. So did it come about that among the two "rival" originally reflexive verbal patterns, which were apt to replace the internal passive of the Arabic first form, the eighth prevailed in Christian-Arabic, since it was more similar to Aramaic *'Eṭpəʿel*. In this case the Aramaic calque did not give rise to a new form, but made one of two existing rival forms preponderate. In later Judaeo-Arabic, however, on which living Aramaic did not exert influence, it was the seventh form that predominated.

4.3.2. *Barrak* "to bless", exhibiting the second verbal pattern, rather than the usual third pattern *bârak*, is attested in Classical Arabic as well (see the dictionaries). In Middle-Arabic, however, its usage is relatively frequent. As to its occurrence in Ancient South Palestinian Christian Arabic, it is due, it seems, to the influence of corresponding *Paʿʿel* in Aramaic (cf. Blau, ChA 156, § 55). Again, the impact of Aramaic did not give rise to a new form, but made one of two existing rival forms prevail. More intricate is, it seems, the origin of *barrak* in Judaeo-Arabic. It might be the continuation of a form that arose owing to Aramaic influence, when Aramaic was still a living language. Yet it is more likely to interpret it as a learned transfer from Hebrew (cf. Blau, Emergence 138–139). Hebrew, which, though being the hallowed tongue of Jews, was no more a living language, utilized the *Piᶜel* (i.e. the verbal pattern corresponding to the Arabic second form) of *brk* for denoting "blessing". In

7 See J. Blau, *Tarbiz* XXXIII (1963/1964), p. 135.

8 See Blau, ChA 150, § 47, where note 24 additional literature is quoted.

9 See Blau, ChA 166, note 115, where additional literature is quoted.

Hebrew, however, *r* is not doubled and, instead, the preceding vowel is lengthened. Thus the imperfect of *brk* is *yəbâreḵ*, phonetically corresponding to Arabic ⌜*yubârik*⌝, the usual form in Arabic, rather than to *yubarrik*, the second verbal pattern. Nevertheless, *barrak* (imperfect ⌜*yubarrik*⌝) is relatively frequent in Judaeo-Arabic. After the grammatical categories *Piʿel* and second (Arabic) form had become identified because of their phonetic and functional resemblence, they were treated as identical even in cases where they differed owing to some phonetic development in one of them (in our case *arr* 〉 *âr*), because people well versed in grammar did not lose sight of their basic identity. The relatively frequent use of *barrak* in Judaeo-Arabic might, therefore, be considered a *learned* calque of Hebrew *Piʿel*.

4.3.3. The perfect and imperative of the fifth form with prosthetic *alif* in Ancient South Palestinian Christian-Arabic, i.e. *'Itfaʿʿal*, might, at the first blush, be due to the impact of Aramaic *'Eṭpaʿʿal*, and this was the opinion of N. Marr (see Blau, ChA 163, note 95). Since, however, this phenomenon occurs in many layers of Arabic, also in those for which Aramaic influence is rather unlikely (see Blau, *loc. cit.*), one should at the most allow for Aramaic influence in giving preference to a form already existent, and even this is not very convincing.

4.4. Concluding this paragraph, I would like to mention the case of a new root arising in Hebrew through the impact of Aramaic (in accordance with Kutscher's wording above, § 4.1). In those Semitic languages which discern *verba tertiae w* from *tertiae y*, *r'y* "to see", as far as attested, belongs to the latter (see, e.g., the biblical dictionaries *s.v.*). In Aramaic, however, *rêw* "appearance" 〈**ri'w* is attested (*ibid.*, *s.v.*), exhibiting final *w*. Brockelmann I, 293 ingeniously suggested that this form is due to the analogical influence of *ḥizwâ* "apparition".[10] If this is true, one will be inclined to interpret *ra'ăwâ* Ezra xxviii 17 "to see" as being due to Aramaic influence, which gave rise to a new root: *r'w* rather than *r'y*.

5. THE GENERAL BACKGROUND of the stress shift in the perfect with *wâw* consecutive

5.1. As far as I am aware, C. H. Gordon was the last who in a stimulating article treated of the stress shift from penult to ultima in the perfect with *wâw*

10 Bauer-Leander, Aram. 184, § 51k' consider *rêw* an ancient Canaanism, because of the absence of the root *r'y* in Aramaic. It would, however, seem that *rêw* is the only residue of this root, which, containing both *alef* and *y*, was especially apt to disappear because it produced exceptionally short forms (cf. its supersession in most modern Arabic dialects, though C. A. Ferguson, *Language* XXXV [1959], item xii overestimates the use of *šâf*). It may even be that the influence of *ḥezwâ* on *rêw* was strengthened, because the "normal" form **rê* 〈 **rêy* was felt as conflicting with the general rhythmical pattern.

consecutive (see *JBL* LVII [1938], pp. 319–325; in this paragraph quoted as Gordon). In contradistinction to most of his predecessors, he payed attention not only to the syllabic structure of the penult, but also of the antepenult. Thus he arrived at the conclusion that (if one takes into consideration forms with *-tâ* and *-tî* suffixes only) the shift occurs when, and only when, (i) the penult is a closed syllable or (ii) the penult and antepenult are both naturally long syllables (i.e., either closed or containing an originally long vowel). One immediately recognizes that, (i) being well known,[1] it is (ii) that constitutes Gordon's contribution. Accordingly, *umillêṯî* (Ezek. xxxii:5), *wəhirbêṯî* (Gen. xvii 20), *wəḥaqqôṯâ* (Ezek. iv 1), *wahăḵînôṯî* (II Sam. vii 12) exhibit stress on the ultimate, although the penult contains long vowel in an open syllable. This is due to the fact that not only the penult but also the antepenult are both naturally long syllables. *Wəqârâṯâ* (e.g. Jer. xix 2), however, displaying a vowel lengthened only by position in the antepenult, continues to be stressed on the penult. If this assumption, in fact, proved correct, it would be of great importance for the history of the Hebrew vowel system. It would demonstrate (as recognized by C. Brockelmann, *ZDMG* XCIV [1940], p. 360) that at the time of the stress shift in the perfect with *wâw* consecutive, there existed still a quantitative difference between vowels long by nature and those long by position only. Since there is no doubt that at this period the latter were long (as proved by their preservation despite our stress shift, as *wəšâḇartî* rather than **ušəbartî*), this would involve the existence of long and half-long vowels (as postulated e.g. by Joüon 21), an assumption apt to revolutionize our idea of the Hebrew vowel system.

5.2. It stands, however, to reason that Gordon exaggerated the importance of naturally long antepenult. Even a partial analysis demonstrates that open penult often preserves the stress, even if the antepenult is naturally long. The main factor promoting the shift of stress is, as has already been suggested above, the penult being closed. If one disregards cases in which factors preserving the stress on the penult acted (*viz.* pause and the retraction of stress because of a following word with the stress on the first syllable; see, e.g., Gordon 324), no cases, it seems, exist, in which the stress did not shift to the perfect suffixes *-tî*/*-tâ* from closed penult. On the contrary, even a cursory inspection hits upon many a case of the preservation of the stress on open penult, although the antepenult is naturally long (i.e., it contains either a closed syllable or an originally long vowel). I have noted the following cases of stress on the penult (without tending at all to exhaust the subject): *wəṣiwwîṯî* Lev.

[1] See, e.g., Ungnad 113, § 295. As a matter of fact, even (ii) was in the main discovered by Lambert (p. 77) as early as 1890, his exellent paper, however, fell almost into oblivion (cf. also below, note 7).

xxv 21 (with *pašṭâ*[2]); *wəḥikkîṭî* Isa. viii 17 (with *pašṭâ*); *wənil'êṭî* Jer. xx 9; *wəhištaḥăwêṭî* II Kgs. v 18 (with *pašṭâ*), I Sam. xv 30 (with *ṭifḥâ*); *wəhištaḥăwîṭâ* Deut. xxx 17 (with *təḇîr*), iv 19, viii 19; *wəniqqêṭî* Joel iv 21 (with *ṭifḥâ*), Ps. xix 14; *wahăṣêrôṭî* Jer. x 18, Zeph. i 17; *wəhôṣêṭâ* Job xv 13. The preservation of stress on open penult as against its quite fixed shift from closed penult, demonstrates, it seems, that Gordon's rule (ii) (*viz.*, the shift occurs when the penult and antepenult are both naturally long) cannot be considered being on the same level as rule (i) (*viz.*, the shift occurs when the penult is a closed syllable). Only rule (i) may be termed a sound shift proper, whereas rule (ii) is only a tendency, counteracted by several exceptions without any apparent reason.

5.3. On the other hand, one readily admits that the tendency of stress shift to the ultimate syllable in the cases of Gordon's rule (ii) really exists, whereas the stress is, as a matter of fact, always,[3] preserved on the penult in the cases enumerated by Gordon in Rubric IX. These cases, all of them belonging to *Qal*, exhibit *qâmâṣ*, long by position, in the antepenult (with the exception of *uḇâṭâ*, in which the verbal form contains two syllables only). The different behaviour of this rubric is displayed, e.g., by Lev. xxvi 9 *ufânîṭî* * *'ălêḵẹm wəhifrêṭî 'ẹṭḵẹm wəhirbêṭî 'ẹṭḵẹm wahăqîmôṭî*, where the first verb, belonging to Rubric IX, preserved the stress on the penult, whereas all the other verbs, exhibiting originally long penult, are stressed on their last syllables. Nevertheless, one doubts that this different behaviour is due to the *qamâṣ* being long by position only. As we have already stated (§ 5.1), this would involve the existence of long and half-long vowels in Hebrew. This is, by no means, impossible. Nevertheless, the tendency of originally long *qâmâṣ* (as in *dayyân* "judge") to behave like that long by position only, does not make this assumption very likely. The different behaviour of verbal forms with *qâmâṣ* in the antepenult might well be due to rhythmical reasons: long vowels (both original ones and long by position only) were, it seems, less long than two phonetic units (i.e., e.g. two vowels). Therefore, the syllable *qâ* (in *wəqârâṭî*) was shorter than, e.g., the syllables *mil*/*hir* (in *umillêṭî*/*wəhirbêṭî*). And as to the cases (Gordon, Rubric VIII) containing a naturally long vowel in the antepenult, they all (with one exception, see below) are preceded by an additional syllable (as *wahăqîmôṭî*), in contradistinction to Rubric IX.[4] Accordingly, this may be the reason for their different behaviour, since forms like *wahăqîmôṭî* were, of course, at least as long as e.g. *wəhirbêṭî*, in contrast with

2 Since the influence of pause is usual only with *zâqêf qâṭân* or with greater distinctive accents, I am quoting cases with smaller distinctive accents as well. Nevertheless, I deemed it appropriate to state the nature of the accent expressly.

3 For reasons for exceptions cf. note 5.

4 Cf. Lambert 77.

wəqârâṯî. There is, to be sure, one exception, exhibiting a naturally long vowel in the antepenult without an additional syllable preceding it (except *wə*), *viz.* the *Hif'îl* of *yṣ'*. There are ten cases of *wəhôṣêṯî* stressed on the last syllable; yet eight do not count, since they are followed by words beginning with '.[5] Accordingly two genuine instances remain, *viz.* Isa. lxv 9; Ezek. xxi 8. *Wəhôṣêṯâ* occurs five times, once stressed on the penultimate (Job xv 13), once preceding ', and three times stressed on the last syllable without special reason. To sum up, there are five conclusive cases of *Hif'îl* of *yṣ'* stressed on the last syllable, and only one on the penult. Nevertheless, one will not pay too much attention to this lonely verb, since the *Hif'îl* of *bw'* (*hêḇêṯî/hêḇêṯâ*) with stress on the *last* syllable, despite the antepenult containing a vowel long by position only, occurs thirty(!) times (in 26 cases, to be sure, preceding '/'/*h*), whereas it is not attested *at all* with stress on the penult.[6] Gordon's own explanation (p. 325), as if the accent belonged properly to the vocalization *wahăḇi'ôṯî/ wahăḇi'ôṯâ*, is, no doubt, fallacious. Gordon himself recognized (*ibid.*) that this meant that the system of musical accent antedated the vocalization. One will, however, rather prefer Bergsträsser's judicious statement (I, 81, § 12q) that vocalization and the system of accents in the main developed simultaneously. Moreover, Bergsträsser (II, 147, § 28k) has made a very strong case for the perfect of *Hif'îl* of *verba mediae infirmae* with direct annexation of suffixes (like *hêḇêṯî*) being more original than those with "separating vowel" (as *hăḇî'ôṯî*). Accordingly, the supersession of the latter by the former in the allegedly late vocalization would reverse the direction of development.

5.4. We have arrived at a conclusion somewhat different from Gordon's. There is only one regular sound shift effecting the transfer of stress from penult to ultima in the perfect with *wâw* consecutive terminating in *-tî/-tâ*, viz. when the penult is a closed syllable. When it is open, no regular shift obtains. There is a tendency (but a tendency only) to shift, when the open penult is preceded by many rhythmical units (i.e., except the *wâw*, by a closed syllable or by two syllables). If, however, it is preceded by an open syllable only, the stress, as a rule, is preserved on the penult.

5.5. Yet the stress shift in the perfect with *wâw* consecutive must not be regarded in isolation. It is a part only of a general tendency, obtaining at a certain period of the history of the Hebrew language, of transferring the stress

[5] For the tendency to shift the stress from the penult to the ultima when the following word commences with '/'/*h*, see König II, 520–521, further also Gordon 324.

[6] On principle, also the shift from penult to ultima in *'ânôḵi* occurs under the same circumstances; see below, § 5.7.5. — It is rather venturesome to suggest that the shift of stress to the ultima in *wəhôṣêṯî/wəhêḇêṯî* is due to impact of regular *Hif'îl* forms (like *wəhirbêṯî*).

from the penult to the ultima, which, in the main, affected the verbal system,[7] but was, by no means, limited to it. In the following we shall attempt to draw the main lines of development, thus illustrating the shift of perfect with *wâw* consecutive as well.

5.6. As has been recognized by many scholars,[8] at a certain period of Hebrew, before the omission of final short vowels, stress was limited to penult. This assumption is corroborated by the fact that if we add to Hebrew words the final short vowels, as they may be reconstructed by comparison with other Semitic languages, *without changing the traditional place of stress*, the great

[7] This was due to the verb, before that period, being more frequently stressed on the penult than other parts of speech, which, originally terminating in *short* vowels, became stressed on their last syllables. For particulars see below.

[8] As far as my knowledge goes, it was M. Lambert who in his masterly paper as early as 1890 first clearly propounded the view of Hebrew stress once being limited to the penult. He also recognized the secondary character of forms like *qâṭəlâ*, *qâṭəlû* (p. 75; cf. below). H. Grimme, *Grundzüge der hebräischen Akzent- und Vokallehre...* (Friburgi Helvetiorum 1896, Collectanea Friburgensia V), p. 21 realized this stress pattern as well, yet (p. 22) he considered *qâṭəlâ*, etc. as belonging to the same stress period; the same applies to Ungnad, 26 ff. J. Cantineau, *Bulletin d'Etudes Orientales de l'Institut Français de Damas* I (1931), pp. 81–98, on the other hand, not only assumed a period of penult stress in Hebrew (and, Biblical Aramaic), but also recognized the secondary character of *qâṭəlâ*, etc. (p. 93; cf. also *ibid.*, II [1932], pp. 141–142). It is a pity that Cantineau did not know of Lambert's paper, although he quoted (I, p. 83, note 1) the latter's *Traité de Grammaire hébraïque*: "Mayer Lambert, *Traité de Grammaire hébraique*, p. 60, a indiqué, en 6 lignes, une opinion du même genre." As a matter of fact, Lambert dealt with this problem *in extenso*, as early as 1890, and limited himself to six lines only in 1931, when the first part of his *Traité* appeared. C. Sarauw, in his masterly *Über Akzent und Silbenbildung in den älteren semitischen Sprachen*, København 1939 (Det Kgl. Danske Videnskabernes Selskab., Historisk-filololgiske Meddelelse XXVI, 8; as a matter of fact, see *op. cit.*, p. 3, this book was in the main written as early as 1908 and its publication was announced the 17th April 1925), pp. 25–26, clearly recognized the general character of the stress shift that, *inter alia*, brought about the ultima stress of forms like *wəqâṭaltî*, *qâṭəlâ*. He came also very near to realizing a period of penult stress, yet instead he assumed for Hebrew (as a matter of fact, for Ancient Semitic; cf. against it C. Brockelmann, *ZDMG* XCIV [1940], pp. 362–363) a stress on the vowel preceding the last consonant. This stress, to be sure, is as a rule identical with penult stress, yet it involves insurmountable difficulties for the explanation of pausal forms like *qâṭâlâ* and the penult stress of the imperfect with *wâw* conversive; see the short, but incisive criticism of Birkeland 125–126. Birkeland himself, as far as Hebrew stress is concerned, relies on Cantineau (see p. 5); he was not aware either of Lambert's pioneer work and, following Cantineau, he speaks of his (and Grimm's) groping remarks ("ahnende Vorbemerkungen") only. For additional literature see Birkeland 1, C. Brockelmann, *ZDMG* XCIV (1940), pp. 332–371, my Hebrew paper in the *H. Schirmann Jubilee Volume*, Jerusalem 1970, p. 27, note 2, and Bergsträsser * I, 113–114. Bergsträsser's own ingenious reconstruction of Hebrew stress, (which was accepted by Z. S. Harris, *Development of the Canaanite Dialects*, New Haven 1939, p. 50, § 23), I pp. 115 ff., fails because it does not account for the pausal stress of verbal forms (cf. Bergsträsser himself I, 163, § 29i).

majority of words exhibit stress on penult. Accordingly, we assume a period of general penult stress. When, however, final short vowels were dropped, words that terminated in them were now stressed on their last syllable (as **qaṭála* "he killed", which now became *qaṭál*), whereas the other words continued to be stressed on their penult (as *qâṭálnû*). Accordingly, the indicative imperfect, which terminated in *-u* (**yaqṭúlu*), became stressed on the ultimate (**yaqṭúl*), whereas the apocopate (which served as jussive and, mainly after *wâw* consecutive, as past tense) preserved penult stress (**yáqṭul*).[9] Therefore, the imperfect forms after *wâw* consecutive stressed on penult, do not exhibit stress shift from the ultima to the penult (as if paroxytone *wayyôḵal* "and he ate" originated in *wayyôḵál*, in accordance with *yôḵál* < **yôkálu*), but reflect the original stress pattern (as against *wâ'ôḵál* "and I ate", displaying shift of stress from the penult to the ultima; on which see below).

The syllable pattern of Hebrew during this period was, in the main,[10] as follows: short vowels in open syllables preceding the main stress were preserved and ultimately lengthened (the so-called "pretonic lengthening"), whereas such vowels in the third (or fifth) syllable from the stress were reduced. We shall see that during the next period this syllable pattern changed, perhaps through the influence of Aramaic,

Yet, at this period, syllable structure admitted short vowels in open stressed syllables (which were lengthened in pausal position only).[11] Accordingly, it stands to reason that the following forms occurred :**qâṭálâ* "she killed" (in pause: *qâṭâlâ*); **qâṭálû* "they killed" (in pause: *qâṭâlû*); **yiqṭólû* "they will kill" (in pause: *yiqṭôlû*); **qəṭólû* "kill!" (in pause *qəṭôlû*); **niqṭólâ* "let us kill" (in pause: *niqṭôlâ*); **dâgéḵâ* "your fish" (in pause: *dâgêḵâ*); **'ánî* "I" (in pause: *'ânî*), all exhibiting short vowels in open stressed syllables (and long stressed vowels in pause).

5.7. It was in the next stress period of Hebrew that in many perfect forms with *wâw* consecutive (which, not having lost their final vowels, were stressed on their penult; like **wəqâṭáltî*) the stress shifted from the penult to the ultima.

[9] Accordingly, one hesitates to concur with R. Hetzron's ingenious proposal, *JSS* XIV (1968), pp. 1ff. (especially pp. 8ff.) that Proto-Semitic "perfect" exhibited the stress pattern *yáqtul*, as against jussive *yaqtúl*. Hebrew, at any rate, one of the main pillars of Hetzron's hypothesis, cannot serve as basis of this assumption, since it is, it seems, established that once a general penult stress prevailed in it, thus eliminating the putative difference between the alleged perfect *yáqtul* and the supposed jussive *yaqtúl*. Therefore, both of them presumably had the form *yáqtul* in Hebrew at least, in accordance with the general penult stress.

[10] We are dealing with syllable pattern only as far as it is necessary for the proper understanding of the stress shift we are concerned with.

[11] We do not deal with the lengthening of short vowels in syllables that became open through the elision of the closing consonant, nor with that of short vowels in originally open syllables, which became closed by the dropping of final short vowels.

This period was characterized by a general tendency of stressing the ultima, rather than the penult,[12] and the changes in the stress pattern of the perfect with *wâw* consecutive exhibit only the results of this general process. It happened rather late, later than pretonic lengthening (because vowels affected by it did not change; as oxytone *wəqâṭaltí*, rather than **uqəṭâltí*) and the opening of syllables originally closed by double laryngals/pharyngals/ *r* (since such syllables behave as open ones, cf. paroxytone *waybârẹḵ* "and he blessed" as against *wayqaddéš* "and he sanctified"). In contradistinction to the preceding periods, short vowels in open syllables, which had become pretonic through the stress shift, were shortened, in accordance with Aramaic syllable patterning and perhaps through its influence.

5.7.1. The stress shift from the penult to the ultima exhibits a tendency only, rather than a veritable sound shift. In one case only does this tendency act with the regularity of a genuine sound shift; with very few exceptions (as *qəṭâlánî* "he killed me", *miḏbárâ* "to the desert"), syllable pattern of this period did not admit of short (full) vowels in open syllables.[13] Accordingly, short vowels in open stressed syllables, the only class of syllables that had preserved short vowels in open syllables (see § 5.6), were either lengthened (presumably mainly through the impact of pausal forms, as *qəṭâlânû* "he killed us"), or, preferably, the vowel remained short. In this case the stress *regularly* shifted to the ultima and the, now pretonic, short vowel in the open penult was shortened. Thus the following forms came into being (instead of those quoted at the end of § 5.6): *qâṭəlâ, qâṭəlû, yiqṭəlû, qiṭlû,*[14] *niqṭəlâ, dâgəḵâ, 'ănî*, all of them stressed on the ultima.

12 *Prima facie*, it stands to reason that only a part of the Hebrew dialects took part in this stress shift. I am inclined to assume that the Dead Sea Scrolls and the Samaritans, whose language exhibits penult stress (see, e.g., Z. Ben-Ḥayyim, *Mélanges de philosophie et de littérature juives* III–V, 1958–1962, pp. 89 ff.), did not partake in this development. Ben-Ḥayyim has proved (see *H. Yalon Jubilee Volume*, Jerusalem 1963, pp. 150 ff., Hebrew) that the penult stress in Samaritan Hebrew is based on the stress pattern described above, § 5.6. He is inclined, however (see *ibid.*, p. 155), not to interpret even features like paroxytone ⌈*qâṭâlû*⌉ as forms reflecting a historical stage prior to Tiberian oxytone *qâṭəlû*. Nevertheless, since, as proved by Ben-Ḥayyim, the stress pattern of Samaritan Hebrew is already exhibited by the Dead Sea Scrolls, i.e. it arose, at the latest, in the last centuries B.C., and since the tendency of the stress shift to the ultima is rather late (see below), it is somewhat unlikely that, during a quite short period, the tendency of ultima stress should have prevailed, to be soon supplanted by penult stress. It is more plausible that in some dialects tendency to ultima stress obtained, in others to penult stress. — Since the language of the Dead Sea Scrolls in many points differs from that reflected in Tiberian vocalization, it cannot be simply considered as the predecessor of the latter (*pace* F. W. Bush, *Revue de Qumran* II (1960), pp. 501–514, quoted also by Ben-Ḥayyim, *Yalon Volume* 150, note 2).

13 See Birkeland 24. Later, however, such syllables again became possible: it was then that the so-called segolization took place (as **na'r* > *na'ar* "boy").

14 For the *i* in the first syllable cf. C. Brockelmann, *ZDMG* XCIV (1940), p. 364, note 2.

5.7.2. There was also a strong tendency to shift the stress to the ultima, if the penult contained a short vowel in closed syllable.[15] In this case, however, this tendency was often contravened by other factors, as the nature of the ultima or the rythm of the word concerned. Otherwise, not only the perfect with *wâw* consecutive would have shifted its stress (as *wəqâṭaltî*), but the ordinary perfect as well (*qâṭaltî*). It was perhaps because of rhythmical reasons[16] (the additional syllable in the perfect with conversive *wâw*; cf. above, § 5.3 and also Lambert 76) that the tendency to stress on the ultima was stronger in the perfect with *wâw* conversive than in the ordinary perfect. Finally, many perfect forms with conversive *wâw* became differentiated by stress on the ultima from ordinary perfect, perhaps also (see, e.g., Birkeland 72–73) through the analogy of *yiqtol* forms stressed on the ultima, which were continued by perfect with *wâw* conversive (as against perfect forms stressed on the penult, which were followed by imperfect form with *wâw* conversive, stressed on the penult as well).

Still the problem remains why *wəqâṭalnû* preserved penult stress. The assumption that it was due to the supersession of the jussive by the cohortative (see Birkeland 72–73), does not suffice, since it does not explain why it was the first person singular that preserved penult stress in the imperfect, but the first person plural in the perfect. It was perhaps due to the tendency not to stress final *-û*. It was owing to this tendency that perfect forms with *wâw* conversive stressed on long penult keep the stress more often when terminating in *-û* than in *-â* (for particulars see Bergsträsser II, 17). Among the pronouns, *'ănaḥnû* "we" preserved the stress on the penult, whereas in *'attâ* "you", *'ânôḵî* "I" it shifted. The same was the case with *pərî* "fruit" ⟨**pérî*, as against *tóhû* "emptiness" (or should one assume that the *o* was lengthened, through the intrusion of the pausal form, and the occurrence of a short vowel in an open syllable avoided ?).

5.7.3. Very similar was the behaviour of the imperfect with *wâw* consecutive. As stated above (§ 5.6), the apocopate imperfect (in contradistinction to the

15 This was the reason that in pause the stress did not shift in the perfect with *wâw* consecutive from closed penult: it contained a long vowel (*wəqâṭâltî* in pause as against *wəqâṭaltî* in context). The reason for the stress on the ultima of imperfect forms with *wâw* consecutive in pause is not clear (see Bergsträsser I, 163, § 29i). At any rate, the differentiation of these pausal forms by the stress is, it seems, secondary.

16 Sarauw 27 (above, note 8), assumes that the stress shifted in context forms strongly connected with the following words, but remained even in small pause. This proposition, though possible, is not very likely. I would rather assume that the Hebrew stress system, as transmitted by the Masoretes, reflects a transition period, during which stress on the ultima had not yet crystallized. (Incidentally, such transition periods, during which sound shifts are not acting uniformly, may be quite long, and one wonders whether or not one may in such cases continue to uphold the very notion of the regularity of sound shifts.)

indicative) was originally stressed on the penult, both when denoting jussive and past (i.e. mainly with *wâw* conversive). Through the influence of the indicative and the general tendency to stress on the ultimate, the stress shifted to the ultima in all the forms of the jussive and a part of the forms with *wâw* conversive, especially in those *containing a short vowel in closed penult*, i.e. * under the very circumstances that brought about stress shift in the perfect with *wâw* consecutive (as *wayqaddéš* "and he sanctified", exhibiting closed penult, as against paroxytone *waybâręk* "and he blessed", with an open one). It is difficult to find the reason for the frequent penult stress in the imperfect with *wâw* conversive, rather than in the jussive. Was it due to the imperfect with *wâw* conversive continuing perfect forms stressed on the penult (see above, § 5.7.2)? Or was it due to rhythmical reasons, as suggested by Lambert 76? The most likely explanation seems to be that the jussive, not differentiated from the ordinary imperfect by *wa-*, was more exposed to its influence than the imperfect with *wâw*-conversive. Similarly, one wonders what was the reason for the shift of stress to the ultima in first person singular of the imperfect with *wâw* conversive, even if the penult was open (as *wâ'êrêd* "and I went down"). As stated above (§ 5.7.2), the supersession of the jussive by the cohortative does not suffice to explain it. It is not easy either to assume rhythmical reasons, as if it were due to the open syllable beginning with *w* in the first person singular (as against closed syllables in the other forms, *wâ'ęqṭol*: *wayyiqṭol*).

5.7.4. The tendency to stress on the ultima, when the penult contained a short vowel in closed syllable, is exhibited by other words as well; again, the pausal forms display the original stress structure: oxytone *'attâ* "you (singular masculine)" (as against pausal paroxytone *'âttâ*); *'attâ* "now" (as against pausal paroxytone *'âttâ*). The etymology of the last case also proves that it was originally stressed on the penult, being **'int* (>*'eṯ* "time") with "terminative" **-ah* (cf. Brockelmann I, 464, note 2): "terminative" **-ah* is unstressed and the shift of *i* to *a* has to be interpreted according to Philippi's law, which affects stressed syllables only.

5.7.5. On the other hand (as stated above, §§ 5.1 and 5.2), this tendency was much weaker when the penult contained a long vowel in an open syllable. We have already seen (*ibid.*) that this is the case in the perfect with *wâw* consecutive. Similarly, the stress does not shift to the ultima from open penult in the imperfect with *wâw* consecutive. The same applies to various verbal and nominal forms with long vowel in open penult, while in corresponding features with closed penult the stress shifted to the ultima: paroxytone *hiqdîšâ* "she consecrated", *hiqdîšû* "they consecrated", *yaqdîšû* "they will consecrate", *haqdîšû* "consecrate!", *naqdîšâ* "let us consecrate", *pîkâ* "your mouth" as against, respectively, oxytone *qâṭəlâ*, *qâṭəlû*, *yiqṭəlû*, *qiṭlû*, *niqṭəlâ*, *dâgəkâ*.

Nevertheless, the shift of stress to the ultima from long vowels in open syllables does occur: we have already quoted some cases in the perfect with *wâw* consecutive (see §§ 5.1–5.4); additional cases in this form with the afformatives *-â*/*-û* are quoted by Bergsträsser II, 17, § 4e (pay attention that many cases of exceptions from the rules fixed by Bersträsser are due to open syllables; thus Bergsträsser states [*ibid.*, §b] that in *Qal* of *verba mediae geminatae* the stress passes to the ultima; from the four exceptions quoted by him, two -*wəḥârâ*, *wəḥâyâ*- contain long vowel in open penult). Similarly, the stress shifted from open penult in first person singular of the imperfect with *wâw* consecutive (see § 5.7.3). Interesting is the shift exhibited in *'ânôḵî* "I" (in pause paroxytone), exhibiting the shift of stress from an open penult preceded by another open syllable, contrary to the tendency dealt with above, § 5.3.

5.8. To summarize: The stress shift in the perfect with *wâw* consecutive must not be regarded in isolation. It is a part only of a general tendency of stress on the ultima that prevailed at a certain period in Hebrew. This tendency developed into a veritable soundshift when the previously stressed penult contained a short vowel in open syllable. It was quite strong, when the penult contained a short vowel in closed syllable, yet admitted of many exceptions and the coexistence of forms with penult and ultima stress even became morphologically significant (in the case of the perfect with *wâw* consecutive, and, to a lesser degree, in the imperfect with *wâw* consecutive, in which the *wâw* had a special form, different from *wâw* copulative; it was also used to differentiate pausal from context forms). On the other hand, long vowels in open penult as a rule preserved the stress, though important exceptions occur even in this case.

6. The Problem of Tenses in Biblical Hebrew

6.1. In a paper written in Hebrew[1] I tried to prove that in Biblical *prose* the Hebrew verbal system denotes tenses, rather than aspects. The central fact inducing scholars to interpret the biblical verbal system as indicating aspects, is, it seems, that both *qâṭal* and *yiqṭol* (the latter, as a rule, with *wâw* consecutive) are to be found in a context in which we would have now applied past; similarly, both *yiqṭol* and *qâṭal* (the latter, as a rule, with *wâw* consecutive) occur in a context in which we would have now used future. Therefore, many scholars inferred that the Hebrew verbal system does not mark tenses at all. According to their view, *qâṭal* and *yiqṭol* denote aspects, and it is only we who, used to tenses, substitute for them sometimes past and sometimes future.

Accordingly, so I argued, if we succeed to point out that the use of *qâṭal* as against *wayyiqṭol*, and of *yiqṭol* as against *wəqâṭal* is due to factors *outside* the verbal system, this will invalidate the main argument for the assumption

* 1 See *In Memory of G. Alon, Essays in Jewish History and Philology* (Tel Aviv 1970), pp. 17–18.

of aspects in Biblical Hebrew. If it can be demonstrated that *qâṭal/wayyiqṭol* refer to a context in which we would have used today past, and that their alternation is due to factors outside the verbal system (and the same applies to *yiqṭol/wəqâṭal* referring to the future), there is no reason to connect them with aspects. If the alternation of the two forms is, in fact, conditioned by factors outside the verbal system, the simplest way to interpret them is by the assumption that there exist two alternating forms according to external factors, for marking each of the tenses.

As to biblical prose, these conditioning factors for the *indicative* tenses are quite obvious. In the vast majority of cases the alternation of forms with and without *wâw* conversive is quite fixed: Whenever the syntactic environment admits of the use of *wâw* copulative, forms with *wâw* conversive are applied; otherwise, the forms without *wâw* consecutive are used. Accordingly, one will assume, for biblical prose at least, a verbal system denoting tenses. *qâṭal/yiqṭol* denote past/future respectively, if the syntactic environment does not allow of the use of *wâw* copulative (or the author does not want to utilize them for stylistic reasons); otherwise, *wayyiqṭol/wəqâṭal* are employed.

6.2. Now I would like to take a further step. I do not claim, of course, that in Prosto-Semitic or even in Proto-Hebrew the verbal system did not denote aspects. What I do claim is that the assumption of aspects during these periods cannot be substantiated even by analysing biblical *poetry*.

We have seen that is stands to reason that in biblical prose verbs denoted tenses. The various usages in poetry, differentiating it from prose,[2] have, no doubt, to be interpreted as archaisms.[3] We have to suppose that poets in biblical times as well as authors writing in prose, spoke a language in which the verbal system denoted tenses. This is demonstrated by the use of verbs in prose.[4] Poets, however, out of archaism, used verbal forms in contexts in which they could not occur in prose language (as *yiqṭol* denoting past, and *qâṭal* marking future). Whatever the reason for this usage, it did not represent a living linguistic system. Poets applied verbal forms, not according to their living linguistic feeling, but out of tradition. It is, of course, very important to collect these poetic usages, as in fact it has been done; yet they do not represent a linguistic system, but scattered intentional archaic features. It is, in my opinion, impossible to infer from these dispersed phenomena what the verbal *system* was like, whether it marked aspects or tenses. Let us, for argument's sake,

[2] See e.g., Bergsträsser II, 29; 34–35.

[3] As far as innovations occur, they have, it seems, to be interpreted as pseudo-archaic features, see below.

[4] I do not claim, of course, that biblical prose was identical with the spoken language. Nevertheless, it stands to reason that the verbal system of the spoken language denoted tenses as well. Otherwise, biblical prose would not have exhibited such a verbal system either.

assume that in Proto-Hebrew the verbal system denoted aspects, to become afterwards a system of tenses (as exhibited by biblical prose). Poets of that time, speaking a language in which the verbal system marked tenses, had lost linguistic feeling for the aspects. Nevertheless, they tried, out of tradition, to utilize verbs in accordance with the bygone system of aspects. One will necessarily assume that they succeeded to some degree only. In many cases, no doubt, they accomplished the correct usage of the aspectual system, in others, however, they violated its rule, applying pseudo-archaic features (as *qâṭal* instead of *yiqṭol*, and *vice versa*, only because biblical prose demanded the other form). It is, therefore, for all practical purposes, impossible to reconstruct the Proto-Hebrew verbal system from these scattered pieces, often, no doubt, wrongly applied. One may even, *mutadis mutandis*, compare the situation of biblical poets in this respect with that of a modern Israeli poet trying to write in biblical language (though, of course, one must not lose sight of the fact that the biblical poet was much nearer to the Proto-Hebrew period both in language and culture). Both of them endeavour to use a verbal system different from their living one. It will be, of course, imprudent to try to reconstruct the biblical verbal system from the poems of such an Israeli poet. It is, with some exaggeration, almost to the same degree impossible to rebuild the Proto-Hebrew verbal system from biblical poetry. One may infer from biblical poetry that, e.g., in Proto-Hebrew no definite article existed, since it is often missing in contexts which would have necessitated it in prose. The very absence of the article in some cases sheds light on Proto-Hebrew usage. On the other side, such an intricate system as the verbal system is, cannot be reconstructed from the linguistic usage of a poet whose mother tongue exhibits a quite different pattern.

6.3. To summarize: Biblical prose exhibits a verbal system that denoted tenses, since the alternation of *qâṭal/wayyiqṭol* and *yiqṭol/wəqâṭal* is due to the syntactic environment (the impossibility/possibility of the use of *wâw* copulative). Accordingly, one will assume a similar system in the spoken language. Deviations in the usage of verbs in biblical poetry have to be interpreted as intentional archaism. Since it is impossible to reconstruct such an intricate system as the verbal system is, from mere archaic features (including, no doubt, pseudo-archaic ones), nothing certain can be inferred from them as to the nature of the Proto-Hebrew verbal system.

7. Syllables in which Short Vowels Were Reduced in Aramaic and Hebrew

7.1. As is well known, short vowels in open unstressed syllables are reduced in certain positions.[1] I am contending that, at least as far as reduction is concerned, only open syllables followed by a syllable containing a full vowel count in Aramaic and Hebrew as phonologically open, while those followed by a(n open) syllable containing a partly reduced vowel count as phonologically closed.[2] Accordingly, in the latter syllables short vowels are preserved both in Aramaic and Hebrew.

7.2. The fact that short vowels in originally open syllables followed by an open syllable containing a partly reduced vowel, were not reduced in Aramaic, is exhibited by the Aramaic incantation in cuneiform found in Uruk.[3] In this text, as a rule, vowels otherwise reduced or dropped appear as full vowels. Yet these vowels have to be interpreted as marking half-vowels,[4] rather than full ones, for the following reasons: (i). In one case the form with vowel

[1] These positions, as is known, differ in Aramaic and Hebrew. This, however, is without importance for the subject treated here.

[2] Perhaps even phonetically; in this case, one would assume that the syllable containing the reduced vowel was pronounced together with the preceding one, thus closing it phonetically.

[3] I have utilized the following papers dealing with this text: C. H. Gordon, *AfO* XII (1937–1939), pp. 105–117 (quoted in this paragraph as Gordon I); idem, *Orientalia* IX (1940), pp. 2–38 (quoted as Gordon II); B. Landsberger, *AfO* XII (1937–1939), pp. 247–257 (quoted as Landsberger); A. Dupont-Sommer, *Revue d'Assyriologie* XXXIX (1942–1944), pp. 35–62 (quoted as Dupont-Sommer).

[4] See also Koehler-Baumgartner xxxix, §d. Therefore, we cannot consent to W. Fischer's vew, *Festigabe für H. Wehr* (Wiesbaden 1969), p. 175, note 2, that there is no evidence whatsoever for the existence of half-vowels (*Murmelvokale*). On the other hand, K. Beyer, in his otherwise instructive paper on the component of Imperial Aramaic in the oldest Syriac literature (*ZDMG* CXVI [1966], pp. 242ff.) goes as far as to claim (p. 245, note 6) that short vowels in open internal syllables were not dropped before the third century C.E.! (the exclamation mark is Beyer's). He bases his supposition on *matres lectionis* in later Imperial Aramaic and cuneiform and Greek transcriptions, interpreting them as exhibiting full vowels. As a matter of fact, however, it brings into relief, all the more, the absurdity of considering every vowel as a full vowel. [Nothing can be inferred, *pace* Beyer, *op. cit.*, p. 245, § 10, from spellings like *'mm'* "nations": between identical consonants the tendency of preserving partly reduced vowels was especially strong, as demonstrated by Mandaic spellings, see Nöldeke, Mand. 31, § 30 (cf. also p. 163; cf. also Schlesinger, *op. cit.* [in § 2.2, note 9], p. 53, note 63. Yet Z. Ben-Ḥayyim, *Lešonenu* XI, 1940/1941 p. 90 regards vowels between identical consonants as full vowels as well).] Gordon I, 115, § 71 thinks that the Uruk text "dates from the time when the tendency to drop short vowels in open, unaccented syllables was first setting in" (and similar is Dupont-Sommer's opinion pp. 60–61), cf. also Gordon II, 33, § 19. Landsberger 250, note 8 wonders whether or not these vowels have to be interpreted as reduced ones. — In my opinion, Landsberger 252, note 18 was wrong in assuming that the Uruk text exhibits short reduced final vowels. He attributed too much weight to genuine Akkadian spelling, as if an Aramaic text written in cuneiform should necessarily be spelt according to it. Cf. against this view Gordon II, 33, § 19 (who also mentions the important claim that final short vowels were earlier eliminated than short vowels in open medial syllables), without, however, agreeing to all his arguments; cf. also Dupont-Sommer 38, note 1, point 2.

(*viz. ga-ba-ri-e* "men [*status constructus*], line 37) is alternating with the vowelless feature (*viz. ga-*[*a*]*b-ri-e*, line 12). This has to be interpreted as exhibiting the alternation of partly reduced and totally dropped vowels, or even different attempts to mark partly reduced vowels. One has also to take into account forms like *ia-ti-ir-ta-'* (lines 17, 42) "superabundant", *ḫa-as-si-ir-ta-a* "deficient" (both fem. sing.), *ḫa-gi-ir-ta-* (lines 16, 41) "lame woman", exhibiting the loss of a short, unstressed vowel before the feminine ending. It is interesting to note that Biblical Aramaic displays in nouns of this pattern (like *bîštâ* "evil") *t*, rather than *ṯ*, as feminine ending, thus demonstrating the eaıly reduction of the vowel preceding the *t* (cf. Bauer-Leander, Aram. 43g, and F. Rosenthal, *A Grammar of Biblical Aramaic*[2], Wiesbaden 1963, p. 13, § 15). [One could, of course, claim that this feature is already Proto-Semitic, see Bauer-Leander 507g; this is, however, not very likely, cf. Brockelmann I, 407, § 225Af3, Remark.] (ii) As a rule, the vowels which we interpret as reduced ones, exhibit their previous quality. Therefore, it is impossible to discern whether or not they have been already reduced. Yet cases occur exhibiting *i*, rather than original *u*, to be interpreted, no doubt, as expressing reduced vowel (see Gordon I, 111, § 35; Landsberger 250, note 8; Koehler-Baumgartner xxxix, §d): *mi-ḫa-aš-še-e* "silencer" (line 28; so Landsberger *ibid.*, following Jensen, accepted by Dupont-Sommer 51 and, hesitatingly, even by Gordon II, 37, despite *ibid.*, note 3) = *məḥaššê* ⟨ **muḥaššê*; presumably also *pi-la-nu* "so and so" (lines 22, 29), ⟨ *pûlân* (despite Landsberger's doubts p. 249, note 4); much less certain is *ri-ḫu-ṭi-'* "run!" (lines 16, 41), because its alleged origin *ruhuṭî* is hypothetical (see Landsberger 250, note 8).[5] Cf. also Greek transcriptions of Aramaic proper nouns, exhibiting ε instead of a reduced *a* in their first syllable, as e.g. Ζεβειδου = Palmyrian **Zəḇîḏâ*, see J. Cantineau, *Grammaire du Palmyrénien épigraphique* (Le Caire 1935), p. 59. Nevertheless, the ε may, theoretically at least, exhibit *imâla* of full vowel. (iii). The early reduction of short vowels in open unstressed syllables in Aramaic is also exhibited by the use of prosthetic *alef* in Biblical Aramaic in *'ištîû* "they drank" Daniel v 3, 4: this presupposes the loss of *a* between *š* and *t*. One will not claim that Proto-Semitic too displays the alternation of a sibilant followed by a short vowel, with prosthetic *alef* preceding the sibilant, imme-

[5] Koehler-Baumgartner (xxxix, §d) consider the *i* in *ti-ḫu-u-ut* "under" (lines 3, 31, 35, 33) as expressing a half-vowel as well. This, however, is proven only if this form arose by analcgy with *'ăḥôrê*, as Baumgartner assumes *s.v. təḥôṯ* (I do not understand the reason for Baumgartner assuming nevertheless *tiḥût* with *i* as original form; in this case, of course, the *i* in Uruk would not prove anything). If, however, the original form is *quṭâl* (see e.g. Brockelm ann I, 351, § 135c*a*), it developed, first by assimilation, to **tuḥôṯ* (see e.g. Brockelmann I, 185, § 68gδ), then, by dissimilation (see Brockelmann, I, 255, § 94r), to **tiḥôṯ*. In this case, of course, the *i* in Uruk could theoretically represent a full vowel.

diately followed by another consonant (cf., e.g., Syriac *ṣeḇʿâ*, Hebrew *'ęṣbaʿ*, Arabic *'iṣbaʿ* "finger"; for other instances see Barth 219, § 148c). This is the case, to be sure, in nouns. In verbs, however, in which patternizing is much stronger, such an alternation is unlikely, and the occurrence of prosthetic *alef* necessarily presupposes the reduction of short vowels in open unstressed syllables. Since Biblical Aramaic exhibits a language from about the third-second century B.C., *i.e.* it is roughly contemporary with the Uruk text, one may consider *'ištîû* an additional proof for the reduction of short vowels.[6]

Accordingly, for the above-mentioned three reasons, it may be taken for granted that short vowels in open unstressed syllables were reduced in the Aramaic of the cuneiform text from Uruk. One will not consent to the view that this text exhibits full vowels on the one hand, totally reduced ones on the other, because the tendency of reducing vowels was first setting in (see above, note 4). In this case, one would be forced to assume, because of *matres lectionis* in later Imperial Aramaic and Greek transcriptions (cf. also, § 7.4), that the coexistence of forms with full vowels and reduced ones continued till the third century C.E. (cf. Beyer's view as to the late reduction of open internal vowels, see above, note 4), and this is more than unlikely. Therefore, it is necessary to suppose that the reduction of short vowels in open unstressed syllables was general: they were either only partly reduced or totally elided, and such forms continued to coexist for a very long time. Originally open syllables, followed by a consonant with reduced vowel, be it totally or partially reduced, were not affected by reduction: these syllables counted as closed, *even if they were followed by a consonant with half vowel* (i.e. the first vowel counted as being in a closed syllable not only in *gabrê* "men [*status constructus*]", i.e. *gab-rê*, but also in *gabărê* with half vowel, since, phonologically at least, it has to be syllabicated into *gabă-rê*). Since the reduced full vowels were often preserved as half vowels, spirantized stops remained spirantized (see for it below, § 7.5).

7.3. Similarly, there are many indications that short vowels in originally

[6] In the opinion of H. H. Schaeder, *Iranische Beiträge*, Schriften der Königsberger Gelehrten Gesellschaft, Geisteswissenschaftliche Klasse, 6. Jahr, Heft 5 (Halle 1930), Vol. I, p. 239 [241], this form goes even back to the sixth-fifth century B.C., since it is attested in the Aramaic ideograms of Pahlavi as well. Accordingly, it has to be attributed to the Babylonian Aramaic of these centuries, being the common origin of Biblical Aramaic and Pahlavi (and of other Eastern Aramaic dialects). Since, however, Schaeder *loc. cit.* interprets the Pahlavi form as imperative, it would not prove any common origin, because, in contradistinction to the perfect, it might have begun with a consonant cluster even in Proto-Semitic and, therefore, the alternation of forms with and without prosthetic *alef* in the imperative is well possible (cf. e.g. Arabic *'uqtul* with Hebrew *qəṭol*). Yet, since Schaeder's assumption of an imperative in Pahlavi is by no means certain (I am indebted to my colleague Dr. S. Shaked for this information), the assumption of such an early origin may nevertheless be correct.

open syllables followed by an open syllable containing a partly reduced vowel, were preserved in different periods of Hebrew.

7.3.1. In the Septuagint, often vowels occur in places in which in Tiberian vocalization *shwa* is attested, be it what is called *shwa medium* or even *shwa quiescens* (see Bergsträsser I 120, § 21p; 135, § 23c; G. Lisowsky, *Die Transkription der hebräischen Eigennamen des Pentateuchs in der Septuaginta*, Inauguaral-Dissertation... Basel, Basel 1940, pp. 138–139), e.g. Αραβωθ (see Lisowsky 94, § 543), Αχοβωρ (see Lisowsky 88, § 512). The latter cases have to be interpreted as exhibiting anaptyctic vowels, see Bergsträsser I, 134–135, § 23c. The former could, on principle, be regarded as preserving full vowels, as if the vowels concerned had not been reduced at all; this, however, is very unlikely. As Bergsträsser (I, 120, § 21p) has convincingly argued, the plethora of vowels corresponding to *shwa*[7] and the frequency of assimilations indicate that the full vowels were not kept in these positions; a very late fixation of the date of reductions would also involve chronological difficulties. Thus, P. Leander (*ZDMG* LXXIV [1920], p. 66), following Ebeling, has made it rather probable that *i* and *u* in open syllables in El-Amarna were subject to reduction.[8] I do not claim that the language history of the different Canaanite dialects reflected in El-Amarna was exactly parallel to that of Hebrew. Nevertheless, if the early reduction of short vowels in El-Amarna proves correct,[9] it would make their very late date in Hebrew quite unlikely. Accordingly, one is inclined to interpret the correspondence of vowels in the Septuagint to the so-called *shwa medium* in the Tiberian vocalization as exhibiting the partial

[7] Cf. also Kutscher 396, note 276, who is taking exception to A. Sperber, *HUCA* 12–13 (1937/1938), p. 135 and quoting forms like Μαναημ, Μανασση, where *a* corresponds, it seems, to original *u*.

[8] Yet the instances adduced for nouns with reduced vowels do not convince: in *zu-ru-uḫ* "arm" the first *u* need not necessarily exhibit *shwa*, but may display full vowel assimilated to the following *u* (cf. cases of vowel harmony in Ugaritic). As to *ba-di-u* "in his hand", it may contain *d* "hand" rather than *yad*, cf. C. Rabin, *The Journal of Jewish Studies* VI (1955), pp. 111–115. The first vowel in infinitive forms need not necessarily exhibit *shwa* either; it may display patterns different from Hebrew (cf. for such patterns in Ugaritic, according to the four-language dictionary, in which Ugaritic is spelt in Akkadian syllabic cuneiform). On the other hand, the first vowels in verbal forms like *ti-dab-bi-ru* "they will expell", *me-ša-li-me* "he who makes peace" presumably reflect *shwa*. [*Obiter dictum*, Leander's interpretation (*loc. cit.*) that "the writer of cuneiform, which lacked special marks of *shwa*, could, of course, sometimes utilize the original full vowel for it" is not necessarily correct. These allegedly full vowels *may* represent reduced vowels, which preserved the qualities of the original ones.]

(pp. 271–72) [9] In *In Memoriam P. Kahle*, ed. M. Black – G. Fohrer (Beihefte zur Zeitschrift für die alttestamentliche Wissenschaft, CIII), pp. 34–35, I claimed that short final vowels had been already dropped in El-Amarna. This would be in harmony with the reduction of short unstressed vowels in open internal syllables.

reduction of short vowels in open unstressed syllables in certain positions, and, thus, the preservation of such vowels in open unstressed syllables preceding the partly reduced ones.[10]

7.3.2. Z. Ben-Ḥayyim[11] has observed the occurrence of vowels in the second column of the Hexapla, corresponding to *shwa* "*medium*" in Tiberian vocalization, *viz.* βιαδαρεθ (Ps. xxix 2) and υαναυαθαχ (Ps. xviii 36), corresponding to בהדרת and וענותך respectively. Ben-Ḥayyim, to be sure, considers it full vowels, which (see §§ 7.3.3; 7.3.4) developed from *shwa* (i.e. from reduced vowels). I do not think that this supposition, despite its possibility, is necessary. At any rate, no matter whether reduced vowels are still preserved or (later) developed to full vowels, the transcriptions of the Hexapla also demonstrate the possibility of *partial* reduction and the preservation of short vowels in originally open syllables preceding a partly reduced vowel. By no means can these vowels be interpreted as exhibiting *original* full vowels, since, as a rule, the second column of the Hexapla displays the total reduction of vowels, see, e.g., E. Brønno, *Studien über hebräische Morphologie und Vokalismus*..., Abhandlungen für die Kunde des Morgenlandes, XXVIII (Leipzig 1943), pp. 322ff.

7.3.3. It stands to reason that spellings with ' in the Dead Sea Scrolls (which are, to be sure, very rare), corresponding to *shwa* "*medium*" in the Tiberian vocalization (cf. Kutscher 396, § 6; see also Ben-Ḥayyim, *ibid.* [above, note 11], who surmises that, as in Samaritan Hebrew [see § 7.3.4], these reduced vowels have developed into full ones), exhibit partial reduction of short vowels in open unstressed syllables in certain positions, and, accordingly, the preservation of such vowels in the syllables preceding them.

7.3.4. Very important is the attestation of this feature in Samaritan Hebrew. As Z. Ben-Ḥayyim has demonstrated (*ibid.*), every *shwa* "*medium*" (as well as *shwa mobile*) shifts into a veritable vowel in Samaritan Hebrew. This demonstrates that in Samaritan Hebrew original vowels (which correspond to *shwa* "*medium*" in Tiberian vocalization) have not been totally reduced. Moreover, short vowels in open unstressed syllables preceding them were not reduced at all.

7.4. The same feature is displayed by Arabic loans from Aramaic exhibiting the pattern *malakût* "kingdom", corresponding to Aramaic *malk̲û* (cf. e.g., Barth 414, note 1). Not only the spirantized *k̲* attests to a vowel preceding it, but also the vowel reproduced by the Arabs.

[10] Accordingly, I do not consent to E. Sievers's criticism on syllables with "*lockerem Schluss*" (see his *Metrische Studien*, Abhandlungen der königlich sächsischen Gesellschaft der Wissenschaften XLVIII, Leipzig 1903, Vol. I, p. 22, §5). It was, in fact, due to Sievers's influence that this notion disappeared from Hebrew grammar.

[11] In *Mélanges*... (see §5.7, note 12), p. 95. Cf. also Kutscher 396, note 277.

* 7.5. Our assumption also solves the well known difficulty of the preservation of spirantization after *shwa* "*medium*" (as *malḵû*, see § 7.4) in both Aramaic and Hebrew. We owe Sievers (cf. for particulars also Bergsträsser I, 121, § 21q) the recognition that this spirantization is due to the vowel now being reduced. Sievers, however, who did not admit the possibility of "lockerer Silbenschluss" (see above, note 10), was forced to transfer spirantization into the earliest period of the history of Hebrew. Although I do not acknowledge (*pace* Bergsträsser *loc. cit.*) the utter impossibility of this assumption, nevertheless, it does not explain the subsistence of spirantization: spirantization continued until the very last stages of Aramaic and Hebrew, as exhibited by its occurrence in *sandhi* in Syriac and Hebrew tradition, by the (partial) supersession of the spirantized consonants by stops in Syriac after the total reduction of the preceding vowel and by the express statement of Saadia ben Joseph al-Fayyûmî * (ninth-tenth century; see his *Commentaire sur le Sefer Yeṣira...*, publ. et trad. * par M. Lambert, Paris 1891, p. 45). Accordingly, had the vowel preceding the *shwa* "*medium*" totally disappeared, it would have, after a certain period of transition, caused the supersession of the spirantized consonants by stops. The only way to solve this difficulty is, in my opinion, the assumption that, during a very long period, forms with half vowels corresponding to *shwa* "*medium*" in Tiberian vocalization alternated with forms with zero, and it was due to the former that the following consonant remained spirantized. Bergsträsser (I, 123, § 21v) has recognized this alternation of half vowels with zero, he has not, however, drawn the necessary conclusions as to the preservation of short vowels in unstressed open syllables preceding syllables containing half vowels.

7.6. To summarize: Syllables with "lockerem Silbenschluss", i.e. short unstressed vowels followed by a consonant and a half vowel, have, phonematically at least, to be considered as closed syllables in Aramaic and Hebrew. Therefore, they were not affected by the reduction of short vowels in open unstressed syllables in certain positions. Such vowels in open unstressed syllables were often only partly reduced, for a long time alternating with totally reduced vowels. These partly reduced vowels, though, phonematically at least, not opening the following syllable, nevertheless were followed by spirantized *b,g,d,k,p,t*, rather than by stops. Indications for these half vowels are to be found in the Aramaic incantation in cuneiform found in Uruk (§ 7.2), in various layers of Hebrew (§ 7.3), as exhibited by the Septuagint, the Hexapla, the Dead Sea Scrolls and Samaritan Hebrew, as well as in Arabic loans from Aramaic (§ 7.4).

REMARK: Gordon I, 112, § 43 has concluded from *za-ki-it* (line 10) "I have won", *za-ka-a-a* (*ibid.*) "victorious" as well as from *ma-zi-ga-'*

(lines 6, 9) "mixer (feminine)" that *b,g,d,k,p,t* after vowels have not yet been spirantized in the Aramaic reflected in the cuneiform text from Uruk, and he has been followed by Beyer, *loc. cit.* (in § 7.2, note 4). This is, however, by no means certain. First, the spelling of *zky* might have been influenced by Akkadian *zakû* (from which it may be borrowed, see, e.g., Koehler-Baumgartner, Aramaic part, *s.v.* "*zkh*"). Second, as to *mzg*, it may well be (see Landsberger 251, note 10, as against Gordon I, 111, §§ 29–30) that *ġayin* had already disappeared from the Aramaic of Uruk. If this proves correct, the only occurrence of *ġ* in this language would be as spirantized *g*. Accordingly, because of its interchange with *g* in Aramaic and its correspondence to Akkadian *g* in many roots, it might have easily been transcribed by *g*. The main reason, however, for the impossibility of drawing any definite conclusions from the transcriptions in Uruk is that spirantized *b,g,d,k,p,t* were allophones only, rather than phonemes. Therefore, they were felt as a part of the archiphonemes *b,g,d,k,p,t* and transcribed accordingly. In this connection, the situation in Eastern Syriac is very instructive. In this dialect, *ḥ* had shifted to *ḫ*. Nevertheless, although this *ḫ*, for all practical purposes, was identical with the spirantized allophone of *k*, these two consonants were not mixed up. The reason for this fact is obvious: if these two consonants were both phonemes, they would have been, no doubt, mixed up. Yet only *ḫ* was an independent phoneme; *ḵ*, on the other hand, was the allophone of *k* (after vowels). Accordingly, the speakers of Syriac were, it seems, conscious of the differences between them.[12] Similarly, the writer of the Aramaic cuneiform text might well have used *k/g* even for spirantized *ḵ/ḡ*, because the latter were allophones of the former, rather than independent phonemes.

ADDENDA

Ad §1.3: For *yûḵal* cf. also M. Lambert, *Revue des Etudes Juives* XXVII (1893), pp. 137–8.

Ad §1.4: I am inclined to derive *mûsâ* "razor" from **miwsâ*, which thus exhibits the shift *iwC* > *ûC* as well (so *pace* Fleisch 508, n. 1, who posits a noun of instrument *mafʿal*, otherwise not attested in Arabic, and derives *mûsâ* from alleged **mawsâ* by an exceptional sound shift).

Ad §3.1, note 1: For Judaeo-Aramaic *ḥṣr* occurring only once, owing to Hebrew influence, v. E. Y. Kutscher, in *Hebräische Wortforschung*, *Fest-*

12 Accordingly, Bergsträsser I, 40, § 6m was wrong in regarding it as proven that the spirantization in Hebrew (and we may add: in Aramaic) was later than the disappearance of *ḫ* and *ġ*; otherwise, he claims, they would have been mixed up with spirantized *k* and *g*. Yet this argumentation loses sight of the difference between phonemes and allophones. For particulars see my paper in the *G. Alon Memorial Volume* (above, § 6, n. 1), p. 16.

schrift W. Baumgartner, Supplements to Vetus Testamentum XVI, Leiden 1967, pp. 171–2 (who, however, considers its occurrence in Sfire as a Canaanism as well).

Ad §7.3.1, note 8: It stands, however, to reason that *ba-di-u* has to be derived from *yad*, v. S. E. Loewenstamm's remark in *Ugarit-Forschungen* II (1970), p. 30, §2.6.

ABBREVIATIONS

AfO — Archiv für Orientforschung.

Barth — J. Barth, *Die Nominalbildung in den semitischen Sprachen*[2] (Leipzig 1894).

Bauer - Leander — H. Bauer - P. Leander, *Historische Grammatik der hebräischen Sprache des Alten Testaments* (Halle 1922).

Bauer - Leander, Aram. — H. Bauer–P. Leander, *Grammatik des Biblisch-Aramäischen* (Halle 1927).

Ben-Yehuda — E. Ben Yehuda, *A Complete Dictionary of Ancient and Modern Hebrew* (Jerusalem–Tel Aviv, Popular Edition, n.d.; Hebrew).

Bergsträsser — G. Bergsträsser, *Hebräische Grammatik* (Leipzig 1918–1929).

Birkeland — H. Birkeland, *Akzent und Vokalismus im Althebräischen..., Skrifter utgitt av Det Norske Videnskaps-Akademi i Oslo, II. Hist.-Filos. Klasse* (Oslo 1940), No. 3.

Blau, ChA — J. Blau, *A Grammar of Christian Arabic Based Mainly on South-Palestinian Texts from the First Millennium*, Corpus Scriptorum Christianorum Orientalium, Subsidia 27–29 (Louvain 1966–1967).

Blau, Emergence — J. Blau, *The Emergence and Linguistic Background of Judaeo-Arabic, A Study of the Origins of Middle Arabic* (Oxford 1965).

Brockelmann — C. Brockelmann, *Grundriss der vergleichenden Grammatik der semitischen Sprachen* (Berlin 1908–1913).

Brockelmann, LS — C. Brockelmann, *Lexicon Syriacum*[2] (Halis Saxonum 1928).

BSOAS — Bulletin of the School of Oriental and African Studies.

Fleisch — H. Fleisch, *Traité de philologie arabe*, vol. I (Beyrouth 1961).

Gesenius-Buhl — F. Buhl, *W. Gesenius' hebräisches und aramäisches Handwörterbuch über das Alte Testament*[17] (unveränderter Neudruck, Leipzig 1921).

Gesenius-Kautzsch — E. Kautzsch, *Gesenius' Hebrew Grammar* (second English edition, revised in accordance with the 28th German edition [1909], Oxford 1910).

HUCA — Hebrew Union College Annual.

JBL — Journal of Biblical Literature.

JSS — Journal of Semitic Studies.

Joüon — P. Joüon, *Grammaire de l'Hébreu biblique*[2] (Rome 1947).

König — F. E. König, *Historisch-kritisches Lehrgebäude der hebräischen Sprache...* (Leipzig 1881–1897).

Koehler - Baumgartner — L. Koehler - W. Baumgartner, *Lexicon in Veteris Testamenti Libros* (Leiden 1953).

Kuryłowicz — J. Kuryłowicz, *L'apophonie en Sémitique...* (Wrocław–Warszawa–Kraków 1961).

Kutscher — E. Y. Kutscher, *The Language and Linguistic Background of the Isaiah Scroll* (Jerusalem 1959) (Hebrew).

Lambert — M. Lambert, "*L'accent tonique en Hébreu*", *Revue des Etudes Juives* XX (1890), pp. 73–77.

Lane — E. W. Lane, *Maddu-l-Ḳamoos, An Arabic-English Lexicon...* (London 1863–1893).

Löw — I. Löw, *Die Flora der Juden* (Wien–Leipzig 1928–1934).

Nöldeke, BSS — Th. Nöldeke, *Beiträge zur semitischen Sprachwissenschaft* (Strassburg 1904).

Nöldeke, Mand. — Th. Nöldeke, *Mandäische Grammatik* (Halle 1875).

OLZ — Orientalistische Literatur-Zeitung.

Rabin — C. Rabin, *Ancient West-Arabian* (London 1951).

Socin-Brockelmann — C. Brockelmann, *A. Socin's arabische Grammatik*⁷, Porta Linguarum Orientalium IV (Berlin 1913).

Ungnad — A. Ungnad, *Hebräische Grammatik* (Tübingen 1912).

ZA — Zeitschrift für Assyriologie und verwandte Gebiete.

ZDMG — Zeitschrift der Deutschen Morgenländischen Gesellschaft.

Additions and Corrections

to **p. 185.***15*: As a matter of fact, ضُوقَى alternates with ضِيقَى (no doubt, the older form), as does الخُورَى 'the best (woman)' with الخِيرَى.

to **p. 186.***10*: So also ريّا › رويا › رُؤْيا 'dream'.

to **p. 186.***13*: It is, as a matter of fact, certain that iKings 22.35 וַיִּצֶק דַּם הַמַּכָּה 'the blood of the wound was spilt', וַיִּצֶק (defective spelling for וַיִּיצֶק) has to be interpreted as a passive form: < וַיֻּיצֶק*. The dictionaries claim that יצק is attested twice only as an intransitive verb 'to flow', yet this erroneous. Our verse contains a passive, and Job 38.38, its other alleged occurrence בְּצֶקֶת עָפָר לַמּוּצָק 'when the dust is poured into clod', is an infinitive, and infinitives may be used both as active and passive. Cf. perhaps also cases of *ktiv* with י, as against *qre* with ו, as Isaiah 12.5 מידעת/מודעת, iiKings 16.18 מיסך/מוסך.

to **p. 187**.*8*: Similarly, תּוּגָה 'grief', נוּגֶה 'grieved', תּוּשִׁיָּה 'sound wisdom', מוּסָר 'discupline', perhaps also מיסך/מוּסָךְ 'covered structure', מוּצָק 'casting', מוּסָד 'foundation' may reflect the shift *iw* > *û*; for theories to explain this *û* see e.g., Barth, *Nominalbildung* 244. n. 2; 266.-4, who uses the somewhat vague term "Trübung".

to **p. 188**.*8, §1.4*: For a more detailed account see my paper 'Arabic *iw* > *ū*, J. Mansour, ed., *Arabic and Islamic Studies*, Ramat-Gan 1973, pp. xiii–xiv, where, in addition to *mûsâ* 'razor' < **miwsâ* , see below p. 217.-6, *tujâh* 'opposite', *turâth* 'inheritance' are derived from **tiwjâh* > **tûjâh, *tiwrâth* > * *tûrâth* by the reduction of the long *û* before another long syllable (and, similarly, by secondary rederivation, *tuhamat* 'suspicion', *tukaʾat* 'walking stick' were formed, by the use of short-vowel-plus-feminine-ending for long vowel without such ending, from **tuhâm* < **tûhâm* < **tiwhâm, *tukâ ʾ* < **tûkâ ʾ* < **tiwkâ ʾ*.

to **p. 201**.*18*: דוד ילין, דקדוק הלשון העברית³, ירושלים תשכ"ג, p. 129, §בב attributes the penult stress to *î* after the second radical (as against *ê*).

to **p. 203**.*n. 8.-5*: = *Hebrew Linguistics*, p. 41, n. 2.

to **p. 207**.*5*: The oxytone stress in וַיּוֹצִא and וַיֵּאָסֵף (e. g. Numeri 11.30) proves that the stress shift from the penult to the ultima also occurred from open penult. As well known, this is the rule in the first person singular, see Bergsträsser, *Hebräische Grammatik*, II, p. 21, §5d.

to **p. 208**.*n. 1*: = *Hebrew Linguistics*, pp. 33–34. For a more detailed analysis see ibid., pp. 109–13.

to **p. 211**.*n. 4.6*: Beyer repeated this view of his in K. Beyer, *Die aramäischen Texte vom Toten Meer*, Göttingen 1984, pp. 128ff.

to **p. 213**.*8*: For cases of prosthetic *alef* in Biblical Aramaic see Bauer-Leander, Aram., p. 44.§12a-c.

to **p. 216**.*1.§7.5*: A more rigorous analysis of the behaviour of plosive and spirantized *b, g, d, k, p, t* suggests that it was in word initial only that these consonants were automatically spirantized in *sandhi* following a closely connected word with vocalic ending; in wordle middle and final, however, spirantization ceased being automatic. This is indicated by the inclination to using quiescent *shwa*, rather than *ḥaṭaf*, preceding *b, g, d, k, p, t* (including the behaviour of verbs iii laryngal/pharyngal in the perfect preceding -תִּי, -תָּ, etc); by forms of the type יָגַעְתְּ; and by the total absence of the elision of the sign of the doubling from *b, g, d, k, p, t* even when followed by a mobile *shwa* (type יִגְּעוּ as against יִסְעוּ). This feature is even more conspicuous in the Babylonian vocalization. For details see *Hebrew Linguistics*, pp. 281ff. Accordingly, nothing may be inferred from the behaviour of *b, g, d, k, p, t* in Biblical Hebrew as to the nature of syllables followed by a consonant with half vowel.

to **p. 216**.*14*: Since Saadia deals with *b, g, d, k, p, t* in *sandhi*; nothing may be inferred as to word middle and final, the more so since he treats Judaeo-Aramaic and not Hebrew.

to **p. 216**.*15*: Read "marked by" for "preceding"!

Marginalia Semitica II

1. AN ARCHAIC FEATURE IN THE DOMAIN OF NUMERALS

The counted noun after the cardinal numbers two/three[1] – ten in Semitic languages, as a rule, stands in the plural. The plural is sometimes substituted by a collective noun, cf. Hebrew, Exod. xxi 37 *ḥămiššā ḇāqār yəšallem taḥat haššōr wə'arbaʿ ṣōn taḥat haśśę* "he shall restore five oxen for an ox, and four sheep for a sheep"; this occurs often in Akkadian with *ṣābum* "people";[2] the same applies to Arabic[3] (where, however, the collective is often governed by the preposition *min* rather than directly dependent on the numeral).[4]

In all these cases we deal with real collectives (cf. the relation of Hebrew *bāqār/ṣōn*, above, with their respective *nomina unitatis šōr/śę*); Reckendorf, *SV*[5] goes as far as to speak (with regard to Arabic) of collective nouns that do not form plurals. Accordingly, one will refrain from confusing this construction with the quite marginal phenomenon of real singular nouns being governed by the numerals two/three – ten. This occurs in Ancient Aramaic (freely alternating with regular plurals): Sfīre I A 22 *šbʿssyh* "seven mares"; 22–23 [*šbʿ*] *šwrh* "seven cows". One can hardly concur with the current view[6] which regards *ssyh/šwrh* as collective nouns. It seems that, as also in other cases,[7] Ancient Aramaic has preserved an archaic feature: in some Semitic languages[8] the numeral "hundred" after two/three – nine (i.e. 200, 300, etc.)

1 If the dual still subsists, "two" governs the dual; otherwise, it governs the plural as well

2 See Soden, p. 194. §h.

3 See, e.g., Wright, II, p. 237; Reckendorf, *SV*, p. 274, Reckendorf, p. 205.

4 See Wright, *ibid*.

5 *Ibid*.

6 See A. Dupont-Sommer, *Les inscriptions Araméennes de Sfiré*...(Paris, 1958), pp. 39, 40; Fitzmyer, pp. 42, 43; H. Donner–W. Röllig, *Kanaanäische und aramäische Inschriften*... (Wiesbaden, 1962–4), II, p. 247; Degen, p. 104. Similarly, A. B. Davidson, *Hebrew Syntax*[3] (Edinburgh, 1901), p. 52, rem. 3, mixed up cases of real collective in Biblical Hebrew with those of genuine singular nouns (for the latter cf. e.g. P. Joüon, *Grammaire de l'Hébreu Biblique*[2] (Rome, 1947), p. 439, n. 4; yet the Hebrew cases of genuine singular are text-critically uncertain, see the commentaries and Kittel-Kahle *ad loc*.).

7 So feminine plural *stat. abs.* still terminates in *-t*. *Obiter dictu*, just as singular after two–ten alternates with plural, the fem. plur. *stat. abs.* *-t* alternates with the later suffix *-n*.

8 Cf. for an overall view Brockelmann, II, p. 274.

occurs in the singular, and this is generally considered to be an archaic feature.[9] One must assume that originally all the numerals, not only those from eleven onwards, governed the counted noun in the singular.[10] Later, after the numerals two/three – ten, the singular was superseded by the plural. Yet the hundreds, being a "closed" syntagma,[11] preserved the archaic construction longer. Traces (p. 293. n. 13) of this construction occur in the archaic Ancient Aramaic inscriptions.[12]

2. PROTO-SEMITIC *'*īθay* AND **yiš* "BEING"

"Being" and its negation are expressed by various particles, which are, externally at least, quite similar and are therefore, as a rule, regarded as being derived from the same Proto-Semitic word:[1] Akkadian *išū* "to have", *laššu* "not to be, not having"[2], Ancient Aramaic *lyš*,[3] Aramaic ⌜*īṭay*⌝, negated ⌜*layt*⌝,[4] Hebrew *yēš*, '*īš*[5], Ugaritic '*iθ*, Arabic (negated) *laysa* (and *lāta*), and perhaps

[9] Cf. e.g. Brockelmann, *ibid.*, Fleisch, I, p. 515, n. 1.

[10] As a matter of fact, the occurrence of the plural after numerals has to be considered a redundant feature, see, e.g., O. Jespersen, *The Philosophy of Grammar* (London, 1924), p. 208.

[11] The preservation of archaic features in closed syntagmas is a well-established fact, cf. * e.g. *lā* "not" in Arabic with perfect in parallel expressions.

[12] On the other hand, not every occurrence of singular instead of plural after numerals need be original; cf. e.g. the secondary development in English and German, see O. Jespersen, *A Modern English Grammar* II (London, 1954 [reprint]), 49–50, H. Paul, *Deutsche Grammatik*, III, Halle 1919, pp. 211–2. Brockelmann (II, p. 275), at any rate seems to consider the use of the singular in Tigre to be secondary. In Christian Arabic, this feature is due to scribal error, see Blau, *ChA*, p. 378, §261. For this feature in Akkadian, see Soden, pp. 194–5; in Ugaritic, see S. E. Loewenstamm, *Proceedings of the International Conference on Semitic Studies* (Jerusalem 1969), pp. 178–9 (add also UT 1126, 1 θ/θ *ktn*).

[1] See, e.g., the current Bible dictionaries, further Brockelmann I, p. 235.

[2] For the affinity of "being" and "having" see M. M. Bravmann, *Studies in Arabic and General Syntax* (Cairo, 1953), pp. 143 ff. According to the testimony of the other Semitic languages "being" was the primary meaning in Akkadian as well (still preserved in the negative form), from which "having" developed. Cf. also Brockelmann I, 501c, II, 107c. *Laššu* (mainly Assyrian) ⟨ (cf. Soden 20, §d) **lāšu* ⟨ (exhibiting *ā* ⟨ *ay*, see I. J. Gelb, quoted by S. Gevirtz, *JNES* XVI, 1957, p. 126, note 22) **layšu* ⟨ *lā išū*.

[3] In Ancient Aramaic *š* reflects both Proto-Semitic *š* and θ.

[4] For the diverse forms occurring in Aramaic see Koehler–Baumgartner[1], Aramaic part, s.v. '*īṭay*.

[5] According to the Massora to 2 Samuel xiv 19, it occurs in this passage, further Micah vi 10, Proverbs xviii 24, in the last passage spelt *plene* with *y*. According to the Tiberian vocalization it is impossible to decide whether the vowel is short or long. I have postulated long *ī* because of the Aramaic form. For Old Canaanite cf. *išū* in the sense of "being(!)" see J. A. Knudtzon, *Die El-Amarna-Tafeln*... (Leipzig, 1915), p. 1430, for "Amorite" the proper noun *la-ši-el-ka-a-bim* "there is no god like Abum", see T. Bauer, *Die Ostkanaanäer*... (Leipzig, 1962), pp. 55; 77.

also Mehri *leh*.[6] Yet the proposed derivation of all these words (even with the exception of Arabic *lāta*, on which see below, *Excursus* 2) from Proto-Semitic **yiθay*[7] meets obstacles, the most serious of which is that Ugaritic and Aramaic indicate *θ* as second radical, as against Proto-Semitic *š́* suggested by Arabic (and perhaps by Mehri). As a rule, scholars content themselves with stating that the Arabic form contravenes regular sound-change,[8] and Brocklemann's attempt (I, p. 235) to interpret Arabic *s* as being due to the dissimilatory effect of *l* is quite unlikely.[9] Moreover, according to the evidence of Old Akkadian (see I. J. Gelb, *Old Akkadian Writing and Grammar* 2, MAD 2, Chicago 1961, p. 185), the Akkadian form reflects Proto-Semitic *š́* as well: it is spelt *isu*, *s* reflecting Proto-Semitic *š́* (see Gelb, p. 37; *š́* spelt in Ur III and adduced by Gelb is a later spelling habit, see Gelb p. 39, J. Aro, *Orientalia*, N.S. XXVIII, 1959, pp. 329–30). There are, however, other difficulties as well for the derivation of these various forms from **yiθay*: it is difficult to account for the interchange of initial *y* and '. As to the Aramaic ', it is explained by Nöldeke (*Mand.*, p. 55, note 5) as a special Aramaic shift, and this is accepted by Brockelmann (I, p. 188). Yet (*pace* Nöldeke, *Mand.*, *ibid.*,) this shift is peculiar to Eastern Aramaic only,[10] and it does not account for the occurrence of ' in the other Aramaic dialects. Therefore, Bauer–Leander, (p. 254, rem. 2) were compelled to assume an Eastern Aramaic loan. This assumption, however, somewhat unlikely in itself, is refuted by the occurrence of ' in Ugaritic

[6] Proto-Semitic *š́* may in Mehri be represented by *h*. For *leh* cf. the literature adduced in Wagner, *Mehri*, p. 34, rem. 1 (yet Wagner postulates, in contradistinction to all his sources, *le*, rather than *leh*, it seems, without justification; accordingly one will not accept the etymology proposed by him, *ibid.*, note 1), further Rundgren, p. 121.

[7] See Nöldeke, *Mand.* p. 293, n. 5, whose view was accepted e.g., by Brockelmann and Bauer–Leander, see below.

[8] See e.g., Nöldeke, *Mand.* p. 293, note 5, further Gesenius-Buhl[16] and BDB, *s.v. yēš*, whereas Koehler-Baumgartner[1] s.v. even refrain from this comment.

[9] His alternative explanation (*ibid.*), that the Arabic form is original whereas Aramaic *t* is due to the dissimilatory effect of *l* in the negative form (incidentally, the alleged dissimilatory effect affected *š́*, rather than θ as adduced by Brockelmann, since in this case Brockelmann postulates original *š́*), is even less likely, and is utterly refuted by the Ugaritic form. Cohen, p. 85, wonders whether *laysa* is due to its character as an accesory word, "to blend" or "to loan". Neither proposition is convincing. As to the assumption that Arabic *laysa* is a (Northwest Semitic) loan, cf. also S. Gevritz, *JNES* XVI (1957), p. 126, note 22 (who also considers Akkadian *išū* a loan [for which see below]); Garbini, p. 172. H. Bauer's assumption (*Islamica* II, 1926–7, pp. 8–9) that **layθa* shifted to *laysa* out of fear from *layθ*, the lion, is, for all its ingenuity, simply absurd.

[10] For Mandaic, see Nöldeke, *Mand.* pp. 55–56; for Syriac, see Brockelmann, *Syr.* p. 45, rem. 4; for the Aramaic of the Babylonian Talmud, see J. N. Epstein, *A Grammar of Babylonian Aramaic* (Jerusalem–Tel Aviv, 1960 [Hebrew]), p. 77, notes 199, 203.

as well. Nor will one postulate Proto-Semitic *'*īθay*[11] and assume the shift of ' to *y* in the negative form (**lā'īθay*>**lāyīθay*; in fact, in many Aramaic dialects the negative form exhibitis *y* as against ' in the positive; see for particulars Koehler–Baumgartner[1], Aramaic part, s.v. *'īṭay*), which was then extended to the positive form. This assumption would not explain Hebrew *yēš*, which is attested after *lō* only in Job ix 33 (and even there the reading is rather uncertain). Accordingly, in Hebrew, the positive form could not have been influenced by the negative.[12] Another difficulty is exhibited by the final *-ay* of **'īθay*, which does not fit in with the Akkadian, Hebrew, and Ancient Aramaic forms. Since in Akkadian *ay* is monophtongized to *ī*, one would have expected **'īθay* to shift to **išī* and therefore to be conjugated according to *verba III infirmae* terminating in preterite G in *-ī*, rather than in *-ū*. As to the Hebrew forms, no traces of any diphtong *ē*<*ay* can be discerned, not even preceding pronominal suffixes. Similarly, the only occurrence of Ancient Aramaic *lyš* is preceding a pronominal suffix: *lyšh*, Barrākib A 16, exhibiting the pronominal suffix of the third person masc. singular. Were *lyš* to have the ending *-ay*, its pronominal suffix would take the plural form *-wh*, just as prepositions terminating in *-ay* have plural suffixes (as ʾ*[l]wh* "to him", Sfīre III 8).[13]

Accordingly, one will not derive all the forms denoting "being" from one Proto-Semitic form,[14] but rather postulate a Proto-Semitic doublet expressing

[11] Garbini, *ibid.*, posits *'*ay*θ as primary form > *'*ayi*θ > *yēš*. Yet a form like '*ay*θ could not have given rise to *ī* in Aramaic '*īṭay*. Moreover, the shift *ay* > *ayi* in Hebrew is very late. Accordingly, one will not accept Garbini's proposal.

[12] For the alleged interchange of *yi* and '*i*/'*ī* in Hebrew, see Blau, *Pseudo-Corrections*, p. 32.

[13] Cf. for this form also F. Rosenthal, *Die Sprache der palmyrenischen Inschriften*, Mitteilungen der Vorderasiatisch-Aegyptischen Gesellschaft (Leipzig, 1936), p. 88. In later Aramaic, according to Brockelmann (I, p. 75, §m), *-ay* was dropped in accordance with the general tendency to drop final long vowels and diphtongs. This tendency, however, is peculiar to Eastern Aramaic, yet '*īṭ* (without final *-ay*) occurs also outside it (cf. the list [Koehler-] Baumgartner,[1] Aramaic part, s.v. '*īṭay*). Accordingly, one will prefer Leander's explanation (p. 119, §h), who considers it backformation from the forms with pronominal suffixes: *-ay* was understood as the plural ending (as it was in the prepositions '*ęl*, ʿ*al*, for instance, which originally also terminated in *-ay*). As to '*īṭā* in the Babylonian Talmud, it may be due to the marginal shift *ay*>*ā* (for which cf., e.g., Nöldeke, *Mand.* 22) or, more likely, to analogy with the synonymous '*ikkā*. — Garbini's supposition (p. 172) that *-ay* is secondary, is unlikely.

[14] This has been suggested frequently, yet without full documentation and argumentation. (pp. 305–6) I myself have shortly treated this problem (*BSOAS* XXXII (1969), pp. 7–8; *Pseudo-corrections*, 32–33), yet in different contexts and, therefore, with different slant. J. Barth, *ZDMG* LXVIII (1914), pp. 361 ff. separated Arabic *laysa* from Aramaic ⌜*layt*⌝, considering *-sa* a demonstrative element, and he was, more or less, followed by V. Christian, *WZKM* XXXI (1924), p. 171, and Rundgren, 119 ff., who postulates, p. 157, Proto-Semitic *š* also for Akkadian *išū* (as to Hebrew *yēš*, '*iš*, he is uncertain, see p. 125). *Obiter dictu*, Christian supposes that *išū* developed from the copule *šu*, just as, according to Friedrich Delitzsch (*sic*!, not Zimmern, as adduced by Christian), *hwy*/*hyy* originated in the copule ⌜*hū*⌝. Since, however, a verb

"being", viz. *'īθay and *yiš (the latter perhaps terminating in a short vowel). From 'īθay are derived Aramaic 'īṯay, Ugaritic 'iθ (presumably to be pronounced 'īθē⟨'īθay) and Hebrew 'īš (because of the initial *alef*; the dropping of the final -*ay* is due, it seems, to the impact of *yēš*, which eventually superseded 'īš altogether).[15] *yiš is represented by Hebrew *yēš* (because of the initial *y* and the total absence of any reflex of final -*ay*,[16] see above), perhaps Mehri *leh* (cf. above note 6), further Ancient Aramaic *lyš(h)* (because of the absence of the reflex of final -*ay*, see above), Akkadian *išū*[17] and Arabic *laysa*, which both reflect Proto-Semitic *š*. The special form of this world in both languages originates in their adaptation to verbs: in Akkadian to the preterite (rarely stative) G of *verba tertiae w*, in Arabic partly to the perfect of the first pattern of *verba mediae infirmae*; it was only in the Ḍabba dialect that *laysa* has been made a "normal" verb by conjugating *lustu* or *listu* (see Rabin p. 191, note 18)[18]. For the elision of the *i* in **lāyisa⟩laysa* cf. *niʿma/biʾsa* (where the initial *i* is due to assimilation because of the following pharyngal/laryngal).

Excursus 1.

1. Hebrew *yēš* with pronominal suffixes. The following forms occur: *yęšḵā*, *yęšḵęm* / *yišḵęm* and *yęšnō*. The last form is difficult, and was emended by

parallel to *hwy* is attested in Akkadian, scil. *ewū*, and Arabic *laysa* (as well as Mehri *leh*) correspond according to Christian himself to *išū*, this would necessitate the very unlikely assumption that ⌈*hū*⌉ served as copule in Akkadian and *šū* in Arabic. F. R. Blake *JAOS* XXXV (1915), pp. 377 ff. and I. Eitan, *AJSL* XLIV (1927/28) pp. 187 ff. derive these particles, as a rule, from Proto-Semitic *š* (Eitan even Ancient Aramaic *lyšh*), whereas for Aramaic they postulate Proto-Semitic *t* and connect it, *inter alia*, with the object-particle ⌈'*iyyāṯ*⌉, *yāṯ*, etc. Since the discovery of Ugaritic had also proved the occurrence of Proto-Semitic θ, Blake later (*JAOS* LXXIII, 1953, pp. 7–8) tentatively suggested that Aramaic might represent either Proto-Semitic *t* or θ, and Hebrew either Proto-Semitic *š* or θ, i.e., he even contemplated the possibility of three(!) different particles denoting "being".

15 Accordingly 'īš is an archaic feature, rather than late Aramaism, as maintained, e.g., by Driver, *Samuel*, p. 309 ("late transcriber"); N. H. Tur-Sinai, *Mishle Shlomo* (Tel Aviv, 1947 [Hebrew]), p. 71; M. Wagner, *Die lexikalischen und grammatikalischen Aramaismen...*, Beihefte *ZAW* XCVI (Berlin, 1966), p. 30.

16 Accordingly, one will reject H. Bauer's ingenious proposal (*ZAW* NS, XLVIII 1930, p. 77, accepted e.g. by Koehler–Baumgartner,[1] s.v. *yēš*, Wagner, *ibid.*) that the proper noun *yišay* reflects the archaic ending -*ay* of *yēš*. Biblical '*Ešbaʿal* does not exhibit our word either, since it corresponds to Ugaritic '*Išbʿl*, see C. Virolleaud, *Le palais royal d'Ugarit*, V (Paris, 1965), p. 156, s.v. It seems too far-fetched to suppose that the Ugaritic name is due to the blend of *yš* and 'iθ.

17 Nothing certain can be stated as to Amorite *laši*, since the *š* may represent both original *š* and θ, and -*i* may be due either to its adaptation to verba III *y* or to monophtongization of -*ay*.

18 Yet *laysa* is also attested in Classical Arabic governing pronominal suffixes, see H. L. Fleischer, *Kleinere Schriften*, I (Leipzig, 1885), p. 147. For its occurrence in Middle Arabic see Blau, *ChA*, 308 and *ibid.* note 26.

C. Brockelmann, *ZA* XIV (1899), pp. 347–8 to **yēšęnnū*. J. Barth, on the other hand (see *ZDMG* XLI, 1887, pp. 642–3; *Sprachwissenschaftliche Untersuchungen...*, I, Leipzig, 1907, p. 7), associates it with *qoḇnō*, Num. xxiii 13; the latter form, however, is very difficult to interpret. As to *yešnō*, I would propose to consider it a Middle Hebrew form that intruded into the Bible text through analogy with its Middle Hebrew antonym *'ēnō* (= Biblical Hebrew *'ēnęnnū*), in which the *n* is, of course, radical.

2. Arabic *lāta*. This word [see: J. Barth, *ZDMG* LXVII (1913), pp. 494–96; *idem*, *ZDMG* LXVIII (1914), 362; A. Fischer, *ZDMG* LXVII (1913), pp. 692–3; G. Bergsträsser, *Verneinungs- und Fragepartikeln... im Kur'ān...*, Leipziger Semitistische Studien V, Leipzig, 1914, pp. 20–21, note 1; Cohen, p. 86; Reckendorf, p. 122, §62.7] does not belong to the group of words dealt with. It is quite rare and denotes "there was no time", both followed by a noun denoting time and without it. The noun denoting time appears in the nominative, accusative or genitive, see Bergsträsser, who rightly stresses the fact that the genitive is, on first sight, so peculiar that its occurrence has to be attributed to tradition rather than to mere fabrication. If this is so, one would expect *lāta* to contain a noun which governs the following genitive (cf. Cohen, who derives it from a phrase parallel to Hebrew *lō ʿeṭ*), rather than a particle (*pace*, Barth). I would tentatively propose to derive it from *lā tawwata* "there is no time" (for *tawwatun* cf. Lane *s.v.*; for the reflex of its root in modern dialects, see W. Fischer, *Die demonstrativen Bildungen der neuarabischen Dialekte*, 's-Gravenhage, 1959, pp. 150 ff). At first, it would seem, it was followed by the genitive of a general noun. Later, the etymology of *lāta* became blurred and it was pleonastically followed by the genitive of a noun denoting time and, afterwards, by accusative/nominative as well.

3. PROTO-SEMITIC *'iš* "FIRE"

As a rule, Hebrew *'eš* is considered to be derived from a triliteral root, and even T. Nöldeke in his classic treatment of the biliteral nouns (*NBSS*, pp. 109–178) does not adduce it. Already W. Gesenius (*Thesaurus*, Lipsiae, 1835 ff. s.v.) mentions, though with qualifications, the possibility of deriving it from the root *'nš*, in accordance with Arabic *'anīsa* "fire". This view became famous, because Lagarde (pp. 68; 190), following J. G. Wetzstein,[1] accepted it. Yet, as BDB s.v. righly observed, Akkadian *išāt*[2] proves that the *dagesh* in the *š*

[1] Lagarde (p. 190) only quoted Wetzstein's opinion, without knowing its exact place. According to Gesenius – Buhl[16] and BDB s.v. it is in Franz Delizsch's *Psalmen*[4], pp. 888–9. I was unable to see this work.

[2] *Sic*!, not *išat*, as quoted by BDB. The same applies to Gʿez and Samaritan Hebrew, see below.

is secondary. Others considered *'eš* to be derived from a root *tertiae infirmae* and the doubling of the *š* secondary; this was, for instance, the opinion of G. Dalman, *Grammatik des jüdisch-palästinischen Aramäisch*² (Leipzig, 1905), p. 202, note 1; J. Barth, *ZDMG* XLI (1887), p. 604; F. Schulthess, *Lexicon Syropalaestinum* (Berolini, 1903), s.v. *'šy*; Bauer–Leander, p. 454, note 1 (who postulate **'išāt* as the original form from which, by misinterpreting *-āt* as feminine plural ending, **'iš* > Hebrew *'eš* was derived by backformation). This derivation, however, is too mechanical.[3] The only way to interpret the various forms of this word, which occurs in the Semitic languages, is, it seems, to derive it from a biliteral root **'iš*,[4] which was in different ways expanded to a triliteral one.

In Akkadian, biliteral *išum* (see the literature quoted in *ZA* LIV [= N.S. XX, 1961], p. 262, especially J. Bottero, *Studi Semitici* 1 (1958), pp. 42–3) is a mere fossil, preserved in proper nouns as a divine name only. The ordinary word for "fire" is *išātum*, exhibiting the addition of the feminine ending to a word feminine by signification: nouns denoting "fire" incline to be feminine (cf. e.g. Brockelmann I 424, §e; M. Feghali–A. Cuny, *Du genre grammatical en Sémitique*, Paris, 1924, p. 79), and there is a general tendency of adding feminine termination to nouns feminine by signification only (see W. Havers, *Handbuch der erklärenden Syntax…*, Heidelberg, 1931, p. 176). This tendency is clearly attested in several semitic languages (cf. e.g. for Ugaritic *'atnt* "she-ass"; for later layers of Arabic: Blau, *ChA* 206, note 36, and in general Brockelmann I 417, 425, where our word is treated as well). Yet the feminine ending has the lengthened form *-āt*, rather than *-at* (*išāt*, rather than **išat*), thus bringing our quite short word into conformity with the general rhythmical patern.[5] Its plural is *išātātum*, with the inclusion of the singular ending *-āt* in the root (already in Old Babylonian, see Soden 77, §1), thus making the root triliteral.

Ugaritic *'išt* exhibits the addition of the feminine ending as well; yet, because * of the lack of vowel signs, nothing more can be stated. Gᶜez *'esāt* (for its traditional pronunciation see, e.g., E. Mittwoch, *Die traditionelle Aussprache des Äthiopischen*, Mitteilungen des Seminars für orientalische Sprachen zu Berlin, Zweite Abteilung, Westasiatische Studien, Berlin 1925, p. 221, verse 7)

3 This was Nöldeke's view (*NBSS*, p. 109) in general on Barth's paper on biliteral nouns, *ZDMG* XLI (1887), pp. 603 ff.

4 So also Koehler–Baumgartner³, s.v., where, however, the derivation from a biliteral root is mixed up with the above-mentioned view of Bauer–Leander, a real *contradictio in adiecto*.

5 Theoretically, it could be claimed that the long *ā* is due to the adding of *y* to the biliteral root, making it triliteral: **'išayat* > *'išāt*, just as Hebrew *'iššę* arose from *'išayu*, see below. Yet this view is less likely.

exhibits the feminine ending *-āt* as well, reflecting long *ā* as in Akkadian. Aramaic *'iššāṭā/'ęššāṭā* (*status absolutus 'iššā/'ęššā*),[6] besides the feminine ending *-āt*, exhibits the presumably secondary doubling of the *š*.[7] The Syriac plural *'eššāṭwāṭā* (see Nöldeke, *Syr.*, p. 53, § 79B2, p. 70, §114)[8] mirrors not only the inclusion of *-āt* in the root, as in Akkadian, but also the formation of the plural with the extended plural morpheme *-wāṭā* (for which cf. Nöldeke, *op. cit.*, pp. 52–3), whereas Mandaic עשאתיא (see Nöldeke, *Mand.* 168) terminates in the ordinary plural suffix. In contradistinction to all the Aramaic dialects, which exhibit ⌜'issāṭā⌝ with feminine ending and lengthened *-ā* in *status emphaticus*, ⌜'iššā⌝ with feminine ending in *status absolutus*, — archaic Ancient Aramaic has *'š*[9] in *status absolutus* (Sfīre I A 35, 37, 37–8), thus indicating again that the addition of the feminine ending is a secondary feature.

In Hebrew our word has been adapted to the triliteral scheme by the doubling of the second radical: *'eš*, *'iššō* ("his fire"). In Babylonian vocalization the ' is followed by *pataḥ/segol* (see P. Kahle, *Der masoretische Text des Alten Testaments*, Leipzig, 1902, p. 68, §2; *idem*, *Masoreten des Ostens*, Leipzig, 1913, p. 196), thus indicating (cf. Bergsträsser I, p. 149) that the doubling of the second radical chronologically precedes Philippi's law. On the other hand, according to the Samaritan pronunciation of Hebrew (in contradistinction to Samaritan Aramaic!) the *š* is not doubled: *ēšu* "his fire" (Ben-Ḥayyim, III, part I, p. 102, note to line 36), *prima facie* a feature older than that mirrored in the other traditions of Hebrew.[10]

It seems quite established that Hebrew *'iššę* "offering" has to be directly derived from *'eš*.[11] According to H. Bauer,[12] its original form was *'iššā*, i.e.

[6] For the various forms in the different Aramaic dialects see (Koehler–)Baumgartner[1], Aramaic Part, s.v. *'ęššā*. In many cases the exact vocalization is unknown and it can be inferred only from the cognate dialects, as is the case in Christian Palestinian (see F. Schulthess, *Grammatik des christlich-palästinischen Aramäisch* (Tübingen, 1924), p. 15, §24.2b). As to the Samaritan form, left by (Koehler–)Baumgartner unvocalized, it is *iššåtå*, Ben-Ḥayyim III, part II, p. 55, line 1. (Koehler–)Baumgartner, *ibid.* also adduces Neo-Syriac *šatha*, a late development.

[7] Cf. e.g. Bauer–Leander, *Aram.*, p. 56c.

[8] In Syriac the meaning of *'eššaṭā* is restricted to "fever".

[9] Koehler–Baumgartner[3] s.v. wrongly state that the addition of the feminine ending is attested already in Ancient Aramaic. The very source on which they rely ("DISO 27") proves the contrary.

[10] Nothing certain can be stated as to Jer. vi 29 *ktību m'štm* (*qrē mē'eš tam*) [see Gesenius-Buhl[16] and BDB s.v. *'eššā*] as to the alleged occurrence of Hebrew *'iššā* with feminine ending. For Bauer's view that *'iššę* arose from *'iššā* see below.

[11] One will not consent with A. B. Ehrlich's view (*Randglossen zur hebräischen Bibel...*, II (Leipzig, 1909), *ad* Lev. i 9; iv 35) that *'iššę*, being independent from *'eš*, is cognate with Arabic *'aθāθ* "goods". Even if *'iššę* need not denote "offering by fire", but can mark any offering, this does not prove that it was not *originally* derived from "fire". For the semantic

'eš with the feminine ending *-at*; it developed into *'iššę* in order to differentiate it from *'iššā* "woman". This view was accepted by Koehler-Baumgartner,[3] *s.v.*, yet it is, despite its ingenuity, rather unlikely.[13] One will prefer to derive *'iššę* from **išayu*, the *y* complementing it to a triliteral root. If this proves * true, *'iššę* is not directly[14] to be derived from *'eš*, with double *š*; the doubling of the *š* is secondary, due to pretonic doubling and/or to the secondary influence of *'eš*. The second supposition seems more likely, in the light of Samaritan Hebrew *ēši* (see Ben-Ḥayyim III, part I, p. 53, verse 18), corresponding to *ēš*, see above.

Excursus 2.

1. The gender of Hebrew *'eš* is, as a rule, feminine. Yet there is one clear case of its use as masculine: Ps. civ 4 עֹשֶׂה מַלְאָכָיו רוּחוֹת מְשָׁרְתָיו אֵשׁ לֹהֵט "who makes his messengers spirits, his servants a flaming fire". In the light of Biblical Aramaic *nūr* "fire", attested not only as feminine, but also Dan. vii 9 as masculine: *nūr dāliq* "flaming fire" (= exactly *'eš lōhēṭ*!), it would be hypercritical to emend the verse because of the masculine usage of *'eš* (the version in the Psalms of Qumran *'eš lōhęṭęt* is clearly *lectio facilior*). Neither should one claim that the plural *məšārəṭāw* "his servants" contradicts the singular *'eš*, and therefore one should read *'eš wālahaṭ* "fire and flame"; even if *'eš* is not used here as some sort of collective noun, the plural *məšārəṭāw* is easily explained by attraction to the preceding parallel plural *mal'āḵāw* "his messengers". Other alleged cases of masculine usage of *'eš* are, to be sure, uncertain: Num. xvi 18 where the second *ʿălēhęm* refers to the fire-holders, rather than to *'eš*; Job xx 26 תְּאָכְלֵהוּ אֵשׁ לֹא־נֻפָּח "a fire not blown will consume him", where *nuppaḥ* is, it seems, an impersonal passive; Jer. xx 9 וְהָיָה בְלִבִּי כְּאֵשׁ בֹּעֶרֶת עָצֻר בְּעַצְמֹתָי "it (*scil.* דְּבַר־ה׳) was in my heart as burning fire, shut up in my bones", where *ʿāṣūr* may be again an impersonal passive (or agree

development fire > offering cf. the use of *'eš* in the sense of "offering" (Num. xviii 9) according to the Septuagint and a quite firmly established Jewish tradition (see Ibn Jānaḥ, Abraham Ibn Ezra).

12 *ZDMG* LXXI (1917), p. 413, §7, *Islamica* II (1926/27), p. 6, cf. also Bauer–Leander, p. 608, note 1.

13 One has also to take into account the difficulty of equating *'iššā* "woman" containing original *a* in the first syllable, giving rise to *i* through attenuation, with alleged **'iššā* "offering" with original *i*.

14 Similarly, Gesenius–Buhl[16] s.v. *'iššę* wanted only to state that, according to the view of Wetzstein–Lagarde (see above), *'iššę* is not *directly* derived from *'eš*. Yet, because they omitted "directly", they are difficult to understand. Barth, p. 388, §237 wonders whether the ending *ę* ⟨*ay* in *'iššę* belongs to the root or is an affirmative; yet p. 375, §230b, he treats it in the chapter dealing with *-ay* as a part of the root.

with 'דְּבַר־ה');[15] Jer. xlviii 45 *'eš yāṣā* "fire will come forth", where *yāṣā* may be accounted to be a variant of feminine *yāṣə'ā*. Nevertheless, the one certain occurrence of *'eš* as masculine (Ps. civ 4) suffices, in the light of Biblical Aramaic masculine *nūr*, to establish the masculine use of *'eš* in Biblical Hebrew. It is a pity that the current Biblical dictionaries,[16] following K. Albrecht's hyper-critical view (in his article on the gender of nouns in Biblical Hebrew,[17] see below), lost sight of this usage altogether.[18]

2. It would be perhaps in general worthwhile to re-examine Albrecht's above mentioned paper on the gender of nouns in Biblical Hebrew, which influenced Biblical lexicography decisively. We shall content ourselves with one example:

Many Semitic languages exhibit *feminine usage of nouns denoting "staff, stick"*. Thus Akkadian *ḫaṭṭu* is feminine (Soden, p. 75, §d), Phoenician *ḥṭr* (Ahīrom 2), Aramaic *ḥoṭrā/ḥuṭrā* (see e.g. P. Kahle, *Die Masoreten des Westens* II, Stuttgart, 1930, p. 24, *ad* Exod. vii 12, Nöldeke, *Syr*., p. 58, according to whom it is more often masc. than fem.),[19] Arabic *ʿaṣan* (see e.g. Fleisch, 334, §f). Moreover, as has been observed by H. Rosenberg (*ZAW* XXV, 1905, p. 334, who also adduced Syriac[20] and Akkadian material), *maqqēl* is used in Mishnaic as feminine only. Nevertheless, Albrecht does not allow for feminine usage of the nouns denoting "staff, stick" in Biblical Hebrew (and he is followed, more or less, by the current Biblical dictionaries). *ZAW* XVI, p. 92 he emends Gen. xxx 37 *bāhen* "in them", referring to (collective) *maqqēl*, with the Samaritan *bāhẹm*,[21] and dismisses the feminine usage of *šeḇeṭ*, because

15 According to Gesenius–Kautzsch, p. 428, §d, sometimes, when two adjectival attributes refer to a feminine noun, only the one next to the noun stands in feminine.

16 BDB, *s.v.*, mentions all the possible masculine usages of *'eš*; yet in the *addenda et corrigenda*, p. 1120b, referring to p. 77a, he accepts Albrecht's analysis.

17 *ZAW* XV (1895), pp. 313–325; XVI (1896), pp. 41–121. With *'eš* he deals *ZAW* XVI, p. 63. — For Albrecht's way of emending texts that did not conform with his views on grammar cf. his article in *ZAW* XLVII (1929), pp. 274 ff., in which he emended *'et* denoting direct object after impersonal passive, despite its frequency and parallel features in other Semitic languages (cf. C. Brockelmann, *ZAW* XLIX, 1931, pp. 147 ff.).

18 Similarly also e.g. M. Lambert, *Traité de grammaire hébraïque* (Paris, 1938), p. 72, note 1.

19 Yet according to Brockelmann, *Lex*. s.v. the feminine usage is more frequent. On the other hand, Brockelmann, *Syr*., p. 55, §98 only states that its usage as to gender is not fixed. — The main usage of *guzʿā* is according to all sources feminine, see Nöldeke, *Syr*., p. 55, Brockelmann, *Syr*., p. 54, §96, Brockelmann, *Lex*., s.v.

20 Read Nöldeke, *Syr*. §87, as does Rosenberg in his *Das Geschlecht der Hauptwörter in der Mischna* (Berlin, 1908), p. 45, being an enlarged version of his article in *ZAW*.

21 This was already taken exception to by Rosenberg, *Das Geschlecht…*, *ibid*. Koehler–Baumgartner[1], s.v. interprets *bāhen* as neutral "threat". This, however, is quite unlikely. One will not claim that in the first part of this verse *maqqēl* is used as masculine, serving as

Ezek. xxi 15, 18 is corrupt; yet even a corrupt passage could have preserved the correct (feminine) usage of nouns occurring in it. *Maṭṭę* is treated by Albrecht not together with the two preceding nouns, but with nouns denoting plants, etc. (*ZAW* XVI, 103–4); he again rejects its feminine usage, because the only occurrence, Micah vi 9, is corrupt; yet, as stated above, the corruptness of a passage does not necessarily imply that the feminine usage of a noun occurring in it is not genuine, if it is established from other sources; the feminine usage of nouns denoting "stick, staff" is, in fact, proved from other Semitic languages and from Middle Hebrew.[22]

3. The gender of *'iššę* is, it seems, masculine. BDB, s.v. adduces as proof Josh. xiii 14 אִשֵּׁי ה׳ אֱלֹהֵי יִשְׂרָאֵל הוּא נַחֲלָתוֹ "the offerings of the Lord God of Israel are their inheritance"; yet *hū* may be due to attraction to ה׳ אֱלֹהֵי יִשְׂרָאֵל, cf. Josh. xiii 33 ה׳ אֱלֹהֵי יִשְׂרָאֵל הוּא נַחֲלָתָם, where ה׳ אֱלֹהֵי יִשְׂרָאֵל is, in fact the subject (as the Septuagint reads also verse 14). Better founded is Albrecht's evidence for its masculine use (*ZAW* XVI, 100), *viz*. Num. xxviii 3 זֶה הָאִשֶּׁה "this is the offering", exhibiting a demonstrative pronoun as subject of a nominal clause, which, as a rule, agrees in number and gender with its predicate — though even this is not always the case, cf. A. Müller, *Hebräische Schulgrammatik*, Halle 1878, p. 260, §508, note a[23]. Nevertheless, the masculine use of *iššę* seems well established. One will not adduce it against our contention above that this masculine *'iššę* is directly derived from mainly feminine *'eš*. As is well known,[24] the same noun may have different genders according to its different meanings. Similarly, *'iššę*, perhaps also because of the influence of masculine synonyms (like *qorbān*),[25] shifted from feminine to masculine.

4. PROTO-SEMITIC *mẓ'/mṭ'* "ARRIVE"

There is a plethora of *verba tertiae alef/infirmae* in the sense of "arriving" and the like that have *m* as their first radical. Small wonder that the opinions of

head of *laḥ* "fresh": *laḥ* refers to *libnę*. Otherwise *laḥ* would separate the *status constructus* from the second and third *nomen rectum*: *maqqal libnę laḥ wəlūz wəʿarmōn* "rods of fresh poplar (see e.g. BDB, s.v. *laḥ*), almond and plane-tree", rather than "fresh rods of..." (so e.g. Koehler–Baumgartner[1], s.v.).

22 Accordingly, one will not agree with A. Bendavid, *Biblical Hebrew and Mishnaic Hebrew*[2], I (Tel Aviv, 1967), p. 150 that the feminine usage of Mishnaic *maqqel* is due to Greek influence.

23 Yet the instance adduced by him, Josh. xiii 14, has to be explained otherwise, see above. As a matter of fact, when looking for exceptions, I did not succeed to detect any. If this proves true, the masculine use of *'iššę* would be established even more firmly.

24 See e.g. Nöldeke, *Syr*. 58, §87, *passim*, further Albrecht, *ZAW* XVI, p. 121, though one will accept his analysis with qualifications only.

25 For other masculine synonyms denoting "offering" cf. Albrecht, *ZAW* XVI p. 100.

scholars diverge as to their etymological connections, and new finds are apt to change the accepted views.

As in so many fields, it was T. Nöldeke who decisively influenced research. He dealt shortly with some of these verbs already in *ZDMG* XXXII (1878), p. 406, and afterwards, following Fr. Delitzsch's criticism (p. 158, note 2), yet rejecting most of his strictures, he proposed the explanation (*ZDMG* XL, 1886, p. 736 and *ibid.*, note 5) which dominated research almost till our very days. He postulated three series of verbs, which, despite the affinity of their significations, are nevertheless to be totally separated:

1. Hebrew *māṣā*, Aramaic *məṣā*, Gᶜez *maṣ'a.*
2. Aramaic *məṭā*, Arabic *'anṭā* (<*'*amṭā*), Gᶜez *maṭṭawa.*
3. Arabic *maḍā.*

As to the first series, its original meaning is "to arrive", as preserved in Gᶜez, from which Hebrew "to find" developed, marginaly attested also in Syriac. In Aramaic it developed to designate "being able", especially in the expression *məṣā ḥaylā də* "to be a match for" (just as *'eškaḥ* "to find" is used in the same sense in the phrase *'eškaḥ* [*bə*]*ḥēl*). As stated above, Nöldeke's view was accepted with relatively few changes and extensions. See e.g. the current Biblical dictionaries, s.v. *mṣ'*, as well as their Biblical Aramaic parts, s.v. *mṭ'*; Driver, *Samuel*, p. 187, *ad* 1 Sam. xxiii 17; Brockelmann, *Lex.* and E.S. Drower–R. Macuch, *A Mandaic Dictionary*, Oxford, 1963, s.v. *mṭ'*, *mṣ'*; Landberg, s.v. *nṭy*. Of greater importance is C. Brockelmann's insight (*Festschrift O. Eissfeldt*, Halle 1947, p. 63) that Aramaic *məṭā* is to be connected with Epigraphic South Arabaian *mẓ'* and Gᶜez *maṣ'a*, rather than with Gᶜez *maṭṭawa.* On the other hand, one will not agree with Brockelmann's view (*ibid*, pp. 62–3) on the derivation of Ugaritic *mġy*, as if the *ġ* corresponded to Proto-Semitic *ḍ* (*v. infra*). Moreover, he did not take into account additional Ugaritic material.

In the following, we shall try to adduce the whole Ugaritic material available. We shall endeavour not only to observe strictly the well-known sound correspondences between the various Semitic languages, but also to separate carefully *verba tertiae alef* from *tertiae infirmae*, as far as the single languages admit of it. One will not deny that even in languages which, as a rule, distinguish between these verbal classes (as Classical Arabic or Biblical Hebrew), cases of interference occur (being either dialectical features or exhibiting the beginning of the merger of these verbal classes, still differentiated by the conservative orthography).[1] Yet these cases of confusion are exceptional. There-

[1] Cf. e.g. Rabin, p. 142, §hh; p. 144, and Bergsträsser, II, pp. 158–9, §§e–h; p. 168, §q.

fore, it seems methodologically unsound to simply connect a verb, always attested as *tertiae alef*, with a verb *tertiae infirmae*, occurring only as such in a language that distinguishes between these verbal classes.

Among *verba tertiae infirmae* there are, it seems, three independent series of verbs:

1. Arabic *mḍy* "to go".
2. Ugaritic *mġy* "to reach, arrive, come".
3. Arabic *mṭw* "to stretch, draw, pull; walk quickly",[2] Epigraphic South- * Arabian *mṭw* "to walk, march, (or something similar);[3] Gʿez (D stem) *maṭṭawa* "deliver".[4]

2 In the dialect of Marazig (V. G. Boris, *Léxique du parler arabe des Marazig*, Paris, 1958, s.v. *mṭy*) its sixth verbal stem (tD) has the sense "stretch out the hand to take something, to take"; a further development is "to steal" (in the ground stem), see (with additional literature) Landberg s.v. — For "stretching" and "going" being related, cf. Hebrew *mšk*, Aramaic *ngd*, see also the Bible dictionaries, s.vv; cf. also the use of *nṭy* Gen. xxxviii 1. According to Arabic, "stretching" is, it seems, the original sense, rather than "arriving", assumed because of related Aramaic *məṭā*.

3 As a rule, the sense "arriving, reaching" is attributed to it (see *Corpus Inscriptionum Semiticarum*, IV, Paris, 1889–1930, Inscription 397, lines 6–7, 9; Conti Rossini, s.v.), yet this is due to its alleged connection with Aramaic *məṭā*, see n. 2. *Corpus... ibid.* "marching" suits the context well (D. H. Müller, *ZDMG* XXX (1876), p. 690, translates "aufbrechen"; the text quoted by Müller, *ibid.* [Reh. IX, line 3,] is broken and nothing can be inferred as to the sense of *mṭw*). A. Jamme, *Sabaean Inscriptions from Maḥram Bilqis* (*Mārib*) (Baltimore, 1962), Inscription 635, lines 9–11 *bnkl.sbʾt. wḍbyʾ sbʾw.wḍbʾ . wmṭw.whʿnn. bʿly.kl. ʾḫms* "from all the encounters and the engagements (which) they have fought and combatted, and they marched (exhibiting either main clause, or continuation of the relative clause, breaking its framework; for this phenomenon cf. Brockelmann II, 583, rem., Blau, *ChA*, p. 575, note 94, where further literature is quoted) and gave aid against all the armies"; Jamme's own explanation *ibid.* "to take part" is not necessary here and impossible *Corpus...*, *ibid.* Rabin's proposal (p. 33, line 1) "to give presents" for *Corpus*, 397, lines 6–7 is possible, yet not necessary. It is, however, less fitting *ibid.*, line 9, and would be very artificial Jamme, *loc. cit.*, whereas "marching" fits all the passages in which *mṭw* occurs.

4 Governing, *inter alia*, two direct objects. For Ethiopic verbs denoting movement and governing direct object see e.g. Brockelmann II, p. 283; therefore "deliver" may govern two direct objects. The sense of "delivering, giving" may well be derived from "stretching", cf., e.g., the use of Hebrew *nṭy* "stretch out" (as transitive *qal* and *hifʿil*) in cases like Gen. xxxix 21 וַיֵּט אֵלָיו חָסֶד וַיִּתֵּן חִנּוֹ בְּעֵינֵי שַׂר בֵּית הַסֹּהַר "and he gave him mercy and gave him favour in the sight of the keeper of the prison"; I Chron. xiii 13 וְלֹא־הֵסִיר דָּוִיד אֶת־הָאָרוֹן אֵלָיו אֶל־עִיר דָּוִיד וַיַּטֵּהוּ אֶל־בֵּית עֹבֵד אֱדֹם "and David did not bring the ark to himself to the city of David, but brought it into the house of Obed-edom". In the light of these and similar passages one will not agree with Nöldeke's ingenious proposal, to derive Arabic *ʾanṭā* "to give" from *ʾamṭā* (see above). One will rather derive it from original *nṭy* with a primary meaning "to stretch out", as preserved in Hebrew *nṭy* and its cognates (see the current Biblical dictionaries), as does also Rabin p. 32.

As to the first two series, they stand alone and cannot be brought into etymological connection either with one another or with other verbs. *ḍ* of Arabic *mḍy* could be represented by *ṣ* in Akkadian and Hebrew (as also in later Gᶜez); yet the allegedly related verbs with *ṣ* terminate in *alef*, thus indicating their different origin. *ġ* in Ugaritic *mġy* could theoretically correspond not only to Proto-Semitic *ġ*, but also to Proto-Semitic *ẓ* (cf. e.g. Gordon, *UT*, §5.8); yet, again, verbs containing *ẓ* or their reflexes (see below) invariably terminate in *alef*. Nor can these two verbs be connected etymologically (*pace* Brockelmann, see above), since Ugaritic *ġ* never corresponds to Proto-Semitic *ḍ*. Accordingly, for the time being at least, these two verbs have to be regarded as isolated etymologically. As to the third series, exhibiting *ṭ* as second radical, its various meanings are perhaps to be derived from original "stretching".[5]

Whereas it is quite simple to separate the various verbs terminating in *w/y*, it is much more intricate to keep apart *verba tertiae alef*. They are clearly divided into two series, one exhibiting *ṣ*, the other *ẓ* as second radical. Since, however, in many Semitic languages Proto-Semitic *ṣ* and *ẓ* are reflected by the same sounds, it is, for all practical purposes, impossible to clearly assign these verbs, in these languages, to one of the two series, so much related in meaning. We shall, therefore, in the following adduce these equivocal verbs in both series, marked by I and II respectively. In case of preference of one of these assignments, we shall adduce the more dubious one in brackets only, whereas in other cases we shall content ourselves with referring a somewhat unlikely assignment to the footnotes.

1. Proto-Semitic *mẓ'*, reflected in: Epigraphic South-Arabian *mẓ'* in various verbal stems, not infrequent "to come, arrive"; Aramaic *məṭā* "to arrive", originally a verb *tertiae alef*, as demonstrated by its spelling in *Reichsaramäisch* (Official Aramaic);[6] Gᶜez I.*mṣ'* "to come", in various verbal stems, frequent;[7]

[5] Cf. the preceding notes.

[6] Though it is obvious that *verba tertiae alef* and *infirmae* had already merged in *Reichsaramäisch* (see H. H. Schaeder, *Iranische Beiträge I*, Halle, 1930, pp. 233 ff.), they are still differentiated in spelling (see W. Baumgartner, *ZAW* XLV, 1927, pp. 112 ff.; cf. also Leander, pp. 62–3): *tertiae alef* are, to be sure, sometimes spelt as *tertiae infirmae*, yet *tertiae infirmae* are not spelt as *tertiae alef*. Since *məṭā* is often spelt as *tertiae alef* (see Baumgartner and Leander, *ibid.*), *alef* being the third radical of *məṭā* is sufficiently demonstrated. Therefore (see above; *pace* Gordon, UT, §1520), it is not to be connected with Ugaritic *mġy*, as if both originated in alleged Proto-Semitic *mẓy*.

[7] It is already attested in the inscription of Aksum, thus making certain that its second radical is *ṣ* (or *ẓ*, see the second series) rather than *ḍ*; see T. Nöldeke, *ZDMG* XL (1886), p. 736, note 5.

Hebrew (I.*mṣ*' "to find"), marginally also "to reach, arrive";[8] Ugaritic *mẓ*' "to arrive, reach, find";[9] Old Akkadian (I.*mṣ*' "to reach").[10]
2. Proto-Semitic *mṣ*', reflected in: Aramaic *mṣ*' "to be able, to be the match of", marginally also (see Nöldeke, above)[11] "to find", presumably < "to arrive";[12] Hebrew II.*mṣ*' "to find", also "to suffice";[13] Gʿez (II. *mṣ*' "to come"),[14] Ugaritic *mṣ*' *D* "to fell"[15]; Old Akkadian (II.*mṣ*' "to suffice?"); Akkadian *maṣū* "to suffice".[16]

8 For "arrive" cf. Job xi 7 הַחֵקֶר אֱלֹהִים תִּמְצָא אִם עַד־תַּכְלִית שַׁדַּי תִּמְצָא "can you reach God's range, or will you arrive until the end of Shadday?"; at least the second *timṣā* may easily be conceived as a calque of Aramaic *mṭ*' in the aramaicising book of Job. On the other hand, it may exhibit the survival of the original Hebrew meaning. I have transferred the use of *mṣ*' in the sense of "suffice" to the second series (although, in principle, it could well belong to the first as well), since it is nearer to Aramaic *mṣ*' to "be able".

9 *mẓ*' is attested in UT 75 only, denoting, as it seems, once "to arrive" (I, line 37; parallel to preceding *mġy*), and twice perhaps "to find" (II, lines 51; 52). As a rule, Ugaritic *ẓ* is unequivocal, invariably corresponding to Proto-Semitic *ẓ*. Yet text 75, because of its archaic character (for particulars see Blau, *JAOS* LXXXVIII, 1968, p. 525), spells Proto-Semitic *ḍ*, (p. 341) with *ẓ*, rather than with *ṣ*, as in other texts. Accordingly, *mẓ* might theoretically correspond to Proto-Semitic *mḍ*'. Moreover, *mṣ*' is once attested in Ugaritic (UT 49:V:4) *ymṣ'i l'arṣ*, by some (Driver, Gordon) parsed as G "he reaches earth", yet presumably to be analysed as D (Ginsberg, Aistleitner) "he fells to earth". If one identifies this *mṣ*' with *mẓ*' (as is generally done; so Gordon, Driver, Aistleitner), one has necessarily to postulate Proto-Semitic *mḍ*', which is represented in "normal" texts (49) by *ṣ*, yet in text 75 by *ẓ*. Gordon, UT §1524, presumably because he realized that *mḍ*' is nowhere attested, assumed (if I am understanding him correctly) Proto-Semitic *mṣ*', which, through conflation with Arabic *maḍā*, had become *mḍ*' (*obiter dictu*, since he — wrongly, see above note 6 — posited Proto-Semitic *mẓy*, he interprets, *ibid.*, Epigraphic South-Arabian *mẓ*' as having arisen through conflation between *mṣ*' and *mẓy*). One need not emphasize how artificial this assumption is in the light of the other Semitic languages. There is no need whatsoever to regard *mẓ*' and *mḍ*' as variants. In such a small-sized literature as is Ugaritic, one need not be surprised that *mẓ*' is attested in text 75 only. It may nevertheless well represent Proto-Semitic *ẓ*, rather than *ḍ* (in the light of the other Semitic languages it in all probability does), and thus, is not related to *mṣ*'.

10 So according to I. J. Gelb, *Glossary of Old Akkadian* (MAD 3, Chicago 1957), s.v. Yet according to Stamm (quoted *ibid.*) it denotes "to suffice", just as Akkadian *maṣūm*, which, because of its greater semantic affinity with Aramaic *mṣ*', I have preferred to adduce in the, second series.

11 It also occurs in *Reichsaramäisch*, if Dupont-Sommer's interpretation is correct, see Semitica II (1949), p. 32.

12 In the light of the testimony of other Semitic languages, one will not consider it a Canaanite loan (see Koehler–Baumgartner[1], Aramaic part, s.v. *mṭ*', where this opinion is not accepted) or an Akkadian one. On the other hand, *šnṣy* "succeed", quoted *ibid.*, is clearly an Akkadian loan-word, see G. R. Driver, *Aramaic Documents*... (Oxford, 1957), p. 54, *ad* line 7.

13 See note 8. 14 See note 7.

15 See note 9. 16 See note 10.

Nothing certain can be stated as to Amorite, because it is impossible to decide whether a name like *Ya-am-ṣú-um* is to be derived from *mṣ'* or *mẓ'*.[17]

As we have seen, there are as many as five separate series of verbs denoting ideas related to "going"; they have as first radical *m*, as second radical *ṣ*, *ẓ*, *ḍ*, *ṭ*, *ġ*, and as third radical ', *w*, *y*. Yet it is clear, pending further evidence, that, at most, three series are Proto-Semitic, viz. *mṭw*, *mṣ'*, *mẓ'* whereas the quite isolated *mḍy* and *mġy* are peculiar to Arabic and Ugaritic respectively. Moreover, even the "Proto-Semitic" verbs were not, presumably, used in the various languages in the same sense at the same time. Besides, not more than three representives of these series are attested in any single language. The following list will clarify the situation:

AKKADIAN: *maṣū* "to suffice", similarly *mṣ'* in Old Akkadian (if it does not denote "to reach"), presumably representing Proto-Semitic *mṣ'*, less likely (also) *mẓ'*.

AMORITE: Reflection of Proto-Semitic *mṣ'* and/or *mẓ'*.

HEBREW: *mṣ'* "to find", sometimes "to suffice", marginally "to reach", representing Proto-Semitic *mṣ'* and/or *mẓ'*.

UGARITIC:
1. *mġy* "to reach, come, arrive", continuing *mġy*.
2. *mṣ' D* "to fell", = Proto-Semitic *mṣ'*.
3. *mẓ'* "to arrive, reach, find", = Proto-Semitic *mẓ'*.

ARAMAIC:
1. *məṭā* "to arrive", representing Proto-Semitic *mẓ'*.
2. *mṣ'* "to be able, to be the match of", marginally also "to find", = Proto-Semitic *mṣ'*.

ARABIC:
1. *mṭw* "to stretch, draw, walk quickly", = Proto-Semitic *mṭw*.
2. *mḍy* "to go", continuing *mḍy*.

EPIGRAPHIC SOUTH ARABIAN:
1. *mṭw* "to march", = Proto-Semitic *mṭw*.
2. *mẓ'* "to come, arrive", = Proto-Semitic *mẓ'*.

GʿEZ:
1. *maṭṭawa* (D) "to deliver", = Proto-Semitic *mṭw*.
2. *mṣ'* "to come", representing Proto-Semitic *mṣ'* and/or *mẓ'*.

5. *θt* > *tt*

In Ancient Aramaic, Proto-Semitic *θ* is represented by *š*, rather than by *t*, as in later Aramaic. Yet the proper noun *ʿtrsmk*, occurring several times in the Sfīre inscription, contains, it seems, the divine name *ʿaθtar* in the form *ʿattar*, rather than *ʿaštar*, i.e. *t* corresponds to *θ*, as in later Aramaic. This

17 See H. B. Huffmon, *Amorite Personal Names in the Mari Texts*... (Baltimore, 1965), p. 232 (who, however, speaks of *mẓy*, rather than *mẓ'*; he also compares Ugaritic *mġy*).

form is, no doubt correctly, considered to be due to assimilation:[1] in Old Aramaic *š* is polyphonic, being pronounced *θ* when corresponding to Proto-Semitic *θ*. Accordingly, the original form was *ʿaθtar*, and *ʿattar* exhibits the shift *θt*〉*tt* through assimilation (as it is also attested in Epigraphic South Arabian, see Beeston, p. 17, §13.4).

There occurs, however, another case of Proto-Semitic *θ* represented by t in Ancient Aramaic: Sfīre I C 24–5 *w'l yrt* (*sic*, not *yrš*) *šršh 'šm* "may his scio[n] inherit no name". No convincing explanation has been forwarded for this exceptional sound shift. Degen (p. 43, §25) accounts it *sandhi* spelling, being due to dissimilation from the immediately following *š*: ⌈*yīraθ šurših*⌉ 〉 [*yīrat šurših*]. One will, however, explain it rather as being due to the above-mentioned assimilation *θt*〉*tt*. Those forms of the perfect that terminated in suffices beginning with *t* (as ⌈*yariθtā*⌉), shifted their *θ* to *t* (⌈*yarittā*⌉), and from these forms *yrt* spread to the whole paradigm.

The influence of the perfect suffixes beginning with *t* on verbs terminating in *θ* is attested in Arabic;[2] yet no cases of the spreading of this phenomenon to other forms are known.[3] On the contrary, as a rule, *θ* is preserved through the influence of the forms not terminating in suffixes beginning with *t*.[4] I am inclined, however, to explain Arabic *bahuta* "to be confounded" etc., as originating in *bhθ*, *θ* having been superseded by *t* through the influence of perfect forms terminating in suffixes beginning with *t*.

According to Lagarde (p. 26) it is this *bahuta* that corresponds to Hebrew *bōš* "to be ashamed" and Aramaic (Syriac) *bəheṯ* (to which, more precisely, Arabic *bahita* corresponds); Lagarde merely remarks that one would have expected *bhθ*, without any further attempt to explain the deviation. Yet T. Nöldeke *ZDMG* XL (1886) p. 157, note 1 ingeniosuly connected Hebrew *bōš* and Aramaic *bəheṯ* with Arabic *buhθa* "fornication", and this view gradually superseded Lagarde's proposition,[5] since it was more likely both seman-

[1] See e.g. Fitzmyer, p. 26. Therefore, one would not accept T. Nöldeke's view (*ZDMG* XLVII, 1893, p. 101) that the occurrence of *ʿtr* in proper nouns demonstrates the common Aramaic shift θ〉*t*.

[2] See e.g. Brockelmann I, p. 172, §dα, J. Cantineau, *Études de linguistique arabe...* (Paris, 1960), p. 42 (in *sandhi*), Fleisch, p. 92.

[3] Yet it is clear that it was in a similar way that, through partial assimilation, *šḥ*θ "to beg" arose from *šḥ*ð : *šaḥaðtạ* 〉 *šaḥa*θ*ta*, see Blau, *ChA*, p. 107, especially note 134.

[4] Cf. Brockelmann *ibid.*

[5] Koehler-Baumgartner[3] *s.v.* only mentions Nöldeke's view. Incidentally, Nöldeke compared the noun *buh*θ*a*, rather than the alleged verb *bahi/u*θ*a*, as Koehler–Baumgartner *ibid.* claim. [Moreover, Aistleitner compares only the Ugaritic noun *b*θ*t* with Hebrew *bōš*, whereas (ibid., §609) he connects the verb *b*θ with Arabic *ba*θθ*a* "to scatter", just as Gray thinks (*pace* Koehler–Baumgartner *ibid.*).]

tically[6] and in sound correspondence.[7] Yet, it seems, *bhθ* and *bht* are a genuine Arabic doublet, *bhθ* being the original form, and *bht* having arisen in perfect forms terminating in suffixes beginning with *t*. Then the *t* spread to the other verbal forms and to the nouns that were felt related, yet not to *buhθa* "fornication", which was semantically isolated.

6. UGARITIC *ibbu*, AN AKKADIAN LOAN-WORD; ON SUBSTANTIVIZED ADJECTIVES IN CONSTRUCT IN UGARITIC

There is general consensus of opinion that Ugaritic *ib*, occurring UT Krt 147; 294 *ib iqni*, is related to Akkadian *ebbu* "pure", and the whole phrase to Akkadian *uqnū ebbu* "pure lapis lazuli". Since, however, word order and the final *i* of *iqni*, reflecting genitive, indicate a construct, *ib* is interpreted as substantive (litterally: gem/lustre of lapis lazuli).[1]

It seems that one can prove that Ugaritic *ib* is not only related to Akkadian *ebbu*, but is its direct continuation, being an Akkadian loan-word. The Akkadian verb connected with *ebbu* is *ebēbu* "to be pure", rather than **abābu*, thus exhibiting $'_{1-3}$ as first radical, i.e. ', *ġ*, or *ḥ*. Accordingly, if **ibbu* were

6 This was stressed by Nöldeke, *ZDMG* XL (1886), p. 741. Yet the semantic gap between "being ashamed" and "being confounded" is not as great as supposed, cf. e.g. Ps. lxxxiii 18 *yēḇōšū* "let them be ashamed" *wəyibbāhălū* "let them be confounded, terrified". The same applies, accordingly, to the active pattern *bahata* "confound, terrify, overcome". Therefore, one will not concur with J. Wellhausen (*ZDMG* LXVII, 1913, p. 633), who separates altogether *bahata* in this meaning from *bōš/bəhet*, whereas he regards *buhtān* "calumny" an Aramaic loan, because, to his mind, *fuʿlān* is genuine Arabic only as infinive, but not as veritable substantive. One will not agree with his view on *buhtān* either. First, genuine substantives of Arabic extraction are attested in this pattern, see some of the nouns adduced by Barth (p. 330, §220a). Moreover, *buhtān* is well attested as infinitive (from *bahata* "to calumniate", as Qur'an iv 20 [24 according to the "royal" Qur'an]). BDB, *s.v. bōs*, consider *bahuta* an Aramaic loan. Yet not only does the vowel of the second radical not correspond, but, because of the spirantized *t* in Aramaic, one would also have expected θ in Arabic rather than *t*. *Obiter dictu*, BDB are, of course, wrong when comparing *bōs* with Epigraphic South Arabian *mhb's*, basing themselves on D. H. Müller (I am quoting in accordance with Müller's transcription); Müller correctly compares it with Arabic *b's* (cf. also Conti Rossini, s.v. *b's*, who, besides correct correspondances to it, also compares Akkadian *bāšu*, and A. Jeffery, *The Foreign Vocabulary of the Qur'ān* (Baroda, 1938), s.v. *buhtān*, who, in the wake of Sprenger and Fränkel, considers it an Aramaic loan, a root connected also with Sabaean *bwš* and Arabic *bwθ* (sic!); in footnote he compares *mhb's* as well). BDB do not quote s.v. *b'š* Epigraphic South-Arabian *b'š* (*b's* according to their transcription).

7 As to the alteration of *verba mediae infirmae* and *mediae h*, see Nöldeke, *ZDMG* XL (1886), p. 741 (*pace* Delitzsch, p. 190, note 1).

1 Cf. the current dictionaries, further Ginsberg, *Keret* p. 39, *ad* line 147.

a genuine Ugaritic word, it would exhibit ʿ, ġ or ḥ as first radical, since pharyngals are preserved in Ugaritic. The *alef* as first radical in Ugaritic clearly indicates *ib* being an Akkadian loan.

This fact, however, gives rise to a new difficulty. Akkadian *ebbu* is an adjective. Therefore, one would have expected Ugaritic *ib* to be an adjective as well. Yet, as stated above, it is used in the construct, namely, *prima facie*, a substantive. Why then did the loan word **'ibbu* pass from its original category of adjectives to that of substantives?

I would suggest, therefore, to consider *ib* as an adjective standing in construct relation to a substantive, being semantically identical with an adjectival attribute following its substantival head. In other words, **'ibbu 'iqni'i*, litterally, "pure of lapis lazuli", is semantically identical with* *'iqni'u 'ibbu*, both meaning "pure lapis lazuli". Accordingly, *ib* is an adjective, rather than a substantive meaning "gem/lustre" (see above), yet it is used in a substantival syntagma, since an adjective in construct relation to a substantive is semantically, and also, it seems, functionally (cf. below), identical with a substantive head followed by an adjectival attribute.

This usage of adjectives is especially frequent in Arabic (see e.g. G. H. A. Ewald, *Grammatica critica linguae arabicae*, Lipsiae, 1831–3, II, p. 24 §533; Brockelmann II, p. 48, and, partly, p. 252, rem. 1; C. Brockelmann, *A. Socins arabische Grammatik*[7], Berlin 1913, p. 133, §138, beginning; Reckendorf, *SV*, p. 128, and Reckendorf, p. 147, §85.2)[2] and has to be separated carefully from attributive (adjectival) usages of adjectives in construct.[3] Pending further material, I have the impression that it is a literary construction,[4] relatively frequent in poetry and late stilted style.[5] One of its origins might have been in adjectives that have developed into substantives.[6] Thus Reckendorf, *ibid.*,

[2] *Ḥuṭayya* 79, 13 *naθīru jumānin*, quoted by Reckendorf, *ibid.* and being rather similar to our example (since the *nomen rectum* denotes material as well), is mistranslated: "durchbohrte Perle". H. Wehr, *Der arabische Elativ* (Wiesbaden, 1953), p. 15 has: *farfaḍḍa damʿī ka'annahū naθīru jumānin baynahunna...* "and my tears were dispersed as if they were *scattered pearls* among which...". (similarly H. Gätje, *Die Sprache* XI, 1965, p. 71 "zerstreute Perle").

[3] As a rule, however, the various usages of adjectives in construct were mixed up, see e.g. Reckendorf, *ibid.* Adjectives in construct governing a genitive of specification (part of the so-called "improper annexation") are, as a rule, adjectival. As to the elative governing an indefinite noun in singular, cf. Wehr, who, p. 15, in our opinion, correctly doubts Reckendorf's view (who connects this construction with our case); see also *loc cit.*, note 4.

[4] According to Wehr, *loc. cit.* this construction is typical of "emotionally stressed style".

[5] It even penetrated the narrative style of dialects, see e.g. J. Blau, *Syntax des palästinensischen Bauerndialekts von Bīr-Zēt* (Hessen, 1960), p. 48, §d, the last but one example. For its occurrence in modern elegant style cf. V. Monteil, *L'arabe moderne* (Paris, 1960), p. 231.

[6] For the usage of substantives in construct instead of adjectives cf. J. Knobloch, *Sprachwissenschaftliches Wörterbuch I* (Heidelberg, 1960), s.v. *Attributverschiebung*. — H. Gaetje's

quotes from *Naqā'iḍ* 406, 15 *najīʿu damin* "coagulated blood". *najīʿ*, as a matter of fact, is attested as adjective in such locution, cf. e.g. *ka'anna daman najīʿan* "as if coagulated blood", yet it is used as a real substantive ("gore", cf. also *Naqā'iḍ*, Glossary, s.v.): *ʿalayhi najīʿun min dami -ljaufi.*[7] Accordingly, *najīʿu damin* might have been considered as a real construct construction, with a genuine substantive as *regens* (corresponding to *najīʿun min damin*); on the other hand, it might have been perceived as containing an adjective in construct (corresponding to *damun najīʿun*) and thus to have given rise to similar constructions with adjectives in construct.[8]

This construction is also attested in Biblical Hebrew, though much less frequently (cf., though with qualifications, Brockelmann II, p. 48,[9] Gesenius-Kautzsch, p. 428, §c, and especially H. Ewald, *Ausführliches Lehrbuch der hebräischen Sprache*...[8], Göttingen, 1870, p. 751. §c). In a case like Ps. cxlv 7 זֵכֶר רַב טוּבְךָ "the memory of your great goodness" the special usage of *rab̲* might be due to the impact of its antonym *məʿaṭ* "fewness", originally a substantive, which developed into a veritable adjective ("few"), in two cases agreeing with the stubstantive even in number (see the Biblical dictionaries, s.v.); accordingly one will refrain from emending *rab̲* into the substantive *rob̲*. The same applies to Isa. xxi 7 רַב־קָשֶׁב "much heed". In a case like Isa. xl 26 מֵרֹב אוֹנִים וְאַמִּיץ כֹּחַ "by the greatness of (his) might and the strength of (his) power (= his strong power)" it is, *prima facie*, easier to read *'omęṣ*, yet one has to bear in mind that *'ammīṣ* is *lectio difficilior*. Quite certain is the use of an adjective in construct Ps. lxviii 14 בִּירַקְרַק חָרוּץ "with green(ish-yellow) gold", since the pattern of *yəraqraq qəṭalṭal* is peculiar to Hebrew adjectives denoting colours (see e.g. Barth, p. 216, §146), whereas substantives of the pattern *qəṭalṭōl* (see Barth, p. 217, §147) are rare in Hebrew and not attested for colours at all. We shall deal again below with the phrase *yəraqraq ḥārūṣ*.

logical and ontological classification (*Die Sprache* XI, 1965, pp. 61 ff., especially pp. 71–2) applies only on synchronical level.

7 For the exact quotations one may refer to the Concordance of Preislamic Poetry of the Hebrew University.

8 Cf. also e.g. Job x 1 *'ădabbərā bəmar nafšī* "I will speak in the bitterness of my soul" with xxi 25 *yāmūt bənęfęš mārā* "he will die with bitter soul".

9 Yet all his examples adduced from Biblical Hebrew exhibit pattern *qəṭol* in construct and *may*, therefore, be interpreted as a development of *quṭl* (> *qoṭęl*), see S. Kogut, *Lešonenu* XXXIV (1969–70), pp. 20–24 [Hebrew, with English summary]. — As to the Syriac examples quoted by Brockelmann, all are of the type *baglē ʿēn* "with open eye", which have perhaps a different historical origin: in the same sense *ʿēn baglē* is attested as well, being (see Brockelmann, II, p. 505, §322) originally an ancient circumstantional clause ("while [the] eye was in the open"), a construction that has almost disappeared in Aramaic. Accordingly, *baglē ʿēn* might exhibit the adjustment of this unusual construction, just as Brockelmann (II, p. 49) quotes Targumic *bərēš gəlē* as against Syriac *baglē rēšā.*

The loan phrase *'ibbu 'iqni'im "pure of lapis lazuli = pure lapis lazuli" corresponds[10] to the genuine Ugaritic phrase UT 51: V:81; 96–7 *bht. ṭhrm .iqnim* (parallel to *bht.ksp. wḫrṣ* "a house of silver and gold"), spelt in the archaic UT 77 (lines 21–22) *išlḥ ẓhrm iqnim*. The passage in 77 clearly shows that *ṭhrm/ẓhrm iqnim* has substantival function. Accordinly, the current dictionaries interpret *ṭhr(m) /ẓhr(m)* as a substantive:[11] (pure glittering) gem. Yet not only is in Hebrew the adjective *ṭāhōr* much more frequent than the substantive *ṭohar* and not only is it the adjective *ṭuuru* (= *tuhuru*, corresponding to Akkadian *ellu*) that is attested in the quadrilingual dictionaries (*Ugaritica* V 130 III 19'; 137 II 1), but the parallel *ib* also indicates that *ṭhr(m)* is an adjective. Accordingly we propose to translate the last passage "I shall send pure lapis lazuli", and the first two: "a house of pure lapis lazuli", interpreting them as a chain of constructs: *bht* stands in *status constructus*, governing *ṭhrm*, which itself (terminating in *-m* suffix, just as *ẓhrm*) stands in construct governing *iqni*. It is necessary to suppose that *bht* is a construct, because, as stated above, a phrase like *ṭhrm iqni* has substantival function.

There is, it seems, an additional case of construct in this function: Krt 126; 138; 250; 269; 283 the phrase *yrq ḫrṣ* is attested, no doubt to be translated, like Hebrew *yəraqraq ḥārūṣ* quoted above, "green(ish yellow) gold", corresponding in meaning, rather than in construction, to Akkadian *ḫurāṣu arqu*.[12] *yrq*, to be sure, is attested as a genuine substantive denoting "gold" (UT 51: IV:6; 11; 1 Aqht 54); yet this substantive developed, no doubt, from the adjectives "green(ish yellow)", rather than from an abstract noun "greenness". Accordingly, one will not interpret *yrq ḫrṣ* as "greenness of gold = green(ish yellow) gold", but rather as an adjective in construct relation to a substantive, semantically and functionally identical with a substantive head followed by an attribute. It is interesting to note that Hebrew and Ugaritic exhibit the

[10] Cf. also Ginsberg, *Keret*, p. 39, *ad* line 147. In his translation of Keret both *ibid.* and ANET[2] Ginsberg interpreted *ib* as substantive "the pureness (of lapis)". Yet *ṭhr(m iqni)* he interpreted, somewhat inconsistently, it seems, as adjective, translating it (ANET[2] *ad loc.*) "most pure (lapis lazuli)". This translation, in itself, is flawless and would be possible in Keret as well. Yet the parallel Akkadian *uqnū ebbu* does not recommend the interpretation of the adjective as superlative.

[11] For ANET[2] see the preceding note.

[12] Cf. Ginsberg, *Keret*, p. 36, *ad* line 53bc–54. Ginsberg, *ibid.*, tentatively suggested that *dm ḫrṣ* UT 51 : I : 33, literally "blood of gold", corresponds to Akkadian *ḫurāṣu sāmu* "red gold". If this proves true, one might suggest that *yrq ḫrṣ* might have been influenced by *dm ḫrṣ* as to its word order and construction. Yet later Ginsberg abandoned this ingenious interpretation and ANET[2] *ad locum* he translated *dm* by "film", following, it seems, Gaster's proposal (cf. also Driver, s.v.), who compared Arabic *damma*.

same construction, in the same phrase (*yəraqraq ḥārūṣ – yrq ḫrṣ*), no doubt another indication of the common Canaanite literary heritage.[13]

7. TWO NOTES ON THE NUMERALS IN UGARITIC

A. S. E. Loewenstamm, in his paper on *The Numerals in Ugaritic*,[1] has dealt extensively with the various morpho-syntactical phenomena in the domain of Ugaritic numerals. In general, one has the impression that many of the peculiarities inherent in Semitic numerals (as the very special use of gender) have been blurred. I would like to add a phenomenon that lies in the same direction, although because of the very limited number of examples the results necessarily remain tentative.

It is as a rule assumed that, as in Arabic, in Proto-Semitic the counted noun stood in the accusative after the numerals 20–90, whereas after the other numbers it stood in the genitive.[2] In the following, I shall quote all the cases I have noted of counted nouns that exhibit their case endings. As is known, in Ugaritic only nouns terminating in *alef* disclose (by the use of the different *alef* signs) their case endings. I have found only two nouns of this sort, viz. *iqnu* "lapis lazuli" and *mru* "commander", after numerals:

UT 1028, 17; 1029, 3; 1030, 6 *ʿšr mrum.*
1106, 12 *θlθm iqnu.*
1106, 16 *ḫmšm iqnu.*
118, 28; 30; 32 *mit iqni.*
1128, 28 *mitm iqnu.*
118, 23 *ḫmš mat iqnu.*
1130, 5 *arbʿ alpm iqni.*

As can be seen, genitive is attested after 100 and 4000, nominative(!) after 10, 30, 50, 200, 500. Since, prima facie, the different behaviour of counted nouns after the hundreds is peculiar, one would, pending further material, assume that, after the hundreds at least, nominative and genitive alternated.[3] Or, from the historical point of view: the original genitive (and, as one would

[13] All the cases proposed for this construction in Ugaritic contain substantives denoting material. Yet in the light of the scantiness of examples and the lack of vowel signs in Ugaritic, one will, pending new material, refrain from reaching any conclusions.

[1] Quoted above, §1, note 12.

[2] I am dealing with the cases of the counted nouns only, rather than with their numbers. These were treated by Loewenstamm, *ibid.*

[3] In other words, it is only accidental that the genitive is attested after 100 and 4000, the nominative after the other numerals.

like to add, accusative) is substituted by the nominative after these numerals.[4] The counted noun is more and more felt as an apposition of the numeral, rather than governed by it. Yet, as we have already stressed, this assumption is based on rather meagre material, and additional examples may change it substantially.

B. There is a tendency in Semitic languages for numeral adjectives to precede their substantival head.[1] Thus in Akkadian ordinal numerals precede the counted noun,[2] and the same applies to Epigraphic South Arabian[3] and to Ugaritic.[4] One phenomenon in Ugaritic, however, deserves special attention: Whereas in Akkadian prepositions precede the numeral followed by the head (as: *ina ḫamuštim šattim* "in the fifth year"), in Ugaritic prepositions may, to be sure, precede the numeral, followed by the head (as: 2Aqht I: 16 *bšbʿ ymm* "on the seventh day"), but they may also stand between the preceding numeral and the head, thus preceding the head alone: 2Aqht V: 3 *šbʿ bymm* "on the seventh day". This word order is, to be sure, not infrequent in Classical languages, especially in Latin,[5] yet in Semitic languages it is quite exceptional. I have encountered something similar in modern South-Arabian only: according to Wagner (*Mehri*, p. 25, §35), in Soqoṭri prepositions stand between the preceding demonstrative and the substantival head: *wulehé-b-ínhor* "and in those days" (and this is exceptionally also the case in Šhauri, see ibid., p. 25, §34ב). One may also, *mutatis mutandis*, compare the precedence of the Hebrew interrogative pronominal element *'ē* to a preposition governing a demonstrative pronoun: *'ē mizzę* "whence", e.g. Gen. xvi 8, and *'ē lāzōt* "upon what ground" Jer. v 7 (as against e.g. Arabic *li-'ayyi šay'in* "why", where the preposition precedes the interrogative pronominal element *'ayy*). Cf. also Ṭūrōyō *i-sāʿa ba-tmōne* "at eight o'clock" (H. Ritter, *Turojo*, A, II, Beirut–Wiesbaden 1969, text 68, 8), *i-sāʿa ba-tarte* "at two o'clock" (*ibid*, text 69, 417), exhibiting the preposition preceding the (cardinal) numeral, which, however, follows the noun.

4 All the examples quoted are taken from lists. Accordingly, the numbers stand in nominative and therefore the counted nouns as well. More accurately this should be expressed as following: the original genitive (accusative), after numerals, is substituted by counted nouns standing in apposition.

1 See Brockelmann, II, p. 202–3. Yet cases like *tāni walad* "the second son" in vulgar Arabic are late and historically quite different; see for them the extensive literature adduced in Blau, *ChA*, p. 379, § 263, notes 48–9. Accordingly, one will not agree with Beeston, who (p. 43, §35.6) assumes a similar case in Epigraphic South Arabian.

2 See Soden, p. 195, §1.

3 See Beeston, *ibid.*, §36.5.

4 Gordon, UT, p. 49, §7.45.

5 V. J. Wackernagel, *Vorlesungen über Syntax...*[2], II, Basel 1926, pp. 200–201.

8. PROTO-SEMITIC *śl*θ "THREE"

"Three" is reflected by Hebrew *šālōš*, Aramaic *təlāṯ* and Arabic *θalāθ*. Since early Semitic linguistics was mainly based on these three languages, one will not be surprised that **θalāθ* was posited as the Proto-Semitic form, to be borne out by forms like Akkadian *šalāš* and especially Ugaritic *θlθ*. And even those few scholars who, owing to new discoveries, took the possibility of Proto-Semitic *ślθ* into consideration (as did Brockelmann, I, p. 236, *in fine*, and later Rundgren, pp. 142–3), finally disregarded it in favour of the established etymology. Yet, it seems, new finds make Proto-Semitic *ślθ* quite likely.

As against Akkadian *šalāš*, Old Akkadian exhibits *salištum* (v. MAD 3, *s.v.*), thus reflecting Proto-Semitic initial *ś*/*š* (spelt in Old Akkadian as *s*, see e.g. MAD 2^2, pp. 28 ff., J. Aro, *Orientalia* N.S. XXVIII, 1959, pp. 321 ff.) and final *θ*.[1] It is Epigraphic South-Arabian (and Gᶜez) that demonstrates that *ślθ*, rather than *šlθ* which) is also possible according to Old Akkadian), * is the original form. As for Epigraphic South-Arabian (see Beeston, p. 40, §35: 4), the early Sabaean form is $s_2l\theta$ (= *ślθ*), and this applies also to Qatabanian, perhaps the Minaean and, it seems, to Hadrami as well (which exhibits s_2ls_3, in which s_3 is due to the confusion of *θ* and s_3 in this dialect; see Beeston, p. 14, §8: 7). Middle and late Sabaean *θlθ* exhibits regressive total assimilation ⟨ *ślθ*. This form is especially important, since it makes it likely that the development was *śalāθ*⟩*θalāθ* in Arabic, Ugaritic and Aramaic (finally ⟩*təlāṯ*) as well, in accordance with the inner shift in Sabaean. Gᶜez exhibits *šallās* (with secondary doubling of the *l*), which, in the light of Old Akkadian and Epigraphic South-Arabian, has to be derived from Proto-Semitic **śalāθ*. It is this *šls* that is exhibited in ancient Gᶜez, in the Aksūm inscriptions, including that describing the expedition against Bega, line 20, where E. Littmann had previously read *slst*. Yet now (see E. Littmann, "*Äthiopische Inschriften*", Sonderabdruck aus *Miscellanea Academica Berolinensia*, Berlin, 1950, pp. 97–127, p. 106) Littmann prefers to read *šlst*, in accordance (cf. *ibid*., p. 105) with its usage in the inscription of the campaign against Nōbā and Kāsū (*ibid*., p. 114 ff.), lines 10 and 16. Thus the only instance for the alleged development *θlθ* ⟩ *ślθ* has disappeared, making the shift *ś*-*θ* ⟩ *θ*-*θ* even more likely. Cf. also the Ugaritic shift *š*-*θ*⟩*θ*-*θ*, as exhibited in the *šafᶜel* of verbs *primae θ* (see UT, p. 34, §5.36) as well as in *θdθ* "sixth" ⟨**šdθ* (which, by a similar progressive assimilation, became in Arabic **šādiš*⟩*sādis*). Accordingly, it is * obvious that the Proto-Semitic form was **śalāθ*.

1. As against Soden, p. 30, §30 f.

ABBREVIATIONS

Barth—J. Barth, *Die Nominalbildung in den semitischen Sprachen*^{2} (Leipzig, 1894).

Bauer–Leander — H. Bauer–P. Leander, *Historische Grammatik der Hebräischen Sprache* (Halle, 1922).

Bauer–Leander, *Aram.* — H. Bauer–P. Leander, *Grammatik des Biblisch-Aramäischen* (Halle, 1927).

Beeston — A.F. L. Beeston, *A Descriptive Grammar of Epigraphic South Arabian* (London, 1962).

Ben-Ḥayyim — Z. Ben Ḥayyim, *The Literary and Oral Tradition among the Samaritans* (Jerusalem, 1957 ff.; Hebrew).

Bergsträsser — G. Bergsträsser, *Hebräische Grammatik* (Leipzig, 1918–1929).

Blau, *ChA* — J. Blau, *A Grammar of Christian Arabic Based Mainly on South-Palestinian Texts from the First Millennium* (Louvain, 1966–1967).

Blau, *Pseudo-Corrections* — J. Blau, *On Pseudo-Corrections in Some Semitic Languages* (Jerusalem, 1970).

Brockelmann — C. Brockelmann, *Grundriss der vergleichenden Grammatik der semitischen Sprachen* (Berlin, 1908–1913).

Brockelmann, *Lex.* — C. Brockelmann, *Lexicon Syriacum*^{2} (Halle, 1928).

Brockelmann, *Syr.* — C. Brockelmann, *Syrische Grammatik*^{7}, (Leipzig, 1955).

Cohen — M. Cohen, *Le système verbal sémitique et l'expression du temps* (Paris, 1924).

Conti Rossini — K. Conti Rossini, *Chrestomathia Arabica Meridionalis Epigraphica* (Rome, 1931).

Degen — R. Degen, *Altaramäische Grammatik...*, Abhandlungen für die Kunde des Morgenlandes XXXVIII, 3 (Wiesbaden, 1969).

Delitzsch — Fr. Delitzsch, *Prolegomena eines neuen hebräisch-aramäischen Wörterbuchs...* (Leipzig, 1886).

Driver, *Samuel* — S. R. Driver, *Notes on the Hebrew Text... of Samuel*^{2} (Oxford, 1913).

Fitzmyer — J. A. Fitzmyer, *The Aramaic Inscriptions of Sefîre* (Rome, 1967).

Fleisch — H. Fleisch, *Traité de philologie arabe* I (Beyrouth, 1961).

Garbini — G. Garbini, *Il Semitico di Nord-Ovest* (Napoli, 1960).

Gesenius–Kautzsch — E. Kautzsch, *Gesenius' Hebrew Grammar*, Second English Edition by A. E. Cowley (Oxford, 1910).

Ginsberg, *Keret* — H. L. Ginsberg, *The Legend of King Keret...*, *BASOR* Supplementary Studies 2–3 (New Haven, 1964).

Lagarde — P. de Lagarde, *Übersicht über die im Aramäischen, Arabischen und Hebräischen übliche Bildung der Nomina* (Göttingen, 1888 [Königliche Geselschaft der Wissenschaften histor.-philolog. Classe, XXXV, 5]).

Landberg — C. de Landberg, *Glossaire Daṯînois* (Leiden, 1920–1942).

Leander — P. Leander, *Laut- und Formenlehre des Ägyptisch-Aramäischen* (Göteborg, 1928).

Nöldeke, *Mand.* — T. Nöldeke, *Mandäische Grammatik* (Halle, 1875).

Nöldeke, *NBSS* — T. Nöldeke, *Neue Beiträge zur semitischen Sprachwissenschaft* (Strassburg, 1910).

Nöldeke, *Syr.* — T. Nöldeke, *Kurzgefasste syrische Grammatik*^{2} (Leipzig, 1898).

Rabin — C. Rabin, *Ancient West-Arabian* (London, 1951).

Reckendorf — H. Reckendorf, *Arabische Syntax* (Heidelberg, 1921).

Reckendorf, *SV* — H. Reckendorf, *Die syntaktischen Verhältnisse des Arabischen* (Leiden, 1895–1898).

Rundgren — F. Rundgren, *Über Bildungen mit s/š und n- t- Demonstrativen im Semitischen...* (Uppsala, 1955).
Soden — W. von Soden, *Grundriss der akkadischen Grammatik* (Rome, 1952).
Wagner, *Mehri* — E. Wagner, *Syntax der Mehri-Sprache...* (Berlin, 1953).
Wright — W. Wright, *A Grammar of the Arabic Language...*[3] (Cambridge, 1896–1898).

Additions and Corrections

to **p. 222**.*n. 11*: Similarly, in some Arabic dialects the (historically older) *y*-imperfect (as against the later *b*-imperfect) was preserved in "protected" position (i. e., in closed syntagmas), see e.g., J. Blau, *Syntax des palästinensischen Bauerndialekts von B īr Zēt*, Walldorf-Hessen 1960, p. 86 (where I would rather not speak of "euphonic" reasons).

to **p. 227**.*-5* : In the meantime, *ʾišt* has been found in syllabic transcription: *i-ši-tu*, i.e., *ʾišītu*; see J. Huehnergard, *Ugaritic Vocabulary in Syllabic Transcription*, Atlanta, Georgia, 1987, p. 110.

to **p. 229**.*4*: : In the light of Ugaritic *ʾišītu*, see the preceding addition, it stands to reason to derive אִשָּׁה from *ʾišiyu*, rather than from *ʾišayu*.

to **p. 233**.*8*: A. F. L. Beeston (private communication from 11.10.1973) is inclined to take as semantic base for Arabic مطو the noun مَطْو 'back', hence مَطِيّة 'camel one whose back one rides', and denominative verbal forms meaning 'ride on the back of' (primarily a camel, but by الحَرِيري used also of embarking in a ship). The contexts in which Epigraphic South-Arabian *mṭw* occurs, do not (in marked contrast to *mẓʾ*, where the contexts practically always say 'to march to such-and-such a place') specify any local objective **to** which a march is made, but something like 'to mount a camel' as initiation of military activities. In the light of these remarks, I would indeed separate Epigraphic South-Arabian *mṭw* and posit for Arabic two roots *mṭw*, one 'to ride', in the wake of Beeston, the other 'to stretch, to draw, to pull' (Beeston dismisses these meanings as "speculations of the Arabic lexicographers", yet I find this attitude overcritical, especially since ramifications of this root are attested in modern dialects, see n. 2).

to **p. 244**.*15*: Modern South-Arabian has a plethora of roots (I am quoting from various dictionaries): *ślṯ*, *ślś*, etc.

to **p. 244**.*-1*: Interesting is also Maghrebine *tlâsa*, see Fischer & Jastrow, p. 84.n. 18, reflecting, it seems, dissimilation.

Marginalia Semitica III*

1. AN INTERNAL PROOF FOR THE RELATIVE CHRONOLOGY OF TIBERIAN *QAMEṢ*[1]

1. One of the main traits of the Tiberian vocalization system is the use of *qameṣ* (which, in all probability, was pronounced as *å*) for marking not only the vowel which originated in Proto-Semitic *u* (the so-called *qameṣ qaṭan*), but also that which stems from Proto-Semitic *a*/*ā* (the so-called *qameṣ gadol*). We do not know the *terminus a quo* for the emergence of *qameṣ gadol*. Since Jerome sometimes transcribes *qameṣ gadol* by *o* and, inversely, as a rule marks *qameṣ qaṭan* by *a*, it has been claimed that in the pronunciation of his teachers *qameṣ qaṭan* and *qameṣ gadol* had already coincided, both being pronounced as *å*.[2] Others, however, attributed the alternation of *a*/*o* to Jerome's deficient phonematization.[3] Under these circumstances, any further datum for the chronology of Tiberian *qameṣ* is of considerable importance, especially since its relative chronology is unknown as well. Bergsträsser, I, §30m, n, considered it to be earlier than the weakening of the laryngals/pharyngals (the earliest indication of which was the loss of their ability of being redoubled, the use of the *ḥaṭafs* being even later). He does not, however, substantiate his claim. In the following I shall attempt to demonstrate that, on the contrary, the shift *ā* > *å*[4] occurred later than the shift of *shwa mobile* after laryngals/pharyngals to *ḥaṭaf*.

* V. *IOS* 1.1–35; 2.57–82.

1 This paper about Tiberian *qameṣ* was submitted to the Seventh World Congress of Jewish Studies and read in Hebrew August, 10, 1977.

2 V. e.g. Bergsträsser, I, §10a, further S. Morag, *Kiryat Sefer* 36. 30 (1968–69). M. Mishor calls my attention to *qameṣ* pronounced as *å* being attested by Elazar ben Qalīr, v. E. Fleischer, *Lĕšonénu* 36. 262–67 (1931–32).

3 V. e.g. J. Barr, *JSS* 12. 30–31 (1967).

4 Although *qameṣ gadol* originates not only in Proto-Semitic *ā*, but, as a rule, in Proto-Semitic *a*, its immediate predecessor was always *ā*, i.e. in the case of Proto-Semitic *a* the development was: Proto-Semitic *a* > Proto-Hebrew *ā* > Tiberian *å*. The few exceptions are due to assimilation (as **mawęt* > *måwęt*; **yam* > *yåm*). For the sake of simplicity, I have contented myself to speak of *ā* > *å* only.

2. We have always to bear in mind[5] that in the Tiberian vocalization the pronunciation of *qameṣ qaṭan* and *qameṣ gadol* totally coincided and any differenciation between the two is alien to this tradition. Therefore one would expect that the phonetic behaviour of *qameṣ gadol*,[6] which was also pronounced *å*, should be identical with that of *qamaṣ qaṭan*. Since *qameṣ qaṭan* influences a following laryngal/pharyngal, originally immediately preceding a consonant, to intercalate a *ḥaṭaf qameṣ* (as פָּעְלוֹ* > פָּעֳלוֹ; טָהְרָה* > טָהֳרָה), one would presume a similar influence of *qameṣ gadol*. Why then is the laryngal/pharyngal after *qameṣ gadol* always followed by a *ḥaṭaf pataḥ*, rather than by a *ḥaṭaf qameṣ* (as פָּעֲלוּ, טָהֲרָה presumably pronounced *på'ălū, ṭåhărā*, rather than **på'ålū, *ṭåhårā*)? The use of the *ḥaṭaf pataḥ* indicates that it was preceded by an *a*-vowel, rather than by *å*, or, more explicitly formulated, that at the time of the shift of *shwa mobile*[7] after laryngals/pharyngals to *ḥaṭaf*, *qameṣ gadol* was still pronounced *ā*, rather than *å*![8] This is, it seems, the most likely explanation for the occurrence of *ḥaṭaf pataḥ* after *qameṣ gadol*, as against *ḥaṭaf qameṣ* after *qameṣ qaṭan*. When later *qameṣ gadol* shifted from *ā* to *å* (as *pā'ălū/ṭāhărā* to *på'ălū/ṭåhărā*), the *ḥaṭaf pataḥ* following the laryngal/pharyngal has already become a stable vowel, not dependent on the preceding vowel, and persisted even after *å*.

3. The explanation proposed for *ḥaṭaf pataḥ* following *qameṣ gadol*, as against *ḥaṭaf qameṣ* following *qameṣ qaṭan*, is, in our opinion, the most powerful one for explaining the different behaviour of the two sorts of *qameṣ*. We shall try to demonstrate it by analysing the only other explanation offered for it (as far as I know; §3.1), further by examining another possible interpretation (which, as far as is known to me, has not yet been propounded; §3.2).

3.1. Bergsträsser, I, §28 l, claimed that *ḥaṭaf* supplanting *shwa mobile*, as a rule, corresponds to the reduced vowel. This accounts for the *ḥaṭaf pataḥ* in forms like פָּעֲלוּ, since, in the light of פָּעַל, the ' should have been followed by *a*. Yet even טָהֲרָה cited above is not accounted for, since the *ḥaṭaf pataḥ* does not match the *e* of טָהֵר. As a matter of fact, outside word initial, it is

[5] V. e.g. Bergsträsser, I, §10a.

[6] I have not taken the *original* length of *qameṣ gadol* into consideration, since it stands to reason that even at a period in which quantitative differences of the length of vowels had not yet become automatic, length did not effect the different phonetic behaviour of *qameṣ gadol*. The more so since, *prima facie*, *qameṣ qaṭan* seems to have more influence on the quality of *ḥaṭaf* than *qameṣ gadol*.

[7] *qameṣ gadol* was originally always followed by *shwa mobile*, *qameṣ qaṭan* invariably by *shwa quiescens* (and *medium*). For the problem of *shwa mobile* cf. also below §3.2.

[8] This also involves that Proto-Semitic *u* developed to *å* (i.e. *qameṣ qaṭan*) before *ā* had shifted to *å* (i.e. *qameṣ gadol*).

almost regularly[9] *ḥaṭaf pataḥ* that supersedes *shwa mobile*, and this is also the case after *qameṣ gadol*, even if the reduced vowel is *e*, rather than *a*, as יְמָאֲנוּ, תְּמָאֲנוּ, הִלָּחֲמוּ, תִּלָּחֲמוּ, וַיִּנָּחֲמוּ, וַיִּצָּעֲקוּ, נִלָּחֲמָה. Without entering into further details, one will *a limine* reject Bergsträsser's thesis, since it simply contravenes the facts.

3.2. Yet it is possible to attempt to account for the different behaviour of *shwa* after *qameṣ gadol* (i.e., of *shwa mobile*) and after *qameṣ qaṭan* (i.e., of *shwa quiescens* and *medium*) by the assumption that *shwa mobile* was earlier superseded by *ḥaṭaf* than *shwa quiescens* (and *medium*). As a matter of fact, alternations of forms preserving laryngals/pharyngals followed by *shwa quiescens* with those exhibiting *ḥaṭaf*, as well as differences between the systems of Ben Asher and Ben Naftali concerning them[10] indicate that the supersession of *shwa quiescens* by *ḥaṭaf* is a very late phenomenon. Accordingly, it could be claimed that, in contradistinction to the proposition propounded by us §2, the emergence of *ḥaṭafs* in general is later than the pronunciation of *qameṣ*, including *qameṣ gadol*, as *å*. In the first period of the emergence of *ḥaṭafs*, when *ḥaṭafs* superseded *shwa mobile* after laryngals/pharyngals, it was *ḥaṭaf pataḥ* that, except in word initial, was used almost regularly. According to this thesis, this was the reason for the *ḥaṭaf pataḥ* in words like טָהֲרָה, פָּעֲלוֹ, although, according to this assumption, every *qameṣ*, including *qameṣ gadol*, was pronounced *å*. In the second period, when *ḥaṭafs* started superseding *shwa quiescens* (and *medium*), the shift of *shwa* changed and it became *ḥaṭaf segol* after *segol* and *ḥaṭaf qameṣ* after *qameṣ* (which in this position was always *qameṣ qaṭan*). At this time, the *ḥaṭaf pataḥ* after *qameṣ gadol*, which had emerged as early as the first period, had already become stable and did not change through the influence of the preceding *qameṣ*.

Yet this proposition, which posits an earlier period in which *shwa mobile* after laryngals/pharyngals shifted to *ḥaṭaf pataḥ*, and a later one in which *shwa quiescens*[11] became *ḥaṭaf segol/qameṣ* through the influence of a preceding *segol/qameṣ* (*qaṭan*), has a serious deficiency. In word initial *ḥaṭaf qameṣ* instead of the original *u* is quite frequent, as אֳנִי, עֳנִי, חֳלִי, חֳרָבוֹת, חֳדָשִׁים. It stands to reason that prior to the weakening of the laryngals/pharyngals these words were pronounced with initial *shwa mobile*,[12] as *חְדָשִׁים, *חְרָבוֹת, *אְנִי, *עְנִי, *חְלִי and when *shwa mobile* became *ḥaṭaf* after laryngals/pharyngals, *ḥaṭaf qameṣ* emerged, not through sound shift, but rather through

9 And not only "often", *pace* Bergsträsser, *ibid.*

10 V. Bergsträsser, I, pp. 153–55.

11 We do not treat here the thorny problem of *shwa medium*, on which opinions are very much divided; cf. e.g. *IOS* 1. 26–32 (1971).

12 As it is attested in many Arabic dialects.

analogy to those forms of these words which contained *qameṣ* (*qaṭan*; as חָדְשִׁי, חָרְבָּה, חָלְיִי, עָנְיִי, אָנְיִי). If at this period *qameṣ gadol* was already pronounced *å*, like *qameṣ qaṭan*, why then shifted words like *הָלַכְתֶּם, *עָנִיִּים, *חָדָשִׁים to חֲדָשִׁים, הֲלַכְתֶּם, עֲנִיִּים; with *ḥaṭaf pataḥ*, despite the expected influence of הָלַךְ, עָנִי, חָדָשׁ with *qameṣ* (*gadol*), allegedly already pronounced *å*?! The only possible answer[13] seems to be that at this time *qameṣ gadol* was still pronounced *ā*. It seems much less likely to assume that חֳדָשִׁים, etc. arose from *ḥådåšīm*, but חֲדָשִׁים, etc. from *ḥadåšīm*, postulating that *shwa mobile* arising from *å* changed to ֳ, in all other cases to ֲ: not only is this assumption more intricate but it also posits that חֳדָשִׁים, חֲדָשִׁים prior to the weakening of the laryngals/pharyngals were pronounced *ḥådåšīm*, *ḥadåšīm*, rather than חֲדָשִׁים*.

4. To sum up: the only explanation for the fact that *qameṣ gadol* influences laryngals/pharyngals to be followed by *ḥaṭaf pataḥ*, rather than by *ḥaṭaf qameṣ*, is that at the period of the supersession of *shwa* by *ḥaṭaf*, *qameṣ gadol* was still pronounced *ā*, rather than *å*.[14] Accordingly the shift of *qameṣ gadol* to *å* is later than the weakening of the laryngals/pharyngals.

2. ORIGINAL MONOSYLLABIC NOUNS MEDIAE ALEF IN BIBLICAL HEBREW STRESSED ON THEIR SECOND SYLLABLE (ON THE BEHAVIOUR OF ALEF IN SYLLABLE FINAL IN BIBLICAL HEBREW).

1. Original monosyllabic nouns in Biblical Hebrew, as a rule, become, by dint of anaptyxis, bisyllabic, yet (in contradistinction e.g. to Aramaic) stress generally remains on the first syllable (as **sipr* 'book' > סֵ֫פֶר, as against Aramaic סְפַר). It is in marginal cases only that stress moves to the second syllable, to the originally anaptyctic vowel (as דְּבַשׁ 'honey', סְבַךְ 'thicket').[1] Among these, admittedly marginal, noun types two groups are standing out, viz. nouns *III y* (types פְּרִי 'fruit', דֳּמִי 'rest') and *II* ʾ (types בְּאֵר 'well', בְּאשׁ

[13] One will not claim that in words of the type חָלְיִ, חֹדֶשׁ the *qameṣ* was more frequent and therefore more apt to exert influence, since in the perfect of *qal* (type הָלַךְ) the *qameṣ* was at least as frequent. Even in words of the type חָדָשׁ one would have expected at least more frequent occurrence of *ḥaṭaf qameṣ* (forms like הָחֳרָבוֹת being quite exceptional). Nor will one interpret פָּעֳלוֹ as being due to the paradigmatic pressure of שָׁמְרוּ pronounced according to Masoretic tradition *šåmåru*: why then was חֳדָשִׁים not influenced by צְרָכִים = *ṣåråḵim*, but חֲדָשִׁים was influenced by דְּבָרִים = *dab̲årim*.

[14] Our assumption also accounts for the dissimilation of *a* > *ẹ* preceding historically doubled laryngals/pharyngals when followed by *å* < *ā* (type הֶחָג), yet not by *å* > *u* (type * הֶחָכְמָה; cf. for particulars M. M. Bravmann, *Lěšonénu* 15. 14–96 [1946–47]): *ā* had not yet shifted to *å*. It does not however explain *ẹ* preceding חֳ (type הֶחֳדָשִׁים).

[1] V. e.g. Bauer-Leander, pp. 579–80.

'stench'). As to nouns *III y*, their different behaviour does not cause problems. Because of the final half-vowel *y*,[2] an anaptyctic vowel emerged earlier than in other nouns, giving rise to a final long vowel in an open syllable (rather than to a short vowel in a closed syllable, as in other nouns), which then attracted the stress. On the other hand, nouns *II* ' pose a problem, which is related, partially or wholly, with the special behaviour of ' (and sometimes of ') in other cases (as תֶּאֶכְלֵהוּ Job xx 26 'it will consume him', תְּאֵהֲבוּ Prov. i 22 'will you love?'). When treating this problem, one must remember that the special behaviour of ' is more frequent in the Babylonian vocalization system than in the Tiberian one, both of the type of *rə'ōš* 'head' and that of *tə'uklēhū*. One has also to pay attention to forms like יואמר, יאומר, רואש, ראוש in the Dead Sea Scrolls, as well as to Samaritan *rē'oš*. Moreover, one must not overlook the Egyptian transcription *Ru-'u-ša-qdš* from the thirteenth century.

2. The explanations given for the exceptional conduct of original monosyllabic nouns *II'* (as well as for the unusual behaviour of ' in syllable final in general) may, in general, be subdivided into three main groups, accounting for the abnormal deportment of ' by the assumption of:

A. Sound shift.
B. Analogical formation.
C. Pseudo-correction (hyper-correction)/restitution.

We shall deal with every group *in extenso*.

3. A. As to the assumption of sound shift, different suggestions were made:

3.1. Lagarde, p. 57, derived בְּאֵר 'well', בְּאֹשׁ 'stench' from oxytone bisyllabic *bi'ír*, *bu'úš*, whereas the parallel Arabic *bi'r*, *bu's*, in his opinion, stem from paroxytone *bí'ir*, *bú'uš*. This assumption, however, unlikely in itself, is decisively refuted by forms like שְׂאֵת 'to bear', which, because of the feminine ending, can only be derived from *śi't*, rather than from *śi'it*. Therefore, we shall in the following disregard Lagarde's theory.

3.2. Other scholars posit that *alef* in syllable final behaved differently after *i/u* and after *a*. After *a*, as is well known, the *alef* was lost with compensatory lengthening, the resulting *ā* being subject to the shift to *ō*: *ra'š* > ראש.[3] On

[2] This does not, however, apply to nouns *III w* (type תֹּהוּ), in which, it seems, the anaptyctic vowel preceding *w* arose comparatively late, so that the final long vowel in open syllable (-*ū*), which eventually emerged, did not attract stress.

[3] The claim sometimes advanced — v. e.g. Lagarde, pp. 58–59, 135, who quotes his earlier *Symmicta* I, Goettingen 1877, p. 113, further J. Friedrich, *Orientalia* 12. 18 (1943) —

the contrary, according to this assumption, after *i*/*u* *alef* in syllable final preceding another consonant was not elided, but rather quite early developed an anaptyctic vowel, which separated it from the following consonant and was strong enough to attract the stress: **bi'r*(*u*) > בְּאֵר, **bu'š*(*u*) > בְּאֹשׁ. This was claimed e.g. by F. Philippi, *BzA* 2.378 (1894); Bauer-Leander, p. 213p, A. Goetze, *JAOS* 59.447, note 55 (1939). Bauer-Leander, to be sure, only consider forms like בְּאֹשׁ, בְּאֵר to be due to sound shift, whereas forms like תְּאֶהֱבוּ 'you love', תְּאָכְלֻהוּ 'you eat him', צֶאנָה 'go out!' (fem. plur.) are regarded by them (*ibid.*, pp. 223–24) as artificial (cf. infra §5). Yeivin, p. 250, following others,[4] on the other hand, compares the special behaviour of *alef* (as well as of ') in Babylonian vocalization in forms of the type of תְּאֶהֱבוּ, etc., in which after ' / ', which originally stood in syllable final after a short vowel, an auxiliary short vowel is inserted, whereas the preceding originally short vowel is shortened to become ultrashort, — with a phenomenon occuring in Bedouin dialects of the Arabian-Syrian desert in which *a* followed by *h*, ', *ġ*, or *x* preceding a consonant (*-aXC*) shifts to *-aXaC*, the second, historically anaptyctic, *a* being stable and even stressed if it is in a stressable position, the older vowel tending to undergo reduction.[5] This comparison, however, cannot be justified: in Babylonian vocalization it is ' (and ') that, so to say, "change the place" of the preceding vowel, whereas *alef* does not have this influence in Bedouin dialects.[6]

Yet the assumption that *alef* closing a syllable after *i*/*u* very early developed an anaptyctic vowel which was strong enough to attract the stress — is as such infelicitous. It is contradicted by forms like יָרֵאתָ 'you were afraid' < **yari'ta*, which (in contradistinction to יָשַׁנְתָּ 'you were asleep' < **yašinta*) were not affected by Philippi's law shifting stressed *i* to *a* in a closed syllable, because ' has been so early dropped that the *i* no longer stood in a closed syllable when Philippi's law acted. Accordingly, one will needs posit **bi'ru* > **bēr*,[7] **bu'šu* > **bōš*,[7] rather than > **bi'ir* > בְּאֵר, > *bu'uš* > בְּאֹשׁ.

that ראשׁ has to be derived from *ru'š*, is unlikely in itself and becomes even more so in the light of Phoenician *ra'š*, as exhibited in the Phoenician place name *ba-'-li-ra'-si* in an Assyrian transcription from the ninth century, representing, it seems, a marginal dialect in which *alef* was preserved in this position, v. Harris, p. 90, *idem*, *Development*, p. 43. One will refrain from assuming that in some Phoenician dialect this word had the original form *ra'š*, in others *ru'š*. Moreover, the omission of *alef* after *a* in this position is also attested by *ṣa'n* > צאן 'small cattle'.

4 V. *ibid.*; cf. also H. Grimme, *OLZ* 17. 221 (1914), *idem*, in: *Festschrift E. Sachau*, Berlin 1915, pp. 134–35.

5 Called by Blanc, p. 14 "the *gaháwah* syndrome"; cf. also Socin, p. 206, §171, J. Cantineau, in: *Annales de la Faculté d'Etudes Orientales, Université d'Alger* 2. 66 (1936).

6 Cf. the similar remark of Bergsträsser, I, p. 159, §28r against Grimme.

7 For *i*/*u* being lengthened to *ē*/*ō* v. e.g. Bergsträsser, I, p. 117, §21k.

REMARK: As to the behaviour of ʾ in syllable final after *a*, three patterns of conduct may be distinguished:[8]

a. *aʾ* > *ā* > *ō*; type אֹכַל 'I shall eat', ראשׁ 'head'.
b. *aʾ* > *ā*; type מָצָאתִי 'I found'.
c. *aʾ* remains (to become later *aʾă*); type מַאֲכָל 'food'.

a. Historically two periods have to be distinguished. Perhaps already in Proto-Semitic ʾ in syllable final was dropped, if the syllable opened with ʾ (type אֹכַל, originally **ʾaʾkul*). In some verbs the first person singular influenced the other forms (as תֹּאכַל), whereas in others the other forms influenced the first person singular, so that e.g. in אֶאֱסֹף 'I shall collect' the ʾ has been restituted.

In other cases it was at a later period in stressed syllable that *aʾ* shifted to *ā* > *ō* (type ראשׁ).[9]

b. Analogical levelling prevented in some cases *aʾ* > *ā* to shift to *ō*. Since in the perfect of *qal* of מָצָאתִי *aʾ* was preserved in the third person, where the ʾ was intervocalic, and in the second person plural, where the *aʾ*, at least in feminine, was unstressed, this *a* influenced (*aʾ* >) *ā* not to shift to *ō*.

c. *aʾ* was preserved in unstressed syllables: **maʾkálu*,[10] later מַאֲכָל.

[8] For particulars v. J. Blau, in: *Kurzweil*, pp. 67–68.

[9] According to Bergsträsser, I, p. 89, §15b, the ʾ was dropped if it constituted the first consonant of a consonant cluster closing the syllable; since case endings first dropped in the construct, Bergsträsser, pp. 163–64, postulated influence of the construct on the absolute. For the difficulties inherent in this assumption v. Birkeland, pp. 40–41 (without, however, consenting to Birkeland's claim that no analogy of the construct can account for nouns like מוֹסֵרוֹת 'bands': Bergsträsser, I, p. 90, himself (!), besides מוֹסֵרוֹת, adduced two additional examples only, from which one, Babylonian שׁאוֹנוֹ, is presumably passive, whereas the other, מוֹפֵת, is etymologically quite opaque. Accordingly, one will consider מוֹסֵרוֹת to exhibit blend of *ʾsr* and *ysr*). Harris, *Development*, p. 42, §15, went in the wake of Bergsträsser, yet p. 73, §53 postulated a later dropping of ʾ in stressed syllable.

[10] If one posits a period of general paroxytone stress in Hebrew (v. e.g. *IOS* 1. 19ff. [1971]), one will attribute the dropping of ʾ in stressed syllables to this period, because it was then that the syllable containing ʾ in **maʾkàlu* was unstressed and, therefore, preserved the ʾ, whereas in the preceding period, according to the usual assumption, *maʾ-* bore the stress. (In this case, one will have to posit that the shift *ā* > *ō* still continued at this period, causing *raʾš* > *rāš* to become *rōš*). Yet if one posits for the first Proto-Hebrew period a stress system similar to that prevailing in ancient Maghrebine dialects (v. *Kurzweil*, pp. 62ff.), then already at this period the syllable containing ʾ in *maʾkalu* was unstressed and, accordingly, the dropping of ʾ could be antedated to this period (and one could postulate that the shift *ā* > *ō* ceased operating during the general penult stress period). This, however, is already outside the scope of this paper.

3.3. Yeivin, p. 196, explains cases like שֵׂאת 'to bear', occurring in a long syllable (*śēt), as being due to double-peak stress; cf. Bergsträsser, I, p. 158,[11] Yalon, p. 29, note 2, Z. Ben-Ḥayyim, in: *Mélanges de Philosophie et de Littérature Juives* 3–5.100 (1958–62). On the other hand, he gives a different explanation for the, externally at least, similar phenomenon in short syllables, v. above § 3.2. In some cases, to be sure, it is difficult to distinguish between long and short syllables (cf. also absolute חַטָּאת 'sin-offering' as against construct חַטַּאת). Nevertheless, this does not demonstrate that Yeivin's assumption as to the twofold origin of this phenomenon is erroneous, although the result of both shifts were quite alike. Yeivin corroborates his thesis by the fact that, despite the *shwa* in the syllable preceding the *alef* in these words, *b, k, l, w* preceding them are vocalized as if they were followed by a full vowel (as לִשְׂאת). Yet also vocalizations fitting the *shwa* occur and Yeivin himself, p. 197, quotes בִּשְׂאת. Moreover, vocalizations of the type לְשֵׂאת *may* be due to the fact that the *alef* was not pronounced, the actual pronunciation being *lāśēt* with long *ē*, but not necessarily exhibiting double-peak stress.

3.4. There is, however, in my opinion one indication that makes the very possibility of phonetic explanations rather unlikely. Kutscher, p. 170,[12] has called attention to the, in our opinion decisive, fact that this transposition of vowel does not occur but in words that are spelled with *alef*. And one must not argue that in words lacking *alef* in spelling it was not possible to mark the double peak stress. Why should, e.g., שׁוֹר 'ox' not be spelt in Babylonian vocalization שֹׁור or שׁוֹר, to be pronounced *šowor*, with *w* as glide?!

4. B. Analogical levelling: this is the simplest explanation for *Ru-'u-š(a)-qdš*, adduced by Albright, p. 35 §III E 6. Nevertheless, one will hardly consent to Albright's view that *Ru-'u-ša* arose from *rōš/rūš* 'head' through the influence of the plural **ra'šīm*, since this blend does not account for the vowel following the *alef*.[13] One will rather posit a plural **ra'ašīm* (in accordance with the well

---

[11] Yet Bergsträsser, I, p. 92, regards forms like שֵׂאת as artificial, and these two explanations, the phonetic one and the assumption of artificial formation, do not fit well. By the way, Bergsträsser, I, p. 158, explains the parallel occurrence of vowel after ', rather than before it, by a parallel feature in Maʿlūla. Yet in Maʿlūla it is the vowel following the ʿ that appears before it, rather than *vice versa*. *Prima facie*, one could interpret this behaviour of ʿ as being due to its disappearance in pronunciation. This, however, is already beyond the scope of this paper.

[12] Cf. also Blau, pp. 28–29.

[13] Albright's transcription posits *ru-'u-ša*, rather than *ru-u'-ša*. Albright, p. 28, §35, rejects Müller's "rückweisendes Prinzip", as if many vowels in syllabic groups do not reflect the vocalization of the syllable in which they are placed, but rather that of the preceding syllable.

known phenomenon that the plural of monosyllabic nouns is bisyllabic, exhibiting *a* in the second syllable), which influenced *rōš/rūš* to become *ru'uš*. Similarly,[14] one may postulate that through the blend of the singular **bēr* (< **bi'r*) with the plural *בְּאָרוֹת (in this position, after *shwa mobile*, the *alef* was more apt to persist), by dint of mutual levelling, בְּאֵרוֹת, בְּאֵר came into being. Yet, though this explanation is quite likely for monosyllabic nouns, it cannot apply to other cases.

5. C. The most powerful explanation of these phenomena is, it seems, the assumption of *pseudo-correction*:[15] since in Biblical Hebrew forms like חֹטְאִים 'sinners' and מֹצְאִים 'finding (masc. plur.)' interchanged, of which the second was considered more correct, pseudo-correct forms like בְּאֵר/בְּאֹשׁ were formed instead of **bēr*/**bōš*, or תְּאָכְלֵהוּ instead of תֹּאכְלֵהוּ ; תְּאֵהָבוּ instead of **ti'hăḇū*.[16] This explains the limitation of this phenomenon to words that exhibit *alef* in spelling: pseudo-correction acted only in those words which were felt as representing vulgar omission of *alef*,[17] and this was the case only in words spelt with *alef*. This accounts, e.g., for the different conduct of *rōš* spelt with *alef*, and of *šōr* spelt without it, in Babylonian vocalization. It also explains Babylonian vocalizations like במאזנים 'in the balances', in a word in which the spelling with *alef* itself is due to popular etymology![18] Even the Egyptian transcription *Ru-'u-ša-qdš* quoted above (§4)[19] may be due to pseudo-correc-

[14] V. Blau, p. 28, where also צֶאֱלִים 'Zizyphus lotus L.' < **ṣi'līm* (rather than > *ṣə'ēlīm*) * is treated and the opinion forwarded that its plural, as frequently in zoological and botanical species, was formed from a monosyllabic stem and therefore it differs from type בְּאֵרוֹת. On the other hand, one must not lose sight from the fact that from בְּאֵרוֹת itself the construct בֶּאֱרוֹת (Gen. xiv 10) is attested.

[15] V. Blau, pp. 28ff. F. R. Blake, *JNES* 10. 250, §21, for instance, calls it "hyper-correct"; P. Haupt (quoted Bauer-Leander, p. 224, note 1) considers such forms to be due to erroneous, artificial formation; Birkeland, pp. 38ff., in accordance with his theory of Biblical Hebrew being a mixed language, speaks of "restitution", the younger layer being, in his opinion, more archaic; P. Kahle posits general restitution of laryngals/pharyngals, v. e.g. Meyer, I, p. 94, II, pp. 24, 72.

[16] Alongside of **ti'hăḇū*, etc. (cf. forms like יֶאֱהַב) vulgar forms as **tēhāḇū* existed (which, it seems, arose through the analogy of the 1st pers. sing.). From the latter the pseudo-correct תְּאֵהָבוּ emerged. Accordingly, there is, it seems, no difference between this phenomenon occurring in allegedly long and short syllables, *pace* Yeivin, above, §§3.2; 3.3. The parallel feature occurring with *'ayin* presumably exhibits pseudo-correction as well, as against vulgar forms in which *'ayin* was not pronounced.

[17] And, in Babylonian vocalization, of *'ayin*.

[18] V. Bergsträsser, I, p. 90, note.

[19] The *u* of *ru-'u-š* already reflects the loss of ': *ra'š* > *rāš* > *rōš* (spelt *rūš*); for the improbability of *ru'š* being the original form, v. above, note 3. A similar pseudo-correct form is exhibited by Ροως (alongside Ρως) in the Septuagint. On the other hand, Kutscher, p. 169, is, in my opinion, right in interpreting Ραως apud Eusebius as an error for Αρως, i.e. Hebrew

tion, influenced by forms in which ʾ still persisted,[20] coexisting with forms without ʾ.

6. To sum up: the most powerful explanation for forms like בְּאשׁ, בְּאֵר, and also such as תְּאֵהָבוּ is the assumption of pseudo-correction. As a matter of fact, it accounts for all forms, both the originally monosyllabic nouns *II*ʾ and other words. This does not, however, exclude possible analogical levelling in some of these forms, in originally monosyllabic nouns *II*ʾ, but not in all cases. Accordingly, the special formation of monosyllabic nouns *II*ʾ is, it seems, due to multiple causation, viz. pseudo-correction and analogical levelling, whereas other forms arose through pseudo-correction only. On the other hand, the assumption of sound shift seems unlikely: the positing of bisyllabic base contravenes forms like שְׂאֵת; the positing of early anaptyctic vowels after *alef* preceded by *i*/*u* is contradicted by the early disappearance of *alef* in forms as יֵרָאת; the transposition of vowels after laryngals/pharyngals in Arabic dialects is different, since it is attested after "strong laryngals", rather than after *alef*; and the assumption of double peak stress does not account for the restriction of this feature to words spelt with *alef*.

3. THE SYSTEM OF TENSES IN BIBLICAL POETRY

1. In a paper submitted to *Studies in Ancient Narrative and Historiography* * in honour of I. L. Seeligmann, to be published in 1977–78, I have attempted to analyse the system of tenses in classical Biblical narrative. In my opinion, the spoken language during the classical period of Biblical Hebrew, prior to the Babylonian exile, possessed a tense system, past being marked by *qtl*/*wayyqtl*, present/future by *yqtl*/*wqtl*. Classical narrative prose,[1] based on this spoken language, yet influenced by literary conventions, restricted the possibility of freer alternation, presumably occurring in spoken language, of simple forms (*qtl*, *yqtl*) and forms with *wāw* consecutive (*wayyqtl*/*wqtl*). As a rule, it marks the indicative tenses by forms with *wāw* consecutive whenever the syntactic environment admits of the use of *wāw* copulative; otherwise the simple forms are used. The fact that classical narrative deliberately abstains

הָרֹאשׁ. Similarly מְאֹד 'wealth, exceedingly' has, presumably, in the light of Akkadian, to be derived from *ma'd > *mād > *mōd > (pseudo-correct) מְאֹד even in the Tiberian vocalization. As to יְאֹר cf. e.g. the proposals of T. O. Lambdin, *JAOS* 73. 151 (1953) and W. Vycichl, most recently in: *Actes du premier Congrès international de Linguistique sémitique et chamito-sémitique Paris* 16-19 *juillet* 1969, ed. A. Caquot-D. Cohen, The Hague-Paris 1974, p. 61.

[20] As attested by the Assyrian transcription *Ba-ʾ-li-ra-ʾ-si*, cited above note 3.

[1] Cf. also *IOS* 1. 24–25 (1971).

from certain forms in some syntactic environment, is demonstrated by the almost exclusive use of *w*-forms in sentence initial in classical narrative, whereas both in poetry and direct speech simple forms in this position are amply attested. Moreover, classical narrative almost totally refrains from *wāw* copulative preceding *qtl* to mark past, although this feature occurs in inscriptions prior to the Babylonian exile.[2]

In the paper cited I mentioned the use of tenses in Biblical poetry only marginally, as counterpart of narration. In the following, I shall attempt to bring out some of the main features of the system of tenses in Biblical poetry in full relief.

2. That the spoken language at the background of Biblical poetry possessed a tense system, is also attested by poetic portions exhibiting the opposition of *qtl* (*wayyqtl*): *yqtl* (*wqtl*) to mark the opposition past: future (present),[3] as: Deut. xxxii 21 הֵם קִנְאוּנִי בְלֹא־אֵל כִּעֲסוּנִי בְּהֶבְלֵיהֶם וַאֲנִי אַקְנִיאֵם בְּלֹא־עָם בְּגוֹי נָבָל אַכְעִיסֵם 'they have made me jealous by that which is not God, they have provoked me to anger with their vanities, and I shall make them jealous with those which are not a people, I shall provoke them to anger with a foolish nation'. Is. vi 7 הִנֵּה נָגַע זֶה עַל־שְׂפָתֶיךָ וְסָר עֲוֹנֶךָ וְחַטָּאתְךָ תְּכֻפָּר 'lo, this has touched your lips, and your iniquity is taken away, and your sin purged'. xiv 20 לֹא־תֵחַד אִתָּם בִּקְבוּרָה כִּי־אַרְצְךָ שִׁחַתָּ 'you will not be joined with them in burial, because you have destroyed your land'. xlii 9 הָרִאשׁוֹנוֹת הִנֵּה־בָאוּ וַחֲדָשׁוֹת אֲנִי מַגִּיד בְּטֶרֶם תִּצְמַחְנָה אַשְׁמִיעַ אֶתְכֶם 'behold the former things have come to pass, and new things I declare, before they spring forth, I shall tell you (of them)'. xlvi 11 אַף דִּבַּרְתִּי אַף אֲבִיאֶנָּה יָצַרְתִּי אַף אֶעֱשֶׂנָּה 'yea, I have spoken, I shall also bring it, I have created it, I shall also do it'. xlvii 7 וַתֹּאמְרִי לְעוֹלָם אֶהְיֶה גְבָרֶת 'and you said "I shall be a lady for ever"'. Hosea viii 14 וַיִּשְׁכַּח יִשְׂרָאֵל אֶת־עֹשֵׂהוּ וַיִּבֶן הֵיכָלוֹת וִיהוּדָה הִרְבָּה עָרִים בְּצֻרוֹת וְשִׁלַּחְתִּי אֵשׁ בְּעָרָיו וְאָכְלָה אַרְמְנוֹתֶיהָ 'and Israel has forgotten his Maker and has built temples, and Judah has multiplied fenced cities, and I shall send fire upon his cities and it shall devour its palaces'. Joel ii 2 כָּמֹהוּ לֹא נִהְיָה מִן־הָעוֹלָם וְאַחֲרָיו לֹא יוֹסֵף 'there has not been ever the like, neither shall be any more after it'.

3. Alongside of such passages, reflecting the opposition past: present/future, very often, especially in late poetry, but also in early poetical passages, the various verbal forms[4] are indiscriminately used referring to all possible shades of time. As the passages with clear tense opposition demonstrate, it would be

[2] V. Y. Aharoni, *Arad Inscriptions*, Jerusalem 1975, p. 18, inscription 3, lines 2–4; p. 32, inscription 16, lines 3–5.

[3] Cf. Bergsträsser, II, pp. 25–26, §6b. c, and also pp. 41–42, §9g. c.

[4] With the exception of the imperative.

erroneous to attempt to base the verbal system of Biblical poetry on the lack of time distinction in other passages. These passages must needs be interpreted as being due to the poet's readiness, because of tradition and literary convention, to abandon the indication of time distinction. One must not lose sight of the decisive fact that redundancy, one of the most outstanding characteristics of every linguistic system, is also inherent in tense system. Not only is time reference often sufficiently indicated by special words (as אֶתְמוֹל 'yesterday', מָחָר 'tomorrow', אַל 'μή', נָא 'pray'), but broader context is very often adequate for the understanding of time reference. This is the reason that modern readers of Biblical prose, with sufficient knowledge of the vocabulary, but without understanding its grammatical finesses, as a rule, do not experience difficulties in perceiving that e.g. וַיִּשְׁמֹר refers to the past, יִשְׁמֹר to the present/future, although they cannot parse them correctly. On this background we interpret the alternation of various verbal forms in many poetical passages as a literary feature deliberately used by the poet, rather than exhibiting a genuine tense system. This interpretation is corroborated by nominal clauses used referring to past and future in Biblical poetry.

4. Some poetical passages exhibiting alternating verbal forms without special time reference, sometimes interchanging with nominal clauses as well:[5] Gen. xlix 10–12 לֹא יָסוּר שֵׁבֶט מִיהוּדָה... אֹסְרִי לַגֶּפֶן עִירֹה... כִּבֵּס בַּיַּיִן לְבֻשׁוֹ... חַכְלִילִי עֵינַיִם מִיָּיִן... 'the sceptre will not depart from Judah... he will bind his foal unto the vine... he will wash his garments in wine... his eyes will be red with wine...'. Ex. xv 4–5 מַרְכְּבֹת פַּרְעֹה וְחֵילוֹ יָרָה בַיָּם... תְּהֹמֹת יְכַסְיֻמוּ יָרְדוּ 'Pharaoh's chariots and his host he has cast into the sea... the depths have covered them, they sank...'. Num. xxiv 17ff. דָּרַךְ כּוֹכָב מִיַּעֲקֹב וְקָם שֵׁבֶט מִיִּשְׂרָאֵל... וְיֵרְדְּ[6] מִיַּעֲקֹב וְהֶאֱבִיד שָׂרִיד מֵעִיר 'a star will come out of Jacob and a sceptre will rise from Israel... out of Jacob (will come he who) will have dominion and he will destroy him who remains from the city'. Deut. xxxii 10ff. יִמְצָאֵהוּ בְּאֶרֶץ מִדְבָּר... יְסֹבְבֶנְהוּ יְבוֹנְנֵהוּ יִצְּרֶנְהוּ כְּאִישׁוֹן עֵינוֹ:... בָּדָד יַנְחֶנּוּ[7] וְאֵין עִמּוֹ אֵל נֵכָר: יַרְכִּבֵהוּ עַל־בָּמֳתֵי אָרֶץ וַיֹּאכַל תְּנוּבֹת שָׂדָי וַיֵּנִקֵהוּ... וְדַם־עֵנָב תִּשְׁתֶּה־חָמֶר: וַיִּשְׁמַן יְשֻׁרוּן 'He found him in the desert... He led him about, He instructed him, He kept him as the apple of His eye... He alone lead him and there was no strange god with Him, He made him ride on the high places of the earth and he ate the crop of the field and He made him suck... and you drank the blood of grapes as wine and Jeshurun became fat'. xxxiii 8–9 אֲשֶׁר נִסִּיתוֹ בְּמַסָּה תְּרִיבֵהוּ

[5] Cf. e.g. Bergsträsser, I, p. 29, §6i; pp. 34–35, §7h.

[6] Pay attention to the short imperfect (called by us *yaqtel* in the following).

[7] Pay attention that *yqtl* governing pronominal suffixes of 3. pers. sg. masc. with *n* alternates with *n*-less suffixes. *n*-suffixes are, as a rule, governed by ordinary *yqtl*, *n*-less suffixes by *yaqtel* (including *wayyqtl*).

עַל מֵי מְרִיבָה: הָאֹמֵר... וְאֶת אֶחָיו לֹא הִכִּיר וְאֶת־בָּנָו לֹא יָדָע כִּי שָׁמְרוּ אִמְרָתֶךָ וּבְרִיתְךָ יִנְצֹרוּ 'whom you proved at Massah and with whom you strove at the waters of Meribah, who said... neither did he acknowledge his brothers nor know his children, for they have observed your word and kept your covenant'. And cf. e.g. Psalm xxix, where *qtl*, *yqtl*, *wayyqtl*, participles and nominal clauses alternate (referring to present).

5. As already stated (§ 3), it was because of tradition and literary convention that poets deviated from the tense system of their spoken language and often used the various verbal forms indiscriminately. We do not, of course, know how these literary conventions came into being. Yet, by comparison with Ugaritic poetry and with the help of what presumably was the Proto-Semitic tense system, we may attempt tentatively to suggest the possible emergence of poetic tradition concerning the use of verbal forms. It stands to reason that the short imperfect (*yaqtel*) for marking the past[8] is an archaic feature inherited from Proto-Semitic. Various features indicate that *yaqtel* in Proto-Semitic marked not only jussive but past as well,[9] and *wayyqtl* (as a matter of fact, as a rule whenever possible, *wayyaqtel*) referring to the past is, it seems, a relic of this usage of *yaqtel*, which has survived in poetry.[10] Another archaic trait, vestiges of which may be found in Semitic languages,[11] is the so-called *perfectum propheticum*. It stands to reason that originally this use of the perfect referring to the future was restricted[12] and spread later[13] because of the literary character of the Bible, containing such a great amount of prophecies. Moreover, *qtl* of stative verbs survived having extratemporal character. Yet not only Proto-Semitic features contributed to the blurring of a clearcut tense system, but literary heritage as well. In Ugaritic epic the use of *yqtl*[14] to

[8] It may be that the use of *yaqtel* for marking the past was the point of departure for the use of *yaqtel* (as well of the cohortative, i.e., *'aqtlā*) for marking indicative present/future, a feature especially frequent in late poetry (v. e.g. Bergsträsser, II, pp. 50–51, §10 l). By blend with *yaqtel* marking (indicative) past, *yaqtel*, used as jussive, referring to the future, started marking indicative future as well. Since *'aqtlā* was used as the jussive of the first person, it also became used for denoting the indicative future (just as *wayyqtl*, formally and also historically identical with *yaqtel*, attracted *'aqtlā* to be used after *wāw* consecutive; cf. e.g. Bergsträsser, II, p. 23, §5f.).

[9] V. e.g. Bergsträsser, II, p. 10, §3b, further *Kiryat Sefer* 51. 474b (1975–76).

[10] As e.g. יַצֵּב 'He set' Deut. xxxii 8.

[11] As in Classical Arabic, further in the Ancient Aramaic of Sham'al, v. *Kiryat Sefer ibid.* (note 9).

[12] To wishes, prayers, curses, etc., as in Arabic (and presumably also in the Aramaic of Sham'al, v. the preceding note).

[13] It stands to reason that the prevalence of *wqtl* to mark future partly originated in this usage, partly being due to contrastive analogy to *wayyqtl*.

[14] The use of *yqtl*, i.e. the "long" imperfect, in this sense is demonstrated by verbs *III'*,

mark the past, presumably originally some sort of *praesens historicum*, is extraordinarily frequent. The influence of this style on Hebrew poetry can be demonstrated: in Ugaritic poetry *yqtl* and *qtl* of the same verb may stand in parallel hemistichs and this occurs in Hebrew poetry as well,[15] thus evincing the historical ties (though not necessarily direct ones) of Ugaritic and Hebrew poetry. Accordingly in Hebrew poetry *yqtl* was used to mark not only present/future and iterative/durative past, as in prose, but also past in general, *yaqtel* was employed not only as jussive, but also as referring to past, *qtl* referred not only to the past, but also to the future. Small wonder that, on the background of this medley of usage, often poets used verbal forms without any special time reference.

4. VESTIGES OF BI-LITERAL ORIGIN OF VERBS *III Y (W)* IN HEBREW AND ARABIC

1. It stands to reason that the bi-literal origin of any formgroup of verbs can only be established when some forms cannot be explained as derived from tri-literal roots. I want to suggest that certain forms of verbs *III y (w)* in Hebrew and Arabic cannot be accounted for by positing tri-literal origin, and, accordingly, partly at least, these verbs have to be derived from bi-literal origin, presumably terminating in a(n anceps) vowel.

2. Yet in spite of the existence of forms which synchronically belong to verbs *III y (w)*, but cannot be accounted for by the assumption of tri-literal origin, one must not take for granted that all verbs *III y (w)* in Hebrew and Arabic have bi-literal derivation.[1] It stands to reason that from the very beginning genuine tri-literal verbs *III y (w)* coexisted with bi-literal ones terminating in vowel. After by certain sound shifts some tri-literal forms had become identical with some bi-literal ones, through analogy the various forms of originally tri-literal and bi-literal verbs became mixed up.

3. It is impossible to derive the imperative (and the related short imperfect) forms without suffixes, of verbs *III y/w* in Arabic, by dint of the assumption of sound shifts, from genuine tri-literal forms. **'udʿuw*, **'ibniy*, **'irḍaw*,

as in the frequent phrase *ynš'u gh* 'he raised his voice', further *tb'u UT* 51: iv: 23, *yml'u*, *UT* ʿnt ii: 25 (perhaps also by verba *III y*).

15 V. M. Held, 'The *yqtl — qtl* (*qtl — yqtl*) Sequence of Identical Verbs in Biblical Hebrew and Ugaritic', *Studies and Essays in Honor of A. A. Neuman*, Leiden 1962, pp. 281–90 (who, in our opinion, exaggerated the importance of this feature in Hebrew).

1 For the whole complex of problems cf. Blau, in: M. Black-G. Fohrer, eds., *In Memoriam Paul Kahle*, Berlin 1968, pp. 42–43.

(pp. 279–80)

***'insay* 'call!, build!, be satisfied!, forget!' should have developed to ***'ud'ū*, ***'ibnī*, ***'irḍaw*, ***'insay*, rather than to *'ud'u*, *'ibni*, *'irḍa*, *'insa*. Brockelmann, I, p. 620, §271Ce, postulated that, presumably already in Proto-Semitic, these forms were shortened, because the long imperfect and the short imperfect have become identical. He surmised (*ibid.*, rem. 1) that this formation was secondary, perhaps through analogy with verbs *II w/y*.

This theory, however, causes considerable difficulties. By no means can the shortening of these forms be attributed to Proto-Semitic. We know now,[2] that the elision of the final *w/y* in verbs *III w/y* did not belong to the Proto-Semitic period, but rather occurred in the single languages. As a matter of fact, the short imperfect/imperative without suffixes in the various Semitic languages is by no means always identical with the Classical Arabic forms. In Ancient Aramaic,[3] for instance, it is the "short" imperfect/imperative that exhibits the third radical (marked by *y*), while the "long" imperfect is, in fact, shortened, terminating in -*ē* (marked by *h*). In Biblical Hebrew in the imperative "long" and "short" forms alternate, viz. type צַוֵּה 'command' < **ṣawwiy*[4] and צַו; the short imperfect, to be sure, only differs from the long imperfect in its shortened forms (type וַיְצַו), whereas its "long" form has become identical with the long imperfect, terminating in הֶ, rather than in the expected הֵ.[5] At any rate, in Biblical Hebrew at least, the difference between the long and the short imperfect was originally marked by the opposition הֶ : הֵ, and there was no need to mark the opposition by the shortening of the short imperfect.[6] Moreover, in Classical Arabic forms like the imperative *qum* of verbs *IIw/y* have phonologically to be interpreted as /*qūm*/, as demonstrated by fem. *qūmī*, whereas *'ud'u*, etc. even phonologically terminate in short vowels.

4. Accordingly, the only possible explanation for the occurrence of short vowels in the termination of the short imperfect/imperative in Classical Arabic as well as for forms of the type צַו/וַיְצַו in Biblical Hebrew is, in my opinion, the assumption that these forms originated in bi-literal roots terminating in vowel. Although most forms of verbs *III y/w* can easily be derived

2 V. especially Birkeland, pp. 41ff.

3 V. R. Degen, *Altaramäische Grammatik*, Wiesbaden 1969, pp. 76ff., §62.

4 Final -*iy* should have shifted to -*ī*, as preserved in the construct of פֶּה 'mouth', viz. פִּי < **piy*. It was through the analogy of final -*ay*, that such words, as a rule, terminate in ֶה.

5 As exhibited by the above mentioned צַוֵּה; for particulars v. Bergsträsser, II, pp. 160–61.

6 Even in Arabic only long and short imperfect forms terminating in -*uw*(*u*)/-*iy*(*u*) coalesced, yet not those ending in -*aw*(*u*)/-*ay*(*u*). These, however, became identical with the 2nd/3rd person plur. masc./2nd. pers. sing. fem. respectively (cf. C. Brockelmann, *Arabische Grammatik*[12], Leipzig 1948, p. 55, §43c).

from tri-literal roots the third radical of which was *y/w*, the occurrence of short vowels in the termination of short imperfect/imperative in Classical Arabic and the existence of shortened forms of these verbal forms in Biblical Hebrew demonstrates that in Proto-Semitic alongside of tri-literal forms also bi-literal ones existed, and it stands to reason that after by sound shifts some of the tri-literal forms had become identical with some bi-literal ones, the latter were felt synchronically to belong to the tri-literal pattern *III y/w*, and the original tri-literal roots *III y/w* and the bi-literal ones terminating in vowel became mixed up.

5. ON THE POSSIBILITY OF MULTILINEAR DEVELOPMENT OF HEBREW *'AQTLĀ*

1. In the main, two derivations have been offered for Hebrew *'aqtlā*. Some identified it with the Arabic subjunctive *yqtla*,[1] others with the Arabic energetic *yqtlan*, which, according to pausal shift characteristic of Arabic, in pause becomes *yqtlā*.[2] Yet W. Moran, 'Early Canaanite *yaqtula*', *Orientalia* 29.1–19 (1960),[3] has convincingly demonstrated that the use of Hebrew *'aqtlā* is sub-
(p. 157) stantially identical with Byblian Amarna *yaqtula*. Therefore, the identity of Hebrew *'aqtlā* with Arabic *yqtla*, which itself has the same origin as Byblian *yaqtula*, is finally proved.

2. This derivation, however, does not account for the preservation of final
* short *-a* in Hebrew *'aqtlā*. Since short final vowels as a rule disappeared in Hebrew, we would have expected the same to happen in **'aqtla* as well, rather than to be lengthened and preserved. In all the other cases of survival of final short vowels in Biblical Hebrew special conditions prevailed. The preservation of the so-called הָ *locale* exhibits a totally different feature, since the *h* was originally consonantal, as proved by Ugaritic spelling. The so-called *ḥireq compaginis* occurs in construct, i.e. in the middle of a com-
* pound noun, and the same applies to *ḥolem*. The preservation of final *a* in *qtl* and the pronominal suffix 2nd pers. sing. masc. is, partly at least, due to the desire to differentiate between the masculine and the feminine (cf. the inverse phenomenon in Aramaic and Arabic dialects, in which it was the feminine form, rather than the masculine one, that preserved the final vowel). The desire to differentiate, however, was much weaker in the case of *'aqtlā*, as demonstrated by the widespread disappearance of the short imperfect. Ac-

[1] V. e.g. Bauer-Leander, p. 273d.
[2] V. e.g. Brockelmann, I, p. 557 (where read *an* > *ā* for *a* > *ă*!), Bergsträsser, II. p. 24.
[3] Cf. also J. Blau, *HUCA* 42. 133–46 (1971).

cordingly, though the derivation of *'aqtlā* from *yqtla* is no doubt correct, it does not explain the preservation of the final *a*.

3. *'aqtlā* is quite often followed by נָא 'pray', as 2Sam. xviii 19 אָרוּצָה נָּא[4] 'let me now run!'. I am tentatively suggesting that it was due to the frequency of this construction, in which *'aqtlā* coalesced with *nā* and, therefore, **a* occurred in word middle, that **a* > *ā* was preserved.

3.1. In § 3 we have attempted to explain the subsistence of *ā* by the coalescence of *'aqtlā* with *nā*. Yet the frequent occurrence of *'aqtlā* with *nā* may also reflect the separation of one word into two: the energetic **'aqtlana*[5] was decomposed into two words, which, however, continued to be one stress unit. Since the first part of the new compound was identified with *'aqtlā* because of their formal and functional similarity,[6] the final *a* of *'aqtlā* was preserved through the influence of *'aqtlā-nā*, in which this *a* was in word middle. According to this thesis, which in my opinion is more likely than that propounded in § 3, Hebrew *'aqtlā* arose through plurilinear development: in the main it continues *yqtla*, yet its final vowel is due to *yqtlana*.[7]

6. UGARITIC IMPERATIVE QAL EXHIBITING THE SAME VOWEL AFTER THE FIRST AND SECOND RADICALS

In Hebrew, Aramaic and Arabic the imperative of *qal* exhibits full vowel only after the second radical, while Akkadian repeats the same vowel after the first and second radicals (type *purus/piris/paras*). There is some indication that in Ugaritic the Akkadian way of forming the imperative of *qal* obtained.

UT, p. 77, §9.20, when reconstructing the imperative of *qal*, puts the vowel after the first radical in brackets, indicating its uncertain existence. Yet the occurrence of *I'* forms with vowels after the ' demonstrates the existence of a

4 The point in the *nūn* is *'ātē mē-raḥīq*, rather than *dageš*, and does not indicate doubling; v. e.g. Bergsträsser, I, p. 65, §10p, A. Dotan, *The diqduqé haṭṭě'amim of Ahăron ben Moše ben Ašér* Jerusalem 1967, p. 387, note 14.

5 I have posited simple, rather than double, *n*, v. the preceding note, contrary to Arabic *'aqtlanna*. There are some indications that in Hebrew other forms of the energetic occurred as well; cf. for the time being my article in the forthcoming volume of *Eretz-Israel* dedicated to H. L. Ginsberg. I have posited original short *a* for *'aqtlā*, since it stands to reason that it was only lengthened at a period which did not tolerate short vowels in open syllables. *

6 This similarity might have been one of the reasons for the decomposition of **'aqtlana*.

7 That Hebrew *'aqtlā* reflects conflation of these two forms has already been surmised, yet for different reasons; v. I. J. Gelb, *Sequential Reconstruction of Proto-Akkadian*, The Oriental Institute of the University of Chicago, Assyriological Studies 18, Chicago 1969, p. 101, and cf. also Lambert, p. 257, note 2.

vowel after the first radical in these forms. Moreover, it can, it seems, be demonstrated that this vowel was originally identical with the vowel after the second radical, yet it has become stabilized.

From *'rš* 'to request' the imperative *'irš* is attested and the *yqtl y'arš/t'arš*.[1] The latter has to be interpreted, in accordance with the Barth-Ginsberg law, as *ya'riš/ta'riš*, the former *'iriš*, exhibiting the same vowel after the second radical as *yqtl*. From *'tw* 'to come', *inter alia*, the imperative *'at* and *yqtl t'ity/t'it*[2] is preserved, the latter to be interpreted as *ti'tayu/ti'tē* < *ti'tay* in accordance with the Barth-Ginsberg law, the former as *'atē* < *'atay*. The fact that after the final *ay* had changed to *ē*, the vowel of the first radical did not change, demonstrates that it had become stabilized.[3]

ABBREVIATIONS

Aistleitner — J. Aistleitner, *Wörterbuch der ugaritischen Sprache*², Berlin 1965.

Albright — W. F. Albright, *The Vocalization of the Egyptian Syllabic Orthography*, New Hav en 1965.

Bauer-Leander — H. Bauer-P. Leander, *Historische Grammatik der hebräischen Sprache des Alt en Testaments*, Halle 1922.

Bergsträsser — G. Bergsträsser, *Hebräische Grammatik*, Leipzig 1918–29.

Birkeland — H. Birkeland, *Akzent und Vokalismus im Althebräischen*, Oslo 1940.

Blanc — H. Blanc, 'The Arabic Dialect of the Negev Bedouins', Jerusalem 1970, The Israel Academy of Sciences and Humanities, *Proceedings*, iv, 7, preprint.

Blau — J. Blau, *On Pseudo-Corrections in Some Semitic Languages*, Jerusalem 1970.

BzA — *Beiträge zur Assyriologie und semitischen Sprachwissenschaft*.

Harris — Z. S. Harris, *A Grammar of the Phoenician Language*, New Haven 1936.

Harris, *Development* — Z. S. Harris, *Development of the Canaanite Dialects*, New Haven 1939.

JAOS — *Journal of the American Oriental Society*.

JNES — *Journal of Near Eastern Studies*.

JSS — *Journal of Semitic Studies*.

Kurzweil — M. Z. Kaddari, *et alii*, eds., *Baruch Kurzweil Memorial Volume*, Ramat-Gan 1975.

Kutscher — E. Y. Kutscher, *Studies in Galilean Aramaic*, Ramat Gan 1976.

Lagarde — P. Lagarde, *Übersicht über die im Aramäischen, Arabischen und Hebräischen übliche Bildung der Nomina*, Göttingen 1889.

1 So Aistleitner s.v.; *UT*, s.v. is wrong in interpreting the *yqtl* form as N-form. He did it, it seems, because according to him (*UT*, p. 31, §5.16) *a'* should have shifted to *e'*. Yet *a'* does occur, v. e.g. *Ugarit-Forschungen* 2. 21–22 (1970).

2 V. Aistleitner, s.v.

3 Just as the prefix vowel of *yqtl qal* has become stabilized, so that *ti'tē* did not change, it seems, to *ta'tē* (although *t'it* may be interpreted as *ta'tē* as well, v. *Ugarit-Forschungen* 2. 21–23 [1970]).

Lambert — M. Lambert, *Traité de grammaire hébraïque*, Paris 1931–38.
Meyer — R. Meyer, *Hebräische Grammatik*, Berlin 1966–72.
OLZ — *Orientalistische Literatur-Zeitung*.
Socin — A. Socin, *Diwan aus Centralarabien*, iii, ed. H. Stumme, Leipzig 1901.
UT — C. H. Gordon, *Ugaritic Textbook*, Analecta Orientalia 38, Roma 1965.
Yalon — H. Yalon, *Studies in the Dead Seas Scrolls*, Jerusalem 1967.
Yeivin — I. Yeivin, *The Babylonian Vocalization...*, Ph.D. Thesis, The Hebrew University 1968.

Additions and Corrections

to **p. 250**.*n. 14.3*: Since the definite article does not behave in the same way when preceding *ḥaṭaf qamaṣ* and *qamaṣ qaṭan* (הֶחֳדָשִׁים as against הַחָכְמָה), it stands to reason that a period existed in which *ḥaṭaf qamaṣ* and *qamaṣ qaṭan* were pronounced differently: *qamaṣ qaṭan*. was pronounced *u* , yet *ḥaṭaf qamaṣ* as *å*; for details see *Hebrew Linguistics*, pp. 23–24, where a more powerful explanation for the shift *ʾa* > *ę* is propounded.

to **p. 255**.*n. 14*: For details on צֶאֱלִים see *Hebrew Linguistics*, pp. 198–99; 209–10, and above p. 191.

to **p. 256**.*–11*: It was published in the *I. L. Seeligmann Volume*, Jerusalem 1983, Hebrew section, pp. 19–23 = *Hebrew Linguistics*, pp. 109–13.

to **p. 262**.*21*: Since, however, these final vowels were, it seems, *anceps* (see e. g. above p. 143. n. 9), no constraint for the omission of the final *a* of *ʾaqtla* existed, because אשמרָה, etc., may be derived from *ʾaqtlā* with final long *a*. Nevertheless, although אשמרה, etc., might have stemmed from *ʾaqtlā* alone, one cannot be sure that the actual process took place exactly along these lines (cf. below pp. 279–80), and it **may** well be that the development was plurilinear, אשמרה, etc., also originating from *ʾaqtlana*.

to **p. 262**.*-7*: For "the preservation of the final *a* of *qtlta* (read so for *qtl* !) and the pronominal suffix 2nd pers. sing. masc." See also above pp. 27–28; 142–43.

to **p. 263**.*n. 5.4*: The paper has been published in *Eretz-Israel* 14.125–131 (1978) = *Hebrew Linguistics*, pp. 94–104, see especially *Eretz-Israel*, p. 127.col. a.11ff. = *Hebrew Linguistics*, pp. 97.10ff. Delete "I have posited original short *a* for *ʾaqtlā* since it stands to reason that it was only lengthened at a period which did not tolerate short vowels in open syllables"; I rather think that the final *a* was *anceps*, see above addition to p. 262.21.

Some Difficulties in the Reconstruction of "Proto-Hebrew" and "Proto-Canaanite"

New finds, not in the least owing to the insight of the late Kahle, have considerably enlarged our knowledge of Hebrew and Canaanite in comparison with the 19th century[1]. Nevertheless, this widening of our horizons with regard to particulars, despite their importance, has not solved the main problems of »Proto-Hebrew« and »Proto-Canaanite«. On the contrary, in some respects it has brought out into relief some of the difficulties which thwart the possibility of establishing this reconstruction on firm ground. In this paper we shall try to treat of some of these difficulties.

1. Defective Knowledge of the Canaanite Dialects

Even our knowledge of Biblical Hebrew, no doubt the best known Canaanite dialect, is rather restricted. The main problem is not the quite limited corpus of texts with their restricted vocabulary, but rather the lack of vowel signs, the vocalization belonging to a much later period[2]. It goes without saying that we possess no indica-

[1] Cf. W. L. Moran, The Bible and the Ancient Near East, Essays in Honor of W. F. Albright, 1961, p. 54ff.

[2] We are in a better position with regard to the vowel system of Syriac. Nevertheless, even it raises problems, cf. the important paper of H. Birkeland, The Syriac Phonematic Vowel Systems, in: Festkrift til Professor O. Broch..., 1947, p. 13ff., dealing, inter alia, with the correspondance of Nestorian *ê* with Jacobite *e* and *i* and assuming that in Nestorian *ê* two sounds, *ệ* and *ȩ̂*, coalesced. (One may add that one has the impression that originally in Proto-Syriac stressed *áj* > *ệ*, but weakly stressed *aj* (as in st. c., prepositions) > *ȩ̂*; this was, however, obscured by many analogical formations. But this problem is already beyond the scope of this paper). — Even Arabic grammatical tradition is deficient in some points. Suffice it to mention the well known fact that we have no knowledge whatever of the role of stress in Arabic. Moreover there is the problem of the so-called *alif maqṣûra bi-ṣûrat al-yâ* (as بَكَى »he wept«), whether or not it represents *-aj* (as claimed for pausal pronunciation by Ch. Sarauw, ZA 21 (1908), p. 38–40; H. Birkeland, Altarabische Pausalformen, 1940, p. 74ff., and even for context forms Ch.

tion of the speech rhythms[3]. As to the Canaanite inscriptions and Ugaritic, we, as well known, do not possess any tradition as to their vowels and depend entirely on *scriptio plena* (in Canaanite) and the diverse *alif*-signs (in Ugaritic).

2. Pitfalls of Transcriptions in Other Languages

For lack of other sources, we are often forced to depend upon transcriptions of Canaanite names and phrases (e.g. in Greek and Latin). It is always, however, rather difficult to derive clear inferences from them, since one has to take into account also the intricacies of both the transcribed and the transcribing languages. We shall illustrate our contention by some examples.

One of the vexing questions of the Hebrew vowel system is the problem of the quantity of originally short vowels in pretonic open syllables (as **maΘal > mAʃâl, *ʿinab > ʿEnâḇ*). Whereas e.g. H.

Rabin, Ancient West Arabian, 1951, p. 115ff. 160; cf. against them H. Fleisch, Traité de Philologie Arabe, I 1961, p. 318). One will not, however, propound a markedly different pronunciation of *alif maqṣûra bi-ṣûrat al-yâ* (as *aj*) as against اَ, since after *yâ* it is spelled *alif*, only in order to avoid two successive *yâ*. Rabin, op. cit., p. 117, it is true, claimed that in this case phonetically *jaj > jâ*. This explanation, however, is contradicted by يا frequently rhyming with ىَ in the Qurân (e.g.—I am quoting according to the »royal« Qurân—20, 71–74 ابقى — موسى — لاولى — ابقى — الدنيا — فصلى — تزكى — يحيى. 87, 13ff. يحيى — ابقى — الدنيا [يحيى is always spelled in the Qurân in this way, even as a verbal form; Rabin's assumption, op. cit., p. 124 n. 32, that this is due to purely graphic confusion with the proper noun, is only possible, if their pronunciation was quite similar!]). Accordingly, for the Qurân one will postulate the pronunciation *ê* for *alif maqṣûra* * *bi-ṣûrat al-yâ*. On the other hand, we do not believe that Arabic orthography was as much influenced by Aramaic (Nabataean) spelling as hinted by A. Spitaler, WZKM 56 (1960), p. 220 n. 25. Had this been the case, one would have expected *tâ ṭawîla* as the spelling of the nominal feminine ending *-at* in *status constructus* (in accordance with Nabataean usage) rather than *tâ marbûṭā*. So the simplest explanation of Arabic orthography remains that every word was spelled as if standing * in *pausa*.

[3] C. Brockelmann, Grundriß der vergleichenden Grammatik der semitischen Sprachen, I 1908, p. 103, 375f., assumes that *mâʿôz*, *mâgên* (and add also *mâsâḵ*) preserve their *â* in the first syllable because they were pronounced slowly (lento forms). This is well possible. On the other hand (v. § 5), these forms may be borrowed from a dialect that preserved *ǎ* even when remote from the stress. In this case the original *pataḥ* changed to *qameṣ*, because in Biblical Hebrew the *pataḥ* could not occur in open syllable. For other interpretations v.e.g. Th. Nöldeke, Mandäische Grammatik, 1875, p. 130 n. 4, who considers *mâ* as a very old form of the prefix *ma*, further J. Barth, Die Nominalbildung in den semitischen Sprachen, 1894[2], p. 234, who considers *mâ* as prolongation of *ma*.

Grimme[4] and P. Joüon[5] regarded them as short[6], now, since C. Brockelmann's paper[7], it is commonplace that these pretonic vowels are long[8]: Brockelmann relies upon Syriac (Nestorian) and Arabic loans of Hebrew proper nouns, which exhibit these pretonic vowels as long. Accordingly, he concludes, these vowels must have been long in Hebrew as well. This inference, however, overlooks the phonetic conditions of Aramaic (Syriac): in Aramaic short vowels in pretonic open syllables cannot subsist. Aramaeans, when borrowing a word like *dawîḏ* »David« (let us, for the argument's sake, assume that the *a* was short), could pronounce it only in one of the following ways: by reduction of the short pretonic vowel (i.e. *dəwîḏ*) — but this form was, it seems, too different from the original; by reduplication of the consonant following the short vowel (i.e. *dawwîḏ*)[9], or by lengthening the short vowel: *dâwîḏ*[10]. Accordingly, the long *â* of Aramaic *dâwîḏ* does not necessarily reflect a long *â* in Hebrew[11]. The same applies to the Arabic loans, as well as to the Arabic place names of Palestine, which continue Hebrew ones, since they were not borrowed directly from Hebrew, but via Aramaic[12].

Nevertheless, we do not claim that these pretonic vowels were not long. All we wanted to demonstrate was how difficult it is to determine the phonetic values of the sounds of a language from transcriptions in another language. As a matter of fact, we even prefer to regard pretonic vowels in open syllables as long[13]. There

[4] Grundzüge der hebräischen Akzent- und Vokallehre, 1896, p. 34.

[5] Grammaire de l'Hébreu biblique, 1923, p. 23.

[6] I.e. the first vowels in *mAʃâl* and *ʿEnâb* have changed their quality only (from *a* and *i* respectively) rather than their quantity. Joüon, it is true, regards *qameṣ* etc. as longer than *pataḥ* etc. (»voyelles moyennes«).

[7] ZA 14 (1899), p. 343.

[8] I.e. *mâʃâl*, *ʿênâḇ*. V. also e.g. Brockelmann, Grundriß ... I, p. 101, G. Bergsträsser, Hebräische Grammatik, I 1918, p. 117.

[9] Cf. e.g. Syriac *ʾattûnâ* < Accadian *atûn*.

[10] Cf. e.g. Syriac *Tâmûz*, representing, it seems, Accadian **Tamûz*; Syriac *kânônâ*, »stove«, corresponding to Middle-Assyrian *kanûnu*.

[11] This oversight on the part of two such great scholars as Brockelmann and Bergsträsser is the more striking, since both of them explain the lengthening of pretonic vowels (v. loc. cit.) by the assumption that Aramaic speaking Jews prolonged these vowels in order not to reduce them in accordance with Aramaic phonetic pattern! We may justly assume the same for Hebrew loans in Aramaic.

[12] V. for them e.g. H. Bauer-P. Leander, Historische Grammatik der hebräischen Sprache ..., 1922, p. 239 j'; F. R. Blake, JAOS 66 (1946), p. 215 note 15; idem, JNES 10 (1951), p. 243, § 3.

* [13] As explanation of this phenomenon, I would prefer the opinion of Ch. Sarauw, Über Akzent und Silbenbildung in den älteren semitischen Sprachen, 1939, p. 66, especially n. 1, and of J. Cantineau, BEOIFD 2 (1932), p. 139, who consider it as a

are, to be sure, no proofs of this assumption from the alternation of such pretonic vowels with short vowels followed by a double consonant[14], since reduplication of consonants after short vowels occurs in many languages, alternating with *short* vowels followed by simple consonants[15]; nor is it borne out by Greek transcriptions as preserved in the second column of the Hexapla: Origines, it is true, transcribes *e* in open pretonic syllables by η, and since η (and ω) occur exactly in the same position as Tiberian *qameṣ*, whereas ε (and o) structurally correspond to Tiberian *pataḥ*, both Sarauw[16] and E. Brønno[17] postulate long η and ω as against short ε and o (and, accordingly, long *qameṣ* as against short *pataḥ*). Yet one has to beware of pitfalls: it stands to reason that, in Origines's system, these vowels only reflect differences of quality.

Origines transcribes long segol (ה ֶ) *by* ε. Accordingly, Sarauw[18] was forced to assume that in these forms (as to his mind everywhere) *segol* is short; for the difficulties of this assumption v. however Brockel-

---

purely phonetic fact. Cantineau loc. cit. adduced some examples from the Arabic dialect of Palmyre, exhibiting *fa'ûl*>*fâ'ûl*; later, however, Cantineau himself (Le Dialecte arabe de Palmyre, I 1934, p. 81) came to regard these cases as due to morphological assimilation of *fa'ûl* to *fâ'ûl* (cf. also Brockelmann, ZDMG 94, 1940, p. 349). Nevertheless, according to T. M. Johnstone, BSOAS 24 (1961), p. 250f., in the Arabic Dôsiri dialect in disyllabic words the ultimate syllable of which contains a long vowel and whose penult is a short open syllable containing the vowel *a*, there is a tendency to lengthen the penult. The unlengthened form is, however, a free variant. Though this feature seems to be quite clear (it occurs not only in *fa'ûl*, like *'âjûz*, *gâ'ûd*, but also in *khâðêt*; so also p. 293 note 1 *sâraḥt*, where the ultimate syllable, though long, does not contain a long vowel), it needs further elucidation, since it is attested in closed (!) syllables as well (*târwa*; so also before a double consonant: p. 292 note 4 *sârraḥt*).

14 V. e.g. Bergsträsser, op. cit. (n. 8) I, p. 117, 139f.

15 Cf. e.g. cases of reduplication in Accadian, v. W. v. Soden, Grundriß der akkadischen Grammatik, 1952, p. 109d, allegedly after secondary stress; p. 114f. as »support of the second vowel (of the imperative) by the reduplication of the third radical consonant«, in Aramaic Brockelmann, Grundriß... I, 69ff., in Maltese Arabic op. cit., p. 66z (and perhaps also op. cit., p. 66w in Classical Arabic, allegedly after stressed short vowel). In the Arabic dialect of Palmyre such a secondary gemination occurs as well. Cantineau, BEOIFD 2 (1932), 139, to be sure, regards it as parallel to pretonic lengthening, but Palmyre (n. 13) I 42 he considers it to be due to the tendency to prevent the reduction of a short vowel in an open syllable.—Bauer-Leander, op. cit. (in n. 12), p. 238i, attribute this secondary gemination in Hebrew to the analogy of *mediae geminatae* or to the tendency to preserve short vowels (if one considered pretonic open syllable as short, one would say: the tendency to preserve the quality of the vowel). *

16 Op. cit. (n. 13), p. 61.

17 Studien über hebräische Morphologie und Vokalismus..., 1943, p. 249f. 346.

18 P. 95ff.; Brønno, op. cit., p. 269, only states that the use of ε is remarkable.

mann, ZDMG 94 (1940), p. 343ff.[19]. Since, in all probability, *segol* in these cases is long, we may explain the use of it by Origines in one of these two ways: either Origines marks quality only or he marks both quality and quantity. In the first case, we have to assume that pretonic vowel lengthening is not mirrored in the Hexapla. Origines marked open *e* by ε, e.g. in final stressed closed syllables in verbs (as ιδαββερ »he will speak«), in nouns from roots *mediae geminatae* (as εμ »mother«) and in *segolata* (as σεθρ »covering«), thus corresponding to ˇ in Babylonian vocalization, as well as in cases of Tiberian חֱ (where the Babylonian vocalization again uses ˇ)[20]. Otherwise, one will have to assume that Origines's system marks both quantity and quality. Since there were at his disposal only two signs, ε and η, to
* mark four sounds, viz. ę, ę̂, ẹ, ệ, he used ε to mark the first three, and η to designate ệ only. Since the first assumption is simpler and explains all the data so far known, one tends, prima facie, to prefer it.

On the other hand, one is inclined[21] to infer the length of pretonic vowels from the Septuagint[22], whose transcriptions, it seems, denote differences of quantity: ε marks a short *e* (corresponding inter alia to short *ṣere* in the Tiberian vocalization and to ˇ in the Babylonian, as in nouns *mediae geminatae* like Χετ and *segolata* like Εδεμ), η long *e* (both long *segol*, like Ιεφοννη, Μανασση[23], and long *ṣere*, as in stressed closed syllables, like Ιαζηρ, and in *pretonic open syllables*, like Ησαυ, Κηδαρ). Accordingly, if this analysis is correct, we possess evidence of the prolongation of pretonic vowels in open syllables from

[19] Who also hints that ε might not have marked a short vowel.—We do not, however, agree with the relevance of Brockelmann's objection that the quantity of Greek vowels has already broken down: the point is how Origines used them, and Sarauw in his brilliant paper has proved that he employed them quite consistently.—It is not clear to me what the intention of Brockelmann (op. cit., p. 346) was, when claiming that one need not accept the consequence of Sarauw's contention that the use of Babylonianˇ for »long *segol*« would prove that *pataḥ* is long too (as if this were impossible). As a matter of fact long *pataḥ* occurs, though rarely, in the Tiberian vocalization as well (v. Bergsträsser, op. cit. [n. 8], I p. 60).

[20] Thus Brønno's argumentation (op. cit., p. 196; v. also Z. Ben-Ḥayyīm, Studies in the Traditions of the Hebrew Language, 1954, p. 54 n. 61) as to the short ε in εχ is not to the point.

[21] I have not analyzed the Septuagint material as thoroughly as necessary; the view propounded is, accordingly, only provisional.

[22] V. especially Sarauw, op. cit., p. 59ff., who however, mixed up the transcriptions of Septuagint and Hexapla, further as to the proper nouns in the Pentateuch, exhibiting the oldest layer of the Septuagint, G. Lisowsky, Die Transkription der hebräischen Eigennamen des Pentateuchs in der Septuaginta, Diss. Basel 1940, whose conclusions, however, p. 124f., have to be corrected, since he did not realize short *ṣere*.

[23] Cf. also Sarauw, op. cit., p. 97 note 1.

the 3rd century B.C. Therefore, one tends to reject Brockelmann's theory[24], accepted by Bergsträsser[25], that this lengthening exhibits an artificial pronunciation of Hebrew, after it had become extinct as a language of communication. Now, after the discovery of the Bar-Kokhba letters, we do know that Hebrew was a living language (true, in its Mishnaic form) until the first part of the second century A.D.; so the Septuagint reflects the prolongation of pretonic vowels in a living language. Nevertheless, this phenomenon *may* be due to Aramaic influence, since bilingual Jews, speaking Aramaic as their first language, might have assumed Aramaic phonetic habits and become unable to pronounce short vowels in open unstressed syllables[26].

3. Features originating in the Author's Mother Tongue and appearing in Texts written in Another Language, because of the Author's Insufficient Mastery of the Latter

An outstanding example of this phenomenon in the domain of Semitic languages is texts intended to be written in Classical Arabic by authors who, for their deficiency in the mastery of Classical Arabic, gave rise to texts teeming with features of Middle Arabic, their mother tongue. Since however the Middle Arabic features alternate freely with Classical and pseudo-Classical ones, the linguist who wants to discern the true Middle Arabic phenomena has to distinguish them from Classical and pseudo-Classical forms by careful investigation of the different groups of texts. Only if a deviation from Classical Arabic occurs quite consistently, does it exhibit, prima facie, a Middle Arabic feature, which crept into the text because of the writer's deficient knowledge of the classical language[27]. *

As well known, the cuneiform tablets of *Tell-el-Amarna* are written in Accadian, but the scribes, because of their deficient mastery of it, inserted not only Canaanite glosses, which translate Accadian words, but also employed Canaanite expressions and forms in the Accadian context. These deviations from correct Accadian enable us to reconstruct *to some extent* the Canaanite mother tongue of these scribes. The pitfalls of this work are, however, manifold.

As a rule, it is assumed that Canaanite nouns in *el-Amarna* have preserved the case endings, at least in the absolute[28] and before

[24] V. ZA 14 (1899), p. 343f.; Grundriß... I, p. 101.

[25] Op. cit. (n. 8), I p. 117.

[26] For pitfalls of loan words cf. also Brockelmann, ZDMG 94 (1940), p. 356.

[27] For particulars v. J. Blau, The Emergence and Linguistic Background of Judaeo-Arabic..., 1965, passim.

[28] V.e.g. Z. S. Harris, Development of Canaanite Dialects, 1939, p. 41, § 14; p. 59, § 35, and especially J. Friedrich, Phönizisch-Punische Grammatik, 1951, §§92ı; 216.

pronominal suffixes[29]. I would, however, rather propound that the use of cases is only due to archaism, whereas in living speech they had already disappeared[30]. If this assumption is correct, it means that, in some Canaanite dialects at least, the case endings had disappeared some 500 prior to standing estimates[31]. This assumption is supported by the fact that[32] in *el-Amarna* the case endings, though often used in accordance with Classical usage, are frequently misused. Now, in contemporary Middle Babylonian and Middle Assyrian the custom was to preserve the case endings[33], and Canaanite scribes were no doubt taught to write in accordance therewith. *Had the Canaanite case endings,* which exactly paralleled the Accadian one, *still been in living usage, the Canaanite scribes would not have encountered any difficulty in learning the Accadian ones.* All they would have had to do is to have added the Canaanite endings to the Accadian nouns. It is difficult to imagine that Canaanite scribes who used case endings in living speech, erred so often in adding the same endings to Accadian nouns. But, of course, this conclusion too is an indirect one, as is everything that is based on texts reflecting in one language the influence of another.

[29] E.g. *ba-di-u* »in his hand«.

[30] Cf. also El-Amarna (ed. Knudzon) 243, 13 the gloss *l[i-e]l* »at night«, without case ending in adverbial usage, as against Biblical-Hebrew *lájla.* The glosses, however, as a rule do have case endings, either in accordance with their syntactic environment (as 74, 20; 46; 79, 36 in genitive) or standing in nominative against the context (as 69, 28; 143, 11).

[31] V. Friedrich, op. cit. (n. 28), § 92 2, who thinks that in the 9th century B.C. the differentiation between nominative/accusative with the pronominal suffix of the first person singular from genitive may have been an archaizing feature.—Similarly, one will suppose that the Egyptian transcriptions of the 19th dynasty showing final vowels after absolute nouns (v.e.g. Harris, op. cit., [n. 28], p. 41f., quoting Burchardt § 173) are archaizing (as far as they reflect the same dialects). The same would presumably apply to the verb in el-Amarna. Thus e.g. the permansive, which was confused with Canaanite perfect, sometimes terminates in el-Amarna in *-a* (v.e.g. E. Ebeling, BzA 8 (1910), p. 56). Since, however, the Accadian permansive has no vocalic ending, one will interpret this *-a* as the Canaanite perfect ending. Nevertheless, it stands to reason that, as the case endings, the short vocalic suffixes disappeared in the verb as well and were kept as archaism only. The same is presumably true as to the *-a* ending of the imperfect (for which v. W. L. Moran, loc. cit. [n. 1], p. 64; Orientalia 29 (1960), p. 1ff.), which are the more difficult to be evaluated syntactically. Cf. also infra n. 46 as to the fallacy of inferring from the absence of final short vowels in verbs that they were dropped: this may be due to Accadian usage.

[32] V. F. M. Th. de Liagre Böhl, Die Sprache der Amarnabriefe, 1909, p. 33.

[33] V.e.g. v. Soden, op. cit. (n. 15), p. 80e.

4. The Problem of Parallel Development

It was A. Meillet who in a famous paper[34] treated of the problem of parallel development in comparative Indo-European grammar. He emphasized that one must not lose sight of this fundamental difficulty, which pertains to the very essence of comparative linguistics. We have dealt with this problem in Arabic dialects[35] and endeavoured to show that they are not to be derived from a *koine*, but have become more and more similar to each other, inter alia, through the »general drift«. We have also tried to demonstrate that the vestiges of *tanwîn* were preserved in Middle Arabic dialects under about the same conditions as hundreds of years later in modern Bedouin vernaculars[36]. Moreover, in a lecture[37] we have expressed the opinion that many features attributed to various »Proto-languages« may have originated in the different dialects through parallel development. Now, the same may be true as to the Canaanite and Hebrew dialects. Features attributed to »Proto-Canaanite«, because they occur in all the Canaanite dialects known to us, may have arisen in them independently. So, for instance, the well known »Canaanite« sound shift *á* > *ô* has not reached Ugaritic[38]; therefore it stands to reason that this feature did not arise in »Proto-Canaanite«, but developed in the various dialects independently[39]. Accordingly[40], assuming parallel development (and contact between the dialects), the variation between the »Canaanite« dialects was apparently greater at the beginning of their history than later.

The possibility that various dialects developed more or less along parallel lines and not necessarily together may even affect our approach to decisive problems of the history of the Canaanite dialects: one of the moot points of Hebrew vocalization is the behaviour of stressed closed syllables in verbs in contrast to nouns. Whereas in nouns these syllables contain long vowels, they exhibit short ones in verbs. Several explanations have been propounded for this phenomenon, such as: the stress was different in verbs[41]; verbs rarely stood

[34] Included in his Linguistique historique et linguistique générale, I: Nouveau tirage 1958, p. 36–43.

[35] V. Blau, op. cit. (n. 27), p. 12ff.

[36] V. Blau, op. cit., p. 167ff.

[37] Delivered at the First International Conference on Semitic Studies, Jerusalem 1965, to be published by The Israel Academy of Sciences and Humanities.

[38] For the problem of the position of Ugaritic among the Canaanite dialects cf. the next §.

[39] Or also by mutual contact, v. the next §.—Therefore, it is always somewhat hazardous to fix the age of a phenomenon according to its occurrence in one or even several dialects (as does Harris, op. cit. [n. 28], e.g. p. 38, § 10).

[40] Pace Harris, op. cit., e.g. p. 91ff.

[41] Bergsträsser, op. cit. (n. 8), I p. 115ff.

in pausal position and therefore, in contradistinction to nouns, pausal forms did not reach them[42]; or, final short vowels disappeared in verbs before they were dropped in absolute nouns, so that the vowel between the second and third radical consonants in verbs came to stand in a closed syllable and was not lengthened[43]. The last explanation is, * it seems, the most plausible one[44]: verbs lost their short vocalic endings in Biblical Hebrew before absolute nouns and their, now, final vowel, standing in a closed syllable (*jirkAb* < **jirkabu*), was not lengthened, in contrast to absolute nouns (*dâḇAr*, which, at this stage, was still **dabaru* etc.)[45]. In *el-Amarna*, however, verbs did not drop their final

[42] Brockelmann, Grundriß... I, p. 106, idem, ZDMG 94 (1940), p. 336; Bauer-Leander, op. cit. (n. 12), p. 187; H. Birkeland, Akzent und Vokalismus im Althebräischen, 1940, p. 20ff.

[43] Grimme, op. cit. (n. 4), p. 51; Cantineau, BEOIFD 2 (1932), p. 141.

[44] Bergsträsser's theory fails since, because of the pausal forms of verbs, he is forced to assume alternative stress patterns of verbs (v. Bergsträsser, op. cit., I p. 162); the theory of regarding long vowels in final closed syllables of nouns as extensions of pausal forms does not hold water because of the occurrence of nouns *mediae geminatae* with short vowel (as *gan* »garden«) alongside with long pausal forms (as *gân*; cf. already Sarauw, op. cit. [n. 13], p. 69 n. 1): one would have expected a long form (as *gân*) in context as well. The occurrence of the short form *gan* < **gannu*, etc. clearly proves that the short vowel is due to the syllable being primarily closed, and one is inclined to assume that verbs exhibited closed final syllables earlier than absolute nouns of similar pattern.

[45] Cf. also *qeṭâlatḵâ* »she killed you«, where the verb with suffixes, which according to Brockelmann, Grundriss..., I p. 108o and Bauer-Leander, op. cit. (n. 12), p. 187, should have been influenced by the pausal form, has penult *pataḥ* rather * than *qameṣ*, presumably owing to the closed syllable.—It stands to reason that in the imperfect short final vowels were dropped early by the impact of the apocopate, and 3rd person masculine singular of the perfect was then influenced by the imperfect devoid of final short vowel, since this vowel was felt as mark of nouns as against verbs (**jiṣḥaqu* [noun] : *jiṣḥaq* [verb] = **jaʃẹnu* [participle] : X; X = *jaʃẹn* [perfect]. Admittedly, nouns like *jiṣḥâq* are quite rare.—Cf. already Grimme, op. cit. (n. 4), p. 51f. By this wording Brockelmann's objection, Grundriß..., I p. 107, becomes unsubstantial).—Prima facie, one would think that *lex Philippi* contradicts the assumption of the early disappearance of final short vowels in verbs: whereas in st. cs. *i* > *a* in final stressed closed syllables (**zaqinu* > *zeqan*), presumably because the final syllable was closed early, this shift does not take place in absolute nouns (**zaqinu* > *zaqện*) and verbs (*zaqina* > *zaqẹn*), on the face of it, because the last syllable was at that time still open. This assumption, however, is fallacious. Just as nouns *mediae geminatae* like *libbu* »heart« change into *läbb* in Babylonian vocalization, λεβ in the Hexapla (cf. Χετ in the Septuagint), apparently through *lex Philippi* (in ultimate closed syllable *with main stress i* > *e*, rather than > *a*, cf. Tiberian *qẹn*, Babylonian **qän* in absolute, as against *qan* in construct), and it is only in the Tiberian system that it becomes ẹ̆ owing to the stress, so also, through *lex Philippi*, it seems, **judabbir* becomes *jᵉdabbär* in Babylonian vocalization (v.e.g. Bergsträsser, op. cit. [n. 8], II p. 95),

short vowels before absolute nouns[46]. Therefore, if we were to consider the disappearance of final short vowels a feature that affected common »Proto-Canaanite«, we would be forced to abandon the theory of the dropping of final short vowels before absolute nouns in Hebrew verbs. On the other hand, if one presumes that the dropping of final short vowels took place at different stages in various Canaanite dialects, owing to parallel (but not entirely identical) development, there is no reason to reject the assumption that in Biblical Hebrew, in contradistinction to dialects mirrored in the texts of *el-Amarna*, final short vowels dropped in verbs earlier than in absolute nouns[47].

5. The Problem of Dialect Contact and Dialect Mixture

Similar features in related dialects may be due not only to common origin and/or parallel development, but also to dialect contact and even to dialect mixture[48]. It is in accordance with modern language theory (prevailing in Indo-European linguistics as far back as the seventies of the last century) to assume that linguistic changes spread, owing to contact between dialects, like waves over a speech area (the so-called »wave theory«). In our opinion, J. Friedrich[49] was right in claiming that, in accordance with the wave theory, the Canaanite lingual type is not the forerunner of the linguistic process, with the various Canaanite dialects splitting off from a more or less

---

ιδαββερ in the Hexapla and only in the Tiberian system *j^edabbeṛ*. Since ˇ stands in the Babylonian system for both Tiberian *pataḥ* and *segol*, in *qal* perfect 3rd person masc. sing. *qaṭal* and *qaṭẹl* became identical. This is the reason that in Babylonian vocalization *qaṭal* has ousted **qaṭil* even more than in the Tiberian system (v.e.g. Bergsträsser, op. cit., II p. 77). As far as *qaṭẹl* occurs in the Babylonian system, it is, it seems, due to the analogy of pausal forms: this assumption is corroborated by the fact that it is in the pause that **qatil* is relatively frequent (v. Bergsträsser op. cit., II p. 76f.). One would presume that it was through the analogy of pausal forms with vocalic afformatives (like *qaṭẹ̄la*)that *qatẹl* persisted in pause rather than in context.

[46] V. supra n. 31. It is even possible that final short vowels in verbs subsisted longer than in nouns, because (v. loc. cit.) it is only because of the apparent breakdown of the case system that one is inclined to assume that final short vowels were dropped in verbs also already at the *el-Amarna* period in living speech (pace Cantineau, BEOIFD 1 (1931), p. 96 n. 1; 2 (1932), p. 141; Birkeland, op. cit. [n. 42], p. 22: the absence of short final vowels in verbs in *el-Amarna* quoted there, corresponds to Accadian usage! Cf. supra n. 31, in fine).

[47] For another case of parallel development cf. Brønno, op. cit. (n. 17), p. 310.

[48] Cf. H. Schuchardt's well known bon mot (H. Schuchardt-Brevier, 1922^1, p. 131) that there is no language not mixed up to some extent. In general cf. e.g. H. Paul, Prinzipien der Sprachgeschichte, 1920^5, p. 390ff.

[49] V. e.g. op. cit. (n. 28), p. 1.

uniform speech (namely »Proto-Canaanite«), but itself emerged only as the consequence of the linguistic development[50]. At any rate, it is * difficult to regard Ugaritic, so closely related to the Canaanite languages, as such *according to the familytree theory*. I do not claim this because of the lack of *á* > *ô* (and similar features) in Ugaritic, since one may consider it a late shift, which did not reach Ugarit, but because of *ð* > *d*, as against Canaanite *ð* > *z*. And one must not profess that Ugaritic *d* is polyphonic[51]. Polyphonic letters occur in alphabets which have been taken over as such by the speakers of a second language without adding new letters to it: if the second language contained additional phonemes, its speakers were forced to mark them by the existing letters which thus became polyphonic[52]. In Ugaritic, however, new letters were added at the end of the alphabet. Accordingly, it seems fallacious to consider Ugaritic *d* as polyphonic[53]. Therefore, since *ð* shifted in Ugaritic to *d* rather than to *z*, the shift *ð* > *z*, at least, must not be regarded as being handed down from »Proto-Canaanite«, but rather as occurring separately in various dialects, spreading by dialect contact and/or (v. § 4) parallel development. And it stands to reason that this may apply to several other »Canaanite shifts« as well[54].

As well known, the notion of dialect mixture has been already employed by linguists dealing with Biblical Hebrew. H. Bauer[55] even claimed that Hebrew is a mixed language; his notion of language mixture, however, was severely criticized[56], and in general correctly. One will not, it is true, concur with claims[57] that the transfer of whole paradigms from one dialect to another is unreasonable[58]; but one will

[50] If this assumption is correct, there does not exist anything like »Proto-Canaanite« (and perhaps »Proto-Hebrew« either). This is the reason that I wrote these two terms between quotation marks throughout this paper.

[51] The use of another sign corresponding in some words to Proto-Semitic *ð* is, it seems, an archaic feature in Ugaritic.

[52] Thus in Biblical Hebrew ש marks both *šîn* and *śîn*, and in Old Aramaic e.g. *z* marks both *z* and *ð*.

[53] One could, however, assume that the new letters were not added to the Ugaritic alphabet until the poliphonic use of *d* was well established. But this seems unlikely.

[54] It was in the same way that modern Arabic dialects developed, v. Blau, op. cit. (n. 27), p. 13ff., and the paper quoted *supra* note 37.

[55] V. e.g. Bauer–Leander, op. cit. (n. 12), passim; H. Bauer, Zur Frage der Sprachmischung im Hebräischen, 1924.

[56] V. especially G. Bergsträsser, OLZ 26 (1923), p. 253ff.; B. Landsberger, OLZ 29 (1926), p. 967ff.

[57] V. OLZ 26 (1923), p. 254; 29 (1926), p. 975.

[58] By transfer of nouns exhibiting e.g. the form *qaṭṭâl* and denoting professions etc., this form *might* have become productive; cf. the frequent occurrence of *qâṭôl* in

hesitate to accept Bauer's view of the cardinal point of his theory of the Hebrew verbal system, viz. that the syntactic characteristics of the verbal systems of two languages mixed have been taken over in the main without alteration[59]. Moreover, in principle, the confrontation of two dialects only, Canaanite and Hebrew[60], is an oversimplification of the linguistic situation of Palestine, which was much more involved, various tribes speaking different dialects influencing each other[61]. Moreover, one must not lose sight of migrations of tri-

Mishnaic Hebrew, as well as of forms of *pi'el* of *mediae infirmae* like *qijjem* (attested already in late Biblical Hebrew, v.e.g. Bergsträsser, op. cit. [n. 8], II p. 151r) or of *hif'il* of these verbs like *hôḇîn* (v.e.g. Brockelmann, Grundriß ..., I p. 616, idem, ZDMG 94 (1940), p. 352; cf. already Biblical Hebrew *hôḇîʃ*; no doubt due to the impact of Aramaic; cf. also U. Weinreich, Languages in Contact, 1953, p. 31ff., for the transfer of morphemes from one language to another). For the mixture of declination and conjugation systems of languages mutually intelligible v. A. Scherer apud C. Mohrmann, etc., Trends in European and American Linguistics 1930–1960, 1962, p. 229, 231. (One has to admit, it is true, that the notion of mutual intelligibility is not always quite clear, v.e.g. Schuchardt-Brevier [v. n. 48], p. 142). Cf. also for morphological mixture in the communal Baghdadi dialects H. Blanc, Communal Dialects in Baghdad, 1964, passim, e.g. p. 106 and notes 97a (belonging to p. 64) and 98a (belonging to p. 66).—Accordingly, *in principle*, even Hebrew *qâm* (instead of expected *qôm*) *might* have been borrowed from another dialect, though it may be explained as due to patterning as well: many items of the paradigms of the perfect and participle of *qal* and *nif'al* of *mediae infirmae* preserved *â* (being unstressed) or even exhibited *ă* (standing in *penult* closed syllable). The original paradigm of *qal*, perfect was perhaps: **qâmâku* > **qâmôku, qămta, qămti, *qâma* > **qôma*, etc. The participle: **qâmu* > **qôm, *qâmatu* > **qôma, qâmîm, qâmôṯ. Nif'al*, perfect: **nasâgâku* > **nasâg̱ôku*, etc. (and similarly the participle, along the same lines as *qal*). Now in *qal* the form with *â/a* prevailed, but in *nif'al* those with *ô*, presumably through the influence of the imperfect *jissôg̱* < **jissâg̱*.

59 V. Bergsträsser, op. cit. (n. 8), II p. III n. 1.

60 Bauer–Leander, it is true, admit other dialectal features as well, v. e.g. op. cit. (n. 12), p. 28ff., 510v, 512d. Nevertheless, they mainly content themselves with these two dialects. The same applies to some extent to Birkeland, op. cit. (n. 42), in spite of his statement, p. 14, that waves of migrations from the desert overflowed Canaan almost in every period: he immediately adds that »such restitutions«, as far as it affects Hebrew, repose upon the Israelitic migrations (which, however, also took place, in his mind, in several stages). As against Birkeland's view that the Jews constituted the nomad element, v.e.g. W. F. Albright, From Stone Age to Christianity, 1957², p. 279. As to dialects cf. also Brockelmann, ZDMG 94 (1940), p. 338; Friedrich, op. cit. (n. 28), p. 2f.; Bergsträsser, op. cit. (n. 8), I p. 11; Ben-Ḥayyîm, op. cit. (n. 20), p. 63.

61 Cf. e.g. Albright, op. cit. (note 60) p. 205, 238ff., 279. E. Schwyzer's words, Griechische Grammatik... I, 1939,¹ p. 75f., on the dialect forming factors of Greece apply, mutatis mutandis, to Canaan as well, but our actual knowledge of the dialects is even more restricted.

bes[62], as well as of the fact that a centre of (linguistic) prestige came into being comparatively late. On the one hand, the political and topographic conditions favoured dialectal partition, on the other, not only did linguistic features spread over this speech area, but literary features as well, as borne out e.g. by literary affinities between Hebrew and Ugaritic[63]. Since our knowledge of the actual linguistic features of these dialects is exceedingly scanty[64], we often grope in the dark, without knowing whether a particular feature is due to sound shift or contact between dialects. Thus[65], it is assumed that Proto-Semitic *ð* preceding *r*/*l* may shift to *d* in Hebrew rather than *z*: *ḥdl, ndr, qdr*[66]. They may, however, be due to borrowing, not only from Aramaic, but also from some Canaanite dialect which, like Ugaritic, has been affected by the shift *ð* > *d*[67]. The same doubts arise as to Hebrew *nṭr* < **nẓr*[68]. Here, however, the possibility of borrowing

[62] As that of Dan. Birkeland, op. cit. (n. 42), often uses the term »restitution«, meaning the introduction of forms already lost in a dialect from a dialect exhibiting a more »primitive« lingual form. (He is, however, not always quite successful when employing this term, v.e.g. Ben-Ḥayyîm, op. cit. [n. 20], p. 16 n. 5. Similarly *lajla* »night« [Birkeland, op. cit., p. 13] is not due to restitution; it represents originally, it seems, *lajl* with the adverbial ending **-ah, -aj* being preserved because standing in an open stressed penult syllable).

[63] Literary features spreading, know even less limits than linguistic ones, cf. the impact of Hebrew Bible and of Greek (v. Schwyzer, op. cit. [n. 61], p. 151) on European languages. In the case of closely related languages as Ugaritic and Hebrew, the literary influence is apt to bring with it direct linguistic impact as well, since e.g. phrases containing related, but not identical words were likely to be taken over as such, thus adding new shades of meaning to these words. (As to cases of »aberrant borrowing« between languages mutually intelligible, cf. L. Bloomfield, Language, 1933, p. 468f.).

[64] Cf. also the fact that we cannot trace Mishnaic Hebrew (exhibiting e.g. the use of demonstrative pronouns, without article attached either to the noun or to the pronoun, as *bajiṯ ze* »this house«, a feature alien to Aramaic and therefore original in Hebrew) to its ancestor in Biblical times. And what do we know e.g. about Moabitic? Cf. in general Harris, op. cit. (n. 28), p. 9ff. and also 38.

[65] I owe this remark to A. Dotan, who is about to deal with this sound shift and to show that its extension is wider than generally assumed.

[66] V. Th. Nöldeke, ZDMG 40 (1886), p. 729 n. 1; S. Fraenkel, ZDMG 70 (1905), p. 252; Brockelmann, Grundriß..., I p. 237; W. Gesenius-F. Buhl,... Handwörterbuch..., 1921[17], s.vv.

[67] Similarly, some scholars regard phenomena as being due to sound shifts, whereas others consider them loans, cf. e.g. Sarauw, op. cit. (n. 13), p. 106, 108, 109f. as against H. Bauer—P. Leander, Grammatik des Biblisch-Aramäischen, 1927, p. 147, 186y, 233f. respectively.

[68] Ancient South-Arabic *nẓr* alternating with *nṣr* does not prove anything (pace Gesenius-Buhl, op. cit. [n. 66], s.v. *nṭr*), because in the later period of that language *ẓ* is apt to become *ṣ*; v. M. Höfner, Altsüdarabische Grammatik, 1943, § 11.

becomes more likely, since, in the sense of »guarding« at least, *nṭr* has the doublet *nṣr*, thus rendering the soundshift *ẓ* > *ṭ* before *r* improbable here.

6. Plurilinear Development[69]

There exists, however, another difficulty which makes it almost impossible to succeed in reconstructing »Proto-Hebrew«, etc. We may well manage to show how a form might have developed, without being, however, sure whether the actual process took place along these lines only. We shall illustrate our case by one example:

One of the central problems of Semitic verbal formation is the question of whether or not the so-called weak verbs are to be traced back to bi-literal roots. Methodologically, Bergsträsser[70] was right in claiming that this problem can only be solved by foregoing a general decision and critically analyzing different formgroups in the various Semitic languages. Accordingly, *verba tertiae infirmae*, for example, which can in all their forms be explained as derived from tri-literal roots, are, as far as Hebrew grammar is concerned, tri-literal[71]. This is, however, by no means sure. The Hebrew verb *galâ* »was clear«, for instance[72], might have developed from »Proto-Hebrew« **galaja*, but *banâ* »built«, for instance, might have been *banâ* in »Proto-Hebrew« as well. Thus it affects Hebrew grammar too whether or not there were bi-literal roots which later developed into *tertiae infirmae*. It may well be (but this cannot be proved) that even forms that *can* be derived from tri-literal roots, actually were bi-literal in »Proto-Hebrew«[73]. Moreover, one is inclined to assume that it was the occurrence of bi-literal roots that served in some cases as a kind of catalyst, affecting tri-literal roots containing a »weak« letter, and, on the other hand, it was the existence of such tri-literal roots that transferred the bi-literal ones into the category of tri-literals. Thus, it has been claimed against the theory of bi-literal roots[74] that it does not stand to reason that e.g. **mawt* «death» and **bajn* »intervening space« are younger than the respective verbs. Moreover, why should the noun of **mît*, **jimât* »to die« be **mawt* rather than **mât*?! We assume,

[69] Cf. for this expression Y. Malkiel, Philology 8 (1954), p. 187.

[70] V. OLZ 26 (1923), p. 477–81; idem, op. cit. (n. 8), II p. 3.

[71] V. Bergsträsser, op. cit. (n. 8), II p. 169.

[72] I am chosing verbs perchance only.

[73] Since our knowledge of Ugaritic morphology is so restricted, one will not venture the suggestion that the occurrence of Ugaritic *tertiae infirmae* with and without *j* is due to tri-literal and bi-literal influences respectively.

[74] V. especially Brockelmann, Grundriß..., I p. 606, who was then a partisan of the tri-literal theory.

however, that *mât* etc. was originally tri-literal: **mawita,* derived from **mawt.* Alongside with these forms there were bi-literal ones, as e.g.[75] *râm, jarûm* »to be high« (or even with short vowel, as perhaps *qăm, jaqŭm* »to stand up«). Now, by some sound shift **jamwut* e.g. developed into *jamût,* thus becoming identical with *jarûm* (and **jamwutna* e.g. into *jamŭtna,* thus becoming identical with *jaqŭmna*). Now, through analogy, the various forms of tri-literal and bi-literal verbs became mixed up. Nevertheless, all one can do is to show how the various forms *might* have developed, without being sure that this was the actual process[76].

7. We have tried to show how unlikely it is that we should actually succeed in reconstructing »Proto-Hebrew« and »Proto-Canaanite« (if they existed at all). In some cases, as in that of the history of the so-called »weak« verbs, we have only endeavoured to show that plurilinear development is probable according to what we know, without being able to show what the actual linguistic process was. In other cases, as in the transliterations of Origines and in the glosses of the *el-Amarna* tables and their deviations from »Classical« Accadian, we have tried to arrive at solutions other than the accepted ones. Yet what we have claimed for the general difficulties of reconstruction, applies to our solutions as well: one only tries to offer the simplest theory that is in accordance with the facts known, without being at all sure that the actual development was not quite different.

[75] I am again chosing verbs perchance only.

[76] Birkeland, op. cit. (n. 42), p. 103, assumes that the Isrealite nomads introduced **qawama* instead of Canaanite **qôm.* Thus he assumes that these forms emanated from two different dialects. According to our assumption, they might have existed together in the same dialect. Nevertheless, we do not regard it as necessary to explain *qâm* (instead of *qôm*) in this way, cf. *supra* note 58.

Additions and Corrections

to **p. 266**.*n. 2. 9*: See now below pp. 299ff.

to **p. 266**.*n. 2.11*: See *Studies* pp. 297–305.

to **p. 267**.*n. 2. 12*: For the possibility of (Nabatean) Aramaic influence on the use of *alif maqṣūra bi-ṣūrat al-yā* in words in which Aramaic *ī* corresponds to Arabic *ā* see *Studies* p. 34 addendum (as also אָחֳרֵי 'other' (fem. sg.), # Arabic أُخْرَى; cf. also for the passive participle of derived verbal themes מְרְמֵי, # Arabic مُزْجًى. On the other hand the Nabatean goddess אלעזא corresponds to Arabic العُزَّى). For the spelling with *alif maqṣūra bi-ṣūrat al-yā* in general see W. Diem, *Orientalia* 48.238–40 (1979).

to **p. 267**.*n. 2, end*: One will rather posit that at first Nabatean Arabic was strongly influenced by Nabatean Aramaic. Then Standard Arabic passed from mere imitation of of Nabatean Aramaic, which gave rise to forms that looked as if representing Standard Arabic pausal forms and were re-interpreted as such, to genuine pausal spelling, spelling *tā marbūṭa* even in construct; see *Studies* 14ff.

p. 268. *n. 13*: For a detailed analysis of the status of pretonic syllables see supra pp. 107ff. The alternation of pretonic lengthening and pretonic doubling (*Grammar*, 32.1ff.) also attests to the length of pretonic open syllables.

to **p. 269**.*n. 15.9*: The tendency to prevent the reduction of a short vowel in an open (unstressed) syllable caused also pretonic lengthening in Hebrew (if one accepts the theory of Aramaic influence, v. infra p. 271.8).

to **p. 270**.*14*: According to this second assumption forms like ηλαυ Psalms 32.6, Θηληχ 32.8 would reflect pretonic lengthening. Yet Field (I, p. lxxi) has for (אמֻנים) שֹׁמֵר Is. 26.2 σωςμηρ, and if this form is indeed in construct (as it seems), it would reflect the transcription of a short *ẹ* by η !

to **p. 271**.*18ff.*: Read for "Middle Arabic" in the whole paragraph "Neo-Arabic", Middle Arabic being the language of texts in which classical, pseudo-classical and vulgar elements alternate, whereas the vulgar features should be called Neo-Arabic.

to p. **272**: A. F. Rainey, *Canaanite in the Amarna Tablets*, Leiden 1996, i, 170 attributes, however, the deviations from the correct use of the case ending attested in El-Amarna by and large simply to scribal errors, mainly caused by the very complex cuneiform script. If one accepts Rainey's argumentation, my claim that the use of cases is only due to archaism, has to be disregarded.

to **p. 273.***n. 35*: Cf. also G. Bergsträsser, *Einführung in die semitischen Sprachen*, München 1928, p. 156, Havers 46.5–7; 136.§115, further G. A. Rendsburg, 'Parallel Development in Mishnaic Hebrew, Colloquial Arabic, and other Varieties of Spoken Semitic', *Leslau Festschrift* , pp. 1265–77; supra pp. 126ff.

to **p. 273.***n. 36*: Cf. also *ZAL* 25 (1993), pp. 95–99

to **p. 273.***n. 37*: See *Studies* pp. 361–67.

to **p. 274.***6* : For details see *ZDMG* 133 (1983) pp. 24–29 = *Hebrew Linguistics*, pp. 72–76.

to **p. 274.***n. 45.4ff.*: For a more powerful explanation see supra p. 32.5

to **p. 276.***3ff.*: For the affinity of Ugaritic to Canaanite see infra pp. 339ff.

to **p. 279.***n. 69*: Malkiel also dubbed it multiple causation. See also Havers 46.5–7; 136§115.

to **p. 280.***10*: Cf. also supra pp. 169ff.; 262–63.

A Misunderstood Medieval Translation of *śered* (Isaiah 44:13) and Its Impact on Modern Scholarship

One of the characteristics of Jacob Milgrom's scholarly work is his knowledge of medieval Jewish tradition. It is for this reason that I am offering him this small treatise dealing with a misunderstood medieval Judeo-Arabic translation that gave rise to a Jewish pseudotradition that ultimately influenced modern scholarship as well.

Saadya Gaon (882–942 C.E.) was one of the greatest figures of medieval Judeo-Arabic society, in which Jewry reached one of its apogees. He was foremost in almost every field of Jewish scholarship and instrumental in the absorption of Islamic-Arabic culture into Judaism. One of his great achievements was the translation of the Bible into Arabic. In a very short time, it became the standard Judeo-Arabic translation, sometimes even accepted by Gentiles, deeply influencing the linguistic usage of later generations.[1] It is against this background of its decisive influence that the spread of the pseudotradition we are dealing with,

1. See J. Blau, "Some Instances Reflecting the Influence of Saadya Gaon's Bible Translation on Later Judeo-Arabic Writings," *Occident and Orient: A Tribute to the Memory of Alexander Scheiber* (ed. R. Dan; Budapest: Akadémiai Kiadó / Leiden: Brill, 1988) 21–29. *

emerging from a misunderstood passage of Saadya Gaon's translation, becomes comprehensible.

The hapax legomenon in Isa 44:13, בַּשֶּׂרֶד (יתארהו) is translated by Saadya Gaon באלרקאן (ויחליה), which means '(he embellishes it) with a plane'. The word رُقان 'carpenter's plane' is a rare Arabic word, absent from ordinary dictionaries, yet cited by I. Löw and S. Fraenkel,[2] derived through Aramaic (including Judeo-Aramaic) from Greek *rykanē*. In Spain in the eleventh century it was already unknown, and therefore Ibn Janah, the greatest Hebrew philologist of the Middle Ages (he died in the first half of the eleventh century at Saragossa) mistook it for the much more usual رِقان 'saffron' (< Aramaic **yarqawnāʾ*).[3] This is Ibn Janah's wording:[4]

יתארהו בשרד ירסמה באלרקאן. ואלתרקין פי כלאם אלערב הו תזיין אלבית באלורס. פאלמעני פי יתארהו בשרד אנמא הו רסם אלנג̇אר באלכ̇יט אלמצבוג באלחמרה̈ מא יריד קטעה מן אלעוד ואכ̇ראג̇ה ענה באלאלה̈ אלתי יקאל להא ענדנא אלמצ̇לע ויסמיהא אלעבראניון מקצוע פי קולה יעשהו במקצועות. ואנמא לכ̇צנא פי בשרד הד̇א אלתלכ̇יץ כלה למא ראינא אלמתרג̇מין יתרג̇מונה באלרקאן ולם נדרי נחן באלרקאן גיר מא ד̇כרנאה. ורבמא כאן תפסיר בשרד באלאלה̈ אלפלאניה̈ אי באלה̈ מא מן אלאלאת כמא קיל ובמחוגה יתארהו.

יתארהו בשרד 'he will draw it with رقان'. The use of رقان in Arabic means 'to embellish the house with saffron'. יתארהו בשרד means that the carpenter marks with a red-dyed[5] cord what he wants to cut from the timber and take out with the tool that we call *miḍlaᶜ*[6] and the Hebrews call מקצוע, as it is

2. I. Löw, *Aramäische Pflanzennamen* (Leipzig: Engelmann, 1881) 10, the note continued from the preceding page; S. Fraenkel, *Die arabischen Fremdwörter im Arabischen* (Leiden: Brill, 1886) 255.

3. Ibid., 149.

4. Abu ʾlwalid Marwan ibn Janaḥ, *The Book of Hebrew Roots [Kitab al-usul]* (ed. A. Neubauer; Oxford: Clarendon, 1873–75) 749, lines 11–18 s.v. *śrd*.

5. 'Red' *ʾaḥmar* includes yellow; see, e.g., W. Fischer, *Farb- und Formbezeichnungen in der Sprache der altarabischen Dichtung* (Wiesbaden: Harrassowitz, 1965) 235.

6. *Miḍlaᶜ*, indeed, means 'plane', as clearly demonstrated by Ibn Janah, *Book of Hebrew Roots*, 642, 14–17 s.v. קצע:

> אלקאף ואלצאד ואלעין יקציע מבית יקשרה. ומן הד̇א אלמעני אשתק לאלה̈ אלנג̇אר אלמסמאה̈ ענדנא מצ̇לעא והי אלאלה̈ אלתי יקשר בהא וג̇ה אלעוד חתי יסאויה וימלסה ויסמי מקצוע כמא קיל יעשהו במקצעות וקאל פיה אלתרגום באזמילא.
>
> קצע: יקציע מבית 'he peels it'. From this meaning derivation is effected for (designating) the carpenter's tool which is called at our place [Spain] *miḍlaᶜ*, and it is the tool with which the surface of timber is peeled till it makes it even and smooth, and it is called מקצוע, as it is said יעשהו במקצעות. And the Targum explained it 'with knife'.

Yet the *miḍlaᶜ* served several purposes, not only for planing and smoothing wood, but also as a knife (see above: וקאל פיה אלתרגום באזמילא 'and the Targum explained it "with

said יעשהו במקצועות ('he will make it with planes'). We have explained all this about שרד only because we saw that the translators[7] translate it by رقان, and as to رقان, we only know what we have mentioned. And perhaps בשרד means 'with such and such a tool', i.e., with a certain tool, as it is said, 'and he will draw it with the compass'.

This lemma clearly reflects Ibn Janah's uneasiness. It is quite obvious that he considered himself forced by tradition to accept the interpretation of שרד as 'saffron', although his fine philological instinct warned him against this understanding and, correctly in my view, suggested to him its comprehension as a carpenter's tool. And even after he had stated that the marking with saffron was followed by the cutting of the timber (and thus introduced the carpenter's tool by the back door) and that he had only accepted the interpretation of שרד because of the (alleged) tradition, he did not refrain from affirming that perhaps (nevertheless) שרד denoted a carpenter's tool, thus giving a new expression to his dissatisfaction with the understanding of שרד as a red-dyed cord.

And indeed, رقان in Saadya Gaon's translation of Isa 44:13 must not be understood as 'saffron', as if it designated a red-dyed cord with which the carpenter marked the timber. This is proven not only by the context, as Ibn Janah's subtle philological sense had taught him, but even more so by David ben Abraham's interpretation of שרד:

יתארהו בשרד והי מן אלאת אלנג̇ארה̈ להא סן חאד יעמל בהא אלחדוד פי אלכ̇שב יקאל לה אלרקאן.

יתארהו בשרד is a carpenter's tool having a sharp point by which the edges of wood are made, called رقان.[8]

---

knife" '), to cut from timber (see Ibn Janah, above, s.v. שרד):

רסם אלנג̇אר באלכ̇יט אלמצבוג באלחמרה̈ מא יריד קטעה מן אלעוד ואכ̇ראג̇ה ענה באלאלה̈ אלתי יקאל להא ענדנא אלמצ̇לע

that the carpenter marks with a red-dyed cord what he wants to cut from the timber and take out with the tool that we call *miḍlaᶜ*

And, indeed, David ben Abraham (see below) describes its synonym رقان as

והי מן אלאת אלנג̇ארה̈ להא סן חאד יעמל בהא אלחדוד פי אלכ̇שב יקאל לה אלרקאן

and it is a carpenter's tool having a sharp point by which the edges of wood are marked, called رقان.

7. The word *mutarjimūn* includes both translators and commentators. It stands to reason that Ibn Janah alludes here, in addition to Saadya Gaon, to commentators, including interpretations contained in biblical dictionaries; cf. the quotation below from David ben Abraham's Bible dictionary (see n. 8).

8. S. L. Skoss, *The Hebrew-Arabic Dictionary of the Bible Known as Kitāb Jāmiᶜ al-Alfāẓ (Agrōn) of David ben Abraham al-Fāsī* (Yale Oriental Series, Researches 20–21; New Haven: Yale University Press, 1936–45) 2.354, lines 105–7.

It even stands to reason that it was Saadya Gaon's translation of the passage in Isaiah that influenced David ben Abraham's interpretation.[9] Nevertheless, Ibn Janah's words, that he only knew رقان as a red-dyed cord, had enough impact that even after David ben Abraham's text had become known, a scholar of Simhah Pinsker's stature was deterred from understanding it correctly, translating יקאל לה אלרקאן by: ונקרא רקאן (הוא מין צמח Henne שצובעין בו אדום) 'And it is called رقان (i.e., a certain plant, henna to dye red)'.[10]

This interpretation of Ibn Janah, based on the misunderstanding of Saadya's translation, influenced Jewish interpretation,[11] which, in its turn, clearly influenced modern scholarship. Among the classical Jewish commentators, Ibn Janah was followed, for example, by Abraham ibn Ezra (ca. 1089, Toledo, through ca. 1164) in his commentary to Isa 44:13;[12] David Qimḥi (Narbonne, 1160–1235), both in his commentary and in his dictionary;[13] and Isaac Abravanel (1437–1508).[14] Here the difference between the master, even if he errs, and epigones is distinctly reflected. Whereas Ibn Janah clearly saw the difficulties inherent in the interpretation of שרד as '(a cord with) dye' and qualified his statement, his epigones disregarded the weakness of this understanding and accepted it without qualification. The impact of this interpretation continued in later Jewish exegesis. Thus, for example, it was simply adopted by Yehiel Hillel Altschul (middle of the seventeenth century) in his lexicological glossary מצודת ציון and by *The Encyclopedia of the World of the Bible, Isaiah*,[15] which cites S. D. Luzzatto, who cites it as the first of two possibilities.[16] It was preferred by S. J. Fin; N. H. Tur-Sinai, the editor of Ben Yehuda's dictionary; S. E. Hartom; *Encyclopaedia Biblica*; and A. Hakham, who (justly) wondered what the linguistic base of this interpretation could be.[17] How

9. For the influence of Saadya's translation on David ben Abraham, cf. Blau, "Instances Reflecting the Influence," passim.

10. S. Pinsker, *Lickute Kadmoniot: Zur Geschichte des Karaismus und der karäischen Literatur* (Vienna: della Torre, 1860) ריב, 2.

11. As also reflected in Pinsker's misinterpretation.

12. He simply defined שרד as a 'dye', מין ממיני צבעונים.

13. In the dictionary s.v. The dictionary has been edited several times; Qimḥi translates Ibn Janah's wording almost literally; see the next note.

14. Isaac Abravanel, *Commentary to the Latter Prophets* (Jerusalem: Tora va-Da^c^at, 1956–57) 2ľ4b, line 5 from bottom. Both Qimḥi and Abravanel exactly follow Ibn Janah. They translate his 'red-dyed cord' אלכ̇יט אלמצבוג באלחמרה̈ by חוט הצבע, literally 'a cord of color', i.e., 'a dyed cord'.

15. *Entsiqlopedya Olam ha-Tanakh, Yesha^c^ya* (ed. M. Haran et al.; Jerusalem and Ramat Gan: Revivim, 1986) 216.

16. S. D. Luzzatto, *Commentary to the Book of Jesaiah* (Tel Aviv: Dvir, 1970).

17. S. J. Fin, *The Thesaurus: The Thesaurus of the Language of the Bible and the Mishnah* (vol. 4; Warsaw: Akhiasaf, 1921); E. ben Yehuda, *A Complete Dictionary of Ancient and Modern Hebrew* (ed. N. H. Tur-Sinai; London: Yoseloff, 1959) 16.7614b n. 3 (on the other

deeply rooted the understanding of שרד as 'dye' in Jewish tradition had become is reflected in Malbim's (Meir Löb ben Yehiel Michael, 1809–79) commentary מקראי קודש on the Prophets and Hagiographa. It consists of two sections, the explanation of words and the explanation of sense. In the first section, on Isa 44:13, Malbim interpreted שרד as שרט, that is, 'to scratch and incise, in order to cut out timber', yet in the explanation of sense he unwittingly spoke of "שרד and dye"![18]

This understanding of שרד was accepted by Christian biblical exegetes as well, mainly because of the deep influence David Qimḥi's works exerted, and later, in the nineteenth century when Ibn Janah's work was rediscovered, also through his impact. In the Authorized Version it is translated by '(he marketh it out with a) line', the line reflecting, it seems, Qimḥi's dyed 'cord'. On the other hand, Luther translated it *Röthelstein* 'red chalk', another development of the *dyed* cord. Luther's translation, of course, influenced modern biblical scholarship, in which German Protestants were prominent.[19] S. Bochartus relied, inter alia, on Qimḥi and translated it *rubrica* 'red earth'.[20] W. Gesenius, in the first edition of his Bible dictionary considered its interpretation as *Röthel, Rothschrift* 'red chalk' to be fitting, his only qualification being that it was absent in the various Semitic languages, and no doubt through Luther's

---

hand, Tur-Sinai cites only the last words of Ibn Janah, in which he proposes to understand שרד as a tool); S. E. Hartom, *Commentary of Isaiah* (17th ed.; Tel Aviv: Yabne, 1965); *EM* 8.389, 1–2; A. Hakham, *Commentary of Isaiah* (Jerusalem: Rav Kook, Daᶜat Miqraᵓ, 1984) vol. 2.

18. There were, of course, also Jewish authors who disregarded this interpretation. See, e.g., S. G. Stern, "Salamonis ben Abrahami Parchon Aragonensis (12th century)," *Lexicon Hebraicum* (Pressburg: von Schmid, 1844) s.v. This is the more remarkable since Parchon relied on Ibn Janah. It is also absent from J. Steinberg, *Neues hebräisch-deutsch-russisches Lexicon zum Urtexte des Alten Testaments* (10th ed.; Tel Aviv: Sreberk, 1937) s.v. See also dictionaries of Modern Hebrew (e.g., Y. Gur, *Dictionary of the Hebrew Language* [5th ed.; Tel Aviv: Dvir, 1945] s.v.; A. Even-Shoshan, *The New Dictionary* [vol. 7; Jerusalem: Kirjath-Sepher, 1970] s.v.; M. Medan, *From Alef to Taw* [2d ed.; Tel Aviv: Akhiasaf, 1973] s.v.; Y. Kenaᶜani, *Thesaurus of the Hebrew Language* (vol. 17; Massada: Givatayim, 1987]). In these dictionaries the interpretation of שרד as 'dye' is, as a rule, missing, and in Modern Hebrew this meaning is indeed unknown. E. ben Yehuda's small dictionary at the beginning of the revival of Hebrew, on the other hand (*Hebrew Dictionary* [Vilna: Pirožnikov, 1901]) attributes to שֶׂרֶד the meaning of 'red dye' as well. See also the next note.

19. It also influenced modern Jewish translations into German, such as M. Obernik, *Translation of Isaiah, with H. Homberg's Commentary* (Vienna: von Schmid, 1818); both the translation and the commentary use *Roethe* 'red chalk'; this is also the case with Jehuda Löb Jeiteles, *Isaiah with New Commentary (Beur)* (Vienna: von Schmid and Busch, 1842). On the other hand, it is often translated *Stift* 'stylus', e.g., by L. Philippson, W. Landau, and S. I. Kaempf, *Die Heilige Schrift* (Leipzig: Nies, 1863); L. Zunz et al., *Die vier und zwanzig Bücher der Heiligen Schrift* (16th ed.; Frankfurt am Main: Kauffmann, 1913).

20. S. Bochartus, *Hierozoicon* (Frankfurt am Main: Zunner, 1675) 2.696.

influence, he ascribed this meaning to Qimḥi (rather than 'dyed cord').[21] Although this inaccuracy was corrected by him in his *Thesaurus*,[22] the very wording of the *Handwörterbuch* was more or less taken over by later dictionaries, such as the dictionaries by S. P. Tregelles, P. Drach, F. E. C. Dietrich, F. Mühlau and W. Volck, and F. Buhl.[23] C. Siegfried and B. Stade consider the interpretation of שרד as 'red chalk' to be "rabbinical."[24] G. Dalman interprets it as *Rotstift?* (i.e., perhaps 'red chalk'),[25] whereas L. Koehler asserts that according to the context it has to be 'red chalk,' Fe_2O_3![26] R. Gradwohl regards this interpretation as possible only (see also A. Brenner).[27] This interpretation is also mentioned by L. Koehler, W. Baumgartner, and J. J. Stamm in their recent dictionary, yet they prefer 'drawing pin', because of the context.[28]

21. W. Gesenius, *Hebräisch-Deutsches Handwörterbuch über die Schriften des Alten Testaments* (Leipzig: Vogel, 1810–12) s.v. Because of this qualification, he suggested the possibility of interpreting שרד as 'awl'.

22. W. Gesenius, *Thesaurus philologicus criticus linguae hebraeae et chaldaeae Veteris Testamenti* (Lipsia: Vogel, 1835–58). Here he cited Saadya, understanding, to be sure, his رقان as a 'dye', Ibn Janah, and also Qimḥi, this time relying on Bochartus, more accurately ('red and yellow cord'). Moreover, he considered its explanation as 'drawing pin' to be more fitting to the context. It is quite interesting that it was his *Handwörterbuch* rather than the *Thesaurus* that influenced later editions.

23. S. P. Tregelles, *Gesenius' Hebrew and Chaldee Lexicon* (London: Bagster, 1846); here, however, its interpretation as 'stylus' is preferred. P. Drach, *Catholicum lexicon hebraicum et chaldaicum* (Paris: Migne, 1848), where both interpretations are described as equal. F. E. C. Dietrich, *Hebräisches und chaldäisches Handwörterbuch* (7th ed.; Leipzig: Vogel, 1868); here the interpretation as 'stylus' is preferred. F. Mühlau and W. Volck, *W. Gesenius' hebräisches und aramäisches Handwörterbuch* (11th ed.; Leipzig: Vogel, 1890): both interpretations are described as equal here. F. Buhl, *W. Gesenius' hebräisches und aramäisches Handwörterbuch* (16th ed.; Leipzig: Vogel, 1915): both interpretations are described as equal here.

24. C. Siegfried and B. Stade, *Hebräisches Wörterbuch zum Alten Testamente* (Leipzig: von Veit, 1893).

25. G. Dalman, *Arbeit und Sitte in Palästina* (Gütersloh: Rufer, 1942) 7.43, 4.

26. L. Koehler and W. Baumgartner, *Lexicon in Veteris Testamenti libros* (Leiden: Brill, 1953) 930b.

27. R. Gradwohl, *Die Farben im Alten Testament* (BZAW 23; Berlin: Töpelmann, 1963) 85–86; A. Brenner, *Colour Terms in the Old Testament* (JSOTSup 21; Sheffield: JSOT Press, 1982) 154.

28. L. Koehler, W. Baumgartner, and J. J. Stamm, *Hebräisches und aramäisches Lexikon zum Alten Testament* (Leiden: Brill, 1990) vol. 4 s.v. Yet the etymology suggested is precarious, since the sibilant does not fit; see already E. König, *Hebräisches und aramäisches Wörterbuch zum Alten Testament* (4th and 5th ed.; Leipzig: Dieterich, 1931) s.v. Also in modern non-Jewish biblical scholarship, there were of course authors who disregarded the interpretation of שרד as 'dye'; e.g., F. Brown, S. R. Driver, and C. A. Briggs, *A Hebrew and English Lexicon of the Old Testament* (Oxford: Clarendon, 1907) 975a; König, *Wörterbuch*; F. Zorell, *Lexicon hebraicum et aramaicum Veteris Testamenti* (Rome: Pontifical Biblical Institute, 1962). Even A. Socin opts for *Reisstift*, i.e., 'drawing pin', s.v. *Röthelstein*, in *Kurzes Bibelwörterbuch* (ed. H. Guthe; Tübingen and Leipzig: Mohr, 1903), in which the lemmata are arranged according to Luther's translation.

I have cited some selected instances of the lasting influence Ibn Janah's misinterpretation of Saadya's رقان had on the history of biblical scholarship regarding the translation of שֶׂרֶד. Yet the understanding of it as a 'dye' (be it a red cord or a red chalk), prima facie, fits into the context less than a carpenter's tool and has no linguistic base whatsoever. It penetrated biblical exegesis only because of Ibn Janah's misunderstanding. Accordingly, now that the error on which it was based has been disclosed, the time has come to discard it altogether.

Additions and Corrections

to **p. 283**.*n. 1*: Yet the thesis that the occurrence of Saadya Gaon's vocabulary in later texts of necessity reflects the influence of his Bible translation, has to be taken *cum grano salis*, since Saadya himself employed the vocabulary of earlier Bible translations, see for the time being J. Blau & S. C. Reif, *Genizah Research after Ninety Years: The Case of Judaeo-Arabic*, Cambridge 1992, pp. 33–34.

Minutiae Aramaicae

A. SOME NOTES ON THE ARAMAIC PART OF THE ACCADIAN-ARAMAIC BILINGUAL INSCRIPTION FROM TELL FEKHERYE[1]

1. *The Representation of Proto-Semitic* ṯ[2] *by* s.

The most conspicuous orthographic feature of this inscription is the representation of Proto-Semitic *ṯ* by *s*, rather than by *š*. In Old Aramaic inscriptions, as well known, Proto-Semitic *ṯ/ḏ/ẓ/ś/ḍ* are represented by *š/z/ṣ/š/q*, i.e., with the notable exception of *ḍ - q*, as in Canaanite writing; in our inscription, however, Proto-Semitic *ṯ/ḏ/ś/ḍ* (*ẓ* is lacking) are reflected by *s/z/š/q*. In the main, three theories have been advanced[3] for the explanation of the Old Aramaic orthography, and we shall examine our inscription in their light:

Proto-Semitic *ṯ/ḏ/ẓ/ś/ḍ* have in fact in Old Aramaic shifted to *š/z/ṣ/š/q*; this assumption is only possible if later Aramaic is not a direct

Max Schloessinger Professor of Arabic, Department of Arabic, The Hebrew University, Jerusalem.

[1] I have perused the edition of A. Abou-Assaf, P. Bordreuil and A. R. Millard (*La Statue de Tell Fekherye et son inscription bilingue assyro-araméene* [Paris: Editions Reserch sur les civilizations, 1982]) and the corrections cited by J. C. Greenfield and A. Shaffer ("Notes on the Akkadian-Aramaic Bilingual Statue from Tell Fekherye," *Iraq* 14 [1983] 109–16). I am obliged to my friend R. Steiner with whom I discussed some of the problems involved.

[2] For typographic reasons, I mark these Proto-Semitic phonemes as is done in Arabic transcriptions, using *ẓ*, *ḍ*, without implying anything as to the actual pronunciation. *Śîn*, wanting in Arabic, is, as usual, marked by *ś*.

[3] See R. Degen, *Altaramäische Grammatik* (Wiesbaden: Steiner, 1969) 32ff. (without accepting his preferences).

continuation of Old Aramaic, since otherwise the later splitting of *š*/*z*/*ṣ*/*q* exactly according to their Proto-Semitic correspondences would be inconceivable. The same applies to our inscription. Only if later Aramaic does not continue the dialect reflected in it, could it represent the actual shift of *ṯ* > *s*.

Proto-Semitic *ṯ*/*ḏ*/*ẓ*/*ś*/*ḍ* still existed in Old Aramaic, and Old Aramaic orthography reflects the attempt to mark them with the letters of Canaanite, in which these Proto-Semitic phonemes had already disappeared, using the letters which seemed to them phonetically closest. Applying this explanation to our inscription, one would claim that to the scribes of the other Old Aramaic inscriptions *ṯ* sounded closer to *š*, whereas the scribe of our inscription perceived it as being closer to *s*.

The most likely explanation, in my opinion,[4] of the orthography of the other Old Aramaic inscriptions is that in Old Aramaic *ṯ*/*ḏ*/*ẓ*/*ś*/*ḍ* have been preserved, and marked, through the influence of Canaanite, by their Canaanite correspondences (with the notable exception of *ḍ* - *q*). This, however, did not, to such an extent, apply to our inscription, being outside the orbit of Canaanite, which, therefore, represents the attempt of marking *ṯ* by what sounded to its scribe phonetically the closest, viz. *s*. As to the representation of *ś*/*ḍ*/ by *š*/*q*, it *may* reflect the partial influence of Canaanite and the other Old Aramaic inscriptions, in the case of *ś* also strengthened by the Accadian shift *ś* > *š*.[5]

2. *Determination and* kln/klm

The most outstanding morpho-syntactic feature of our inscription is the increase in the use of the absolute, at the expense of the emphatic state. The latter occurs only four(!) times: 1 *dmwtʾ zy hdysʿy* 'the statue of H.'; 15 *dmwtʾ zʾt* 'this statue'; 16 *mʾnyʾ zy bt hdd* 'the objects of the temple of Adad'; 22 *wmn qlqltʾ llqṭw* 'may they scavenge from the rubbish dumps' (in this last case the article is generic, and the absolute could have been used as well; cf. 22 *tnwr* 'oven'). In the following cases, too, the emphatic state could have been used as well instead of the absolute which actually occurs (which is used as a kind of proper noun): 2 *šmyn wʾrq* 'heaven and earth,' cf. Zkr B 25, 26, Sfire I A 26; 5 *ʾlh rḥmn*

[4] Cf. J. Blau, *On Pseudocorrections in Some Semitic Languages* (Jerusalem: Israel Academic Press, 1970) 45.

[5] *If* Proto-Semitic *ghayn* still existed (cf. F. Rosenthal, *Die Sprache der palmyrenischen Inschriften* [Leipzig: Hinrichs, 1936] 24, n. 1), the use of ʿ for *gh* (21 *ʿylm* "child") *may* be due to Canaanite influence.

'merciful god'; 6 *mrʾ rb mrʾ* 'the great lord, the lord' (if this interpretation of the second *mrʾ* is correct and it does not have to be emended to *mrʾh* 'his lord,' it exhibits the use of the absolute to express individual determination); 12 *hdd gbr* 'the valiant Adad.' 4 *lʾlhyn klm* 'to the gods in their entirety' (see below for *klm*) is also remarkable, since *kl* is expected to occur only with *determinate* plural; yet *kl* with indeterminate plural is also attested in Elephantine.[6]

One is immediately reminded of the incantation of Uruk (about third century B.C.), in which there is a similar increase in the use of the absolute at the expense of the emphatic state.[7] Although at least about half a millennium separates between these two inscriptions, it stands to reason that both reflect independently the influence of Akkadian. At this period in Akkadian, too, nouns without ending were used in both determinate and indeterminate position, and through their influence in Aramaic the use of the absolute, being without any ending, prevailed.[8]

In *ʾlhyn klm*, cited above, *klm* follows an (at least formally) indeterminate plural. After an indeterminate singular it occurs 4 *gwgl nhr klm* 'controller of every river.' *kln* in this position is attested 3, 4 *mt kln* 'every land.' The assumption[9] that *m/n* have to be interpreted as 3 pl. m./f. pronominal suffixes explains, to be sure, the interchange of *m/n*, yet it presupposes not only the fixed construction *ad sensum* of a plural referring to a singular, but also the loss of the *h* of the pronoun, which seems quite unlikely in the light of the preservation of the *h* not only in the singular, but also in the imperfect of *hqṭl*: *lhynqn*, 'may they satiate,' 20, 21. Therefore, it stands to reason to parse *klm/kln* (the selection between which was *perhaps also* influenced by the gender of the preceding noun) as an adverb 'in its entirety.' Such adverbial usage is well attested in

[6] H. Bauer and P. Leander, *Grammatik des Biblisch-Aramäischen* (Halle/Salle: Niemeyer, 1927) 308–9.

[7] C. H. Gordon, "The Aramaic Incunabula in Cuneiform," *AfO* 12 (1937/9) 114, par. 61; J. Blau, "Studies in Semitic Pronouns Including the Definite Article," *H. Yalon Memorial Volume* (ed. E. Y. Kutscher et al.; Jerusalem: Bar Ilan University, 1974) 17–45, * nn. 18 and 18a (in Hebrew; English summary pp. x–xi).

[8] This, to be sure, makes the probability that the emphatic state prevailed in Eastern Aramaic through the influence of Akkadian, less likely. Cf. Blau, "Studies in Semitic * Pronouns," 33–34 and S. A. Kaufmann, *The Akkadian Influences on Aramaic* (Chicago and London: University of Chicago, 1974) 133–35. In our opinion, it is unlikely that our inscriptions reflect a transitional stage from the absence of the definite article (as preserved in Yaʾudian Aramaic) to its optional use. This is contradicted by the occurrence of the generic definite article, on the one hand, and its occurrence with the demonstrative pronoun, on the other (if, indeed, the absence of the article, as preserved in Canaanite and Rabbinical Hebrew, is more original).

[9] Abou-Assaf et al., *La Statue*, 29.

Semitic languages: Bible Aramaic *kollâ*,[10] Syriac *kul*,[11] *kul kullêh*,[12] Arabic *jamîᶜan, kâffatan*, etc., Akkadian *kališ*.[13]

B. ON TENSE STRUCTURE IN THE ARAMAIC PARTS OF DANIEL

Tense structure in the Aramaic parts of Daniel is characterized by the extensive use of the imperfect[14] and the participle when referring to the past. I have used the expression "when referring to the past," rather than "when marking the past" on purpose, because the past is marked by a

[10] The *synchronic* usage of *kollâ* is both adverbial (at least as a possibility) and nominal (its main usage); in the last case, it has to be interpreted as ultimately stemming from the emphatic state. Yet its penultimate stress clearly attests to the adverbial usage being one of its sources. Therefore, it has to be analysed as being due to the blend of nominal usage (with original ultimate stress) and an adverbial one (with original penultimate stress). J. A. Fitzmyer, ("The Syntax of *kl*, *klᵓ* in the Aramaic Texts from Egypt and in Biblical Aramaic," *Bib* 38 [1957] 170–84, repeated in his *A Wandering Aramean* [SBL Monograph Series 25; Missoula: Scholars, 1979] 205–7) confounded synchronical and diachronical approaches and inferred from its synchronic usage to its historial origins. His view was accepted by Y. E. Kutscher, "Aramaic," *Current Trends in Linguistics* 6 (The Hague: Mouton, 1971) 380.

[11] C. Brockelmann (*Grundriss der vergleichenden Grammatik der semitischen Sprachen* [Berlin: Reuther and Reichard, 1908/13] 2. 253 (who, however, also takes the possibility of ellipsis into account. The last example, at any rate, is erroneous. (Read T. Nöldeke, *Mändaische Grammatik* [Halle: Verlag des Waisenhauses, 1875] par. 217 for 210!) See also Brockelmann, 2:215 *ṭĕlâyê kol* "all the young men" which *may* reflect adverbial usage.

[12] C. Brockelmann, *Lexicon Syriacum* (2nd ed.; Halle: Niemeyer, 1928; reprinted Hildesheim: Olms, 1966), s.v.

[13] In passing, I would like also to mention, in my opinion, another archaic feature in our inscription. In Sfire (see Degen, *Altaramäische Grammatik*, 104–5) the counted noun after *šbᶜ*, "seven," may be in the singular (alternating with the plural; see J. Blau, "Marginalia Semitica II," *Israel Oriental Studies* 2 [1972] 57–58). Such an alternation of (pp. 221–22) singular with plural is also attested in our inscription after *mᵓh*, 'hundred,' 20ff. This singular has not, therefore, to be emended to the plural (*pace* Greenfield and Shaffer, "Notes on the Akkadian-Aramaic Bilingual Statue") although it alternates with the plural, the more so, since the singular after "hundred" is well attested in Semitic languages (always in Classical Arabic, often in Hebrew).

[14] I do not deal with the jussive. *Obiter dictu*, the supersession of the jussive *yfᶜlû/tfᶜlî* by the indicative *yfᶜlûn/tfᶜlîn* could be interpreted as (partly) reflecting the inclination to add *-n* after final long vowels. As is well known (see recently A. Tal, *The Samaritan Targum of the Pentateuch* 3 [Tel Aviv: University of Tel Aviv, 1983] 85–86) the nasalization of such vowels prevails in later Palestinian Aramaic, and beginnings of this phenomenon could have added to the prevalence of the imperfect ending with *-n* (without losing sight of the fact that in some Arabic Bedouin dialects the endings with *-n* prevailed without this inclination; other dialects, as Iraqi *geltu* dialects, might have been influenced by the Aramaic substratum). One could interpret similarly forms like *himmôn*, *illên*, Syriac *anaḥnan*.

preceding perfect[15] and/or temporal adverbial[16] referring to the past. Some references are Dan 4:8–9 (where not only imperfect forms,[17] but also the nominal clauses at the beginning of v 9 are transferred to the past by the preceding perfect); 5:6–7; 3:7; 4:31,[18] 33.

Though this usage of the imperfect and the participle is especially conspicuous in Daniel, it is, to some extent, attested in other Aramaic dialects as well. In Mandaic, the participle continuing the perfect is very frequent,[19] and verbs denoting saying in the imperfect may refer to the

[15] So, e.g., Brockelmann (*Grundriss*, 2. 163) who understands it this way both after the perfect and adverbs; yet he interprets the imperfect as marking durative action in the past (2.152, n. 1). For an opposing view, see below n. 17. F. Rosenthal (*A Grammar of Biblical Aramaic* [Wiesbaden: Harrassowitz, 1961] 55) argues similarly both for the participle and the imperfect, yet after the perfect only; he considers other occurrences of the participle in this sense (in the only example cited the participle is preceded by the temporal adverbial *bêdayin*, 'thereupon') to be "free use" due to further development. Bauer and Leander (*Grammatik*, 280, 292) regard the imperfect in this usage after the perfect (expressed actually or imagined by the speaker) as durative or iterative, the participle as continuing a shorter or longer time. The participle not preceded by the perfect (p. 294; they do not mention the imperfect in this position), in their opinion, reflects special development, and they disregard the fact that it is always preceded by a temporal adverbial referring to the past. S. Segert (*Altaramäische Grammatik* [Leipzig: Verlag Enzyklopädie, 1975], 373ff.) is of the opinion that to a great extent it is the context that determines the time reference of the verbal forms. Yet, although he describes the imperfect as marking continued/iterative action (p. 379) and the participle as referring to continued action (p. 381), in Daniel he regards the participle as an independent marker of the past (p. 383) because, in his opinion, continued action is designated by the periphrastic perfect with the participle. He recognizes, however, that "often" time is marked by temporal adverbials (the only alleged counter-example adduced by him, viz. Dan 5:7, continues v 6, where the past is marked both by a temporal adverbial and the perfect).

[16] Cf. the bibliography cited in the preceding note. See also M. Cohen, *Le Système verbal sémitique et l'expression du temps* (Paris: Leroux, 1924) 142.

[17] Among which *yimṭê* is a clear case of momentaneous past. Segert (*Altaramäische Grammatik*, 380), on the other hand, interpreted it as an incomplete action ("it almost reached"), which is in our opinion mere linguistic sophistry. E. Vogt (*Lexicon Linguae Aramaicae Veteris Testamenti* [Rome: Pontifical Biblical Institute, 1971] ad loc.) parses it as a consecutive clause; yet the limits are rather blurred.

[18] Segert (*Altaramäische Grammatik*, 380) suggested that *yĕtûb*, being an imperfect, marks *gradual* return, again this seems to be mere linguistic sophistry. Vogt (*Lexicon*, ad loc.) parsed it as a circumstantial clause, yet it occurs in v 33 as well, where it clearly marks the main action.

[19] Nöldeke (*Mandäische Grammatik*, 375). Yet the participle is also attested as sentence initial. The view expressed there, that the imperfect after the "conversive" *waw* reflects basically the same phenomenon, must be rejected since originally the apocopate was used in this position. The apocopate marked not only the jussive, but also the past, as reflected by Akkadian *iprus*, Arabic *lam yaktub* and also by Yaʾudian Aramaic (see J. Blau, "Review of P. E. Dion, *La Langue de Yaʾudi*," *Kirjath Sepher* 51 [1975/6] 474b; *pace* J. C. L. Gibson, *Textbook of Syrian Semitic Inscriptions, ii, Aramaic Inscriptions* [Oxford: University Press, 1975] 15).

past.[20] ᵓ*mr* in the participle referring to the past occurs in Christian Palestinian Aramaic,[21] as well as in Syriac and Jewish Palestinian Aramaic.[22] The participle and the imperfect referring to the past are attested in the Genesis apocryphon of Qumran cave i. Fitzmyer[23] cites occurrences of the imperfect referring to the past, after a perfect, yet without connecting them with our phenomenon. As to the use of the participle as past reference in the Genesis apocryphon it is hard to identify, since in Qal singular it cannot be distinguished from the perfect in unvocalized texts. Yet in one case it occurs in the plural: col. 22.4 (p. 64) *ngdw mlky*ᵓ . . . *wšbyn wbzyn wmḥyn wqṭlyn w*ᵓ*zlyn lmdynt drmšq*, translate 'the kings set out . . . and took captives, plundered, destroyed, killed and set out (for ᵓ*zl* 'to set out' cf. col. 21.15) toward the province of Damascus'. Imperfect after a temporal adverb referring to the past occurs Ezra 5:5, and participle after the perfect in this function Ezra 4:12, 5:3, 6:13–14.

It stands to reason[24] that basically the imperfect and the participle in this construction mark action occurring simultaneously with the time of the preceding perfect or temporal adverb. That this is the case at least synchronically is demonstrated by the fact that (see above par. 1) nominal clauses as well may refer to the past when preceded by the perfect or a temporal adverb marking the past. Clauses with participial predicate are indeed basically nominal clauses. The use of the imperfect as marker of simultaneous action is even more archaic.[25] The alternation of the imperfect and the participle referring to the past[26] reflects, it seems, the

[20] Nöldeke, *Mandäische Grammatik*, 371. *d* plus *nym*ᵓ*r* is very interesting since it is a case of true ellipsis.

[21] Bauer and Leander, *Grammatik*, 295, n. 2.

[22] Ibid., 296, n. 1 and 2.

[23] *The Genesis Apocryphon of Qumran Cave I* (Rome: Pontifical Biblical Institute, 1966), 202, *in medio*. The first two examples of the imperfect continuing the perfect are certain. The reading of the third example is not entirely clear; see T. Muraoka, "Notes on the Aramaic of the Genesis Apocryphon," *RevQ* 8 (1972) 27; although ᵓ*dḥl* may refer to the past, as well as to the present. Cf., e.g., Dan 2:10, *yûkhal*.

[24] See the literature cited above, n. 15.

[25] See Rosenthal, *A Grammar of Biblical Aramaic*, 55, par. 178. It stands to reason that the use of the imperfect as marker of simultaneous action has been, *inter alia*, preserved because of the frequency of circumstantial clauses. This usage was especially emphasized by Bauer and Leander (*Grammatik*, 281ff.) who went so far as to consider that the imperfect referring to the past after the perfect usually exhibited a circumstantial clause. Yet this assumption does not account for the parallel use of the imperfect after temporal adverbials; cf. also H. B. Rosén's convincing arguments in "On the Use of the Tenses in the Aramaic of Daniel," *JSS* 6 (1961) 183–84. Already Nöldeke (*Mandäische Grammar*, 371) took this usage of the imperfect into consideration.

[26] Cf., e.g., Dan 5:6 (cited above, par. 1) the alternation of the imperfect and the participle, as well as the alternation of nominal clauses, the participle and the imperfect (7:9–10). Cf. also 5:6, *yĕḇahălunnêh*, as against 5:9, *mitbâhal*.

blend of two systems marking simultaneous action, the earlier one with the imperfect and the later one with the participle.[27]

As we have seen, the system of clauses referring to the past is quite intricate in Daniel, due to long historical development. Besides the perfect,—the imperfect, the participle, as well as nominal clauses are attested, which, as it seems, basically mark simultaneous action with the preceding perfect or temporal adverbials. The supposition of such a complicated system, consisting of several parallel subsystems, is, of course, not "elegant," and any theory which succeeds in discovering the conditioning of the various subsystems, is preferable to it. An ingenious attempt in this direction was made by H. B. Rosén[28] and his main results are shown in Figure 1.

	Linear aspect verb	Point aspect verb
Future-volitive:	*lehĕwe dâʾar*	*yippul*
Present:	*dâʾar (!)*	*îtay nâp̄el*
Narrative-constative:	*yĕdûr*	*nâp̄el*
Subordinative:	*hawa dâʾar (!)*	*nĕp̄al* (also perfect)

FIGURE 1

By "subordinative" a sort of "cleft sentence" is meant, in which the verb is the psychological subject (topic; the rest of the sentence being the psychological predicate, the comment).[29]

In my opinion, this brilliant article[30] nevertheless has to be rejected mainly because in most instances in which Rosén analyses the verb as psychological subject ("subordinative"), such is not the case. Cf. e.g., 3:22 *gub̲rayyâ illêk̲ . . . qaṭṭil himmōn . . .* '(it) killed . . . those men,' where the fact of being killed exhibits the novelty (the psychological predicate). It cannot be claimed that it is 'those men' that serve as psychological predicate, the novelty being that *they* were killed and not Shadrach, Meshack, and Abed-nego, since according to v 21 Shadrach and his friends were cast into the burning fiery furnace (a fact which is repeated in v 23) and we are still made to believe that they are dead. Similarly 5:30 *bêh bĕlêlĕyâ qĕṭîl*, 'in the same night he was killed,' the novelty is not that

[27] For the special status of *ʿnh wʾmr* see Bauer and Leander, *Grammatik*, 295. Dan 7:28 is difficult. Perhaps the nominal clause, opening the verse, refers to the past because of the opening (local!) adverbial. It is followed by two imperfects referring to the past, followed by a final(!) perfect.

[28] Rosén, "On the Use of the Tenses in the Aramaic of Daniel," 183–203.

[29] If these are indeed identical. For other terms, cf., e.g., J. Blau, *An Adverbial Construction in Hebrew and Aramaic* (Jerusalem: Central Press, 1971), 5, n. 11.

[30] Cf. Kutscher's enthusiastic appraisal in "Aramaic," 378–79.

the killing took place in that night, but rather that he, the great king, was killed, 'in the same night' being a marginal detail only. Further 5:19 *kol ᶜamĕmayyâ ummayyâ wĕliššânayyâ hăwô zâyĕᶜîn wĕdâḥălîn*, 'all people, nations, and languages trembled and feared,' the verbs clearly serve as the psychological predicate (as well). Therefore, Rosén's differentiation between "narrative-constative" and "subordinative" does not work (the more so since he admits that *Nĕphal* occurs not only as the alleged subordinative, but as "perfect" as well), and since nominal clauses, imperfect forms and participles alternate without visible functional difference (see above, n. 24), we are forced to return to the less elegant supposition that these constructions, basically marking simultaneous action, after the perfect and temporal adverbials may refer to the past without any functional distinction.

C. THE ORDER OF THE ARAMAIC ALPHABET BORROWED FROM CANAANITE

The Ancient Aramaic script is so closely linked with the Canaanite that it can properly be called "Phoenician-Aramaic."[31] Moreover, the Aramaic abecedary has the same order as the Hebrew one.[32] And it can be demonstrated that its order has been taken over from Canaanite.

In the Aramaic abecedaries the last but one letter is *š*, as in Canaanite (Hebrew). As Loewenstamm[33] has demonstrated, from the point of view of the alphabet, *š* corresponds to (Ugaritic) *ṯ*. This anomaly clearly shows that the Hebrew alphabet was invented by speakers of a Canaanite dialect who did not distinguish between *š* and *ṯ* (as well as *ś*). Accordingly since in Aramaic *ṯ* has not coincided with *š*,[34] the order of the Aramaic abecedaries has to be regarded as borrowed from Canaanite.

[31] J. Naveh, *The Development of the Aramaic Script* (Jerusalem: Ahva, 1970) 8.

[32] J. B. Segal, *Aramaic Texts from North Saqqâra* (London: Egypt Exploration Society, 1983) 141.

[33] S. E. Lowenstamm, *Comparative Studies in Biblical and Ancient Oriental Literatures* (Neukirchen-Vluyn: Neukirchner Verlag, 1980) 8–9.

[34] This would only be the case, if one assumed that the marking of Protosemitic *ṯ* by Old Aramaic *š* reflects a phonetic process. See above, A.1.

Additions

to **p. 292**.*n.7.4*: The passage referred to is p. 33. nn. 18 and 18a = *Hebrew Linguistics*, p. 361, nn. 18 and 18a.

to **p. 292**.*n.8.3*: = *Hebrew Linguistics*, pp. 361–62.

to **p. 293**.*2*: Cf. also Zechariah 4.2 וְהִנֵּה מְנוֹרַת זָהָב כֻּלָּהּ ‘and behold, a candlestick of gold in its entirety’, cf. F. E. König, *Historisch-kritisches Lehrgebäude der hebräischen Sprache*, ii, 2, Leipzig 1897, p. 400.7.

The Origins of Open and Closed *e* in Proto-Syriac

1. As is well known,[1] the Eastern (or Nestorian) vocalization of Syriac (henceforth ES) consistently distinguishes between *ē* and *ī*, whereas the Western (or Jacobite) tradition (henceforth WS), although having both *e* and *i*,[2] also has in many cases (originally long) *e* coinciding with (originally long) *i*. The question arises of how it happened that in some cases (originally long) *e* was preserved, whereas in others it shifted to *i*. Brockelmann and Birkeland [3] were, no doubt, correct in assuming that in Proto-Syriac (henceforth PS) there existed two long *e* sounds, *ẹ̄* and *ę̄*.[4] In ES vocalization these two sounds were not differentiated,[5] whereas in WS (originally long) *ę* was preserved, but *ẹ̄* shifted to *i*. Only the assumption of two different forms of *ē* in PS can account for the twofold representation of original *ē* in WS, by both *ę* and *i*.[6]

The aim of this paper is to investigate the sound shifts that gave rise to these two *ē* sounds in PS. The analysis of this feature, as offered by Brockelmann, *Gram.*, 28–9, § 47a, b, is not clear enough. Brockelmann, it is true, recognized that *a'* shifted to *ę̄*, but *i'* to *ẹ̄*,[7] yet in other cases he did not propose any solution as to why *ay* shifted to both *ę̄* (*v.* Brockelmann, *Gram.*, § 47 *aβ*) and *ẹ̄* (*v.* Brockelmann, *Gram.*, § 47b*a*, and also § 53). Similarly (*v.* § 47aδ, bδ),

[1] *v.* the standard Syriac grammars, viz. T. Nöldeke, *Kurzgefasste syrische Grammatik*, second ed., Leipzig, 1898 (henceforth Nöldeke, *Gram.*), 7–8, C. Brockelmann, *Syrische Grammatik*, seventh ed., Leipzig, 1955 (henceforth Brockelmann, *Gram.*), 9–10, and the important paper by H. Birkeland, 'The Syriac phonematic vowel systems' (henceforth Birkeland), *Festskrif til O. Broch . . .*, Oslo, 1947, 13 ff. Cf. also S. Morag, *The vocalization systems of Arabic, Hebrew, and Aramaic*, 's-Gravenhage, 1962, 49 ff.

[2] In this vocalization system quantitative differences have altogether disappeared, *v.* especially Birkeland, 15. Therefore, *ĕ*/*ē* and *ĭ*/*ī* respectively are marked by the same vowel signs. Here, however, we are concerned with WS *e* and *i* corresponding to historical long vowels only.

[3] *v.* especially Brockelmann, *Gram.*, 14–15. Brockelmann's original thesis, as it was expressed in earlier editions of his grammar (*v.* also Brockelmann, *Grundriss der vergleichenden Grammatik der semitischen Sprachen*, Berlin, 1908–13 (henceforth Brockelmann, *Grundriss*), I, 37–8, 562g) was elaborated by Birkeland, 19 ff.

[4] It stands to reason that they were only phonetically different, but did not represent separate phonemes; cf. Birkeland, *passim*, and Brockelmann, *Gram.*, 15.

[5] Nevertheless, one is inclined to assume that they subsisted as phonetic variants, but, being phonematically not differentiated, they were not marked by special signs.

[6] According to Nöldeke, *ZDMG*, XXXV, 1881, 224, the original *ę̄* is preserved in the West Syriac Neo-Aramaic dialect of Ṭūr 'Abdīn, the only exceptions being *rīšō* 'head' and *šīdō* 'devil', the latter perhaps a loan-word from the ecclesiastical language. It would be easy to explain *rīšō* phonetically, as influenced by the following *š*, *v.* A. Siegel, *Laut- und Formenlehre des neu-aramäischen Dialekts des Ṭūr Abdîn* (Beitrage zur Semitischen Philologie und Linguistik, 2), Hannover, 1923 §§ 14e, 15b (and even *šīdō* owing to the preceding *š*). However, *ẹ̄* > *ī* occurs in Ṭūr 'Abdīn in some other cases (*v.* Siegel, op. cit., 87, O. Jastrow, *Laut- und Formenlehre des neuaramäischen Dialekts von Miḏin im Ṭur 'Abdin. Inaugural-Dissertation . . . Universität des Saarlandes*, Bamberg, 1967, 179): *bīrō* 'well', *fīrō* 'fruit'. Should one assume dialect mixture? This assumption, however, does not seem necessary for old WS, *v. infra*.

[7] cf. also Birkeland (whose paper and the above-mentioned paragraphs in Brockelmann, are together the most important contributions to our subject), 26.

he makes pausal lengthening responsible for both *ẹ̄* and *ę̄*. We shall endeavour to define these sound shifts more exactly, not forgetting, however, that they were blurred by various analogical formations. Even the tradition as to which variant of *ē* to employ is not always fixed, *v.* for particulars e.g. Nöldeke, *Gram.*, pp. 32, 34, 112, n. 1, 115, n. 2, further *idem, Neue Beiträge zur semitischen Sprachwissenschaft*, Strassburg, 1910, p. 152, n. 4.

2. As stated above, it stands to reason that non-final *i'* shifted to PS *ẹ̄* (WS *i*), *a'* to PS *ę̄* (WS *e*). These shifts are exhibited by the prefixes of the imperfect *pə'al* of *verba primae ālaf*: from the presupposed two original themes *yiqṭal* and *yaqṭil*,[8] the theme *niqṭal* appears in WS as *niṭal* (e.g. *nimar* 'he will speak'),[9] whereas *naqṭul* has the form of *neṭul* (e.g. *neḵul* 'he will eat'), thus reflecting the shift *i'* > PS *ẹ̄* > WS *i* (**ni'mar* > PS **nẹ̄mar* > WS *nimar*) as against *a'* > PS *ę̄* > WS *e* (**na'kul* > PS **nę̄kul* > WS *neḵul*). The infinitives (WS) *meḵal/mimar* follow the analogy of the imperfect,[10] but nouns with the prefix *ma*, in accordance with the regular sound shift *a'* > WS *e*, exhibit WS *me*, as *metyo*, *meṯiṯọ* 'coming',[11] *mepiṯọ* 'baking', in spite of the WS imperfects *niṯe*,[12] *nipe*.[13] It goes without saying that **ma'kūltā* shifts to WS *meḵultọ* 'food'; similarly **pella'tā* > *pelleṯọ* 'proverb', **ga'wūtā* > *gewuṯọ* 'pride', **ša'ileṯ* (*sic*, *pace* Brockelmann, *Gram.*, § 46) > *ša'leṯ* > *šeleṯ* 'I asked'. *i'* > WS *i* is also shown by **bi'rā* > WS *birọ* 'well', *di'bā* > WS *diḇọ* 'wolf', *ki'bā*[14] > *kiḇo* 'pain'. Similarly, in accordance with Hebrew *ḥāṣīr* 'herbage' and *ḥāṣēr* 'court', containing original *ī* and *i* respectively, one is inclined to interpret WS *ḥirọ* 'reed' and *ḥirṯọ* 'camp' as *qiṭl*: **ḥiḏr(t)ā* > **ḥi'r(t)ā* > **ḥi'r(t)ā* > *ḥir(t)ọ* (so *pace* Brockelmann, *Gram.*, 23-4).

Some cases, however, cause difficulties.

2.1. WS *riš* = ES *rēš* 'head'. As a rule, *ra'š* is considered to be the Proto-Semitic form, which, however, should have given rise to WS *reš*. The usual

[8] For the themes *yiqṭal* as against *yaqṭul* (*yaqṭil*) cf. e.g. H. Ewald, *Ausführliches Lehrbuch der hebräischen Sprache des Alten Bundes*, eighth ed., Göttingen, 1870, § 138b; J. Barth, *ZDMG*, XLVIII, 1894, 1 ff.; Brockelmann, *Grundriss*, I, 562; H. L. Ginsberg, *Orientalia*, VIII, 1939, 319 ff.; A. Bloch, *ZDMG*, CXVII, 1, 1967, 22 ff.

[9] *Verba primae w(y)* also follow this pattern as well, e.g. WS *nilaḏ* 'he will bear', cf. Nöldeke, *Gram.*, § 175A, *pace* Brockelmann, *Grundriss*, I, 601gβ, Brockelmann, *Gram.*, § 181E, F, G.

[10] *v.* Brockelmann, *Gram.*, 91. One assumes the existence of one original infinitive form *miqṭal*, rather than postulating two different vowels in the first syllable in accordance with the imperfect prefixes.

[11] So Nöldeke, *Gram.*, 74; R. Payne Smith, *Thesaurus syriacus*, Oxford, 1879–1901 (henceforth Payne Smith), s.v.; as against *mi* . . . , Brockelmann, *Lexicon syriacum*, second ed., Halle/Saale, 1928 (henceforth Brockelmann, *LS*), s.v.

[12] Even the infinitive of *'ty* is, according to Payne Smith s.v., *meṯọ*, presumably because the influence of the imperfect, terminating in *-e* as against the final *ọ* in the infinitive (*v. infra* p. 7, n. 55), was less conspicuous.

[13] Thus Nöldeke, *Gram.*, 124, yet A. Moberg (ed.), *Le Livre des splendeurs : le grande grammaire de Grégoire Barhebraeus*, Lund, 1922 (henceforth Bar Hebraeus), p. 125, l. 25, and Payne Smith s.v., read *nepe*. In some cases, however, even nouns beginning with original *ma-* are influenced by the imperfect: *mizlọ*, *mizalṯọ* 'going', *mimrọ* 'saying'.

[14] Not **ka'bā*, *pace* G. Bergsträsser, *Einführung in die semitischen Sprachen*, München, 1928, 61.

explanation,[15] according to which the original *a* became *e* by assimilation to the following *š*, thus ultimately giving rise to WS *i* rather than to *e*, holds good for Syriac, where *aš* regularly shifts to *eš*; [16] it does not, however, apply to Biblical Aramaic (and perhaps to other Aramaic dialects),[17] where this shift is only marginally attested.[18] Accordingly one wonders if it is not more likely that in Proto-Semitic *ra'š* and *ri'š* alternated.[19]

2.2. *Mānā*, WS *mǫnǫ*, spelt with *ālaf* after the *mīm*, if it is in fact derived from *'ny*,[20] thus exhibiting the shift of **ma'nā* to *mānā* rather than to **mēnā*, is due, it seems, to an older sound shift *a'* > *ā* (WS *ǫ*). It was perhaps the great frequency of *mānā* that caused the early disappearance of the glottal stop.[21] In other cases, it was the occurrence of a preceding ' that occasioned the early dissimilation of the *ālaf*, and therefore these nouns too exhibit the early shift *a'* > *ā*: [22] **ḍa'na* > *'*a'nā* > '*ānā* (WS '*ǫnǫ*) 'small cattle'; **ḍa'lā* > *'*ā'lā* > '*ālā* (WS '*ǫlǫ*) 'thorny lotus'.[23]

2.3. WS *'eštęlaṯ* 'she was asked', as against ES *'eštalaṯ* shows the regular sound shift from **'ešta'laṯ*, whereas the ES form is presumably due to re-patterning in accordance with the strong verb. The same applies to WS *šęlūn* 'they asked us', though Bar Hebraeus, 235, 20 prefers ES *šalūn*.

3.1. Whereas *ay* in open syllable is preserved, it shifts in closed syllable to *ẹ̄* (> WS *i*). This gave rise to the morphological alternation of *ay* in *status determinatus* with ES *ē*, WS *i* in *status absolutus/constructus* in nouns like WS '*aynǫ* (where the syllable is open) : '*in* (where the syllable is closed) 'eye'; [24] *ḥaylǫ* : *ḥil* 'power'; *qayso* : *qis* 'timber'. (A somewhat different alternation

[15] *v.* e.g. Brockelmann, *Grundriss*, I, 202c; H. Bauer and P. Leander, *Grammatik des Biblisch-Aramäischen*, Halle/Saale, 1927 (henceforth Bauer and Leander), 60 f.; Brockelmann, *Gram.*, §§ 47bβ, 58 [*sic*].

[16] *v.* e.g. Brockelmann, *Gram.*, § 58.

[17] *Pace* Bauer and Leander, 60 f.

[18] *v.* Bauer and Leander, 41s.

[19] cf. also Hebrew *rēšiṯ* 'beginning' and perhaps Ugaritic *riš* as well. But one would not go as far as J. Friedrich, *Orientalia*, XII, 1943, 18.

[20] *v.* Brockelmann, *Grundriss*, I, 266, 379; Bauer and Leander, 59c; Brockelmann, *LS*, s.v., where, however, the possibility of another derivation is indicated.

[21] For the special status of *mānā* cf. also Brockelmann, *Grundriss*, I, 379, § 198c; *v.*, however, also Brockelmann, *Grundriss*, I, 266, § ζ, where a more likely solution is offered, and, following him, Bauer and Leander 194r. This ancient sound shift is perhaps shown also by *bāṯar*, WS *bǫṯar*, if it is to be derived from **ba'tar* (rather than from *bə'aṯar*, from which the later *baṯar* arose). This would, however, presuppose an ancient construct form *'*tar*, rather than '*aṯar*. As a rule, however, it is derived from **ba'aṯar*. On the other hand, *qərā* < **qara'*, etc., is regular, because it occurs in final syllable, and final *a'* > *ā*.

[22] This seems more likely than the assumption (*v.* Brockelmann, *Gram.*, § 59) that owing to the influence of the ', *a'* shifted to *ā* rather than to *ē*.

[23] cf. also A. Spitaler, *BO*, XI, 1, 1954, p. 32, n. 5. As to '*ā'yāṯā* 'pinnacle', *v.* Brockelmann, *LS*, s.v. (and the literature quoted there), as against Nöldeke, *Gram.*, 38, § 53. *ḥannā* 'bosom' < **ḥa'nā* < **ḥa'nā* < **ḥaḏnā* the glottal stop was assimilated to the immediately following *n*, *v.* Brockelmann, *Gram.*, 23, § 35, remark.

[24] For the (relatively late) analogical spread of *i* in '*in* in prepositional use *v.* Brockelmann, *Gram.*, 33, Anm. 2, where other cases of analogical formation are also mentioned. This phenomenon is also exhibited by WS *kəminǫ* 'ambush' and *rətitǫ* 'trembling', derived from the theme *quṭayl*, *v.* Brockelmann, *Grundriss*, I, § 137.

of *ay* : *i* is exhibited by WS *lilyo,*[25] *status absolutus layle*[26] ‘ night ’.) Other cases of *ay* > *ę̄* (> WS *i*) in open syllables are shown by[27] WS *mekil* (ES *mekkēl*), *hǫḵil* ‘ now ’, *‘ədakil* (ES *‘ədakkēl*) ‘ still ’ ;[28] *kiṯ* ‘ so ’, *’awkiṯ* ‘ i.e.’ ; *rəmiṯ* ‘ I threw ’.[29]

3.2. Similarly, it seems, non-final *ayi/awi*[30] shifted to *ę̄* > WS *i*. Nöldeke, *Mandäische Grammatik*, Halle/Saale, 1875, 108–9, was correct when adducing against this derivation the fact that most of the nouns that seem to belong to this class are spelt in Hebrew defectively, and in Syriac too as a rule *ālaf* rather than *yōdh* is used as *mater lectionis*. Nevertheless, even he preferred to analyse them as theme *qaṭil*. The simplest explanation of the facts seems to be that these nouns (p. 23, n. 8) derive from original triliteral nouns *mediae w/y* on the one hand, and biliteral nouns on the other. In these triliteral nouns of the theme *qaṭil* (thus containing *awi/ayi*), forms with medial *ę̄* (= WS *i*) arose, and the biliteral nouns were adapted to them. It was perhaps due to the relatively great number of originally * biliteral nouns that these nouns, as a rule, exhibit *scriptio defectiva* in Hebrew and are not spelt with *yōdh* in Syriac.[31]

To these nouns belong : WS *riḥǫ* ‘ odour ’ ; since this noun is spelled with *yōdh* in both Hebrew and Syriac, *v.* Nöldeke, *Mandäische Grammatik*, p. 108, * n. 2, it presumably belongs to an originally triliteral noun.[32] Further : *piqǫ* ‘ dumb ’[33] ; *kinǫ* ‘ just ’[34] ; *ḥifǫ* ‘ force ’.[35] *Pirǫ* ‘ fruit ’, originally from the

[25] But also *lelyo*, *v.* Nöldeke, *Gram.*, 91.

[26] For this form, instead of the expected *laylay*, which still occurs (*v.* Nöldeke, *Gram.*, 91), with *ay* in the final *open* syllable, *v.* p. 7, n. 54.

[27] Some of the cases may show original *ayi*, *v. infra*, § 3.2.

[28] So according to Payne Smith, s.vv. ; Nöldeke, *Gram.*, 97, § B. Brockelmann, *LS*, s.vv. is inexact.

[29] As against *rəmayt* ‘ you threw (masc./fem.) ’, where the final vowel disappeared later, thus preserving the diphthong in the originally *open* syllable.

[30] For *ayī*, *v. infra*, p. 6, n. 48.

[31] One will not try to disprove the shift *ayi/awi* > *ę̄* (> WS *i*) by citing the occurrence of forms like ES *mīṯ* ‘ dead ’, ‘*īr* ‘ awake ’, as a rule regarded as also belonging to the theme *qaṭil* (cf. Nöldeke, *Neue Beiträge zur semitischen Sprachwissenschaft*, Strassburg, 1910 [henceforth *NBSS*], 209), thus allegedly exhibiting *awi* > *ī* (i.e. **mawit* > *mīṯ*, *‘*awir* > ‘*īr*). They may reflect the lengthening of originally biliteral words (to whose pattern originally triliteral words might have been adapted). The same *may* apply to WS ‘*eqaṯ leh* (but ES ‘*āqaṯ*) ‘ to loathe ’, *v.* Bar Hebraeus, 236, 28. Biblical Aramaic *rę̄m* ‘ was high ’ according to the Babylonian vocalization need not be due to Canaanite influence, as Bauer and Leander, 145j, assume, but may exhibit the regular sound shift.

[32] One will not regard it as diminutive of *rūḥā*, *pace* Brockelmann, *LS*, s.v., or as exhibiting *rayḥ*, *pace* Brockelmann, *Gram.*, 33, Anm. 2, since its root is *rwḥ*, but as belonging to the scheme *qaṭil*, *v.* Brockelmann, *Grundriss*, I, 348, Anm., Bauer and Leander, 186w, *pace* J. Barth, *Nominalbildung* . . . , 79. One cannot, however, agree with Bauer and Leander, loc. cit., that *qaṭil* shifted to both *qāl* and *qēl*. One prefers to regard *qāl* as being due to lengthening of originally biliteral nouns.

[33] One derives this word from a root *mediae infirmae*, rather than from *pqq*, *pace* Brockelmann, *LS*, s.v., who, because of its medial *ē* (= WS *i*), is inclined to consider it a loan from Akkadian : this conclusion arises from circuitous reasoning.

[34] Our assertion in the preceding note that nothing indicates an Akkadian loan applies (because of Hebrew *kę̄n*) even more to this word, *pace* Brockelmann, *LS*, s.v., Brockelmann, *Gram.*, 29, § bε, *v.* e.g. Brockelmann, *Grundriss*, I, § 51a. WS *zipǫ* ‘ falsity ’, however, is perhaps of Akkadian origin.

[35] This, however, corresponds to Arabic *ḥayf*.

root *pry*, was transferred to this class of nouns, cf. Brockelmann, *ZDMG*, XCIV, 3, 1940, 351. The same would seem to apply to *ḥirǫ* ‘free’, its original root being *ḥrr* and its theme *quṭl*: first, **ḥurrūṯā* ‘freedom’ by dissimilation became **ḥerrūṯā*, from which **ḥerrā* was then abstracted. It was then transferred to the class of nouns with which we deal, perhaps especially by the influence of *rišǫ* ‘head’, *v.* Brockelmann, *Gram.*, 30, and especially Brockelmann, *LS*, s.v. *ḥrr*.[36]

3.3. *ẹ̆* is sometimes lengthened into *ẹ̄* = WS *i*. This is the case[37] when *ẹ̆* is lengthened because of total dissimilation of *l/n*: **šelšaltā* > WS *šišaltǫ* ‘chain’, **qenqənā* > WS *qiqənǫ* ‘plough’.[38]

4. In some cases, however, open *ē* occurs where one would have expected closed *ē* = WS *i*:

4.1. This is the case in words bearing secondary stress only. Thus *ay* in such words shifts to *ę̄* in WS *təḥeṯ* ‘under’ < **tuḥayt*,[39] which, being a preposition, bears secondary stress only; further *beṯ*, the *status constructus* of *bayto* ‘house’: since the *status constructus* of this word, bearing secondary stress and thus containing open *e*, was very frequent,[40] it was not affected by the analogy of the nouns (*v.* § 3.1) exhibiting *ay* in *status determinatus* as against *ẹ̄* = WS *i* in *status constructus/absolutus*. Besides, in this case the *status absolutus* (*bay*) was also different. Moreover, it might have been influenced by *beṯ* ‘between’ < **baynt*, which, as a preposition, also has *ę̄*.[41] Whatever the derivation of *ṣeḏ* ‘apud’ is,[42] its open *ę̄* = WS *e* is due to the secondary stress of this preposition.

4.2. In some cases, by assimilation to a following *r*, *l*, *h*, and especially *n*,[43] occurring in the same syllable, *ę̄* occurs instead of the expected *ẹ̄*. This assimilation, however, was not so strong as to dissociate nouns from the usual nominal themes. Thus **perī* > **per* was not lengthened to **pẹ̄r*, *status determinatus*

[36] One may consider this form also to be due to dissimilation of *r* and subsequent lengthening. In cases of dissimilation of *r*, it is true, the following consonant is doubled (as **gargartā* > *gaggartā* ‘throat’, *v.* Brockelmann, *Gram.*, § 31); in our case, however, there is a double *r*.

[37] *v.* Brockelmann, *Gram.*, § 31, and cf. also § 47bγ; Brockelmann, *Grundriss*, I, 247, § e. Cf. also the preceding note.

[38] On the other hand, nothing can be inferred from WS *məniqiṯǫ* ‘sacred bowl’, *pace* Brockelmann, *Gram.*, 29, § bγ, since it is a loan-word < Hebrew *mənaqqīṯ*. Similarly, nothing can be inferred from many loan-words containing WS *i/e*, since they may depend upon the timbre of the vowel in the original language. Cf. also Bar Hebraeus, p. 237, l. 3, for WS *e* alternating with ES *ẹ̆*, all of them loan-words. Forms like *haykəlā* ‘palace’ owe their *ay* perhaps to the timbre of *ē* in the original language, *pace* Brockelmann, *Gram.*, 30, Anm. 3.

[39] *Pace* C. Sarauw, *Über Akzent und Silbenbildung in den älteren semitischen Sprachen*, København, 1939, p. 121, n. 1.

[40] As against ‘*aynā* ‘eye’, which seems to have been less frequent in the *status constructus*; accordingly, it developed differently, *v. supra*, p. 3, n. 24.

[41] One could, however, claim that **baynt* shifted to **bęnt* through assimilation to the *n* (§ 4.2) and *beṯ*, the *status constructus* of *baytā*, was influenced by it. This assumption, however, does not explain the (open) *e* of *ṣeḏ*.

[42] Presumably < **ṣadd*, *v.* Nöldeke, *Gram.*, § 21C, Brockelmann, *ZDMG*, XCIV, 3, 1940, 351.

[43] For the influence of *r* and *l* cf. Brockelmann, *Gram.*, § 56β; for *r* also cf. Bauer and Leander, 42u; for *h*, cf. Bauer and Leander, 39–40, Brockelmann, *Gram.*, § 60; for *n*, cf. Bauer and Leander, 41t.

**pęrā* = WS **perǫ*, but to *pẹ̄rā* = WS *pirǫ* 'fruit', in accordance with the nominal class dealt with *supra*, § 3.2.[44] Similarly, the *status constructus/absolutus* WS *'in* 'eye' does not appear as **'en*, owing to the influence of the above-mentioned nominal class. Outside of these analogical influences, however, *ę̄* appears: **hāydayn* > WS *hǫyden* 'then'; [45] **dayn* > WS *den* 'then, but'; **gayr* > WS *ger* 'in fact, for'; **hālayn* [46] > WS *hǫlen* 'these'; *'aylen* 'which (pl.)'; further, the few remnants of the dual ending *-ayn* > WS *-en*: *təren* 'two', *maṯen* '200'.[47] *-ayīn* > WS [48] *-en* is exhibited by WS *rǫmen* 'throwing (masc. pl.)', etc., *termen* 'you (fem. sing.) throw', etc. Originally short *ę* is lengthened to *ę̄* (WS *e*) before following *n*, *r*, *h*, and *l*: [49] *hennēn*, WS *henen* 'they (fem.)'; *'attēn*, WS *'aten* 'you (fem. pl.)'; *-ḵēn*, WS *-ḵen* 'you(r) (fem. pl.)'; *-hēn*, WS *-hen* 'them, their (fem. pl.)'; *-ēh*, WS *-eh* 'her', after nouns in plural, spelt with *yōdh* as *mater lectionis* before the *h*; presumably also *-eh* 'his', spelt, it is true, defectively, but vocalized in ES with *Rəbhāṣā karyā* [50]: as to the causes of the lengthening of these pronouns cf. e.g. Brockelmann, *Grundriss*, I, 302ε; 576i; Bauer and Leander, 70 l, 81z. On the other hand, WS *ber* 'my son', *'en* 'yes' are due to pausal lengthening. If *men šel* 'suddenly' (*v.* Brockelmann, *ZDMG*, XCIV, 3, 1940, 351) really belongs to this category, its open *e* may be influenced by the final *l*.[51]

5. Final *-iy*, originally followed by a vowel belonging to the nominal or verbal suffix, shifted to *ẹ̄*, WS *e* [52]: **rāmiy(u)* > WS *rǫme* 'throwing', etc.; **nirmiy(u)* > *nerme* 'he will throw', etc.[53]; *təmāniy(u)* > *təmǫne* 'eight'. On the other hand, final *ay* was preserved, both when followed by an original final

[44] Yet *gērā*, WS *gerǫ* 'arrow', has open *e*, perhaps influenced by the *r*, as against WS *ḥirǫ* 'free', *v.* § 3.2. Its derivation from *grr* is not generally accepted, *v.* e.g. Brockelmann, *LS*, s.v. (whose etymology, however, is very doubtful); yet it is borne out by *girrā* according to Targum Aramaic and the Yemenite reading tradition of Babylonian Aramaic (*v.* S. Morag, 'Oral traditions and dialects', offprint from *Proceedings of the International Conference on Semitic Studies, Jerusalem, 1965*, p. 10, n. 26). According to some (admittedly inferior) traditions it was pronounced WS *girǫ*, *v.* Bar Hebraeus, p. 230, ll. 16 ff.

[45] *Hǫydęḵ* 'then' is influenced by *hǫydęn*.

[46] cf. e.g. Bauer and Leander, 83j.

[47] *Saṯīn* (also in ES) 'two measures' is presumably influenced by the masc. pl. ending, *v.* Brockelmann, *LS*, s.v., Nöldeke, *NBSS*, 131, as against Brockelmann, *Grundriss*, I, 458. The same occurs with *maṯīn* '200', *v.* Nöldeke, *NBSS*, p. 152, n. 4.

[48] One is not inclined to assume that *ayī* shifted to *ę̄*, as against *ayi* shifting to *ẹ̄* (*v.* § 3.2).

[49] For the ordinary lengthening of *ẹ* to *ẹ̄* (WS *i*) *v.* § 3.3, where, however, slightly different cases are quoted.

[50] cf. also Bauer and Leander, 78-9, who consider this *e* to be long (but one cannot consent to the proofs adduced by them), as against Brockelmann, *Grundriss*, I, 312.

[51] At this stage of our knowledge, one should not rely too heavily on the fluctuation of ¨ and ⁚ in ES MSS, *v.* Nöldeke, *Gram.*, p. 8, l. 3; Brockelmann, *ZDMG*, XCIV, 3, 1940, 350; J. B. Segal, *The diacritical point and the accents in Syriac*, London, 1953, 30-1. The same applies perhaps to the use of *matres lectionis* in words like *šeṯ* 'six', *v.* Sarauw, op. cit. (above, p. 5, n. 39), 113, Nöldeke, *Gram.*, § 47, Brockelmann, *ZDMG*, XCIV, 3, 1940, 351.

[52] It may be argued that this *ē* was a closed one; it did not, however, shift to *i* in WS in final position. Since thus *ẹ̄* could occur in WS in final position only, where no *ę̄* was to be found, the differences between these two variants of *ē* continued to be non-phonematic, and were, accordingly, marked by the same vowel sign. Nevertheless, this seems less likely.

[53] As against **rəmiy* > *rəmī* 'throw!', having final *-iy* not followed by an original vowel.

vowel, like *marmay* ' thrown ', *salway* ' quail ',[54] and when in absolute final position, as *bīshay* (masc. pl., *stat. constr.*) ' bad ' as well as the WS imperative *'eṯpə'el 'eṯrəmay*. Nevertheless, since the differences between forms terminating in *-ay* and *-iy* are often neutralized (as with *qaṭyā* being the *status determinatus* of both *qaṭiy* and *qaṭay*), by the analogy of nouns terminating in *-iy*(*u*) >-*ē*, nouns originally ending in *-ay* may terminate in *ē* as well : *qənay*(*u*) > *qənē* ' stalk '.[55]

6. To sum up : we have to assume that in PS two variants of *ē* existed (though presumably not two phonemes). In WS *ẹ̄* remained, whereas *ẹ̄* shifted to *i* (a different phoneme, comprising both ancient *ī* and *i*, since quantitative differences disappeared in WS). In ES the situation remained as in PS, i.e. presumably the phonetic differences between the two variants of *ē* subsisted, but they were marked by the same sign, since no phonematic differences between them existed. *ẹ̄* arose in PS from non-final *ay* in closed syllables in words bearing principal stress, from non-final *ayi* and from *i'*, as well as by lengthening from *ĕ* because of total dissimilation of *l*/*n*. *ę̄* arose from non-final *ay* in closed syllables in words bearing secondary stress, from final *iy plus* vowel, from *a'*, as well as in place of *ẹ̄* by assimilation to a following tautosyllabic *h*, *r*, *l*, and *n*. Though these principal features are quite clear, they were rather blurred by analogical formation.[56]

Excursus

1. As we have seen (§ 2.1) in the case of *riš*, in principle, a form occurring in several Aramaic dialects must not be explained according to a sound shift attested in only one of them (if one does not assume that it was borrowed from that particular dialect by the others). This applies also to Aramaic *'īṯ*(*ay*) ' there is ' : if one postulates Proto-Semitic **yiṯay*,[57] the initial *'ī* is regular in Eastern Aramaic, including Syriac,[58] but not, e.g., in Biblical Aramaic (*pace*

[54] One would not claim with Birkeland, 24, that *mərammay* cannot be due to analogical formation (cf. *qəṭull* : *rəmayt* = *maqaṭṭal* : *X*), but a form like *salway* exhibits, no doubt, original *-ay*. *Laylę̄* ' night ' < **laylay* (cf. p. 4, n. 26) is not only due to the analogy of nouns terminating in *-iy* (*qashyā* : *qəshē* = *lilyā* : *X*), but to dissimilation as well.

[55] *Pace* Birkeland, 23, *qənę̄* = Arabic *qanan*, *qanāt* has to be analysed as *quṭal*. The plural *-ēn* of nouns ending in original *-iy* is presumably due to the analogy of nouns terminating in original *-ay*, *v.* e.g. Bauer and Leander, 64y. For another explanation *v.* E. Kutscher, *Studies in Galilean Aramaic* (in Hebrew), Jerusalem, 1952, p. 28, n. 1. On the other hand, forms like infinitive *p'al* WS *mermǫ* ' to throw ' < **mermay* are due to the analogy of the perfect, *v.* Brockelmann, *Grundriss*, I, 379.

[56] One has, however, to admit that Syriac grammars and MSS sometimes contain pronunciation systems different from what is known to us both from ES and WS standard vocalization. We stand only at the beginning of these investigations, cf. for the time being the important observations of Segal, *The diacritical point, passim*, especially 28 ff., 152–3. Accordingly, further investigations may alter the conclusions reached.

[57] *v.* Nöldeke, *Mandäische Grammatik*, p. 293, n. 5.

[58] *v.* e.g. Nöldeke, *Mandäische Grammatik*, 55–6 (who, op. cit., p. 293, n. 5, in my opinion exaggerates when stating that the shift *yə* > *'ī* occurs ' more or less ' in every Aramaic dialect ; it is not impossible that his words are based on the occurrence of *'īṯ*) ; Brockelmann, *Gram.*, p. 45, Anm. 4 ; for the Aramaic of the Babylonian Talmud e.g. J. N. Epstein, *A grammar of Babylonian Aramaic* (in Hebrew), Jerusalem, Tel-Aviv, 1960, p. 77, n. 199, 203.

Brockelmann, *Grundriss*, I, 188h*a*). Therefore, Bauer and Leander, p. 254, Anm. 2, saw themselves compelled to assume an Eastern Aramaic loan. This, however, is precluded by Ugaritic *iṯ*. Accordingly, one prefers to postulate two independent words [59] (which were later confused) expressing existence: **'īṯay* and **yiš*. Arabic *laysa* 'is not' is a continuation of the latter (the final *a* perhaps being due to its being carried over to the category of verbs in the perfect) as well as Hebrew *yeš*, whereas the rare Hebrew *'iš*, Ugaritic *iṯ* (presumably to be read **'iṯē*), and Aramaic *'īṯ(ay)* relate to the former.

2. The best explanation so far offered for the masc. pl. *status determinatus* ending *-ę̄* is that of J. Cantineau, *BEOIFD*, I, 1931, p. 92, n. 1: *-áy'a* > *-ay'* > *ę̄*.` One would like to add that *-ay* in *status constructus* masculine plural was preserved, because it occurred in an open syllable. *'esrę̄* '10 (fem., in the series 11–19)' instead of the expected **esray* has to be derived from **'esrayh*, so that *ay* stood in a closed syllable. Cf. in Ugaritic (with its consonantal spelling in which *h* as *mater lectionis* never occurs) *'šrh* = **'išrēh*, further Hebrew עֶשְׂרֵה (*sic*, with *h* as *mater lectionis*) with closed final *ē*: **'eśrayh* > **eśrẹ̄h* (cf. nouns like *ḥẹ̄q* < **ḥayq* 'bosom') > *'eśrẹ̄*.[60] One wonders, however, how to explain the final *h*. Is it a demonstrative element ?[61] At any rate, one cannot agree with Brockelmann's view (*Gram.*, 60-1, *v.* also Brockelmann, *Grundriss*, I, 412–13) that, besides *-ay*, a fem. ending *-ē* also existed, shown by *'esrē* as well as by *ḥrēn*, WS *ḥrin* 'other'. As to *ḥrēn/ḥrin*, if one follows Brockelmann's argument, loc. cit., one will assume that the original masc. form was **'oḥrān*, the fem. form **'oḥray* [*sic*]. To the latter form, in which the fem. ending was no longer recognized as such, the usual fem. ending of the *status determinatus* was added: **'oḥraytā*, on the basis of which the masc. *status absolutus* **'oḥrayn*/*status determinatus* **'oḥraynā* was formed. **'oḥrayn* shifted to **'oḥrēn*, WS **oḥrin*,[62] because *ay* stood in a closed syllable, from which then *ḥərēn*, WS *ḥərin* developed. Later *ḥərin* influenced the *status determinatus*, which became *ḥərinǫ*, through the influence of which again the feminine *ḥəriṯǫ* arose.

3. *Hāḏę* 'this (fem.)' is difficult to explain. It *may* be due to dissimilation < **hāḏā*, still preserved in *hāḏay* 'this is'; it *may* have originated from **hadiya*, cf. Arabic *hiya* 'she', further Phoenician **z'*, *v.* Brockelmann, *Grundriss*, I, 321, J. Friedrich, *Phönizisch-punische Grammatik*, Roma, 1951,

[59] This had been proposed by other scholars, even before the discovery of Ugaritic *iṯ*, *v.* e.g. F. R. Blake, *JAOS*, XXXV, 1915, 377 ff.; I. Eitan, *AJSL*, XLV, 1928–9, 138.

[60] Final *-ay* followed by the case vowel should have shifted to *ę̄*, cf. H. Birkeland, *Über Akzent und Vokalismus im Althebräischen*, Oslo, 1949, 6.

[61] cf. for the addition of demonstrative elements to numerals J. Barth, *Sprachwissenschaftliche Untersuchungen*, II, Berlin, 1911, 2 ff. The only other Hebrew noun terminating in *status absolutus* in *ę̄* is *'aryę̄* 'lion'. Is it a loan-word from Aramaic ? This is, at any rate, the opinion of Bauer and Leander, p. 193, n. 2, M. Wagner, *Die lexikalischen und grammatikalischen Aramaismen im alttestamentlichen Hebräisch*, Berlin, 1966, 29–30. *Yošpē* is attested both with *ę̄* and *ẹ̄*.

[62] The closed *ē* was not assimilated to the following *n*, because of the analogy of nouns like *'aynā* : *'ę̄n* = **'oḥraynā* : *X*.

48–9, partly, perhaps, to be interpreted **zi'a*, Moabite *z't* (Mesha 3), Gəʿez *zīʾa* with pronominal suffix to mark possessive pronoun, *di'a* in the Aramaic incantation text from Nippur in cuneiform, ll. 2, 4; it *may*, however, reflect Proto-Semitic *ē*: though I do not believe in the existence of Proto-Semitic *ē* as a phoneme,[63] one will not deny that it did exist phonetically, and in isolated words like the demonstrative pronoun, *ē* in the single languages may be a direct continuation of Proto-Semitic *ē*. The same may apply to *kẹmaṯ* 'that is', for which, however, J. Barth, *Die Pronominalbildung in den semitischen Sprachen*, Leipzig, 1913, p. 89, n. 1, claims foreign extraction, a distinctly unlikely assertion. As to the adhortative particle *nē*, WS *ni*, one has to bear in mind the special character of interjections. Moreover, one has perhaps to take into account Bar Hebraeus' assertion (p. 160, l. 18; p. 204, l. 11) that it is a Hebrew word.

[63] For the vast literature about this subject cf. H. Fleisch, *Traité de philologie arabe*, I, Beyrouth, 1961, 69; cf. also S. Moscati (ed.), *An introduction to the comparative grammar of the Semitic languages*, Wiesbaden, 1964, 46–7.

Additions

to **p. 302**.*15*: It is quite interesting that in the more archaic version iiSamuel 22.29 נֵירִי is spelt, as against the later version Psalms 18.29 נֵרִי.

to **p. 302**.*-2*: The spelling with *y* **may** be influenced by the iiy verb in both Hebrew (הֵרִיחַ) and Syriac (*râḥ*.).

to **p. 306**.*4*: For details see supra pp. 222ff.

Hebrew and North West Semitic: Reflections on the Classification of the Semitic Languages

*

1. AS IS WELL KNOWN, the comparative method has been elaborated upon with reference to the Indo-European languages. For more than a century, it has been customary to view them from the angle of both the family-tree theory and the wave hypothesis. As far as the continuity of the territory of Indo-European languages can be posited, it is the wave hypothesis that best explains the relation of the languages involved. Yet the position of the Indo-European languages in historical times presupposes migrations, and the linguistic situation due to them is best interpreted in the light of the family-tree theory.[1]

2. One immediately recognizes that the wave hypothesis is much more convincing if applied to the Semitic languages. Even a hasty glance at the map of the Semitic tongues, in the past and in our own day, more or less reveals the continuity of the domain of these languages. Moreover, close contact between various Semitic idioms is well attested throughout history, the more so since Semitic languages surprisingly often were established as *linguae francae*, used in preference to the spoken language. This was the case not only with the language of a great power, viz., Akkadian, in which, e.g., Canaanite princes wrote their diplomatic correspondence with Pharaoh around 1400 B.C.E. (the Tel el-Amarna letters), but also with Phoenician, used in Karatepe and Zen-

1. See, e.g., Porzig (1954, p. 28).

jirli, and especially with Aramaic. The status of the latter as an international language is mirrored in the Hebrew Bible in the demand of Hezekiah's officials from Rab-Shakeh to speak Aramaic, rather than Akkadian (2 Kgs 18:26). Cultural contact is well attested outside the domain of the *lingua franca* as well, one of its outstanding examples being the affinity of poetic structure in Hebrew and Ugaritic. Accordingly, linguistic phenomena were apt to spread to Semitic dialects which had different origins and histories, which thus eventually give the impression that they historically belonged to a separate branch of the Semitic languages, which had earlier seceded from the other branches of the Semitic speech community. In fact, however, the similarity of these dialects is due to contact and parallel development.

2.1 The possibility of parallel development is, it seems, a factor to be taken into consideration even more in Semitic than in Indo-European languages. The importance of the fundamental difficulty of distinguishing between initial identity and parallel development, which pertains to the very essence of comparative linguistics, was stressed for comparative Indo-European grammar by Meillet in a famous paper (1958, pp. 36–43). Because of the very close affinity of Semitic tongues, which are not less similar to each other than languages belonging to one branch of Indo-European, constituting a very similar starting point for the various Semitic languages, one must allow for the possibility of parallel development on a larger scale than in Indo-European linguistics.[2]

2. Accordingly, it is very difficult to distinguish between the diffusion of linguistic elements, in accordance with the wave hypothesis, and parallel (and even convergent) development. Thus, the features interpreted by Rabin in his important and stimulating paper (1963) as due to linguistic diffusion, are, to my mind, rather cases of parallel development, the assumption of linguistic diffusion being contravened by the fact that most of the features adduced by Rabin extend over very long periods. Constant attention to the possibility of parallel development may save the scholar from pitfalls such as Kutscher's suggestion (1971, pp. 389–390) that, if during the centuries of its coexistence with Canaanite-Hebrew, Aramaic has jettisoned those (consonantal) phonemes that were alien to Canaanite-Hebrew, one can think of only one reason—the fact that the Canaanite-Hebrew substratum was able to assert itself, imposing its phonemic set upon the Aramaic substratum. This assumption, however, though possible, is by no means necessary. The (synchronic) identity of the stock of consonantal phonemes of Official Aramaic with that of Canaanite-Hebrew may well be due to convergent development. Setting aside the special development of the laryngals/pharyngals, due to the Sumerian substratum, Akkadian has developed exactly the same stock of consonantal phonemes as Canaanite-Hebrew, and, with the partial exception of the shift ś>š, even the individual sound shifts were identical with that of Canaanite-Hebrew, as against the different sound shifts in Aramaic! Therefore, the (synchronically) identical stock of consonantal phonemes in Canaanite-Hebrew and Aramaic may well be due to the general drift, which exerted its influence on Akkadian as well.

2.2 The importance of contact and parallel development in Semitic comparative grammar does not, of course, entirely dispense with the need for the model of the family-tree diagram. The basic dvision of the Semitic languages into East Semitic (=Akkadian) and West Semitic is best explained by the assumption of the early separation of Akkadian from the rest of the Semitic tongues, in accordance with the family-tree model. Later, to be sure, Akkadian came into close contact with various Semitic languages, influencing them[3] and being influenced by them,[4] so that even for Akkadian, the family-tree model does not suffice.[5]

3. Introductions to comparative linguistics almost invariably mention the more favorable case, where the parent language is known from written records,[6] viz., the Romance dialects. Therefore, it will be convenient to start with such a case among the Semitic languages, viz., the modern Arabic dialects. One will take care, to be sure, not to simply identify Classical Arabic[7] or even its pre-Islamic predecessor with the parent language of the Arabic dialects or to consider pre-Islamic standard Arabic and the parent language of the Arabic dialects as if they were "mother" and "daughter." It stands to reason that they were rather "sister" languages, closely related and mutually intelligible, so that it is not too difficult to reconstruct the proto-language of the Arabic dialects which, to be sure, was by no means homogeneous (cf. Fischer, 1959, p. vii). The same applies, however, to Proto-Romance as well (see Hall, 1972): Classical Latin differs in various respects from Proto-Romance and is decidedly not its direct ancestor, and one must take into account the dialectal division in Proto-Romance as well. And just as the comparative study of the Romance languages is especially important because of the light it sheds on the value of our inferences in the cases in which no record of the proto-language is available, so is the comparative study of the Arabic dialects.

3. See, e.g., Zimmern (1917), Kutscher (1971, pp. 386–387), and Kaufman (1974).

4. See, e.g., for Aramaic influence: Rimalt (1932) and Kutscher (1971, pp. 356–358); for "Amorite" influence: Moran (1965, p. 62) and Kaufman (1974, pp. 22–27), who also mentions Aramaic influence; in general: Ungnad-Matouš (1964, pp. 7–8).

5. Yet even a model like Southworth's (1964), which takes into account independent isoglosses, does not suffice, since it loses sight of changes due to contact.

6. So, e.g., Bloomfield (1933, pp. 300ff).

7. I do not claim, of course, that Arabic has especially preserved the Proto-Semitic language type. In my opinion (see already Bergsträsser, 1928, pp. 134ff), in the main, Arabic mirrors the late Semitic language type. Similarly, nobody will claim that Latin, rather than any other Indo-European language, mirrors the ancient Indo-European language structure. Yet both Latin and Arabic have the great advantage of, more or less, serving as proto-languages.

3.1 Before starting with a (rather cursory) overall comparative view of the Arabic dialects (see Section 3.2 below), it will be expedient to adduce some features in which pre-Islamic standard Arabic and the parent language of the Arabic dialects (at least partly) differ. Whereas Classical Arabic uses *'ī* ("yes"), both *'ē* (see, e.g., Barthélemy, 1935–69, s.v.) and *'aywā* (<*'ay wallāhi*; see, e.g., Dozy, 1881, s.v.,[8] also borrowed into Turkish, which again influenced some Arabic dialects), occurring in some dialects, attest to **'ay*. As against Classical Arabic *hākaðā*, many dialects suggest an etymon *hākiðā* (see Blanc, 1964, p. 199, note 161). Whereas the perfect forms of *verba mediae geminatae* terminating in suffixes beginning with a consonant are built like *ḥalalt(u)* in Classical Arabic, in dialects *ḥallayt* and its developments prevail, already attested as ancient dialectal forms (see Kofler, 1941, p. 65; Wright, 1896–1898, I, p. 69). *

3.2 Relying on features like *ḥallayt* mentioned above, Ferguson (1959) posited a relatively homogeneous *koiné* in the first centuries of the Muslim era, from which most modern sedentary dialects stem, especially those outside Arabia. Yet this theory has to be rejected, especially since the history of the Arabic dialects lacks a single linguistic center of prestige and communication (for particulars see Blau, 1965a, pp. 12–17 and forthcoming, §§6.5, 6.6). * Moreover, Bedouin dialects, even from Arabia, frequently evince features that are generally considered as peculiar to the sedentary vernaculars and in other cases fluctuate between what is presumably old Bedouin usage and a new one which corresponds to that of the sedentary dialects, thus revealing the imprint of the latter and/or convergent development. Thus the *koiné* stands at the end of the linguistic development, rather than at its beginning, being due to the general drift and the diffusion of linguistic features. The main lesson to be learned from the growth of the modern Arabic dialects is the understanding of the extent of the diffusion of language forms, also favored by the basic similarity of the various dialects (which also facilitated parallel development). Not only phonetic features, like the shift of *q* to ', spread over a vast dialect area, as well as lexemes, like *hayk* ("so"; see Blau, 1965a, p. 14), but morphological innovations as well, as *ḥallayt* quoted above. It is generally assumed (see, e.g., Weinreich, 1953, pp. 31–37, 43–44 and Kaufman, 1974, p. 122), that, under favorable circumstances, even bound morphemes may be transferred from language to language; and in the case of the Arabic dialects (as well as in the case of close contact between Semitic languages), the

8. Féghali (1919, p. 15, note 5) offers a much less plausible etymology. This, however, does not affect the derivation of *'ay* from **'ay*, rather than from **'ī*.

circumstances were favorable indeed: because of the great similarity between these tongues the diffusion of even bound morphemes was made possible. Accordingly, even unmotivated morphological innovations[9] shared by Semitic languages being in close contact are not necessarily valid for genetic classification, since they *may* be due to the diffusion resulting from close contact. This, of course, makes genetic classification that much more difficult.

4. It seems that the basic division of the Semitic languages into East (= Akkadian) and West Semitic is sound. Akkadian is characterized in a positive way by the far-reaching influence of the Sumerian substratum, phonetically mirrored in the weakening of the laryngals/pharyngals, and in a negative way by the absence of the West Semitic perfect *qatala* and the internal passive. It could have happened, to be sure, that some Semitic dialect exhibiting the Akkadian type stative **qatila/*qatula* (rather than the West Semitic type perfect *qatala* and passive *qutila* etc.) developed the West Semitic forms through close contact with a Western type dialect rather than by genetically belonging to the West Semitic type (cf. Hetzron, 1975, p. 108); and Hetzron (1976, p. 105) even considers the possibility of independent innovation. Yet, in my opinion, the existence of *qatala* and *qutila* in all the Semitic languages[10] with the exception of Akkadian makes the assumption of a separate historical West Semitic entity for at least most of them absolutely imperative, in accordance with the theory accepted by most scholars.

4.1 An additional feature, *historically* a part of the structure of the West Semitic languages, yet *perhaps* originally absent from Akkadian, is the indicative "imperfect" *yqtlu*.[11] Some scholars, to be sure, posited it for Proto-

9. For the importance of morphological features for genetic classification cf., e.g., Meillet (1958, pp. 91–92), Polotsky (1964, p. 360, note 10), and especially Hetzron (1974, pp. 181–194; 1975, pp. 107–108; 1976, pp. 89–108).

10. During the development of the West Semitic languages some, in turn, *lost qatala* and *qutila*. *qatala*, e.g., is absent from modern East Aramaic dialects, and in many Semitic languages the internal passive has been superseded by former reflexive verbal themes. In the latter case, however, the category of the passive is still present, although its formal expression has changed. Moreover, in both cases, these languages exhibit later developments, after they had historically possessed *qatala/qutila*. In Akkadian, however, the use of the stative mirrors a stage in which the perfect *qatala* and the passive had *not yet* developed.

11. Again, it is absent from many West Semitic languages. This, however, was due to historical development as well, during which the imperfect *yqtlu* disappeared. We shall deal later (in Section 5) with the hypothesis that *yqtlu* formed a part of "Central" Semitic only. Here, we are concerned only with the question of whether or not *yqtlu* was a part of the Proto-Akkadian verbal structure as well, i.e., whether it was a Proto-Semitic or rather a West Semitic feature.

Semitic (Soden, 1959, as punctual, as against durative *yaqattil,* both Proto-Semitic in his opinion), whereas Kuryłowicz (1961, pp. 55ff; cf. also p. 49) considered *yqtlu* the original imperfect in Akkadian as well, which was later replaced in Akkadian by *yaqattal,* etc. and confined to secondary functions, viz., as *modus relativus* (in relative clauses, etc.). Since the relegation of ancient features to secondary features (I would rather speak of their preservation in closed syntagmemes)[12] is very well attested, this proposition is quite attractive. One must not, however, lose sight of the fact that, synchronically at least, the alleged continuation of Proto-Semitic **yaqtulu,* i.e., Akkadian *iprusu,* does not denote the indicative imperfect in relative clauses, etc., but rather the preterite in this syntactic environment, the imperfect (present) being marked by *iparrasu.* Accordingly, if one adheres to the view that *iprusu* originates in the Proto-Semitic indicative imperfect *yaqtulu,* one has to postulate that, through the impact of the Akkadian preterite *iprus,* the use of *iprusu* became that of *modus relativus* of the preterite (and then the *modus relativus* ending *-u* was transposed to the other indicative forms as well).[13] This supposition is, to be sure, possible, yet rather intricate. On the other hand, there are internal Akkadian indications which may suggest the (comparatively) late date of the emergence of Akkadian *iparras* (=*yaqattal*): many "weak" verbs[14] exhibit "weak" formation of *iparras* (see Soden, 1952, pp. 126ff) and this may indicate that these forms were built according to the preterite forms, exhibiting *yaqtul* etc. This assumption would, e.g., explain the present *ubbal* (from *wabālum,* "to carry"), formed according to the preterite *ūbil* (alongside "strong" D *uwaššar*; one will interpret "weak" D forms as being influenced by the "weak" G forms). This interpretation is, *prima facie,* buttressed by the fact that in Old Akkadian original I pharyngals/laryngals behave as "strong" verbs (see Gelb, 1961, p. 181), thus suggesting that their later "weakness" is due to the influence of *verba I w/y* etc. Accordingly, one would fix the time of

12. For the relegation of ancient features to closed syntagmemes (cf. Blau, 1961-62, pp. 70–71) see Arabic *yqtl* in the sense of the past used only after *lam* and in conditional clauses, Hebrew *yqtl* after *wa-* ("and"); Arabic *lā* preceding *qtl* in parallel negations; *yktb* (as against *bktb*) in some modern Arabic dialects as subjunctive; Arabic *'aḥad* (as against *wāḥid*) after negation etc., as the first member of construct structures and in certain numerals; in modern Aramaic dialects the participle without *ko* is used in subordination (Cohen, 1924, p. 216). Cf. also Blau (1960, p. 100).

13. For the productivity of the *-u* suffix cf. its Middle Babylonian (sometimes also Old Babylonian) addition to the third person singular feminine ending of the stative (cf. Soden, 1952, p. 108). Sarauw (1912, p. 68) posits an original *modus relativus iparrasu*, from which the *u* was then transferred to *iprus*.

14. I do not take into account *verba mediae w/y*, because the doubling of the last radical, rather than of *w/y*, may be due to the aversion to double *w*, attested in several Semitic languages (see Blau, 1971, pp. 147ff).

(pp. 169ff.)

the emergence of *iparras after* the "weak" formation of G *iprus* of *I w/y* (as demonstrated by *ubbal* built according to *ūbil*), but before I pharyngals/laryngals had become "weak" (as hinted by "strongly" formed *iparras* of these verbs in Old Akkadian). If the assumption of the late date of *iparras* should, in fact, turn out to be true,[15] it would make the notion of an early Akkadian **yaqtulu* much more palatable.

4.2 There are, however, rather strong indications that *yaqattal* etc. is a Proto-Semitic, or even a "Hamito-Semitic" feature, being attested in Ethiopic and Berber (see Polotsky, 1964, pp. 110–111). Parallel development, to be sure, is a very frequent feature in Semitic languages (see Section 2.1 above) and it has been assumed for *yaqattal* by many scholars (see the literature adduced by Polotsky, 1964, p. 358, note 29). Yet one has to admit that the existence of a strange feature such as gemination outside D,[16] occurring in Akkadian, Ethiopic and Berber makes it much more likely to assume that Akkadian *iparras* (as well as its Ethiopic[17] and Berber parallels) continue a Proto-(Hamito-)Semitic feature, although it is not easy to understand its "weak" formation in the Akkadian weak verb.

Nevertheless, this assumption does not necessarily imply that the Akkadian *modus relativus iprusu* cannot be the continuation of Proto-Semitic *yaqtulu* etc. One could postulate (with Soden, 1957) that in Proto-Semitic two present/future forms coexisted, viz., punctual *yaqtulu* etc., and durative *yaqattil* etc. In Akkadian *yaqattil* superseded *yaqtulu*, which was preserved only in closed syntagmemes, i.e., in relative clauses etc.

5. In Ethiopic and modern South Arabic no traces of *yaqtulu* etc. can be detected, and we do not know how to vocalize the prefix tense forms in Epigraphic South Arabic.[18] The so-called North West Semitic languages as

15. Cf. also Bergsträsser, 1918-29, II, p. 12.

16. Cf. Sarauw (1912, p. 67). On the other hand, I do not agree with his assumption that, were *yaqtulu* early, *yaqtulu* and *yaqtul* would have to be interpreted as moods of one tense. The "imperfect" *yaqtulu* and the preterite *yaqtul* are different tenses, and it is only between *yaqtulu* and the jussive *yaqtul* that a relationship of moods obtains.

17. No certain traces of *yaqattal* etc. have been detected in North West Semitic languages. In "Amorite," because of its close contact with Akkadian, such forms, especially in proper names, could well exhibit Akkadian influence. Biblical Hebrew reflects no vestiges of it (despite Meyer, 1966-72, I, p. 19; II, pp. 121, 134–135), nor does Ugaritic (see Gordon, 1965, p. 67, §9.2, following H. L. Ginsberg). Cf., in general, Fenton (1970).

18. The subjunctive of *verba III w/y* clearly evinces that it terminated in a vowelless *w/y*. As to the controversy on the origins of the Main Verb-Markers in the Northern Gurage verb, see the exposition and the literature adduced by Hetzron (1977, pp. 88–92). At any rate, even according to Hetzron's view, the Main Verb-Markers do not attest to Proto-West Semitic *yaqtulu*.

well as Arabic, on the other hand, attest to *yaqtulu*. Therefore, Hetzron (1974, p. 189; 1975, p. 107; 1976, p. 105; 1977, pp. 14–15), who regarded *yaqtulu* as an innovation, posited a Central Semitic branch, consisting of Arabic, Canaanite and Aramaic, sharing the morphological innovation *yaqtulu* (cf. also Polotsky, 1964, p. 110), thus restricting South Semitic to South Arabic and Ethiopic, which, like Akkadian, did not share the innovated *yaqtulu*.

One can hardly consider the claim that *yaqtulu* was absent from Proto-South Arabic (from which Ethiopic as well branched off) as proven. *If* Proto-Semitic in fact had two forms marking the present/future, viz., punctual *yaqtulu* and durative *yaqattil*, these forms were threatened because of their similarity in function, on the one hand, and because of their formal similarity to *yaqtul* and the D prefix form, on the other. Therefore, the total absence of one of them from any language does not prove that it did not occur in a preceding stratum. Thus the total disappearance of the short imperfect from rabbinic Hebrew, as opposed to the ordinary imperfect, could be interpreted as an indication of the total absence of *yaqtulu* in the linguistic strata preceding rabbinic Hebrew; yet biblical Hebrew, exhibiting the short imperfect as opposed to the ordinary one, attests to the existence of *yaqtulu*. Similarly, nothing must be inferred from the lack of any indication of *yaqtulu* in modern South Arabic and Ethiopic for Proto-South Arabic. Furthermore, as to Epigraphic South Arabic, although it is very difficult to state anything certain because of the total lack of vocalization, the possibility of *w/y* used as *matres lectionis* (see Beeston, 1962, p. 5; Jamme, 1962, p. 80b, line 7), and the uncertainty as to the classes of verbal themes, I nevertheless have the feeling that it is easier to interpret various forms by the assumption that, presumably alongside *yaqattil* etc., Epigraphic South Arabic also had *yaqtulu* etc. Thus the simplest way to account for verbs *II w/y* spelled without *w/y* in indicative function (like *yknn*; see Beeston, 1962, p. 26) is to postulate *yakûnunna*, *yakûnanna*, i.e. an "energetic" form derived from *yaqtul*. Yet one may interpret such forms in accordance with Akkadian forms exhibiting doubling of the last, rather than of the middle radical (like *ikunnū*). The same may apply (cf. Jamme, 1962, no. 577, line 5) to *wyh'nw* ("and they helped," root *'wn*), which, however, may also exhibit short imperfect denoting the past (yet cf. *ibid.*, line 12 *ylfyhmw*, also referring to the past, and because of the *y* presumably not to be interpreted as short imperfect). On the other hand, *yhqðw* (with assimilation of the *n*, root *nqð*, "he carried away"; Jamme, 1962, no. 586, line 22) by necessity exhibits a vowelless first radical (because of the assimilation of the *n*) and is, therefore, presumably to be interpreted as *yaqtulu* (this is more likely than its interpretation as short imperfect referring to the past, cf. *ylfyhmw* quoted above). If the *b*-imperfect is in fact indicative (see Höfner, 1943, pp. 79–81; Beeston, 1962, pp. 24–25), *bymd* (root *mdd*; Beeston, 1976, p. 420, line 72) exhibits *yaqtulu*. Höfner (1943, p. 90) interprets *yhzḥ* as *yuhaziḥḥu*, and I am inclined to interpret similarly the *h*-causatives of *ṣrr* and $s_3l\,l$ referring to the past (see Jamme, 1962, s.vv. *hṣr* and *hšl* [!]). I have also noted imperfect forms terminating in (energetic?) *n* in relative clauses in indicative function, without, however, losing sight of the fact that in Epigraphic South Arabic there seems to be formal affinity between the use of the imperfect in relative clauses and the jussive (see Beeston, 1962, p. 24): *yknn* (see above, root *kwn*) in Jamme (1962, no. 750, line 14); *yz'n* (root *wz'*, "he will continue"), *ibid.*, no. 577, line 18; *ymrn* (root *mrr*, "it occurs (?)"), *ibid.*, no. 711, line 5. Cf. also Jamme (1962) no. 669, line 10; no. 729, line 9 *yldn* ("he will be born," in conditional clauses), root *wld*; no. 577, line 15 *yθrw* ("they leveled", root *wθr*). These examples (which can easily be augmented), although they can be explained in various ways, nevertheless give the impression that they at least partly attest to the existence of *yaqtulu* in Epigraphic South Arabic. At any rate, there is no indication for its absence from Epigraphic South Arabic. Accordingly, one ought rather to abstain from transferring Arabic to the "innovating Central Semitic" branch because of the alleged absence of *yaqtulu* etc. in Proto-South Arabic.

5.1 Nor do the other alleged innovations of Arabic, shared with Canaanite and Aramaic, prove that Arabic is closer to Canaanite and Aramaic than to South Arabic and Ethiopic, and that, accordingly, it has to be grouped with the former as Central Semitic, rather than with the latter as South Semitic.

5.1.1 There exist positive indications of shared innovations common to South Arabic, Ethiopic, and Arabic. The most outstanding among these are the "broken plurals." One must not claim that they mirror a common retention (so Hetzron, 1975, p. 102): even if the notion of broken plurals should turn out to be an ancient Hamito-Semitic feature, it is not the existence of broken plurals as such that proves the close affinity of Arabic, South Arabic and Ethiopic, but rather their widespread formal identity; cf., e.g., Arabic *qital*, Ge'ez *qətal;* Arabic *qatalat*, Ge'ez *qatalt*, both denoting plurals of participles and *nomina agentia*; Arabic *qitāl*, Ge'ez *qətāl*; Arabic *qutūl*, Ge'ez *qətūl*; Arabic *'aqtul*, *'aqtilat*, Ge'ez *'aqtəl*, *'aqtəlt*; Arabic and Ge'ez *'aqtāl*; Arabic *maqātil*, *maqātilat*, Ge'ez *maqātəl*, *maqātəlt*. The occurrence of some scattered parallels to these broken plurals in other Semitic languages must not be considered remnants, but rather the primary elements from which the South Semitic languages, including Arabic, built their broken plurals. The comparatively late age of the broken plurals is proven by their invariable tri-radical form, whereas the "sound plural" has sometimes preserved its bi-literal form: cf. Arabic *banūna* ("sons"), formed from the bi-radical basis *ban*, as against the tri-radical broken plural *'abnā* (cf. Blau, 1965, p. 278).[19] *

5.1.2. Another important morphological innovation shared by the South Semitic languages is the development of the verbal theme *qātala*. *qātala*, it seems, is a general West Semitic innovation, yet its development in quite a similar manner in Arabic and Ethiopic (see Fleisch, 1944, especially his general conclusion on pp. 417ff) has, in all probability, to be interpreted as an additional proof for the inclusion of Arabic in the South Semitic group. *

5.1.3 I consider the broken plurals and *qātala* as the main morphological proof for the affinity of Arabic and South Arabic (including Ethiopic). Other real or alleged shared features are less cogent. Nothing can be inferred from the existence of *f*, instead of northern *p*, because the shift *p*>*f*, without necessarily applying to other stops, is a universal feature (see Vendryès, 1972, p. 110). In both Arabic and Ge'ez *š* shifted to *s*, and *ś to š*. This, however, is another case of surprising parallel developments, so often occurring in Semitic languages: it has been proven that in Epigraphic South Arabic and modern South Arabic these shifts have not occurred (see the literature cited in Blau, 1970, note 4, and further in Beeston, 1977). The use of *qātil* for ordinal numbers in Arabic, Ge'ez, modern (and presumably also Epigraphic) South Arabic may be due to shared innovation; it might, however, also be the result of parallel development and contact. Arabic *tanwīn* corresponds to Epigraphic South Arabic *tamyīm*; yet no clear indication for its general use in Ethiopic can be detected. All the South Semitic languages, even those which do not form the causative by **š*, form the *t*-form of the causative by **št*. This, however, may be due to phonetic reasons. Whereas no phonetic reasons opposed the replacement of the *š*-causative by the *h/'*-causative, there were phonetic reasons not only for the preservation of the *t*-form of the *š*-causative, but even for the replacement of the *t*-form of the *h/'*-causative (which sub-

19. Hetzron (1974, p. 183, following Lambert and Greenberg), considers the broken plurals to be a common (Hamito-) Semitic feature, regarding the *a*-plural of the segolate nouns in Hebrew a remnant of the broken plural as well. This view, however, is not convincing. Forms parallel to these *a*-plurals are well attested in Arabic, as *'aradūna* from *'arḍ* ("land"), *ḍarabāt* from *ḍarb* ("blow"), and they must not be interpreted as ancient broken plurals with later addition of the sound plural suffixes, since in Classical Arabic it is the broken plural that expands to the detriment of the sound plurals. Accordingly, the type *ġuraf* ("rooms") has to be regarded as later than *ġurafāt*. Therefore the *a*-plurals of the monosyllabic ("segolate") nouns have to be considered as original sound plurals, rather than broken plurals with later addition of the plural suffixes.

sisted in Aramaic only; for a different interpretation see Bravmann, 1977, pp. 201–202). For shared lexical features between Arabic and Ethiopic cf., e.g., Littmann (1954, p. 353).

5.1.4 On the other hand, other indications for the alleged special affinity of Arabic with Canaanite and Aramaic, adduced by Hetzron (and following him by Rabin in a lecture delivered at the Seventh World Congress of Jewish Studies, August 1977), are not convincing. Hetzron (1976, pp. 92–93) has rightly stressed what he calls "the principle of archaic heterogeneity" (cf. also, e.g., Blau, 1972a, pp. 90, 120), according to which the relatively most heterogeneous system is considered to be the most archaic, the more homogeneous ones being assumed to have risen as a result of simplification. Yet he does not sufficiently take into consideration that such simplifications may arise independently in various languages as a result of linguistic drift. Hetzron (1974, p. 191; 1975, pp. 93–94) posits two innovative groups: Central Semitic—including Canaanite, Aramaic, and Arabic; and South Semitic—consisting of South Arabic and Ethiopic; Central Semitic having innovated *t*-suffixes in the perfect in a homogeneous way, South Semitic *k*-suffixes, whereas Akkadian has preserved heterogeneous *k* and *t*. That the heterogeneous system of Akkadian has been made homogeneous in all the other Semitic languages is quite understandable. Yet, there were only two ways in which this could be achieved: by the preponderance of either *t* or *k*. Since the chances in each direction were fifty percent, the chances of independent development are extraordinarily high,[20] so that it must not be used for genetic grouping.

Hetzron (1974, pp. 189–190; 1976, pp. 94–95) has, quite ingeniously, called attention to the heterogeneity of the prefix-vowels in the prefix tense of G in Akkadian, as against their uniformity in the other Semitic languages. These split into two branches: South Semitic (= South Arabic and Ethiopic), which completely eliminated the open vowel *a* from the system; and "Central Semitic," which originally used *a* before thematic *i/u*, but *i* before thematic *a*; later Arabic generalized *a* and "the rest submitted the prefix vowels to a reduction process."[21] Again, it is very difficult to use this feature for genetic classification. It is not even quite certain that the heterogeneity of Akkadian is

20. Through the influence of the corresponding pronominal suffixes, new suffixes penetrated into the second person of the perfect in various dialects (see Nöldeke, 1904b, pp. 21–22), an additional indication for the wide range of independent parallel development.

21. So Hetzron (1976, p. 95). This, to be sure, is not entirely accurate in Hebrew, but this fact does not affect the problem treated.

archaic. Hetzron himself (1976, p. 93) cautioned against using heterogeneity as an indication of an archaic feature if one can find a clear conditioning for differentiation. This, indeed, can be detected in this case: the prefix *ni* might have been originally *na,* which later became *ni* through the impact of the corresponding separate personal pronoun **niḥnū* (see Ungnad, cited by Hetzron, 1974, p. 190, note 10); whereas *i* might have risen from *ya* through assimilation (for *ya* >*i* in Old Akkadian, see Gelb, 1961, p. 122). Yet even if the Akkadian heterogeneity turns out to be archaic, nothing may, in my opinion, be inferred from it for the genetic classification of West Semitic. First, it may well be that the opposition *yiqtal*:*yaqti/ul* is a general West Semitic phenomenon, characteristic not only of "Central" Semitic, but of South Semitic as well. As is well known, this opposition disappeared also in "Central" Semitic, leaving a few vestiges in Hebrew and only slight traces in Aramaic and Arabic. Accordingly, its absence in most branches of South Semitic (Ethiopic, modern South Arabic) may well be due to later development, just as it totally disappeared in modern Arabic dialects, whereas we do not know anything of the prefix vowels in Epigraphic South Arabic, the only other alleged branch of South Semitic. On the other hand, this opposition might have emerged independently in different dialects. It is not unreasonable to assume that in some dialects the prefix vowel *a* prevailed, to become *i*, through dissimilation, when preceding *a*,[22] thus giving rise to *yiqtal*:*yaqtul*. Yet the development might have been much more involved; the possible intricacy of this process may easily be learned from Grotzfeld's attempts (1964, pp. 28–31) to explain the shift of original *a* to *i* (and later, in certain positions, its reduction) in the dialect of Damascus both medially and in affixes. At any rate, one should rather refrain from using the differences in the prefix-vowels of the prefix-tense G as an indication for genetic classification.

Even less convincing is Hetzron's suggestion (1976, p. 103) to group Arabic and Hebrew together within his alleged Central Semitic, on the grounds that these two languages are "innovative" as against the more archaic Aramaic, insofar as the feminine plural endings in the second and third persons of the verbal conjugations are concerned. The ending is *-ā* in Akkadian and Ethiopic, *-ān* (with an added *-n*) in Aramaic, whereas Arabic and Hebrew exhibit *-na/nā*. There is, in my mind, no doubt whatsoever that Arabic and Hebrew reflect independent parallel development. Hetzron himself saw the reasons for the Hebrew and Arabic innovation quite clearly (in note 25): it was necessitated by the homonymy with the dual ending, and was based on the ending of the corresponding independent pronouns. He even

22. For such a dissimilation in later biblical Hebrew, see Blake (1950).

adduced parallel cases from modern South Arabic, which he rightly considered to be independent innovations. Exactly in the same way, the Hebrew and Arabic innovations were also independent.

5.1.5 So far we have dealt with the features adduced by Hetzron for the alleged genetic grouping of Arabic with Canaanite and Aramaic. In the following section we shall adduce some features, not hitherto proposed—shared by Arabic, Canaanite, and Aramaic—which cannot, in my opinion, be used for genetic classification either.

An outstanding feature is, *prima facie*, the shift of the feminine suffix *-at* * to *-ah/-a/-ā*, attested in North West Semitic and Arabic. Yet a closer look reveals that this surprising conformity is by no means complete, and because of the different dates at which these suffixes occurred, has to be interpreted as due to parallel development. This shift is totally absent from Ugaritic, yet occurs in Hebrew in both nouns and verbs. In Phoenician it is attested in the verb yet absent in the noun.[23] In Aramaic and modern Arabic dialects, on the other hand, it is absent in the verb,[24] yet attested in the noun. In Classical Arabic it occurs in nouns in the pausal forms[25] (in the form *-ah*), but is absent in verbs and in nouns in context forms. The gap in the dates at which this phenomenon occurs in the various languages is even greater. In Classical

23. In Moabite, too, *prima facie -at* is preserved in nouns; no examples of the third person feminine singular of the suffix tense are attested. It was in late Punic only that *t* was omitted in nouns as well (see Friedrich, 1951, p. 99). The reason for the preservation of the *t* in nouns in Phoenician seems to be that this shift operated in Phoenician in a period in which nouns had still kept case vowels. Therefore the *t* in nouns was not yet in a final position and, accordingly, not affected by the shift, in contradistinction to the vowelless third person feminine singular of the tense suffix (see Friedrich, 1951, p. 19, note 2). In el-Amarna, *-at* in verbs is still preserved (see Friedrich, 1951, p. 19).

24. Birkeland (1940, p. 97) explained the preservation of *-at* in the verb by differentiation (*darabat*>**darabah* would have been taken for <*darabahū*). This explanation, however, is not convincing, since similar forces operated in the realm of the noun as well (**malikat*>*malikah* could be mistaken for *malikahū*). I would tentatively propose, for both Aramaic and Arabic, that *-at* shifted to *-a(h)*, whereas *-āt* (cf. the feminine plural ending in nouns) was preserved. As is well known, the influence of verbs with a final weak consonant on the other verbal classes is quite conspicuous (cf., e.g., Brockelmann, 1908-13, pp. 567, 574), whereas that of nouns with a final weak consonant is much more restricted. It was through the influence of verbs *III w/y*, which exhibited *-āt* in the 3rd person fem. sing., that *t* was preserved in verbs. On the other hand, nouns *III w/y* terminating in **-āt* shifted to *-āh* through the influence of nouns with the **-at*>*ah* ending.

25. By no means should one posit pausal orthography outside Arabic. In Arabic itself, it is due to historical chance: since Arabic orthography continued Nabatean Aramaic and the Nabatean forms were mostly identical with the Arabic pausal ones, they were reinterpreted as pausal forms. For particulars see Blau, forthcoming, §4.3.

Arabic, as stated, until about 700 A.D., *-at* was preserved in bound forms,[26] whereas, much more than a millennium earlier, it had already disappeared in the oldest Phoenician and Aramaic inscriptions (in the verb and the noun, respectively). Accordingly, this case may be considered a *locus classicus* for the extent of proven parallel development.

Hebrew, Ugaritic, Aramaic, and Arabic have, in various degrees, preserved indications for the forming of the plural of monosyllabic nouns (including those with a feminine ending) by the insertion of *a* between the second and third radicals.[27] However, this feature, in all likelihood, is not only an archaism, but it is attested in Ge'ez as well (though only after liquids, where it *may* also be anaptyctic; see Nöldeke, 1904a, p. 70).

Nor should one attribute too much importance to the word "what" being expressed by *mā/mah* in Ugaritic, Canaanite, Aramaic and Arabic (cf. Loewenstamm, 1958–59, p. 74), not only because it may exhibit an archaic feature, but also because a lexical feature such as this may easily be borrowed from dialect to dialect (cf. Singer's summary, 1958, pp. 257–258, as to the interrogative pronouns in the Arabic dialects).

5.2 Not only does Arabic share innovative features with South Arabic (see Sections 5.1.1 and 5.1.2 above), whereas its features common with Canaanite and Aramaic are due to inheritance or parallel development (see Sections 5.1.3 and 5.1.4 above), but it also lacks features characteristic to North West Semitic. Because of the close contact between the Semitic languages, and the large extent of parallel development, one must not claim that these features cogently prove that the North West Semitic dialects once formed a unity in which these features developed. On the contrary, in some cases these features are shared by other Semitic languages as well, thus making the possibility of parallel development even more likely. On the other hand, synchronically at least, the lack of these features in Arabic differentiates it from North West Semitic, making its closer affinity with Canaanite and Aramaic (even historically) rather unlikely.

In North West Semitic, Proto-Semitic *w* in initial position is represented by *y*. I do not claim that this feature could not have developed independently

26. Even later is the shift *-at*>*-oh*/*-əh* in modern South Arabic, since it occurs only in one dialect, in Socotri (see Johnstone, 1975, p. 20). The final *h* that exists not only in Arabic, but in this dialect as well, makes it quite likely that in the other Semitic languages *t* first shifted to *h*, to become afterwards zero.

27. For Hebrew, Aramaic and Arabic, see Nöldeke (1904a, p. 70); for Ugaritic cf., e.g., *rìš* ("head"), plural *r'ašm*. Ginsberg (1970, p. 102) was therefore wrong in restricting this feature to Canaanite (including Ugaritic) and Aramaic only. Cf. also note 19 above.

as well, especially since in Arabic also some isolated roots exhibit both *w* and *y* as the first radical (see Nöldeke, 1910, pp. 203–206). Nevertheless, it is quite a strong (admittedly phonological) piece of evidence for the unity of North West Semitic, since it is not easy to explain it phonetically (see Nöldeke, 1910, p. 202).

On the other hand, the total assimilation of vowelless *n* to the following consonant, characteristic of North West Semitic, might have easily emerged independently. It is a well-established feature of Akkadian and is sporadically attested in South Semitic as well. In Classical Arabic it is well attested in *sandhi*; and for Epigraphic South Arabic cf. Beeston (1962, pp. 16–17). Less convincing is the absence of *lqḥ* ("take"), imperfect *yqḥ* in Arabic, as against its attestation in North West Semitic, in Ugaritic, Hebrew, Moabite *and* Aramaic (see Degen, 1969, p. 79 and Hoftijzer, 1965, s.v.).

5.3 It has been claimed several times that South Arabic and Ethiopic (excluding Arabic) exhibit special ties with East Semitic (see the literature cited by Cantineau, 1932, p. 178; and Hetzron, 1974, pp. 183–184). This claim has been refuted by Cantineau (1932) and Leslau (1959). It will suffice to refer the reader to these papers, though I do not agree with every item adduced. Thus (in spite of Soden, 1957), I would posit (for "twenty") Proto-Semitic **ʿiśrā*, terminating in an original dual ending (= "twice ten"), and for the other tens the plural suffix *-ūn(a)/-īn(a)*. In Akkadian and Ethiopic (in the latter it is the only remnant of the nominative dual ending, as against *-ē* in other cases), as well as in modern South Arabic, if one is entitled to infer such from remnants in Socotri (as cited by Johnstone, 1975, p. 24), *-ā* analogically spread over the whole paradigm, whereas in the other Semitic languages it was the plural ending that prevailed. Verbal themes occurring in both Akkadian and Ethiopic formed by a combination of morphemes are, in all likelihood, due to late parallel development; cf., e.g., Middle Hebrew *nitqattēl* as well as similar formations in Arabic dialects (see Brockelmann, 1908–1913, pp. 540–541; Littmann, 1954, p. 359). On the other hand (*pace* Leslau, 1959, p. 252), the semantic independence of the Ethiopic forms is, in all likelihood, a late development. As to the causative *š*, as well as *ʿšt* ("one"), these forms are, as we know now, attested in Ugaritic as well. For *-ku* marking the first person singular of the suffix tense/stative in Akkadian and Ethiopic/South Arabic, cf. Hetzron (1974, p. 191 and 1976, pp. 93–94); for *yaqattal* etc., see Section
(p. 244) 4.2 above; for Proto-Semitic *śl θ*, see Blau (1972b, p. 80).

5.4 Accordingly, one may retain the "accepted" grouping of South Arabic, Ethiopic, and Arabic as South (West) Semitic. Within South (West) Semitic,

Ethiopic and South Arabic form a unit, as opposed to Arabic (see, e.g., Cantineau, 1932, pp. 178–185; Hetzron, 1977, p. 12; cf. also the glottalized pronunciation of emphatics in modern South Arabic and Ethiopic [Johnstone, 1975, pp. 6–7]), dubbed by Leslau South East Semitic.

6. Having arrived at the conclusion that Arabic does not form a unit with North West Semitic, we may now proceed to subdivide the North West Semitic languages. We shall not deal with so-called "Amorite," not only because our knowledge is too restricted for any linguistic classification, but also because of our knowledge of the language of Ebla at this time, and it would not be prudent to rush to any conclusions. Taking the accepted division into Canaanite and Aramaic for granted (without broaching the question whether these linguistic groups arose in accordance with the family-tree theory or the wave hypothesis, although we tend to accept the latter; see Sections 2 and 3 above), we shall proceed to the linguistic position of Ugaritic.

6.1 It is now (see Gordon, 1965, p. 144, who cites additional literature) more or less generally accepted that Ugaritic is a North West Semitic language, yet disagreement exists as to whether to consider it a separate subdivision of North West Semitic or rather to group it within Canaanite. Recently, in a brilliant essay, Ginsberg (1970, especially pp. 102 and 104–106) grouped Ugaritic within Canaanite together with Phoenician, as opposed to Hebraic (consisting of Hebrew and Moabite). I think that Ginsberg has proven his point that Ugaritic is more closely related to Canaanite than to Aramaic. On the other hand, in my opinion, Phoenician and Hebraic belong together ("Canaanite"), as opposed to Ugaritic.[28]

6.2 From the features distinguishing Canaanite and Ugaritic from Aramaic adduced by Ginsberg (1970, pp. 103–104), I have not found any that cannot be reasonably attributed either to archaism or parallel development and/or

28. One could dub Ugaritic and Canaanite as "Canaanaic." Yet not only is this a mere play of words, but it also implies genetic affinity in accordance with the family-tree theory (cf. Section 6.2 below). Contrary to Ginsberg (1970, p. 105), I would not simply group the Canaanisms and Canaanite glosses in the Akkadian letters from el-Amarna with Phoenician. It stands to reason that, according to their places of provenance, some were closer to Phoenician, and others closer to Hebrew. Thus, in my opinion, it is not due to mere chance that it is in a letter from Palestinian Gezer that *banītī* ("I built," in accordance with Hebrew), is attested (el-Amarna 292, 29) as against Phoenician *-ētī* (cf. Friedrich, 1951, p. 77). The Canaanite material in these letters, however, is much too restricted to enable us to make these subdivisions.

contact. Nevertheless, one will readily admit that synchronically, Ugaritic exhibits special affinity to Canaanite, though presumably it did not form a genetic group with it within North West Semitic; but rather, in accordance with the wave hypothesis, it more or less developed in the same direction through contact and/or parallel development.

In Canaanite and Ugaritic a suppletive paradigm *hlk~ylk* ("to go") exists. Yet not only does Akkadian *alākum* exhibit the apophony *a* ~ *i*, as in verbs *I w* (see Soden, 1952, p. 128) and Aramaic exhibits suppletive *hlk/hwk*, but the spread of suppletive *hlk/ylk* < *wlk* may be due to mutual contact and/or parallel development. Such parallel development might have started from the imperative **hlik* >*lik*, on the one hand, or from the causative **hahlak* >*hōlak* in the dialects with *h*-causative (i.e., with the exclusion of Ugaritic), on the other.

The lexical parallels between Ugaritic and Canaanite adduced by Ginsberg are rather impressive. Yet, partly at least, they may well be due to the cultural relation of Ugaritic poetry with Canaanite (Hebrew) poetry.

Nothing must be inferred from the *t* prefix of the third person feminine plural of the prefix tense. Such an analogical formation, due to the impact of the singular, might well have emerged independently, as it emerged in ancient Arabic dialects (see, e.g., Brockelmann, 1908–13, I, p. 568), in Epigraphic South Arabic (see Beeston, 1962, p. 23) and modern South Arabic (see Johnstone, 1975, pp. 16–17).

Quite a conspicuous isogloss connecting Hebrew with Ugaritic is the merger (synchronically at least) of the D of *II w/y* and the *pōlēl* forms etc. The extent of this phenomenon surely gives the impression of later innovation. Parallel development, however, must not be excluded. Several Semitic languages exhibit aversion to doubling *w/y* (i.e., *pawwel, payyel*), resorting instead to the doubling of the third radical (for Arabic *baynūna, daymūma,*
(p. 169) Akkadian *tukinnā,* cf. Blau, 1971, p. 147, note 63; for Aramaic *'etbawrar* etc., cf. *ibid.*, p. 148). With this background one has to take into consideration also the possibility of convergent development.

In Canaanite (for Phoenician, cf. Friedrich, 1951, pp. 61, 72) certain active participle forms are simply the stem of the perfect (!) inflected as a noun. Such features, however, are not completely absent from other Semitic languages either. In Arabic, adjectives (not real participles) such as *ẖāf* ("afraid") from roots *II w/y* are attested (see Nöldeke, 1910, pp. 210–216). Similarly, *qatil* serves as verbal adjective from intransitive verbs of the *qatila* pattern (see Wright, 1896–98, I, p. 132) and is, as a matter of fact, much more frequent than the "real" participle *qātil*. For Aramaic, cf. *śāḇ* ("elder"). Accordingly, Nöldeke's cautious remark (1910, p. 209) concerning roots *II w/y*, that this formation "for all that" be considered Proto-Semitic is quite convincing and thus one may regard this feature as an archaism that has been preserved (and perhaps expanded, to some extent).

For the use of the prefix vowel *a* preceding the thematic vowel *i/u* of the prefix tense, of the prefix vowel *i* preceding *a*, see Section 5.1.4 above.[29]

6.3 The features adduced by Ginsberg (1970, pp. 105–106) as distinguishing Phoenician, el-Amarna, and Ugaritic from Hebrew and Moabite are not convincing. Lexical features, especially those that are attested in Hebrew as well, though rare and/or poetic, can scarcely be used as decisive proof for genetic classification, the more so when the Ugaritic word *pa'n* ("foot") differs from the Phoenician and Hebrew *pa'm* (rare in Hebrew). The possibility not only of contact, but even of parallel development is considerable: cf., e.g., for "to be," Phoenician, Ugaritic, *and* Arabic *kwn*, Hebrew *hyy/hwy*, *and* Aramaic *hwy*, as cited by Ginsberg himself. *ytn* ("to give") in Ugaritic and Phoenician, is, it seems, due to later independent development, starting from the imperative *tin*, which, because of its identity with verbs *I w*, was transferred into that verbal class. Nor is the Hebrew use of perfect and imperfect consecutive suitable for genetic classification. It is due to the special Hebrew (and Moabite) development of elements to be found in Phoenician as well, as so ably demonstrated by Ginsberg; cf. also for the consecutive imperfect the *'ḥrm* inscription line 2 *wygl*, continuing the perfect *'ly*. This development surely distinguishes Hebrew and Moabite from Phoenician, being due to a later, presumably shared, innovation; it does not, however, group Ugaritic with Phoenician. A quite conspicuous feature connecting Ugaritic with el-Amarna is the use of *tqtlū* for the third person masculine plural. This feature, however, is absent not only from Hebrew, but presumably from Phoenician as well (see Friedrich, 1951, p. 54, note 1).

6.4 On the other hand, important isoglosses distinguish Ugaritic from Hebrew and Phoenician, thus separating these languages (as the Canaanite group) from Ugaritic. Not all the features, to be sure, are equally apt for genetic classification; together, however, in my opinion, they sufficiently warrant a Canaanite group not including Ugaritic.

In my opinion, Ugaritic clearly exhibits the shift *ð* > *d*. The attempt to interpret the Ugaritic *d* as polyphonic, marking both *d* and *ð* is, to my mind

29. Ginsberg (1970, p. 104) also adduces causative forms like *heḥbī* ("he hid"), occurring in Hebrew, Phoenician and el-Amarna. In my opinion. this form has to be considered an archaism, its corresponding form *šuprus* being attested in Akkadian also; cf. Blau (1971, pp. 152–158).

(p. 340) fallacious (for particulars, see Blau, 1968). The assumption of polyphony does not fit the character of the Ugaritic script, which exhibits added symbols at its end. This sound shift clearly separates Ugaritic from all the Canaanite dialects known.

It seems that a dialect of Ugaritic also exhibited the shift ð̣ > ṭ. Dietrich *et al.* (1975) have cited seven words (in ten occurrences) exhibiting the spelling with ð̣ for ṭ. Five of these occur in one group of texts. In the dialect underlying these texts, ð̣ had shifted to ṭ; accordingly, there was no difference in whether the sound ṭ was marked by the letter ṭ or ð̣. In this group of texts it was, from the point of view of the history of the alphabet, the *letter* ð̣ that prevailed, just as in Ge'ez the letter ẓ continued South Arabic ð̣, rather than ẓ, and š in the Canaanite alphabet occupies the place of θ, as demonstrated by the Ugaritic alphabet. Two words occur in the archaizing text (Gordon, 1965, text 77) in which ð̣ also had shifted to ṭ. In this text the use of the letter ð̣ is due to some sort of pseudo-archaism. At any rate, it seems that in at least one Ugaritic dialect, ð̣, contrary to Canaanite, had shifted to ṭ (whereas the weak sound shift ð̣ > ǵ exhibits a different dialect). These sound shifts, in my opinion, clearly distinguish Ugaritic from Canaanite.

Other important features common to Hebrew and Phoenician, yet absent from Ugaritic, are: the definite article *ha-*, the shift *ā* > *ō*,[30] and the relative pronoun *'ăšer/šel/'š* (for its absence in Ugaritic, see Rainey, 1965-66, pp. 261–263). The first two features are, in my opinion, quite important, whereas I would not attach too much importance to the relative pronoun. I also mention here, somewhat with hesitation (since Aramaic and Arabic parallels are not lacking[31]), *yt/'t/'et/'ōt* denoting the definite direct object in Canaanite dialects and lacking in Ugaritic (so far, at least).

7. We have tried to show that the wave hypothesis is much more convincing for the understanding of the classification of the Semitic languages than the family-tree theory (Section 2) and that parallel development characterizes the Semitic languages even more than the Indo-European ones (Section 2.1). This may also be inferred from the modern Arabic dialects, the proto-language of which can relatively easily be reconstructed with the help of Classical Arabic (Sections 3, 3.1, 3.2): they attest even to the transfer of unmotivated mor-

30. Since "I" is transcribed in Ugaritic *a-na-ku* in the quadrilingual word list, it stands to reason that, contrary to Canaanite (and perhaps even Aramaic, see Lipiński, 1976, p. 233a/b), the first person singular of the suffix tense terminated in *-tu*, rather than in *-ti/-tī*, as in the Canaanite dialects.

31. See Dion (1974, pp. 164–165).

phological innovations (Section 3.2). The basic division of the Semitic languages into East and West Semitic is well established (Section 4). It stands to reason that *yaqtulu* was a part also of the verbal system of Proto-South East Semitic (Section 5), and perhaps even of that of Akkadian, and thus Proto-Semitic (Sections 4.1, 4.2). Arabic has to be grouped with South Arabic and Ethiopic as "South (West) Semitic" (Section 5.1), because of shared innovations between them (Sections 5.1.1, 5.1.2, 5.1.3), whereas the isoglosses connecting Arabic with North West Semitic are not relevant for genetic classification (Sections 5.1.4, 5.1.5). Moreover, Arabic lacks features characteristic of North West Semitic (Section 5.2). Since South Arabic and Ethiopic do not evince special ties connecting them with Akkadian (Section 5.3), one should retain the "accepted" grouping of Arabic, South Arabic, and Ethiopic as "South (West) Semitic," within which the last two groups form a unit ("South East Semitic"; Section 5.4). West Semitic consists of South (West) Semitic and North West Semitic, the last being sub-divided (disregarding "Amorite") into Ugaritic, Canaanite (including, *inter alia*, Hebrew and Phoenician), and Aramaic (Section 6.1). Ugaritic is closer to Canaanite than to Aramaic; it cannot, however, be regarded as a Canaanite dialect proper (Section 6). Though the isoglosses marking off Canaanite and Ugaritic from Aramaic do not prove the genetic unity of Canaanite and Ugaritic, nevertheless they demonstrate, at least synchronically, quite a conspicuous affinity (Section 6.2). The isoglosses separating Ugaritic from Hebrew and Phoenician (including el-Amarna) (Section 6.4) are more relevant than those distinguishing Phoenician (including el-Amarna) and Ugaritic from Hebrew (and Moabite) (Section 6.3).

BIBLIOGRAPHY

Barthélemy, A. 1935-69. *Dictionnaire arabe-français*. Paris.

Beeston, A. F. L. 1962. *A Descriptive Grammar of Epigraphic South Arabian*. London.

———. 1976. "Notes on Old South Arabian Lexicography X." *Le Muséon* 89:4.

———. 1977. "On the Correspondence of Hebrew *s* to Epigraphic South Arabian s^2." *Journal of Semitic Studies* 22:50–57.

Bergsträsser, G. 1918-29. *Hebräische Grammatik*. Leipzig.

———. 1928. *Einführung in die semitischen Sprachen*. München.
Birkeland, H. 1940. *Altarabische Pausalformen*. Oslo.
Blake, F. R. 1950. "The Apparent Interchange between *a* and *i* in Hebrew." *Journal of Near Eastern Studies* 9:76–83.
Blanc, H. 1964. *Communal Dialects in Baghdad*. Cambridge.
Blau, J. 1960. *Syntax des palästinensischen Bauerndialekts von Bīr-Zēt*. Walldorf-Hessen.
———. 1961-62. Review of Kuryłowicz (1961). *Ləšonenu* 26:68–74.
———. 1965a. *The Emergence and Linguistic Background of Judaeo-Arabic*. Oxford.
———. 1965b. Review of A. E. Murtonen, *Broken Plurals*. *Ləšonenu* 29: 275–278.
———. 1968. "On Problems of Polyphony and Archaism in Ugaritic Spelling." *Journal of the American Oriental Society* 88:523–526.
———. 1970. *On Pseudo-Corrections in Some Semitic Languages*. Jerusalem.
———. 1971. "Studies in Hebrew Verb Formation." *Hebrew Union College Annual* 42:133–158.
———. 1972a. *Torat hahege vəhaccurot*. Tel Aviv.
———. 1972b. "Marginalia Semitica II." *Israel Oriental Studies* 2:57–82.
———. forthcoming. "The Beginnings of the Arabic Diglossia." *Afroasiatic Linguistics*.
Bloomfield, L. 1933. *Language*. New York.
Bravmann, M. M. 1977. *Studies in Semitic Philology*. Leiden.
Brockelmann, C. 1908-13. *Grundriss der vergleichenden Grammatik der semitischen Sprachen*. Berlin.
Cantineau, J. 1932. "Accadien et sudarabique." *Bulletin de la Société de Linguistique de Paris* 33:175–204.
Cohen, M. 1924. *Le Système verbal sémitique et l'expression du temps*. Paris.
Degen, R. 1969. *Altaramäische Grammatik*. Wiesbaden.
Dietrich, M., O. Loretz, and J. Sanmartín. 1975. "Untersuchungen zur Schrift- und Lautlehre des Ugaritischen (III)." *Ugarit-Forschungen* 7:103–108.
Dion, P.-E. 1974. *La Langue de Ya'udi*. Otava.
Dozy, R. P. 1881. *Supplément aux dictionnaires arabes*. Leyde.
Féghali, M. T. 1919. *Le parler de Kfar ʿabīda (Liban-Syrie)*. Paris.
Fenton, T. L. 1970. "The Absence of a Verbal Formation **yaqattal* from Ugaritic and North West Semitic." *Journal of Semitic Studies* 15: 31–41.
Ferguson, C. A. 1959. "The Arabic *koiné*." *Language* 35:616–630.

Fischer, W. 1959. *Die demonstrativen Bildungen der neuarabischen Dialekte*. 's-Gravenhage.

Fleisch, H. 1944. *Les verbes à alongement vocalique interne en sémitique*. Paris.

Friedrich, J. 1951. *Phönizisch-punische Grammatik*. Rome.

Gelb, I. J. 1961. *Old Akkadian Writing and Grammar*. Chicago.

Ginsberg, H. L. 1970. "The Northwest Semitic Languages." *The World History of the Jewish People, II, Patriarchs*, pp. 102–124. Tel Aviv.

Gordon, C. H. 1965. *Ugaritic Textbook*. Rome.

Grotzfeld, H. 1964. *Laut- und Formenlehre des Damaszenisch-Arabischen*. Wiesbaden.

Hall, R. A. 1972. "The Reconstruction of Proto-Romance." *A Reader in Historical and Comparative Linguistics*, pp. 25–48. Ed. A. Keiler. New York.

Hetzron, R. 1974. "La division des langues sémitiques." *Actes du Premier Congrès International de Linguistique Sémitique et Chamito- Sémitique*, pp. 182–194. Eds. D. Cohen and A. Caquot. The Hague.

———. 1975. "Genetic Classification and Ethiopian Semitic." *Hamito-Semitica*, pp. 103–127. Eds. J. and T. Bynon. The Hague.

———. 1976. "Two Principles of Genetic Reconstruction." *Lingua* 38: 89–108.

———. 1977. *The Gunnän-Gurage Languages*. Napoli.

Höfner, M. 1943. *Altsüdarabische Grammatik*. Leipzig.

Hoftijzer, J. and C. F. Jean. 1965. *Dictionnaire des inscriptions sémitiques de l'ouest*. Leiden.

Jamme, A. 1962. *Sabaean Inscriptions from Maḥram Bilqis (Mârib)*. Baltimore.

Johnstone, T. M. 1975. "The Modern South Arabian Languages." *Afroasiatic Linguistics* I, 5:1–29.

Kaufman, S. A. 1974. *The Akkadian Influences on Aramaic*. Chicago.

Kofler, H. 1940-42. "Reste altarabischer Dialekte." *Wiener Zeitschrift zur Kunde des Morgenlandes* 47 (1940):61–130, 233–262; 48 (1941):52–88, 247–274; 49 (1942):14–30, 234–256.

Kuryłowicz, J. 1961. *L'apophonie en sémitique*. Wrocław.

Kutscher, E. Y. 1971. "Aramaic." *Current Trends in Linguistics 6, Linguistics in South West Asia and North Africa*, pp. 347–412. The Hague.

Leslau, W. 1959. "The Position of Ethiopic in Semitic: Akkadian and Ethiopic." *Akten des 24. internationalen Orientalisten-Kongresses, München 28 August-4 September*. Wiesbaden.

Lipiński, E. 1976. Review of Dion (1974). *Bibliotheca Orientalis* 33: 231–234.

Littmann, E. 1954. "Die äthiopische Sprache." *Handbuch der Orientalistik, III, Semitistik,* pp. 350–375. Leiden.

Loewenstamm, S. E. 1958-59. "Lətorat hakkinnuyim bə'ugaritit lə'or hakkəna'anit." *Ləšonenu* 23:72–84.

Meyer, R. 1966-72. *Hebräische Grammatik*. Berlin.

Meillet, A. 1958. *Linguistique historique et linguistique génerale I*. Paris.

Moran, W. J. 1965. "The Hebrew Language and its Northwest Semitic Background." *The Bible and the Ancient Near East*, pp. 59–84. Ed. G. E. Wright. New York.

Nöldeke, T. 1904a. "Zur semitischen Pluralendung." *Zeitschrift für Assyriologie und verwandte Gebiete* 18:68–72.

———. 1904b. *Beiträge zur semitischen Sprachwissenschaft*. Strassburg.

———. 1910. *Neue Beiträge zur semitischen Sprachwissenschaft*. Strassburg.

Polotsky, H. J. 1964. "Semitics." *The World History of the Jewish People*, I, 1, *The Dawn of Civilization*, pp. 99–111, 357–358. Tel Aviv.

Porzig, W. 1954. *Die Gliederung des indogermanischen Sprachgebiets*. Heidelberg.

Rainey, A. F. 1965-66. "Kelim ḥadašim ləḥeqer ha'ugaritit." *Ləšonenu* 30: 250–272.

Rabin, C. 1963. "The Origin of the Subdivision of Semitic." *Hebrew and Semitic Studies presented to Godfrey R. Driver*, pp. 104–115. Oxford.

Rimalt, E. S. 1932. "Wechselbeziehangen zwischen dem Aramäischen und Neubabylonischen." *Wiener Zeitschrift zur Kunde des Morgenlandes* 39:100–122.

Sarauw, C. 1912. "Das altsemitische Tempussystem." *Festschrift für Vilhelm Thomsen*, pp. 59–69. Leipzig.

Singer, H. -R. 1958. *Neuarabische Fragewörter. Inaugural-Dissertation Erlangen*. Erlangen.

Soden, W. von. 1952. *Grundriss der akkadischen Grammatik*. Rome.

———. 1957. "Die Zahlen 20–90 im Semitischen und der status absolutus." *Wiener Zeitschrift zur Kunde des Morgenlandes* 57:24–28.

———. 1959. "Tempus und Modus im Semitischen." *Akten des 24. internationalen Orientalisten-Kongresses, München, August 28-September 4*. Wiesbaden.

Southworth, F. C. 1964. "Family-Tree Diagrams." *Language* 40:557–567.

Ungnad, A. and L. Matouš. 1964. *Grammatik des Akkadischen*. München.

Vendryès, J. 1972. "Some Thoughts on Sound Laws." *A Reader in Historical and Comparative Linguistics*, pp. 109–120. Ed. A. Keiler. New York.
Weinreich, U. 1953. *Languages in Contact*. New York.
Wright, W. 1896-98. *A Grammar of the Arabic Language*³. Cambridge.
Zimmern, H. 1917. *Akkadische Fremdwörter als Beweis für babylonischen Kultureinfluss*². Leipzig.

Additions

to **p. 308**.*2*: A plethora of studies in the classification of the Semitic languages, especially in the position of Arabic, have been published. I am quoting five of them, and the reader may find additional researches in the bibliography referred to in these articles: G. Goldenberg, 'The Semitic Languages of Ethiopia and Their Classification', *BSOAS* 40.461–507 (1977), especially pp. 473 ff.; W. Diem, 'Die geneologische Stellung des Arabischen in den semitischen Sprachen. Ein ungelöstes Problem der Semitistik', *Studien aus Arabistik und Semitistik*, Wiesbaden 1980, pp. 65–85; A. Zaborski, 'The Position of Arabic within the Semitic "Dialect Continuum"', *Proceedings of the Colloquium on Arabic Grammar*, Budapest 1991, pp. 365–75; J. Rodgers, 'The Subgrouping of the Semitic Languages', *Semitic Studies in Honor of W. Leslau*, Wiesbaden 1991, pp. 1323–36; D. L. Appleyard. 'Ethiopian Semitic and South Arabian, towards a Re-Eximation of a Relationship', *IOS* 16.203–28 (1996). I still rely on the classification propunded here, admitting, however, that these experiments in classification are, to a great extent, intellectual speculations.

to **p. 309**.*12*: I disagree with Zaborski's (ibid., p. 368.7) claim that "since alleged 'independent developments' by definition, i.e., a priori) cannot be verified, i. e., distinguished from shared (or 'dependent') developments of the original inherited elements, the use of the concept of 'independent innovation' as a scientific tool is none." On principle, even if it were true that independent and dependent developments are indistinguishable, the mere assumption of the possibility of parallel development is important, since it keeps us from rushing to conclusions and take shared changes for granted. Moreover, the existence of parallel development can be proven, if it takes place in various languages at different times and reflects differences in details; for a clear example see above pp. 126–37 and below in this paper §5.1.5, further *ZAL* 25 (1993), pp. 95–99.

to **p. 311**.*1* : For details cf. my paper 'On Some Proto-Neo-Arabic and Early Neo-Arabic Features Differing from Classical Arabic', *Studies* , pp. 368–80; a quite conspicuous feature is Classical *qittîl*, etc., as against modern *qattîl*, etc.

to **p. 311**.*19*: = *Studies* , pp. 25ff. §§6.5; 6.6.

to **p. 317**.*3*: Read "(Blau,) 1965b" for "1965"!

to **p. 317**.*9*: S. Hopkins proposed as an additional feature shared by Arabic and G^{c}ez, the conjugation of the basic theme of verbs iiw/*y qumtu, sirtu* # *nômkû, sêmkû*. On the other hand, Modern South Arabian (Mehri), at least, exhibits *matki* "I died'.

to **p. 320**.*10ff*.: For details see above pp. 126ff.

Some Ugaritic, Hebrew, and Arabic Parallels

1. In the following I shall deal with three small topics connected with Biblical Hebrew, using Ugaritic as point of departure and utilizing Arabic as well. First, I shall treat a morpho-syntactic feature (§2), to continue with etymological problems connected with two Biblical roots (§§3; 4).

2. In 1955, S. E. Loewenstamm published his magisterial paper on the development of the term "first" in the Semitic languages, in Hebrew,[1] and in 1980 he translated it into English with a few added notes.[2] He convincingly demonstrated that Proto-Semitic did no express the concept "first" at all, using instead in enumerations the counted noun without adding any numeral to it. This primitive stage has been preserved by Ugaritic in the type *ym wthn thlth rbᶜ ym* . . . 'day (i.e. the first day) and the second, third, fourth day . . .'. A later development was the use of the cardinal numeral "one" to mark the concept of "first". This stage is e.g.[3] preserved in Hebrew in the type *yôm eḥâd* . . . *yôm shênî* 'the first day . . . the second day' (Gen. 1, 5, 8) or *hâ-eḥâd* . . . *ha-n-nâhâr ha-sh-shênî* 'the first . . . the second river' (Gen. 2, 11, 13). It was only in the last stage of development that the various Semitic languages developed the special notion

[1] *Tarbiz* 24 (1955), 249-51. *

[2] In: S. E. Loewenstamm, *Comparative Studies in Biblical and Ancient Oriental Literatures*, Alter Orient und Altes Testament 204, Neukirchen-Vluyn 1980, pp. 13-16.

[3] In a short Hebrew note (*Shnaton* 1 [1975], pp. 29-31) I called attention to the fact that the use of "one" instead of "first" is attested in various languages, when the sequence of the counted nouns is arbitrary and it is possible to begin with their enumeration with any of them; as when Julius Caesar opens his *Bellum gallicum* with "Gallia est omnis divisa in partes tres, quarum *unam* incolunt Belgae, aliam Aquitani, tertiam . . .". In this case, of course, the enumeration could have as well have started with the part inhabited by the Aquitans, rather than by that of the Belgians. I adduced examples for this feature also from English, German and medieval Judeo-Arabic. I would like to point out that I have found the use of *wâḥid* 'one' in the sense of "first" in medieval Judeo-Arabic also in a case in which the sequence is not arbitrary: in the commentary of the Sayings of the Fathers attributed to R. David Maimonides, *Sepher pirqê abhôt ᶜim pêrûsh belâshôn ᶜarâbhî*, ed. B. H. Ḥânân, Alexandria 1900-01, p. 27b, 8 ff. the chairs of honour surrounding the throne of Divine Majesty are described: *wa-karâsî fî -l-wâhid minhom Abhrâhâm âbhînû* . . . *wa-th-thânî li-sayyidinâ Môshê rabbênû* . . . *wa-th-thâlith li-l-gêrîm alladhîn yatagayyarûn min dhât nafsihom war-râbiᶜ li-xâyifîn Allâh* 'and chairs, in the first of which is our father Abraham . . . and the second is for our master Moses . . . and the third for proselytes who became proselytes of their own accord and the fourth for pious men'. Abraham, being the ancestor of the children of Israel and preceding Moses in time, precedes him in rank as well, and both of them come before the great mass of righteous men, among whom again proselytes, who joined God of their own accord, have preference. – By the way, H. Fleisch, *Traité de philologie arabe*, I. Beyrouth 1961, p. 521, n. 2, rightly in our opinion, considered *wâhid*, having the form *fâᶜil* like ordinal numbers, to be originally an ordinal number. I wonder whether the alternation of "one"/"first" in enumerations could not have been one of the reasons for the passage of *wâḥid* to cardinal numbers.

"first", and since this development took place in the various Semitic languages separately, "first" is derived from different roots having no connection between them, as a rule without connection with the cardinal number "one".

In the following an attempt will be made to find vestiges of the first stage in Biblical Hebrew, viz. of the use of the counted noun without adding either ordinal "first" or cardinal "one" to it. I have found one case in which the counted noun, without the addition of any numeral, is expressly marked by the definite article:[4] Ex. 38, 14-15 *qelâᶜîm ḥamesh-ᶜeśrê ammâ el-ha-k-kâtêph . . . we-la-k-kâtêph ha-sh-shênît* . . . "the hangings were fifteen cubits for the (first) side . . . and for the second side . . .'. In additional cases it is only in the vocalization that the definite article (following *be-, le-*)[5] is marked: Ex. 27, 14-15 (parallel to 38, 14-15, cited above) *wa-ḥamesh ᶜeśrê ammâ qelâᶜîm lakkâtêph . . . we-la-k-kâtêph ha-sh-shênît* . . .; 36, 17 *wa-y-yaᶜaś lûlâ'ôt ḥamishshîm ᶜal śephat ha-yrîᶜâ ha-q-qîṣônâ ba-m-maḥbâret wa-ḥamishshîm lûlâ'ôt ᶜâśâ ᶜal-śephat ha-yrîᶜâ ha-ḥôbheret ha-sh-shênît* 'and he made fifty loops upon the uttermost edge of the curtain in the (first) coupling, and fifty loops he made upon the edge of the second coupling curtain'; I King 6, 27 (where counted noun with *eḥâd* alternates with a mere counted noun) *wa-t-tiggaᶜ kenaph-hâ-eḥâd ba-q-qîr u-khnaph ha-k-kerûbh ha-sh-shênî nôgaᶜat ba-q-qîr ha-sh-shênî* 'and the wing of the first (literally: of the one) touched the (first) wall, and the wing of the second cherub touched the second wall'.[6] I have also noticed one case of an indefinite counted noun without attributive numeral used in the sense of "first":[7] Ex. 28, 17-18 = 39, 10-11 *arbâᶜâ ṭûrîm* (39, 10 *ṭûrê*) *âbhen ṭûr odem piṭdâ u-bhâreqet ha-ṭ-ṭûr hâ-eḥâd, we-ha-ṭ-ṭûr ha-sh-shênî* . . . 'four rows of stone: (the first) row[8] a sardius, a topaz, and a carbuncle, the first row, and the

[4] In Ugaritic, as well known, no definite article exists.

[5] M. Lambert, as early as 1898 (v. *REJ* 37, 208-209), has brought out in full relief the complexity of the addition of the definite article to *be-, le-* (and *ke*) by the punctuators and cautioned against its acceptance at its face value.

[6] I have excluded Zec. 11, 7, 10, 14 *wâ-eqqaḥ-lî shenê maqlôt le'aḥad qârâtî noᶜam ul'aḥad qârâtî ḥôbhelîm . . . wâ-eqqaḥ et-maqlî et-noᶜam . . . wâ-egdaᶜ et-maqlî ha-sh-shênî et ha-ḥôbhelîm* 'and I took unto me two rods, the one I called delightfulness and the other (literally: and one) union . . . and I took the rod the delightfulness . . . and I cut my second rod, the union', since *et-maqlî* in verse 10 is sufficiently defined by *et-noᶜam*, which makes the addition of "one/first" superfluous (yet in verse 14 the ordinal number is added, although the name of the rod is mentioned as well).

* [7] V. *Shnaton* 1(1975), p. 30, n. 18a. Even with the ordinal number the counted noun may remain indefinite, v. Gen. 1, where verses 8, 13, 19, 23 indefinite *yôm shênî. yôm shelîshî, yôm rebhîᶜî, yôm ḥamîshî* occur, as against definite *yôm ha-sh-shishshî* verse 31 (with the article added to the number only). I have, of course, excluded cases like Gen. 30, 5, 7 or 30, 10, 12, where *ben* (as against *ben shênî*), must not be interpreted as "the first son", but rather as 'a son', since at this stage it is not yet known whether or not a second son will be born.

[8] It seems much less likely to interpret *ṭûr* as construct 'a row of sardius . . .' (against the accents).

second row . . .'. According to this interpretation, "the first row" is twice expressed, once by an archaic construction *(ṭûr)*, once by a later pattern *(ha-ṭ-ṭûr hâ-eḥâd)*.[9]

It stands to reason that, in the main, the use of the counted noun not only without mentioning "first", but even without "one", continues the archaic Proto-Semitic construction, as preserved in Ugaritic.[10]

3. Most Biblical dictionaries base their etymological analysis of the root * *qṣ*^{c} on W. Robertson Smith's paper "On the Hebrew Root *qṣ*^{c} and the Word *miqṣôa*^{c}."[11] Since some scholars[12] dealing with Ugaritic connected this root * (or a part of it) with Ugaritic *qṣ*^{c}*t*, it seems appropriate to survey the etymological part of Robertson Smith's paper.[13]

R. Smith connects *yaqṣîa*^{c} 'he shall scrape off', *maqṣûa*^{c} 'scraping tool' (and also *qeṣîa*^{c} '"powdered" fragrant bark') with Arabic *quḍâ*^{c}*(a)* 'fine dust', whereas *miqṣôa*^{c} 'corner, etc.'[13] as well as its derivation *mehuqṣâ*^{c}*ôt*, etc., he groups with Arabic (and Aramaic) *qaṭa*^{c}*(a)* 'break off, cut off', originally, in his opinion, *qḍ*^{c}. Since, with exception of *yqḍ* 'to be awake', *qḍ* does not occur in Arabic roots, he posits that *qḍ*^{c} shifted to *qṭ*^{c} (as did *sqḍ* 'to fall' to *sqṭ*, according to him related to Hebrew *shqṣ* 'to detest').

Both etymologies, especially the second, and the division itself of this root into two homonymes, are very dubious. Even the surface similarity between *yaqṣia*^{c} 'to scrape off' and *quḍâ*^{c}*(a)* 'fine dust' is not as convincing as it seems at the first blush: in Arabic,[14] the form *fu*^{c}*âl(a)* denotes small portions which are broken off or thrown away, and this accounts for the meaning of *quḍâ*^{c}*(a)*; yet the meaning of 'scrape off' is totally absent from Arabic. It seems easier to derive the Hebrew meaning from an original 'to cut', since "to cut off from the wall" does denote "to scrape it". If *miqṣôa*^{c} 'corner' were in fact connected with *qṭ*^{c} 'to cut, to break', we could connect the whole root of Hebrew *qṣ*^{c} with it.[15] Yet it is impossible to derive Arabic

[9] This, however, does not of necessity indicate that *ha-ṭ-ṭûr hâ-eḥâd* is a gloss to explain *ṭûr*. Redundancy is a quite usual feature of the Bible.

[10] In some cases, however, it may well be an independent stylistic feature. Thus Ex. 36, 23 *wa-y-ya*^{c}*aś et-ha-q-qerâshîm la-m-mishkân* ^{c}*eśrîm qerâshîm li-ph'at negebh têmânâ* 'and he made the boards for the tabernacle, twenty boards for the south corner southward' the "side" is mentioned implicitly only; only in verse 25 does it occur explicitly with "second": ***u-l-ṣela***^{c} ***ha-m-mishkân ha-sh-shênîth li-ph'at ṣâphôn*** ^{c}***âśâ*** ^{c}***eśrîm qerâshîm*** 'and for the second side of the tabernacle toward the north corner he made twenty boards'.

[11] *The Journal of Philology* 16 (1888), 71-81.

[12] For details see below.

[13] We do not deal with the archaeological part of this paper.

[14] V. e.g. W. Wright, *A Grammar of the Arabic Language*,[3] Cambridge 1933, I, p. 176B.

[15] With the possible exception of *qeṣî*^{c}*â* 'cassia', the origin of which is obscure, v.e.g. É. Masson, *Recherches sur les plus anciens emprunts sémitiques en Grec*, Études et commentaires lxvii, Paris 1967, p. 49, note 5.

qṭᶜ from *qð̣ᶜ*![16] Already C. Brockelmann, *Lexicon Syriacum*², Halle 1928, p. 660a, s.v. refuted Robertson Smith's view; yet, admittedly, his refutation is not totally cogent. It is based on a secondary meaning of *qṭᶜ*, rather than on its main meaning "to cut, to break". In Syriac, *qeṭᶜat lî* 'be disgusted' occurs, and Brockelmann connects with it Gᶜez *taqᵘaṭᶜa* 'to be impatient, utterly disgusted'. If indeed *ṭ* is attested in Gᶜez as well, the derivation of this root from *qð̣ᶜ* becomes impossible, since in Gᶜez *ð̣* shifts to *ṣ*. Yet my main reason for not accepting Robertson Smith's derivation of *qṭᶜ* from *qð̣ᶜ* is that he mistook empirically stated incompatibility,[17] reflecting empty slots due to the low frequency of phonemes involved and being thus accidental, with phonemically pertinent incompatibility.[17] Thus the lack of *ð̣* as second radical after most consonants functioning as first radical is clearly due to the relative rarity of this consonant,[18] and this is the reason for the rarity of *qð̣* in Arabic. Therefore, any assumption of the shift *qð̣* > *qṭ* is totally unfounded.

Yet as early as 1916,[19] H. Torczyner (= N. H. Tur-Sinai), in a review of the 16th edition of W. Gesenius' *Handwörterbuch* edited by F. Buhl, has called attention to the possibility to connect *maqṣûᶜâ* with *maqṣaᶜ* 'coin en fer pour fendre la pierre', occurring in the Arabic dialect of Hadramaut from the South of the Arabian Peninsula. In this dialect[20] as well as in that of Dathina[21] also the verb *qṣᶜ* 'to split, to cut' occurs, as well as presumably in Epigraphic South Arabian.[22] Cf. also Classical Arabic *miqṣaᶜ* 'sharp'. It is easily *possible* to derive all the occurrences of the root *qṣᶜ*[15] from this *qṣᶜ* 'to cut', both *yaqṣiaᶜ*, *maqṣûaᶜ* and *miqṣôaᶜ*. Pending further discoveries it seems appropriate to posit only one root *qṣᶜ* for Biblical Hebrew, containing Proto-Semitic *ṣ*.

Prima facie, one will derive Ugaritic *qṣᶜt* from this *qṣᶜ* and connect it with

[16] This applies even more to the semantically very twisted connection of Arabic *sqṭ* 'to fall' with Hebrew *shqṣ* 'to detest'. In fact, *sqṭ* simply corresponds to Hebrew *shqṭ* 'to be quiet, undisturbed'; for this semantic correspondence cf. e.g. *VT* 6 (1956), 244, n. 5 (with further literature).

[17] For these terms see J. Kuryłowicz, *Studies in Semitic Grammar and Metres*, London 1973, pp. 19; 27.

[18] V. Kuryłowicz, *ibid.*, who (p. 21) cites G. Herdan's calculation (*Word* 18 [1962], 267), according to whom *ð̣* has the least frequency in Arabic verbal roots. According to J. Cantineau's (*Études de linguistique arabe*, Paris 1960, p. 179) rather preliminary calculation of the frequency of Arabic consonants too, *ð̣* belongs to the least frequent consonants (though more frequent than ɣ and *ṯ*).

[19] *ZDMG* 70 (1916), 559, also accepted by I. Löw, *Die Flora der Juden* I, Wien-Leipzig 1926, p. 243.

[20] V. C. de Landberg, *Études sur les dialectes de l'Arabe méridionale, I, Hadramoût*, Leide 1901, p. 692.

[21] V. *idem, Glossaire datînois*, Leiden 1920-42, s.v.

[22] V. K. Conti Rossini, *Chrestomathia arabica meridionalis epigraphica*, Roma 1931, p. 233b.

the Hebrew root.[23] Since *qṣ^ct* follows and parallels *qsht* 'bow', it has to denote 'bow' as well[24] or 'darts, arrows'.[25] It is, of course, very easy to derive 'darts, arrows' from cutting. But even a carved bow may without difficulty be connected with cutting, so that no decision can be made based on etymology.[26]

Accordingly, pending further finds, we shall consider *qṣ*ᶜ 'to cut' as the etymon of Ugaritic *qṣᶜt*, no matter whether it means 'bow' or 'darts', and of Hebrew *yaqṣīaᶜ*, *maqṣûaᶜ*, *miqṣôaᶜ*, etc.

4. The etymon of Hebrew *shtᶜ* 'to fear' //*yr'* (Is. 41, 10, 23d), also attested in Phoenician (Azitawadd A II, 4) and Ammonite (Citadel inscription 6), is clearly *thtᶜ*, as attested in Ugaritic (also //*yr'*!).[27] I. Eitan, who was the first who established this *shtᶜ* not only in Is. 41, 10, but also 41, 23, connected it[28] with Arabic *shatiᶜa* 'to be sad and agitated'.[29] This was before the discovery of Ugaritic, which disproved Arabic *shtᶜ* to be the cognate of Hebrew *shtᶜ*. Yet as it happens in the history of scholarly work, the ballast of earlier discoveries is not always cast overboard. Even a phonetic reason for Arabic *shtᶜ*, rather than *thtᶜ*, was found: dissimilation due to the following *t*.[30]

Thus Arabic *shtᶜ* continued its existence as cognate of Hebrew *shtᶜ*, despite discrepancy in both meaning ('to be sad and agitated' as against 'to fear') and form (*sh* as against *th*). As a matter of fact, however, Arabic *shtᶜ*

[23] It was connected (interpreted as 'arrow') with Hebrew *mequssâᶜ* and Arabic *miqsaᶜ* by G. R. Driver, *Canaanite Myths and Legends*, Edinburgh 1956, p. 143, n. 18, and with the same Hebrew word by A. Caquot, M. Sznycer, A. Herdner, *Textes ougaritiques*, I, Paris 1974, p. 427, n. q.

[24] So e.g. Gordon, *UT*, J. Aistleitner, *Wörterbuch der Ugaritischen Sprache*², Berlin 1965, s.v.

[25] See e.g. note 23, further H. L. Ginsberg, *ANET*, e.g. 151a, v. 14.

[26] Context does not convey any clue. Gordon's (*UT*, s.v.) claim that *qsᶜt* follows *qsht* climactically and 'arrow' would be anticlimactic after 'bow' does not convince, since 'arrow' need not be anticlimactic. Caquot, et alii, *ibid.*, base their translation 'darts' on the rather dubious assumption that the governing verb *ashrbᶜ (qsᶜt)* means 'I shall supply many (darts)'. Some attempts at etymology are more than doubtful, as is Gordon's (*ibid.*) that *qsᶜt* 'bow' is to be connected with Classical Arabic *qsᶜ* 'to crush, bruise' and is an epithet of *qsht*, meaning 'the crusher, bruiser'. Aistleitner, s.v., who explained 'bow' as 'the bent one' like German 'biegen – Bogen', connected *qsᶜt* with Gᶜ*ez qasᶜa*, allegedly meaning 'to bend'. Yet Aistleitner mistranslated 'incurvare', which means not only 'to bend', but also 'to subdue'. The Gᶜez verb (v. Dillmann, s.v.) means 'humiliare, subigere, incurvare', i.e. 'to subdue', so that no etymological base for the exclusive interpretation of *qsᶜt* as 'bow' can be provided.

[27] For convenience cf. J. C. Greenfield, *HUCA* 29 (1958), 226-28, H. R. C. Cohen, *Biblical Hapax Legomena in the Light of Akkadian and Ugaritic*, SBL Dissertation Series 37, Ann Arbor 1978, p. 44.

[28] I. Eitan, *A Contribution to Biblical Lexicography*, New York 1924, p. 8.

[29] According to the state of knowledge at that time, Eitan should have inferred from Arabic *shtᶜ* that Hebrew *shtᶜ* should be rather vocalized *śtᶜ*. As a matter of fact, Eitan (*ibid.*, note 15) also tried to compare Arabic *stᶜ*; yet its meaning ('toujours agile et infatigable') does not fit.

[30] V. Greenfield, *ibid.*, p. 226, n. 7, following H. L. Ginsberg.

'to be sad and agitated' is a ghost-word. The *Qâmûs*[31] defines *shati^{c}a* as follows: *jazi^{c}a min maraḍin aw jû^{c}in* 'he was impatient (worried, concerned, sad) because of disease or hunger'. This definition, though not impossible, is not completely satisfactory. Why is this impatience, sadness, etc., restricted to malady and famine, to the exclusion of other disasters? Yet further checking of the *Qâmûs* discovers a variant reading: *xari^{c}a* instead of *jazi^{c}a*: 'he became weak (because of disease or hunger)'. It goes without saying that 'to become weak because of disease or hunger' is much more fitting than 'to become impatient, sad, etc., because of them'. Moreover, *xari^{c}a*, a verb much rarer than *jazi^{c}a*, is definitely a *lectio difficilior* and therefore preferable. In Arabic script *jazi^{c}a/xari^{c}a* are for all practical purposes identical, but for the diacritical point under the *jîm* (whether the point is above the *ḥâ*, thus making it a *xâ*, or the *râ*, cannot be discerned in ordinary Arabic script). So it is easily understandable how the *lectio facilior jazi^{c}a* arose from *xari^{c}a*, to supersede it in most dictionaries. Yet, both because its smoother meaning and being a *lectio difficilior*, *xari^{c}a* has to be recognized as the authentic reading. Accordingly, *shati^{c}a* 'to be impatient, sad, etc.' is a ghost-word and must not be adduced as cognate of Hebrew *sht^{c}*.

Additions

to **p. 333**.*n. 3.1*: = *Hebrew Linguistics*, pp. 216–20.
to **p. 334**.*n. 7.1*: = *Hebrew Linguistics*, p. 219.n. 18א.
to **p. 335**.*7*: See also *Hebrew Linguistics*, p. 211.
to **p. 337**.*9*: See also *Hebrew Linguistics*, pp. 211–12.

[31] M. Fîrûzâbâdhî, *Al-Qâmûs al-muḥîṭ*^{3}, Cairo 1933, s.v.

On Problems of Polyphony and Archaism in Ugaritic Spelling[1]

1. As is well known, Proto-Semitic phonemes are, in Ugaritic, sometimes represented by two, or more letters. Thus Proto-Semitic δ is, as a rule, represented by Ugaritic *d*.[2] Sometimes however,[3] especially in texts 75 and 77,[4] Proto-Semitic *d* is represented by the 16th letter of the Ugaritic alphabet. But this letter occurs mostly in Hurrian words, presumably denoting a sound like ʒ.[5]

2. The question, whether or not the representation of Proto-Semitic δ by *d* demonstrates the shift of δ to *d* in Ugaritic, is one of the most important problems of Ugaritic historical phonetics. Most shifts wherein Canaanite dialects differ from Ugaritic (as that of stressed *â* to *ô*, absent in Ugaritic), may be explained (in spite of chronological difficulties, such as the occurrence of stressed *â* to *ô* in El-Amarna) by the assumption that Ugaritic exhibits an ancient stage of Canaanite, which has not yet been affected by the changes typical of *late* Canaanite dialects. If however, as we think, the shift $\delta > d$ turns out to be genuine Ugaritic, corresponding to Aramaic and contrasting with the Canaanite shift $\delta > z$, it will be impossible to class Ugaritic simply as a dialect emerging from

[1] A lecture delivered at the 27th Congress of Orientalists at Ann Arbor, August 1967. I had the privilege of discussing these problems with my friends and colleagues, Prof. S. E. Loewenstamm and Prof. J. C. Greenfield, who also furnished me with important material.

[2] We dispense with the documentation of well-known phenomena, and as a rule refer to C. H. Gordon's *Textbook*.

[3] V. *Textbook*, §5.3.

[4] The texts 75 and 77 use the 16th letter even in words in which the other texts employ *d*. Contrariwise, the other texts utilize the 16th letter in special words only. In these texts there are no sure cases of words spelled both with *d* and with the 16th letter.

[5] The 16th letter also occurs in the Semitic word *k-16-d*= 'to strive for', alternating with *kšd* (v. M. Held, in *Studies and Essays in Honor of* A. A. *Neuman*, Leiden 1962, p. 285, n. 4), thus exhibiting a similar pronunciation (assimilation of *š* to *d*). Cf. also presumably *šd* 'field', also *16-d* (yet one has to take into account the possibility that *16-d* represents Akkad. *šadū*). Even more complicated is *16-d* 'breast', since for this "nursery word" not only *θd* but also *zd* and Hebrew *dad* are attested. Cf. also D. N. Freedman, *BASOR* 175 (1964), p. 49 *a-16-ddy*, if = Hebrew אַשְׁדוֹדִי. At any rate, *pace* F. M. Cross, *Harvard Theological Review* 55 (1962), p. 249, cases of sign 16 corresponding to *š* and not preceding *d* (as *16-rt* 'vision', allegedly Hebrew שור) are completey uncertain. The same pronunciation is reflected by the Akkadian transliterations of the personal name *16-mrhd* by *ši-im-rad-du* and *zi-im-rad-du*, v. *Palais Royal d'Ugarit* IV, p. 250, *s.v.*

an alleged Proto-Canaanite language. This despite its close lexical and grammatical affinities with the Canaanite languages. One will no longer claim that the Canaanite dialects constituted, *at first*, a quite homogeneous body of closely related dialects, which were differentiated only by later divergent development.[6] On the contrary, one will then concur with J. Friedrich opinion[7] that the characteristics of the Canaanite dialects did not emerge in a Proto-Canaanite prehistoric period, but arose in historical times — presumably directly from Northwest Semitic, through parallel development and mutual contact in accordance with the so-called wave-theory. Accordingly, the term Canaanite applies to the result of the linguistic development, but not to the development itself. Ugaritic, however, because of its early extinction, was not affected by this later development, and so exhibits features alien to the later Canaanite dialects, e.g., the preservation of long stressed *a* and the shift $\delta > d$.

3. The current view is that Ugaritic *d* is polyphonic:[8] it designates not only *δ*, but also *d*, just as Old Aramaic *z* marks not only *z*, but also *δ*. Nevertheless, this comparison with Old Aramic is, it seems, fallacious. Aramaic took over the Canaanite alphabet, and was therefore obliged to designate its sounds with the inventory of the Canaanite alphabet. Ugaritic, however, added new letters at the *end* of its original alphabet. Accordingly, if *δ* had been preserved in common Ugaritic pronunciation, a corresponding letter would have been added at the end of the alphabet. Moreover, the sixteenth letter, which sometimes designates *δ*, stands in the middle of the alphabet. Now, if *δ* were originally represented by polyphonic *d*, the sixteenth letter would have primarily denoted a foreign sound, which occurred mainly in Hurrian words. The only other letter marking an original foreign sound, however, stands at the end of the Ugaritic alphabet, and it seems reasonable that the sixteenth letter, had it originally denoted a foreign sound, would have been placed there as well.

4. Similarly, it seems difficult to assume that the majority of texts exhibit a dialect different from that reflected in those texts which designate *δ* by the sixteenth letter, as if in the latter *d* had survived, while in the former it had shifted to *d*.[9] This assumption is contradicted by the fact that the the sixteenth letter,

[6] As does e.g., Z. S. Harris, *Development of the Canaanite Dialects*, New Haven 1939, *passim*.

[7] V. e.g., *Scientia* 84 (1949), pp. 220–23, and his *Phönizisch-punische Grammatik*, Roma 1951, p. 1, and cf. also P. Fronzaroli, *La fonetica Ugaritica*, Sussidi eruditi 7, Roma 1955, pp. 76, 85; further G. Garbini, e.g., in *Linguistica Semitica: Presente e futuro*, Studi Semitici 4 (Centro di Studi Semitici, Università di Roma), Roma 1961, pp. 55ff., cf. especially p. 61, where additional literature is quoted.

[8] V. e.g., H. L. Ginsberg, *Journal of the Palestine Oriental Society* 16 (1936), p. 139, as to the polyphony of *d* and *ḍ*, further *idem*, *BASOR*, Supplementary Studies, nos. 2–3 (1946), pp. 48–49. So also Gordon, *Manual*, pp. 22–23.

[9] This is *perhaps* C. Brockelmann's view, *Festschrift O. Eissfeldt*, Halle an der Saale 1947, p. 61.

denoting δ, occurs alongside of *d*, allegedly denoting δ.[10] Accordingly, the only valid explanation seems to be that the sixteenth letter denoting δ is an archaic feature:[11] δ shifted to *d* only after the invention of the Ugaritic alphabet.[12] Before this shift, δ was denoted by the sixteenth letter, which, accordingly, stood in the middle of the alphabet. After δ had disappeared, it ceased to be used for this purpose and was employed to mark a similar foreign sound. Nevertheless, the spelling with the sixteenth letter to mark original δ survived as an archaic feature in certain words,[13] whereas the archaic texts 75 and 77 continued designate *d* by it in almost every word.[14] In other texts, however, Proto-Semitic δ is marked by Ugaritic *d*, thus exhibiting the shift $\delta > d$ contrary to the Canaanite dialects, in accordance with Friedrich's theory about the emergence of Canaanite.

5. The archaic character of text 75[15] is also exhibited by its marking Proto-Semitic *ḍ* by *ẓ*.[16] Again, it seems unlikely that *ḍ*, to which, as a rule, Ugaritic *ṣ* corresponds, persisted in Ugaritic, as if Ugaritic *ṣ* had been polyphonic, marking both *ṣ* and *ḍ*. One would rather assume that *ḍ*, not represented in the Ugaritic alphabet, had already disappeared before its invention. A trace of it, presumably through some sort of tradition,[17] was preserved only in the archaic text 75, where it was represented by the (in all likelihood) phonetically related *ẓ*.

6. Nevertheless, one is inclined to assume that, in process of time, *ẓ* too disappeared in Ugaritic. This happened, however, comparatively late, as may be inferred from the fact that, as a rule, *ẓ* is marked by a special letter. As to the disappearance of *ẓ*, the Ugaritic texts reflect two different dialect groups.[18] In one of them, *ẓ* shifted to *ġ*: this is reclected by the spelling of *ẓ* with *ġ* in some

[10] Even texts 75 and 77 exhibit $d < \delta$: 75 I 3 *darṣ* (?); 77, 38 *dašr* (v. e.g., *Syria* 23 [1942/3], p. 283), as against 77, 45 *16-pid*. Gordon, *Textbook*, §5.3, did not succeed in establishing a sound shift responsible for the respective use of *d* and the 16th letter representing Proto-Semitic δ.

[11] So tentatively already E. Ullendorff, *JSS* 7 (1962), pp. 350ff.

[12] Cf. also F. M. Cross, *Harvard Theological Review* 55 (1962), p. 249, further P. Fronzaroli, *op. cit.*, e.g., p. 29, who wonders whether the 16th letter representing *d* is a dialectical feature or an archaism.

[13] Such archaic spellings may subsist in certain words. Thus, e.g., in literary Arabic *â* is not marked by *alif* in some words, in accordance with archaic orthography.

[14] For exceptions v. n. 10.

[15] In text 77 no letter corresponding to Proto-Semitic *ḍ* occurs. Because of the archaic character of this text, one will not agree with C. Brockelmann's view, *Festschrift O. Eissfeldt*, pp. 61–63, that the use of *ẓ* for *ḍ* exhibits a different dialect.

[16] As *yẓḥq* (I, 12) and *ẓi* (I, 14), v. *Textbook*, §5.7. *ẓ* may, of course, denote *ẓ* as well (77, 2 *qẓ*). In one doubtful case (I, 3 *darṣ*) Proto-Semitic *ḍ* may be represented by *ṣ*.

[17] It was perhaps due to a similar sort of tradition that the Septiagint to some extent distinguished between *ḥ* and *x*, as well as between ᶜ and *ġ* . [Cf. now J. Blau, *On Polyphony in Biblical Hebrew*, The Israel Academy of Sciences and Humanities, Proceedings, VI:2, Jerusalem 1982].

words of some texts.[19] The phonetic process was, *mutatis mutandis*, like that by which Proto-Semitic *ḍ* was affected in Old Aramaic, where it is spelled with *q*, presumably exhibiting *ġ*, which afterwards shifted to *ᶜayn*.[20] In the other dialect group *ẓ* shifted to *ṭēṭ*. This is exhibited by the single passage RS 24.244, line 67–68 *mġy. ḥrn. lbth. yštql. lḥṭrh* (and not *ḥẓrh* 'his court', as attested parallel to *hkl* and *bt*) 'HRN reaches his house, he turns to his court'. This shift is also corroborated by text 77, which twice uses *ẓ* instead of original *ṭ*.[21] The ony possible explanation of this strange phenomenon seems to be that it reflects hyper-correction, thus exhibiting the intentional archaic character of text 77 (and the orthographically related text 75): *ẓ* had already shifted to *ṭ*, but text 77, in accordance with its archaic spelling, strove to mark it with a special letter. Nevertheless, its scribe overshot the mark and used the special letter of *ẓ* to denote original *ṭ* as well: since he was used to spelling *ẓ* and pronouncing *ṭ*, he applied *ẓ* even to cases in which even archaic orthography demanded *ṭ*.[22]

7. The purpose of this paper is to show that the assumption of archaism explains various strange features in Ugaritic orthography[23] which would otherwise remain unexplained. I propose that, approximately at the time of the invention of the Ugaritic alphabet, several sound shifts affected Ugaritic: at first, preceding the invention of the alphabet, *ḍ* shifted to *ṣ*, and, accordingly, was not represented in the alphabet (with the exception of archaic 75, where it is indirectly marked by *ẓ*). Immediately after its invention δ coalesced with *d* and was only in some special words, and in 75/77, marked by its special sign, which had become, as a rule, the sign of a similar foreign sound. Even later was the disappearance of *ẓ*, being, as a rule, expressed by a special sign. Some texts,

[18] Cf. Brockelmann, op. cit., pp. 61–63, who assumes, however, three dialects — cf. n. 15.

[19] In spite of O. Rössler, *ZA* 54 (1961), pp. 158ff. [See above sin 70–72]

[20] So A. Jirku, *ZDMG* 113 (1963), pp. 481–82.

[21] *ẓhrm* '(pure) gems' (21), *lẓpn* 'Lṭpn' (44), v. *Textbook*, §5.11. Cf. J. Cantineau, *Syria* 21 (1940), p. 46.

[22] Because of Rš 24.244, 67–68 and since 77 already exhibits the shift *ẓ* > *ṭ* and and it stands to reason that 75 and 77 belong to the same dialect group, one will not derive *mġy*, occurring also 75 I 36, from *mẓy* (contrary to C. Brockelmann op. cit., 62–3). For the differenties of its etymology cf. e.g., Noldeke *ZDMG* 40 (1886), p. 736, note 5; C. Brockelmann, *Lex. Syr.*², *s.vv. mṣy, mṭy*; Koehler-Baumgartner, Aramaic part, *s.v. mṭy*.[Cf. now above *marg II* 67–72] — One *may* similarly analyze the restricted alphabet, as used e.g., by text 74, exhibiting one sign for *š* and Θ and employing *ḥ* for *h*. Accordingly, one may claim that Θ and *ḥ* disappeared in Ugaritic and their retention in ordinary orthography is due to archaic spelling. On the other hand, this alphabet may well reflect a different dialect.

[23] Cf. *mutatis mutandis*, the spelling of Egyptian Aramaic, v. P. Leander, *Laut- und Formenlehre des Ägyptisch-Aramäischen*, Göteborg 1928, pp. 8–10, as to the representation of Proto-Semitic δ and *ḍ* by *z*/*d* respectively. For hyper-correction in this dialect see E. Kutscher, *JAOS* 74 (1954). p. 235. [For the whole scope of hyper-corrections and their occurrence in Semitic languages, cf. now J. Blau, *On Pseudo-Corrections in Some Semitic Languages*, Jerusalem 1970.]

however, exhibit its shift to ġ one, its coalescence with ṭ. This latter feature is also reflected by text 77, which applies ẓ for original ṭ, thus clearly attesting its intentional archaic character. At any rate, the shifts δ to *d*, ẓ to ġ/ṭ, clearly differ from those attested in the Canaanite dialects (δ to *z*, ẓ to ṣ) and corroborate Friedrich's theory that the Canaanite dialects did not constitute a homogeneous body from their very beginnings, but developed in historical times through pa-rallel development and mutual contact.

Short Philological Notes on the Inscription of Mešaᶜ

1. In a recent, important article, W. Diem[1] has, I believe, presented decisive arguments that mimation, not nunation, was originally characteristic of the singular in the Semitic languages. In contrast, nunation typified the dual and the masculine plural. This original distinction of mimation / nunation is perhaps preserved in Moabite, offering corroboration of Diem's thesis.

In Moabite, the dual (*Mešaᶜ* = *KAI* 181:20 *m*ʾ*tn* "200") and the m. pl. (e.g., line 8 ʾ*rb*ᶜ*n* "40") terminate in *n*. Accordingly, *hṣhrm* (line 15), "the noon," (Hebrew *hṣhrym*) cannot be explained as dual.[2] Since one can scarcely consider it possible that *hṣhrm* ends in an ossified pronominal suffix,[3] one should analyze the form as a singular noun terminating in the original adverbial ending *-aym* > *ēm*, which originally preceded a (short)

1. W. Diem, "Gedanken zur Frage der Mimation and Nunation in den semitischen Sprachen," *ZDMG* 125 (1975): 239-258.

2. So, e.g., Carl Brockelmann, *Grundriss der vergleichenden Grammatik der semitischen Sprachen* (2 vols.; Berlin: Reuther & Reichard, 1908-1913): 1.458; *pace* T. Nöldeke ("Glossen zu H. Bauers semitischen Sprachproblemen," *ZA* 30 [1915-1916]: 160-170) who, in his argument for the interpretation of *hṣhrm* as dual, did not take into account the decisive proof for *-m* not being a dual suffix, viz. the form *m*ʾ*tn*.

3. As claimed by H. Bauer, see e.g. Hans Bauer and Pontus Leander, *Historische Grammatik der hebräischen Sprache des Alten Testaments* (Halle: Niemeyer, 1922): 518.

vowel.[4] In all likelihood this *m*, which originally functioned as a part of an adverbial ending,[5] is identical with mimation: Since in languages with mimation in the singular, common nouns[6] terminate in adverbial endings containing *m*,[7] whereas in classical Arabic, where the singular exhibits nunation, adverbs terminate in *-n*,[8] we can suggest an analogous situation for Moabite. Accordingly, in the light of *hṣhrm*, we can posit original mimation for the singular in Moabite. Thus Moabite originally exhibited

4. For this adverbial ending see, e.g., Brockelmann (N 2): 393-394, 458. He (hesitatingly) calls it a locative ending. Brockelmann, however, mixes up three different categories. The locative ending proper is limited to place names, as Ar. *Baḥrayn*, South Arabian *Yabrīn*, Heb. *Dōtān, Dōtayin, Šōmərōn, Ḥōrōnayim*. As these examples demonstrate, Hebrew, though originally a language with mimation in the singular, exhibits the locative ending with both *-m* and *-n*; cf. also J. Barth (*Die Nominalbildung in den semitischen Sprachen* [2nd ed.; Leipzig: Hinrich, 1894]: 319-320); cf. also Moabite *qrytn* (line 10), *ḥrnn* (31,32) *bt.dbltn* (30). The second category contains our temporal adverb *ṣhrym*, and one may also add the Hebrew temporal adverb *ywmm* 'by day' and the Hebrew adverbs of manner *rqm* 'emptily, vainly', *ḥnm* 'in vain'; the three latter examples terminate in *-ām*. It stands to reason that the adverbs belonging to these first two categories originally terminated in a vowel after *m* / *n*. Such a vowel is expressly attested in El-Amarna 137:21 *ri-ka-mi*. It is also suggested by the final stress in the Hebrew words (without taking late segholization into account. For segholization as a late development, cf. Joshua Blau, *A Grammar of Biblical Hebrew* [*Porta Linguarum Orientalium* N.S. xii; Wiesbaden: Harrassowitz, 1976]: 34). Hebrew forms with ultimate stress generally bear witness to a final vowel being omitted, since at one time penult stress prevailed in Hebrew (cf. ibid., p. 30). Moreover, the long *ā* in *-ām* is, in all likelihood, due to compensatory lengthening of an originally short *a* for an omitted following vowel (cf. ibid., p. 31). The third category cited by Brockelmann (p. 394), viz. Akkadian adverbials terminating in *-ān* (as *el*[*l*]*ân* 'above'), does not belong to the class of adverbials discussed here at all. These Akkadian adverbials originally terminate in *-ânum*, with the locative ending *-um*, the forms without *-um* exhibiting late development (cf. *GAG:* 167, §115b).

5. Yet in the Mešaᶜ inscription, *hṣhrm* already functions as a substantive. Substantival usage of adverbial forms is not infrequent, cf. Hebrew *lylh*, Moabite *llh* 'at night'>'night,' as well as the substantival usage of Hebrew *ywmm* (as Jer 33:20) and *ḥnm* (as 1 Kgs 2:31).

6. Yet the locative ending, added to place names, may contain *n* even in languages with mimation in the singular; see note 4.

7. For Hebrew, see the second category of adverbials cited in note 4. For Epigraphic South Arabian, see A. F. L. Beeston, *A Descriptive Grammar of Epigraphic South Arabian* (London: Luzac, 1962): 52, §42:4, who cites the adverbial ending *-hm*.

8. Cf. Arabic *yawman* 'one day,' which, however, is already adjusted to the accusative and lacks the final vowel.

mimation in the singular, but nunation in the dual and the m. pl., in accordance with Diem's reconstruction of Proto-Semitic.

2. Moabite *hlk* 'to go' lacks the first radical in the imv. *lk* (line 14), yet has retained it in the impf. *wʾhlk* (lines 14-15).[9] It stands to reason that the (at least synchronic) elision of the first radical in the imv. antedates its elision in the impf.[10] Traces of this situation are, to some extent, still recognizable in Biblical Hebrew: in the imv., forms without *h* prevail (about 240 cases), *h* being attested only once (*hilkū* Jer 51:50). In the impf., too, the great majority of forms is built without *h* (about 635 cases), a small minority exhibiting radical *h* (11 cases).[11] Nevertheless, the occurrences of the *h*-impf. (11/635 = .017) are significantly more frequent than those of the *h*-imv. (1/240 = .004). One can postulate that the development of the elision of the *h* started in the imv.:[12] the monosyllabic[13] imv. **hlik* shifted to **lik.*[14] Moabite

9. Since the impf. form is immediately preceded by the G-stem imv. *lk* (*lk.ʾḥz.ʾt.nbh. ᶜl.yśrʾl.wʾhlk* " 'Go, take Neboh from Israel!' So I went."), it has to be interpreted as a G rather than a D.

10. Similarly, it stands to reason that, in verbs I*w*, originally only the G imv. was formed with the elision of the *w*, whereas the impf. originally retained the *w*. Only this assumption explains the frequency of Hebrew I*w* H forms, as against Ugaritic G; for particulars see J. Blau ("Der Übergang der bibelhebräischen Verba *I w* (*y*) von Qal in Hifᶜil im Lichte des Ugaritischen," *UF* 5 [1973]: 275-277). In Moabite, too, one case of I*w* G as against Hebrew H is attested: *lspt* (line 21) 'to add'; for vestiges of Hebrew G in this verb see ibid., 276 n. 4.

11. The count was made according to S. Mandelkern's *Concordance*.

12. Before the discovery of Ug. it was assumed (so, following F. Praetorius, "הלך and ילך," *ZAW* 2 [1882]: 310-312, e.g., *GKC*: 192, §69, *GKB*, I: 94, §16a, Bauer and Leander [N 3]: 384, §55e) that the passage of *hlk* to *ylk* started in H: the pf. **hahlaka* through complete dissimilation of the second *h* became **hālaka*>**hōlaka*, and from the latter form other forms of the type *ylk* were built by analogy to I*w* verbs. Thus this theory posits that G forms, built according to the pattern of verbs I*w* (*lek*, *yēlek*), arose through the paradigmatical impact of the H. However, in Ugaritic, where such G forms are well attested (*lk*, (*b*)*lkt*, *ylk*), the causative verbal stem preserved the radical *h*: *ašhlk*. Since Ugaritic has the Š causative, not H, no dissimilation of the radical *h* could occur. (see *UT*, *WUS* s.v.). Accordingly, Praetorius's theory, despite its simplicity, has to be regarded as refuted.

13. It is reasonable to assume that the G imv. was originally bisyllabic, repeating the same vowel after the first and second radical (as preserved in Akkadian and Ugaritic; see J. Blau, "Marginalia Semitica III," *Israel Oriental*
(pp. 263–64) *Studies* 7 [1977]: 30-31), yet in Hebrew (as well as in Aramaic and Arabic) it was adjusted to the impf., thus becoming (phonemically, at least) monosyllabic.

14. But the imv. only prevailed in *hlk*, presumably because of its frequency in speech. In other verbs I*h* the *h* of the imv. was restored through the influence of the

still reflects a stage in which the imperfect has not yet been influenced by the imv. and has preserved its *h,* whereas in Biblical Hebrew, as a rule, the impf. exhibits the impact of the imv.[15]

3. As a rule, it is claimed[16] that the pf. first person singular ending (**-ku*>) **-tu* shifted to *-tī* in Canaanite in general and in Hebrew in particular due to the influence of the corresponding pronominal suffix. Likewise, it is argued that **ʾanāku* 'I' became *ʾānōkī* due to the influence of the pronominal suffix.[17] Yet we encounter here one of the inherent difficulties of linguistic reconstruction: an explanation given for the emergence of a form may, on principle, be sufficient, yet one cannot be sure if the actual process took place only along these lines or was rather due to what Y. Malkiel termed "pluralinear development," the explanation given being only one of the factors bringing about the form discussed.[18] And if an additional explanation is more

impf. In Ugaritic, however (see *UT*: 86-87) *hlm* 'to beat' has the impf. *ylm,* with elision of the *h*. Accordingly, it seems likely that the imv. was without *h* as well, viz., **lm.* I am therefore inclined to interpret *hlm* in 2.4[68]. 14, 21 as an inf. abs. denoting order, rather than as an imv., and the same applies to *hlmn* in line 21, cf. 18[3 AQHT].4.33 (*pace* André Caquot, Maurice Sznycer and Andrée Herdner, *Textes ougaritiques, Tome I: mythes et légendes, introduction, traduction, commentaire* [Littératures anciennes du Proche-Orient 7; Paris: Cerf, 1974]: 439, n.b), which has to be parsed as inf. "abs." with pronominal suffix; compare the infinitival constructions with suffixes in the Phoenician Karatepe inscription *KAI* 26 A I:20 *yrdm ʾnk yšbm ʾnk* "I have brought them down and established them." For still further material, cf. the literature cited by W. L. Moran ("The Hebrew Language and its Northwest Semitic Background," in *The Bible and the Ancient Near East, Essays in Honor of William Foxwell Albright* [G. E. Wright, ed.; New York: Anchor, 1965]: 59-84, esp. 81-82, n. 77.

15. In Hebrew the passage of *hlk* to *ylk* was accelerated by the dissimilation of the *h* in the H-stem (cf. note 12).

16. See, e.g., Brockelmann (N 2): 1.573; Bauer and Leander (N 3): 310, §42j; *GKB*: 2.19 §4g; Sabatino Moscati, Anton Spitaler, Edward Ullendorff and Wolfram von Soden, *An Introduction to the Comparative Grammar of the Semitic Languages, Phonology and Morphology,* (Sabatino Moscati, ed.; *Porta Linguarum Orientalium* N.S. VI; Wiesbaden: Harrassowitz, 1964): 139, §16.45. I have not differentiated between the "accusative" pronominal suffix *-nī* and the "genitive" pronominal suffix *-ī*, though such differences have been noted in the sources cited.

17. See, e.g., Brockelmann (N 2): 1.298, Bauer and Leander (N 3): 248, Moscati (N 16): 103-104, §13.7. Again (cf. n. 16), I have not differentiated between *-nī* and *-ī*.

18. Cf. J. Blau, "Some Difficulties in the Reconstruction of 'Proto-Hebrew' and 'Proto-Canaanite' " in *In Memoriam Paul Kahle* (BZAW 103; Matthew Black and Georg Fohrer, eds.; Berlin: Töpelmann, 1968): 29-43, esp. 42-43. (pp. 279–80)

forceful, accounting, for instance, for the distribution of the form involved, one may wish to give preference to that explanation, without, however, ignoring the possibility of the influence of additional factors, along the lines suggested by the first explanation. This seems the case with Hebrew **ʾanāku*>*ʾānōkī* and **-tu* > *-tī*. The usual explanation does not account for the distribution of these shifts. Why is it that these shifts are attested only in languages in which the shift *ā*>*ō* obtains?[19] Naturally, an interpretation that links the shifts **ʾanāku*>*ʾānōkī* and **-tu*> *-tī* with the shift *ā*>*ō* would be much more powerful and convincing than the standard explanation (although one would not discard the latter entirely but rather view it as an additional contributing factor). In fact, such an interpretation exists: first, **ʾanāku* shifted to **ʾanōku,* which, however, contains *ō* preceding *u*. In this vowel sequence one of the two similar vowels is, in Hebrew, regularly dissimilated:[20] this was the reason that **ʾanōku* shifted to **ʾanōkī* (and later to *ʾānōkī*). Now, not only the pronominal suffixes *-nī* / *-ī* terminated in *-ī*, but **ʾanōkī* as well, and their joint impact was strong enough to affect **ʾana* / **-tu*, which became **ʾanī* (later *ʾānī*) / *-tī*.[21] Accordingly, if a Semitic dialect

19. In some Arabic dialects, to be sure, Old Arabic *ʾanā* is reflected as *ʾanī*, etc.; cf., e.g., Brockelmann (N 2): 297, §104B. But here we should assume that *-nī* gave rise to *ʾanī*, influencing *ʾanā* also because of the *n* preceding *-ī*. Yet one has to bear in mind that, as far as known to me, in no Arabic dialect was the pf. ending *-tu* influenced by *-ī*, presumably because the extension of the *-ī* ending was limited to *-nī* (*-nī*, *ʾanī*). In the Canaanite languages, on the other hand, it was the ending *-ī*, rather than *-nī*, that was extended; accordingly, it reached *-tu* as well. Nothing * certain can be stated as to *ʾnky* in the Panamu inscriptions (*KAI* 214:1, 215:19), since it may be a Canaanite loan.

20. In general, when *u*/*ū*/*ō* precedes *u*/*ū*/*o*/*ō* in the next syllable, one of the vowels is dissimilated (though exceptions like *kuttonet* 'tunic' do occur); cf., e.g., *GKB:* 1.151, §27h, Blau, *Grammar* (N 4): 29, §8.4; for the dissimilation of short *u* cf. also Eduard Y. Kutscher, *The Language and Linguistic Background of the Isaiah Scroll (1QIsa*[a]*)* (Leiden: Brill, 1974): 452-496. For regressive dissimilation cf. *šibbolet, qippod.* Such dissimilation in cases like *tīkōn, ḥīṣōn* has a special reason: progressive dissimilation would have destroyed the suffix morpheme *-ōn*. Progressive dissimilation is reflected by *lūlē, yōḥez*; in these cases the product of the dissimilation is *e*, rather than *i*. In the case of *ʾanōkī* the final *-ī*, rather than *-ē*, is also due to the influence of the pronominal suffix.

21. In the pf., *-tu* shifted to *-tī* not only by analogy, but, in the case of some forms of verbs II*w*/*y* and *mediae geminatae* exhibiting the "connecting vowel" *-ō-* (*haqīmōtī, sabbōtī, hasibbōtī*), also directly through dissimilation.

exhibits the first person s. pf. ending *-tī*, this can be taken as a proof that it exhibits the shift *ā*>*ō* as well. And since in Moabite the pf. first person s. in fact terminates in *-ty* (cf., e.g., lines 2-3 *mlkty*), i.e. in *-tī*, this indicates that in Moabite *ā* had already shifted to *ō* and that *ʾnk* (e.g., in line 1) exhibits **ʾanōkī*.[22] The shift *ā*>*ō*, for chronological reasons, has long been posited for Moabite,[23] yet not proved. In the light of the pf. ending *-tī*, it may be regarded as demonstrated.

4. The interpretation of the *ʾ* of *zʾt* 'this' (line 3) is of importance for the use of *matres lectionis* in Moabite.[24] Analysis of the *ʾalep* vowel letter must proceed on the basis of its Northwest Semitic background. In Hebrew orthography, *ʾalep*, when employed as *mater lectionis*, betrays the existence of an original (i.e., consonantal) *ʾalep*.[25] Therefore, most scholars[26] postulate a radical *ʾ* for Hebrew *zʾt*, as well as for Moabite *zʾt*, Phoenician and Aramaic **dʾ*>*zʾ*. In the light of Proto-Semitic *huʾa*/**hiʾa*[27] 'he/she,' containing the pronominal element *ʾa*, I would posit a derivation for Canaanite *zʾ* from an original **zaʾa*, and for *zʾt*, **zaʾat*>**zāt*>*zōt*. This is, at least, the case for Hebrew, whereas for Moabite one may posit both **zaʾat* with consonantal *ʾalep* still subsisting, or, in accordance with Heb. *zōt*, the *ʾalep* already serving as *mater lectionis*. The exceptional omission of intervocalic *ʾalep* in *zaʾat* in a demonstrative should

22. Whether *ʾnk* without final *y* already reflects the dropping of the final *-ī* or *ʾanōkī* still subsisted in Moabite, is a moot question; cf. recently S. Segert, "Die Sprache der moabitischen Königsinschrift," *ArOr* 29 (1961): 197-267, esp. 217, n. 91. At any rate, it does not affect our problem.

23. Cf., e.g., Zellig S. Harris, *Development of the Canaanite Dialects* (AOS 16; New Haven: American Oriental Society, 1939): 43-45.

24. Cf. recently Segert (N 22): 215, §3:362.

25. The only seeming exception is *ṣwʾr* 'neck,' pronounced *ṣawwar*. However, the standard interpretation of *ṣwʾr* as a form exhibiting *scriptio plena* in order to differentiate it from *sūr* 'rock' (so Eduard König, *Historisch-kritisches Lehrgebäude der hebräischen Sprache* [3 vols.; Leipzig: Hinrichs, 1881-1897]: 2.90; cf. *BDB*: 848 [s.v. צוּר I], *KB*²: 796), seems to me unlikely. Rather, derive the form from *sawʾar* (with Theodor Nöldeke, *Mandäische Grammatik* [Halle: Buchhandlung des Weisenhauses, 1875): 127-128, esp. 128, n. 1).

26. Cf., e.g., Brockelmann, (N 2): 1.321; *KAI* 2.171; Johannes Friedrich and Wolfgang Röllig, *Phönizisch-punische Grammatik* (AnOr 46; Roma: PBI, 1970): 51-52.

27. For the sake of simplicity, I do not take forms with initial *š* into consideration, since they do not affect our problem.

not be surprising: exceptional sound shifts in demonstratives are well attested.[28]

5. Biblical *mēdəbāʾ* (with final quiescent *ʾalep*) corresponds to Moabite *mhdbʾ* (lines 8, 30?). Since in both places the spelling with *ʾalep* is consistent, the *ʾalep* has to be considered an original radical, once (at least) pronounced (cf. 4 above). The *mh* element of Moabite *mhdbʾ* was regarded by G. Kampffmeyer[29] as denoting 'water,' which, in his opinion, was hebraized to *mē* in this biblical form *mēdəbaʾ*; LXX Μαιδαβα, Μηδαβα. A similar view was expressed, presumably independently, by E. König;[30] König's view was accepted by S. Segert,[31] who is cited, more or less with assent, by *KAI:* 2.173, *KB³*: 545ab, *s.v. mēdəbaʾ*. Yet had the Hebrews, even by popular etymology, derived *mē* in *mēdəbaʾ* from 'water,' they would have spelled it, in a manner consistent with place names beginning with *mē* 'water' (cf. *mē zāhāb* Gen 36:39, 1 Chr 1:50, *mē hayyarqōn* Josh 19:46), as a separate word: *mē dəbaʾ*.[32] I would suggest that in Moabite *mhdbʾ* the *h* represents a glide: a strongly accented vowel was split into two vowels, between which a glide *h* developed.[33] Whatever the

28. Cf., e.g., recently Otto Jastrow, *Die mesopotamisch-arabischen qəltu-Dialekte, Band I: Phonologie und Morphologie* (Abhandlungen für die Kunde des Morgenlandes XLIII, 4; Wiesbaden: Steiner, 1978): 101, §3b, where the exceptional dropping of initial *h* in demonstratives is mentioned.

29. G. Kampffmeyer, "Alte Namen im heutigen Palästina und Syrien, I. Namen des Alten Testaments (Schluss)," *ZDPV* 16 (1893): 1-71, esp. 49.

30. König (N 25): 2.345; idem, "Ist die Mesa-Inschrift ein Falsifikat," *ZDMG* 59 (1905): 233-251, esp. 235-236; idem, "Mesa-Inschrift, Sprachgeschichte und Sprachkritik," *ZDMG* 59 (1905): 743-756, esp. 747.

31. Segert (N 22): 216-217; 249.

32. In the light of these place names it seems quite improbable that in the Masoretic transmission of **mē dəbāʾ* these allegedly original two words wrongly coalesced. On the contrary, popular etymology was apt to interpret this name as containing *mē* 'water.'

33. Along the lines suggested, on the basis of a parallel feature in Modern South Arabian dialects, for Epigraphic South Arabian by Nikolaus Rhodokanakis in his comprehensive study *Studien zur Lexikographie und Grammatik des Altsüdarabischen*, I (Sitzungsberichte der Akademie der Wissenschaften, philosophisch-historische Klasse 178/4; Wien: Hölder, 1915): 12-56. Rhodokanakis's view is generally accepted, cf. Maria Höfner, *Altsüdarabische Grammatik* (Porta Linguarum Orientalium, xxiv; Leipzig: Harrassowitz, 1943): 27, Beeston (N 7): 11 §4:7. This phenomenon is attested in Northwest Semitic as well; cf. the transition of verbs II*w*/*y* into II*h* (where, however, one has to take into account the tendency to triliterality as an additional factor). Thus, we can note *mwl*/*mhl* 'to

etymology of this place name, it first had the form **maydabaʾ*, from which Hebrew *mēdəbaʾ* can easily be derived.[34] A strong stress split the first *a*[35] into **aha*, giving rise to **mahaydabaʾ*, which developed to **mahēdabaʾ*, the Moabite form. Or was the development **maydabaʾ*> *mēdabaʾ*>*mēhēdabaʾ*?

6. *The direct object marker ʾt in Mešaᶜ*. As in Hebrew, the direct object marker in Moabite has the form *ʾt,* as against *ʾyt* in the older layer of Phoenician. Because of the close affinity of these languages, it seems likely[36] that they have to be derived from one proto-form. Z. Harris[37] postulates *ʾiyāt.* However, we should probably assume that the Arabic marker of the pronominal direct object *ʾiyyā-* (without final *-t*, no doubt an additional demonstrative element) is related to our word,[38] and one has to account for the double *y* in Arabic. One can posit secondary doubling[39] in Arabic, yet the preservation of simple intervocalic *y* in a preposition, as it would then occur in Phoenician (and Old Aramaic) *ʾyt,* is quite surprising. I would, accordingly,[40] prefer to

circumcise' (perhaps also *Abrām*/*Abrahām*) in Hebrew, *bht* 'to be ashamed' in Aramaic (as against Heb. *bwš*). For further examples see F. Buhl, *Wilhelm Gesenius' hebräisches und aramäisches Handwörterbuch über das Alte Testament* (16th edition; Leipzig: Vogel, 1915): 171a. For this feature in Arabic see Wolfdietrich Fischer, *Farb- und Formbezeichnungen in der Sprache der altarabischen Dichtung* (Leipzig: Harrassowitz, 1965): 330, n. 4.

34. It is not easy to account for the modern Arabic place name *Mādaba.* In the modern dialect in the environs of *Mādaba* (cf. Andrzej Czapkiewicz, *Sprachproben aus Mādabā* [Polska Akademia Nauk, Komisja Orientalistyczna, Prace monograficzne 2: Kraków 1960]) the shift *ā*>*ē* (the so-called *ʾimāla*) does not occur. One could suggest that **mēdabaʾ* was first taken over as such in a dialect with *ʾimāla,* later, however, when the dialect without *ʾimāla* prevailed, it was interpreted as exhibiting *ʾimāla* and, therefore, *mādaba* was wrongly restored. This, however, is rather intricate.

35. The first *a* was stressed, if in Moabite a stress system prevailed, as assumed for Hebrew by Blau, *Grammar* (N 4): 30, §9.1.1.

36. Cf. Harris (N 23): 43, §16.

37. Ibid.

38. Cf. Brockelmann (N 2): 1.314. Otherwise Jakob Barth (*Die Pronominalbildung in den semitischen Sprachen,* Leipzig: Hinrichs, 1913): 93-94. I do not deal with the etymology of the Akkadian free accusatival pronoun *yātī*, etc., because P. Haupt's theory, cited by Brockelmann (1.314), is, despite its ingenuity, rather dubious. Barth (pp. 24-27), at any rate, considers this feature original and very ancient.

39. For this phenomenon cf. Brockelmann (N 2): 1.59; S. Morag, "*Lbᶜyt hkplwtm šl hgyy hmᶜbr,*" *Tarbiz* 23 (1952): 236-239.

40. Cf. also, e.g., Friedrich and Röllig (N 26): 128-129.

derive the Hebrew, Phoenician and Moabite (as well as the Old Aramaic) forms from **ʾiyyāt*. The double *y* persisted in ancient Phoenician; yet in Hebrew, Moabite and later Phoenician it was, despite its doubling, elided,[41] not unexpectedly in such a frequent grammatical marker.[42] The alternation of Hebrew (and presumably also Moabite) *ʾet, ʾōtō, ʾetkem,* etc., can easily be accounted for. Since Canaanite *ā* did not shift to *ō* except in a stressed position, one should posit stressed *a* preceding most pronominal suffixes (e.g. **ʾiyyấtahū* "him">(by elision of *yy*) **ʾấtahū*>**ʾṓtahū* >*ʾṓtaw*>*ʾōtô*). Before nouns (and the so-called "heavy" pronominal suffixes), however, the *a* was unstressed. Therefore, *ʾāt* persisted, to be shortened (as not unexpected in a marker as common as *ʾt*) to *ʾat*, which later, through the inclination of *ʾa* to *ʾe*,[43] shifted to *ʾet*.

More intricate than the etymology of *ʾt* is the analysis of its usage in the inscription of Mešaᶜ. Even a glance at the inscription clearly demonstrates that its usage is facultative. However, because of the restricted size of this inscription, it is very difficult to determine the limits of its use. Still, one central fact seems clearly to be established: as emphasized by Segert,[44] *ʾnk* plus pf. is never followed by *ʾt* (cf. lines 21-29); Segert designates this, correctly in my

41. Beginnings of this elision are attested, it seems, already in the ancient layer of Phoenician. Thus, in my opinion, *wqrʾ ʾnk ʾt rbty* "I have been calling my mistress," (*KAI* 10:2-3) and *kmʾš qrʾt ʾt rbty,* "as I called my mistress" (line 7) both are clauses in which *qrʾ* clearly governs the direct object, since "to call *with*" is quite unlikely. The fact that *rbty* is in the genitive (as against the accusative **rbt*) does not prove that it is governed by the preposition *ʾt* 'with,' rather than by the direct object marker *ʾt* (*pace KAI:* 2.14, where wrongly *bᶜlty* is cited for *rbty*). Already in the first edition of his grammar, Johannes Friedrich (*Phönizisch-punische Grammatik* [AnOr 32; Roma: Pontificium Institutum Biblicum, 1951]: 101) has rightly called attention to the fact that the direct object marker is itself a preposition (and, indeed, *lə*, when used as direct object marker, remains a preposition as well!). The other certain case of ancient Phoenician *ʾt* as direct object marker is in an inscription published by M. Lidzbarski (*Ephemeris für Semitische Epigraphik* [3 vols.; Giessen: Töpelmann, 1902-1915]): 1.170, where *ʾt* is governed by *ḥzy* 'to see.' For the whole problem cf., e.g., Zellig Harris, *A Grammar of the Phoenician Language* (AOS 8; New Haven: American Oriental Society, 1936): 84; Friedrich, 118 §255; Friedrich and Röllig (N 26): 128-129; *DISO s.v. ʾt* I.

42. In later Aramaic, the *yāt* direct object marker arose through the dropping of the initial syllable.

43. As in *teʾesop*/ *ʾeḥšob* over against *taḥšob*.

44. Segert (N 22): 236, §6:12.

opinion, as a stylistic feature. So clear is the absence of *ʾt* in this construction that, with Segert,[45] one must refrain from reading *wʾnk.bnty.[ʾt.mhd]bʾ* in lines 29-30 and should rather restore something like *[bt.mhd]bʾ*. I would like to emphasize that the absence of *ʾt* is not caused by the preceding perfect alone but by the whole stylistic feature *ʾnk* plus perfect. After the perfect third person m. s., without a preceding personal pronoun, *ʾt* is attested: lines 18-19 *wmlk.yśrʾl.bnh ʾt / yhṣ* "and the king of Israel had built Yahaz." Therefore, Segert[46] overstresses the part of the consecutive imperfect in the government of *ʾt*. I would rather say that, in the part of the inscription where Mešaᶜ's deeds are recounted in the consecutive impf., all verbal forms, including the perfect (line 18; cf. above), the ordinary imperfect (cf. line 6: *ʾᶜnw.ʾt.mʾb* "I shall humble Moab") and the imperative (cf. line 14: *ʾḥz.ʾt.nbh* "take Nebo!") may govern definite direct objects marked by *ʾt*.

Are there any constraints on the use of *ʾt*? H. B. Rosén[47] had the stimulating idea that in Moabite *ʾt* does not mark nouns determined by the definite article. Yet if one takes into consideration the above mentioned stylistic difference, viz. that *ʾnk* plus pf. never governs *ʾt*, his proof for the absence of *ʾt* is rather meager, the only cases being line 3 *wʾᶜś.hbmt.zʾt* "and I made this high place," and line 9 *wʾᶜs.bh.hʾšwḥ*, "and I made the reservoir in it." The other two cases in which *ʾt* is omitted before the definite article occur after *ʾnk* plus pf.: line 25 *wʾnk.krty.hmkrtt* "and I cut the beams(?)," and line 26 *ẘʾnk.ᶜśty.hmslt* "and I made the highway(s)."

Therefore, I would tentatively suggest a different analysis of the use of *ʾt*: that *ʾt* is only utilized preceding persons as direct objects. As is well known, there is a special tendency for differentiating subject from object when both are persons, since otherwise the two can be confused. One can similarly understand the fact that in Indo-European the neuter exhibits the same ending in the nominative and the accusative, since it is normally the object of the action of the verb, rather than the subject. For the same reason, in Spanish and Rumanian only *persons* serving as objects are introduced by special markers (by *a* and *pe* respectively). In the Semitic languages the tendency of marking

45. Segert (N 22): 209, §2:32.
46. Segert (N 22): 236, §6:12.
47. Ḥayim B. Rosen, *Hᶜbryt šlnw* (Tel-Aviv: Am oved, 1956-1957): 18, §3.

personal objects is especially reflected in Biblical Aramaic, where, as a rule, *lə* introduces determinate[48] personal objects.[49] This is, it seems, the case in the inscription of Mešaᶜ as well, though with one important, but easily understandable development: *ʾt* also marks the names of countries and towns used as direct objects. The probable reason for this is because place names are frequently expanded in application to denoting, not simply countries and towns, but their respective populations as well (cf. the numerous examples in Biblical Hebrew).[50] As such, the place names can be said to function as collective personal nouns. In the Mešaᶜ inscription *mʾb* 'Moab' occurs six times, twice as direct object introduced by *ʾt* (line 5 *wᶜnw.ʾt.mʾb* "and he humbled Moab"; line 6 *ʾᶜnw.ʾt.mʾb* "I shall humble Moab"). In four passages, including the two just cited (lines 1, 2, 5, 6), *mʾb*

48. W. Baumgartner, in the Aramaic part of *KB¹* (*s.v. l*, p. 1089a) is wrong in analyzing Dan 2:10 *lʾ šʾl lkl-ḥrṭm wʾšp wkšdy* "he did not ask any magician and enchanter and astrologer," as exhibiting an indeterminate direct object introduced by *lə*. Such phrases introduced by *kol* have to be considered determinate. This is the reason why *lə* in Syriac (cf. Theodor Nöldeke, *Kurzgefasste syrische Grammatik* [2nd ed.; Leipzig: Tauchnitz, 1898]: 221), *li* in Ancient South-Palestinian Christian Arabic (cf. Joshua Blau, *A Grammar of Christian Arabic Based mainly on South-Palestinian Texts from the First Millennium* [Corpus Scriptorum Christianorum Orientalium 267, 276, 279, Louvain, 1966-1967]: 415-416) and *ʾt* in Biblical Hebrew (e.g., Gen 8:21 *ʾt kl ḥy*, "everything living") are used to introduce *kul / kol / kull*-phrases; for in these languages, too, only determinate direct objects are especially marked.

49. Exceptions are rare; cf. M. Lambert, "De l'emploi du Lamed en Araméen biblique devant le complément direct," *REJ* 27 (1893): 269-270, Hans Bauer and Pontus Leander, *Grammatik des Biblisch-Aramäischen* (Halle: Niemeyer, 1927): 339-341 (where Lambert's paper is wrongly cited from *REJ* 54), Baumgartner, *KB¹* (n. 48) (where German *sächlich*, used here in the sense of denoting things, i.e. non-persons, is wrongly translated by "neuter"). Lambert assumed that these exceptions reflected the author's whim or clerical error, but this is hardly correct. Following Bauer and Leander (*ibid. in extenso*) one should rather admit that, although in Biblical Aramaic *lə*, as a rule, introduces personal direct objects, it is sometimes used with non-persons as well.

50. Cf., e.g., 1 Sam 6:13 *wbyt šmš qṣrym* "and (the people of) Beth-shemesh were reaping"; Ex 1:13 *wyᶜbdw mṣrym ʾt bny yśrʾl bprk* "and (the people of) Egypt made the children of Israel to serve with harshness." Cf. also the examples cited by König (N 25): 3.455, §346k. The names of nations may be understood as m. s., the name being that of the personal ancestor; as pl.; or as f. s., when the reference is to the country or when the population is treated as a collective, often personified; cf. A. B. Davidson, *Hebrew Syntax* (3rd ed.; Edinburgh: Clark, 1901): 161, rem. 5. See further Brockelmann (N 2): 2.177-179.

may be interpreted as denoting both the land and the people; whereas in line 12, and especially in line 20, it seems to designate the people alone.[51] We can further note lines 14-16 *ʾḥz.ʾt. nbh . . . wʾḥzh.wʾhrg.kl*[*h/m*] "take Nebo . . . and I took it and killed all [its/their] (population)" and line 28 *ky. kl.dybn.mšmᶜt* "because all Dibon is (my) loyal dependency." With this personal aspect of place names thus established, it is easy to see how, in an instance like the Mešaᶜ inscription, *ʾt* could be extended to mark the names of lands and towns in general as personal direct objects. Similar developments are found in other languages. Thus in Ancient Spanish the personal object marker *a* is also found in this environment. A. Zauner[52] quotes "sacastes a Castiella de gran cutividat" "you redeemed Castile from a great misfortune."

If it is correct to see *ʾt* as a marker of personal objects, including land and town names, we may employ this principle as a guide for restoring passages, as well as for elucidating to some degree the meaning of difficult words. Thus in lines 12-13 *wʾšb.mšm.ʾt.ʾrʾl. dwdh.wʾ*[*s*]*ḥbh.lpny.kmš* "and I brought back/took captive from there ʾRʾL DWDH and [dra]gged it / him before Chemosh," the use of *ʾt* before *ʾrʾl dwdh* suggests that the latter denotes a person.[53] In lines 17-18 the usual restoration is *wʾqḥ.mšm. ʾ*[*t.k*]*ly. YHWH* "I took from there YHWH's [ves]sels." This restoration, however, contradicts the assumption of *ʾt* introducing personal objects. Therefore, I am inclined to posit that *lqḥ* governs a personal object.[54] This is the more likely assumption in

51. The double usage of Moab is well attested in Biblical Hebrew as well: it denotes land, e.g., in Num 21:11, nation in Num 21:29.

52. Adolf Zauner, *Altspanisches Elementarbuch* (Sammlung romanischer Elementar- und Handbücher, Reihe I, 5; Heidelberg: Winter, 1921): 96. It *may* well be that this phenomenon is attested in Biblical Aramaic as well. According to the accents the passage *ᶜlynʾ ʾtw lyršlm qrytʾ mrdtʾ wbʾyštʾ bnyn* in Ezra 4:12 has to be translated "they have come to us to Jerusalem, building the rebellious and bad city"; yet Bauer and Leander ([N 49]: 341, with n. 3, following Ch. C. Torrey and Baumgartner, *KB*[1] (N 48), following Bauer and Leander, interpret it, against the accents, "they have come to us, building Jerusalem, the rebellious and bad city." If one accepts this interpretation, one will not analyze *lə* as introducing non-persons (*pace* Bauer and Leander; Baumgartner) but rather as an extension of the use of *lə* from personal objects to towns, as in our inscription.

53. Cf., e.g., W. F. Albright, in *ANET*: 320-321.

54. Heb. *malqoᵃḥ* 'booty' is, to be sure, differentiated from captives in Num 31:12, yet includes them in Num 31:11, 26-27, 32. Accordingly, *lqḥ* may well refer to persons.

the light of our discussion above on line 12, where we have proposed that *sḥb* governs a personal object. For this same *sḥb* occurs in line 18, the immediate sequel of the passage cited from line 17; viz. *wʾsḥb.hm.lpny.kmš* "and I dragged them before Chemosh." This suggests that, since the pronominal *hm* is the object of *sḥb,* it is probably a personal pronoun, just as *ʾrʾl dwdh* is the personal object of *sḥb* in line 12. Moreover, it follows that the antecedent of *hm* in line 17 should be personal as well and hence introduced by *ʾt.*[55] The problem remains, however, to restore after it a cstr. pl. noun terminating in *-ly.*[56]

The two main proposals[57] for the reading and restoration in lines 30-31 are *wʾśʾ.šm.ʾt.m̊ʿ̊[dny.hbqr.wʾt.myṭb.]ṣʾn.hʾrṣ* "and I set there the be[st cattle and the best] small cattle of the earth," and *wʾśʾ.šm.ʾt.n̊q̊[dy.hbqr.wʾt.rʿy.]ṣʾn.hʾrṣ* "and I set there the rai[ser of the cattle and the shepherds] of the small cattle of the earth." Because of the theory that *ʾt* marks personal objects only, we shall prefer the second interpretation.

At this juncture, it may be appropriate to list all the occurrences of direct objects in the inscription of Mešaʿ[58] in light of the preceding discussion (omitting the restorations proposed).

THE USE OF *ʾT*, NOT OCCURRING AFTER *ʾNK* PLUS PERFECT

ʾt preceding place names: line 5 *wyʿnw.ʾt.mʾb* "he humiliated Moab"; line 6 *ʾʿnw.ʾt.mʾb* "I will humiliate Moab" (in both instances *mʾb* can also be interpreted as the name of a people);

55. This, however, is not absolutely necessary; cf. *infra* the absence of *ʾt* preceding personal objects even when not after *ʾnk* plus pf.

56. I have played with the thought of restoring line 17 *ʾ[t.šʾ]ly.YHWH, šōʾel* denoting some sort of priests, as suggested (e.g., for Deut 18:11) by M. Jastrow, Jr., "The name of Samuel and the stem *šʾl*," *JBL* 19 (1900): 82-105 (without agreeing to all the items suggested by him). I have even thought of reading *ʾ[t.ʿg]ly.* with *ʿgly* equated to Hebrew *ʿeglê*, and referring to the calves set up in Israel. If this restoration is correct, we might explain the use of *ʾt* as occasioned by the fact that calves are conceived as deities, i.e., persons.

57. See, e.g., Segert (N 22): 209, nn. 58, 59.

58. Bruce Zuckerman kindly called my attention to *ʿśty. ʾt* preceding a lacuna in a broken context in line 3 of the el-Kerak inscription. *Prima facie,* one would assume that the direct object introduced by *ʾt* refers to a non-person, i.e. an altar or something similar built by the king. Yet, on second view, because of the broken context, this is by no means certain. The form *ʿśty* may be used in the sense of appointing someone (cf., e.g., 1 Kgs 12:31). Besides, *ʾt may* be the preposition

lines 7-8 *wyrš.ʿmry.ʾt.k̊[l.ʾr]ṣ.mhdbʾ* "and Omri took possession of the who[le lan]d of Mahdeba" (note that both here and twice in lines 13-14 a place name serves as the second member of a cstr. phrase); line 9 *wʾbn.ʾt.bʿlmʿn* "and I built Baalmeon"; lines 9-10 *wʾb̊[n] ʾt.qrytn* "and I built Qiryatên"; lines 10-11 *wybn.lh.mlk. yśrʾl.ʾt.ʿṭrt* "and the king of Israel had built Ataroth for himself"; line 13 *bis* (-14) *wʾšb.bh.ʾt.ʾš.šrn.wʾt.ʾš̊ m̊ḥrt* "and I settled there men of SHRN and men of MḤRT."

ʾt preceding a proper noun (? cf. above): 12 *wʾšb.mšm.ʾt.ʾrʾl.dwdh* "and I took captive from there ʾRʾL DWDH."

ʾt preceding a kl ("all")–phrase referring to persons: line 11b *wʾhrg.ʾt.kl. hʿm* "and I killed all the people."

ʾt missing before a kl *("all")–phrase referring to persons:* line 16 *wʾhrg.kl[h/m]* "and I killed all [its/their] (population)"; perhaps also line 20 *[w]ʾqḥ.mmʾb.mʾtn.ʾš.kl.ršh* "and I took from Moab two hundred men, his whole division (?)" if the final *h* of *ršh* is a pronominal suffix and this form therefore determinate.

ʾt missing before impersonal objects preceded by the definite article: line 3 *wʾʿś.hbmt.zʾt* "and I have made this high place[23]; line 9 *wʾʿś.bh.hʾšwḥ* "and I made the reservoir in it."

DIRECT OBJECTS GOVERNED BY *ʾNK* PLUS PERFECT

ʾt missing before place names: line 21 *ʾnk.bnty.qrḥh* "and I built QRḤH"; line 26 *ʾnk.bnty.ʿrʿr* "I built Aroer"; line 27 *bis ʾnk.bnty.bt.bmt. . .ʾnk.bnty.bṣr* "I built Beth-bamoth. . .I built Bezer"; lines 29-30 *ter* (yet before the first of the three parallel terms there is a lacuna; v. above) *wʾnky.bnty.[ ]bʾ. wbt d̊bltn.wbt̊.bʿlmʿn* "and I built [ ]Bʾ and Bet-Dibatên and Bet-Baalmeon."

ʾt missing before impersonal objects with pronominal suffix: line 22 *bis wʾnk.bnty.šʿryh.wʾnk.bnty.mgdlth* "and I built its gates and I built its towers."

ʾt missing before definite impersonal objects in cstr.: line 23

'with,' as attested in Hebrew (e.g., Gen 24:49). Moreover, *ʾt* may be the beginning of a noun, denoting the thing built (cf. Heb. *ʾtyq*, e.g., in Ezek 42:3).

wᵓnk.ᶜśty.klᵓy.hᵓšẘ[ḥ] "and I made both (?) of its reservoirs."[59]

ᵓt missing before impersonal objects with the definite article: line 25 *wᵓnk.krty.hmkrtt* "and I cut the beams(?)"; line 26 *ẘᵓnk. ᶜśty.hmslt* "and I made the highway(s)."[60]

ᵓt missing before an indefinite impersonal object: lines 24-25 *ᶜśw.l̊km.ᵓš.br.bbyth* "let each of you make a cistern for himself in his house."

If this thesis of *ᵓt* denoting personal (definite) direct objects (including place names) proves true, it follows that, at the time of the inscription of Mešaᶜ, the case system in Moabite had already disappeared, since it is only when the subject and the direct object are no longer distinguished by endings that the necessity for distinguishing subjects from personal objects arises.

59. Interesting is line 23 *wᵓnk.bnty.bt.mlk* "and I built the king's house," where one would have rather expected determinate *bt.hmlk*.

60. If one interprets *hmslt* as sg., it would prove that the feminine ending *-at* still persisted in Moabite, since after the double *l* of *mslt* (root *sll*) the feminine ending *-t* cannot be assumed. Still, the form may easily be analyzed as a pl. All the other occurrences of feminine *-t* in the Mešaᶜ inscription *may* be interpreted as exhibiting *-t*, rather than *-at*, contrary to the *communis opinio* (cf., e.g., Segert [N 22]: 220, §4231). The form *št* 'year' (lines 2, 8) clearly does not attest to the preservation of *-at*, since the form undoubtedly reflects the assimilation of an original *n* (**šant*>**šatt*) and hence exhibits the f. ending *-t*. Nor is *-at* clearly attested in *mšmᶜt* (line 28); cf. Hebrew *mišmáᶜat*, or in *(h)šḥrt* (line 15); cf. Middle Hebrew *šaḥărit*. The somewhat dubious *ryt* (line 12) may be vocalized *rīt*, and the equally dubious *mᵓt* (line 29) may reflect *miᵓt* (cf. Ugaritic **mit*, rather than **mat*, Geᶜez *məᵓət*). Even *(h)bmt* (line 3) could be vocalized *bāmt* / *bamt* (cf. Akkadian *bāmtu*). Accordingly, contrary to scholarly opinion, there is no direct proof for the preservation of the f. ending *-at* in Moabite. One can only adduce an *argumentum ex silentio:* had *-at* really shifted to *-aʰ* in Moabite, one would expect to encounter it in the inscription of Mešaᶜ. Yet, in fact, the only possible case of the f. ending *-h* (=*aʰ*) could be *qrḥh* (lines 3, 21, 24, 25), which, if this ending really existed in Moabite, could be interpreted as *qorḥaʰ*, rather than *qorḥōʰ* (cf. line 14 *nbh* = Heb. *nəbō*). In this case the pun in Isa 15:2 *bəkol rōšāw qorḥāʰ*, "on all their heads will be baldness," referring to Moab, would be even more powerful, since it plainly alluded to the Moabite town **qorḥaʰ*. I have dealt with this feature in my paper "The Parallel Development of the Feminine Ending -*at* in Hebrew and Some Other Semitic Languages," to appear in *HUCA*. (pp. 126–37)

Addition

to **p. 348**.*n. 19.8*: The spelling *KAI* 214:1 is אנכ (perhaps reflecting the influence of Canaanite orthography), 215:19 אנכי (may be exhibiting genuine Ya'udi spelling habit).

Abbreviations

Brockelmann = C. Brockelmann, *Grundriss der vergleichenden Grammatik der semitischen Sprachen*, Berlin 1908–13.

BSOAS = *Bulletin of the School of Oriental and African Studies.*

Emergence = J. Blau, *The Emergence and Linguistic Background of Judaeo-Arabic*², Jerusalem 1981.

Fischer & Jastrow = W. Fischer & O. Jastrow, *Handbuch der arabischen Dialekte*, Wiesbaden 1980.

Grammar = J. Blau, *A Grammar of Biblical Hebrew*², Wiesbaden 1993.

Havers = W. Havers, *Handbuch der erklärenden Syntax*, Heidelberg 1931.

HAR = *Hebrew Annual Review.*

Hebrew Linguistics = יהושע בלאו, עיונים בבלשנות עברית, ירושלים תשנ"ו

HUCA = *Hebrew Union College Annual.*

IOS = *Israel Oriental Studies.*

JAOS = *Journal of the American Oriental Society.*

JSAI = *Jerusalem Studies in Arabic and Islam.*

JSS = *Journal of Semitic Studies.*

Leslau Festschrift = A. S. Kaye, ed., *Semitic Studies in Honor of W. Leslau*, Wiesbaden 1991.

Nöldeke, *Syriac* = T. Nöldeke, *Kurzgefasste syrische Grammatik*², Leipzig 1898.

Polyphony = J. Blau, *On Polyphony in Biblical Hebrew*, Jerusalem 1982.

Sivan = D. Sivan, *Ugaritic Grammar*, Jerusalem 1993 (in Hebrew).

Studies = J. Blau, *Studies in Middle Arabic and Its Judaeo-Arabic Variety*, Jerusalem 1988.

ZAL = *Zeitschrift für arabische Linguistik.*

ZDMG = *Zeitschrift der Deutschen Morgenländischen Gesellschaft.*

* Used in the Additions and corrections.

List of Sources

The Monophthongization of Diphthongs as Reflected in the Use of Vowel Letters in the Pentateuch. Z. Zevit, S. Gitin, M. Sokoloff, eds., *Solving Riddles and Untying Knots, Biblical, Epigraphic, and Semitic Studies in Honor of J. C. Greenfield*, Winona Lake, Ind.: Eisenbraun, 1995, pp. 7–11.

Non-Phonetic Conditioning of Sound Change and Biblical Hebrew. *HAR* 3 (1979), pp. 7–15.

On Pausal Lengthening, Pausal Stress Shift, Philippi's Law and Rule Ordering in Biblical Hebrew. *HAR* 5 (1981), pp. 1–13.

"Weak" Phonetic Change and the Hebrew *śîn*. *HAR* 1 (1977), pp. 67–119.

Hebrew Stress Shifts, Pretonic Lengthening, and Segolization: Possible Cases of Aramaic Interference in Hebrew Syllable Structure. *IOS* 8 (1978), pp. 91–106.

Some Remarks on the Prehistory of Stress in Biblical Hebrew. *IOS* 9 (1979). pp. 49–54.

The Parallel Development of the Feminine Ending *-at* in Semitic Languages. *HUCA* 51 (1980), pp. 17–28.

Remarks on the Development of Some Pronominal Suffixes in Hebrew. *HAR* 6 (1982), pp. 61–67.

Redundant Pronominal Suffixes Denoting Intrinsic Possession. *The Journal of the Ancient Near Eastern Society of Columbia University* 11 (1979), pp. 31–37.

Studies in Hebrew Verb Formation. *HUCA* 42 (1971), pp. 133–58.

On Some Vestiges of Univerbalization of the Units and Tens of the Cardinalia 21–99 in Arabic and Hebrew. *Bar-Ilan Departmental Researches: Arabic and Islamic Studies*, II, Ramat Gan 1978, pp. ix–xii

Marginalia Semitica I. *IOS* 1 (1971), pp. 1–35.

Marginalia Semitica II. *IOS* 2 (1972), pp. 57–82.

Marginalia Semitica III. *IOS* 7 (1977), pp. 14–32.

Some Difficulties in the Reconstruction of "Proto-Hebrew" and "Proto-Canaanite". M. Black & G. Fohrer, eds., *In Memoriam Paul Kahle*, Berlin: A. Töpelmann, 1968, pp. 29–43

A Misunderstood Medieval Translation of *śered* (Isaiah 44:13) and Its Impact on Modern Scholarship. D. P. Wright, *et al.*, eds., *Pomegranates and Golden Bells, Studies... in Honor of J. Milgrom*, Winona Lake, Ind.: Eisenbraun, 1995, pp. 689–95

Minutiae Aramaicae. E. W. Conrad–E. G. Newing, eds., *Perspectives on Language and Text, Essays and Poems in Honor of F. I. Anderson...*, Winona Lake, Ind.: Eisenbraun, 1987, pp. 3–10.

List of Sources

The Origins of Open and Closed *e* in Proto-Syriac. *BSOAS* 32 (1969), pp. 1–9.

Hebrew and North West Semitic: Reflections on the Classification of the Semitic Languages. *HAR* 2 (1978), pp. 21–44.

Some Ugaritic, Hebrew, and Arabic Parallels. *Journal of Northwest Semitic Languages* 10 (1982), pp. 5–10.

On Problems of Polyphony and Archaism in Ugaritic Spelling. *JAOS* 88 (1968), pp. 523–26.

Short Philological Notes on the Inscription of Mešaᶜ. *Maarav* 2 (1979–80), pp. 143–57.

It seems appropriate to mention here some books and papers of mine not included in this volume, although partly dealing with the same topics. I have published the following books dealing with related subjects: *On Pseudo-Corrections in Some Semitic Languages*, Jerusalem 1970; *A Grammar of Biblical Hebrew*, Wiesbaden, [1]1976,[2] 1993; 'An Adverbial Construction in Hebrew and Arabic: Sentence Adverbials in Frontal Position Separated from the Rest of the Sentence'. *Proceedings of the Israel Academy of Science and Humanities*, 6:1 (1977), pp. 1–103; *The Renaissance of Modern Hebrew and Modern Standard Arabic: Parallels and Differences in the Revival of Two Semitic Languages*, Berkeley 1981; 'On Polyphony in Biblical Hebrew'. *Proceedings of the Israel Academy of Science and Humanities*, 6:2 (1982), pp. 105–83.

Summaries were, as a rule not included in this volume, although often treating related subjects, e.g., 'Hebrew Language, Biblical', *Encyclopedia Judaica* [2], XVI (supplement entries), cols. 1568–83; 'The Historical Periods of the Hebrew Language', in H. H. Paper, ed., *Jewish Languages*, Cambridge, Mass. (1978), pp. 121–31.

Since some of the papers dealing with general Arabic linguistics (which, therefore, were not included in the *Studies in Middle Arabic Linguistics* ...) are tied in with papers published in this volume, it is appropriate to give a more or less complete list of them here: 'To Which Dialect Group did Sicilian Arabic belong', *JAOS* 88 (1968), pp. 522–23; 'Arabic *iw* > *ū*, J. Mansour, ed., *Arabic and Islamic Studies*, Ramat-Gan 1973, pp. xlii–xlv; 'Remarks on Some Syntactic Trends in Modern Standard Arabic', *IOS* 3 (1973), pp. 172–231; 'Notes on Syntactic Phenomena in Classical Arabic as exhibited by *Jaḥiẓ's Kitāb al-Buxalāʾ*', *IOS* 5 (1975), pp. 277–98; 'Some Additional Observations on Syntactic Trends in Modern Standard Arabic', *IOS 36.158–90* (1976); 'Studies in Arabic Morphology and Syntax', *JSAI* 2 (1980), pp. 351–64 (1980); 'The *Jāhiliyya* and the Emergence of the Neo-Arabic Lingual Type', *JSAI* 7 (1986), pp. 35–43; 'Two Studies in Sibawayhi's Kitâb, *JSAI* 12 (1989), pp.1–30. The following papers of mine dealing with Middle Arabic were not included in the *Studies* : 'L'apparition du type linguistique néo-arabe, *Revue des études Islamiques* 37, fasc. 2 (1969), pp. 191–201; 'Littérature judéo-arabe', Histoire des littératures, I: Littératures anciennes, orientales at orales, *Encyclopédie de la Pléiade*, Paris 1977, pp. 732–39; 'The contribution of Middle Arabic to the Vocabulary of Modern Standard Arabic', *Logos Islamicos*, Toronto

1984, pp. 9–20; 'Classical Arabic *versus* Post-Classical Arabic as Viewed from the Vantage Point of Judaeo-Arabic',*JSAI* 13 (1990), pp. 218–24; 'Notes on the Use of Different Registers of Judeo-Arabic by One Author', *Hebrew Annual Review* 9 (1995), pp. 75–78; 'On Two Works Written in Middle Arabic Literary Standard', *Studies in Islamic History and Civilization*, Jerusalem–Leiden 1986, pp. 447–71; 'Some Instances Reflecting the Influence of Saadya Gaon's Bible Translation on Later Judeo-Arabic Writings', *Occident and Orient*, Budapest–Leiden 1988, pp. 21–30; 'A Poem on the Decalogue Attributed to Saadiah Gaon', *The Ten Commandments in History and Tradition*, Jerusalem 1990, pp. 355–61; 'Anmerkungen zum Gebrauch der Pronomina in mittelarabischen Texten', *Festgabe für Hans-Rudolf Singer,* Frankfurt 1991, pp. 143–49; '"At Our Place in al-Andalus", "At Our Place in the Maghreb"', *Perspectives on Maimonides: Philosophical and Historical Studies*, Oxford 1991, pp. 293–94; 'On a Fragment of the Oldest Judaeo-Arabic Bible Translation Extant', *Genizah Research after Ninety Years: The Case of Judaeo-Arabic*, Cambridge 1992, pp. 31–39; 'A Melkite Arabic Literary *lingua franca* from the Second Half of the First Millennium, *BSOAS* 57 (1994), 14–16; 'Vernacular Arabic as Reflected by Middle Arabic', *Proceedings of the 14th Congress of the Union Européenne des Arabisants et Islamisants*, II, Budapest 1995, pp. 11–15; 'On the Inaccurate Use of Participles in Medieval Judaeo-Arabic, *JSAI* 19 (1995), pp. 233–39.

Index of Notions

a vowel, stability of 19, 27, 262–63, 265

ā > *ō* 12, 16–17, 24, 120–22, 128[3], 170, 190–91, 253, 273, 277[58], 326, 339, 348–49, 352

Adverbial endings 29, 291–93, 345

Akkadian 12, 58, 62[37], 65, 71, 88, 131, 148, 151, 152, 160, 162, **163–64**, 166, 169[63], 175, 178, 179, 222ff., 238ff., 243, 244, 252[3], 268[9, 10], 269[15], 280, 309, 310, 312–14, 318–19, 345[4]. See also (El-)Amarna

Alef 190–91, 250–56; elision of 253, 349–50; *maqṣūra* 266–67[3], 281; prosthetic 213, 220, 250. See also nouns, ii *alef*; verbs, i/iii *alef*

Alienable (possession), see intrinsic (possession)

Allophone 16, 30, 31[21]

(El-)Amarna 130, 152, **157–63**, 176, 178–79, 214. 218, 271–72, 274–75, 281–82, 308, 339, 345[4]

Arabic 12, 15, 27, 28, 29, 52, 57, 58, 59, 61, 63, 64, 65, 66[54, 56], 67, 68, 69, 71–72, **75–83**, 87, 103, 107, 108, 109, **131–35**, 137, **138–45**, 143, 145, 146ff., 149[10], 151–52, 153–54, **164–65**, **166–68**, 169[63], 175, 177, 180, **181–84**, **188–89**, 190, 219, 232ff., 238[6], 239–40, 242, 243, 244, 246, 252, 259[11, 12], 260–262, 262, 266–67[3], 268, 268–69[13], 269[15], 271, 273, 281, 293[13], **310–12**, 318–19, 320–21, 341[12], 345, 348[19], 354[48], **333–38**; stress system 105–06[3], **121–22**, 124[10], 128[3]. See also Semitic.

Aramaic 11, 13, 14, 17, 18, 21, 27, 29, 42, **52–53**, 56, 59, 61, 62, 63, 64, 65, 67, 68, 69, 71, **83–86**, **86–87**, 88, **90–93**, **104–119**, 131, **135–36**, 138–143, 147, 148, 151, 153[24], **170–73**, 176[100], 196–99, 210–17, 217–18, 220, 221–22, 222–25, 228, 232, 233[3], 234, 235, 236, **236–38**, 243, 244, 259[11, 12], 261, 262, 268, 281, **290–98**, 309, 316, 318, 319, 320, 321, 340, 342[23], 352[42], 354[48], 355[52]. See also Semitic; Syriac

Assimilation 35, 39[9], 51, 108, 109[5], 236–38, 247[4], 322

Attenuation 18, 35, 49, 176.

aw > *ō* 21–25

ay > *ē* 21–2

Index of Notions

Selected Index of Words